BAKE

THE AUSTRALIAN
Women's Weekly

BAKE

CELEBRATING THE TIME-HONOURED TRADITION OF HOME BAKING

acp
books

Contents

SPECIAL FEATURES

Baking conjures up many wonderful images for me. I can recall my great-grandmother, Elizabeth, making a big batch of scones for the visitors, usually my parents with us three kids, who'd arrived on the doorstep unannounced. I can see grandma turning the scone dough out of a great big bowl onto a scrubbed wooden kitchen table in the middle of a small hot kitchen, the fuel stove was in full flight. I remember being mesmerised by the way grandma handled the dough, in no time flat the scones were in and out of that oven. There was home-made jam, strawberry of course, dolloped onto the hot scones, followed by lashings of cream skimmed from the milk from the resident cow, and, this was all happening in the mid 1950s just 10 kilometres from Sydney's CBD.

I don't know if grandma's scones influenced me or not with my career choice, but I like to think they did. I make good scones, but not as good as those stashed away in my memory bank.

I love to bake, and now I'm busily teaching my two granddaughters the finer points. I'm determined that they'll be able to whip up a cake, a slice, a batch of biscuits or scones, without any fuss or bother. It doesn't take much time, just a bit of practice. If you're just starting out, make notes on the recipe about how the mixture feels and looks, to refresh your memory next time. The ingredients for baked goodies are fairly finely balanced, it's all about chemistry and science, so measure and follow the recipes carefully. After you've gained some skills and confidence, start experimenting, you'll be surprised at what you can do.

I have loved putting together this collection of my favourite baking recipes. They have all been triple-tested in *The Australian Women's Weekly* Test Kitchen, so you know they really will work. I think *Bake* is destined to become a book you'll love and cherish and I hope it inspires another generation of home bakers.

Pamela Clark

Pamela Clark
Director
The Australian Women's Weekly Test Kitchen

Filling the Tins

AN INTRODUCTION TO THE HISTORY OF BAKING BY MARY MOODY

There was a period in Australian domestic history when a woman's worth was measured by her capabilities on 'baking day'. The well-filled cake tin and biscuit jar sent a subliminal message to the family and to the neighbours about the competence of the wife and mother who was running the home. It seems incredible to imagine that cooking for the family could be deemed competitive, but that's exactly how life was for a woman of a certain status in the days before females ventured outside the home to take up independent careers.

Just as amazing is the notion that routine household chores were assigned to particular days of the week. Monday was washing day. Tuesday was ironing. Wednesday was mending. Thursday was shopping. Friday was for cleaning and Saturday was baking day. Then Sunday was the day of rest. That's if you don't include cooking the whole family a big Sunday lunch after church! And, no doubt, cleaning up afterwards.

Of necessity, a woman's life was structured this way before labour-saving devices took the drudgery out of the more menial aspects of housework. Washing took an entire day, depending on the size of the family and the same was true of ironing, which was hot and tedious work. Women planned their weekly menus so that the less fussy meals could be prepared on the busiest of days, with recipes such as 'Busy Day Pudding' an example of a good dessert to serve on a Monday evening after a day spent leaning over a wood-fired copper.

The fact that baking was so highly prized was reflected in rural and regional fairs and agricultural shows where the displays of local homemade baked items — bread, cakes, slices, scones and preserves — were a major attraction, with women vying for the sought-after blue ribbon that confirmed that THEIR sponge really was the lightest and most delicious in the district. These 'baking displays' at our farming shows have virtually disappeared over the last few decades, reinforcing the fact that women don't want to compete on that level anymore. And also, even more significantly, that most women these days are just too busy to bake — in spite of all our modern kitchen gadgets and labour-saving devices.

This is a great shame because bread, cakes, pies and pastries that are baked at home are not only healthier — made from fresh, raw ingredients without all the colourings, flavourings and preservatives of mass-produced foods — but they also taste completely different. They are simply better in every way. It's a bit like comparing the taste of an organically homegrown tomato with one from the supermarket shelf that has been picked green and kept in cold storage for a month.

BAKING IN HISTORY

Cakes and biscuits evolved as an adjunct to the making of bread. It was a way in which the baker or the cook could utilise any leftover dough as well as make good use of the oven while it was still hot after the baking of the bread. By adding sugar or honey, plus fruit, spices and seeds to the dough they produced nourishing and tasty 'sweet' breads that could be eaten fresh (cake) or baked hard and stored for longer periods (biscuits).

Often described as 'the staff of life', bread has been one of the principal forms of food for humans for more than 8,000 years, since the time when grain crops were first cultivated, harvested and ground to make flour. In most countries during summer, the grain was grown and the flour was made and stored for the baking of bread to carry the population through the colder winter months. From early times, bread was made both domestically and on a large scale — in Pompeii, for example, there were public baking ovens where the poor could bring their meagre loaves for cooking.

Also from Greek and Roman times the colour of the bread determined status. The wealthier preferred bread made from highly refined flour — white bread — while the peasants had to be satisfied with a coarser loaf. So the preference for white bread is certainly not a modern fad. In rural Europe when people still cooked most of their meals over an open fire, each hamlet constructed a communal bread oven (usually in a barn) that was fired up two or three times a week to cook large numbers of loaves economically. Interestingly, in the major cities the ruling classes did their upmost to keep bread prices as low as possible, knowing that a rebellion usually followed a famine. Keeping the peasants comfortably 'on the breadline' helped to prevent insurgence.

Traditionally, bread was made using yeast as the raising agent. This was quite a complicated process for individual households who had to make and maintain their own yeast by boiling hops and malt and storing the active organism in bottles for weeks at a time. Mrs Beeton devotes several pages of her wonderful book of household management just to the preparation, storage and use of yeast, cautioning readers that stale yeast 'flavours the bread and makes it disagreeable, the result being a heavy, unwholesome loaf.'

In time the situation improved with the introduction of commercial mass-produced compressed yeast, which greatly simplified the bread making process for home cooks. In modern times of course, the use of dried, granulated yeasts has made life even easier, allowing for much greater accuracy of measurements.

THE BAKING POWDER REVOLUTION

Cakes, as we know them today, would never have reached such a high level of refinement had it not been for the invention of an alternative raising agent to yeast. The earliest cakes were 'seed cakes' that were based on yeast dough with sugar and caraway seeds added for flavour. This concept was refined and made lighter and more spongy with the addition of eggs which, when beaten and frothy, introduce their own raising qualities. While the addition of eggs and shortening (butter or dripping) was helpful, it was not until the 1840s when an English chemist developed a yeast-free raising mixture of bicarbonate of soda (also known as baking soda), cream of tartar and a moisture absorber (cornflour) that produced excellent results. Since that time it was known, generically, as 'baking powder'.

Around the same period, tea was being introduced into British society. The upper and middle classes took to the tradition of a late afternoon 'light' meal of dainty sandwiches, delicate cakes and other 'niceties', all served with pots of steaming hot tea. The notion of 'high tea' was born, and its influence spread to all the colonies and affected how meals were taken and how ovens were utilised to produce a wonderful range of baked goods that were to become a staple part of what was considered a 'civilised' diet. High tea eventually evolved into a much more substantial and elaborate ceremony, often held on a Sunday afternoon, replacing the evening meal (although there was probably still a late supper served with simple fare such as eggs and toast). There was a great deal of snobbery and class distinction associated with afternoon tea and the upper classes turned it into a formal occasion, with hand-written invitations and a prescribed tea pouring ceremony where the hostess was always the centre of attention. Also during this era tea dances became popular and remained so right up until World War II.

Like cake, biscuits also evolved from bread-making, but they were not what we know them to be today. The earliest biscuits were very crisp rusks, made from the previous day's leftover bread, which was baked a second time, again making use of the last heat in the oven. Hence the name bis cuit — meaning twice cooked. Biscuits were deliberately baked until hard as a method of ensuring they were less prone to attack by weevils and this also meant they could be stored and used as sustenance on long journeys. The so-called 'ship's biscuits' were carried as the staple diet for sailors for centuries until the invention of preserved food in tins, which allowed meats and other protein-rich foods to be carried and stored for long periods.

BAKING IN AUSTRALIA

The first settlers brought with them an English diet of meat, vegetables, flour, sugar and tea (plus rum of course). After the first few years of struggling against the harsh Australian climate and soil, agriculture was established and houses were built — initially slab huts and rudimentary dwellings of wattle and daub using sticks and clay for the walls. In many of these early houses the kitchen was a separate building out the back — it was separated as a way of preventing the entire dwelling from burning down should the kitchen catch on fire. There were no stoves for baking, and cooking was done over an open flame and eaten in the kitchen during winter, and often outside in summer.

It was ironical that bread was a staple part of the diet as so many of the first settlers were convicts who had been sent to Australia for stealing bread. Flour was issued from

Government stores. The first bakery in Sydney was well equipped and had a windmill to generate power for grinding not just wheat, but also corn and barley.

As settlers moved further west, fresh bread wasn't available and there were certainly no ovens in which to bake. So 'damper' was eaten instead of bread. This was a mixture of flour and water flavoured with salt and baked in cast iron 'camp ovens' over hot coals. Some pioneers improvised, making rudimentary ovens out of old metal drums boxed in with clay bricks, but these were very basic and it was extremely difficult to control the oven temperature and not scorch the bread or the roast of mutton.

The role of women during these early days of settlement should never be underestimated. While many had come from the slums of London, there were also many genteel women who would have been (quite rightly) culture-shocked at the standard of living and the hardships to be endured in the colonies. One commentator at the time wrote:

'Married women, more deeply versed in ballroom gossip than in the arts of boiling or frying, should set their faces against emigration, unless they intend to turn over a new leaf. Unmarried girls may emigrate, but they must condescend to become useful as well as agreeable. Many good, honest settlers have been ruined by having fine ladies for wives.'

For many of these women mastering domestic skills was a question of survival. In rural areas they cooked not just for the family, but also for farm labourers and sometimes for teams of visiting shearers. The baking of bread, cakes, biscuits and puddings was essential to bulk out the largely meaty diet — vegetables were more difficult to procure, especially during times of drought, and the diet was high in fat, carbohydrate and sugar and often low in vitamins.

The open fireplaces in most colonial kitchens were enormous and generally more than one fire was going at a time — meals were often 'one pot' affairs cooked over the open flames — the pot would be suspended from a tripod — and there may also have been a small brick oven at one end for baking. Wood was plentiful and the fires were quite extravagant in their use of fuel compared to the UK. Families simply loved to gather around the 'open flame' even though accidents with fires were quite common.

Cast iron colonial stoves that were set into a simple chimney were available from around the 1840s, but many families resisted them because they 'hid the fire'. There was a perception that these stoves were unattractive 'iron monsters' which took the family away from a 'cheerful fireside'. They also were quite tricky for baking because again the temperature was hard to control — there was no damping-down mechanism — and it took a lot of practice and experience to get good results.

The situation began to improve in the mid to late 19th century when more sophisticated cooking stoves were imported from America. These were quite expensive and only the wealthier families could afford to have them installed. Again there was scepticism about the effectiveness of a closed oven, with a common belief that it was difficult to obtain even heat, resulting in the food burning on the top while remaining uncooked at the bottom. Eventually Australian manufacturers started producing similar appliances and they gradually gained acceptance and became part of the Australian domestic scene, eventually replacing the old open hearth as the heart of the home.

HOT OVEN TIPS

With no thermostat to indicate oven temperatures, women had to be experienced and creative to avoid burning the precious food. One cookbook advised that when the handle of the oven was too hot to touch, it was then the correct temperature for baking a cake (I wonder how many women had burnt fingertips working this one out). My own grandmother taught my mother that if the stove was too hot it helped to put an ordinary house brick in the oven for 15 minutes — it absorbed the heat and lowered the oven temperature.

With the introduction of the more efficient wood- and coal-burning stoves, the look of the average Australian kitchen changed. The table was often relocated into a separate 'dining' room and there was a belief by middle class families that eating together around this table was essential for family bonding — the concept of matching plates, silverware, glasses and table napkins established family unity and set a certain (slightly higher) standard of living. The kitchen was seen as a more functional working area and less as a place for the family to gather.

The new stoves allowed meals to become more complex with two or three courses now possible because there was both an oven and a cooking top that could be used simultaneously. Meals were no longer seen merely for 'survival' but as being central to a woman's role in the home and the essential ingredient of a happy marriage. Printed cookbooks became popular and were always given to the new bride — the first one specifically written for Australian conditions was *The English and Australian Cookery Book* (1864). Before that, most women simply kept detailed notebooks of handwritten recipes passed down from mother to daughter and circulated among friends. *The Antipodean Cookery Book* (1895) emphasised the close link between a well-fed man and a happy home:

'Man must be cooked for. He'll do without shirt buttons, and he'll do without his slippers but he will not do without his dinner... The husband is a creature of appetite, believe me, and not to be approached upon any important matter, such as a new bonnet or a silk dress, on an empty stomach.'

THE JOYS OF BAKING

Eventually, in the early 19th century, electric and gas stoves were introduced and again this made a dramatic change to the appearance of kitchens. Cleanliness and hygiene became an important factor and most housewives were pleased to see the end of dusty wood and dirty coal as part of their daily way of life. Kitchens were 'planned' with purpose-built cupboards for storage and life became easier in so many ways.

Women felt an elemental joy in baking, in filling their cake tins, because they earnestly believed they were providing essential and nutritious food for their families. Which, of course, they were. The basic ingredients of flour, butter, eggs, milk and sugar were all important to the health of their growing children who were much more physically active than children are today. While we feel obliged to restrict our intake of refined and processed breads, cakes and biscuits they felt no similar anxiety.

BAKING TINS AND UTENSILS

Compared with modern kitchens filled with labour-saving gadgets and appliances, pre-1950s kitchens were equipped only with a range of simple bowls, wooden spoons for mixing, metal whisks for beating egg whites, sieves for sifting flour, baking trays for biscuits and cake tins and moulds in various shapes and sizes. The English and Dutch were the only nationalities to bake their bread in moulds or tins — other European countries preferred crusty loaves baked on a terracotta slab or directly on the stone base of the brick bread oven. The early bread moulds were earthenware, glazed only on the inside, until after the industrial revolution when tin bread baking moulds became available. A square loaf of bread, which could be easily sliced, was very popular.

The English cake moulds were often very fancy and made from beaten copper which had to be maintained carefully — polished after use and stored in a dry place. One of the favourite moulds was for a popular cake in Victorian times — called a Balmoral cake it was made from flour, butter, milk, eggs, sugar and caraway seeds with a little baking powder to make it rise. It was cooked in a most elaborate mould then, when cooled, it was sliced and toasted over an open fire. There were also moulds for making ring cakes, with a hole in the centre; nut roll tins, which were cylindrical with lids fitted at each end; plus trays with scooped moulds for cooking traditional French Madeleines.

The heaviest cooking moulds were made from cast iron and used for making gem scones, which is a simple mix that is cooked very quickly at high heat. The moulds, weighing up to 1.35kg, are put into the oven first to heat up, and then a small dab of butter is placed in each mould before the batter is added with a sizzle. The gem irons are put back in the oven for only four to six minutes, the cast iron retaining the heat required for fast cooking. Similar in concept is the griddlecake or scone, which again is a basic mix that is dropped onto an extremely hot, greased griddle pan, then flipped and cooked on the other side.

In colonial Australia people improvised, making their baking containers from old cocoa tins or even 'spirit tins' that were beaten flat and then remade into squares or rectangles for baking bread and cakes. Tinware became popular, with the brand 'Willow' being the biggest seller in Australia. The company is still making baking tins to this day, although now they are light aluminum, often with a non-stick coating — unlike the heavy tin trays and moulds that were fashionable at the turn of the 20th century.

A CENTURY OF LAMINGTONS

Australia has only a handful of recognised 'national' baked recipes apart from damper, lamingtons and pavlova — and there are wildly differing versions of how (and where) they originated. New Zealand also lays claim to the last two. However Queensland proudly insists that lamingtons were invented in Brisbane in 1901 when the housemaid of the then Governor of Queensland, Lord Lamington, accidentally dropped some freshly baked sponge cake into a bowl of melted chocolate icing. To avoid wasting her mistake, it is claimed, she chopped the cake into squares and rolled it in desiccated coconut so they could be eaten daintily, without chocolate sticking to the fingers. Lord Lamington was suitably impressed and the cake was served often at Government House, and the recipe subsequently spread interstate.

Regardless of the truth of the matter, these cakes have been popular for at least 100 years and they have been used, not just for filling tins on a Saturday, but also for fundraising for schools and various community organisations. Known as a 'lamington drive', it's a tradition that involves a group of women getting together and baking, en masse, literally hundreds of these squares to sell at a profit for charity.

WARS AND DEPRESSION

Australia was a prosperous young country in the years leading up to World War I. Food was plentiful, meat was cheaper and much more readily available than in the UK and Europe. Of course keeping food fresh was always a problem in the days before refrigeration, particularly with our hot summer climate. In the cities people shopped daily for meat, milk and cream. These, along with butter and other perishables could be kept in a simple Coolgardie safe or an ice chest. The Coolgardie safe was a basic cupboard made with shelves and wire mesh, with hessian bags hanging on the sides. Water was allowed to drip down the hessian, with breezes creating a cooling effect inside. The ice chest was not dissimilar, but used ice for cooling. This was delivered every few days in large blocks by 'the iceman' who had a leather pad on his shoulder where he carried the ice, lifting it with metal hooks.

Countrywomen lived without the luxury of an ice chest but they had greater access to fresh milk, butter and cream and this allowed them to be more creative — even lavish — with their cake baking for the family. They also continued making their own bread for much longer than their city sisters, as 'trips to town' for shopping were only done once a fortnight or monthly, depending on the distances.

In 1922 the first meeting of the Country Women's Association was held at the Sydney Royal Agricultural Show (more commonly known these days as the Easter Show). They banded together with the aim of providing better health, education and services for countrywomen and their children. Although essentially quite a conservative group, the members worked hard to improve conditions by lobbying for baby health centres in rural areas, and for benefits such as cheaper rail fares to the coast so that country children could enjoy holidays at the seaside. Cooking, and baking in particular, was always an important part of the CWA although they definitely view themselves as being much more than 'tea and scones'. They encouraged women to bake and exhibit their wonderful cakes, scones and preserves at rural agricultural shows and they used baking as a fundraising exercise, which is a tradition that has continued until this day. Indeed, the CWA tea room at the Easter Show remains one of the most popular attractions, with queues forming from early morning to enjoy the legendary Devonshire Teas and other baked delicacies. CWA members worked tirelessly to support Australian forces during both wars, through fundraising and by cooking for men in rural training camps. After the war, the CWA took an interest in welcoming new migrants meeting at least two ships a month and providing meals for between 1,000 and 2,500 people at a time.

The basic ingredient of baking — the flour — was often bought in bulk and stored in airtight hopper bins under the kitchen bench or in the pantry. Many women made their own self-raising flour by adding baking powder to the basic flour in small quantities. Sugar was bought and stored in bulk too, and if weekly shopping lists of the period are anything to go by, jam and treacle or golden syrup were also consumed in very large quantities. It would appear that instead of the packaged biscuits and snack food that we use today, between-meal fillers for hungry children would have been large slabs of bread and butter smothered in jam or treacle. For poor folk, dripping would have been used instead.

World War I brought many changes to Australia. Initially there was economic prosperity because Britain cancelled trade with Germany and Austria and subsequently Australian companies won contracts to supply minerals for armaments as well as primary produce. There was tremendous enthusiasm among young Australian men who were keen to support 'the mother country' and married women were left behind to keep the home fires burning. During this period many women joined the workforce, either to replace the men who had enlisted or to be involved in efforts that supported the war. A lot of women became engaged to enlisted men just before they left for overseas service, and many of these women never saw their young fiancés again. It was a sad time for everyone.

In the trenches, the men were fed an unpalatable diet of dried beef and hardtack army biscuits that were so tough as to be almost impossible to chew. Some men ground them up and ate them like cereal. Anxious wives and mothers at home made food and clothing parcels to send to their men, with warm knitted clothing and the now famous Anzac biscuits that were sent to augment the scant army catering. There are many contradictory stories about the original recipe for these biscuits, which in fact evolved from a very similar mix to the army ration with the addition of oatmeal, desiccated coconut and golden syrup. This was a slightly more palatable biscuit, and it could be made to last for weeks if kept in an airtight biscuit tin. Because it contained no butter, eggs or fresh milk, it had excellent keeping qualities yet wasn't as tough or tasteless as the army issue. The modern version of this biscuit does contain butter and therefore doesn't keep as well as the ones sent lovingly from home during both wars, and it tastes a lot better.

At home there were food shortages, and even though the overall economy was prosperous there was an attitude of frugality in the sense that it was deemed unpatriotic to be wasteful during a time of war. The wages of soldiers were also quite low and families at home often had to survive by living as economically as they could. Women took their role as dedicated homemakers very seriously in the belief that maintaining a warm and welcoming home was a comfort during such difficult times, providing a safe and comfortable place for their soldier to return to.

The 1920s were another period of prosperity, and women became more liberated and less chained to the kitchen sink. Although Australian women had been given the vote in 1902 (New Zealand women were the first in the world to vote in 1893) they were still not emancipated in terms of education or working outside the home. Gradually, however, they started to enter universities and join the professions; this was the era of the 'flapper' where women wore shorter skirts and could be seen openly drinking, smoking and dancing wildly in public. On the home front, however, the domestic goddess was still highly valued with the husband still generally viewed as the breadwinner and head of the household.

Belts were tightened yet again in the 1930s, with the Great Depression causing greater hardship and suffering in Australia and New Zealand than in Europe. Men took to the road in search of work, walking from city to country with a swag on their back (they were known as the swaggies) in the hope of earning money to send home to their families. There were no social security payments for the unemployed; instead, the families of unemployed were given meagre food vouchers that could be handed to the corner store or butcher in exchange for basics such as flour, butter, sugar, milk and meat. In the suburbs, people transformed their backyards into small farms with fruit trees, choko and passionfruit vines, chicken runs and small vegetable gardens. It was all a question of survival.

People had a great sense of pride (or shame) and were embarrassed to admit that they were struggling financially. My grandfather was unemployed for nearly five years and he worked tirelessly in the backyard to produce fresh fruit, vegetables and eggs for the family. My grandmother, who was frail, would ask my mother (aged about 11) to walk several miles to the next suburb to exchange the vouchers for food so that the local shopkeepers would not know that the family had no income. In spite of their poverty, she always set an extra place at the table for 'the stranger' as it was not uncommon for swaggies to knock on the kitchen door at mealtimes offering to do odd jobs in return for a meal. It turns out that my grandmother's front gate had been marked by one of her guests with a notch in the wood that told other swaggies they would be welcome at her table.

Women baked bread and various pudding-like recipes as starchy fillers to augment the frugal rations. Bread was served with every meal, and this is when dumplings and Yorkshire puddings came into their own as a way of filling gaps in hungry bellies. Nothing was wasted or thrown away in those years, and women developed the skill of baking various meals at one time to save gas or electricity (or wood if they still had an old-fashioned stove).

Cakes, biscuits and scones were cooked at the same time as the family roast and stored in airtight tins to be handed out carefully during the week. Leftovers were eaten as breakfast or turned into soup.

Life for farmers and their families was tough during the depression too. The price for wheat dropped from 4/- a bushel down to 1/10d a bushel and they could no longer afford the wages of their farm workers. The women often had to hang up their aprons to go and help in the paddocks or with the rounding up of the livestock.

World War II again brought hard times to Australia. Basic foods were rationed and coupons were issued for each family member in an effort to control and reduce food consumption. This was done as part of the war effort, to ensure there was a plentiful supply for our servicemen and for the British people when their supplies were cut off from other sources.

Tea was the first food to be rationed. This was quite a blow, because tea was drunk with every meal — and between meals as well. The fashion for inviting neighbours in for tea and scones was one of the first pleasantries to be abandoned.

Sugar was next to be rationed, and this really hit hard. People used sugar extensively in baking and jam-making and the initial ration was 1 lb (450g) per person a week, which sounds like an awful lot, but was considered very little in those days. Sugar was soon followed by butter rationing, which made baking even more difficult. The diet of most Australians before the war was high in fats and sugar — people often ate meat three times a day and smothered their cooked vegetables in butter. A clever invention of the time was the butter curler that sliced the butter paper thin and made it appear to go further.

New products were advertised to help overcome some of the shortages — for example sandwiches could be made using a commercial mayonnaise or cheese spread instead of butter, although most families preferred to use dripping. Dripping was also used as shortening instead of butter for baking cakes and biscuits, but first it had to be clarified (boiled and strained) to reduce the meaty flavour. Copha, which is a solidified form of coconut oil, was also used as shortening instead of butter for the baking of cakes and puddings, and sugar replacements included honey and corn syrup or golden syrup and molasses. Packaged and prepared desserts such as junket and custard were also popular as were various concoctions that featured powdered and condensed milk. Women's magazines and the women's pages of the newspapers featured rationing recipes including an eggless, butterless, milkless 'War Cake' made from flour, raisins, lard and baking powder.

Eventually meat was also rationed, with each person entitled to 2½lbs (1.25kg) per week. Ironically, the compulsory reduction in consumption of meat and butter, combined with an increased intake of vegetables (people were again encouraged to grow vegetables in their own backyards), meant that the overall health of the population improved and this continued for several years after the war until rationing was finally abandoned.

A NEW AUSTRALIA

In the years immediately after the war, people continued to live quite frugally and it wasn't until the mid to late 1950s that financial confidence grew to the point that there was a consumer revolution. Manufacturers flooded the market with new and exciting products and appliances, and this was reflected in the advertising pages of women's magazines. Colourful ads for streamline refrigerators and stylish new stoves encouraged families to upgrade their kitchens and at the same time many new food products emerged, often aimed at saving time and effort for the housewife. There were tinned and packet soups and pre-mixed pastry as well as packaged cereals, powdered and evaporated milk, baby food and jellies. Women were encouraged not to feel guilty about taking shortcuts in the kitchen, with one ad using the copy line: 'tell them they're not letting their own family down when they serve them packet soup.'

There was also a growing emphasis on the need for women to remain slender, with crispbreads and 'slimmers' which were basically diet biscuits, also being heavily promoted. It's a good reminder that there's nothing new in the obsession with being thin.

Local bakeries still existed, but small supermarkets started to spring up around the suburbs, selling mass-produced sliced bread wrapped in plastic and a vast range of processed bakery goods including biscuits and packaged cakes. The message to women was 'why bother' baking at home when there are so many excellent products available on the supermarket shelves. Those women who still wanted to bake for the family were encouraged to reach for a new product — the cake mix — a concept imported from America, that made it possible to whip up a cake for the family in a matter of minutes by just adding milk and an egg to the contents of the package. This could have spelled the end of baking, except for the hardline views of a few dedicated home cooks who refused to allow 'cake mix' cakes to be entered in local shows or fairs.

During this post-war period, the make up of our population was also undergoing a dramatic change, with an influx of migrants from western and central Europe bringing with them an entirely new cuisine and way of life. How culture-shocked they must have been to encounter doughy white sliced bread and packaged lamingtons, not to mention a scarcity of wine and only carrots, potatoes, onions and cabbage on the greengrocer's shelves. Migrants also had to confront the successful marketing push that encouraged us to eat more 'exotic' food in the form of tinned pineapple, which seemed to dominate the cooking pages of every women's magazine. There was virtually no recipe — sweet or savoury — that couldn't be improved by the addition of a can of pineapple.

There's no doubt that Australia underwent a significant cultural change as we embraced these newcomers (sometimes with suspicion) and eventually changed the way we cooked and ate (and drank) forever. Delicatessens became popular, selling rye and sourdough breads, salamis, olives and biscuits that were very different from those produced at the Arnott's factory. Zucchini, garlic and eggplant started to feature in recipe books along with pasta and rice dishes.

During the 1970s there was a renewed interest in promoting more healthy eating habits, although shortcut meals were still heavily advertised. Tinned foods, frozen vegetables and prepared 'TV dinners' took a lot of the hard work out of cooking and, subsequently, many Australian women lost some of the skills and experience needed to prepare meals from scratch using raw ingredients.

The fact that during this period so many women were rejoining the workforce once their children reached school age, created an increased demand for 'convenience foods' and takeaways that would allow them to spend less time in the kitchen.

This is a situation that has continued to this day, although over the past decade there has, fortunately, been an increased knowledge and understanding about the importance of freshly cooked meals. This is reflected in the proliferation of television cooking programs and gourmet magazines and glossy cookbooks that encourage both men and women (and children) to get back into the kitchen and enjoy the simple pleasures of creating healthy family food. The next influx of migration from Asia also changed the way we cooked and ate, producing a unique Australian cuisine that is now recognised and highly regarded internationally.

These days, the baking of bread, cakes, biscuits and slices is undertaken for sheer pleasure rather than necessity. Given that most of us live busy and often stressful lives, the simple joy of baking a cake on a Saturday afternoon is one that will reunite us with our heritage and reconnect us with some of the basic values of our pioneering forebears. Knowing that the results of our baking will be so much healthier and taste superior to anything bought from a shop or a supermarket shelf is an added incentive. And there is nothing more comforting than the sweet, rich aroma of homemade bread, cake or biscuits, wafting from the oven. ▭

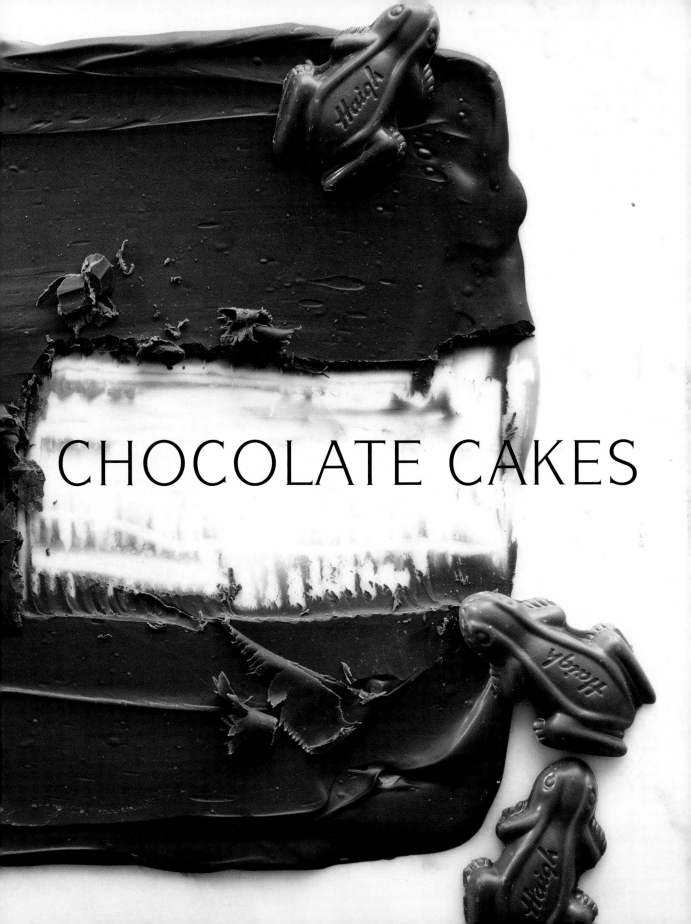

CHOCOLATE CAKES

Chocolate Cakes

The prodigious offspring of the southern and central American cacao tree, chocolate is made by fermenting, drying, roasting and shelling the cacao bean and extracting chocolate liquor or paste from its nibs or meat. The liquor is made up of cocoa solids, which provide chocolate's rich bitter flavour and cocoa butter, which contributes to the smooth mouth-feel. Cocoa butter is unique among vegetable fats in that it's solid at room temperature, but melts in the mouth, which accounts for the many rapturous descriptions of the sensation of eating chocolate. Bar chocolate is made by blending varying quantities of cocoa butter and solids with sugar, flavourings such as vanilla, milk and milk products and sometimes emulsifiers.

The Spanish conquistadors encountered chocolate as the beverage favoured by the Mayan Indians of central America. They prized the drink they called *xocoatl*, a combination of chocolate, water and spices, so highly that cacao beans were used for trade, thus setting the centuries-old tradition of buying favours with chocolate treats. The explorers brought this drinking chocolate back to Europe in the 15th century but it wasn't until 1847 that chocolate as we know it in bar form was commercially produced. In that year the Fry's chocolate factory of Bristol in England released the first bars, closely followed by the chocolate cream bar which is still produced to the present day.

The old adage that you get what you pay for certainly applies to chocolate. The better quality chocolate you use in cooking, the better the results. The more bitter the chocolate, the higher the content of cocoa solids and more intense the chocolate flavour. Bittersweet and semisweet chocolate have less sugar than milk chocolate, in which milk or milk products replace some of the solids. White chocolate doesn't contain any cocoa solids and therefore purists argue that it isn't chocolate at all. It's made from cocoa butter, sugar, milk and vanilla. Couverture, from the French word for "covering" is the chocolate professional chocolate makers and patissièrs use. Its high proportion of cocoa butter makes it extremely glossy. However, to maintain that glossy finish, couverture must be tempered, a tricky process of heating and quickly cooling the chocolate to exact temperatures measured with a sugar (or candy) thermometer. If not tempered properly the chocolate can appear dull and streaky. Cocoa powder is made from ground and sieved cocoa solids. Dutch cocoa powder is alkalinised by the addition of bicarbonate of soda, which neutralises the cocoa's natural bitterness.

For most of these recipes we recommend you use good-quality eating chocolate. By and large we avoid anything labelled compound chocolate in which some of the cocoa butter is replaced with other vegetable fats such as palm, coconut or soya oil. The result is a waxy tasting chocolate — think of the worst Easter eggs you can remember ever eating. Exceptions to this rule are when the recipes call for chocolate Melts or Choc Bits. Chocolate Melts are made from compound chocolate and are sometimes used when chocolate has to be piped or used for dipping. Because of the higher vegetable oil content, melted chocolate Melts don't set as quickly as better quality chocolate. Choc Bits, sometimes specified in cookies or muffins, also contain less cocoa butter than quality chocolate, so will keep their shape when they're baked.

Chocolate should be stored in cool, dry conditions. If it becomes too warm, the cocoa butter rises to the surface and a white-ish grey film or "bloom" develops. The chocolate will still taste the same and once it's melted it will usually return to its original colour. If the chocolate has been refrigerated or frozen, bring it to room temperature before using.

Melting chocolate is not difficult if you follow a few guidelines. Everything you use when melting chocolate, from the pan and the stirring spoon to your hands, must be absolutely dry: the slightest amount of water in the chocolate will make it seize, that is, turn lumpy or gritty and an unappealing grey in colour (see also *Baking Techniques* page 642).

The secret to successfully melting chocolate in the microwave oven is to break or cut it into small evenly-sized chunks and to select a good microwave-safe dish. Even sizes will result in even melting, and a good dish will conduct heat more efficiently than a plastic container, also allowing the chunks to melt at the same rate. Place the chopped chocolate in a microwave-safe bowl; heat on MEDIUM power (55%) for 15- to 20-second intervals, pausing to stir gently a few times. The chocolate will hold its shape even after it's melted, so the stirring is important. When the chocolate is almost melted, remove from the microwave oven and allow it to sit for a minute or two to complete the melting process.

The cooktop melting method is more time consuming than the microwave, but it is also a bit easier to judge when the chocolate has been sufficiently heated. Place a little water in a small saucepan, making sure that the water won't touch the bottom of the heatproof bowl (glass or china is best), or saucepan (such as the top of a double boiler) that you place on top of the pan. Bring the water to the boil and sit the bowl or top saucepan, uncovered (a lid would trap steam, the drops would fall onto the chocolate and ruin it), over the simmering water, stirring from time to time until the chocolate is melted.

We're firm believers that there's no such thing as too much of a good thing, so some of these recipes call for chocolate decorations as finishing touches. To grate chocolate make sure that the piece of chocolate you intend to grate is cool and firm. Grate on a hand grater, cleaning the grater often so the chocolate doesn't clog the teeth of the grater. To make chocolate curls use a sharp vegetable peeler and scrape along the long side of a block of room-temperature eating-quality chocolate. For larger curls, spread melted chocolate evenly and thinly onto a clean, flat oven tray, cutting board, or ideally, a slab of marble; stand until just set, but not hard. Scrape a flat knife or ice-cream scoop across the chocolate, pulling curls off with every movement. If the curls start to break up, the chocolate is too cold and you need to clean the board off, re-melt the chocolate and start again. The curls can be stored in an airtight container at room temperature until required — if the weather is hot, keep them in the refrigerator. See also *Chocolate tricks & techniques* pages 40 & 41.

Mississippi mud cake with chilli cherries

PREPARATION TIME 25 MINUTES   **COOKING TIME** 1 HOUR 35 MINUTES (PLUS COOLING TIME)   **SERVES** 12

In the Test Kitchen, we get many requests for recipes. Mud cake is our most requested recipe of all. Bourbon is a traditional ingredient in this recipe, but you can use any other type of whisky or even brandy rum or sherry. If you don't want to use alcohol, use the same amount of milk instead.

250g butter, chopped

200g dark eating chocolate, chopped coarsely

2 cups (440g) caster sugar

1 cup (250ml) milk

1 teaspoon vanilla extract

⅓ cup (80ml) bourbon

1½ cups (225g) plain flour

¼ cup (35g) self-raising flour

¼ cup (25g) cocoa powder

2 eggs

CHILLI CHERRIES

2 cups (500ml) water

¾ cup (165g) caster sugar

1 fresh small red thai chilli, halved lengthways

1 star anise

6 black peppercorns

10cm piece orange peel

300g frozen cherries

DARK CHOCOLATE GANACHE

⅓ cup (80ml) cream

200g dark eating chocolate, chopped coarsely

1 Preheat oven to 170°C/150°C fan-forced. Grease deep 22cm-round cake pan; line base with baking paper.

2 Combine butter, chocolate, sugar, milk, extract and bourbon in medium saucepan; stir over low heat until smooth. Transfer mixture to large bowl; cool 15 minutes. Whisk in sifted flours and cocoa, then eggs.

3 Pour mixture into pan; bake about 1½ hours.

4 Meanwhile, make chilli cherries.

5 Stand cake 5 minutes; turn, top-side up, onto wire rack to cool.

6 Meanwhile, make dark chocolate ganache.

7 Spread cold cake with ganache; serve with chilli cherries.

CHILLI CHERRIES Stir the water, sugar, chilli, star anise, peppercorns and peel in medium saucepan over low heat, without boiling, until sugar dissolves. Bring to the boil; boil 2 minutes. Add cherries; simmer 5 minutes or until cherries are tender. Cool cherries in syrup. Remove cherries from pan with a slotted spoon; bring syrup to the boil. Boil 10 minutes or until syrup thickens slightly; cool. Return cherries to pan.

DARK CHOCOLATE GANACHE Bring cream to the boil in small saucepan. Remove from heat; add chocolate, stir until smooth.

This is one of these recipes that came about by accident. We added chopped Cherry Ripe bars (among other things) to a favourite recipe, thinking the pieces would sink to the bottom — they didn't, and the cake is delicious.

Cherry coconut mud cake

PREPARATION TIME 35 MINUTES (PLUS STANDING TIME) **COOKING TIME** 2 HOURS **SERVES** 12

250g butter, chopped

1 tablespoon instant coffee granules

1⅔ cups (400ml) coconut milk

200g dark eating chocolate, chopped coarsely

2 cups (440g) caster sugar

1 cup (150g) plain flour

¾ cup (110g) self-raising flour

¼ cup (25g) cocoa powder

2 eggs

1 teaspoon vanilla extract

2 x 85g Cherry Ripe bars, chopped coarsely

200g dark eating chocolate, chopped coarsely, extra

125g unsalted butter, chopped, extra

CHOCOLATE PANELS

300g dark chocolate Melts

1 teaspoon vegetable oil

1 Preheat oven to 150°C/130°C fan-forced. Grease deep 22cm-round cake pan; line base and side with baking paper.

2 Melt butter in large saucepan; add coffee, coconut milk, chocolate and sugar. Stir over heat until chocolate melts and sugar dissolves; cool to room temperature.

3 Whisk in sifted flours and cocoa, then eggs and extract; stir in half of the Cherry Ripe. Pour mixture into pan. Top with remaining Cherry Ripe; bake about 1¾ hours. Stand cake 10 minutes; turn, top-side up, onto wire rack to cool.

4 Meanwhile, make chocolate panels.

5 Stir extra chocolate and extra butter in small saucepan over low heat until smooth. Refrigerate until mixture is spreadable.

6 Spread chocolate mixture all over cake; place chocolate panels around side of cake.

CHOCOLATE PANELS Stir chocolate and oil in medium heatproof bowl over medium saucepan of simmering water until smooth. Cut two 6cm x 50cm strips of baking paper. Spread chocolate evenly over strips; lift strips to allow chocolate to drip off paper. Allow chocolate to set, then, using ruler as guide, cut chocolate into 4cm panels with sharp knife. Carefully peel away baking paper.

Marbled chocolate mud cake

PREPARATION TIME 25 MINUTES **COOKING TIME** 1 HOUR **SERVES** 12

250g butter, softened

1 teaspoon vanilla extract

1¼ cups (275g) caster sugar

3 eggs

2¼ cups (335g) self-raising flour

¾ cup (180ml) buttermilk

¼ cup (25g) cocoa powder

¼ cup (60ml) milk

½ cup (95g) white Choc Bits

½ cup (95g) dark Choc Bits

CHOCOLATE BUTTER CREAM

125g butter, softened

1½ cups (240g) icing sugar

2 tablespoons milk

2 tablespoons cocoa powder

1 Preheat oven to 180°C/160°C fan-forced. Grease deep 22cm-round cake pan; line base with baking paper.

2 Beat butter, extract and sugar in small bowl with electric mixer until light and fluffy. Beat in eggs, one at a time. Transfer mixture to large bowl; stir in sifted flour and buttermilk, in two batches.

3 Divide cake mixture between two bowls. Blend sifted cocoa with milk; stir into one of the bowls of mixture with white Choc Bits. Stir dark Choc Bits into other bowl.

4 Drop alternate spoonfuls of mixtures into pan, then pull skewer back and forth through cake mixture several times to achieve a marbled effect.

5 Bake cake 1 hour. Stand cake in pan 5 minutes; turn, top-side up, onto wire rack to cool.

6 Meanwhile, make chocolate butter cream.

7 Drop alternate spoonfuls of the two butter cream mixtures onto cake; spread over top and side of cake.

CHOCOLATE BUTTER CREAM Beat butter in small bowl with electric mixer until light and fluffy. Gradually beat in half of the icing sugar, then milk, then remaining icing sugar. Transfer half of the mixture to another small bowl; stir sifted cocoa into one of the bowls.

Chocolate banana cake

PREPARATION TIME 25 MINUTES **COOKING TIME** 1 HOUR 15 MINUTES **SERVES** 12

⅔ cup (160ml) milk

2 teaspoons lemon juice

150g butter, softened

1 cup (220g) caster sugar

2 eggs

2 cups (300g) self-raising flour

½ teaspoon bicarbonate of soda

1 cup mashed banana

100g dark eating chocolate, grated finely

CREAMY CHOC FROSTING

200g dark eating chocolate, chopped coarsely

1 cup (160g) icing sugar

½ cup (120g) sour cream

It is important to use overripe well-mashed banana in cakes. The natural sugar in the ripe fruit contributes to the correct balance of the ingredients.

1 Preheat oven to 170°C/150°C fan-forced. Grease deep 22cm-round cake pan; line base with baking paper.

2 Combine milk and juice in small jug; stand 10 minutes.

3 Meanwhile, beat butter and sugar in small bowl with electric mixer until light and fluffy. Beat in eggs, one at a time. Transfer mixture to large bowl; stir in sifted flour and soda, banana, chocolate and milk mixture. Spread mixture into pan.

4 Bake cake about 1 hour 10 minutes. Stand cake in pan 5 minutes; turn, top-side up, onto wire rack to cool.

5 Meanwhile, make creamy choc frosting; spread cold cake with frosting.

CREAMY CHOC FROSTING Melt chocolate in medium heatproof bowl over medium saucepan of simmering water; gradually stir in sugar and sour cream.

Buttermilk can be found in cartons in the dairy section of the supermarket. If you can't find it, use the same amount of milk instead, or a mixture of yogurt and milk.

Chocolate buttermilk cake

PREPARATION TIME 20 MINUTES (PLUS COOLING AND CHILLING TIME) **COOKING TIME** 1 HOUR **SERVES** 10

185g butter, chopped

1 teaspoon vanilla extract

1½ cups (330g) caster sugar

4 eggs, separated

¾ cup (110g) self-raising flour

⅓ cup (35g) cocoa powder

¾ cup (180ml) buttermilk

CHOCOLATE FILLING

400g dark eating chocolate, chopped coarsely

250g butter, melted

½ cup (80g) icing sugar

1 Preheat oven to 180°C/160°C fan-forced. Grease deep 20cm-round cake pan; line base with baking paper.

2 Beat butter, extract and sugar in small bowl with electric mixer until light and fluffy. Beat in egg yolks, one at a time. Transfer mixture to large bowl; stir in sifted flours and cocoa, and buttermilk.

3 Beat egg whites in small bowl with electric mixer until soft peaks form; fold into cake mixture, in two batches. Pour cake mixture into pan.

4 Bake cake about 1 hour. Cool cake in pan.

5 Make chocolate filling; reserve about 1 cup.

6 Split cake into three layers. Place one layer on serving plate, spread thinly with some of the remaining chocolate filling; repeat layering with remaining cake layers and filling. Spread reserved filling all over cake. Refrigerate 3 hours before serving.

CHOCOLATE FILLING Stir chocolate and butter in medium saucepan over low heat until smooth. Remove from heat; stir in sifted icing sugar. Cool filling to room temperature; beat with wooden spoon until thick and spreadable.

Low-fat chocolate cake

PREPARATION TIME 15 MINUTES **COOKING TIME** 50 MINUTES (PLUS COOLING TIME) **SERVES** 10

½ cup (160g) plum jam

½ cup (110g) firmly packed brown sugar

½ cup (50g) cocoa powder

¾ cup (180ml) skim evaporated milk

2 teaspoons instant coffee granules

50g butter

2 eggs

½ cup (110g) caster sugar

1 cup (150g) self-raising flour

⅓ cup (50g) plain flour

2 teaspoons icing sugar

1 Preheat oven to 180°C/160°C fan-forced. Grease 20cm baba cake pan well.

2 Stir jam, brown sugar, sifted cocoa, milk, coffee and butter in medium saucepan over low heat until smooth. Cool.

3 Beat eggs and caster sugar in small bowl with electric mixer until thick and pale. Transfer mixture to large bowl; fold in sifted flours and chocolate mixture. Pour mixture into pan.

4 Bake cake about 45 minutes. Stand cake in pan 5 minutes; turn, top-side up, onto wire rack to cool. Serve cake dusted with sifted icing sugar.

A 20cm ring cake pan or two 8cm x 26cm bar cake pans can be used instead of the baba pan if you like. The ring cake will take the same baking time as the baba cake, the bar cakes will take slightly less time to cook.

Rich chocolate meringue cake

PREPARATION TIME 15 MINUTES **COOKING TIME** 1 HOUR 30 MINUTES **SERVES** 8

8 egg whites

1 cup (220g) caster sugar

60g dark eating chocolate, chopped finely

¼ cup (60g) finely chopped glacé figs

¼ cup (50g) finely chopped seeded prunes

¾ cup (45g) stale breadcrumbs

¼ cup (25g) cocoa powder

1 tablespoon icing sugar

1 tablespoon cocoa powder, extra

1 Preheat oven to 120°C/100°C fan-forced. Grease 22cm springform tin; line base and side with baking paper.

2 Beat egg whites in medium bowl with electric mixer until soft peaks form. Add sugar, 1 tablespoon at a time, beating until sugar dissolves between additions. Fold in chocolate, fruit, breadcrumbs and sifted cocoa.

3 Spoon mixture into tin; bake about 1½ hours. Cool in oven with door ajar.

4 Dust cake with combined sifted icing sugar and extra cocoa; serve with cream, if desired.

This cake is fragile, which is why we've baked it in a springform tin. There's no need to turn it right-side up.

1 LOW-FAT CHOCOLATE CAKE **2** RICH CHOCOLATE MERINGUE CAKE
3 DOUBLE-DECKER MUD CAKE [P 36] **4** DEVIL'S FOOD CAKE [P 36]

Double-decker mud cake

PREPARATION TIME 30 MINUTES (PLUS STANDING AND COOLING TIME) **COOKING TIME** 1 HOUR **SERVES** 10

It's best to use deep (not sandwich) cake pans here. The higher sides of the pans will help to prevent the cake from developing a thick crust.

250g butter, chopped

150g white eating chocolate, chopped coarsely

2 cups (440g) caster sugar

1 cup (250ml) milk

1 ½ cups (225g) plain flour

½ cup (75g) self-raising flour

1 teaspoon vanilla extract

2 eggs

2 tablespoons cocoa powder

600g milk eating chocolate, chopped coarsely

1 cup (250ml) cream

1 Preheat oven to 150°C/130°C fan-forced. Grease two deep 20cm-round cake pans; line bases and sides with baking paper.

2 Stir butter, white chocolate, sugar and milk in medium saucepan over low heat until smooth. Transfer mixture to large bowl; cool 15 minutes.

3 Whisk sifted flours into white chocolate mixture then whisk in extract and eggs; pour half of the mixture into one of the pans. Whisk sifted cocoa into remaining mixture; pour into other pan.

4 Bake cakes about 50 minutes. Stand cakes in pans 5 minutes; turn, top-side up, onto wire rack to cool.

5 Stir milk chocolate and cream in medium saucepan over low heat until smooth. Transfer mixture to medium bowl. Cover; refrigerate, stirring occasionally, until mixture is spreadable. Reserve 1 cup of the chocolate mixture.

6 Split each cooled cake in half. Centre one layer of cake on serving plate; spread with ½ cup of the remaining milk chocolate mixture. Repeat layering, alternating colours. Cover top and sides of cake with reserved chocolate mixture.

Devil's food cake

PREPARATION TIME 20 MINUTES **COOKING TIME** 45 MINUTES **SERVES** 10

Be aware that just about every brand of food colouring available will be a different strength. Start colouring with a tiny amount, and increase it as necessary.

185g butter, softened

1 ¾ cups (385g) caster sugar

3 eggs

1 ½ cups (225g) self-raising flour

½ cup (75g) plain flour

½ teaspoon bicarbonate of soda

⅔ cup (70g) cocoa powder

3 teaspoons instant coffee granules

½ teaspoon red food colouring

½ cup (125ml) water

½ cup (125ml) milk

300ml thickened cream

RICH CHOCOLATE FROSTING

60g dark eating chocolate, chopped coarsely

60g butter, chopped

1 Preheat oven to 180°C/160°C fan-forced. Grease two deep 20cm-round cake pans; line bases with baking paper.

2 Beat butter and sugar in small bowl with electric mixer until light and fluffy. Beat in eggs, one at a time. Transfer mixture to large bowl; fold in sifted flours, soda and cocoa with combined coffee, colouring, water and milk, in two batches. Pour mixture into pans.

3 Bake about 45 minutes. Turn cakes, top-side up, onto wire racks to cool.

4 Meanwhile, make rich chocolate frosting.

5 Join cold cakes with whipped cream; top with frosting.

RICH CHOCOLATE FROSTING Stir chocolate and butter in small heatproof bowl over small saucepan of simmering water until smooth. Cool at room temperature until spreadable, stirring occasionally.

Brandied apricot and chocolate cake

PREPARATION TIME 20 MINUTES (PLUS REFRIGERATION TIME) **COOKING TIME** 1 HOUR **SERVES** 10

125g dark eating chocolate, chopped coarsely

½ cup (125ml) water

125g butter, softened

1 cup (220g) firmly packed brown sugar

2 eggs

½ cup (120g) sour cream

1⅓ cups (200g) plain flour

⅓ cup (50g) self-raising flour

½ cup (160g) apricot jam

2 tablespoons brandy

300ml thickened cream

CHOCOLATE ICING

90g dark eating chocolate, chopped coarsely

15g butter

The texture of this cake is quite firm and fine — this is because of the very little raising agent used and the addition of sour cream.

1 Preheat oven to 160°C/140°C fan-forced. Grease deep 20cm round cake pan; line base with baking paper.

2 Stir chocolate and the water in small saucepan over low heat until smooth. Cool.

3 Beat butter and sugar in small bowl with electric mixer until light and fluffy. Beat in eggs, one at a time. Transfer mixture to large bowl; stir in chocolate mixture, sour cream and sifted flours in two batches. Spread mixture into pan.

4 Bake cake 1 hour. Stand cake in pan 5 minutes; turn, top-side up, onto wire rack to cool.

5 Meanwhile, make chocolate icing.

6 Combine jam and brandy in small bowl. Beat cream in small bowl until soft peaks form. Split cold cake into four layers; join layers with jam mixture and cream. Spread cake with icing; refrigerate until set.

CHOCOLATE ICING Stir chocolate and butter in small heatproof bowl over small saucepan of simmering water until smooth and spreadable.

If you want a plain cake simply leave out the citrus rinds; add 1 teaspoon vanilla extract instead.

Lemon and lime white chocolate mud cake

PREPARATION TIME 20 MINUTES

COOKING TIME 1 HOUR 50 MINUTES (PLUS COOLING AND REFRIGERATION TIME) **SERVES** 12

250g butter, chopped

2 teaspoons finely grated lemon rind

2 teaspoons finely grated lime rind

180g white eating chocolate, chopped coarsely

1 ½ cups (330g) caster sugar

¾ cup (180ml) milk

1 ½ cups (225g) plain flour

½ cup (75g) self-raising flour

2 eggs

COCONUT GANACHE

140ml can coconut cream

360g white eating chocolate, chopped finely

1 teaspoon finely grated lemon rind

1 teaspoon finely grated lime rind

1 Preheat oven to 170°C/150°C fan-forced. Grease deep 20cm-round cake pan; line base with baking paper.

2 Stir butter, rinds, chocolate, sugar and milk in medium saucepan over low heat until smooth. Transfer mixture to large bowl; cool 15 minutes.

3 Stir sifted flours and eggs into mixture; pour into pan.

4 Bake cake about 1 hour 40 minutes. Cool cake in pan.

5 Meanwhile, make coconut ganache.

6 Turn cake, top-side up, onto serving plate; spread ganache over cake.

COCONUT GANACHE Bring coconut cream to the boil in small saucepan. Place chocolate and rinds in medium bowl, add hot cream; stir until smooth. Cover; refrigerate, stirring occasionally, about 30 minutes or until ganache is spreadable.

Chocolate tricks & techniques

It's one thing to make a cake, but it's quite another to make it look wonderful. Here are some easy decorating tricks.

SPREADING CHOCOLATE
Spread melted chocolate evenly over a cold surface, such as a flat oven tray, a laminated chopping board, or, best of all marble. Leave to almost set at room temperature.

MAKING CURLS
There are many ways of making curls, here we've used a melon baller, just drag the baller smoothly and evenly across the surface of the chocolate. Remember you can always re-melt your mistakes.

USING CURLS
This spectacular looking cake looks far more difficult than it really is. Cut a mud cake made in a large cake pan into a star-shape, spread with ganache, then top with white and dark chocolate curls.

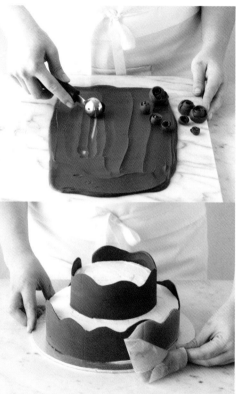

MAKING SCALLOPED BANDS
Cut out several strips of baking paper to fit around and up the side(s) of the cake. Cut a scalloped edge on the paper strips, making sure the joins will meet. Spread the paper strips evenly, all over, with melted chocolate.

POSITIONING SCALLOPED BANDS
Have the cake ready (iced, frosted etc) for the positioning of the bands. When the chocolate strips are starting to set, lift the strips, and carefully wrap each one around the side of the cake, then peel the paper away.

FINISHING TOUCHES
We've used two cakes, each with scalloped bands, stacked on top of each other, then decorated with fresh mixed berries. Note the join in the scalloped bands on the bottom cake, where the two strips of chocolate have joined up neatly.

MAKING WAVES
Cut out a circle of baking paper, the same size as the top of the cake you want to decorate, then cut it into four pieces. Using a small spatula, spread each piece with melted chocolate.

SHAPING WAVES
Line up cylindrical shapes, over which to dry the waves, we used two candles to dry two wave shapes. Carefully pick up each chocolate wave while they are still soft, and drape them over the candles to set at room temperature.

USING WAVES
Peel the paper away from each chocolate wave, then position the waves on top of the iced cake. The waves are easy to handle, move then around until they all "fit" together. Dust with sifted cocoa.

COMBING CHOCOLATE
Melted white chocolate colours well, here we've used pink food colouring. Spread the coloured chocolate out evenly, then use a pastry comb (bought from chef or cake decorating suppliers) to make the "stripes" in the chocolate. When it is almost set, spread with more melted white chocolate.

MAKING STRIPED CURLS
When the chocolate is almost set, drag the blade of a large sharp knife, held at about a 45° angle, across the chocolate to make candy-striped curls. This technique takes some practice, do this with plain melted chocolate until you've mastered it. Re-melt the mistakes. The trick is to have the chocolate at just the right stage, if it has set too much, the curls will break, if it's not set enough, the chocolate won't curl.

SIMPLE CURLS
The simplest of all chocolate-curl making is done with a vegetable peeler. You will only be able to make small curls, but they're quick and easy, and you can curl the chocolate straight onto the surface of the cake. Use a large bar or piece of chocolate, at room temperature, and drag the peeler along the side of the bar.

Nutty choc-orange cake

PREPARATION TIME 30 MINUTES (PLUS COOLING AND REFRIGERATION TIME)

COOKING TIME 1 HOUR 15 MINUTES **SERVES** 16

As an alternative, changed the type of nuts used. Hazelnuts, for example, taste great with the orange flavour.

1½ cups (240g) blanched almonds

2½ cups (250g) walnuts

200g dark eating chocolate, chopped coarsely

250g butter, softened

1 teaspoon vanilla extract

1 cup (220g) caster sugar

5 eggs, separated

1 tablespoon finely grated orange rind

1 tablespoon icing sugar

1 Preheat oven to 150°C/130°C fan-forced. Grease deep 23cm-square cake pan; line base and sides with baking paper.

2 Blend or process nuts and chocolate until chopped finely.

3 Beat butter, extract and sugar in small bowl with electric mixer until light and fluffy. Beat in egg yolks, one at a time. Transfer mixture to large bowl; stir in chocolate mixture and rind.

4 Beat egg whites in small bowl with electric mixer until soft peaks form; fold into chocolate mixture, in two batches. Pour mixture into pan.

5 Bake cake about 1¼ hours. Cool in pan. Cover; refrigerate 3 hours or overnight.

6 Cut cake into squares; serve squares dusted with sifted icing sugar.

Cream cheese chocolate cake

PREPARATION TIME 20 MINUTES **COOKING TIME** 50 MINUTES **SERVES** 10

Finish this cake by dusting with a little sifted icing sugar and cocoa, or top with a chocolate icing (see page 37).

125g cream cheese, softened

60g butter, softened

½ cup (110g) caster sugar

½ cup (100g) firmly packed brown sugar

1 egg

½ cup (60g) chopped pecans

¾ cup (180ml) milk

1 cup (150g) plain flour

⅓ cup (50g) self-raising flour

2 tablespoons cocoa powder

½ teaspoon bicarbonate of soda

1 Preheat oven to 180°C/160°C fan-forced. Grease deep 20cm-round cake pan; line base with baking paper.

2 Beat cheese, butter, sugars and egg in small bowl with electric mixer until light and fluffy. Transfer mixture to medium bowl; stir in nuts, milk and sifted dry ingredients, in two batches. Spoon mixture into pan.

3 Bake cake about 50 minutes. Stand cake in pan 5 minutes; turn, top-side up, onto wire rack to cool.

NUTTY CHOC-ORANGE CAKE

Don't be alarmed when you see how runny this cake mixture is, it's meant to be that way.

Family chocolate cake

PREPARATION TIME 20 MINUTES **COOKING TIME** 50 MINUTES (PLUS COOLING TIME) **SERVES** 16

2 cups (500ml) water

3 cups (660g) caster sugar

250g butter, chopped

⅓ cup (35g) cocoa powder

1 teaspoon bicarbonate of soda

3 cups (450g) self-raising flour

4 eggs

FUDGE FROSTING

90g butter

⅓ cup (80ml) water

½ cup (110g) caster sugar

1 ½ cups (240g) icing sugar

⅓ cup (35g) cocoa powder

1 Preheat oven to 180°C/160°C fan-forced. Grease deep 26.5cm x 33cm (3.5-litre/14-cup) baking dish; line base with baking paper.

2 Stir the water, sugar, butter and sifted cocoa and soda in medium saucepan over heat, without boiling, until sugar dissolves; bring to the boil. Reduce heat; simmer, uncovered, 5 minutes. Transfer mixture to large bowl; cool to room temperature.

3 Add flour and eggs to bowl; beat with electric mixer until mixture is smooth and pale in colour. Pour mixture into pan.

4 Bake cake about 50 minutes. Stand cake in pan 10 minutes; turn, top-side up, onto wire rack to cool.

5 Meanwhile, make fudge frosting. Spread frosting over cold cake.

FUDGE FROSTING Stir butter, the water and caster sugar in small saucepan over low heat, without boiling, until sugar dissolves. Sift icing sugar and cocoa into small bowl then gradually stir in hot butter mixture. Cover; refrigerate about 20 minutes or until frosting thickens. Beat frosting with wooden spoon until it is spreadable.

This is quite a dense cake. If you prefer, bake the mixture in a loaf pan. It will take about another 10 minutes to cook.

Chocolate fruit cake

PREPARATION TIME 20 MINUTES **COOKING TIME** 1 HOUR (PLUS REFRIGERATION TIME) **SERVES** 12

125g butter, chopped

¾ cup (150g) firmly packed brown sugar

50g dark eating chocolate, chopped coarsely

½ cup (125ml) water

¼ cup (60ml) dark rum

¼ cup (30g) coarsely chopped walnuts

½ cup (75g) dried currants

1 cup (160g) sultanas

1 cup (170g) coarsely chopped raisins

¼ cup (40g) mixed peel

¾ cup (110g) plain flour

2 tablespoons self-raising flour

2 tablespoons cocoa powder

½ teaspoon mixed spice

2 eggs

CHOCOLATE FROSTING

80g dark eating chocolate, chopped coarsely

¼ cup (60g) sour cream

1 Preheat oven to 150°C/130°C fan-forced. Grease 20cm-ring pan; line base with baking paper.

2 Stir butter, sugar, chocolate and the water in medium saucepan over heat until sugar dissolves. Remove from heat; stir in rum, nuts, fruit and peel. Stir in sifted dry ingredients and eggs. Spoon mixture into pan; bake cake about 1 hour. Cool cake in pan.

3 Meanwhile, make chocolate frosting.

4 Place cake onto serving plate, top with frosting; refrigerate until set.

CHOCOLATE FROSTING Stir ingredients in small heatproof bowl over small saucepan of simmering water until smooth.

Chocolate peppermint cake

PREPARATION TIME 20 MINUTES (PLUS REFRIGERATION TIME) **COOKING TIME** 1 HOUR **SERVES** 20

125g unsalted butter, chopped

2 teaspoons instant coffee granules

¾ cup (180ml) water

100g dark eating chocolate, chopped coarsely

1 cup (220g) caster sugar

1 egg

¾ cup (110g) self-raising flour

½ cup (75g) plain flour

2 tablespoons cocoa powder

PEPPERMINT CREAM

125g unsalted butter, softened

3 cups (480g) icing sugar

2 tablespoons milk

½ teaspoon peppermint essence

green food colouring

CHOCOLATE GANACHE

300g dark eating chocolate, chopped coarsely

1 cup (250ml) cream

This cake looks wonderful when it's cut. It's important to have the ganache at the right temperature. It needs to be warm enough to flow evenly over the cake, but, if it's too warm it will melt the peppermint cream.

1 Preheat oven to 150°C/130°C fan-forced. Grease two 8cm x 26cm bar cake pans; line bases and sides with baking paper.

2 Stir butter, coffee, the water, chocolate and sugar in medium saucepan over heat until smooth. Transfer mixture to medium bowl; whisk in egg with sifted flours and cocoa. Pour mixture equally between pans.

3 Bake cakes about 45 minutes. Stand cakes in pans 5 minutes; turn, top-side up, onto wire rack to cool.

4 Make peppermint cream.

5 Using serrated knife, split cakes in half. Place bottom layers on wire rack over tray. Spread each with about a quarter of the peppermint cream; top with cake tops. Place remaining peppermint cream in piping bag fitted with 2cm fluted tube. Pipe remaining cream along centre of each cake top; refrigerate 1 hour.

6 Meanwhile, make chocolate ganache.

7 Using metal spatula and working quickly, pour ganache over cold cakes, smoothing sides. Stand at room temperature until ganache sets.

PEPPERMINT CREAM Beat butter in small bowl with electric mixer until pale. Gradually beat in sifted icing sugar, milk, essence and enough of the colouring to tint pale green.

CHOCOLATE GANACHE Stir ingredient in small saucepan over low heat until smooth.

1 2

3 4

Caramel mud cake

PREPARATION TIME 20 MINUTES (PLUS COOLING TIME) **COOKING TIME** 1 HOUR 40 MINUTES **SERVES** 12

Good caramel mud cake recipes are not easy to find; this is our favourite.

180g white eating chocolate, chopped coarsely

185g butter, chopped coarsely

1 cup (220g) firmly packed brown sugar

1/3 cup (80ml) golden syrup

1 cup (250ml) milk

1 1/2 cups (225g) plain flour

1/2 cup (75g) self-raising flour

2 eggs

WHITE CHOCOLATE GANACHE

1/2 cup (125ml) cream

360g white eating chocolate, chopped coarsely

1 Preheat oven to 160°C/140°C fan-forced. Grease deep 22cm-round cake pan; line base and side with baking paper.

2 Stir chocolate, butter, sugar, syrup and milk in large saucepan over low heat until smooth. Cool 15 minutes. Whisk sifted flours and eggs into chocolate mixture; pour into pan.

3 Bake cake about 1 1/2 hours. Cool cake in pan.

4 Meanwhile, make white chocolate ganache.

5 Turn cake, top-side up, onto serving plate; spread with ganache.

WHITE CHOCOLATE GANACHE Bring cream to the boil in small saucepan, remove from heat; add chocolate, stir until smooth. Refrigerate about 30 minutes or until spreadable.

Chocolate coconut cakes

PREPARATION TIME 25 MINUTES **COOKING TIME** 30 MINUTES **MAKES** 6

If you like, make 12 smaller patty cakes — they will take about 20 minutes to cook.

2/3 cup (150g) firmly packed brown sugar

1/4 cup (25g) cocoa powder

1/2 cup (75g) self-raising flour

1/2 cup (75g) plain flour

1/3 cup (25g) desiccated coconut

125g butter, melted

1 egg

1/3 cup (80ml) milk

CHOCOLATE BUTTER CREAM

70g butter, softened

1 tablespoon milk

3/4 cup (120g) icing sugar

2 tablespoons cocoa powder

1 Preheat oven to 160°C/140°C fan-forced. Grease 6-hole texas (3/4-cup/180ml) muffin pan.

2 Sift sugar, cocoa and flours into medium bowl; stir in coconut, butter and combined egg and milk. Divide mixture among pan holes.

3 Bake cakes about 35 minutes. Stand 5 minutes; turn, top-side up, onto wire rack to cool.

4 Make chocolate butter cream; spread over cold cakes.

CHOCOLATE BUTTER CREAM Beat butter, milk and sifted dry ingredients in small bowl with electric mixer until light and fluffy.

1 CARAMEL MUD CAKE 2 CHOCOLATE COCONUT CAKES
3 MINI CHOCOLATE HAZELNUT CAKES [P 48] 4 BOILED RAISIN CHOCOLATE CAKE [P 48]

Try this recipe using either ground almonds, walnuts or pecans in place of the hazelnut meal. Change the liqueur to match the nut — Grand Marnier is good.

Mini chocolate hazelnut cakes

PREPARATION TIME 35 MINUTES **COOKING TIME** 25 MINUTES (PLUS STANDING TIME) **MAKES** 12

100g dark eating chocolate, chopped coarsely

¾ cup (180ml) water

100g butter, softened

1 cup (220g) firmly packed brown sugar

3 eggs

¼ cup (25g) cocoa powder

¾ cup (110g) self-raising flour

⅓ cup (35g) hazelnut meal

WHIPPED HAZELNUT GANACHE

⅓ cup (80ml) cream

180g milk eating chocolate, chopped finely

2 tablespoons hazelnut-flavoured liqueur

1 Preheat oven to 180°C/160°C fan-forced. Grease 12 x ½-cup (125ml) oval friand pans.

2 Make whipped hazelnut ganache.

3 Meanwhile, combine chocolate and the water in medium saucepan; stir over low heat until smooth.

4 Beat butter and sugar in small bowl with electric mixer until light and fluffy. Beat in eggs, one at a time (mixture might separate at this stage, but will come together later). Transfer mixture to medium bowl; stir in sifted cocoa and flour, hazelnut meal and warm chocolate mixture.

5 Divide mixture among pans; bake about 20 minutes. Stand cakes 5 minutes; turn, top-side up, onto wire rack to cool. Spread ganache over cakes.

WHIPPED HAZELNUT GANACHE Stir cream and chocolate in small saucepan over low heat until smooth. Stir in liqueur; transfer mixture to small bowl. Cover; stand about 2 hours or until just firm. Beat ganache in small bowl with electric mixer until mixture changes to a pale brown colour.

A bundt pan is a heavily decorated ring pan. You can buy them from cookware shops. Make sure you grease the pan well; we prefer to use butter. If you don't have a bundt pan, the cake mixture can be made in two 20cm ring or baba pans. Each will take about 40 minutes to cook.

Boiled raisin chocolate cake

PREPARATION TIME 20 MINUTES

COOKING TIME 1 HOUR 20 MINUTES (PLUS COOLING AND STANDING TIME) **SERVES** 12

2 cups (300g) raisins

2 cups (500ml) water

1 teaspoon bicarbonate of soda

⅓ cup (35g) cocoa powder

2 teaspoons ground cinnamon

½ teaspoon ground clove

1 teaspoon vanilla extract

250g butter, softened

1½ cups (330g) caster sugar

4 eggs

1½ cups (225g) plain flour

1 cup (150g) self-raising flour

CHOCOLATE GLAZE

200g dark eating chocolate, chopped coarsely

100g butter, chopped

1 Preheat oven to 180°C/160°C fan-forced. Grease 24cm bundt pan well.

2 Place raisins and the water in medium saucepan; bring to the boil. Reduce heat; simmer, uncovered, 10 minutes. Remove from heat; stir in sifted soda and cocoa, spices and extract. Cool to room temperature.

3 Beat butter and sugar in medium bowl with electric mixer until light and fluffy. Beat in eggs, one at a time. Stir in sifted flours and raisin mixture, in two batches. Spread mixture into pan.

4 Bake cake about 1 hour 10 minutes. Stand cake in pan 5 minutes; turn onto wire rack to cool.

5 Make chocolate glaze. Pour glaze over cake; stand 30 minutes before serving.

CHOCOLATE GLAZE Stir ingredients in medium heatproof bowl over medium saucepan of simmering water until smooth.

Microwave chocolate hazelnut cake

PREPARATION TIME 15 MINUTES **COOKING TIME** 15 MINUTES **SERVES** 8

125g butter, chopped

1 cup (220g) caster sugar

1 cup (250ml) water

1 cup (150g) self-raising flour

⅓ cup (35g) cocoa powder

½ teaspoon bicarbonate of soda

½ cup (55g) hazelnut meal

2 eggs

1 teaspoon vanilla extract

¼ cup (35g) roasted hazelnuts, chopped coarsely

CHOCOLATE GANACHE

250g dark eating chocolate, chopped coarsely

¾ cup (180ml) cream

It's all about timing with cakes cooked in the microwave oven. All ovens are slightly different, you simply have to watch the cake carefully during cooking — it will overcook in a flash.

1 Grease 21cm microwave-safe ring pan; line base with baking paper.

2 Combine butter, sugar and the water in large microwave-safe bowl; heat, uncovered, on HIGH (100%) about 4 minutes, stirring once. Cool.

3 Whisk sifted flour, cocoa and soda into butter mixture, then hazelnut meal. Whisk in eggs and extract. Pour mixture into pan; place on a microwave-safe rack in microwave oven.

4 Cook cake, uncovered, on MEDIUM-HIGH (70-80%) about 10 minutes or until almost cooked in the centre. Stand cake in pan 5 minutes; turn onto wire rack to cool.

5 Make chocolate ganache; spread ganache all over cake and sprinkle with nuts.

CHOCOLATE GANACHE Combine chocolate and cream in medium microwave-safe bowl; cook, uncovered, on HIGH (100%) for 1½ minutes. Stir until mixture is smooth. Refrigerate, stirring occasionally, until spreadable.

Sticky chocolate date cake

PREPARATION TIME 15 MINUTES (PLUS STANDING TIME) **COOKING TIME** 1 HOUR **SERVES** 10

1⅓ cups (200g) coarsely chopped dried dates

1¾ cups (430ml) water

1 teaspoon bicarbonate of soda

80g butter, softened

⅔ cup (150g) caster sugar

2 eggs

1 cup (150g) self-raising flour

⅓ cup (35g) cocoa powder

⅔ cup (70g) roasted pecans, chopped

BUTTERSCOTCH SAUCE

1¼ cups (280g) firmly packed brown sugar

80g butter

300ml cream

1 Preheat oven to 180°C/160°C fan-forced. Grease deep 22cm-round cake pan; line base with baking paper.

2 Combine dates and the water in small saucepan; bring to the boil. Remove from heat, add soda; cover, stand 5 minutes. Blend or process until smooth.

3 Beat butter and sugar in small bowl with electric mixer until combined. Beat in eggs, one at a time (mixture will curdle at this stage). Transfer mixture to large bowl; stir in sifted flour and cocoa, then stir in nuts and warm date mixture, in two batches. Pour mixture into pan.

4 Bake cake about 1 hour. Stand cake in pan 10 minutes; turn onto serving plate.

5 Make butterscotch sauce; serve hot sauce with cake and whipped cream, if desired.

BUTTERSCOTCH SAUCE Stir ingredients in saucepan over heat, without boiling, until sugar dissolves. Simmer, without stirring, 3 minutes.

The chocoholic's chocolate cake

PREPARATION TIME 35 MINUTES

COOKING TIME 2 HOURS (PLUS COOLING, STANDING AND REFRIGERATION TIME) **SERVES** 16

Your reputation as a cake-maker will reach giddy heights when you show off this cake. The stars are incredibly simple to make and look really effective.

250g butter, chopped

1 tablespoon instant coffee granules

1 ½ cups (375ml) water

2 cups (440g) caster sugar

1 teaspoon vanilla extract

100g dark eating chocolate, chopped coarsely

2 eggs

1 ½ cups (225g) self-raising flour

1 cup (150g) plain flour

¼ cup (25g) cocoa powder

180g white eating chocolate, melted

2 x 45g packets Maltesers

CHOCOLATE GANACHE

100g dark eating chocolate, chopped coarsely

⅓ cup (80ml) cream

1 Preheat oven to 150°C/130°C fan-forced. Grease deep 19cm-square cake pan; line base and sides with baking paper.

2 Heat butter, coffee, the water, sugar, extract and dark chocolate in large saucepan, stirring until smooth. Transfer mixture to large bowl; cool 20 minutes. Stir in eggs and sifted dry ingredients, in two batches. Pour mixture into pan.

3 Bake cake about 1 hour 50 minutes. Stand cake in pan 15 minutes; turn, top-side up, onto wire rack to cool.

4 Meanwhile, make chocolate ganache.

5 Spread white chocolate into 15cm x 20cm rectangle onto baking paper; stand until just set. Using 3cm- and 5cm-star cutter, cut as many stars as possible from chocolate. Stand about 30 minutes or until firm.

6 Spread cake with ganache; decorate with stars and Maltesers.

CHOCOLATE GANACHE Stir ingredients in small saucepan over low heat until smooth. Cover; refrigerate 1 hour or until spreadable.

Sacher torte

PREPARATION TIME 30 MINUTES (PLUS STANDING TIME)

COOKING TIME 40 MINUTES (PLUS COOLING TIME) **SERVES** 12

150g dark eating chocolate, chopped

1 tablespoon water

150g butter, softened

½ cup (110g) caster sugar

3 eggs, separated

1 cup (150g) plain flour

2 tablespoons caster sugar, extra

1 cup (320g) apricot jam

CHOCOLATE ICING

125g dark eating chocolate, chopped coarsely

125g butter, chopped coarsely

1 Preheat oven to 180°C/160°C fan-forced. Grease deep 22cm-round cake pan; line base with baking paper.

2 Stir chocolate in small heatproof bowl over small saucepan of simmering water until melted. Stir in the water; cool.

3 Beat butter and sugar in small bowl with electric mixer until light and fluffy. Beat in egg yolks, one at a time. Transfer mixture to large bowl; stir in chocolate mixture, then sifted flour.

4 Beat egg whites in small bowl with electric mixer until soft peaks form. Gradually add extra sugar, beating until dissolved between additions; fold into chocolate mixture, in two batches. Spread mixture into pan.

5 Bake cake about 30 minutes. Stand cake in pan 5 minutes; turn, upside-down, onto wire rack to cool.

6 Split cake in half; place half, cut-side up, on serving plate. Heat and strain jam; brush half of the jam over cake. Top with remaining cake, brush cake all over with remaining jam. Stand 1 hour at room temperature to allow jam to set.

7 Make chocolate icing; spread all over cake, set at room temperature.

CHOCOLATE ICING Stir ingredients in small heatproof bowl over small saucepan simmering water until smooth. Cool at room temperature, stirring occasionally, until spreadable.

Chocolate butterscotch cake

PREPARATION TIME 20 MINUTES (PLUS REFRIGERATION TIME) **COOKING TIME** 1 HOUR **SERVES** 10

¼ cup (25g) cocoa powder

1¼ cups (185g) self-raising flour

250g butter, softened

1 cup (200g) firmly packed dark brown sugar

2 eggs

1 tablespoon golden syrup

½ cup (125ml) milk

MASCARPONE CREAM

250g mascarpone cheese

300ml thickened cream

CARAMEL ICING

60g butter

½ cup (100g) firmly packed dark brown sugar

¼ cup (60ml) milk

1½ cups (240g) icing sugar

1 Preheat oven to 180°C/160°C fan-forced. Grease deep 20cm-round cake pan; line base and side with baking paper.

2 Sift cocoa and flour into large bowl; add remaining ingredients. Beat with electric mixer on low speed until combined. Increase speed to medium; beat until mixture has changed to a paler colour. Pour mixture into pan.

3 Bake cake about 1 hour. Stand cake in pan 10 minutes; turn, top-side up, onto wire rack to cool.

4 Make mascarpone cream. Make caramel icing.

5 Split cake into three layers. Centre one layer on serving plate; spread with one-third of the mascarpone cream and one-third of the caramel icing. Repeat with second layer and half of the remaining mascarpone cream and half of the remaining icing; top with remaining cake layer. Cover top cake layer with remaining mascarpone cream then drizzle with remaining icing. Swirl for marbled effect; refrigerate 30 minutes or until icing is firm.

MASCARPONE CREAM Whisk ingredients in small bowl until soft peaks form.

CARAMEL ICING Heat butter, brown sugar and milk in small saucepan, stirring constantly, without boiling, until sugar dissolves; remove from heat. Stir in sifted icing sugar.

Upside-down chocolate caramel nut cake

PREPARATION TIME 15 MINUTES **COOKING TIME** 1 HOUR 20 MINUTES **SERVES** 10

2 tablespoons finely chopped, roasted macadamias

2 tablespoons finely chopped, roasted pistachios

2 tablespoons finely chopped, roasted walnuts

125g butter, softened

1 cup (220g) firmly packed brown sugar

3 eggs

1 cup (150g) self-raising flour

¼ cup (35g) plain flour

¼ teaspoon bicarbonate of soda

⅓ cup (35g) cocoa powder

100g dark eating chocolate, melted

¾ cup (180ml) milk

CARAMEL TOPPING

40g butter

¼ cup (55g) brown sugar

2 tablespoons cream

It's important to let the cake and its topping settle before turning it out of the pan. Serve the cake warm as a dessert, maybe with some cream or ice-cream.

1 Preheat oven to 160°C/140°C fan-forced. Grease deep 20cm-round cake pan; line base with baking paper.

2 Make caramel topping; pour hot topping over base of pan, sprinkle with combined nuts. Freeze while preparing cake mixture.

3 Beat butter and sugar in small bowl with electric mixer until light and fluffy. Beat in eggs, one at a time. Transfer mixture to large bowl; stir in sifted flours, soda and cocoa, then chocolate and milk. Spread cake mixture over caramel in pan.

4 Bake about 1 hour 10 minutes. Stand cake 15 minutes; turn onto wire rack to cool.

CARAMEL TOPPING Stir ingredients in small saucepan over low heat, without boiling, until sugar dissolves. Bring to the boil; remove from heat.

Caramel choc-chip mud cakes

PREPARATION TIME 10 MINUTES (PLUS COOLING TIME) **COOKING TIME** 25 MINUTES **MAKES** 9

90g white eating chocolate, chopped coarsely

90g unsalted butter, chopped coarsely

½ cup (110g) firmly packed brown sugar

2 tablespoons golden syrup

½ cup (125ml) milk

¾ cup (110g) plain flour

¼ cup (35g) self-raising flour

1 egg

2 tablespoons milk Choc Bits

2 teaspoons icing sugar

1 Preheat oven to 160°C/140°C fan-forced. Grease 9-hole (⅓-cup/80ml) friand pan; line bases of holes with baking paper.

2 Stir chocolate, butter, brown sugar, syrup and milk in medium saucepan over low heat until smooth. Cool 15 minutes.

3 Whisk sifted flours and egg into chocolate mixture; stir in Choc Bits. Divide mixture among pan holes.

4 Bake cakes about 25 minutes. Stand cakes in pan 5 minutes; turn, top-side up, onto wire rack to cool. Serve dusted with sifted icing sugar.

Milk chocolate beetroot cake

PREPARATION TIME 20 MINUTES **COOKING TIME** 40 MINUTES **SERVES** 16

Beetroot, like carrots, are quite high in natural sugars, so are a natural ingredient for cakes. The beetroot softens a little, but will hold its shape and colour during baking.

250g butter, softened

1 cup (220g) caster sugar

4 eggs

1 cup (150g) plain flour

1 cup (150g) self-raising flour

¼ cup (25g) cocoa powder

100g milk eating chocolate, chopped coarsely

3 small fresh beetroot (300g), peeled, grated coarsely

FLUFFY CHOCOLATE GANACHE

200g dark eating chocolate, chopped coarsely

½ cup (125ml) thickened cream

1 Preheat oven to 170°C/150°C fan-forced. Grease 20cm x 30cm lamington pan; line with baking paper, extending paper 5cm over long sides.

2 Beat butter and sugar in small bowl with electric mixer until light and fluffy. Beat in eggs, one at a time. Transfer mixture to medium bowl; stir in sifted flours and cocoa, then chocolate and beetroot. Spread mixture into pan.

3 Bake cake about 40 minutes. Stand cake in pan 5 minutes; turn, top-side up, onto wire rack to cool.

4 Make fluffy chocolate icing; spread over cake.

FLUFFY CHOCOLATE GANACHE Stir ingredients in small heatproof bowl over small saucepan of simmering water until smooth. Cool. Refrigerate until spreadable.

Chocolate, apricot and hazelnut cake

PREPARATION TIME 30 MINUTES (PLUS COOLING AND REFRIGERATION TIME)

COOKING TIME 2 HOURS **SERVES** 12

1⅔ cups (250g) dried apricots, chopped finely

½ cup (125ml) water

250g butter, softened

2 cups (440g) firmly packed brown sugar

6 eggs

1 cup (150g) plain flour

½ cup (75g) self-raising flour

¼ cup (25g) cocoa powder

1 cup (110g) hazelnut meal

⅔ cup (160ml) buttermilk

CHOCOLATE BUTTERMILK CREAM

300g milk eating chocolate, chopped coarsely

½ cup (125ml) buttermilk

1 cup (160g) icing sugar

1 Combine apricots and the water in small saucepan; bring to the boil. Reduce heat; simmer, covered, about 10 minutes or until apricots are soft. Cool.

2 Preheat oven to 180°C/160°C fan-forced. Grease deep 22cm-round cake pan; line base with baking paper.

3 Beat butter and sugar in small bowl with electric mixer until light and fluffy. Beat in eggs, one at a time. Transfer mixture to large bowl; stir in apricot mixture, sifted flours and cocoa, hazelnut meal and buttermilk, in two batches. Spread mixture into pan.

4 Bake cake about 1 hour 50 minutes. Stand cake in pan 10 minutes; turn, top-side up, onto wire rack to cool.

5 Meanwhile, make chocolate buttermilk cream.

6 Split cake into three layers; sandwich layers with two-thirds of the chocolate buttermilk cream. Spread cake with remaining chocolate buttermilk cream. Top with dark chocolate curls, if desired.

CHOCOLATE BUTTERMILK CREAM Stir chocolate and buttermilk in small heatproof bowl over small saucepan of simmering water until smooth. Gradually stir in sifted icing sugar. Refrigerate mixture, stirring occasionally, about 30 minutes or until spreadable.

You can buy dried apricots already chopped from the supermarket, otherwise, use scissors for chopping them. Buttermilk gives both the cake and the cream a velvety texture, and takes the edge off the richness and sweetness of both too.

BUTTER CAKES

Butter Cakes

In the days before electric mixers, making a cake was a laborious task indeed. What is now the simple process of beating butter, adding in sugar and beating eggs to introduce enough air to create a light, melt-in-the-mouth texture was a daunting task when the only kitchen aids were a bowl, a wooden spoon and plenty of elbow grease. Early cooking manuals sing the praises of the cook who could beat eggs for an hour without tiring while another recommends that the butter and sugar business is best done by a manservant.

Many cooks believe the butter or pound cake to be the mother of all cakes and indeed it has been around so long and spawned so many variations that it deserves the title. The term pound cake comes from the balance of major ingredients — a pound of each. The French version is called *quatre quarts* (four quarters) because it contains equal weights of the major ingredients: eggs, butter, flour and sugar. Other variations include fruit with the addition of dried mixed fruit, currants or sultanas; orange or lemon in which rind and juice are added instead of the milk and vanilla; chocolate, which incorporates grated chocolate; seed, in which the traditional poppy and caraway seeds are added; and marble, in which portions of the mixture are coloured and blended to give a swirly multi-coloured effect.

Most butter cakes begin with the creaming process in which the butter is beaten until it is light and creamy. This is best achieved with a hand-held or benchtop electric mixer — a food processor simply won't aerate the mixture sufficiently. Rinse the bowl and beaters under hot water before mixing ingredients; dry thoroughly. Have all ingredients at room temperature and use either regular table (salted) butter or unsalted butter.

Beat the butter first with any flavouring such as fruit rinds or extracts and essences that are included in the recipe. The fat in the butter will absorb the flavour and give the fullest flavour to the baked cake. The butter should be beaten until it is as light in colour as possible. Add the sugar, beat until the mixture is light and fluffy in appearance; the sugar should not be completely dissolved in the butter.

Add unbeaten eggs one at a time and beat each egg into the mixture before adding the next. If the eggs are added too quickly or if they are cold, the mixture can curdle. This will also happen if the eggs are too large or added too slowly. Excessive beating will break the fat down, causing curdling. We use 60g eggs in all our recipes. In any case, the world is not going to stop revolving if the mixture does curdle; it generally reconstitutes when you add the dry ingredients. At worst, it may cause the baked cake to crumble a little.

If you have been using a small bowl for mixing, transfer the mixture to a larger bowl before adding the dry ingredients. Add about half the sifted dry ingredients, then half the liquid and mix the ingredients together lightly. Add the remaining dry ingredients and liquid and mix lightly once again. At this stage the mixture will look coarse in texture; give a quick beating to make the texture finer and smoother.

Sifted dry ingredients and liquid can be added using the electric mixer, but it must be done carefully; there is a tendency to overmix which will toughen the mixture. Add half the sifted dry ingredients and half the liquid to the creamed mixture, turn the mixer to the lowest speed, beat only until the ingredients are combined; scrape the mixture down from the side of the bowl. Turn the mixer off, add the remaining dry ingredients and liquid, carefully mix and scrape again. Then increase the speed a little and beat for about 30 seconds or until the mixture is smooth. See also *Butter cake basics* on pages 74 & 75.

TROUBLE SHOOTING

- If the cake sinks in the centre after baking it probably means that it is undercooked. Check the cake just after the suggested baking time; it should be brown and starting to shrink from the side(s) of the pan. Feel the top with your fingertips; it should feel firm. You may want to insert a thin skewer into the deepest part of the cake from the top to the base (we prefer to use a metal skewer rather than wooden as any mixture adhering to it is easier to see). As the skewer is removed, it shouldn't have any uncooked mixture adhering to it.
- If the cake sinks in the centre while still baking, it could be that the oven is too hot and the mixture has been forced to rise too quickly then fall.
- If it has a sugary crust, the butter and sugar have not been beaten sufficiently or there is too much sugar in the recipe.
- White specks on top indicate undissolved sugar. In a light butter cake it is better to use caster sugar, which dissolves easily during baking.
- Excessive shrinking indicates that the cake has been baked at too high a temperature for too long.
- If the cake sticks to the pan, it may be because there is too much sugar or sweetening in the recipe. If a recipe contains honey or golden syrup, or if you're using a new pan, it is wise to line the evenly greased pan with baking paper.
- If the cake rises and cracks in the centre, it could be because the cake pan is too small for the amount of mixture; most cakes baked in loaf, bar or ring pans crack slightly due to the confined space of the pan.
- A collar around the top outside edge of the cake suggests the cake was baked at too high a temperature.
- If the cake is pale on top, this can be caused by too large a pan or having the lining paper too far up the sides of the pan.
- If there are coloured streaks on top, this indicates that the ingredients have not been mixed together enough. Bowl scrapings should be mixed thoroughly into the cake mixture.
- Uneven rising suggests that the mixture has not been spread evenly into the pan. Or that the oven shelf has not been set straight or the oven is not level on the floor.
- Holes in a baked cake occur when the butter, sugar and egg mixture is not beaten sufficiently or the oven is too hot.

Marmalade polenta cake

PREPARATION TIME 20 MINUTES **COOKING TIME** 1 HOUR 45 MINUTES (PLUS STANDING TIME) **SERVES** 10

You can serve this cake
warm with a dollop of
lemon- or orange-flavoured
mascarpone: whisk
together 1 cup (250g)
mascarpone cheese,
2 teaspoons finely grated
lemon or orange rind,
1 tablespoon lemon or
orange juice and about
2 tablespoons sifted icing
sugar in a small bowl until
smooth. Taste the mixture
to see if it needs a bit
more sugar. Be careful
with mascarpone, don't
overbeat it, or it will curdle.
A serrated knife will help
you to cut through the rinds
of the citrus fruit.

¾ cup (165g) caster sugar

1¼ cups (310ml) water

1 medium unpeeled orange (240g), sliced thinly

1 large unpeeled lemon (180g), sliced thinly

¼ cup (60ml) water, extra

125g butter, softened

1 tablespoon finely grated lemon rind

1 cup (220g) caster sugar, extra

3 eggs

½ cup (60g) almond meal

½ cup (75g) plain flour

½ cup (75g) self-raising flour

¾ cup (120g) polenta

⅓ cup (80g) sour cream

¼ cup (60ml) lemon juice

1 Preheat oven to 180°C/160°C fan-forced. Grease deep 20cm-round cake pan; line base and side with baking paper.

2 Stir sugar and the water in large frying pan over heat, without boiling, until sugar dissolves; bring to the boil. Reduce heat; simmer, without stirring, uncovered, about 5 minutes or until syrup thickens slightly. Add orange and lemon slices; simmer gently, uncovered, 7 minutes or until rind is tender, turning slices halfway through cooking time.

3 Remove syrup mixture from heat. Carefully lift alternate orange and lemon slices directly from syrup to cover base and side of pan. Reserve syrup.

4 Return reserved syrup to heat, add the extra water; bring to the boil. Reduce heat; simmer, uncovered, without stirring, about 5 minutes or until syrup is a light honey colour. Pour hot syrup over orange and lemon slices in cake pan.

5 Beat butter, rind and extra sugar in small bowl with electric mixer until light and fluffy. Beat in eggs, one at a time. Transfer mixture to large bowl; stir in almond meal, sifted flours, polenta, sour cream and juice. Spread mixture into pan.

6 Bake cake about 1¼ hours. Stand cake in pan 15 minutes; turn onto serving plate, serve at room temperature.

Orange cake

PREPARATION TIME 10 MINUTES **COOKING TIME** 40 MINUTES **SERVES** 10

150g butter, softened

1 tablespoon finely grated orange rind

⅔ cup (150g) caster sugar

3 eggs

1 ½ cups (225g) self-raising flour

¼ cup (60ml) milk

¾ cup (120g) icing sugar

1 ½ tablespoons orange juice

1 Preheat oven to 180°C/160°C fan-forced. Grease deep 20cm-round cake pan.

2 Beat butter, rind, caster sugar, eggs, flour and milk in medium bowl with electric mixer at low speed until combined. Increase speed to medium, beat about 3 minutes or until mixture is smooth and changed to a paler colour. Spread mixture into pan.

3 Bake cake about 40 minutes. Stand cake in pan 5 minutes; turn, top-side up, onto wire rack to cool.

4 Combine sifted icing sugar and juice in small bowl; spread over cake.

Passionfruit buttermilk cake

PREPARATION TIME 20 MINUTES **COOKING TIME** 45 MINUTES (PLUS COOLING TIME) **SERVES** 12

250g butter, softened

1 cup (220g) caster sugar

3 eggs, separated

2 cups (300g) self-raising flour

¾ cup (180ml) buttermilk

¼ cup (60ml) passionfruit pulp

PASSIONFRUIT ICING

1 ½ cups (240g) icing sugar

¼ cup (60ml) passionfruit pulp

1 Preheat oven to 180°C/160°C fan-forced. Grease and lightly flour 24cm bundt pan; tap out excess flour.

2 Beat butter and sugar in small bowl with electric mixer until light and fluffy. Beat in egg yolks, one at a time. Transfer mixture to large bowl; stir in sifted flour, buttermilk and passionfruit, in two batches.

3 Beat egg whites in small bowl with electric mixer until soft peaks form. Fold into cake mixture in two batches. Spread mixture into pan.

4 Bake cake about 40 minutes. Stand cake in pan 5 minutes; turn onto wire rack to cool.

5 Make passionfruit icing; drizzle over cake.

PASSIONFRUIT ICING Sift icing sugar into heatproof bowl; stir in enough passionfruit to form a firm paste. Stand bowl over small saucepan of simmering water, stir until icing is a pouring consistency.

Mixed nut cake

PREPARATION TIME 25 MINUTES **COOKING TIME** 1 HOUR 15 MINUTES **SERVES** 12

125g butter, softened

1 teaspoon finely grated lemon rind

1¼ cups (275g) caster sugar

3 eggs

½ cup (75g) self-raising flour

1 cup (150g) plain flour

¼ teaspoon bicarbonate of soda

½ cup (125ml) milk

1 tablespoon lemon juice

2 tablespoons finely chopped pistachios

2 tablespoons finely chopped walnuts

2 tablespoons finely chopped slivered almonds

2 teaspoons icing sugar

NUT TOPPING

2 tablespoons coarsely chopped pistachios

2 tablespoons coarsely chopped walnuts

2 tablespoons slivered almonds

There is a mixture of nuts in this cake as well as on top of it. The nut topping is added prior to cooking so that it's finished after the cake is cooked and cooled.

1 Preheat oven to 180°C/160°C fan-forced. Grease deep 22cm-round cake pan; line base and side with baking paper.

2 Make nut topping.

3 Beat butter, rind and caster sugar in small bowl with electric mixer until light and fluffy. Beat in eggs, one at a time. Transfer mixture to large bowl; stir in sifted dry ingredients and milk, in two batches. Stir in juice and nuts. Spoon mixture into pan, level surface of cake mixture with wet metal spatula; sprinkle with nut topping.

4 Bake cake about 30 minutes. Cover loosely with foil; bake further 45 minutes. Stand cake in pan 5 minutes; turn onto wire rack, top-side up, to cool.

5 Dust cake with sifted icing sugar.

NUT TOPPING Combine ingredients in small bowl.

1 2

3 4

Cut-and-keep butter cake

PREPARATION TIME 15 MINUTES **COOKING TIME** 1 HOUR 15 MINUTES (PLUS COOLING TIME) **SERVES** 10

125g butter, softened

1 teaspoon vanilla extract

1¼ cups (275g) caster sugar

3 eggs

1 cup (150g) plain flour

½ cup (75g) self-raising flour

¼ teaspoon bicarbonate of soda

½ cup (125ml) milk

1 Preheat oven to 160°C/140°C fan-forced. Grease deep 20cm-round cake pan; line base with baking paper.

2 Beat ingredients in medium bowl on low speed with electric mixer until combined. Increase speed to medium; beat until mixture is smooth and changed to a paler colour. Spread mixture into pan.

3 Bake cake about 1¼ hours. Stand cake in pan 5 minutes; turn, top-side up, onto wire rack to cool. Serve dusted with sifted icing sugar, if desired.

We like this cake baked in a slab or lamington pan too. It will take about 40 minutes to cook. Spread it with a simple glacé icing (see page 220) and sprinkle it with hundreds and thousands before the icing sets. It will be a big hit with the kids. Try substituting the caster sugar with brown sugar for a light caramel flavour.

Lemon cake

PREPARATION TIME 20 MINUTES **COOKING TIME** 1 HOUR **SERVES** 10

125g butter, softened

2 teaspoons finely grated lemon rind

1¼ cups (275g) caster sugar

3 eggs

1½ cups (225g) self-raising flour

½ cup (125ml) milk

¼ cup (60ml) lemon juice

LEMON MASCARPONE FROSTING

300ml thickened cream

½ cup icing sugar

2 teaspoons finely grated lemon rind

150g mascarpone cheese

1 Preheat oven to 180°C/160°C fan-forced. Grease deep 20cm-round cake pan; line base with baking paper.

2 Make lemon mascarpone frosting. Cover; refrigerate until required.

3 Beat butter, rind and sugar in small bowl with electric mixer until light and fluffy. Beat in eggs, one at a time. Transfer mixture to large bowl; stir in sifted flour, milk and juice, in two batches. Pour mixture into pan.

4 Bake cake about 50 minutes. Stand cake in pan 5 minutes; turn, top-side up, onto wire rack to cool.

5 Split cold cake into three layers, place one layer onto serving plate, cut-side up; spread with one-third of the frosting. Repeat layering process, finishing with frosting.

LEMON MASCARPONE FROSTING Beat cream, sifted icing sugar and rind in small bowl with electric mixer until soft peaks form. Fold cream mixture into mascarpone.

**1 CUT-AND-KEEP BUTTER CAKE 2 LEMON CAKE
3 COCONUT CAKE [P 68] 4 MADEIRA CAKE [P 68]**

Coconut cake

PREPARATION TIME 25 MINUTES **COOKING TIME** 40 MINUTES **SERVES** 16

125g butter, softened
½ teaspoon coconut essence
1 cup (220g) caster sugar
2 eggs
½ cup (40g) desiccated coconut
1 ½ cups (225g) self-raising flour
1 ¼ cups (300g) sour cream
⅓ cup (80ml) milk

COCONUT ICE FROSTING
2 cups (320g) icing sugar
1 ⅓ cups (100g) desiccated coconut
2 egg whites, beaten lightly
pink food colouring

1 Preheat oven to 180°C/160°C fan-forced. Grease deep 23cm-square cake pan; line base and sides with baking paper.
2 Beat butter, essence and sugar in small bowl with electric mixer until light and fluffy. Beat in eggs, one at a time. Transfer mixture to large bowl; stir in coconut, sifted flour, sour cream and milk, in two batches. Spread mixture into pan;
3 Bake cake about 40 minutes. Stand cake in pan 5 minutes; turn, top-side up, onto wire rack to cool.
4 Make coconut ice frosting; drop alternate spoonfuls of white and pink frosting onto cake, marble over top of cake.

COCONUT ICE FROSTING Sift icing sugar into medium bowl; stir in coconut and egg white. Place half the mixture in small bowl; tint with pink colouring.

Madeira cake

PREPARATION TIME 15 MINUTES **COOKING TIME** 1 HOUR **SERVES** 10

185g butter, softened
2 teaspoons finely grated lemon rind
⅔ cup (150g) caster sugar
3 eggs

¾ cup (110g) plain flour
¾ cup (110g) self-raising flour
⅓ cup (55g) mixed peel
¼ cup (35g) slivered almonds

1 Preheat oven to 160°C/140°C fan-forced. Grease deep 20cm-round cake pan; line base with paper.
2 Beat butter, rind and sugar in small bowl with electric mixer until light and fluffy. Beat in eggs, one at a time. Transfer mixture to large bowl; stir in sifted flours. Spread mixture into pan.
3 Bake 20 minutes. Remove cake from oven; sprinkle with peel and nuts. Return to oven; bake about 40 minutes. Stand cake in pan 5 minutes; turn, top-side up, onto wire rack to cool.

Caramel butter cake

PREPARATION TIME 15 MINUTES **COOKING TIME** 50 MINUTES **SERVES** 10

125g butter, softened

1 teaspoon vanilla extract

1 cup (220g) firmly packed brown sugar

2 eggs

1 tablespoon golden syrup

1 cup (150g) plain flour

½ cup (75g) self-raising flour

1 teaspoon ground cinnamon

½ cup (125ml) milk

CARAMEL ICING

1 cup (220g) firmly packed brown sugar

60g butter

2 tablespoons milk

¾ cup (120g) icing sugar

2 teaspoons milk, extra

You could use honey or treacle in place of the syrup if you like. Don't over-measure the syrup — all of our spoon measurements are level.

1 Preheat oven to 180°C/160°C fan-forced. Grease deep 20cm round cake pan; line base with paper.

2 Beat butter, extract and sugar in small bowl with electric mixer until light and fluffy. Beat in eggs, one at a time; beat in golden syrup. Transfer mixture to large bowl; fold in sifted dry ingredients and milk. Pour mixture into pan.

3 Bake cake about 50 minutes. Stand cake in pan 5 minutes; turn, top-side up, onto wire rack to cool.

4 Make caramel icing; spread icing over cold cake before serving.

CARAMEL ICING Stir sugar, butter and milk in small saucepan over heat without boiling until sugar dissolves; bring to the boil. Reduce heat; simmer, uncovered, 3 minutes, without stirring. Remove from heat; stir in sifted icing sugar. Stir in extra milk.

Cardamom almond cake

PREPARATION TIME 15 MINUTES **COOKING TIME** 50 MINUTES **SERVES** 10

185g butter, softened

¾ cup (165g) firmly packed brown sugar

2 eggs

2 cups (300g) self-raising flour

2 teaspoons ground cardamom

¼ cup (30g) almond meal

½ cup (175g) golden syrup

½ cup (125ml) milk

See the warning above about measuring golden syrup (or honey, treacle etc.) — be accurate. Coat the inside of the cup or spoon measure lightly with cooking-oil spray and the syrup will slip out nicely.

1 Preheat oven to 180°C/160°C fan-forced. Grease 20cm baba pan well.

2 Beat butter and sugar in small bowl with electric mixer until light and fluffy. Beat in eggs, one at a time. Transfer to large bowl; stir in sifted flour and cardamom, almond meal and combined syrup and milk, in two batches. Pour mixture into pan.

3 Bake cake about 50 minutes. Stand cake in pan 5 minutes; turn, top-side up, onto wire rack to cool. Serve dusted with sifted icing sugar, if desired.

Pink, green and white also make a pretty marble cake. If this is your preference, delete the cocoa powder and extra milk from this recipe. See page 630 for tips on marbling.

Marble cake

PREPARATION TIME 30 MINUTES (PLUS COOLING TIME) **COOKING TIME** 1 HOUR **SERVES** 12

250g butter, softened

1 teaspoon vanilla extract

1¼ cups (275g) caster sugar

3 eggs

2¼ cups (335g) self-raising flour

¾ cup (180ml) milk

pink food colouring

2 tablespoons cocoa powder

2 tablespoons milk, extra

BUTTER FROSTING

90g butter, softened

1 cup (160g) icing sugar

1 tablespoon milk

1 Preheat oven to 180°C/160°C fan-forced. Grease deep 22cm-round or deep 19cm-square cake pan; line base and side(s) with baking paper.

2 Beat butter, extract and sugar in medium bowl with electric mixer until light and fluffy. Beat in eggs, one at a time. Stir in sifted flour and milk, in two batches.

3 Divide mixture among three bowls; tint one mixture pink. Blend sifted cocoa with extra milk in cup; stir into second mixture. Drop alternate spoonfuls of mixtures into pan. Pull a skewer backwards and forwards through cake mixture.

4 Bake cake about 1 hour. Stand cake 5 minutes; turn, top-side up, onto wire rack to cool.

5 Make butter frosting; spread over top of cake.

BUTTER FROSTING Beat butter in small bowl with electric mixer until light and fluffy; beat in sifted icing sugar and milk, in two batches. Tint frosting pink with colouring.

This is a good old stand-by recipe which is ideal for patty cakes too.

Basic butter cake

PREPARATION TIME 30 MINUTES **COOKING TIME** 1 HOUR **SERVES** 12

250g butter, softened

1 teaspoon vanilla extract

1¼ cups (275g) caster sugar

3 eggs

2¼ cups (335g) self-raising flour

¾ cup (180ml) milk

1 Preheat oven to 180°C/160°C fan-forced. Grease deep 22cm-round or deep 19cm-square cake pan; line base and side(s) with baking paper.

2 Beat butter, extract and sugar in medium bowl with electric mixer until light and fluffy. Beat in eggs, one at a time. Stir in sifted flour and milk, in two batches.

3 Spread mixture into pan; bake about 1 hour. Stand cake in pan 5 minutes; turn, top-side up, onto wire rack to cool.

MARBLE CAKE

Caramelised apple butter cake

PREPARATION TIME 20 MINUTES **COOKING TIME** 1 HOUR **SERVES** 10

2 medium apples (300g)
80g butter
¾ cup (165g) firmly packed
brown sugar
125g butter, softened, extra
⅔ cup (150g) caster sugar
1 teaspoon vanilla extract

2 eggs
1 cup (150g) self-raising flour
⅔ cup (100g) plain flour
½ teaspoon bicarbonate of soda
1 cup (250ml) buttermilk
¾ cup (180ml) cream

1 Preheat oven to 180°C/160°C fan-forced. Grease 20cm bundt pan well.
2 Peel, core and quarter apples; slice thinly. Melt butter in large frying pan; cook apple about 5 minutes or until browned lightly. Add brown sugar; cook, stirring, about 5 minutes or until mixture thickens slightly. Strain apples over medium bowl. Reserve apples and cooking liquid.
3 Beat extra butter, caster sugar and extract in small bowl with electric mixer until light and fluffy. Beat in eggs, one at a time; transfer mixture to large bowl. Stir in sifted dry ingredients and buttermilk, in two batches.
4 Spread two-thirds of the mixture into pan. Top with apples, leaving a 2cm border around the edge; cover with remaining mixture. Bake about 50 minutes. Stand cake in pan 5 minutes; turn, top-side up, onto wire rack to cool.
5 Meanwhile, return reserved apple liquid to large frying pan, add cream; bring to the boil. Reduce heat; simmer, uncovered, about 15 minutes or until sauce thickens.
6 Serve warm cake with caramel sauce.

A 20cm ring or baba pan can be used instead of a bundt pan. Most types of apples are fine to use, but granny smith and golden delicious are definitely the best for cooking.

Cinnamon teacake

PREPARATION TIME 15 MINUTES **COOKING TIME** 30 MINUTES **SERVES** 8

60g butter, softened
1 teaspoon vanilla extract
⅔ cup (150g) caster sugar
1 egg
1 cup (150g) self-raising flour

⅓ cup (80ml) milk
10g butter, extra, melted
1 teaspoon ground cinnamon
1 tablespoon caster sugar, extra

1 Preheat oven to 180°C/160°C fan-forced. Grease deep 20cm-round cake pan; line base with baking paper.
2 Beat butter, extract, sugar and egg in small bowl with electric mixer until light and fluffy. Stir in sifted flour and milk. Spread mixture into pan.
3 Bake cake about 30 minutes. Stand cake in pan 5 minutes; turn, top-side up, onto wire rack. Brush top of cake with melted butter, sprinkle with combined cinnamon and extra sugar.

The secret to making a perfect cinnamon teacake is to beat the butter, sugar and egg mixture in a small bowl until it's as light and white as possible.

CARAMELISED APPLE BUTTER CAKE

Butter cake basics

Most cakes made in a home kitchen are butter cakes of some sort. These finer points will make them perfect every time.

SOFTENING BUTTER
Butter should be soft, not melted. Have butter at room temperature. Chop it coarsely into an appropriate-sized bowl. If the kitchen is cold, stand bowl in warm water for a while.

GRATING BUTTER
If you forget to take the butter out of the fridge, grate it into an appropriate-sized mixing bowl, using the coarsest side of the grater. If you heat the grater under hot water, then dry it well, the butter will slip off the grater easily.

ADDING FLAVOURING
If recipes call for grated citrus rind, essence or extract, beat the flavouring with the butter. The butter will "hold" the flavouring from the mixing stage right through to eating the cake.

ADDING EGGS
The eggs should be at room temperature. Beat the first egg into the butter/sugar mixture only until it is absorbed. Beat in the remaining eggs, one at a time, and only until they are absorbed, over-beating will cause curdling. Some mixtures have more egg content than the butter/sugar mixture can absorb, these mixtures will curdle.

MIXING
It's usually best to transfer the butter/sugar/egg mixture to a larger bowl to make it easier and more efficient to mix in the remaining ingredients. If you're making a small cake, then, often, the small bowl will be large enough to mix in the remaining ingredients. We will advise you what to do in our recipes.

SIFTING DRY INGREDIENTS
Mostly we sift half the dry ingredients over the butter/sugar/egg mixture in the larger mixing bowl, then add half the liquid. Once again, if you're making a small cake, then we might advise you to add all the dry ingredients and liquid at once. For some really large mixtures, we might advise you to add the ingredients in even more than two batches.

BEATING BUTTER

The most thorough way of making a butter cake, is to beat the butter (and flavouring), until it is paler in colour. The bowl needs to be of a size that will let the beaters work in the butter.

ADDING SUGAR

Once the butter is creamy, add all the sugar to the mixing bowl. Caster sugar is finer than regular white crystal sugar, and will give a finer-textured cake, but one can be substituted for the other. Beat until light and fluffy.

BUTTER/SUGAR MIXTURE

This is what the mixture should look like before you start adding the egg(s) — light in colour, creamy in texture. Don't dissolve the sugar grains in the butter, this breaks the mixture down too much.

MIXING

Usually a wooden spoon is the best utensil for mixing butter cakes at this stage. There is no need to beat the mixture now, just stir the wet and dry ingredients together until everything is evenly mixed. You can do this mixing stage with an electric mixer, but do it on a low speed, and only until the ingredients are mixed, over-beating will toughen the cake.

ADDING FINAL INGREDIENTS

Sift the rest of the dry ingredients over the mixture, add the liquid, stir the ingredients together, until they're evenly mixed. You'll see that the mixture looks a bit lumpy and coarse, so give it a beating until it noticeably changes from a coarse to a finer texture. This can be done with an electric mixer, but you do have to be careful to avoid over-beating.

GETTING READY TO BAKE

Dollop spoonfuls of the mixture into the prepared pan, spread the mixture out evenly to the side(s) of the pan. Tap the pan firmly on the bench to break any large air bubbles, then smooth the surface of the mixture with a spatula. Bake as directed in the recipe.

Spices of the orient teacake

PREPARATION TIME 20 MINUTES **COOKING TIME** 25 MINUTES **SERVES** 10

60g butter, softened

1 teaspoon vanilla extract

½ cup (110g) caster sugar

1 egg

1 cup (150g) self-raising flour

⅓ cup (80ml) milk

20g butter, melted, extra

SPICED NUTS

2 tablespoons finely chopped pistachios

2 tablespoons finely chopped blanched almonds

2 tablespoons finely chopped pine nuts

¼ cup (40g) icing sugar

½ teaspoon ground allspice

½ teaspoon ground cardamom

1 teaspoon ground cinnamon

1 Preheat oven to 180°C/160°C fan-forced. Grease deep 20cm-round cake pan.

2 Beat butter, extract, sugar and egg in small bowl with electric mixer until light and fluffy. Stir in sifted flour and milk. Spread mixture into pan.

3 Bake cake 25 minutes. Stand cake in pan 5 minutes; turn, top-side up, onto wire rack.

4 Meanwhile, make spiced nuts.

5 Brush cooled cake with extra butter; sprinkle with spiced nuts. Serve warm.

SPICED NUTS Rinse nuts in strainer under cold water. Spread wet nuts onto oven tray, sprinkle with sifted dry ingredients. Roast in oven about 10 minutes or until dry.

Hazelnut, plum and sour cherry cake

PREPARATION TIME 15 MINUTES **COOKING TIME** 1 HOUR **SERVES** 12

125g butter, softened

1 teaspoon vanilla extract

1¼ cups (275g) firmly packed brown sugar

3 eggs

¾ cup (110g) plain flour

¾ cup (110g) self-raising flour

½ cup (125ml) milk

½ cup (50g) hazelnut meal

6 small (270g) plums, halved, seeded

¼ cup (40g) drained sour cherries

¼ cup (35g) coarsely chopped roasted hazelnuts

1 Preheat oven to 160°C/140°C fan-forced. Grease 20cm x 30cm lamington pan; line base and sides with baking paper.

2 Beat butter, extract, sugar, eggs, flours, milk and hazelnut meal in medium bowl on low speed with electric mixer until combined. Increase speed to medium, beat 2 minutes or until smooth and changed to a paler colour.

3 Spread mixture into pan; top with plums, cherries and nuts. Bake 1 hour. Cool in pan.

Pecan sour cream cake

PREPARATION TIME 15 MINUTES **COOKING TIME** 1 HOUR **SERVES** 12

250g butter, softened

1 teaspoon vanilla extract

¾ cup (165g) caster sugar

2 eggs

300g sour cream

1½ cups (225g) plain flour

½ cup (75g) self-raising flour

1 teaspoon bicarbonate of soda

½ cup (60g) finely chopped pecans

2 tablespoons brown sugar

½ teaspoon ground cinnamon

1 Preheat oven to 180°C/160°C fan-forced. Grease deep 22cm-round cake pan.

2 Beat butter, extract and sugar in small bowl with electric mixer until light and fluffy. Beat in eggs, one at a time. Transfer mixture to large bowl; stir in sour cream then sifted flours and soda.

3 Spread half the cake mixture into pan; sprinkle with half the combined nuts, brown sugar and cinnamon. Spread with remaining cake mixture; sprinkle with remaining nut mixture, pressing gently into cake mixture.

4 Bake cake 1 hour. Stand cake in pan 5 minutes; turn, top-side up, onto wire rack to cool.

Use full-fat sour cream for the best flavour and texture.

Orange yogurt cake

PREPARATION TIME 25 MINUTES **COOKING TIME** 2 HOURS **SERVES** 10

125g butter, softened

1 tablespoon finely grated orange rind

1 cup (220g) caster sugar

3 eggs, separated

½ cup (85g) mixed peel

2 cups (300g) self-raising flour

¼ cup (60ml) orange juice

1 cup (250g) yogurt

ORANGE ICING

1½ cups (240g) icing sugar

30g butter, softened

2 tablespoons orange juice, approximately

1 Preheat oven to 150°C/130°C fan-forced. Grease 14cm x 21cm loaf pan; line base and sides with baking paper.

2 Beat butter, rind and sugar in small bowl with electric mixer until light and fluffy. Beat in egg yolks, one at a time. Transfer mixture to large bowl; stir in peel. Stir in sifted flour and combined juice and yogurt, in two batches.

3 Beat egg whites in small bowl with electric mixer until soft peaks form; fold gently into cake mixture, in two batches. Pour mixture into pan.

4 Bake cake 2 hours. Stand cake in pan 5 minutes; turn, top-side up, onto wire rack to cool.

5 Make orange icing; spread over cake.

ORANGE ICING Combine sifted icing sugar and butter in small bowl; stir in enough juice to make icing spreadable.

Yogurt, like sour cream, contributes to the richness and texture of butter cakes. Just for a change, try using buttermilk instead.

Almond butter cake

PREPARATION TIME 20 MINUTES **COOKING TIME** 1 HOUR **SERVES** 16

250g butter, softened

1 teaspoon almond essence

1 cup (220g) caster sugar

4 eggs

1 cup (150g) self-raising flour

½ cup (75g) plain flour

¾ cup (90g) almond meal

1 Preheat oven to 180°C/160°C fan-forced. Grease deep 19cm-square cake pan; line base with baking paper.

2 Beat butter, essence and sugar in medium bowl with electric mixer until light and fluffy. Beat in eggs, one at a time. Fold in sifted flours and almond meal, in two batches. Spread mixture into pan.

3 Bake 30 minutes. Reduce oven to 170°C/150°C fan-forced; bake further 30 minutes. Stand cake in pan 5 minutes; turn onto wire rack to cool.

Everybody loves a plain almondy butter cake — a light lemon or orange icing finishes it off nicely. Don't be surprised at how stiff this cake batter is when you spread it into the pan.

Cinnamon almond coffee cake

PREPARATION TIME 25 MINUTES **COOKING TIME** 50 MINUTES **SERVES** 16

185g butter, softened

1 cup (220g) caster sugar

2 eggs

1½ cups (225g) self-raising flour

1 cup (150g) plain flour

½ teaspoon bicarbonate of soda

1½ cups (375ml) milk

CINNAMON ALMOND TOPPING

90g butter, softened

¼ cup (55g) brown sugar

¾ cup (110g) plain flour

¼ cup (35g) roasted slivered almonds

2 teaspoons ground cinnamon

1 Preheat oven to 180°C/160°C fan-forced. Grease deep 23cm-square cake pan; line base with baking paper.

2 Make cinnamon almond topping.

3 Beat butter and sugar in small bowl with electric mixer until light and fluffy. Beat in eggs, one at a time. Transfer mixture to large bowl; stir in sifted flours and soda and milk, in two batches. Spread mixture into pan; sprinkle with topping.

4 Bake cake about 50 minutes. Stand cake in pan 5 minutes; turn, top-side up onto wire rack to cool.

CINNAMON ALMOND TOPPING Beat butter and sugar in small bowl with electric mixer until light and fluffy. Stir in sifted flour, nuts and cinnamon.

This cake is not flavoured with coffee, rather it is designed to be served with a cup of coffee.

Lemon sour cream cake

PREPARATION TIME 15 MINUTES **COOKING TIME** 1 HOUR (PLUS COOLING TIME) **SERVES** 16

250g butter, softened

1 tablespoon finely grated lemon rind

2 cups (440g) caster sugar

6 eggs

¾ cup (180g) sour cream

2 cups (300g) plain flour

¼ cup (35g) self-raising flour

½ cup (80g) pine nuts

1 tablespoon demerara sugar

¼ cup (90g) honey

1 Preheat oven to 170°C/150°C fan-forced. Grease deep 23cm-square cake pan; line base and sides with baking paper, extending paper 5cm over sides.

2 Beat butter, rind and caster sugar in medium bowl with electric mixer until light and fluffy. Beat in eggs, one at a time. Stir in sour cream and sifted flours, in two batches. Spread mixture into pan; bake 15 minutes.

3 Meanwhile, combine pine nuts and demerara sugar in small bowl.

4 Carefully remove cake from oven; working quickly, sprinkle evenly with nut mixture, pressing gently into cake. Return cake to oven; bake further 45 minutes. Stand cake in pan 5 minutes; turn, top-side up, onto wire rack.

5 Heat honey in small saucepan; drizzle hot honey evenly over hot cake. Cool.

If you can't find demerara sugar use raw sugar or coffee crystals instead.

Coco-berry-nut cake

PREPARATION TIME 20 MINUTES **COOKING TIME** 50 MINUTES **SERVES** 9

250g butter, softened

1 teaspoon vanilla extract

1¼ cups (275g) caster sugar

3 eggs

⅔ cup (100g) plain flour

1 cup (150g) self-raising flour

½ cup (55g) hazelnut meal

150g frozen raspberries

COCONUT TOPPING

⅓ cup (50g) plain flour

2 tablespoons caster sugar

40g butter

⅓ cup (15g) flaked coconut, chopped coarsely

1 Preheat oven to 180°C/160°C fan-forced. Grease deep 23cm-square cake pan; line base with baking paper.

2 Make coconut topping.

3 Beat butter, extract and sugar in small bowl with electric mixer until light and fluffy. Beat in eggs, one at a time. Transfer mixture to large bowl; stir in sifted flours and hazelnut meal.

4 Spread mixture into pan; sprinkle evenly with raspberries, then coconut topping.

5 Bake 50 minutes. Stand cake in pan 5 minutes; turn, top-side up, onto wire rack to cool.

COCONUT TOPPING Combine ingredients in small bowl; rub in butter with fingertips.

Frozen berries work best in this cake, they keep their shape and don't "bleed" into the cake mixture too much. Use any frozen berry.

LEMON SOUR CREAM CAKE

Golden syrup coconut cake

PREPARATION TIME 15 MINUTES **COOKING TIME** 45 MINUTES **SERVES** 12

125g butter, chopped coarsely

½ cup (125ml) golden syrup

1 cup (250ml) milk

2 eggs

½ cup (35g) shredded coconut

2 cups (300g) self-raising flour

¼ cup (55g) caster sugar

1 Preheat oven to 180°C/160°C fan-forced. Grease 21cm baba cake pan.

2 Stir butter and syrup in medium saucepan over low heat until butter is melted; do not boil. Remove from heat; stir in milk, eggs, coconut and sifted flour and sugar. Pour mixture into pan.

3 Bake cake about 40 minutes. Stand cake in pan 5 minutes; turn onto wire rack to cool.

You have to love a cake you can make in a saucepan. For a darker coloured cake, use treacle — or even molasses (if you like the flavour) instead of golden syrup. The hardest part of this recipe is greasing the cake pan — use melted butter, brush it evenly over the patterned surface of the pan.

Raspberry butter cake

PREPARATION TIME 15 MINUTES **COOKING TIME** 1 HOUR **SERVES** 10

125g butter, softened

¾ cup (165g) caster sugar

2 eggs

1½ cups (225g) self-raising flour

½ cup (125ml) milk

¾ cup raspberries

1 Preheat oven to 180°C/160°C fan-forced. Grease deep 20cm round cake pan; line base with baking paper.

2 Beat butter and sugar in small bowl with electric mixer until light and fluffy. Beat in eggs, one at a time. Transfer mixture to medium bowl; stir in sifted flour and milk, in two batches. Fold ¼ cup raspberries into mixture.

3 Spread three-quarters of cake mixture into pan; sprinkle with remaining raspberries. Spread remaining cake mixture over raspberries.

4 Bake cake about 1 hour. Stand cake in pan 5 minutes; turn, top-side up, onto wire rack to cool.

Use either fresh or frozen raspberries in this cake — or you can use strawberries, blueberries, boysenberries or any type of berry you like.

Greek yogurt cake

PREPARATION TIME 25 MINUTES **COOKING TIME** 35 MINUTES (PLUS COOLING TIME) **SERVES** 40

125g butter, softened	½ teaspoon bicarbonate soda
1 cup (220g) caster sugar	¼ cup (40g) finely chopped blanched almonds
3 eggs, separated	
2 cups (300g) self-raising flour	1 cup (280g) yogurt

1 Preheat oven to 180°C/160°C fan-forced. Grease 20cm x 30cm lamington pan; line with baking paper, extending paper 2cm over long sides.

2 Beat butter and sugar in small bowl with electric mixer until light and fluffy. Beat in egg yolks, one at a time. Transfer mixture to large bowl; stir in sifted flour and soda, in two batches. Stir in nuts and yogurt.

3 Beat egg whites in small bowl with electric mixer until soft peaks form. Fold egg whites into yogurt mixture in two batches. Spread mixture into pan.

4 Bake cake about 35 minutes. Turn cake, top-side up, onto wire rack to cool.

Coffee walnut streusel cake

PREPARATION TIME 30 MINUTES **COOKING TIME** 30 MINUTES **SERVES** 12

1 tablespoon instant coffee granules	**WALNUT STREUSEL**
¼ cup (60ml) boiling water	⅔ cup (100g) self-raising flour
125g butter, softened	100g butter, chopped finely
1 teaspoon vanilla extract	⅔ cup (150g) firmly packed brown sugar
1 cup (220g) caster sugar	
2 eggs	1 cup (120g) coarsely chopped walnuts, roasted
⅔ cup (160g) sour cream	
1¼ cups (185g) plain flour	
¼ cup (35g) self-raising flour	
¼ teaspoon bicarbonate of soda	

1 Make walnut streusel.

2 Preheat oven to 180°C/160°C fan-forced. Grease 20cm x 30cm lamington pan; line with baking paper, extending paper 2cm over long sides.

3 Dissolve coffee in the boiling water in small bowl. Cool 5 minutes.

4 Beat butter, extract and sugar in small bowl with electric mixer until light and fluffy. Beat in eggs, one at a time. Transfer mixture to large bowl; stir in sour cream and sifted flours and soda, in two batches. Stir in coffee mixture. Spread mixture into pan; sprinkle with walnut streusel, then remaining walnuts.

5 Bake cake about 30 minutes. Cool cake in pan.

WALNUT STREUSEL Sift flour into medium bowl; rub in butter with fingertips, until mixture resembles coarse breadcrumbs. Stir in sugar and half the walnuts.

We love butter cakes that have sour cream, yogurt or buttermilk as ingredients. The texture and keeping qualities are improved by these additions.

SPONGE CAKES

Sponge Cakes

The mythology surrounding the sponge can make attempting to bake this light, airy classic seem daunting. However, dire warnings about opening the oven door during baking causing the sponge to collapse before your eyes and the need for a mystical "light touch" in the mixing are frankly, over the top. Making a sponge may need patience for the extended beating, but it's not such a delicate operation that you need a cordon bleu diploma to attempt it.

A classic sponge uses plain flour only and contains no raising agent as the rising occurs from the air which is incorporated into the eggs during the beating time, usually taking somewhere between 10 and 15 minutes. Some sponges use a mixture of cornflour and plain flour, while others use custard powder, which also contains cornflour and is therefore lighter than plain flour. Purists, however, frown on these additions and use only plain flour which has been sifted at least three times. Hold the sifter as high as possible (without dusting the entire benchtop) to incorporate as much air as possible into the flour. The final sifting should be over the egg mixture, ready for folding through.

The small, high-sided bowl of an electric mixer is the ideal vessel for beating the eggs to their greatest volume. Start to beat the eggs at a low speed and, as they thicken, increase the speed to moderately high.

Add the sugar a tablespoon at a time, beating until the grains dissolve after each addition and continue until all the sugar is used. Scrape the mixture down from the side of the bowl and around the top of the bowl and beaters to avoid any undissolved sugar. When all the sugar has been incorporated and dissolved, quickly transfer the mixture to a larger, wide-topped bowl to make it easier to fold in the remaining ingredients.

Experience will teach you how to fold the ingredients into a sponge. Use a metal spoon, a knife or a plastic or rubber spatula. We prefer to fold the dry ingredients in by hand. Use your hand with the fingers splayed like a rake, dragging the flour up through the egg mixture and wiping the side of your hand around the edge of the bowl.

Liquid is usually the last ingredient to be added to sponges. Some recipes have no liquid (beyond the eggs), others contain milk or water and sometimes a little butter. Most recipes specify melted butter and hot liquid; melt the butter in the liquid and leave to cool slightly. If the liquid is too hot, it will toughen the sponge; if too cool it's more difficult to fold through the egg and flour mixture.

CAKE PANS

Deep-sided pans will give the best results as the high sides protect the delicate sponge mixture and prevents a crisp crust developing. Aluminium pans are best. Cake pans which are made from tin, or are anodised or coated with a non-stick surface cook more rapidly and it is wise to lower the oven temperature by 10°C (25°F). Unless recipes state otherwise, a light but even greasing using a pastry brush dipped in melted butter will give the best results.

When you're dividing a sponge mixture between the pans, gently spread the mixture to the edge of the pan; the mixture will not spread in the heat of the oven. The last scrapings from the bowl in which the sponge was mixed should be placed around the edge of the pan; this is the heaviest part of the mixture and if it's placed in the centre of the sponge it will make a dark heavy patch in the centre. To break large air bubbles, run a knife through the sponge mixture several times or tap the sponge pans once on the bench.

OVEN POSITIONS

As a general rule, sponges cook best when the tops of the pans are in the centre of the oven. If the sponges are being cooked on different shelves it will be necessary to swap them around after half the cooking time to make sure the cakes cook evenly. They won't be adversely affected if you move fairly quickly and handle the pans carefully after half the cooking time has expired. Opening the oven door does decrease the temperature and can affect the cake's rising if you do it during the early stages of cooking.

TO TEST IF COOKED

When cooked, the sponge will be beginning to shrink from the side of the pan and it should feel slightly springy to the touch. Turn sponges out immediately; if you leave them in the pan, they will continue to cook and dry out. Turn onto a wire rack and then turn up the right way immediately to prevent the wire racks from marking the tops.

STORAGE

Sponges are best made on the day of serving. Refrigerate the sponge if it is to be filled more than an hour ahead. The unfilled cakes can be frozen for up to one month.

TROUBLE SHOOTING

- Small white specks on the top of the sponges point to undissolved sugar. Caster sugar dissolves more readily than regular white sugar.
- If the sponge shrinks in the oven, the cake may have been baked at too high a temperature or for too long.
- If it shrinks and wrinkles while it's cooling, it may not have been baked for long enough.
- If the cake is flat and tough, the flour and liquid have not been mixed correctly.
- A pale and sticky top suggests the sponge has been baked at too low a temperature.
- If the top is crusty, this indicates that the sponge has been baked at too high a temperature or in the wrong oven position.
- If the cake sinks in the centre it could be that the pan is too small.
- Streaks on top of the sponge suggest the scrapings from the mixing bowl have not been mixed in properly; scrapings are always slightly darker than the full amount of mixture.

Featherlight sponge

PREPARATION TIME 20 MINUTES **COOKING TIME** 20 MINUTES **SERVES** 8

If you want even higher sponges, bake the mixture in two deep 20cm-round cake pans — they'll take a few more minutes to cook.

4 eggs

¾ cup (165g) caster sugar

⅔ cup (100g) wheaten cornflour

¼ cup (30g) custard powder

1 teaspoon cream of tartar

½ teaspoon bicarbonate of soda

⅓ cup (110g) apricot jam

300ml thickened cream, whipped

1 Preheat oven to 180°C/160°C fan-forced. Grease and flour two deep 22cm-round cake pans.

2 Beat eggs and sugar in small bowl with electric mixer until thick and creamy and sugar is dissolved. Transfer mixture to large bowl; gently fold in triple-sifted dry ingredients. Divide mixture between pans.

3 Bake about 20 minutes. Turn sponges, top-side up, onto baking-paper-lined wire rack to cool. Sandwich sponges with jam and cream.

Grated chocolate roll

PREPARATION TIME 25 MINUTES **COOKING TIME** 12 MINUTES **SERVES** 10

Sponge rolls, also known as swiss rolls and roulades, are easy to make and more "forgiving" than sponge cakes. Be careful not to over cook the mixture or the sponge will split when you roll it. follow the instructions in the recipe when rolling. Today, baking paper sprinkled with sugar is most commonly used to roll the sponge but you can also use a clean tea towel, sprinkled with sugar.

4 eggs, separated

½ cup (110g) caster sugar

2 tablespoons hot water

60g dark cooking chocolate, grated

½ cup (75g) self-raising flour

2 tablespoons caster sugar, extra

VANILLA CREAM

¾ cup (180ml) thickened cream

2 teaspoons icing sugar

1 teaspoon vanilla extract

1 Preheat oven to 180°C/160°C fan-forced. Grease 25cm x 30cm swiss roll pan; line base and sides with baking paper, extending paper 5cm over long sides.

2 Beat egg yolks and sugar in small bowl with electric mixer until thick and creamy. Transfer mixture to large bowl; fold in hot water and chocolate, then triple-sifted flour.

3 Beat egg whites in small bowl with electric mixer until soft speaks form; fold into chocolate mixture. Spread mixture into pan; bake about 12 minutes.

4 Meanwhile, place a piece of baking paper cut the same size as pan on bench; sprinkle evenly with extra caster sugar. Turn sponge onto paper; peel lining paper away. Cool; trim all sides of sponge.

5 Beat ingredients for vanilla cream in small bowl with electric mixer until soft peaks form; spread cream over sponge. Using paper as a guide, roll sponge from long side.

FEATHERLIGHT SPONGE

Tiramisu roulade

PREPARATION TIME 35 MINUTES **COOKING TIME** 20 MINUTES (PLUS REFRIGERATION TIME) **SERVES** 10

2 tablespoons coffee-flavoured liqueur

¼ cup (60ml) water

2 tablespoons caster sugar

1 tablespoon instant coffee granules

1 tablespoon boiling water

3 eggs

½ cup (110g) caster sugar, extra

½ cup (75g) plain flour

2 tablespoons flaked almonds

COFFEE LIQUEUR CREAM

250g mascarpone cheese

½ cup (125ml) thickened cream

2 tablespoons coffee-flavoured liqueur

1 Preheat oven to 220°C/200°C fan-forced. Grease 25cm x 30cm swiss roll pan; line base and two long sides with baking paper, extending paper 5cm over long sides.

2 Place liqueur, the water and sugar in small saucepan; bring to the boil. Reduce heat; simmer, uncovered, without stirring, about 5 minutes or until syrup thickens slightly. Remove from heat, stir in half of the coffee; reserve syrup.

3 Dissolve remaining coffee in the boiling water.

4 Beat eggs and extra sugar in small bowl with electric mixer about 5 minutes or until thick, creamy and sugar dissolves. Transfer mixture to large bowl; fold in dissolved coffee. Fold in triple-sifted flour. Spread mixture into pan; sprinkle with nuts. Bake 15 minutes.

5 Meanwhile, place a piece of baking paper cut the same size as pan on bench; sprinkle evenly with about 2 teaspoons caster sugar. Turn sponge onto paper; peel lining paper away. Trim all sides of sponge. Using paper as a guide, roll sponge from long side; cool.

6 Meanwhile, beat ingredients for coffee liqueur cream in small bowl with electric mixer until firm peaks form. Unroll sponge, brush with reserved syrup. Spread cream over sponge then re-roll sponge. Cover roulade with plastic wrap; refrigerate 30 minutes before serving.

Passionfruit sponge roll

PREPARATION TIME 40 MINUTES **COOKING TIME** 25 MINUTES (PLUS COOLING TIME) **SERVES** 10

3 eggs

½ cup (110g) caster sugar

1 teaspoon vanilla extract

¾ cup (100g) wheaten cornflour

¾ teaspoon cream of tartar

½ teaspoon bicarbonate of soda

¼ cup (10g) flaked coconut

¼ cup (55g) caster sugar, extra

½ cup (125ml) thickened cream

1 teaspoon icing sugar

PASSIONFRUIT CURD

⅓ cup (80ml) passionfruit pulp

⅔ cup (150g) caster sugar

2 eggs, beaten lightly

125g unsalted butter, chopped

1 Preheat oven to 180°C/160°C fan-forced. Grease 25cm x 30cm swiss roll pan; line base with baking paper, extending paper 5cm over long sides.

2 Beat eggs, caster sugar and extract in small bowl with electric mixer until sugar is dissolved. Fold in triple-sifted cornflour, tartar and soda. Spread mixture into pan; sprinkle with coconut. Bake about 12 minutes.

3 Meanwhile, place a piece of baking paper cut the same size as pan on bench; sprinkle evenly with extra caster sugar. Turn sponge onto paper; peel lining paper away. Cool; trim all sides of sponge.

4 Meanwhile, make passionfruit curd.

5 Whip cream and icing sugar in small bowl with electric mixer until soft peaks form. Unroll sponge; spread with half the passionfruit curd, top with cream. Using paper as a guide, roll sponge from long side.

PASSIONFRUIT CURD Stir ingredients in medium heatproof bowl over medium saucepan of simmering water about 10 minutes or until thickened slightly. Remove from heat; cool.

Lamington roll

PREPARATION TIME 30 MINUTES **COOKING TIME** 12 MINUTES (PLUS REFRIGERATION TIME) **SERVES** 10

Most rolls and roulades are trimmed, rolled fairly loosely, cooled, unrolled, filled, then re-rolled; however there are some recipes that cool the cake unrolled. Be guided by individual recipes.

3 eggs

½ cup (110g) caster sugar

¾ cup (110g) self-raising flour

2 tablespoons hot milk

¾ cup (65g) desiccated coconut

FILLING

90g unsalted butter, softened

1 teaspoon vanilla extract

1 cup (160g) icing sugar

1 tablespoon milk

ICING

1 cup (160g) icing sugar

¼ cup (25g) cocoa powder

1 teaspoon butter

2 tablespoons milk

1 Preheat oven to 180°C/160°C fan-forced. Grease a 25cm x 30cm swiss roll pan; line base with baking paper, extending paper 5cm over long sides.

2 Beat eggs in small bowl with electric mixer until thick and creamy. Gradually add sugar, beating until sugar dissolves between additions. Transfer mixture to large bowl; fold in triple-sifted flour and milk. Spread mixture into pan. Bake about 12 minutes.

3 Meanwhile, place piece of baking paper cut the same size as pan on bench; sprinkle with 2 tablespoons of the coconut. Turn sponge onto paper; peel lining paper away. Cool; trim all sides of sponge.

4 Make filling and icing.

5 Spread sponge with filling. Using paper as a guide, roll sponge from long side. Place on wire rack over tray; pour icing over roll. Press remaining coconut onto roll; refrigerate until set.

FILLING Beat butter and extract in small bowl with electric mixer until pale and creamy. Gradually beat in sifted icing sugar and milk until light and fluffy.

ICING Sift icing sugar and cocoa into small heatproof bowl; stir in butter and milk. Stir over small saucepan of simmering water until icing is pourable.

Brown sugar sponge

PREPARATION TIME 30 MINUTES **COOKING TIME** 20 MINUTES (PLUS COOLING TIME) **SERVES** 10

4 eggs

¾ cup (165g) firmly packed
dark brown sugar

1 cup (150g) wheaten cornflour

1 teaspoon cream of tartar

½ teaspoon bicarbonate of soda

300ml thickened cream

PRALINE

⅓ cup (75g) sugar

¼ cup (60ml) water

½ teaspoon malt vinegar

⅓ cup (45g) roasted hazelnuts

1 Preheat oven to 180°C/160°C fan-forced. Grease two deep 22cm-round cake pans.
2 Beat eggs and sugar in small bowl with electric mixer until thick and creamy and sugar is dissolved. Transfer mixture to large bowl; fold in triple-sifted dry ingredients. Divide mixture between pans.
3 Bake cakes about 18 minutes. Turn cakes, top-side up, onto baking-paper-covered wire rack to cool.
4 Meanwhile, make praline.
5 Beat cream in small bowl with electric mixer until firm peaks form; fold in praline. Place one sponge on serving plate; spread with half of the cream mixture. Top with remaining sponge; spread with remaining cream mixture.

PRALINE Stir sugar, the water and vinegar in small saucepan over heat, without boiling, until sugar dissolves; bring to the boil. Reduce heat; simmer, uncovered, without stirring, about 10 minutes or until syrup is golden brown. Add nuts; pour praline mixture onto baking-paper-lined tray. Cool about 15 minutes or until set. Break praline into pieces then blend or process until mixture is as fine (or coarse) as desired.

Dark brown sugar is best for this recipe simply for the colour of the finished sponge. The sugar is always available around Christmas baking time, but often hard to find the rest of the year. The regular brown sugar can be substituted with success — the sponge will be a little pale.

Coconut sponge cake

PREPARATION TIME 15 MINUTES **COOKING TIME** 30 MINUTES **SERVES** 12

185g butter, softened

¾ cup (165g) caster sugar

3 eggs

⅔ cup (60g) desiccated coconut

1½ cups (225g) self-raising flour

1 teaspoon baking powder

⅓ cup (80ml) milk

1 Preheat oven to 180°C/160°C fan-forced. Grease 20cm x 30cm lamington pan; line base with baking paper.
2 Beat ingredients in medium bowl with electric mixer on low speed until combined. Increase speed to medium, beat until mixture is smooth and changes to a paler colour. Spread mixture into pan.
3 Bake cake about 30 minutes. Turn cake, top-side up, onto wire rack to cool.

The coconut sponge cake is more like the buttery victoria sponge than the light fluffy version.

BROWN SUGAR SPONGE

Splitting & layering cakes

No need to worry about splitting and layering cakes any more, these tips will help you perfect the techniques.

SPLITTING WITH A KNIFE
Use a sharp serrated knife to split a cake into layers. This is quite easy to do if the cake is firm, but if it's soft, use the next two suggested methods for better results.

USING SKEWERS OR TOOTHPICKS
Bamboo skewers are good to use as a guide for the knife as you split the cake. If the cake is large, long skewers can be pushed through the cake, from one side to the other. If the cake is small, use toothpicks to mark the layer.

SPLITTING THE CAKE
Use a sharp serrated knife to split the cake. Cut the cake barely above the bamboo skewers or toothpicks, you should feel the knife touch the skewers as you cut through the cake.

JOINING THE SPONGE CAKES
If you don't want to roll the side of the sponge cakes as we have, then now is the time to put the cake on the serving plate. Position the cake with the cream, on the plate, then position the top cake. Gently twist the top cake around until you get the cake as even as possible, there's always some unevenness to contend with.

CREAMING THE SIDE OF A SPONGE
Spread the whipped cream (or frosting etc) as evenly as you can around the side of the cake, don't worry if crumbs get in the cream. The coconut will hide any crumbs.

ROLLING THE SIDE OF A SPONGE
Have the coconut or nuts etc on a flat tray, ready for the rolling. Slide the cake onto one hand, hold the cake between both hands. Roll the side of the cake, like a wheel, in the coconut.

SPLITTING WITH COTTON

This method is quick, neat and efficient. Use a length (enough to hold both ends as you cut through the cake) of strong cotton or dental floss, pull the cotton firmly through the cake towards you.

SPREADING A SPONGE WITH JAM

If you want to ice the top of a sponge sandwich (two layers of sponge cake), as we're doing here, spread jam over the top sides of both sponge cakes. If you like, you can warm the jam, then strain it, for a smooth effect.

SPREADING A SPONGE WITH CREAM

Spread whipped cream over one of the sponge cakes. Whipped thickened cream is more stable than regular pouring cream. Cream can be flavoured with vanilla and sifted icing sugar.

ICING THE SPONGE

Place the cake on a serving plate, make a glacé icing (see page 220). Pour the warm icing quickly all over the top of the cake, spreading the icing quickly to the edge of the cake. Don't worry if the icing runs over the side of the cake, it can be removed easily when the icing sets.

TRIMMING THE ICING

Glacé icing will set quite hard, if there is no butter or oil in it (or only a little). If you really want to neaten the edge, leave the icing to set at room temperature, use a small sharp knife to cut the drips of icing away from the side of the cake.

CUTTING A ROUND CAKE

This is a useful tip for efficient cake cutting, particularly if the cake is large. Mark a circle in the centre of the cake to be cut, then cut down into the cake around the marking. Don't remove the round centre piece of cake. Cut pieces of cake, they'll be almost wedge-shaped, right up to the round of cake.

1

2

3　4

Sponge roll with jam and cream

PREPARATION TIME 25 MINUTES (PLUS REFRIGERATION TIME) **COOKING TIME** 12 MINUTES **SERVES** 8

3 eggs

²⁄₃ cup (150g) caster sugar

½ cup (75g) wheaten cornflour

2 tablespoons custard powder

¾ teaspoon cream of tartar

½ teaspoon bicarbonate of soda

⅓ cup (110g) raspberry jam

¾ cup (180ml) thickened cream, whipped

1 Preheat oven to 180°C/160°C fan-forced. Grease 25cm x 30cm swiss roll pan; line base with baking paper, extending paper 5cm over long sides.

2 Beat eggs and ½ cup of the sugar in small bowl with electric mixer until thick and creamy and sugar is dissolved. Fold in triple-sifted dry ingredients.

3 Spread mixture into pan; bake about 12 minutes.

4 Meanwhile, place piece of baking paper cut the same size as pan on bench; sprinkle with remaining caster sugar. Turn sponge onto paper; peel lining paper away. Cool; trim all sides of sponge.

5 Spread sponge with jam then cream. Using paper as a guide, roll sponge from short side. Cover with plastic wrap; refrigerate 30 minutes.

Lemon butter sponge cake

PREPARATION TIME 25 MINUTES **COOKING TIME** 25 MINUTES (PLUS COOLING TIME) **SERVES** 10

4 eggs

¾ cup (165g) caster sugar

1 cup (150g) self-raising flour

1 tablespoon cornflour

2 teaspoons soft butter

⅓ cup (80ml) hot water

⅓ cup (110g) lemon butter

¾ cup (180ml) thickened cream, whipped

1 tablespoon icing sugar

1 Preheat oven to 180°C/160°C fan-forced. Grease two deep 20cm-round cake pans.

2 Beat eggs in small bowl with electric mixer until thick. Gradually beat in sugar until dissolved. Transfer mixture to large bowl; fold in triple-sifted flours. Pour combined butter and the water down side of bowl; fold through egg mixture. Spread mixture into pans.

3 Bake sponges 25 minutes. Turn sponges, top-side up, onto baking-paper-covered wire rack to cool.

4 Place one sponge on serving plate, spread with lemon butter and cream. Top with remaining cake, dust with sifted icing sugar.

You'll notice most sponge recipes call for triple-sifted flour. We sift the dry ingredients three times onto a piece of greaseproof paper — why create washing up by using a bowl — this sifting not only mixes the ingredients thoroughly, but also incorporates some air into the flour. Hold the sifter up high as you sift. The dry ingredients should be sifted over the egg mixture, seconds before you start folding the ingredients together.

1 SPONGE ROLL WITH JAM AND CREAM 2 LEMON BUTTER SPONGE CAKE
3 GENOISE SPONGE [P 98] 4 GINGER FLUFF ROLL [P 98]

Genoise sponge

PREPARATION TIME 35 MINUTES (PLUS REFRIGERATION TIME)
COOKING TIME 30 MINUTES (PLUS COOLING TIME) **SERVES** 8

4 eggs
½ cup (110g) caster sugar
⅔ cup (100g) plain flour
60g butter, melted
300ml thickened cream

1 tablespoon icing sugar
¼ cup (80g) strawberry jam, warmed
500g strawberries, sliced thinly
1 tablespoon icing sugar, extra

1 Preheat oven to 180°C/160°C fan-forced. Grease deep 20cm-round cake pan; line base with baking paper.
2 Place eggs and sugar in large heatproof bowl over large saucepan of simmering water. Do not allow water to touch base of bowl. Beat with electric mixer until thick and creamy, about 10 minutes. Remove bowl from pan; beat mixture until it returns to room temperature.
3 Sift half of the triple-sifted flour over egg mixture, carefully fold in flour; fold in remaining sifted flour. Quickly fold in cooled butter. Pour mixture into pan.
4 Bake sponge about 20 minutes. Turn sponge, top-side up, onto baking-paper-covered wire rack to cool.
5 Beat cream and sifted icing sugar in small bowl with electric mixer until soft peaks form. Split sponge in half; place one half, cut-side up, on serving plate. Spread with jam and cream; top with strawberries, then remaining sponge half. Dust with extra sifted icing sugar.

Ginger fluff roll

PREPARATION TIME 25 MINUTES (PLUS REFRIGERATION TIME) **COOKING TIME** 12 MINUTES **SERVES** 10

3 eggs
⅔ cup (150g) caster sugar
⅔ cup (100g) wheaten cornflour
1 teaspoon cream of tartar
½ teaspoon bicarbonate of soda
1 teaspoon cocoa powder

2 teaspoons ground ginger
½ teaspoon ground cinnamon
¾ cup (180ml) thickened cream
2 tablespoons golden syrup
1 teaspoon ground ginger, extra

1 Preheat oven to 180°C/160°C fan-forced. Grease 25cm x 30cm swiss roll pan; line base with baking paper, extending paper 5cm over long sides.
2 Beat eggs and ½ cup of the sugar in small bowl with electric mixer until thick and creamy and sugar is dissolved. Transfer mixture to large bowl; fold in triple-sifted flour, cream of tartar, soda, cocoa, ginger and cinnamon. Spread mixture into pan; bake about 12 minutes.
3 Meanwhile, place piece of baking paper cut the same size as pan on bench; sprinkle with remaining sugar. Turn sponge onto paper; peel lining paper away. Cool; trim all sides of sponge.
4 Beat cream, syrup and extra ginger in small bowl with electric mixer until firm peaks form; spread over sponge. Using paper as a guide, roll sponge from long side. Cover with plastic wrap; refrigerate 30 minutes.

Chocolate sponge

PREPARATION TIME 20 MINUTES **COOKING TIME** 25 MINUTES **SERVES** 10

3 eggs

½ cup (110g) caster sugar

¼ cup (35g) cornflour

¼ cup (35g) plain flour

¼ cup (35g) self-raising flour

2 tablespoons cocoa powder

300ml thickened cream, whipped

COFFEE ICING

3 teaspoons instant coffee granules

2 tablespoons milk

1½ cups (240g) icing sugar

1 teaspoon soft butter

1 Preheat oven to 180°C/160°C fan-forced. Grease deep 22cm-round cake pan; line base with baking paper.

2 Beat eggs in small bowl with electric mixer until thick and creamy. Gradually add sugar, beating until dissolved between each addition. Transfer mixture to large bowl; gently fold in triple-sifted dry ingredients. Spread mixture into pan.

3 Bake 25 minutes. Turn sponge, top-side up, onto baking-paper-lined wire rack to cool.

4 Make coffee icing.

5 Split sponge in half; join with cream. Spread top with icing; leave to set before cutting.

COFFEE ICING Stir coffee and milk in small bowl until dissolved. Sift icing sugar into small bowl; stir in butter and enough of the coffee mixture to give a firm paste. Stir over hot water until icing is spreadable; do not over-heat. Use immediately.

If you like, drop the coffee from this icing recipe and use 1 tablespoon cocoa powder instead. Sift it in with the icing sugar. Add the milk with the butter.

Lamingtons

PREPARATION TIME 25 MINUTES **COOKING TIME** 35 MINUTES **MAKES** 16

6 eggs

⅔ cup (150g) caster sugar

⅓ cup (50g) cornflour

½ cup (75g) plain flour

⅓ cup (50g) self-raising flour

2 cups (160g) desiccated coconut

ICING

4 cups (640g) icing sugar

½ cup (50g) cocoa powder

15g butter

1 cup (250ml) milk

1 Preheat oven to 180°C/160°C fan-forced. Grease 20cm x 30cm lamington pan; line base with baking paper, extending paper 5cm over long sides.

2 Beat eggs in medium bowl with electric mixer about 10 minutes or until thick and creamy; gradually beat in sugar, dissolving between additions. Fold in triple-sifted flours. Spread mixture into pan.

3 Bake cake about 35 minutes. Turn cake onto baking-paper-covered wire rack to cool.

4 Meanwhile, make icing. Cut cake into 16 pieces; dip each square in icing, drain off excess. Toss squares in coconut. Place lamingtons onto wire rack to set.

ICING Sift icing sugar and cocoa into medium heatproof bowl; stir in butter and milk. Set bowl over medium saucepan of simmering water; stir until icing is of a coating consistency.

Just for a change, try a mocha variation: Add 1 tablespoon cocoa powder to dry ingredients for the cake; fold into the egg mixture. Combine 1 tablespoon instant coffee granules with 1 tablespoon boiling water; fold into the cake mixture then follow instructions from step 3 of the lamington recipe. Beat 300ml thickened cream with 2 tablespoons coffee-flavoured liqueur until firm peaks form. Once the icing has set, halve the lamingtons horizontally then sandwich cakes with the whipped cream.

Friand pans are oval in
shape and are available —
in varying quality — from
cookware shops, chain
stores and supermarkets.
You can use muffin
pans instead.

Little chocolate and coconut sponges

PREPARATION TIME 35 MINUTES **COOKING TIME** 15 MINUTES **MAKES** 18

4 eggs

¾ cup (165g) caster sugar

⅔ cup (100g) self-raising flour

⅓ cup (35g) cocoa powder

90g butter, melted

1 tablespoon hot water

⅔ cup (160ml) thickened cream

2 tablespoons caster sugar, extra

⅓ cup (15g) flaked coconut

CHOCOLATE GANACHE

200g dark eating chocolate,
chopped coarsely

⅔ cup (160ml) thickened cream

1 Preheat oven to 180°C/160°C fan-forced. Grease two 9-hole friand pans.

2 Beat eggs in small bowl with electric mixer until thick and creamy. Gradually add sugar, a tablespoon at a time, beating until sugar is dissolved between additions. Transfer mixture to large bowl; fold in sifted flour, cocoa, then butter and hot water. Spoon mixture into pans.

3 Bake cakes 12 minutes; turn out immediately onto wire racks to cool.

4 Meanwhile, make chocolate ganache.

5 Beat cream and extra sugar in small bowl with electric mixer until soft peaks form. Split cooled sponges in half. Spread bases with cream; replace tops. Spread ganache over cakes, sprinkle with coconut.

CHOCOLATE GANACHE Stir ingredients in small saucepan over low heat until smooth. Remove from heat; stand until thickened.

This loaf cake is not as
light as a traditional
sponge cake, it's more like
a spicy victorian sponge.

Spicy sponge cake

PREPARATION TIME 20 MINUTES **COOKING TIME** 40 MINUTES **SERVES** 10

3 eggs

¾ cup (165g) caster sugar

1½ cups (225g) self-raising flour

1 teaspoon ground cinnamon

1 teaspoon ground ginger

1 teaspoon ground clove

1 teaspoon ground cardamom

125g butter, melted

⅓ cup (80ml) milk

1 Preheat oven to 180°C/160°C fan-forced. Grease 15cm x 25cm loaf pan; line base with baking paper.

2 Beat eggs and sugar in small bowl with electric mixer until thick and creamy and sugar is dissolved. Transfer mixture to large bowl; fold in triple-sifted dry ingredients then butter and milk. Pour mixture into pan.

3 Bake sponge 40 minutes. Turn sponge, top-side up, onto baking-paper-covered wire rack to cool. Serve slices topped with whipped cream.

Honey spice sponge cake

PREPARATION TIME 15 MINUTES **COOKING TIME** 10 MINUTES **SERVES** 8

2 eggs	½ teaspoon cream of tartar
½ cup (110g) caster sugar	¼ teaspoon bicarbonate of soda
⅓ cup (50g) wheaten cornflour	300ml thickened cream
1½ tablespoons custard powder	2 tablespoons honey
1 teaspoon mixed spice	1 tablespoon icing sugar

1 Preheat oven to 180°C/160°C fan-forced. Grease 25cm x 30cm swiss roll pan; line base with baking paper, extending paper 5cm over long sides.
2 Beat eggs and ⅓ cup of the caster sugar in small bowl with electric mixer 10 minutes or until thick and creamy and sugar is dissolved. Gently fold in triple-sifted dry ingredients.
3 Spread mixture into pan. Bake sponge 10 minutes.
4 Place a piece of baking paper cut the same size as pan on bench; sprinkle evenly with remaining sugar. Turn cake onto sugared paper; peel lining paper away. Cool.
5 Beat cream and honey in small bowl with electric mixer until firm peaks form.
6 Trim edges from all sides of sponge then cut widthways into three rectangles. Place one piece of sponge on plate; spread with half the cream mixture. Top with second piece of sponge and remaining cream. Top with remaining sponge; dust with sifted icing sugar.

Strawberry jelly cakes

PREPARATION TIME 25 MINUTES **COOKING TIME** 35 MINUTES (PLUS REFRIGERATION TIME) **MAKES** 20

6 eggs	⅓ cup (50g) self-raising flour
⅔ cup (150g) caster sugar	80g packet strawberry jelly
⅓ cup (50g) cornflour	2 cups (160g) desiccated coconut
½ cup (75g) plain flour	½ cup (125ml) thickened cream

1 Preheat oven to 180°C/160°C fan-forced. Grease 20cm x 30cm lamington pan; line with baking paper, extending paper 5cm over long sides.
2 Beat eggs in medium bowl with electric mixer about 10 minutes or until thick and creamy; gradually beat in sugar, dissolving between additions. Fold in triple-sifted flours.
3 Spread mixture into pan; bake about 35 minutes. Turn cake immediately onto a baking-paper-covered wire rack to cool.
4 Meanwhile, make jelly according to manufacturer's instructions. Refrigerate until set to the consistency of unbeaten egg white.
5 Cut cake into 20 squares; dip each square into jelly then coconut. Refrigerate 30 minutes.
6 Meanwhile, beat cream in small bowl with electric mixer until firm peaks form. Cut cakes in half; sandwich with cream.

Jelly cakes are loved by kids of all ages – even grown-up kids. Change the flavour of the jelly to suit yourself. The coating of jelly and coconut keep them moist inside and out. Store them in an airtight container, in a single layer, in the refrigerator.

HONEY SPICE SPONGE CAKE

Don't worry about the mixture standing while you're baking the first batch of puffs. The second batch won't be quite as light as the first, but no one will even notice.

Strawberry powder puffs

PREPARATION TIME 25 MINUTES **COOKING TIME** 15 MINUTES **MAKES** 36

2 eggs

⅓ cup (75g) caster sugar

2 tablespoons cornflour

2 tablespoons plain flour

2 tablespoons self-raising flour

½ cup (125ml) thickened cream

2 tablespoons icing sugar

½ cup (65g) finely chopped strawberries

1 Preheat oven to 180°C/160°C fan-forced. Grease and flour two 12-hole shallow round-based patty pans.

2 Beat eggs and sugar in small bowl with electric mixer until thick, creamy and sugar dissolves. Gently fold in triple-sifted flours. Drop 1 teaspoon of mixture into holes of pans.

3 Bake puffs about 7 minutes; turn immediately onto wire racks to cool. Wash, grease and flour pans again; continue using mixture until all puffs are baked.

4 Beat cream and half the sifted icing sugar in small bowl with electric mixer until firm peaks form; fold in strawberries.

5 Sandwich puffs with strawberry cream just before serving. Dust with remaining sifted icing sugar.

Pomegranate and raspberry flavours are delicious together. If you've never eaten pomegranates before, you're going to be pleasantly surprised at their unique taste and prettiness.

Raspberries and cream sponge cake

PREPARATION TIME 30 MINUTES **COOKING TIME** 25 MINUTES **SERVES** 9

4 eggs

¾ cup (165g) caster sugar

⅔ cup (100g) wheaten cornflour

2 tablespoons custard powder

1 teaspoon cream of tartar

½ teaspoon bicarbonate of soda

1 medium pomegranate (320g)

300ml thickened cream

1 tablespoon icing sugar

½ teaspoon vanilla extract

240g fresh raspberries

1 Preheat oven to 180°C/160°C fan-forced. Grease and flour deep 23cm-square cake pan.

2 Beat eggs and caster sugar in small bowl with electric mixer until thick, creamy and sugar dissolves. Transfer mixture to large bowl; gently fold in triple-sifted flour, custard powder, tartar and soda. Pour mixture into pan.

3 Bake cake about 25 minutes. Turn cake, top-side up, onto baking-paper-covered wire rack to cool.

4 Remove seeds from pomegranate. Discard flesh.

5 Beat cream, sifted icing sugar and extract in small bowl with electric mixer until firm peaks form. Place sponge on serving plate; top with cream mixture, raspberries and pomegranate seeds.

Berry cream roulade

PREPARATION TIME 15 MINUTES **COOKING TIME** 12 MINUTES **SERVES** 10

3 eggs

½ cup (110g) caster sugar

½ cup (75g) wheaten cornflour

1 tablespoon custard powder

1 teaspoon cream of tartar

½ teaspoon bicarbonate of soda

1 tablespoon caster sugar, extra

1 tablespoon icing sugar

BERRY CREAM

¾ cup (180ml) thickened cream

1 teaspoon vanilla extract

1 tablespoon icing sugar

1 cup (150g) frozen blackberries, chopped coarsely, thawed

1 Preheat oven to 180°C/160°C fan-forced. Grease 25cm x 30cm swiss roll pan; line base with baking paper, extending paper 5cm over long sides.

2 Beat eggs and caster sugar in small bowl with electric mixer about 5 minutes or until thick, creamy and sugar dissolves. Transfer mixture to large bowl.

3 Gently fold in triple-sifted flour, custard powder, tartar and soda. Spread mixture into pan; bake about 12 minutes.

4 Meanwhile, place a piece of baking paper cut the same size as pan on bench; sprinkle evenly with extra caster sugar. Turn sponge onto paper; peel lining paper away. Cool; trim all sides of sponge.

5 Meanwhile, make berry cream.

6 Spread berry cream over sponge. Using paper as a guide, roll sponge from long side. Dust with sifted icing sugar.

BERRY CREAM Beat cream, extract and sifted icing sugar in small bowl with electric mixer until soft peaks form; fold in berries.

Use any berries you like in this recipe — fresh or frozen — if they're a bit bland in flavour, fold a tablespoon of similar flavoured jam through the cream as well.

Victoria sponge sandwich

PREPARATION TIME 20 MINUTES **COOKING TIME** 30 MINUTES **SERVES** 10

250g butter, softened

1 teaspoon vanilla extract

1 cup (220g) caster sugar

4 eggs

⅓ cup (80ml) milk

2 cups (300g) self-raising flour

⅓ cup (110g) strawberry jam

1 tablespoon icing sugar

1 Preheat oven to 180°C/160°C fan-forced. Grease two deep 20cm-round cake pans; line base with baking paper.

2 Beat butter, extract and caster sugar in small bowl with electric mixer until light and fluffy. Beat in eggs, one at a time; beat in milk. Transfer mixture to large bowl. Stir in sifted flour, in two batches. Divide mixture evenly between pans.

3 Bake sponges about 30 minutes. Turn sponges, top-side up, onto baking-paper-covered wire rack to cool. Sandwich sponges with jam; serve dusted with icing sugar.

This classic recipe is buttery and light all at the same time. Make sure you beat the butter, sugar and egg mixture thoroughly.

Mango and coconut jelly cakes

PREPARATION TIME 30 MINUTES (PLUS REFRIGERATION TIME)

COOKING TIME 10 MINUTES (PLUS REFRIGERATION TIME) **MAKES** 24

1 small mango (300g)

85g packet mango jelly crystals

1 ¼ cups (310ml) boiling water

2 eggs

⅓ cup (75g) caster sugar

½ cup (75g) self-raising flour

2 teaspoons cornflour

10g butter

2 tablespoons boiling water, extra

1 ½ cup (110g) shredded coconut

300ml thickened cream

1 Blend or process about half of the mango until smooth (you need ⅓ cup pulp). Combine jelly and the boiling water in medium bowl until jelly dissolves; stir in mango pulp. Strain; refrigerate until set to the consistency of unbeaten egg white.

2 Preheat oven to 180°C/160°C fan-forced. Grease two 12-hole shallow round-based patty pans.

3 Beat eggs in small bowl with electric mixer until thick and creamy; gradually beat in sugar, dissolving between additions. Fold in triple-sifted flours then combined butter and the extra boiling water. Spoon mixture into pan holes.

4 Bake cakes about 10 minutes. Turn cakes immediately onto baking-paper-covered wire rack to cool.

5 Dip each cake into jelly then toss in coconut. Refrigerate 30 minutes.

6 Meanwhile, beat cream in small bowl with electric mixer until firm peaks form. Chop remaining mango finely; fold into cream. Cut cakes in half; sandwich with cream.

Ginger powder puffs with orange cream

PREPARATION TIME 25 MINUTES **COOKING TIME** 10 MINUTES **MAKES** 12

2 eggs

⅓ cup (75g) caster sugar

2 tablespoons cornflour

1 tablespoon plain flour

2 tablespoons self-raising flour

1 teaspoon cocoa powder

1 ½ teaspoons ground ginger

¼ teaspoon ground cinnamon

2 teaspoons icing sugar

ORANGE CREAM

⅔ cup (160ml) thickened cream

2 tablespoons icing sugar

1 teaspoon finely grated orange rind

1 Preheat oven to 180°C/160°C fan-forced. Grease and flour two 12-hole shallow round-based patty pans.

2 Beat eggs and caster sugar in small bowl with electric mixer until thick, creamy and sugar dissolved. Fold in triple-sifted dry ingredients. Divide mixture among pan holes.

3 Bake cakes about 8 minutes; turn immediately onto wire racks to cool.

4 Make orange cream.

5 Sandwich puffs with orange cream just before serving. Dust with sifted icing sugar.

ORANGE CREAM Beat ingredient in small bowl with electric mixer until firm peaks form.

Passionfruit curd sponge cakes

PREPARATION TIME 25 MINUTES **COOKING TIME** 12 MINUTES **MAKES** 12

3 eggs

½ cup (110g) caster sugar

¾ cup (110g) self-raising flour

20g butter, melted

¼ cup (60ml) hot water

2 teaspoons icing sugar

PASSIONFRUIT CURD

⅓ cup (80ml) passionfruit pulp

⅔ cup (150g) caster sugar

2 eggs

125g unsalted butter, chopped coarsely

1 Make passionfruit curd.

2 Preheat oven to 180°C/160°C fan-forced. Grease 12 x ½-cup (125ml) oval friand pans.

3 Beat eggs in small bowl with electric mixer until thick and creamy. Beat in caster sugar, a tablespoon at a time, until dissolved. Transfer mixture to large bowl; fold in triple-sifted flour then combined butter and the water. Divide mixture among pans.

4 Bake friands about 12 minutes; turn immediately, top-side up, onto wire racks to cool.

5 Split sponges in half; sandwich with passionfruit curd. Dust with sifted icing sugar.

PASSIONFRUIT CURD Stir ingredients in small heatproof bowl over small saucepan of simmering water about 10 minutes or until thickened slightly. Cool.

Passionfruit curd is even better if it's made with unsalted butter. If you want to make larger quantities of curd — maybe for gifts — increase the size of the bowl and pan to keep the curd mixture quite shallow. This way you'll be able to get it to thicken in 10 minutes or so, despite the larger quantity.

FRUIT CAKES

Fruit Cakes

The earliest fruit cake recipes date from ancient Rome and included pomegranate seeds, pine nuts and raisins mixed into a barley mash with a texture probably more like a pudding than cake as we know it today. By medieval times the fruit cake had developed into a baked cake containing honey, spices and preserved fruits. Perhaps because of its high sugar content and also because of the nuts which were incorporated into the recipe, the fruit cake evolved into festive fare to celebrate the year's harvest. Its relatively long keeping qualities meant that the cake could be prepared at the time of the harvest but saved to be consumed months or even years later.

The most popular form of this celebration fruit cake is the traditional dark fruit cake and some of our most famous recipes and tips for making them are included in *Christmas Baking* which begins on page 570.

Lighter-style cakes based on fruit are enjoying a new wave of popularity as they straddle the divide between cake and dessert; they can be prepared ahead and generally keep well. Moist and flavour-packed thanks to the fruit that inspires them, these cakes are often teamed with a nut that complements their main ingredient. Some of these recipes can be made using canned fruit so it makes good sense to have a few cans on stand-by in the pantry for those occasions when you need to turn out a sweet treat with little advance warning. If the fruit needs to be cooked before being incorporated in the recipe, it's often possible to speed the process up by lightly stewing or cooking it in the microwave oven. Some of these recipes also provide a great opportunity for using up bananas that are perhaps a little past peak eating condition.

Some fruit, particularly stone fruit, needs to be peeled before adding to the recipe. The techniques are covered in *Friands* (see page 416). Apricots, nectarines, plums and cherries don't need to be peeled before use, but they should be washed and dried and the stones removed. Easier said than done sometimes as clingstone fruit don't give up their seeds easily. The best method of attack is to cut them in half and twist the two halves against each other until they come apart, then using a small sharp knife, cut around the stone until you can lift it out. A cherry pitter is a godsend when it comes to removing stones from this fruit. And they're not just for cherries — most cherry pitters work equally well on olives.

PREPARING PANS

To grease a cake pan use either a light, even coating of cooking-oil spray or a pastry brush to brush melted butter or margarine lightly over the base and side(s) of the pan. Sometimes a recipe calls for a greased and floured pan. Simply grease the pan evenly (melted butter is best in this case) and allow it to set for a minute or two before sprinkling a little flour evenly over the greased surface. Invert the pan and tap it several times on the bench to remove any excess flour.

Cakes that are high in sugar, or that contain golden syrup, treacle or honey have a tendency to stick to pans, so we recommend lining the base and/or sides of the pans — we indicate in the recipes where this is necessary. Trace around the base of the pan with a pencil onto greaseproof or baking paper; cut out the shape, slightly inside the pencil mark, so the paper fits snugly inside the greased pan. It is not necessary to grease baking paper once it's in position. See *Baking Techniques* pages 632 & 633 for further tips.

As a guide, cakes requiring one hour or longer to bake should have a baking paper "collar" extending about 5cm above the edge of the pan, to protect the top of the cake. The following method for lining round or square pans allows for this, using greaseproof or baking paper. For side(s), cut three paper strips long enough to fit around the inside of the pan and 8cm wider than the depth of the pan. Fold strips lengthways about 2cm from the edge and make short diagonal cuts about 2cm apart, up to the fold. This helps ease the paper around the curves or corners of the pan, with the cut section fitting around the base. Using the base of the pan as a guide, cut three paper circles or squares as instructed above and position in the pan after lining the sides.

COOLING CAKES

Our recipes suggest the times needed for cooling cakes before turning out onto wire racks to cool further. The best way to do this, after the standing time has elapsed, is to hold the cake pan firmly and shake it gently, to loosen the cake in the pan. Turn the cake, upside-down, onto a wire rack, then turn the cake top-side up immediately using a second rack (see *Baking Techniques* page 631) — unless directed otherwise. We indicate when it is best to cool cakes in the pans in which they were baked; generally fruit cakes are cooled in this way and should be covered with foil before cooling.

KEEPING AND STORING

Most cakes keep well for two or three days depending on the climate and type of cake. As a general rule, the higher the sugar content, the longer the cake can be kept. Make sure your cake is at room temperature before storing it in an airtight container as close in size to the cake as possible to minimise the amount of air around the cake which can either dry it out, or cause deterioration.

For cakes which are suited to freezing, it's usually better to freeze them unfilled and un-iced because icing can crack during the thawing process. Wrap or seal the completely cooled cake in plastic wrap or a freezer bag, expelling as much air as possible before placing it in the freezer. It's best to thaw cakes overnight in the refrigerator. If you want to reheat a cake to serve it as a dessert, or even just slightly warmed, bring the cake to room temperature, wrap it in aluminium foil to stop it drying out and place it in a slow oven for about 15 minutes, depending on the size of the cake.

Glacé fruit cake with limoncello cream

PREPARATION TIME 30 MINUTES **COOKING TIME** 45 MINUTES (PLUS REFRIGERATION TIME) **SERVES** 24

Limoncello is a lemon flavoured liqueur; you could use Cointreau, Curaçao or Grand Marnier instead. Not everyone likes rich fruit cake and this is the perfect cake for those who prefer a lighter cake. Mix and match the glacé and dried fruit and nuts to suit your taste, but this combination is particularly pretty. The syrup gives the cake quite another dimension when compared with a traditional rich fruit cake.

90g butter, softened

1 tablespoon finely grated lemon rind

¾ cup (165g) caster sugar

2 eggs

¾ cup (110g) plain flour

½ cup (75g) self-raising flour

⅓ cup (80ml) milk

⅔ cup (150g) coarsely chopped glacé pineapple

⅔ cup (170g) coarsely chopped glacé apricots

⅔ cup (170g) coarsely chopped glacé peaches

¾ cup (110g) coarsely chopped dried pears

¾ cup (110g) roasted shelled pistachios

LEMON SYRUP

½ cup (125ml) lemon juice

1 cup (220g) caster sugar

LIMONCELLO CREAM

300ml thickened cream

2 tablespoons limoncello

1 Preheat oven to 160°C/140°C fan-forced. Line 20cm x 30cm lamington pan with baking paper, extending paper 3cm over long sides.

2 Beat butter, rind and sugar in small bowl with electric mixer until light and fluffy. Beat in eggs, one at a time. Transfer mixture to large bowl; stir in sifted flours, milk, fruit and nuts. Spread mixture into pan.

3 Bake cake about 45 minutes.

4 Meanwhile, make lemon syrup.

5 Remove cake from oven; pour hot syrup over hot cake in pan. Refrigerate overnight.

6 Make limoncello cream.

7 Cut cake into squares; serve with limoncello cream.

LEMON SYRUP Stir ingredients in small saucepan over heat, without boiling, until sugar dissolves; bring to the boil. Reduce heat; simmer, uncovered, without stirring, about 10 minutes or until thickened slightly.

LIMONCELLO CREAM Beat ingredients in small bowl with electric mixer until soft peaks form.

Lumberjack cake

PREPARATION TIME 30 MINUTES **COOKING TIME** 1 HOUR 10 MINUTES **SERVES** 16

2 large apples (400g), peeled, cored, chopped finely

1 cup (200g) finely chopped dried dates

1 teaspoon bicarbonate of soda

1 cup (250ml) boiling water

125g butter, softened

1 teaspoon vanilla extract

1 cup (220g) caster sugar

1 egg

1 ½ cups (225g) plain flour

TOPPING

60g butter

½ cup (100g) firmly packed brown sugar

½ cup (125ml) milk

⅔ cup (50g) shredded coconut

1 Preheat oven to 180°C/160°C fan-forced. Grease deep 23cm-square cake pan; line base and sides with baking paper.

2 Combine apple, dates and soda in large bowl, add the water. Cover; stand 10 minutes.

3 Meanwhile, beat butter, extract, sugar and egg in small bowl with electric mixer until light and fluffy. Add butter mixture to apple mixture; stir in sifted flour, in two batches.

4 Pour mixture into pan; bake 50 minutes.

5 Make topping. Remove cake carefully from oven. Carefully spread warm topping evenly over cake; bake a further 20 minutes or until topping has browned.

6 Stand cake 5 minutes then turn onto wire rack; turn cake top-side up to cool.

TOPPING Stir ingredients in medium saucepan over low heat until butter melts and sugar dissolves.

Mango cake

PREPARATION TIME 20 MINUTES **COOKING TIME** 1 HOUR 15 MINUTES **SERVES** 10

185g butter, softened

1 cup (220g) caster sugar

3 eggs

½ cup (125ml) mango puree

⅓ cup (80ml) sour cream

1 ¾ cups (260g) self-raising flour

½ cup (100g) chopped dried mango

1 Preheat oven to 160°C/140°C fan-forced. Grease 15cm x 25cm loaf pan; line base and two long sides with baking paper, extending paper 2cm above edges.

2 Beat butter and sugar in medium bowl with electric mixer until light and fluffy. Beat in eggs, one at a time; stir in mango puree, cream, flour and dried mango. Pour mixture into pan.

3 Bake cake about 1 ¼ hours. Stand cake in pan 5 minutes; turn, top-side up, onto wire rack to cool.

Rhubarb and almond cakes

PREPARATION TIME 20 MINUTES **COOKING TIME** 40 MINUTES **MAKES** 6

½ cup (125ml) milk

¼ cup (40g) blanched almonds, roasted

80g butter, softened

1 teaspoon vanilla extract

½ cup (110g) caster sugar

2 eggs

1 cup (150g) self-raising flour

POACHED RHUBARB

250g trimmed rhubarb, chopped coarsely

¼ cup (60ml) water

½ cup (110g) white sugar

1 Preheat oven to 180°C/160°C fan-forced. Grease 6-hole texas (¾-cup/180ml) muffin pan.

2 Make poached rhubarb.

3 Meanwhile, blend or process milk and nuts until smooth.

4 Beat butter, extract and sugar in small bowl with electric mixer until light and fluffy. Beat in eggs, one at a time. Stir in sifted flour then almond mixture.

5 Spoon mixture equally among muffin pan holes; bake 10 minutes. Carefully remove muffin pan from oven; divide drained rhubarb over muffins, bake further 15 minutes.

6 Stand muffins in pan 5 minutes; turn, top-side up, onto wire rack to cool. Serve warm or cold with reserved rhubarb syrup.

POACHED RHUBARB Stir ingredients in medium saucepan over medium heat; bring to the boil. Reduce heat; simmer, uncovered, about 10 minutes or until rhubarb is just tender. Drain rhubarb over medium bowl; reserve rhubarb and syrup separately.

Almond milk is the ingredient that gives this cake its wonderful flavour. You can make this nut-flavoured milk from any nut you like. Always roast the whole nuts to bring out the best flavour. Cashews are good and go beautifully with poached pears or apples, maybe with some dates added during the poaching.

Glacé peach and almond cake

PREPARATION TIME 20 MINUTES **COOKING TIME** 1 HOUR (PLUS COOLING TIME) **SERVES** 6

185g butter, softened

½ teaspoon almond essence

¾ cup (165g) caster sugar

3 eggs

1 cup (250g) finely chopped glacé peaches

⅓ cup (40g) almond meal

1 ½ cups (225g) self-raising flour

½ cup (75g) plain flour

½ cup (125ml) milk

2 tablespoons brandy

1 Preheat oven to 180°C/160°C fan-forced. Grease 21cm baba cake pan well.

2 Beat butter, essence and sugar in medium bowl with electric mixer until light and fluffy. Beat in eggs, one at a time. Stir in peaches, almond meal, sifted flours, milk and brandy, in two batches. Spread cake mixture into pan.

3 Bake cake about 1 hour. Stand cake in pan 5 minutes; turn, top-side up, onto wire rack to cool.

Quince and blackberry crumble cake

PREPARATION TIME 30 MINUTES **COOKING TIME** 2 HOURS 15 MINUTES (PLUS COOLING TIME) **SERVES** 16

185g unsalted butter, softened

¾ cup (165g) caster sugar

2 eggs

2¼ cups (335g) self-raising flour

¾ cup (180ml) milk

2 cups (300g) frozen blackberries

2 teaspoons cornflour

POACHED QUINCE

3 cups (750ml) water

¾ cup (165g) caster sugar

1 cinnamon stick

1 tablespoon lemon juice

3 medium quinces (1kg), each cut into 8 wedges

CINNAMON CRUMBLE

¾ cup (110g) plain flour

2 tablespoons caster sugar

½ cup (110g) firmly packed brown sugar

100g cold unsalted butter, chopped coarsely

1 teaspoon ground cinnamon

Quinces are a wonderful old-fashioned fruit which develop a rich rosy colour after long slow cooking. It's almost impossible to give an accurate cooking time, as each quince will take a different time to turn pink. Don't give up, just keep simmering until they turn pink; you can't really overdo it.

1 Make poached quince.

2 Preheat oven to 180°C/160°C fan-forced. Grease deep 23cm-square cake pan; line base and sides with baking paper.

3 Beat butter and sugar in small bowl with electric mixer until light and fluffy. Beat in eggs, one at a time. Transfer mixture to large bowl; stir in sifted flour and milk, in two batches. Spread mixture into pan; bake 25 minutes.

4 Meanwhile, make cinnamon crumble.

5 Remove cake from oven. Working quickly, toss frozen blackberries in cornflour to coat. Top cake with drained quince then blackberries; sprinkle cinnamon crumble over fruit. Return cake to oven; bake further 20 minutes. Stand cake in pan 5 minutes; turn, top-side up, onto wire rack. Serve cake warm or cold with reserved quince syrup.

POACHED QUINCE Stir the water, sugar, cinnamon and juice in medium saucepan over heat until sugar dissolves. Add quince; bring to the boil. Reduce heat; simmer, covered, about 1½ hours or until quince is tender and rosy in colour. Cool quince in syrup to room temperature; strain over medium bowl. Reserve quince and syrup separately.

CINNAMON CRUMBLE Blend or process ingredients for cinnamon crumble, pulsing until ingredients come together.

Plum and hazelnut upside-down cake

PREPARATION TIME 15 MINUTES **COOKING TIME** 1 HOUR **SERVES** 10

50g butter, chopped coarsely

½ cup (110g) firmly packed brown sugar

6 medium plums (680g), halved, seeded

185g butter, softened, extra

1 cup (220g) firmly packed brown sugar, extra

3 eggs

½ cup (50g) hazelnut meal

½ cup (75g) self-raising flour

½ cup (75g) plain flour

1 Preheat oven to 180°C/160°C fan-forced. Grease deep 22cm-round cake pan; line base with baking paper.

2 Stir butter and sugar in small saucepan over low heat until smooth; pour over cake pan base. Place plums, cut-side down, over pan base.

3 Beat extra butter and extra sugar in small bowl with electric mixer until creamy. Beat in eggs, one at a time. Transfer mixture to large bowl; stir in hazelnut meal and sifted flours. Spread mixture into pan.

4 Bake cake about 1 hour. Stand cake in pan 5 minutes; turn onto serving plate.

You really need to use fresh — ripe, but not too soft — plums for this cake, canned plums are too soft. Fresh peaches, apricots or nectarines can be used instead. Serve this cake warm with whipped cream, ice-cream, custard or, best of all, crème fraîche.

Boiled passionfruit and orange fruit cake

PREPARATION TIME 20 MINUTES (PLUS COOLING TIME) **COOKING TIME** 1 HOUR 35 MINUTES **SERVES** 20

½ cup (125ml) strained passionfruit pulp

500g mixed dried fruit

¼ cup (60ml) orange juice

1 cup (220g) caster sugar

125g butter, chopped coarsely

3 eggs, beaten lightly

¾ cup (110g) plain flour

¾ cup (110g) self-raising flour

1 teaspoon mixed spice

1 Stir passionfruit pulp, mixed fruit, juice, sugar and butter in saucepan constantly over heat, without boiling, until sugar is dissolved; bring to the boil. Reduce heat; simmer, uncovered, 3 minutes. Remove from heat; transfer mixture to large bowl, then cool to room temperature.

2 Preheat oven to 160°C/140°C fan-forced. Grease deep 20cm-round cake pan; line base and side with baking paper.

3 Stir eggs and sifted dry ingredients into cold fruit mixture. Pour mixture into pan; bake about 1½ hours. Cover cake with foil; cool in pan.

Mixed fruit varies in price and quality and, like most things, you get what you pay for. Be aware that often the glacé cherries in the cheaper mixed fruit are not cherries at all. The best way around the problem of inferior mixed fruit is to mix your own. Generally you'd expect to find sultanas, raisins, currants, mixed peel and glacé cherries in store-bought mixed fruit — but please yourself about the combination.

Carrot and banana cake

PREPARATION TIME 20 MINUTES **COOKING TIME** 1 HOUR 15 MINUTES (PLUS COOLING TIME) **SERVES** 10

1 ¼ cups (185g) plain flour

½ cup (75g) self-raising flour

1 teaspoon bicarbonate of soda

1 teaspoon mixed spice

½ teaspoon ground cinnamon

1 cup (220g) firmly packed brown sugar

¾ cup (80g) coarsely chopped roasted walnuts

3 eggs

2 cups coarsely grated carrot

1 cup mashed banana

1 cup (250ml) vegetable oil

CREAM CHEESE FROSTING

90g cream cheese

90g butter, softened

1 cup (160g) icing sugar

1 Preheat oven to 170°C/150°C fan-forced. Grease base and side of 24cm-round springform tin; line base with baking paper.

2 Sift flours, soda, spices and sugar into large bowl. Stir in nuts, eggs, carrot, banana and oil. Pour mixture into tin.

3 Bake cake about 1 ¼ hours. Cool cake in tin.

4 Meanwhile, make cream cheese frosting. Top cake with frosting.

CREAM CHEESE FROSTING Beat cream cheese and butter in small bowl with electric mixer until as white as possible; gradually beat in sifted icing sugar.

You will need about four medium carrots (480g) and two large overripe bananas (460g) for this recipe. This moist cake will quickly become a family favourite and good old stand-by, it's so quick to mix in just one bowl.

Apricot chocolate chip cake

PREPARATION TIME 30 MINUTES (PLUS STANDING TIME)

COOKING TIME 1 HOUR 15 MINUTES (PLUS COOKING TIME) **SERVES** 8

1 cup (150g) chopped dried apricots

1 cup (250ml) apricot nectar

125g butter, softened

⅔ cup (150g) raw sugar

2 eggs, separated

1 ½ cups (120g) desiccated coconut

1 ½ cups (225g) self-raising flour

½ cup (95g) dark Choc Bits

1 Combine apricots and nectar in medium bowl; stand 1 hour.

2 Preheat oven to 180°C/160°C fan-forced. Grease deep 20cm-round cake pan; line base with baking paper.

3 Beat butter and sugar in small bowl with electric mixer until light and fluffy. Beat in egg yolks. Transfer mixture to large bowl; stir in coconut then sifted flour and apricot mixture, in two batches. Stir in Choc Bits.

4 Beat egg whites in small bowl with electric mixer until soft peaks form; fold into apricot mixture. Spread mixture into pan.

5 Bake cake about 1 ¼ hours. Stand cake in pan 10 minutes; turn, top-side up, onto wire rack to cool.

Change the fruit and nectar to suit yourself. The cake is good made with dried peaches or mango and their accompanying juice or nectar.

Dried & glacé fruit

Dried and glacé fruit are the central ingredients in fruit cakes, but have a variety of uses in modern cooking.

GLACE FRUIT
Glacé is a method of preservation using sugar syrup to stop the production of microorganisms. Fruit preserved in this way is very sweet and juicy and will last for years.

DRIED FRUIT
Drying has been used as a food preservation method since about 2000 BC, and it is still going strong. Dried fruit is eaten all over the world, particularly in ancient cuisines such as Middle Eastern and Indian.

DRIED DATES
Dates are the fruit of the palm tree, which grows in desert conditions. Plump, and thin-skinned with a honey-sweet flavour and sticky texture. De-seed before using in cooking.

MIXED PEEL
Sometimes referred to as candied citrus rind in recipes, mixed peel adds some citrus punch to your Christmas cake or can be dipped in melted chocolate for a special after-dinner treat.

DRIED FRUIT MIX
Dried fruit mix is an essential ingredient in Christmas cake. It is a mixture of sultanas, raisins, currants, mixed peel and glacé cherries. A traditional fruit cake involves soaking dried fruit for a month, so prepare well in advance for your cake making.

GLACE CHERRIES
Glacé cherries are boiled in heavy sugar syrup, then dried to make these beautiful, sweet and colourful baubles. Use in cakes, breads, sweets, as decoration on a banana split, or in a cocktail.

PRUNES

Prunes are plums that have been either commercially or sun dried. They are very sweet and sticky. Adds an acidic flavour to stewed fruit, a Moroccan tagine, or piquant desserts.

DRIED FIGS

Dried figs add the honey-sweet and nutty fig flavour to cakes, muffins and breads without the moist and delicate texture of fresh figs. Dried fruit lasts for at least a year in an airtight container in the refrigerator.

DRIED CRANBERRIES

Dried cranberries are also called craisins. Use in baking for a sweet, tangy flavour; add to salads. Stewed fruit, fruit mince pies, Christmas dried fruit mix or include in your turkey stuffing.

DRIED GRAPES

Currants are dried, tiny grapes native to Corinth, Greece. Used in jams, jellies and sauces. Raisins are dried muscatel grapes; great on a cheese platter. Add sultanas to slow cooked savoury meals for a juicy, sweet explosion of flavour.

DRIED APRICOTS

Australian dried apricots are dried halved, and are of deeper colour and flavour and have a chewy texture. Turkish apricots are dried whole and are plumper, with a very sweet, slightly tangy flavour.

SEMI-DRIED FRUIT

Dried apples, pineapples, pears and bananas are intensely flavoured and packed with nutrients. Add to a cheese platter, or make a spiced fruit mix for a special Christmas gift.

Sticky date cake with butterscotch sauce

PREPARATION TIME 20 MINUTES **COOKING TIME** 55 MINUTES **SERVES** 20

3¾ cups (635g) dried pitted dates

3 cups (750ml) water

2 teaspoons bicarbonate of soda

185g butter, softened

2¼ cups (500g) firmly packed brown sugar

6 eggs

3 cups (450g) self-raising flour

½ cup (60g) coarsely chopped walnuts

½ cup (60g) coarsely chopped pecans

BUTTERSCOTCH SAUCE

2 cups (440g) firmly packed brown sugar

500ml thickened cream

250g butter, chopped coarsely

1 Preheat oven to 180°C/160°C fan-forced. Grease 26cm x 36cm baking dish; line with two thicknesses baking paper, extending paper 5cm above long sides of dish.

2 Combine dates and the water in medium saucepan; bring to the boil. Remove from heat; stir in soda. Cover; stand 5 minutes. Blend or process date mixture until smooth.

3 Beat butter and sugar in large bowl with electric mixer until light and fluffy. Beat in eggs, one at a time. Stir in date mixture and sifted flour, in two batches. Spread mixture into dish; sprinkle with nuts.

4 Bake cake about 50 minutes. Stand cake in dish 10 minutes; turn, top-side up, onto wire rack to cool.

5 Meanwhile, make butterscotch sauce.

6 Brush surface of hot cake with ⅓ cup of the hot butterscotch sauce. Serve with remaining sauce.

BUTTERSCOTCH SAUCE Stir ingredients in medium saucepan over medium heat, without boiling, until sugar dissolves; bring to the boil. Reduce heat; simmer 3 minutes.

Sticky date cake (or pudding) suffers from an identity crisis — it never knows if it's a cake or a dessert. In fact it doubles happily as both. This recipe will serve at least 20 people. If by chance you have leftovers, freeze the cake in portion sizes and keep the sauce in a jar in the fridge. Then, reheat both separately in the microwave oven for an instant dessert.

It's important bananas be well and truly ripe for use in any cake, the natural sugars in overripe bananas are part of the ingredient balance. You need at least one medium-sized banana for each ½ cup of well-mashed banana. Toss any overripe bananas in the freezer — no need to wrap them — for future use.

Tropical papaya and banana cake

PREPARATION TIME 20 MINUTES   **COOKING TIME** 1 HOUR   **SERVES** 10

125g butter
¾ cup (165g) caster sugar
2 eggs
½ cup mashed banana
½ cup (100g) chopped fresh papaya
1½ cups (225g) self-raising flour
½ cup (45g) desiccated coconut
¼ cup (60ml) milk

1 Preheat oven to 180°C/160°C fan-forced. Grease deep 20cm round cake pan; line base with baking paper.
2 Beat butter and sugar in small bowl with electric mixer until light and fluffy. Beat in eggs, one at a time. Transfer mixture to large bowl; stir in banana and papaya. Stir in sifted flour, coconut and milk, in two batches. Sread mixture into pan.
3 Bake cake 1 hour. Stand cake in pan 5 minutes; turn, top-side up, onto wire rack to cool.

Banana cake with passionfruit icing

PREPARATION TIME 35 MINUTES   **COOKING TIME** 50 MINUTES   **SERVES** 10

125g butter, softened
¾ cup (165g) firmly packed brown sugar
2 eggs
1½ cups (225g) self-raising flour
½ teaspoon bicarbonate of soda
1 teaspoon mixed spice
1 cup mashed banana
½ cup (120g) sour cream
¼ cup (60ml) milk

PASSIONFRUIT ICING
1½ cups (240g) icing sugar
2 tablespoons passionfruit pulp, approximately

1 Preheat oven to 180°C/160°C fan-forced. Grease 15cm x 25cm loaf pan; line base with baking paper.
2 Beat butter and sugar in small bowl with electric mixer until light and fluffy. Beat in eggs, one at a time. Transfer mixture to large bowl; stir in sifted dry ingredients, banana, sour cream and milk. Spread mixture into pan.
3 Bake cake about 50 minutes. Stand cake in pan 5 minutes; turn, top-side up, onto wire rack to cool.
4 Meanwhile, make passionfruit icing. Spread cake with icing.

PASSIONFRUIT ICING Sift icing sugar into small bowl; stir in enough of the passionfruit to give a thick pouring consistency.

Upside-down toffee date and banana cake

PREPARATION TIME 20 MINUTES **COOKING TIME** 1 HOUR 10 MINUTES **SERVES** 12

1½ cups (330g) caster sugar

1½ cups (375ml) water

3 star anise

2 medium bananas (400g), sliced thinly

1 cup (140g) dried seeded dates

¾ cup (180ml) water, extra

½ cup (125ml) dark rum

1 teaspoon bicarbonate of soda

60g butter, chopped

½ cup (110g) firmly packed brown sugar

2 eggs

2 teaspoons mixed spice

1 cup (150g) self-raising flour

½ cup mashed banana

300ml thickened cream

1 Preheat oven to 180°C/160°C fan-forced. Grease deep 22cm-round cake pan; line base with baking paper.

2 Stir caster sugar, the water and star anise in medium saucepan over low heat, without boiling, until sugar dissolves. Bring to the boil; boil syrup, uncovered, without stirring, about 5 minutes or until thickened slightly. Strain ½ cup of the syrup into small heatproof jug; reserve to flavour cream. Discard star anise.

3 To make toffee, continue boiling remaining syrup, uncovered, without stirring, about 10 minutes or until golden brown. Pour hot toffee into cake pan; top with sliced banana.

4 Place dates, the extra water and rum in small saucepan; bring to the boil, remove from heat. Stir in soda; stand 5 minutes. Process date mixture with butter and brown sugar until almost smooth. Add eggs, spice and flour; process until just combined. Stir in mashed banana. Pour mixture into pan.

5 Bake cake about 40 minutes. Turn cake, in pan, onto serving plate; stand 2 minutes. Remove pan then peel away baking paper.

6 To make star anise cream, beat cream in small bowl with electric mixer until firm peaks form. Stir in reserved syrup.

7 Serve cake warm or at room temperature with star anise cream.

Everybody loves an upside-down cake, especially served warm as a dessert. If you'd prefer to make this cake in a square cake pan — for easier cutting and serving — use a deep 19cm-square cake pan. The oven temperature and baking time will be the same.

Blueberry and olive oil cake

PREPARATION TIME 25 MINUTES **COOKING TIME** 1 HOUR (PLUS STANDING TIME) **SERVES** 16

3 eggs

1¼ cups (275g) caster sugar

2 tablespoons finely grated orange rind

½ cup (125ml) olive oil

⅓ cup (80ml) milk

1 cup (150g) plain flour

1 cup (150g) self-raising flour

100g frozen blueberries

¼ cup (80g) apricot jam, warmed, strained

Olive oil replaces butter in this recipe. Avoid using a full-flavoured extra virgin olive oil — as the flavour would dominate the cake. Use a regular olive oil for the best results.

1 Preheat oven to 180°C/160°C fan-forced. Grease deep 19cm-square cake pan.

2 Beat eggs, sugar and rind in small bowl with electric mixer until sugar is dissolved. Transfer mixture to large bowl; fold in combined oil and milk, and sifted flours, in two batches. Pour mixture into pan.

3 Bake cake 20 minutes. Carefully remove from oven; sprinkle surface evenly with blueberries. Return cake to oven; bake further 40 minutes.

4 Stand cake in pan 10 minutes; turn, top-side up, onto wire rack to cool. Brush warm cake with jam.

Economical boiled fruit cake

PREPARATION TIME 15 MINUTES (PLUS COOLING TIME) **COOKING TIME** 1 HOUR 30 MINUTES **SERVES** 20

2¾ cups (500g) mixed dried fruit

½ cup (125ml) water

1 cup (220g) firmly packed brown sugar

125g butter, chopped coarsely

1 teaspoon mixed spice

½ teaspoon bicarbonate of soda

½ cup (125ml) sweet sherry

1 egg

1 cup (150g) plain flour

1 cup (150g) self-raising flour

⅓ cup (55g) blanched almonds

2 tablespoons sweet sherry, extra

1 Stir fruit, the water, sugar, butter, spice and soda in large saucepan over low heat, without boiling, until sugar dissolves and butter melts; bring to the boil. Reduce heat; simmer, covered, 5 minutes. Remove from heat; stir in sherry. Cool.

2 Preheat oven to 160°C/140°C fan-forced. Grease deep 20cm-round cake pan; line base and side with two layers of baking paper, extending paper 5cm above side.

3 Stir egg and sifted flours into fruit mixture. Spread mixture into pan; decorate with nuts.

4 Bake cake about 1½ hours. Brush top of hot cake with extra sherry. Cover cake with foil; cool in pan.

1 BLUEBERRY AND OLIVE OIL CAKE **2** ECONOMICAL BOILED FRUIT CAKE
3 APPLE STREUSEL CAKE [P 128] **4** MOIST WHOLE ORANGE CAKE [P 128]

Try baking this popular cake in either a 23cm slab cake pan or a deep 23cm-square cake pan. It's best to line whichever pan you use. Bake the cake at the same temperature we suggest here, but reduce the baking time to about 20 minutes in steps 3 and 5. The cake is not as deep and won't rise much, but it's slightly more manageable to cut.

Apple streusel cake

PREPARATION TIME 25 MINUTES (PLUS FREEZING TIME) **COOKING TIME** 50 MINUTES **SERVES** 12

200g butter, softened

2 teaspoons finely grated lemon rind

⅔ cup (150g) caster sugar

3 eggs

1 cup (150g) self-raising flour

½ cup (75g) plain flour

⅓ cup (80ml) milk

5 medium apples (750g)

25g butter, extra

⅓ cup (75g) firmly packed brown sugar

STREUSEL

½ cup (75g) plain flour

¼ cup (35g) self-raising flour

⅓ cup (75g) firmly packed brown sugar

½ teaspoon ground cinnamon

80g butter, chopped finely

1 Preheat oven to 180°C/160°C fan-forced. Grease deep 22cm-round cake pan; line with baking paper.

2 Make streusel; wrap in plastic wrap, freeze about 1 hour or until firm.

3 Meanwhile, beat butter, rind and caster sugar in small bowl with electric mixer until light and fluffy. Beat in eggs, one at a time. Transfer to large bowl; stir in sifted flours and milk, in two batches. Spread mixture into pan; bake 25 minutes.

4 Meanwhile, peel, core and quarter apples; slice thinly. Melt extra butter in large frying pan; cook apple, stirring, about 5 minutes or until browned lightly. Add brown sugar; cook, stirring, about 5 minutes or until mixture thickens slightly. Remove from heat.

5 Remove cake from oven. Working quickly, top cake with apple mixture; coarsely grate streusel over apple. Return to oven; bake about 25 minutes. Stand cake 10 minutes; turn, top-side up, onto wire rack to cool. Serve cake warm or cold.

STREUSEL Process flours, sugar and cinnamon until combined. Add butter; process until ingredients come together.

Moist whole orange cake

PREPARATION TIME 30 MINUTES **COOKING TIME** 2 HOURS 45 MINUTES (PLUS COOLING TIME) **SERVES** 12

2 medium oranges (480g)

⅔ cup (110g) blanched almonds, roasted

1 cup (220g) caster sugar

1 teaspoon baking powder

6 eggs

2 cups (250g) almond meal

2 tablespoons plain flour

1 Place unpeeled oranges in medium saucepan; cover with cold water, bring to the boil. Boil, covered, 30 minutes; drain. Repeat process with fresh water, boil about 1 hour or until oranges are tender. Remove oranges from pan; cool.

2 Preheat oven to 180°C/160°C fan-forced. Grease deep 22cm-round cake pan; line base and side with baking paper.

3 Process roasted almonds with 2 tablespoons of the sugar until finely chopped.

4 Trim and discard ends from oranges. Halve oranges; discard seeds. Process oranges, including rind, with baking powder until pulpy.

5 Beat eggs and remaining sugar in medium bowl with electric mixer until thick and pale in colour. Fold in almond mixture, almond meal, sifted flour and orange pulp. Pour mixture into pan.

6 Bake cake about 1 hour. Cool cake in pan; turn onto serving plate. Dust with sifted icing sugar, if desired.

Hummingbird cake

PREPARATION TIME 35 MINUTES **COOKING TIME** 40 MINUTES (PLUS COOLING TIME) **SERVES** 16

450g can crushed pineapple in syrup

1 cup (150g) plain flour

½ cup (75g) self-raising flour

½ teaspoon bicarbonate of soda

½ teaspoon ground cinnamon

½ teaspoon ground ginger

1 cup (220g) firmly packed brown sugar

½ cup (45g) desiccated coconut

1 cup mashed banana

2 eggs

¾ cup (180ml) vegetable oil

CREAM CHEESE FROSTING

30g butter, softened

60g cream cheese, softened

1 teaspoon vanilla extract

1½ cups (240g) icing sugar

It's really important to drain the canned pineapple thoroughly in this recipe. If you don't the cake will be soggy. Cream cheese frosting is a favourite, but, if you prefer, top the cake with a simple icing made using some of the pineapple syrup. Sift 2 cups icing sugar into a bowl, stir in 2 teaspoons vegetable oil, then about 2 tablespoons pineapple syrup. The mixture should be pasty in texture. When the cake is turned out of the pan to cool, spread the icing onto the hot cake. It will set when the cake is cold.

1 Preheat oven to 180°C/160°C fan-forced. Grease deep 23cm-square cake pan; line base with baking paper.

2 Drain pineapple over medium bowl, pressing with spoon to extract as much syrup as possible. Reserve ¼ cup (60ml) syrup.

3 Sift flours, soda, spices and sugar into large bowl. Stir in drained pineapple, reserved syrup, coconut, banana, eggs and oil. Pour mixture into pan.

4 Bake cake about 40 minutes. Stand cake in pan 5 minutes; turn, top-side up, onto wire rack to cool.

5 Make cream cheese frosting; spread cold cake with frosting.

CREAM CHEESE FROSTING Beat butter, cream cheese and extract in small bowl with electric mixer until light and fluffy; gradually beat in sifted icing sugar.

Boiled whisky fruit cake

PREPARATION TIME 35 MINUTES (PLUS STANDING TIME) **COOKING TIME** 3 HOURS **SERVES** 24

1½ cups (250g) raisins

1½ cups (210g) dried seeded dates

1½ cups (250g) seeded prunes

1½ cups (250g) sultanas

⅓ cup (70g) red glacé cherries, quartered

⅓ cup (55g) mixed peel

2 tablespoons caster sugar

30g butter

½ cup (125ml) whisky

250g butter, chopped, extra

1 cup (220g) firmly packed dark brown sugar

½ teaspoon bicarbonate of soda

½ cup (70g) slivered almonds

2 cups (300g) plain flour

2 teaspoons mixed spice

5 eggs

¼ cup (60ml) whisky, extra

1 Chop raisins, dates and prunes the same size as the sultanas; combine in large bowl with sultanas, cherries and peel.

2 Place caster sugar in large heavy-based saucepan over medium heat; turn pan occasionally until sugar is melted. Add butter and whisky; stir over low heat until mixture is smooth.

3 Add extra butter, brown sugar and fruit to pan, stir over heat until butter melts; bring to the boil. Remove from heat; stir in soda. Transfer mixture to large bowl, cover; stand overnight at room temperature.

4 Preheat oven to 150°C/130°C fan-forced. Grease deep 19cm-square cake pan; line base and sides with two layers of brown paper then baking paper, extending paper 5cm over sides.

5 Add nuts, sifted flour and spice, then eggs to fruit mixture; stir until well combined. Spoon mixture into corners of pan then spread remaining mixture into pan. Tap pan on bench to settle mixture and break any large air bubbles; level surface of cake with wet spatula. Bake about 3 hours.

6 Brush hot cake with extra whisky. Cover hot cake tightly with foil; cool in pan.

Light and dark fruit cake

PREPARATION TIME 30 MINUTES (PLUS STANDING TIME) **COOKING TIME** 2 HOURS **SERVES** 40

2 cups (340g) seeded dates, chopped coarsely

1 cup (170g) seeded prunes, chopped coarsely

1 cup (150g) dried currants

⅓ cup (80ml) dark rum

40g butter, softened

½ cup (100g) firmly packed brown sugar

2 eggs

½ cup (50g) finely chopped pecans

40g dark eating chocolate, grated finely

½ cup (75g) plain flour

½ teaspoon bicarbonate of soda

200g marzipan

2 tablespoons icing sugar

¼ cup (60ml) dark rum, extra

LIGHT LAYER

90g butter, softened

⅔ cup (150g) caster sugar

2 eggs

1 cup (150g) plain flour

⅓ cup (80ml) dark rum

¾ cup (120g) sultanas

½ cup (85g) mixed peel

¼ cup (55g) finely chopped glacé pineapple

½ cup (50g) finely chopped pecans

You need only slender small servings of this ultra-rich cake, which is why we've chosen to bake it in a lamington pan. The layer of marzipan in the middle keeps the cake moist as well as adding to the flavour. Buy the best marzipan (or almond paste) you can find.

1 Combine fruit and rum in medium bowl. Cover; stand overnight.

2 Line 20cm x 30cm lamington pan with baking paper, extending paper 3cm over long sides of pan.

3 Beat butter, sugar and eggs in small bowl with electric mixer until pale in colour (mixture will curdle, but will come together later). Add butter mixture to fruit mixture; stir in nuts, chocolate and sifted flour and soda. Spread mixture in pan.

4 Roll out marzipan on icing-sugared surface to 20cm x 30cm rectangle; place in pan over dark cake layer.

5 Preheat oven to 150°C/130°C fan-forced.

6 Make light layer; spread mixture evenly over marzipan.

7 Bake cake about 1 hour. Cover with foil; bake further 1 hour. Brush cake top with extra rum. Cover with foil; cool in pan.

LIGHT LAYER Beat butter, sugar and eggs in small bowl with electric mixer until pale in colour (mixture will curdle, but will come together later). Stir in sifted flour, rum, fruit and nuts.

Fresh ginger cake with golden ginger cream

PREPARATION TIME 15 MINUTES **COOKING TIME** 1 HOUR (PLUS STANDING TIME) **SERVES** 12

250g butter, chopped

½ cup (110g) firmly packed brown sugar

⅔ cup (230g) golden syrup

12cm piece fresh ginger (60g), grated finely

¾ cup (180ml) thickened cream

1 cup (150g) plain flour

1 cup (150g) self-raising flour

½ teaspoon bicarbonate of soda

2 eggs

GOLDEN GINGER CREAM

300ml thickened cream

2 tablespoons golden syrup

2 teaspoons ground ginger

1 Preheat oven to 180°C/160°C fan-forced. Grease deep 22cm-round cake pan.

2 Melt butter in large saucepan, add sugar, syrup and ginger; stir over low heat until sugar dissolves. Remove from heat; whisk in cream, then sifted flours and soda, and eggs. Pour mixture into pan.

3 Bake cake about 50 minutes. Stand cake in pan 10 minutes; turn, top-side up, onto wire rack to cool.

4 Meanwhile, beat ingredients for golden ginger cream in small bowl with electric mixer until soft peaks form. Serve cake with cream.

Pear and almond cake with passionfruit glaze

PREPARATION TIME 30 MINUTES **COOKING TIME** 50 MINUTES **SERVES** 12

185g butter, softened

½ cup (110g) caster sugar

3 eggs

1½ cups (185g) almond meal

¼ cup (35g) plain flour

420g can pear halves in natural juice, drained

PASSIONFRUIT GLAZE

⅓ cup (80ml) passionfruit pulp

⅓ cup (80ml) light corn syrup

1 tablespoon caster sugar

1 Preheat oven to 160°C/140°C fan-forced. Grease 22cm springform tin; line base and side with baking paper.

2 Beat butter and sugar in medium bowl with electric mixer until light and fluffy. Beat in eggs, one at a time; stir in almond meal and flour. Spread mixture into tin; top with pears.

3 Bake cake 50 minutes. Stand cake in pan 5 minutes; remove from tin.

4 Make passionfruit glaze; pour over cake.

PASSIONFRUIT GLAZE Stir ingredients in small saucepan over heat, without boiling, until sugar dissolves; bring to the boil. Reduce heat; simmer, uncovered, without stirring, about 2 minutes or until thickened slightly; cool.

Almond carrot cake

PREPARATION TIME 20 MINUTES **COOKING TIME** 1 HOUR 15 MINUTES **SERVES** 12

5 eggs, separated

1 teaspoon finely grated lemon rind

1¼ cups (275g) caster sugar

2 cups (480g) coarsely grated carrot

2 cups (240g) almond meal

½ cup (75g) self-raising flour

2 tablespoons roasted slivered almonds

CREAM CHEESE FROSTING

100g cream cheese, softened

80g butter, softened

1 teaspoon lemon juice

½ cup (80g) icing sugar

Almond is the main flavour in this cake, the carrot adds texture, colour and a little taste. The cake is light, almost spongy — unlike the average carrot cake.

1 Preheat oven to 180°C/160°C fan-forced. Grease deep 19cm-square cake pan; line base with baking paper.

2 Beat egg yolks, rind and sugar in small bowl with electric mixer until thick and creamy. Transfer mixture to large bowl; stir in carrot, almond meal and sifted flour.

3 Beat egg whites in small bowl with electric mixer until soft peaks form; fold into carrot mixture, in two batches. Pour mixture into pan.

4 Bake cake about 1¼ hours. Stand cake in pan 5 minutes; turn, top-side up, onto wire rack to cool.

5 Meanwhile, make cream cheese frosting.

6 Spread cold cake with cream cheese frosting; sprinkle with slivered almonds.

CREAM CHEESE FROSTING Beat cream cheese and butter in small bowl with electric mixer until light and fluffy; gradually beat in juice and sifted icing sugar.

Caramelised apple teacakes

PREPARATION TIME 25 MINUTES **COOKING TIME** 35 MINUTES **MAKES** 12

Serve these little cakes warm, topped with thick or whipped cream, or ice-cream. Serve as a dessert or as an afternoon tea treat.

125g butter, softened

1 teaspoon vanilla extract

⅔ cup (150g) caster sugar

2 eggs

1¼ cups (185g) self-raising flour

½ cup (75g) plain flour

1 teaspoon mixed spice

½ teaspoon ground cinnamon

1 cup (250ml) buttermilk

1 large apple (200g), peeled, grated coarsely

CARAMELISED APPLES

2 small apples (260g)

80g butter, chopped

⅓ cup (75g) firmly packed brown sugar

1 Make caramelised apples.

2 Preheat oven to 180°C/160°C fan-forced. Grease 12-hole (⅓-cup/80ml) muffin pan.

3 Place one slice caramelised apple in base of each pan hole. Spoon caramel sauce into pan holes.

4 Beat butter, extract and sugar in small bowl with electric mixer until light and fluffy. Beat in eggs, one at a time. Transfer mixture to large bowl; stir in sifted flours and spices and buttermilk, in two batches. Stir in apple. Spoon mixture into pan holes.

5 Bake cakes about 30 minutes. Stand cakes in pan 5 minutes; turn upside-down onto serving plates.

CARAMELISED APPLES Slice unpeeled apples crossways into 1cm thick slices. Stir butter and sugar in large frying pan over low heat until sugar dissolves. Add apple slices; cook, turning occasionally, about 3 minutes or until browned lightly.

Ginger sticky date pudding with butterscotch sauce

PREPARATION TIME 10 MINUTES **COOKING TIME** 45 MINUTES **SERVES** 8

Prunes go just as well as dates with ginger. Try and get some dark brown sugar to use in this dessert cake — it adds more colour and flavour. Use unsalted butter in both the cake and sauce if you have it.

1 cup (140g) seeded dried dates

¼ cup (55g) glacé ginger

1 teaspoon bicarbonate of soda

1 cup (250ml) boiling water

50g butter

½ cup (110g) firmly packed brown sugar

2 eggs

1 cup (150g) self-raising flour

1 teaspoon ground ginger

BUTTERSCOTCH SAUCE

300ml cream

¾ cup (165g) firmly packed brown sugar

80g butter, chopped coarsely

1 Preheat oven to 200°C/180°C fan-forced. Grease deep 20cm-round cake pan; line base with baking paper.

2 Place dates, glacé ginger and soda with the water in food processor; place lid in position, stand 5 minutes. Add butter and sugar; process until mixture is almost smooth. Add eggs, flour and ground ginger; pulse until combined. Pour mixture into pan.

3 Bake pudding about 45 minutes. Stand 10 minutes before turning onto serving plate.

4 Meanwhile, make butterscotch sauce. Serve pudding warm with butterscotch sauce.

BUTTERSCOTCH SAUCE Stir ingredients in medium saucepan over low heat until smooth.

Rhubarb cake

PREPARATION TIME 20 MINUTES **COOKING TIME** 1 HOUR 30 MINUTES **SERVES** 12

60g butter, softened

1 teaspoon finely grated lemon rind

1½ cups (300g) firmly packed brown sugar

2 eggs

1 cup (150g) self-raising flour

1 cup (150g) plain flour

1 teaspoon ground cinnamon

1 cup (250ml) sour cream

500g rhubarb, trimmed, chopped coarsely

⅓ cup (75g) firmly packed brown sugar, extra

1 teaspoon ground cinnamon, extra

1 Preheat oven to 180°C/160°C fan-forced. Grease deep 22cm-round cake pan; line base with baking paper.

2 Beat butter, rind and sugar in small bowl with electric mixer until light and fluffy. Beat in eggs. Transfer mixture to large bowl; stir in sifted flours and cinnamon and cream, in two batches. Stir in rhubarb. Spread into pan; sprinkle with combined extra sugar and extra cinnamon.

3 Bake cake about 1½ hours. Stand cake in pan 5 minutes; turn, top-side up, onto wire rack to cool.

The butter, sugar and egg mixture will curdle — the fat content of this cake comes not only from the butter, but from the sour cream as well. So, use a full-fat sour cream for the best results. If you're using frozen rhubarb, thaw it and drain it well before mixing it in. Orange goes well with rhubarb too — try it next time, instead of the lemon.

SYRUP CAKES

Syrup Cakes

The English may have invented the butter cake, but we have the people of the countries of the eastern Mediterranean — Greece, Turkey, Syria, Lebanon and Jordan — to thank for the serendipitous act of transforming a simple cake into something truly splendid by drenching it in sugar syrup.

The Polish, meanwhile, developed their own syrup cake, the baba, using a leavened dough (a bit like brioche) and a syrup flavoured with rum or kirsch. In the 19th century the French Julien brothers, came up with their own interpretation which they called a savarin, as a tribute to Jean-Anthelme Brillat Savarin, the French gastronome and story-teller who was supposed to have shared the secret of making the sugar syrup with the Juliens. A savarin is soaked in syrup then filled with whipped cream or crème pâtissière (custard) and fruit.

Thanks to the syrup, these cakes are delightfully moist and intensely sweet. Because of their high sugar content they keep well in an airtight container if the weather is cool, or in the refrigerator if it is not.

Unless otherwise specified in the recipe, the hot syrup should be poured over the cake while it's still hot to increase the absorption of the syrup. Some recipes suggest piercing the top of the cake with a skewer to further enhance the syrup absorption. Turn the cake onto a wire rack, then use another wire rack to turn the cake the right way up. Stand the cake on the rack over a tray or dish to catch any excess syrup. The excess can be poured back over the cake, or served, separately, in a jug. (See *Baking Techniques* page 631.)

If you want to make a syrup cake in advance, you can freeze it un-syruped and store the syrup in a separate container in the refrigerator for up to a week. Defrost the cake in the refrigerator, heat the syrup in a saucepan and the foil-wrapped cake in a slow oven, then pour the syrup over the cake as directed in the recipe. A butter cake which is no longer at peak freshness can be revived by heating it gently and pouring a warm syrup over it. In the Middle East, syrup cakes are served with kaymak, a kind of clotted cream which is made by slowly simmering milk and cream, then standing until the thickened cream rises to the surface and the excess milk is poured off. While whipped or heavy cream, thick yogurt or ice-cream are the most obvious accompaniments, you could also poach some complementary fruits in the excess (or extra) syrup to serve with the cake as an accompaniment.

At its most basic, sugar syrup is a simple combination of sugar or honey and water, heated and stirred to dissolve the sugar, then boiled to reduce it to a sticky consistency. Most also include a measure of orange, lemon or lime juice and perhaps some peeled rind to enhance the flavouring. You could also add a liqueur such as orange-flavoured Cointreau or Grand Marnier, hazelnut-flavoured Frangelico, almond-flavoured Amaretto or brandy, rum or whisky to the syrup. Syrup cake makers can also access an apothecary's cabinet of flavourings and aromatics that lend flavour and intrigue to the cake. They include:

STAR ANISE, a dried star-shaped pod whose seeds have an astringent aniseed flavour.

CARDAMOM, a spice native to India and used extensively in its cuisine. It can be purchased in pod, seed or ground form and has a distinctive aromatic, sweetly rich flavour.

VANILLA BEAN, the dried, long, thin pod from a tropical golden orchid grown in central and South America and Tahiti. Its minuscule black seeds are used to impart a luscious flavour in baking and desserts. To release the seeds you will need to split the bean and scrape the seeds out.

CINNAMON, available both in the piece (called sticks or quills) and ground into powder. It's the dried inner bark of the shoots of the Sri Lankan native cinnamon tree. However, much of what is sold as the real thing is in fact cassia, or Chinese cinnamon, from the bark of the cassia tree. Less expensive to process than true cinnamon, it is often blended with Sri Lankan cinnamon to produce the type of "cinnamon" most commonly found on supermarkets shelves.

NUTMEG, a strong and very pungent spice ground from the dried nut of an evergreen tree native to Indonesia. Usually found ground but the flavour is more intense from a whole nut, available from spice shops, so it's best to grate your own.

ORANGE FLOWER WATER, a natural extract made from the distillation of orange blossoms, which imparts an orange fragrance to Mediterranean desserts.

ROSE WATER, an extract made from crushed rose petals, called gulab in India; used for its aromatic quality in many desserts.

SAFFRON is the stigma of a member of the crocus family. It is available ground or in strands and imparts a yellow-orange colour and rich honeyed flavour to food once infused. The quality can vary greatly; the best is the most expensive spice in the world.

The most natural drink to serve with syrup cakes is the strong black coffee variously described as arabic, turkish, lebanese or greek coffee. Made from pulverised, rather than ground coffee, this thick, usually sweet brew is commonly made in a long-handled aluminium, brass or enamelled pot. Allow approximately a teaspoon of sugar and a teaspoon of ground coffee per person. Add the sugar and about a shot glass of water to the pot. Bring to the boil to dissolve the sugar — it is the guest of honour's prerogative to dictate how sweet the coffee is — then add the coffee to the boiling water. As the coffee mixture returns to the boil, foam rises to the top of the pot. When this happens, remove the pot from the heat and give it a sharp tap to reduce the foam. Repeat the process two or three times and after the final boiling, add a few drops of cold water to settle the grounds. Serve immediately in small coffee cups. It's customary to leave the residue in the bottom of the cup. A strong espresso or short black would make a worthy substitute. A glass of water, to counteract both the sweetness of the cake and the strength of the coffee, is usually a welcome gesture.

Orange and brandy marry well together. Handle the baked cake gently, it's quite fragile.

Orange syrup cake

PREPARATION TIME 25 MINUTES **COOKING TIME** 1 HOUR 10 MINUTES **SERVES** 12

1 large orange (300g)

2 cups (500ml) water

2 cups (440g) caster sugar

²⁄₃ cup (160ml) brandy

250g unsalted butter, softened

1 cup (220g) caster sugar, extra

4 eggs

1 ½ cups (225g) self-raising flour

2 tablespoons cornflour

1 Preheat oven to 160°C/140°C fan-forced. Grease deep 22cm round cake pan; line base and side with baking paper.

2 Peel orange. Chop both the peel and the flesh of orange finely; discard seeds. Place flesh and peel in medium saucepan with the water, sugar and brandy; stir over medium heat until sugar dissolves. Bring to the boil. Reduce heat; simmer, uncovered, 15 minutes or until orange skin is tender. Strain syrup into heatproof jug; reserve solids, cool.

3 Beat butter and extra sugar in small bowl with electric mixer until light and fluffy. Beat in eggs, one at a time. Transfer mixture to large bowl; stir in sifted flours and reserved orange solids. Pour mixture into pan; bake about 50 minutes.

4 Meanwhile, simmer reserved syrup over heat in small saucepan until thickened slightly.

5 Stand cake in pan 5 minutes; turn, top-side up, onto wire rack over tray. Pour hot syrup over hot cake; serve warm.

There's no need to line the cake pan for this recipe. Use either a 23cm slab cake pan or a deep 23cm-square cake pan.

Cinnamon and walnut syrup cake

PREPARATION TIME 20 MINUTES **COOKING TIME** 40 MINUTES **SERVES** 12

3 eggs

¾ cup (165g) caster sugar

¾ cup (110g) self-raising flour

3 teaspoons ground cinnamon

185g butter, melted

¾ cup (120g) coarsely chopped walnuts

SUGAR SYRUP

1 cup (220) caster sugar

¾ cup (180ml) water

1 Preheat oven to 180°C/160°C fan-forced. Grease deep 23cm-square cake pan.

2 Beat eggs in small bowl with electric mixer until thick and creamy. Gradually add sugar; beat until dissolved. Beat in sifted flour and cinnamon, in two batches; beat in butter, stir in walnuts. Pour mixture into pan.

3 Bake cake about 30 minutes. Stand cake in pan 5 minutes; turn onto wire rack over tray, leave cake upside down.

4 Make sugar syrup; pour hot syrup over hot cake. Serve cake warm or cold.

SUGAR SYRUP Stir ingredients in small saucepan over heat, without boiling, until sugar is dissolved; bring to the boil. Reduce heat; simmer, uncovered, 5 minutes.

ORANGE SYRUP CAKE

Pistachio butter cake with orange honey syrup

PREPARATION TIME 20 MINUTES **COOKING TIME** 50 MINUTES **SERVES** 16

2 cups (280g) pistachios, chopped coarsely

185g butter, softened

1 tablespoon finely grated orange rind

¾ cup (165g) caster sugar

3 eggs

¼ cup (60ml) buttermilk

1½ cups (225g) self-raising flour

¾ cup (110g) plain flour

ORANGE HONEY SYRUP

1 cup (220g) caster sugar

1 cup (250ml) water

1 tablespoon honey

1 cinnamon stick

1 teaspoon cardamom seeds, bruised

3 star anise

3 strips orange rind

1 Make orange honey syrup; cool.

2 Preheat oven to 180°C/160°C fan-forced. Grease deep 23cm-square cake pan; line base and sides with baking paper, extending paper 2cm above sides. Sprinkle nuts evenly over base of pan.

3 Beat butter, rind and sugar in small bowl with electric mixer until light and fluffy. Beat in eggs, one at a time. Transfer mixture to large bowl; stir in buttermilk and ⅓ cup of the orange honey syrup, and sifted flours, in two batches. Spread mixture into pan.

4 Bake cake about 40 minutes. Stand cake in pan 5 minutes; turn, top-side up, onto baking-paper-covered wire rack. Brush surface of hot cake with half of the remaining heated syrup.

5 Cut cake into squares, serve warm, drizzled with remaining heated syrup.

ORANGE HONEY SYRUP Stir ingredients in small saucepan over low heat, without boiling, until sugar dissolves; bring to the boil. Remove from heat; cool 15 minutes then strain.

Choc-chip orange syrup cake

PREPARATION TIME 20 MINUTES **COOKING TIME** 1 HOUR **SERVES** 10

185g butter, softened

2 teaspoons finely grated orange rind

1¼ cups (275g) caster sugar

4 eggs

100g dark Choc Bits

¾ cup (180g) sour cream

2 cups (300g) plain flour

½ teaspoon bicarbonate of soda

ORANGE SYRUP

½ cup (110g) caster sugar

¼ cup (60ml) orange juice

1 Preheat oven to 170°C/150°C fan-forced. Grease and flour 20cm baba pan, shaking away any excess flour.

2 Beat butter, rind and sugar in medium bowl with electric mixer until light and fluffy. Beat in eggs, one at a time. Stir in Choc Bits and sour cream, then sifted flour and soda. Spread mixture into pan.

3 Bake cake about 55 minutes. Stand cake in pan 5 minutes; turn, top-side up, onto wire rack over tray.

4 Meanwhile, make orange syrup; pour hot syrup over hot cake.

ORANGE SYRUP Stir sugar and juice in small saucepan over heat, without boiling, until sugar dissolves; bring to the boil. Remove from heat.

Lime coconut syrup cake

PREPARATION TIME 30 MINUTES **COOKING TIME** 55 MINUTES **SERVES** 8

125g butter, softened

1 tablespoon finely grated lime rind

1 cup (220g) caster sugar

3 eggs

1 ¾ cups (260g) self-raising flour

1 cup (90g) desiccated coconut

½ cup (125ml) yogurt

½ cup (125ml) milk

TANGY LIME SYRUP

⅓ cup (80ml) lime juice

¾ cup (165g) caster sugar

¼ cup (60ml) water

1 Preheat oven to 180°C/160°C fan-forced. Grease 20cm baba pan well.

2 Beat butter, rind and sugar in medium bowl with electric mixer until light and fluffy. Beat in eggs, one at a time. Stir in sifted flour, coconut, yogurt and milk, in two batches. Spread mixture into pan.

3 Bake cake about 45 minutes. Stand cake in pan 5 minutes; turn, top-side up, onto wire rack over tray.

4 Make tangy lime syrup; drizzle hot syrup over hot cake.

TANGY LIME SYRUP Stir ingredients in small saucepan over heat, without boiling, until sugar dissolves. Simmer, uncovered, without stirring, 3 minutes.

Baba pans are simply fluted ring pans; they hold more mixture than a 20cm ring pan. Baba pans need to be greased well and evenly. We prefer to use melted butter for greasing. Sometimes recipes suggest flouring the greased pan too. To do this, simply sprinkle some plain flour over the greased area, shake the pan until the flour is distributed evenly, then tap the upside-down pan to get rid of the excess flour. (See Baking Techniques page 630.)

Mixed berry cake with vanilla bean syrup

PREPARATION TIME 20 MINUTES **COOKING TIME** 40 MINUTES **SERVES** 10

125g butter, softened

1 cup (220g) caster sugar

3 eggs

½ cup (75g) plain flour

¼ cup (35g) self-raising flour

½ cup (60g) almond meal

⅓ cup (80g) sour cream

1 ½ cups (225g) frozen mixed berries

½ cup (100g) drained canned seeded black cherries

VANILLA BEAN SYRUP

½ cup (125ml) water

½ cup (110g) caster sugar

2 vanilla beans

1 Preheat oven to 180°C/160°C fan-forced. Grease 20cm baba pan well.

2 Beat butter and sugar in small bowl with electric mixer until light and fluffy. Beat in eggs, one at a time. Transfer mixture to large bowl; stir in sifted flours, almond meal, sour cream, berries and cherries. Pour mixture into pan.

3 Bake cake about 40 minutes. Stand cake in pan 5 minutes; turn onto wire rack over tray.

4 Make vanilla bean syrup; pour hot syrup over hot cake.

VANILLA BEAN SYRUP Place the water and sugar in small saucepan. Split vanilla beans in half lengthways; scrape seeds into pan then add pods. Stir over heat, without boiling, until sugar dissolves. Simmer, uncovered, without stirring, 5 minutes. Discard pods.

You can leave the cherries out of this cake, just increase the frozen berries to 2 cups to compensate. This cake mixture will curdle after the third egg is added. don't worry — it's fine — and will come together later in the mixing.

Semolina and yogurt lemon-syrup cake

PREPARATION TIME 15 MINUTES **COOKING TIME** 50 MINUTES **SERVES** 10

250g butter, softened

1 tablespoon finely grated lemon rind

1 cup (220g) caster sugar

3 eggs, separated

1 cup (150g) self-raising flour

1 cup (160g) semolina

1 cup (280g) yogurt

LEMON SYRUP

1 cup (220g) caster sugar

⅓ cup (80ml) lemon juice

1 Preheat oven to 180°C/160°C fan-forced. Grease and flour 20cm baba pan, shaking away any excess flour.

2 Beat butter, rind and sugar in small bowl with electric mixer until light and fluffy. Beat in egg yolks. Transfer mixture to large bowl; stir in sifted flour, semolina and yogurt.

3 Beat egg whites in small bowl with electric mixer until soft peaks form; fold egg whites, into cake mixture, in two batches. Spread mixture into pan; bake about 50 minutes. Stand cake in pan 5 minutes; turn onto wire rack over tray, pierce all over with skewer.

4 Make lemon syrup; pour hot syrup over hot cake.

LEMON SYRUP Stir ingredients in saucepan over heat until sugar dissolves; bring to the boil without stirring.

Semolina, which is made from durum wheat, is more coarsely ground than regular wheat flour. This gives the cake an interesting texture.

1 MIXED BERRY CAKE WITH VANILLA BEAN SYRUP **2** SEMOLINA AND YOGURT LEMON-SYRUP CAKE
3 LEMON SYRUP CAKE [P 148] **4** WHOLE TANGELO CAKE [P 148]

Lemon syrup cake

PREPARATION TIME 15 MINUTES **COOKING TIME** 50 MINUTES **SERVES** 12

250g butter, softened

1 tablespoon finely grated lemon rind

1 cup (220g) caster sugar

3 eggs

1 cup (250ml) buttermilk

⅓ cup (80ml) lemon juice

2 cups (300g) self-raising flour

LEMON SYRUP

⅓ cup (80ml) lemon juice

¼ cup (60ml) water

¾ cup (165g) caster sugar

1 Preheat oven to 180°C/160°C fan-forced. Grease 24cm baba pan well.

2 Beat butter, rind and sugar in small bowl with electric mixer until light and fluffy. Beat in eggs, one at a time. Transfer mixture to large bowl; fold in buttermilk, juice and sifted flour, in two batches. Spread mixture into pan.

3 Bake cake about 50 minutes — cover cake with foil if browning too quickly. Stand cake in pan 5 minutes; turn onto wire rack over tray.

4 Meanwhile, make lemon syrup; pour hot syrup over hot cake. Serve warm.

LEMON SYRUP Stir ingredients in small saucepan over heat, without boiling, until sugar dissolves. Simmer, uncovered, without stirring, 5 minutes.

Whole tangelo cake

PREPARATION TIME 20 MINUTES **COOKING TIME** 45 MINUTES **SERVES** 12

2 medium tangelos (420g)

125g butter, softened

1½ cups (330g) caster sugar

2 eggs

1 cup (150g) self-raising flour

½ cup (75g) plain flour

½ cup (45g) desiccated coconut

TANGELO SYRUP

1 cup (220g) caster sugar

rind of 1 tangelo, sliced thinly

⅔ cup (160ml) tangelo juice

⅓ cup (80ml) water

1 Place tangelos in medium saucepan; cover with cold water. Bring to the boil; drain. Repeat process twice; cool to room temperature.

2 Preheat oven to 180°C/160°C fan-forced. Grease deep 22cm-round cake pan; line base and side with baking paper.

3 Halve tangelos; discard seeds. Blend or process tangelo until pulpy; transfer to large bowl.

4 Beat butter, sugar and eggs in small bowl with electric mixer until light and fluffy. Stir butter mixture into tangelo pulp. Stir in sifted flours and coconut. Pour mixture into pan.

5 Bake cake about 45 minutes. Stand cake in pan 5 minutes; turn, top-side up, onto wire rack over tray.

6 Make tangelo syrup; pour hot syrup over hot cake. Serve cake warm.

TANGELO SYRUP Stir ingredients in small saucepan over heat, without boiling, until sugar dissolves; bring to the boil. Reduce heat; simmer, uncovered, without stirring, 2 minutes.

Orange almond cakes with cardamom syrup

PREPARATION TIME 15 MINUTES (PLUS STANDING TIME) **COOKING TIME** 20 MINUTES **MAKES** 6

80g butter, softened

2 teaspoons finely grated orange rind

½ cup (110g) caster sugar

3 eggs

1½ cups (185g) almond meal

⅓ cup (50g) rice flour

⅓ cup (25g) flaked almonds, chopped finely

CARDAMOM SYRUP

1 medium orange (240g)

½ cup (110g) caster sugar

½ cup (125ml) water

6 cardamom pods, bruised

1 Preheat oven to 180°C/160°C fan-forced. Grease six ½-cup (125ml) oval or rectangular friand pans; place on oven tray.

2 Beat butter, rind and sugar in small bowl with electric mixer until light and fluffy. Beat in eggs, one at a time; stir in almond meal, flour and nuts. Divide mixture among pans.

3 Bake cakes about 20 minutes. Stand cakes in pans 5 minutes; turn, top-side up, onto wire rack over tray.

4 Meanwhile, make cardamom syrup; pour hot syrup over hot cakes.

CARDAMOM SYRUP Remove rind from orange; shred rind finely. Juice the orange; place ⅓ cup (80ml) of juice in small saucepan with shredded rind, sugar, the water and cardamom. Stir over heat, without boiling, until sugar dissolves; bring to the boil. Boil, uncovered, without stirring, 10 minutes or until mixture thickens slightly; discard cardamom.

Here's a wheat-flour-free cake, the almond meal — along with a little rice flour — makes up for the lack of flour. You can buy almonds already ground (almond meal) or you can buy blanched almonds, roast them for about 5 minutes, cool, and then grind them finely either in a blender or food processor. The mixture will curdle after the second egg is added, carry on, the curdling won't affect the finished cakes.

Pretty plates

Present your baked treats on the perfect plate and turn delicious into special.

FEATURE FOCUS
A funky feature amongst a set of elegant white crockery adds personality and pizzazz to your place settings. Avoid overdoing it by mixing it into a set of basic whites.

ORGANIC
In tune with current trends focussing on beauty in nature, incorporate a modern design with smooth edges and delicate detail that reflects the mood for a subtle endorsement of the organic.

HANDMADE
Search vintage stores and flea markets for beautiful bespoke pieces like this simple, yet oh-so-elegant handmade set. Look for slightly uneven edges and quirky textures for a unique finish.

VINTAGE
1950s' designs that almost jive off the plate bring movement, colour and a touch of quirkiness to your place settings. Balance sweet colours and funky patterns with basic white.

TEXTURE
When plates feature a textured surface such as this gorgeous soft design with reference to sand dunes you have a special plate that doesn't overwhelm with colour. Dish up colourful salads or cakes for maximum effect.

CLEAN & CRISP
Match your crockery to your occasion; clean, crisp design and colour whisper thoughts of sea breeze and brunch or a late Sunday breakfast on a sunny balcony with friends.

OPULENCE

Many of the classic tableware houses such as Missoni, Wedgewood or Royal Doulton detail their plates with platinum, gold or silver gilt-edged glamour for elegant sophistication.

FINE BONE CHINA

Generally accepted as the premium material for tableware, fine bone china is actually made with bone ash, rendering it incredibly tough and brilliantly white, yet so fine as to be almost tanslucent.

CLASSIC SHAPES

Rustic French design is characterised by soft colours and a scalloped edge. The motif is carried from the plate through to cutlery and linen for classic casual French style.

BASIC WHITE SET

Nothing is as elegant or as easy as a basic white plate set and no home should be without one. Choose a renowned brand; should anything break, it can be easily replaced, even years after you made the original purchase.

GLAZES

We owe thanks to Egyptian and Chinese ingenuity for ceramic glazes, the earliest of which date back to about 2000BC. Play with degrees of gloss or matt, variegation, surface finishes and colour for a look that suits your taste and occasion.

STATEMENT COLOUR

The rich, strong colour and high gloss glaze make this simple plate a statement that will turn your table into a jewel-studded masterpiece; a perfect backdrop for a special meal.

Pistachio and polenta cake with blood orange syrup

PREPARATION TIME 10 MINUTES **COOKING TIME** 1 HOUR 15 MINUTES **SERVES** 10

125g butter, softened

1 cup (220g) caster sugar

300g sour cream

2 cups (300g) self-raising flour

½ teaspoon bicarbonate of soda

⅔ cup (110g) polenta

1 teaspoon finely grated blood orange rind

¾ cup (180ml) water

⅔ cup (100g) shelled pistachios

BLOOD ORANGE SYRUP

1 cup (250ml) blood orange juice

1 cup (220g) caster sugar

1 cinnamon stick

1 Preheat oven to 160°C/140°C fan-forced. Grease deep 20cm-round cake pan; line base and side with baking paper.

2 Make blood orange syrup.

3 Beat butter, sugar, sour cream, sifted flour and soda, polenta, rind and the water in large bowl on low speed with electric mixer until combined. Increase to medium speed, beat until mixture changes to a paler colour. Stir in nuts. Spread mixture into pan.

4 Bake cake about 1 hour. Stand cake in pan 10 minutes; turn, top-side up, onto wire rack to cool. Serve cake warm or cold with strained blood orange syrup.

BLOOD ORANGE SYRUP Stir ingredients in small saucepan; bring to the boil. Reduce heat; simmer, uncovered, about 15 minutes or until syrup thickens. Cool.

Mocha syrup cake

PREPARATION TIME 15 MINUTES **COOKING TIME** 40 MINUTES **SERVES** 10

3 teaspoons instant coffee granules

1 tablespoon hot water

150g butter, softened

¾ cup (165g) firmly packed brown sugar

2 eggs

1 cup (150g) self-raising flour

½ cup (75g) plain flour

1 tablespoon cocoa powder

½ cup (125ml) milk

75g dark eating chocolate, chopped finely

COFFEE SYRUP

½ cup (110g) caster sugar

½ cup (125ml) water

3 teaspoons instant coffee granules

1 Preheat oven to 180°C/160°C fan-forced. Grease 20cm-round cake pan; line base and side with baking paper.

2 Combine coffee and the water in small bowl.

3 Beat butter and sugar in small mixing bowl with electric mixer until light and fluffy. Beat in eggs, one at a time. Transfer mixture to large bowl; stir in flours and combined milk and coffee mixture, in two batches. Stir in chocolate. Spread mixture into pan.

4 Bake cake about 40 minutes.

5 Meanwhile, make coffee syrup.

6 Turn hot cake onto wire rack over tray; pierce all over with wooden skewer. Drizzle hot syrup over hot cake.

COFFEE SYRUP Stir sugar and the water in small saucepan over heat until sugar dissolves. Bring to the boil; simmer 4 minutes. Remove from heat; stir in coffee.

If you happen to have some good strong coffee leftover use it in place of the water and instant coffee granules in both the cake and the syrup.

Banana butterscotch syrup cake

PREPARATION TIME 30 MINUTES **COOKING TIME** 1 HOUR 10 MINUTES **SERVES** 9

125g butter, softened

¾ cup (165g) caster sugar

2 eggs

1 cup mashed banana

¾ cup (110g) self-raising flour

¾ cup (110g) plain flour

½ teaspoon bicarbonate of soda

¾ cup (110g) finely chopped roasted hazelnuts

BUTTERSCOTCH SYRUP

½ cup (100g) firmly packed brown sugar

30g butter

¾ cup (180ml) water

For an even more butterscotch flavour, substitute brown sugar (firmly packed) for the caster sugar. Remember to use overripe bananas whenever they're a cake ingredient.

1 Preheat oven to 180°C/160°C fan-forced. Grease deep 19cm-square cake pan; line base with baking paper.

2 Beat butter and sugar in small bowl with electric mixer until light and fluffy. Beat in eggs, one at a time. Stir in banana, then sifted flours and soda, and nuts. Spread mixture into pan.

3 Bake cake about 1 hour. Stand cake in pan 5 minutes; turn, top-side up, onto wire rack over tray.

4 Make butterscotch syrup; slowly drizzle hot syrup over hot cake.

BUTTERSCOTCH SYRUP Stir sugar and butter in small saucepan over heat until butter melts. Stir in the water; bring to the boil, stirring.

Ginger and lime cake

PREPARATION TIME 45 MINUTES **COOKING TIME** 45 MINUTES (PLUS REFRIGERATION TIME) **SERVES** 12

250g butter, chopped coarsely

½ cup (110g) firmly packed dark brown sugar

⅔ cup (230g) golden syrup

12cm piece fresh ginger (60g), grated

¾ cup (180ml) cream

2 eggs

1 cup (150g) plain flour

1 cup (150g) self-raising flour

½ teaspoon bicarbonate of soda

1 cup (50g) flaked coconut

LIME SYRUP

½ cup (125ml) lime juice

½ cup (125ml) water

½ cup (110g) caster sugar

MASCARPONE CREAM

250g mascarpone cheese

300ml thickened cream

2 tablespoons icing sugar

2 teaspoons finely grated lime rind

1 Preheat oven to 180°C/160°C fan-forced. Grease deep 22cm-round cake pan; line base and side with baking paper.

2 Melt butter in medium saucepan; remove pan from heat. Stir in sugar, golden syrup and ginger; stir until sugar dissolves. Whisk in cream, eggs and sifted flours and soda. Pour mixture into pan.

3 Bake cake about 40 minutes.

4 Meanwhile, make lime syrup.

5 Pierce hot cake, still in pan, all over with skewer; drizzle hot syrup over hot cake. Cover; refrigerate about 3 hours or until cold.

6 Meanwhile, make mascarpone cream.

7 Remove cake from pan; line base and side of same cleaned pan with plastic wrap. Split cake into three layers; return one layer of cake to pan. Spread layer with 1 cup of the mascarpone cream; repeat with second cake layer and another 1 cup of mascarpone cream, then top with third cake layer. Cover; refrigerate 2 hours. Cover remaining mascarpone cream; refrigerate until required.

8 Remove cake from pan to serving plate, spread remaining mascarpone cream around side and top of cake; press coconut onto side of cake.

LIME SYRUP Stir ingredients in small saucepan over heat, without boiling, until sugar dissolves; bring to the boil. Reduce heat; simmer, uncovered, without stirring, 2 minutes.

MASCARPONE CREAM Whisk ingredients in small bowl until soft peaks form. Refrigerate until required.

Mascarpone is really a cheese — it's seriously rich. It's important not to overbeat it or it could curdle. If you'd prefer to make a square cake, this mixture will fit into a deep 19cm-square cake pan. The baking time and temperature will be the same.

Passionfruit and lemon syrup cake

PREPARATION TIME 20 MINUTES **COOKING TIME** 1 HOUR **SERVES** 9

⅔ cup (160ml) passionfruit pulp

250g butter, softened

1 tablespoon finely grated
lemon rind

1 cup (220g) caster sugar

3 eggs

1 cup (250ml) buttermilk

2 cups (300g) self-raising flour

LEMON SYRUP

⅓ cup (80ml) lemon juice

¼ cup (60ml) water

¾ cup (165g) caster sugar

1 Preheat oven to 180°C/160°C fan-forced. Grease deep 19cm-square cake pan;
line base and sides with baking paper.

2 Strain passionfruit over medium jug; reserve both juice and seeds separately.

3 Beat butter, rind and sugar in small bowl with electric mixer until light and fluffy.
Beat in eggs, one at a time. Transfer mixture to large bowl; stir in buttermilk, passionfruit
juice and sifted flour, in two batches. Spread mixture into pan.

4 Bake cake about 1 hour.

5 Make lemon syrup.

6 Stand cake in pan 5 minutes; turn, top-side up, onto wire rack over tray. Pour hot syrup
over hot cake. Serve warm.

LEMON SYRUP Stir juice, the water, sugar and half of the reserved passionfruit seeds
in small saucepan over heat, without boiling, until sugar dissolves. Simmer, uncovered,
without stirring, 5 minutes.

A lot of people love the flavour of passionfruit but hate the seeds. Just leave the seeds out completely, if you prefer.

Lime and poppy seed syrup cake

PREPARATION TIME 20 MINUTES **COOKING TIME** 1 HOUR **SERVES** 16

¼ cup (40g) poppy seeds

½ cup (125ml) milk

250g butter, softened

1 tablespoon finely grated
lime rind

1¼ cups (275g) caster sugar

4 eggs

2¼ cups (335g) self-raising flour

¾ cup (110g) plain flour

1 cup (240g) sour cream

LIME SYRUP

½ cup (125ml) lime juice

1 cup (250ml) water

1 cup (220g) caster sugar

Poppy seeds are quite an old-fashioned ingredient, but they have made a bit of a comeback in cakes, particularly in citrus-flavoured cakes.

1   Preheat oven to 180°C/160°C fan-forced. Grease deep 23cm-square cake pan.

2   Combine poppy seeds and milk in small jug; soak 10 minutes.

3   Beat butter, rind and sugar in small bowl with electric mixer until light and fluffy. Beat in eggs, one at a time. Transfer mixture to large bowl; stir in sifted flours, cream and poppy seed mixture, in two batches. Spread mixture into pan.

4   Bake cake about 1 hour. Stand cake in pan 5 minutes; turn, top-side up, onto wire rack over tray.

5   Meanwhile, make lime syrup; pour hot syrup over hot cake.

LIME SYRUP Stir ingredients in small saucepan over heat, without boiling, until sugar dissolves. Simmer, uncovered, without stirring, 5 minutes.

Pumpkin citrus syrup cake

PREPARATION TIME 25 MINUTES **COOKING TIME** 1 HOUR 10 MINUTES **SERVES** 12

250g butter, softened

2 tablespoons finely grated orange rind

2 tablespoons finely grated lemon rind

1 cup (220g) caster sugar

3 eggs, separated

2 cups (300g) self-raising flour

1 cup mashed pumpkin

CITRUS SYRUP

2 tablespoons lemon juice

2 tablespoons orange juice

¾ cup (165g) caster sugar

1   Preheat oven to 180°C/160°C fan-forced. Grease deep 22cm-round cake pan; line base with baking paper.

2   Beat butter, rinds, sugar and egg yolks in small bowl with electric mixer until light and fluffy. Transfer mixture to large bowl; stir in sifted flour and pumpkin, in two batches.

3   Beat egg whites in small bowl with electric mixer until soft peaks form; fold into cake mixture. Spread mixture into pan.

4   Bake cake about 1 hour.

5   Meanwhile, make citrus syrup.

6   Pour hot syrup over hot cake in pan. Stand cake in pan 10 minutes; turn, top-side up, onto wire rack to cool.

CITRUS SYRUP Stir ingredients in small saucepan, over heat, without boiling, until sugar is dissolved; bring to the boil. Reduce heat; simmer, without stirring, 2 minutes.

Cakes which have pumpkin as an ingredient are always a lovely golden colour and are always moist. The best flavour and colour comes from the normal large round pumpkins available all year. Make sure it is cooked through, drained well, mashed finely and is at room temperature before using in a cake. Pushing the pumpkin through a fine sieve will give the best results.

Almond honey spice cake

PREPARATION TIME 20 MINUTES

COOKING TIME 40 MINUTES (PLUS COOLING, REFRIGERATION AND STANDING TIME) **SERVES** 10

125g butter, softened

⅓ cup (75g) caster sugar

2 tablespoons honey

1 teaspoon ground ginger

1 teaspoon ground allspice

2 eggs

1½ cups (180g) almond meal

½ cup (80g) semolina

1 teaspoon baking powder

¼ cup (60ml) milk

SPICED SYRUP

1 cup (220g) caster sugar

1 cup (250ml) water

8 cardamom pods, bruised

2 cinnamon sticks

HONEY ORANGE CREAM

¾ cup (180ml) thickened cream

1 tablespoon honey

2 tablespoons finely grated orange rind

1 Preheat oven to 180°C/160°C fan-forced. Grease deep 20cm-round cake pan; line base and side with baking paper.

2 Beat butter, sugar, honey and spices in small bowl with electric mixer until light and fluffy. Beat in eggs, one at a time. Transfer mixture to medium bowl; fold in almond meal, semolina, sifted baking powder and milk. Spread mixture into pan.

3 Bake cake about 40 minutes. Stand cake in pan 5 minutes.

4 Meanwhile, make spiced syrup.

5 Pour strained hot syrup over hot cake in pan; cool cake in pan to room temperature. Turn cake, in pan, upside-down onto serving plate; refrigerate 3 hours or overnight.

6 Remove cake from refrigerator. Make honey orange cream. Remove pan from cake; serve cake at room temperature with honey orange cream.

SPICED SYRUP Stir ingredients in small saucepan over heat, without boiling, until sugar dissolves; bring to the boil. Boil, uncovered, without stirring, about 5 minutes or until syrup thickens slightly.

HONEY ORANGE CREAM Beat ingredients in small bowl with electric mixer until soft peaks form.

Orange and blueberry cake

PREPARATION TIME 20 MINUTES **COOKING TIME** 1 HOUR **SERVES** 10-12

125g butter, softened

1 tablespoon finely grated orange rind

½ cup (110g) caster sugar

2 eggs

1¾ cups (260g) self-raising flour

½ cup (125ml) yogurt

¼ cup (60ml) orange juice

1 cup (150g) frozen blueberries

ORANGE SYRUP

¾ cup (165g) caster sugar

½ cup (125ml) orange juice

¼ cup (60ml) water

1 tablespoon grated orange rind

1 Preheat oven to 180°C/160°C fan-forced. Grease deep 20cm-round cake pan; line base and side with baking paper.

2 Beat butter, rind and sugar in medium bowl with electric mixer until light and fluffy. Beat in eggs, one at a time; stir in sifted flour then yogurt and juice, in two batches. Stir in blueberries. Spread mixture into pan.

3 Bake cake about 1 hour. Stand cake in pan 5 minutes; turn, top-side up, onto wire rack over tray.

4 Meanwhile, make orange syrup; drizzle hot syrup over hot cake.

ORANGE SYRUP Stir sugar, juice and the water in small saucepan over heat, without boiling, until sugar dissolves. Stir in rind; simmer, uncovered, without stirring, 5 minutes.

Caramel cake with whole-spice syrup

PREPARATION TIME 20 MINUTES **COOKING TIME** 1 HOUR **SERVES** 10

185g butter, softened

¾ cup (150g) firmly packed brown sugar

⅓ cup (80ml) golden syrup

2 eggs

⅓ cup (40g) almond meal

½ cup (125ml) milk

2 cups (300g) self-raising flour

1 teaspoon ground cinnamon

1 teaspoon ground nutmeg

1 teaspoon ground ginger

WHOLE-SPICE SYRUP

1 medium lemon (140g)

¾ cup (165g) caster sugar

¼ cup (60ml) water

4 cardamom pods, crushed

1 cinnamon stick

1 vanilla bean, split

One-bowl cakes are popular and easy to make. For the best results have all the ingredients for the cake at room temperature, particularly the butter. Always beat the ingredients together, scraping the side of the bowl down often, on a low speed in an electric mixer. Then gradually increase the speed to medium, and beat until the ingredients are smooth and slightly paler in colour than when you started mixing at medium speed.

1 Preheat oven to 180°C/160°C fan-forced. Grease 20cm baba pan.

2 Beat ingredients in medium bowl with electric mixer on low speed until combined. Increase speed to medium, beat about 5 minutes or until mixture is paler in colour. Spread mixture into pan.

3 Bake cake about 1 hour. Stand cake in pan 5 minutes; turn, top-side up, onto wire rack over tray.

4 Meanwhile, make whole-spice syrup. Drizzle hot syrup over hot cake. Serve cake warm or cold.

WHOLE-SPICE SYRUP Peel thin slices of lemon rind; cut slices into 1cm strips. Squeeze lemon; reserve ⅓ cup (80ml) juice. Combine rind and juice with remaining ingredients in medium saucepan. Stir over heat, without boiling, until sugar dissolves. Simmer, uncovered, without stirring, 3 minutes; strain.

Espresso syrup cake

PREPARATION TIME 20 MINUTES **COOKING TIME** 40 MINUTES **SERVES** 10

3 teaspoons instant coffee granules

1 tablespoon hot water

3 eggs

¾ cup (165g) caster sugar

1 cup (150g) self-raising flour

1 tablespoon cocoa powder

150g butter, melted

ESPRESSO SYRUP

¾ cup (165g) caster sugar

¾ cup (180ml) water

3 teaspoons instant coffee granules

1 Preheat oven to 180°C/160°C fan-forced. Grease 20cm baba pan.

2 Dissolve coffee in the water in small jug.

3 Beat eggs in small bowl with electric mixer about 8 minutes or until thick and creamy. Gradually add sugar, beating until dissolved between additions. Transfer mixture to large bowl; fold in sifted flour and cocoa, then butter and coffee mixture. Pour mixture into pan.

4 Bake cake about 40 minutes. Stand cake in pan 5 minutes; turn onto wire rack over tray.

5 Meanwhile, make espresso syrup; reserve ¼ cup (60ml) syrup. Drizzle remaining hot syrup over hot cake. Serve cake with reserved syrup.

ESPRESSO SYRUP Stir ingredients in small saucepan over heat, without boiling, until sugar dissolves. Bring to the boil; remove from heat.

Beating eggs until thick and creamy takes a surprisingly long time — somewhere between 5 and 10 minutes depending on the type and strength of the mixer you're using.

LOAF CAKES

Loaf Cakes

Midway between cake and fruit bread, loaf cakes and nut rolls are great to have on standby for lunch box treats, morning and afternoon teas and just about any occasion when a nourishing sweet snack is required. High in fibre, thanks to fruit and nut content and the addition of bran, wholemeal flour and occasionally oats, loaf cakes are that rare category of treat that can be said to taste good and be good for you as well.

SUGAR AND SUBSTITUTES

Apart from the obvious function of sweetening, sugar retains moisture in cakes and prolongs freshness. We use coarse, granulated table sugar, also known as crystal sugar, unless otherwise specified. However, in this chapter other types of sugar or sweetening agents are used to impart particular flavours and textures to the recipe. They include:

BROWN SUGAR which is an extremely soft, fine granulated sugar that retains molasses for its characteristic colour and flavour. Available in both dark and light versions, dark brown sugar is less refined than light.

GOLDEN SYRUP is a by-product of refined sugarcane. Golden syrup and treacle (a thicker, darker syrup), also known as flavour syrups, are similar sugar products made by partly breaking down sugar into its component parts and adding water. Treacle is more viscous, and has a stronger flavour and aroma than golden syrup.

MAPLE SYRUP is distilled from the sap of maple trees and found only in Canada and parts of North America. Maple-flavoured syrup is not an adequate substitute for the real thing.

HONEY is an ancient sweetener, prized for its distinctive flavours imparted by the flowers of the particular trees the bees feed upon.

NUTS

Nuts provide texture, flavour, protein and fibre. Commonly used nuts include:

ALMONDS flat, pointy-tipped nuts with a pitted brown shell enclosing a creamy white kernel which is covered by a brown skin. Blanched almonds have the brown skin removed.

WALNUTS with their crinkly bitter-tasting kernels contained in a shiny outer shell, contain the beneficial omega-3 fatty acids.

PECANS natives of the US, pecans are golden brown, buttery and rich kernels enclosed in a shiny oval shell.

CASHEWS plump, kidney-shaped, golden-brown nuts with a distinctive sweet, buttery flavour and about a 48 per cent fat content. Because of this high fat content, they should be kept, sealed tightly, under refrigeration to prevent them from becoming rancid.

FRUITS

Fruits lend distinctive flavour, moisture, sweetness and texture to these recipes. Fresh, canned, dried and preserved fruits are used. They include:

RAISINS, SULTANAS AND CURRANTS are all dried forms of grapes.

DATES the intensely sugary and sticky fruit of the date palm tree.

PRUNES commercially sun-dried plums which are prized for their high fibre and iron contents.

GLACE OR GLAZED fruit are preserved in sugar syrup.

MIXED DRIED FRUIT means a combination of sultanas, raisins, currants, cherries and mixed peel.

MIXING TIPS

As a rule we don't recommend mixing cakes, biscuits or slices in blenders or food processors. Use an electric mixer to mix the cake, then a spatula, your hand or a spoon to work in the other ingredients. Overmixing can affect the gluten, making the cake tough.

Always have all ingredients at room temperature. Melted or extremely soft butter will alter the texture of the finished baked product. When measuring liquids, always stand the marked measuring jug on a flat surface and check at eye level for accuracy. Spoon and cup measurements should be levelled off with a knife or spatula. When measuring ingredients such as honey, oil the spoon or cup lightly before adding the sticky liquid. It will slide out of the container readily, resulting in an accurate measurement. Be fussy about levelling spoons when you're measuring honey etc. — more is not better in this case.

PANS AND TINS

We used loaf pans, bar cake pans and nut roll tins in this chapter. If you don't have a nut roll tin, you can make a serviceable substitute using a juice can, which has had the lid removed with a can opener that takes the rim off as well as the lid. Grease the can well, add the mixture and cover the open end firmly with several layers of foil, which have been pierced in the centre with a skewer. For ease of transfer in and out of the oven, stand nut roll tins on an oven tray or in a baking dish. The mixture will expand considerably, so only half fill. As the tins stand upright in the oven, you will need to adjust the oven shelves. See *Loaves & nut rolls* on pages 170 & 171 for tips.

STORING AND FREEZING

Most of the cakes in this chapter will keep moist for up to a week. Cool the cake to room temperature, store in an airtight container that is close in size to the cake to minimise exposure to the air. Most of these cakes can be sliced and frozen so you can take out as many slices as you want at a time. Separated slices will thaw in a matter of minutes. If you want to freeze a whole loaf, wrap the cold cake in plastic wrap or a freezer bag, expelling as much air as possible. It is best to thaw overnight in the refrigerator.

Kumara and pecan loaf

PREPARATION TIME 20 MINUTES **COOKING TIME** 1 HOUR 40 MINUTES **SERVES** 10

Kumara will keep the loaf moist. If the weather is hot or humid store the loaf in the fridge.

200g butter, softened

¾ cup (165g) firmly packed brown sugar

2 eggs

¾ cup (90g) coarsely chopped pecans

½ cup (40g) desiccated coconut

1 cup mashed kumara

1½ cups (225g) self-raising flour

½ cup (125ml) milk

1 Preheat oven to 170°C/150°C fan-forced. Grease 14cm x 21cm loaf pan; line base and long sides with baking paper, extending paper 2cm over sides.

2 Beat butter, sugar and eggs in small bowl with electric mixer until combined. Transfer mixture to large bowl; fold in nuts, coconut and kumara. Stir in sifted flour and milk, in two batches. Spread mixture into pan.

3 Bake loaf about 1 hour 40 minutes. Stand loaf in pan 10 minutes; turn, top-side up, onto wire rack to cool.

Zucchini and walnut loaf

PREPARATION TIME 15 MINUTES **COOKING TIME** 1 HOUR 15 MINUTES **SERVES** 12

We like to leave the skin on the zucchini; this way, the loaf will be flecked with green. If the zucchini seems to be particularly wet after grating, strain it, and press out any excess liquid with the back of a spoon.

3 eggs

1½ cups (330g) firmly packed brown sugar

1 cup (250ml) vegetable oil

1½ cups finely grated zucchini

1 cup (110g) coarsely chopped walnuts

1½ cups (225g) self-raising flour

1½ cups (225g) plain flour

1 Preheat oven to 180°C/160°C fan-forced. Grease 15cm x 25cm loaf pan; line base and long sides with baking paper, extending paper 2cm over sides.

2 Beat eggs, sugar and oil in large bowl with electric mixer until combined. Stir in zucchini, nuts and sifted flours, in two batches. Spread mixture into pan.

3 Bake loaf about 1¼ hours. Stand loaf in pan 5 minutes; turn, top-side up, onto wire rack to cool.

KUMARA AND PECAN LOAF

Banana, honey and seed loaf

PREPARATION TIME 15 MINUTES **COOKING TIME** 1 HOUR **SERVES** 10

1 tablespoon toasted sesame seeds

¼ cup (35g) sunflower seeds

¼ cup (50g) pepitas

½ cup (125ml) extra light olive oil

⅓ cup (75g) firmly packed brown sugar

¼ cup (90g) honey

2 eggs

½ cup mashed banana

½ cup (125ml) buttermilk

¼ cup (20g) quick-cook oats

¼ cup (35g) coarsely chopped raisins

1 ¼ cups (185g) self-raising flour

1 teaspoon ground cinnamon

2 tablespoons honey, extra

1 Preheat oven to 180°C/ 160°C fan-forced. Grease 14cm x 21cm loaf pan; line base and long sides with baking paper, extending paper 2cm over sides.

2 Combine seeds in small bowl.

3 Place oil, sugar, honey, eggs, banana, buttermilk, oats, raisins, sifted flour and cinnamon and two-thirds of seed mixture into large bowl; stir until combined. Pour mixture into pan; sprinkle top with remaining seed mixture.

4 Bake loaf about 1 hour. Stand loaf in pan 10 minutes; turn, top-side up, onto wire rack. Brush top with extra honey.

Choc-chip almond loaf

PREPARATION TIME 20 MINUTES **COOKING TIME** 1 HOUR **SERVES** 10

125g butter, softened

1 teaspoon vanilla extract

1 cup (220g) caster sugar

3 eggs

¼ cup (30g) almond meal

¾ cup (110g) plain flour

¼ cup (35g) self-raising flour

⅓ cup (80g) sour cream

½ cup (90g) dark Choc Bits

½ cup (80g) almond kernels, roasted, chopped coarsely

1 Preheat oven to 160°C/140°C fan-forced. Grease 14cm x 21cm loaf pan; line base and long sides with baking paper, extending paper 2cm over sides.

2 Beat butter, extract and sugar in small bowl with electric mixer until light and fluffy. Beat in eggs, one at a time. Transfer mixture to large bowl; stir in almond meal, sifted flours, sour cream, Choc Bits and nuts, in two batches. Spread mixture into pan.

3 Bake loaf about 1 hour. Stand loaf in pan 10 minutes; turn, top-side up, onto wire rack to cool.

Lemon crumble loaf

PREPARATION TIME 25 MINUTES **COOKING TIME** 1 HOUR **SERVES** 10

125g butter, softened

2 teaspoons finely grated lemon rind

¾ cup (165g) caster sugar

2 eggs

¾ cup (110g) plain flour

½ cup (75g) self-raising flour

¼ cup (60ml) milk

LEMON CRUMBLE

2 tablespoons white sugar

2 tablespoons plain flour

30g butter, chopped

2 teaspoons finely grated lemon rind

2 tablespoons flaked almonds

1 Preheat oven to 160°C/140°C fan-forced. Grease 14cm x 21cm loaf pan; line base and long sides with baking paper, extending paper 2cm over sides.

2 Make lemon crumble.

3 Beat butter, rind and sugar in a small bowl with electric mixer until light and fluffy. Beat in eggs, one at a time. Transfer mixture to large bowl; stir in sifted flours and milk, in two batches. Spread mixture into pan; sprinkle evenly with lemon crumble.

4 Bake loaf about 1 hour. Stand loaf in pan 10 minutes; turn, top-side up, onto wire rack to cool.

LEMON CRUMBLE Place sugar and flour in small bowl; rub in butter with fingertips. Stir in rind and nuts.

Change the flavour of this loaf to any citrus flavour you like, the same goes for the nuts — orange with hazelnut, and lime with macadamias also make good combinations.

Fig, walnut and ginger loaf

PREPARATION TIME 20 MINUTES **COOKING TIME** 1 HOUR 15 MINUTES **SERVES** 10

185g butter, softened

¾ cup (165g) caster sugar

3 eggs

½ cup (95g) finely chopped dried figs

⅓ cup (65g) finely chopped glacé ginger

½ cup (50g) finely chopped walnuts

½ cup (75g) plain four

½ cup (75g) self-raising flour

⅓ cup (65g) sour cream

1 Preheat oven to 170°C/150°C fan-forced. Grease 14cm x 21cm loaf pan; line base with baking paper.

2 Beat butter and sugar in small bowl with electric mixer until light and fluffy. Beat in eggs, one at a time. Transfer mixture to large bowl; stir in figs, ginger and nuts, then sifted flours and sour cream. Spread mixture into pan.

3 Bake loaf about 1¼ hours. Stand loaf in pan 5 minutes; turn, top-side up, onto wire rack to cool.

Most loaf-shaped cakes split during baking, either down the centre, or one side, or sometimes even both long sides of the top of the loaf. This is normal, it's only due to the narrow confines of the loaf pan.

Loaves & nut rolls

Just about everyone loves loaves and nut rolls, especially with a little butter. Here are some extra tips for making them.

LINING A LOAF PAN

Grease pan with cooking oil spray or melted butter. Cut a strip of baking or greaseproof paper, long enough to cover the sides, base and extend over the edges of the pan.

PREPARING TO BAKE

Pour or spread the mixture into the pan, level the mixture with a spatula if necessary. Some mixtures are wet and sticky with golden syrup, honey etc, and it might be necessary to line all four sides of the pan with paper strips.

CRACKED LOAVES

Most loaf-shaped cakes crack during baking. This is because the mixture is forced up by heat, in a narrow pan. Stand the loaf about 5 minutes before turning it out of the pan to cool.

HOME-MADE NUT ROLL TINS

Make your own nut roll tins from tall 850ml (8cm x 17cm) fruit juice cans. You'll need to remove one end from each can by using a can opener that cuts just below the rims. Wash and dry the cans thoroughly before greasing.

FILLING NUT ROLL TINS

Because of the narrow confined area of the tins or cans, these rolls double in height during baking. Half-fill the tins, tap them firmly on the bench, then, if you're using the traditional nut roll tins, place the top lid in position, ready for baking.

PREPARING TO BAKE

Stand the tins or cans upright on an oven tray, make sure there is enough head room in the oven for the tall tins. If you're using the fruit juice cans, you'll need to cover the tops of the cans with a piece of strong foil (a doubled piece if the foil is fine) and secure it with string. Slash a hole in the foil tops, to allow the steam to escape during the baking.

OVEN-STEAMING LOAVES

If you have a recipe that gets a thick crust, you can minimise it — pleat a strip of foil and place it over the pan. The foil will steam and soften the crust. Remove foil for last 10 minutes of baking.

NUT ROLL TINS

These tins always came in pairs, and were popular years ago, so might be hard to buy now — try second-hand shops. Remove the lids from both ends of the tins. Some tins have lids with holes, these are the top lids.

GREASING NUT ROLL TINS

Put the bottom lids (without holes) on the tins, grease inside the tins and the bottom lids thoroughly and evenly with melted butter. Grease inside the top lids (with the holes).

COOLING NUT ROLLS

Most rolls take an hour to bake, let them stand for 5 minutes, then gently shake the cans or tins until you feel each roll is loose. Remove the foil and string from the juice cans, or the lids from both ends of the tins. Gently shake the rolls from the tins or cans onto a wire rack to cool. Some of the older tins open down the sides as well, making it even easier to get the rolls out.

SERVING NUT ROLLS

They're at their best eaten on the day of baking, either warm or cold, sliced and spread with butter. Since the rolls are quite small, there are usually no leftovers, but they will keep in an airtight container at room temperature for a day, or they freeze well.

FREEZING NUT ROLLS

You can freeze the whole uncut rolls in plastic, foil, freezer bags or airtight containers. Or, slice the rolls, then interleave the slices with plastic or freezer wrap, reshape the rolls and freeze them. This way you can use as many slices as you like when you need them.

Wholemeal banana and prune bread

PREPARATION TIME 15 MINUTES **COOKING TIME** 1 HOUR **SERVES** 10

1 ½ cups (240g) wholemeal self-raising flour

1 teaspoon ground cinnamon

2 teaspoons finely grated lemon rind

100g butter, softened

¾ cup (165g) firmly packed dark brown sugar

2 eggs

1 ½ cups mashed banana

1 cup (170g) seeded prunes, chopped coarsely

1 Preheat oven to 180°C/160°C fan-forced. Grease 14cm x 21cm loaf pan; line base and long sides with baking paper, extending paper 2cm over sides.
2 Sift flour and cinnamon into large bowl; add rind, butter, sugar and eggs. Beat with electric mixer on low speed until ingredients are combined. Increase speed to medium; beat mixture until smooth. Stir in banana and prunes. Spread mixture into pan.
3 Bake bread about 1 hour. Stand bread in pan 5 minutes; turn, top-side up, onto wire rack to cool.

All wholemeal flour will give you quite a firm bread, ideal for toasting. If you want to make the bread a little lighter in colour and texture, use half white self-raising flour with its wholemeal cousin.

One-bowl sultana loaf

PREPARATION TIME 15 MINUTES **COOKING TIME** 1 HOUR 30 MINUTES **SERVES** 12

125g butter, melted

½ cup (110g) firmly packed brown sugar

2 eggs

750g (4¾ cups) sultanas

2 tablespoons marmalade

¼ cup (60ml) sweet sherry

¾ cup (110g) plain flour

¼ cup (35g) self-raising flour

¾ cup (120g) blanched almonds

1 Preheat oven to 150°C/130°C fan-forced. Grease 15cm x 25cm loaf pan; line base with baking paper.
2 Stir butter, sugar, eggs, sultanas, marmalade, sherry and sifted flours in large bowl until combined. Spread mixture into pan; decorate top with nuts.
3 Bake loaf about 1 ½ hours. Cover with foil; cool in pan.

Here's a loaf that's rich in sultanas. We often suggest this loaf to our readers to make at Christmas time in place of a richer fruit cake. It will keep well for about 2 weeks if stored in an airtight container.

WHOLEMEAL BANANA AND PRUNE BREAD

Date and maple loaf

PREPARATION TIME 20 MINUTES **COOKING TIME** 50 MINUTES **SERVES** 10

¾ cup (110g) finely chopped dates

⅓ cup (80ml) boiling water

½ teaspoon bicarbonate of soda

¼ cup (90g) maple syrup

90g butter, softened

⅓ cup (75g) firmly packed brown sugar

2 eggs

¾ cup (120g) wholemeal self-raising flour

½ cup (75g) plain flour

MAPLE BUTTER

125g butter, softened

2 tablespoons maple syrup

Use proper maple syrup for a wonderful flavour as the imitation is just that. This is another recipe that will curdle after the second egg is added -- don't worry about it.

1 Preheat oven to 180°C/160°C fan-forced. Grease 14cm x 21cm loaf pan.

2 Combine dates and the water in medium heatproof bowl. Stir in soda; cover, stand 5 minutes. Stir in maple syrup.

3 Meanwhile, beat butter and sugar in small bowl with electric mixer until light and fluffy. Beat in eggs, one at a time. Add butter mixture to date mixture; stir in sifted flours, in two batches. Spread mixture into pan.

4 Bake loaf about 50 minutes. Stand loaf in pan 10 minutes; turn, top-side up, onto wire rack to cool.

5 Meanwhile, make maple butter. Serve loaf with maple butter.

MAPLE BUTTER Whisk ingredients together in small bowl until combined.

Yogurt fruit loaf

PREPARATION TIME 20 MINUTES **COOKING TIME** 1 HOUR 30 MINUTES **SERVES** 10

100g butter, softened

2 teaspoons finely grated orange rind

¾ cup (165g) caster sugar

2 eggs

2 cups (320g) wholemeal self-raising flour

1 cup (280g) yogurt

⅓ cup (80ml) orange juice

1 cup (200g) finely chopped dried figs

1 cup (150g) coarsely chopped raisins

Yogurt is not only a nutritionally-sound ingredient to add to a loaf, but it helps produce a lovely texture. Try slices of this loaf toasted and buttered lightly.

1 Preheat oven to 180°C/160°C fan-forced. Grease 14cm x 21cm loaf pan.

2 Beat butter, rind, sugar, eggs, flour, yogurt and juice in medium bowl with electric mixer, on low speed, until combined. Stir in fruit. Pour mixture into pan; cover with foil.

3 Bake loaf 1¼ hours. Remove foil; bake further 15 minutes. Stand loaf in pan 10 minutes; turn, top-side up, onto wire rack to cool.

1 DATE AND MAPLE LOAF **2** YOGURT FRUIT LOAF
3 PINEAPPLE SULTANA LOAF [P 176] **4** COFFEE WALNUT LOAF [P 176]

Pineapple sultana loaf

PREPARATION TIME 15 MINUTES **COOKING TIME** 55 MINUTES **SERVES** 10

The most tedious part of making this recipe is draining the pineapple well. Once the obvious syrup is drained away from the strainer, press the pineapple firmly with the back of a spoon to try and make the pineapple as dry as possible. Chill and drink the juice later. The rest of the recipe is easy, toss everything into a bowl, mix with a fork or spoon, ignore the lumps, then bake it.

440g can crushed pineapple in syrup, drained
1 cup (150g) self-raising flour
½ cup (110g) caster sugar
1 cup (80g) desiccated coconut
1 cup (160g) sultanas
1 egg, beaten lightly
½ cup (125ml) milk

1 Preheat oven to 180°C/160°C fan-forced. Grease 14cm x 21cm loaf pan; line base and long sides with baking paper, extending paper 2cm over sides.

2 Combine ingredients in large bowl. Pour mixture into pan.

3 Bake loaf about 50 minutes. Stand loaf in pan 10 minutes; turn, top-side up, onto wire rack to cool.

Coffee walnut loaf

PREPARATION TIME 25 MINUTES **COOKING TIME** 45 MINUTES **SERVES** 10

⅔ cup (70g) roasted walnuts
125g butter, chopped
1 cup (220g) caster sugar
½ cup (125ml) milk
2 tablespoons instant coffee granules
1⅓ cups (200g) self-raising flour
2 teaspoons ground cinnamon
2 eggs, beaten lightly

COFFEE ICING
1 tablespoon boiling water
2 teaspoons instant coffee granules
2 teaspoons butter
1 cup (160g) icing sugar

1 Preheat oven to 160°C/40°C fan-forced. Grease 14cm x 21cm loaf pan; line base and long sides with baking paper, extending paper 2cm over sides.

2 Chop half of the nuts.

3 Stir butter, sugar, milk and coffee in small saucepan over low heat until smooth. Sift flour and cinnamon into medium bowl; stir in butter mixture, egg and chopped walnuts. Pour mixture into pan.

4 Bake loaf 15 minutes. Sprinkle with remaining nuts; bake further 30 minutes. Stand loaf in pan 10 minutes; turn, top-side up, onto wire rack to cool.

5 Make coffee icing; drizzle icing over loaf.

COFFEE ICING Combine the water, coffee and butter in small heatproof bowl; stir in sifted icing sugar to form a firm paste. Place bowl over small saucepan of simmering water, stir until icing is spreadable.

Gingerbread loaves

PREPARATION TIME 35 MINUTES **COOKING TIME** 25 MINUTES (PLUS COOLING TIME) **MAKES** 16

200g butter, softened

1¼ cups (275g) caster sugar

¾ cup (270g) treacle

2 eggs

3 cups (450g) plain flour

1½ tablespoons ground ginger

3 teaspoons mixed spice

1 teaspoon bicarbonate of soda

¾ cup (180ml) milk

VANILLA ICING

3 cups (500g) icing sugar

2 teaspoons butter

½ teaspoon vanilla extract

⅓ cup (80ml) milk

1 Preheat oven to 180°C/160°C fan-forced. Grease two eight-hole (½-cup/125ml) petite loaf pans or line 22 muffin pan holes (⅓-cup/80ml) with paper cases.

2 Beat butter and sugar in small bowl with electric mixer until light and fluffy. Add treacle, beat 3 minutes. Beat in eggs, one at a time. Transfer mixture to large bowl; stir in sifted dry ingredients and milk, in two batches. Divide mixture among pans.

3 Bake loaves about 25 minutes. Stand loaves in pans 5 minutes; turn, top-side up, onto wire rack to cool.

4 Meanwhile, make vanilla icing; spread over loaves.

VANILLA ICING Sift icing sugar into heatproof bowl; stir in butter, extract and milk to form a smooth paste. Place bowl over simmering water; stir until spreadable.

When it's baked in a loaf pan, this mixture is just so buttery and sweet with treacle that it sometimes rises like a dream, then sinks in the middle. To guarantee great results, try making the little loaves or the muffins we suggest. Measure the bicarbonate of soda accurately, by levelling off the metric 5ml teaspoon. Too much soda will cause the loaves to taste soapy, but can also cause the cake to rise then fall.

Walnut and raisin loaf

PREPARATION TIME 10 MINUTES **COOKING TIME** 35 MINUTES (PLUS COOLING TIME) **SERVES** 15

⅓ cup (55g) raisins

90g butter

½ cup (100g) firmly packed brown sugar

⅓ cup (80ml) water

½ teaspoon bicarbonate of soda

2 eggs

½ cup (60g) chopped walnuts

½ cup (75g) plain flour

½ cup (75g) self-raising flour

1 Stir raisins, butter, sugar and the water in medium saucepan; bring to the boil. Remove from heat; stir in soda. Cool 15 minutes.

2 Preheat oven to 150°C/130°C fan-forced. Grease 8cm x 26cm bar cake pan; line base with baking paper.

3 Stir eggs and nuts into raisin mixture; stir in sifted flours. Pour mixture into pan.

4 Bake loaf about 35 minutes. Turn, top-side up, onto wire rack to cool.

Rhubarb and coconut cake

PREPARATION TIME 25 MINUTES **COOKING TIME** 1 HOUR 30 MINUTES **SERVES** 10

1 ½ cups (225g) self-raising flour

1 ¼ cups (275g) caster sugar

1 ¼ cups (110g) desiccated coconut

125g butter, melted

3 eggs

½ cup (125ml) milk

½ teaspoon vanilla extract

1 cup (110g) finely chopped rhubarb

5 trimmed rhubarb stalks (300g)

2 tablespoons demerara sugar

1 Preheat oven to 150°C/130°C fan-forced. Grease 14cm x 21cm loaf pan; line base with baking paper.

2 Combine sifted flour, caster sugar and coconut in medium bowl; stir in butter, eggs, milk and extract. Spread half of the mixture into pan; sprinkle evenly with chopped rhubarb, spread remaining cake mixture over rhubarb.

3 Cut rhubarb stalks into 12cm lengths. Place rhubarb pieces over top of cake; sprinkle with demerara sugar.

4 Bake cake about 1 ½ hours. Stand cake in pan 5 minutes; turn, top-side up, onto wire rack to cool.

Upside-down cashew and maple loaf

PREPARATION TIME 25 MINUTES **COOKING TIME** 1 HOUR **SERVES** 12

90g butter, softened

½ cup (100g) firmly packed brown sugar

2 tablespoons maple syrup

1 cup (150g) unsalted roasted cashews, chopped coarsely

125g butter, softened, extra

¾ cup (150g) firmly packed brown sugar, extra

2 eggs

1 cup (150g) self-raising flour

½ cup (75g) plain flour

½ teaspoon mixed spice

½ cup (125ml) sour cream

2 tablespoons maple syrup, extra

1 Preheat oven to 180°C/160°C fan-forced. Grease 15cm x 25cm loaf pan; line base and long sides with baking paper, extending paper 2cm over sides.

2 Beat butter, sugar and syrup in small bowl with wooden spoon until smooth; spread over base of pan. Sprinkle with nuts.

3 Beat remaining ingredients in medium bowl with electric mixer on low speed until combined. Increase speed to medium, beat until mixture is smooth and changed to a lighter colour. Spread cake mixture into pan.

4 Bake loaf about 1 hour. Stand loaf in pan 10 minutes; turn, top-side up, onto wire rack to cool.

RHUBARB AND COCONUT CAKE

Date and walnut loaf

PREPARATION TIME 15 MINUTES **COOKING TIME** 50 MINUTES (PLUS COOLING TIME) **SERVES** 20

60g butter

1 cup (250ml) boiling water

1 cup (180g) finely chopped dried dates

½ teaspoon bicarbonate of soda

1 cup (220g) firmly packed brown sugar

2 cups (300g) self-raising flour

½ cup (60g) coarsely chopped walnuts

1 egg, beaten lightly

1 Preheat oven to 180°C/160°C fan-forced. Grease two 8cm x 19cm nut roll tins; line bases with baking paper. Place tins upright on oven tray.

2 Stir butter and the water in medium saucepan over low heat until butter melts. Remove from heat; stir in dates and soda, then remaining ingredients. Spoon mixture into tins; replace lids.

3 Bake loaves about 50 minutes. Stand loaves in tins 5 minutes; remove ends (top and bottom), shake tins gently to release loaves onto wire rack to cool.

My grandmother used to make this recipe, it's an oldie, but a goodie. If you can't buy new nut roll tins, look around in some second-hand shops or garage sales, you might be lucky. They will rust if they're not looked after properly, as they're made from tin. You can use fruit juice tins as a substitute (see pages 170 & 171).

Apricot loaf

PREPARATION TIME 15 MINUTES **COOKING TIME** 1 HOUR 25 MINUTES (PLUS COOLING TIME) **SERVES** 10

200g (1⅓ cups) dried apricots, chopped coarsely

½ cup (125ml) apricot nectar

½ cup (110g) caster sugar

½ cup (110g) firmly packed brown sugar

250g butter, chopped

3 eggs

1 cup (150g) plain flour

¾ cup (110g) self-raising flour

1 Preheat oven to 150°C/130°C fan-forced. Grease 14cm x 21cm loaf pan; line base and long sides with baking paper, extending paper 2cm over sides.

2 Bring apricots, nectar and sugars to the boil in medium saucepan. Reduce heat; simmer, covered, 5 minutes, stirring occasionally. Remove from heat; add butter, stir until melted. Transfer mixture to large bowl; cover, cool to room temperature.

3 Stir in eggs and sifted flours into apricot mixture. Spread mixture into pan.

4 Bake loaf about 1¼ hours. Cover loaf with foil; cool in pan.

Whole dried apricots are quite expensive, sometimes you can buy already-chopped dried apricots, which are less expensive. Avoid buying the pale apricots that appear to be "plumped", they are cheaper, but lack the flavour of properly dried apricots.

DATE AND WALNUT LOAF

Fig jam and raisin loaf

PREPARATION TIME 20 MINUTES **COOKING TIME** 50 MINUTES (PLUS COOLING TIME) **SERVES** 20

You can bake this recipe in one 15cm x 25cm loaf pan if you like. It will take about 1 ¼ hours to cook at the same temperature as for the nut roll tins. If the loaf begins to brown too much on top — due to the jam — cover the pan loosely with a piece of foil.

125g butter, softened

½ cup (100g) firmly packed brown sugar

2 eggs

1½ cups (225g) self-raising flour

½ cup (160g) fig jam

1 cup (170g) finely chopped raisins

½ cup (125ml) milk

1 Preheat oven to 180°C/160°C fan-forced. Grease two 8cm x 19cm nut roll tins; line bases with baking paper. Place tins upright on oven tray.

2 Beat butter and sugar in small bowl with electric mixer until light and fluffy. Beat in eggs, one at a time. Transfer mixture to medium bowl; stir in sifted flour, jam, raisins and milk, in two batches. Spoon mixture into tins; replace lids.

3 Bake loaves about 50 minutes. Stand loaves in tins 5 minutes; remove ends (top and bottom), shake tins gently to release loaves onto wire rack to cool.

Glacé fruit loaf with ginger syrup

PREPARATION TIME 20 MINUTES **COOKING TIME** 2 HOURS 30 MINUTES **SERVES** 10

Ginger wine does contain alcohol and is available at hotels and bottle shops.

185g butter, softened

½ cup (110g) caster sugar

3 eggs

1 cup (250g) finely chopped glacé apricots

½ cup (80g) finely chopped glacé oranges

½ cup (90g) finely chopped glacé ginger

¾ cup (210g) finely chopped glacé fig

1½ cups (225g) plain flour

½ cup (75g) self-raising flour

½ cup (125ml) milk

¼ cup (60ml) ginger wine

GINGER SYRUP

¼ cup (60ml) ginger wine

¼ cup (60ml) water

¼ cup (55g) caster sugar

2 teaspoons lemon juice

1 Preheat oven to 150°C/130°C fan-forced. Grease 14cm x 21cm loaf pan; line base and long sides with baking paper, extending paper 2cm over sides.

2 Beat butter and sugar in small bowl with electric mixer until combined. Beat in eggs, one at a time. Transfer mixture to large bowl; stir in fruit then sifted flours, and combined milk and wine, in two batches. Spread mixture into pan.

3 Bake loaf about 2½ hours.

4 Make ginger syrup; pour hot syrup over hot cake in pan. Cover with foil; cool in pan.

GINGER SYRUP Stir ingredients in small saucepan over low heat until sugar dissolves; bring to the boil. Boil, without stirring, about 2 minutes or until syrup thickens slightly.

Chocolate walnut log

PREPARATION TIME 30 MINUTES **COOKING TIME** 50 MINUTES (PLUS REFRIGERATION TIME) **SERVES** 20

125g butter, softened

¾ cup (165g) caster sugar

2 eggs

½ cup (75g) plain flour

¾ cup (110g) self-raising flour

¼ cup (25g) cocoa powder

⅓ cup (80ml) milk

½ cup (50g) coarsely chopped walnuts

CHOCOLATE BRANDY CREAM

125g unsalted butter

¼ cup (40g) icing sugar

200g white eating chocolate, melted

2 tablespoons brandy

1 Preheat oven to 180°C/160°C fan-forced. Grease two 8cm x 19cm nut roll tins; line bases with baking paper. Place tins upright on oven tray.

2 Beat butter and sugar in small bowl with electric mixer until light and fluffy. Beat in eggs, one at a time. Transfer mixture to medium bowl; stir in sifted flours and cocoa with milk and nuts in two batches. Spoon mixture into tins; replace lids.

3 Bake loaves about 50 minutes. Stand loaves in tins 10 minutes; remove ends (top and bottom), shake tins gently to release loaves onto wire rack to cool.

4 Make chocolate brandy cream.

5 Cut loaves into 1cm slices; join slices together with thin layer of chocolate brandy cream, reassembling as you go into one long log shape. Place on serving plate; refrigerate 2 hours.

6 Spread log with remaining chocolate brandy cream. Serve log sliced diagonally.

CHOCOLATE BRANDY CREAM Beat butter and sifted icing sugar in small bowl with electric mixer until light and fluffy; beat in chocolate and brandy. Refrigerate, stirring occasionally until spreadable.

We baked this cake in nut roll tins so we could make a long "log" from them. It would be just as easy to arrange the cakes to look like a yuletide log or bûche de Noël. Use either dark or milk chocolate in place of the white for a more log-like look. Once the log is covered with the brandy cream, pull the fork through the cream to make it look like bark. You could make some chocolate leaves, by brushing the backs of ivy leaves with melted chocolate. When they're set, simply peel away the real leaves, and use the chocolate leaves to decorate the log. A dusting of sifted icing sugar at the last minute would just finish it off.

Mini choc-chip banana loaves

PREPARATION TIME 10 MINUTES **COOKING TIME** 20 MINUTES **MAKES** 8

1 cup (460g) mashed overripe banana

¾ cup (165g) firmly packed brown sugar

2 eggs

60g butter, melted

¼ cup (60ml) buttermilk

⅔ cup (100g) self-raising flour

⅔ cup (100g) wholemeal self-raising flour

½ cup (95g) milk Choc Bits

1 Preheat oven to 180°C/160°C fan-forced. Grease 8-hole (¾-cup/180ml) mini loaf pan; line base and two short sides of each hole with strips of baking paper.

2 Combine banana and sugar in large bowl; stir in eggs, butter and buttermilk, then sifted flours and Choc Bits. Divide mixture among pan holes.

3 Bake loaves about 20 minutes. Stand loaves in pans 5 minutes; turn, top-side up, onto wire rack to cool.

English malt loaf

PREPARATION TIME 15 MINUTES **COOKING TIME** 1 HOUR 45 MINUTES **SERVES** 12

4 cups (640g) wholemeal plain flour

½ cup (100g) firmly packed brown sugar

1½ cups (250g) sultanas

1 teaspoon bicarbonate of soda

1 tablespoon hot water

1¼ cups (310ml) milk

1 cup (250ml) liquid malt

½ cup (125ml) treacle

1 Preheat oven to 160°C/140°C fan-forced. Grease 15cm x 25cm loaf pan; line base with baking paper.

2 Sift flour into large heatproof bowl; add sugar and sultanas. Combine soda and the water in medium jug; stir in milk.

3 Stir malt and treacle in medium saucepan, over heat until mixture begins to bubble; add milk mixture. Stir foaming milk mixture into flour mixture. Spread mixture into pan.

4 Bake loaf about 1¾ hours. Stand loaf in pan 5 minutes; turn, top-side up, onto wire rack to cool.

Lime and pineapple loaves

PREPARATION TIME 30 MINUTES (PLUS REFRIGERATION TIME) **COOKING TIME** 30 MINUTES **MAKES** 8

100g butter, softened

1 tablespoon finely grated lime rind

½ cup (110g) caster sugar

2 eggs

¾ cup (110g) self-raising flour

2 tablespoons milk

½ small (450g) pineapple

LIME GANACHE

180g white eating chocolate, chopped coarsely

2 tablespoons lime juice

¼ cup (60ml) thickened cream

1 Preheat oven to 150°C/130°C fan-forced. Grease 8-hole (¾-cup/180ml) mini loaf pan; line bases with baking paper.

2 Beat butter, rind, sugar, eggs, flour and milk in medium bowl with electric mixer at low speed until combined. Increase speed to medium, beat about 3 minutes or until mixture is smooth and changed to a paler colour. Spoon mixture into pan holes; cover pan loosely with foil.

3 Bake cakes about 25 minutes. Stand cakes in pan 5 minutes; turn, top-side up, onto wire rack to cool.

4 Meanwhile, make lime ganache.

5 Peel and core pineapple; slice thinly.

6 Split loaves in half. Spread cut sides of loaves with about half the ganache. Sandwich loaves with about half of the pineapple slices. Top loaves with remaining ganache and pineapple.

LIME GANACHE Stir chocolate, juice and cream in small heatproof bowl over small saucepan of simmering water until smooth. Refrigerate until spreadable.

These are delicate little lime-flavoured butter cakes — very special. Make sure the fresh pineapple you use is ripe, sweet and full of flavour. And it's also important to slice it finely.

RICH DESSERT
CAKES

Rich Dessert Cakes

The custom of sharing a cake to spread the good fortune and happiness of the occasion has been around since at least ancient Roman times, when wedding guests shared the crumbs of a loaf of bread which was broken over the bridal couple's heads as a symbol of abundance and good times ahead. There are a host of reasons why a cake makes a great celebratory dessert. It becomes a festive centrepiece for the party table and it can be prepared well in advance, leaving the cook free to attend to the myriad other tasks of hosting a party. With simple layering, yummy fillings and easy decorations it's possible to turn even the most humble cake into a special occasion dessert. Allow yourself sufficient time and go step by step and you'll turn out gateaux and tortes like a professionally trained pâtissier.

CUTTING A CAKE INTO LAYERS

A turntable will make cake decorating and assembly easier, but if you don't have one, you can improvise using a footed cake plate, or a cake board or flat plate standing on a bowl for stability. You need a long, serrated knife to split a cake cleanly into layers. If you want to cut the cake in half or quarters, start at a point midway up the side of the cake, place one hand on top of the cake and, holding the knife parallel with the plate, make an incision about 2cm deep all round the cake, turn the plate as you go. Continue turning and cutting until you feel the resistance of the cake against the knife ease off, then gently remove the top layer. For quarters, split each half in half again. You can slide a piece of thin cardboard under the top layer to make lifting it off easier if you think the cake is in danger of breaking. Some cooks believe that the easiest and neatest way to cut cakes is by dragging a long piece of strong thick cotton or dental floss across the middle of the cake. (See also *Splitting & layering cakes* on pages 94 & 95.)

ASSEMBLING AND ICING A LAYER CAKE

Position the bottom layer in the middle of the serving plate or cake board. Pile the filling in the centre of the layer; using a flexible spatula, work the filling to the outside of the cake, turning the cake as you go. Repeat with the remaining layers and filling. To cover the sides, put a quantity of frosting on the top end of the spatula and press it into the sides of the cake, spreading it out as you work. Rotate the cake and continue applying the frosting until the whole cake is covered. Cover the top of the cake the same way you did the layers, taking extra care not to pick up crumbs. If you do end up with crumbs, remove them with the tip of a knife blade. To smooth the top and edges, dip the spatula in hot water, dry it, then run it across the surface, working from one side to the other. Wipe the exposed plate surrounding the cake with a clean damp cloth to remove any frosting or filling which may have dropped onto the plate; finish the edge close to the cake by wiping it with a finger which has been covered in a tissue. (See also *Splitting & layering cakes* on pages 94 & 95.)

TRANSFERRING THE CAKE TO ANOTHER PLATE

Place a broad, flexible spatula under one side of the cake and move it until you can lift one side of the cake sufficiently to slide one hand under it. Balance the cake on this hand, then, with the serving plate as close as possible, transfer the cake to the plate.

TOFFEE TIPS

Toffee is great for decorating cakes, whether it's as fruit or nuts dipped in toffee, shards of toffee speared into the cake surface, or spun toffee over the top. The method is not difficult, but you must exercise great care not to get the boiling toffee on your fingers or hands as it will produce a nasty burn.

Combine the sugar and water as specified in the recipe in the recommended sized heavy-based saucepan and place over medium to high heat. To prevent crystallisation or graininess, the sugar must be completely dissolved before the mixture boils. Stir constantly until the sugar dissolves and if any sugar grains stick to the sides of the pan, brush them down with a pastry brush that has been dipped in water. Once the sugar syrup comes to the boil, stop stirring. Reduce the heat and simmer the syrup, uncovered, for about 10 minutes or until the mixture is golden brown. The longer you cook the toffee the deeper the colour and the harder it will set.

The state described as "hard crack", when the toffee sets pretty much instantly is achieved between 138°C and 154°C on a candy thermometer. If you don't have one, you can drizzle some of the hot toffee mixture into a container of cold water. If it sets immediately and can be snapped between the fingers, the mixture is at "hard crack"; if not, it should be boiled for a few minutes more. Always remove the pan from the heat and allow the bubbles to subside before testing. Once "hard crack" is achieved, fruit or nuts can be dipped into the toffee. Stand to set on a baking-paper-lined tray.

To make toffee shards, use a wooden spoon to drizzle toffee over a baking-paper-lined tray. When the toffee sets, break it and position on the cake.

To create a spun toffee topping over a cake, hold a fork in each hand and dip them in the hot toffee. Bring the backs of the forks together over the cake, draw them apart, dragging the toffee onto the cake. Repeat until you've achieved a "nest" of spun toffee. See also page 203 for tips on toffee strands and shapes.

SUGAR COATING

Sugared fruit also looks pretty piled on top of a cake — you can apply the same technique to rose petals and edible whole flowers such as violets, pansies and nasturtiums (make sure they're free from insecticides). Rinse and pat dry the fruit or flowers to be coated. Beat an egg white lightly with a fork, then, using a fine artists brush, lightly brush the fruit with egg white. Roll in a saucer of caster sugar, then place on a baking-paper-lined tray. Leave about one hour or until the sugar feels dry to the touch before placing on the cake. (See also page 203.)

Muscat prune shortcake

PREPARATION TIME 30 MINUTES **COOKING TIME** 25 MINUTES (PLUS COOLING AND REFRIGERATION TIME)
SERVES 8

200g butter, softened

1 teaspoon finely grated lemon rind

⅓ cup (75g) caster sugar

¼ cup (50g) rice flour

¾ cup (110g) self-raising flour

¾ cup (110g) plain flour

300ml thickened cream

1 tablespoon caster sugar, extra

MUSCAT PRUNES

1 cup (170g) coarsely chopped seeded prunes

1 cup (250ml) muscat

1 Preheat oven to 180°C/160°C fan-forced. Grease three 20cm-round sandwich pans.

2 Beat butter, rind and sugar in medium bowl with electric mixer until light and fluffy. Fold in sifted flours, in two batches. Press mixture evenly into pans.

3 Bake shortcakes about 20 minutes. Stand shortcakes in pans; cool to room temperature.

4 Meanwhile, make muscat prunes.

5 Beat cream in small bowl with electric mixer until firm peaks form. Place one shortcake into deep 20cm-round cake pan or 20cm springform tin; spread with half of the prune mixture then half of the whipped cream. Top with another shortcake; spread with remaining prune mixture then remaining whipped cream. Top with remaining shortcake, cover; refrigerate overnight.

6 Remove from pan; serve sprinkled with extra sugar.

MUSCAT PRUNES Stir prunes and muscat in small saucepan over heat, without boiling, until prunes soften. Cool to room temperature.

Celebration cake

PREPARATION TIME 1 HOUR 30 MINUTES (PLUS COOLING TIME)

COOKING TIME 2 HOURS 15 MINUTES (PLUS REFRIGERATION TIME) **SERVES** 12

This cake is a labour of love, but well worth the effort if you're after something that is memorable and special. The little pockets of white chocolate custard scattered throughout the rich dark mud cake will surprise and delight.

250g butter, chopped

200g dark eating chocolate, chopped coarsely

1½ cups (375ml) water

2 eggs

2 teaspoons vanilla extract

2 cups (440g) caster sugar

¾ cup (110g) self-raising flour

1¼ cups (185g) plain flour

¼ cup (25g) cocoa powder

50g white eating chocolate, melted

WHITE CHOCOLATE CUSTARD

¾ cup (180ml) milk

1 vanilla bean

2 egg yolks

1½ teaspoons gelatine

2 tablespoons water

130g white eating chocolate, melted

⅓ cup (80ml) cream

CHOCOLATE TRUFFLES

75g dark eating chocolate

½ cup (125ml) cream

CHOCOLATE GANACHE

200g dark eating chocolate, chopped coarsely

⅓ cup (80ml) cream

1 Preheat oven to 160°C/140°C fan-forced. Grease deep 22cm-round cake pan; line base and side with baking paper.

2 Stir butter, dark chocolate and the water in medium saucepan over low heat until smooth. Transfer mixture to large bowl; cool 10 minutes.

3 Meanwhile, beat eggs, extract and sugar in small bowl with electric mixer until thick and creamy; stir into chocolate mixture. Stir in sifted dry ingredients; pour into pan. Bake about 1¾ hours. Stand cake 10 minutes; turn cake, top-side up, onto wire rack to cool. Enclose cake with plastic wrap; refrigerate 3 hours or overnight.

4 Split cake horizontally a third of the way from the top. Place bottom two-thirds of cake on serving plate; using small teaspoon or melon baller, scoop about 14 deep holes (at equal distances apart and not through to bottom of cake) out of cake, reserving 1¼ cups of scooped-out crumbled cake pieces for truffles.

5 Make white chocolate custard; pour immediately into holes in cake. Replace top of cake, cover; refrigerate 2 hours.

6 Meanwhile, make truffles then chocolate ganache.

7 Spread chocolate ganache over cake; decorate with truffles. Drizzle truffles with white chocolate; refrigerate 1 hour before serving.

WHITE CHOCOLATE CUSTARD Place milk in small saucepan. Split vanilla bean in half lengthways, scrape seeds into saucepan, then add pod; bring to the boil. Cool 10 minutes; discard pod. Whisk in egg yolks; transfer mixture to medium heatproof bowl. Place custard mixture over medium saucepan of simmering water, stir over heat about 10 minutes or until mixture thickens slightly and coats the back of a spoon. Remove custard mixture from heat. Sprinkle gelatine over the water in small heatproof jug; stand jug in same saucepan of simmering water. Stir until gelatine dissolves. Stir gelatine mixture into custard mixture, cover; cool 5 minutes. Add chocolate and cream; stir until smooth.

CHOCOLATE TRUFFLES Stir chocolate and cream in small saucepan over low heat until smooth. Stir in reserved scooped-out cake, cover; refrigerate until firm. Roll level teaspoons of the mixture into balls, place on trays, cover; refrigerate until firm.

CHOCOLATE GANACHE Stir ingredients in small saucepan over low heat until smooth.

Tiramisu torte

PREPARATION TIME 30 MINUTES **COOKING TIME** 25 MINUTES (PLUS REFRIGERATION TIME) **SERVES** 16

6 eggs

1 cup (220g) caster sugar

½ cup (75g) plain flour

½ cup (75g) self-raising flour

½ cup (75g) cornflour

¼ cup (10g) instant coffee granules

1½ cups (375ml) boiling water

¾ cup (180ml) marsala

¼ cup (60ml) coffee-flavoured liqueur

300ml thickened cream

½ cup (80g) icing sugar

750g mascarpone cheese

500g vienna almonds, chopped coarsely

Tiramisu means "pick-me-up", and the dessert has become increasingly popular over the last 20 years or so. We've turned a couple of modest sponge cakes into a stunning cake with all the flavours of the well-known dessert. Vienna almonds are toffee-coated almonds, available in specialty nut and confectionery shops. If you can't find them, you can cover the cake with roasted flaked almonds, then drizzle the nuts with toffee.

1 Preheat oven to 180°C/160°C fan-forced. Grease two deep 22cm-round cake pans; line bases with baking paper.

2 Beat eggs in medium bowl with electric mixer about 10 minutes or until thick and creamy. Add sugar, about 1 tablespoon at a time, beating until sugar is dissolved between additions. Gently fold in triple-sifted flours. Divide cake mixture evenly between pans.

3 Bake cakes about 25 minutes. Turn cakes, top-side up, onto wire racks to cool.

4 Meanwhile, dissolve coffee in the water in small heatproof bowl. Stir in marsala and liqueur; cool.

5 Beat cream and sifted icing sugar in small bowl with electric mixer until soft peaks form; transfer to large bowl. Stir in mascarpone and ½ cup of the coffee mixture.

6 Split cooled cakes in half. Centre half of one cake on serving plate; brush with a quarter of the remaining coffee mixture then spread with about 1 cup of mascarpone cream. Repeat layering until last cake half is covered with mascarpone cream. Spread remaining mascarpone cream around side of cake; press almonds onto side and top of cake. Refrigerate 1 hour.

1

2

3

4

Maple pecan cake

PREPARATION TIME 15 MINUTES **COOKING TIME** 1 HOUR **SERVES** 10

1 cup (100g) pecans

⅓ cup (80ml) maple syrup

1¼ cups (235g) coarsely chopped dried figs

1¼ cups (310ml) boiling water

1 teaspoon bicarbonate of soda

60g butter, chopped coarsely

¾ cup (150g) firmly packed brown sugar

2 eggs

1 cup (150g) self-raising flour

MAPLE BUTTERSCOTCH SAUCE

1 cup (250ml) maple syrup

½ cup (125ml) cream

100g butter, chopped coarsely

1 Preheat oven to 180°C/160°C fan-forced. Grease deep 20cm-round cake pan; line base with baking paper. Coat paper with cooking-oil spray.

2 Arrange nuts over base of pan; drizzle with maple syrup.

3 Place figs, the water and soda in bowl of food processor. Cover with lid; stand 5 minutes. Add butter and sugar; process until almost smooth. Add eggs and flour; process until just combined. Pour mixture into pan.

4 Bake cake about 55 minutes. Stand cake in pan 5 minutes; turn onto wire rack.

5 Make maple butterscotch sauce. Serve with warm cake and ice-cream, if desired.

MAPLE BUTTERSCOTCH SAUCE Stir ingredients in small saucepan over heat until smooth; bring to the boil. Boil, uncovered, about 2 minutes or until mixture thickens slightly.

This cake resembles the much-loved sticky date cake or pudding, here we've used figs, pecans and maple syrup flavours. Use a proper maple syrup – not an imitation – for the best flavour.

Rich truffle mud cake

PREPARATION TIME 15 MINUTES **COOKING TIME** 1 HOUR (PLUS REFRIGERATION TIME) **SERVES** 12

6 eggs

½ cup (100g) firmly packed brown sugar

400g dark eating chocolate, melted

1 cup (250ml) thick cream (48% fat content)

⅓ cup (80ml) lemon-flavoured liqueur

1 Preheat oven to 180°C/160°C fan-forced. Grease deep 22cm-round cake pan; line base and side with baking paper.

2 Beat eggs and sugar in large bowl with electric mixer until thick and creamy. Beat in melted chocolate until combined. Using metal spoon, gently fold in combined cream and liqueur. Pour mixture into pan. Place pan in baking dish; pour enough boiling water into dish to come halfway up side of pan.

3 Bake 30 minutes. Cover with foil; bake further 30 minutes. Discard foil; remove cake pan from baking dish; cool cake in pan. Turn cake onto serving plate, cover; refrigerate overnight.

Rich is the word that best describes this cake – it is mousse-like in texture and cuts beautifully into slender wedges. Use whatever flavour liqueur you like, maybe orange (Grand Marnier) or Tia Maria or Kahlua. It's important to use cream that has a high fat content – at best 48% fat content. Also, you must give the cake at least 12 hours refrigeration for it to settle and set properly. Serve it dusted with some good quality sifted cocoa powder.

1 MAPLE PECAN CAKE **2** RICH TRUFFLE MUD CAKE **3** FLOURLESS CHOCOLATE DESSERT CAKE [P 196] **4** STICKY DATE ROLL WITH BUTTERSCOTCH SAUCE [P 196]

Flourless chocolate dessert cake

PREPARATION TIME 20 MINUTES **COOKING TIME** 45 MINUTES (PLUS REFRIGERATION TIME) **SERVES** 10

Almond meal (finely ground almonds) replaces the flour in this recipe, making it rich and luscious. As a bonus it is an ideal dessert for dinner guests who have a gluten intolerence. The cake is quite fragile, so handle it carefully, it does become firmer after refrigeration. Use a hot dry sharp knife to cut this cake. Serve it with whipped cream.

100g dark eating chocolate, chopped coarsely

100g butter, chopped coarsely

2 tablespoons marsala

½ cup (110g) caster sugar

⅔ cup (80g) almond meal

1 tablespoon instant coffee granules

1 tablespoon hot water

3 eggs, separated

STRAWBERRY COULIS

250g strawberries, hulled

¼ cup (40g) icing sugar

1 Preheat oven to 180°C/160°C fan-forced. Grease deep 20cm-round cake pan; line base and side with baking paper.

2 Stir chocolate and butter in small saucepan over low heat until smooth.

3 Combine marsala, sugar, almond meal and combined coffee and the water in large bowl; stir in chocolate mixture. Stir in egg yolks.

4 Beat egg whites in small bowl with electric mixer until soft peaks form; gently fold into chocolate mixture, in two batches. Pour mixture into pan.

5 Bake cake about 45 minutes. Cool in pan, cover; refrigerate several hours or overnight.

6 Make strawberry coulis.

7 Dust cake with sifted icing sugar; serve with strawberry coulis.

STRAWBERRY COULIS Blend or process ingredients until smooth.

Sticky date roll with butterscotch sauce

PREPARATION TIME 15 MINUTES **COOKING TIME** 30 MINUTES (PLUS COOLING TIME) **SERVES** 10

Yet another version of the sticky date cake or pudding. The cake takes about 10 minutes to make, only 15 minutes to bake and about 5 minutes to cool ready for filling. So you can whip this popular dessert up ready to serve in 35 minutes.

1 cup (160g) seeded dates

¾ cup (180ml) boiling water

1 teaspoon bicarbonate of soda

50g butter, chopped coarsely

⅔ cup (150g) firmly packed brown sugar

2 eggs

¾ cup (110g) self-raising flour

2 tablespoons white sugar

300ml thickened cream

BUTTERSCOTCH SAUCE

½ cup (100g) firmly packed brown sugar

⅔ cup (160ml) cream

100g butter, chopped coarsely

1 Preheat oven to 180°C/160°C fan-forced. Grease 25cm x 30cm swiss roll pan; line base with baking paper, extending paper 5cm over long sides.

2 Place dates, the water and soda in bowl of food processor. Cover with lid; stand 5 minutes. Add butter and brown sugar; process until almost smooth. Add eggs and flour; process until combined. Pour mixture into pan; bake about 15 minutes.

3 Meanwhile, place a piece of baking paper cut the same size of pan on bench; sprinkle evenly with caster sugar. Turn cake onto paper; peel lining paper away. Trim all sides of cake. Using paper as a guide, roll cake from long side; hold for 30 seconds then unroll. Cover cake with tea towel; cool.

4 Meanwhile, make butterscotch sauce.

5 Beat cream in small bowl with electric mixer until firm peaks form. Fold ¼ cup of the butterscotch sauce into cream. Spread cake evenly with cream mixture. Using paper as a guide, roll cake from long side. Serve drizzled with remaining warmed sauce.

BUTTERSCOTCH SAUCE Stir ingredients in small saucepan over heat until sugar dissolves and butter melts.

Black forest cake

PREPARATION TIME 35 MINUTES **COOKING TIME** 1 HOUR 50 MINUTES (PLUS COOLING TIME) **SERVES** 12

Originally from Swabia in Germany's Black Forest region, this cake has become popular all over the world. We like to use canned black cherries – already seeded.

250g butter, chopped coarsely

1 tablespoon instant coffee granules

1½ cups (375ml) water

200g dark eating chocolate, chopped coarsely

2 cups (440g) caster sugar

1½ cups (225g) self-raising flour

1 cup (150g) plain flour

¼ cup (25g) cocoa powder

2 eggs

2 teaspoons vanilla extract

600ml thickened cream

¼ cup (60ml) kirsch

2 x 425g cans cherries, drained, halved

1 Preheat oven to 150°C/130°C fan-forced. Grease deep 22cm-round cake pan; line base and side with baking paper.

2 Melt butter in medium saucepan, stir in combined coffee and the water, then chocolate and sugar; stir over low heat, without boiling, until smooth. Transfer mixture to large bowl; cool until mixture is warm. Beat mixture on low speed with electric mixer; gradually beat in sifted dry ingredients, in three batches. Beat in eggs, one at a time, then extract. Pour mixture into pan.

3 Bake cake about 1¾ hours. Stand cake in pan 5 minutes; turn, top-side up, onto wire rack to cool.

4 Beat cream until firm peaks form.

5 Trim top of cake to make it flat. Split cake into three layers. Place one layer of cake on serving plate; brush with one-third of the kirsch. Spread with one-third of the cream, then top with half of the cherries. Repeat layering process, finishing with layer of cake. Brush top of cake with remaining kirsch; spread with remaining cream.

Blackberry and orange mascarpone cake

PREPARATION TIME 30 MINUTES **COOKING TIME** 50 MINUTES (PLUS REFRIGERATION TIME) **SERVES** 12

We don't use blackberries
very often, but they are
delicious. Use any berries
you like in this cake, they
will all marry happily
with the orange flavour.
Mascarpone needs to
be handled carefully,
overwhipping, stirring,
beating or whisking
can cause it to curdle
and separate — rendering
it useless.

185g butter, softened

1 tablespoon finely grated orange rind

1 cup (220g) caster sugar

3 eggs

1 cup (150g) self-raising flour

⅓ cup (40g) almond meal

½ cup (125ml) orange juice

350g blackberries

⅓ cup (110g) blackberry jam, warmed

1 tablespoon orange-flavoured liqueur

1 tablespoon icing sugar

MASCARPONE CREAM

1 cup (250g) mascarpone cheese

⅓ cup (55g) icing sugar

1 teaspoon finely grated orange rind

1 tablespoon orange-flavoured liqueur

⅔ cup (160ml) thickened cream

1 Preheat oven to 160°C/140°C fan-forced. Grease deep 22cm-round cake pan; line base and side with baking paper.

2 Beat butter, rind and caster sugar in medium bowl with electric mixer until light and fluffy. Beat in eggs, one at a time. Stir in sifted flour, almond meal and juice, in two batches. Pour mixture into pan.

3 Bake cake about 50 minutes. Stand cake in pan 5 minutes; turn, top-side up, onto wire rack to cool.

4 Meanwhile, make mascarpone cream.

5 Reserve 12 blackberries. Split cake into three layers. Place one layer of cake on serving plate; spread with half of the combined jam and liqueur. Spread with half of the mascarpone cream, then top with half of the blackberries. Repeat layering process, finishing with layer of cake. Cover; refrigerate 1 hour.

6 Serve cake dusted with sifted icing sugar and reserved blackberries.

MASCARPONE CREAM Combine mascarpone, sifted icing sugar, rind and liqueur in medium bowl. Beat cream until soft peaks from; fold into mascarpone mixture.

Berry-mousse cake

PREPARATION TIME 40 MINUTES **COOKING TIME** 20 MINUTES (PLUS REFRIGERATION TIME) **SERVES** 12

4 egg whites

¾ cup (165g) caster sugar

1½ cups (240g) almond meal

¼ cup (35g) plain flour

300ml thickened cream

450g fresh raspberries

½ cup (160g) raspberry jam, warmed

¼ cup (60ml) coconut-flavoured liqueur

RASPBERRY MOUSSE

200g fresh raspberries

3 teaspoons gelatine

2 tablespoons water

125g white eating chocolate, melted

2 egg yolks

¼ cup (55g) caster sugar

1 tablespoon coconut-flavoured liqueur

300ml thickened cream

1 Preheat oven to 180°C/160°C fan-forced. Grease two 22cm springform tins; line bases with baking paper.

2 Beat egg whites in medium bowl with electric mixer until soft peaks form. Gradually add sugar, beating between additions, until sugar dissolves. Fold in dry ingredients. Spread mixture equally between tins; bake about 20 minutes. Stand cakes in tins 5 minutes. Remove from tins to wire racks; cool at room temperature.

3 Make raspberry mousse. Line base and side of clean 22cm springform tin with baking paper; return one cake to tin. Pour mousse over cake; top with remaining cake. Cover; refrigerate 3 hours or overnight, until mousse sets.

4 Remove cake from tin. Beat cream in small bowl with electric mixer until soft peaks form; spread all over cake. Place raspberries on top of cake; brush raspberries with combined strained jam and liqueur.

RASPBERRY MOUSSE Push raspberries through sieve into large bowl; discard seeds. Sprinkle gelatine over the water in small heatproof jug. Stand jug in small saucepan of simmering water; stir until gelatine dissolves. Stir gelatine mixture, chocolate, egg yolks, sugar and liqueur in small bowl until smooth. Beat cream in small bowl with electric mixer until soft peaks form; fold cream and chocolate mixture into raspberry puree.

Vanilla pear almond cake

PREPARATION TIME 30 MINUTES (PLUS COOLING TIME) **COOKING TIME** 2 HOURS 15 MINUTES **SERVES** 8

8 corella pears (800g)

2½ cups (625ml) water

1 strip lemon rind

1¾ cups (385g) caster sugar

1 vanilla bean

125g butter, softened

3 eggs

⅔ cup (160g) sour cream

⅔ cup (100g) plain flour

⅔ cup (100g) self-raising flour

¼ cup (40g) blanched almonds, roasted, chopped coarsely

40g dark eating chocolate, chopped coarsely

½ cup (60g) almond meal

1 Peel pears, leaving stems intact.

2 Combine the water, rind and 1 cup of the sugar in medium saucepan. Split vanilla bean in half lengthways; scrape seeds into pan, then add pod. Stir over heat, without boiling, until sugar dissolves. Add pears; bring to the boil. Reduce heat; simmer, covered, 30 minutes or until pears are just tender. Transfer pears to medium bowl; bring syrup to the boil. Boil, uncovered, until syrup reduces by half. Cool completely.

3 Preheat oven to 160°C/140°C fan-forced. Insert base of 23cm springform tin upside down in tin to give a flat base; grease tin.

4 Beat butter and remaining sugar in medium bowl with electric mixer until light and fluffy. Beat in eggs, one at a time; beat in sour cream. Stir in 2 tablespoons of the syrup, then sifted flours, nuts, chocolate and almond meal. Spread mixture into tin; place pears upright around edge of tin, gently pushing to the bottom.

5 Bake cake about 1 hour 35 minutes. Stand cake in tin 10 minutes; remove from tin. Serve cake warm, brushed with remaining syrup.

Coffee hazelnut torte

PREPARATION TIME 20 MINUTES (PLUS COOLING TIME) **COOKING TIME** 1 HOUR 30 MINUTES **SERVES** 16

6 egg whites

1¼ cups (275g) caster sugar

½ cup (75g) roasted hazelnuts, chopped coarsely

1 cup (80g) roasted flaked almonds

1 tablespoon cocoa powder

COFFEE CREAM

⅔ cup (160ml) water

1 cup (220g) caster sugar

1 teaspoon gelatine

2 tablespoons milk

1 tablespoon instant coffee granules

250g unsalted butter, softened

1 teaspoon vanilla extract

Unsalted butter will make this coffee cream velvety smooth. Beat the butter and extract until it is as white as possible, before gradually beating in the coffee syrup mixture.

1 Preheat oven to 150°C/130°C fan-forced. Line three oven trays with baking paper; draw a 22cm-diameter circle on each tray.

2 Beat egg whites in medium bowl with electric mixer until soft peaks form. Gradually add sugar, beating after each addition, until sugar dissolves; fold in hazelnuts.

3 Spread mixture equally on drawn circles; bake about 1 hour or until firm. Cool meringues in oven with door ajar.

4 Make coffee cream. Place one meringue on serving plate; spread with a quarter of the coffee cream. Top with another meringue; spread with a third of the remaining coffee cream. Top with last meringue; spread side of cake with remaining coffee cream. Press almonds over cream all around torte; dust top with sifted cocoa.

COFFEE CREAM Stir the water, sugar, gelatine, milk and coffee in small saucepan over heat, without boiling, until sugar and gelatine dissolve. Cool to room temperature. Beat butter and extract in small bowl with electric mixer until light and fluffy. With motor operating, gradually beat in sugar mixture until fluffy (this will take about 10 minutes).

Frills

Cakes and desserts benefit from some sort of edible decoration, here are some easy ideas.

GLAZING FRUIT

For added gloss and flavour, brush washed and dried strawberries with warmed sieved jam. Apricot jam is our favourite; warm in a microwave oven, then push through a fine sieve.

SHAPING CREAM

Shaping thick heavy cream into quenelle (oval) shapes, is easy and looks professional. Use two dessertspoons to shape the cream as you transfer a spoonful of cream from one dessertspoon to the other.

PIPING CHOCOLATE

Piping chocolate onto serving plates adds style. It's easy to make your own paper piping bag (pages 642 & 643). Fill the bag with melted chocolate, cut a tiny piece from the tip of the bag.

PIPING SHELL EDGING

Piping is a bit old-fashioned these days, but it's handy to be able to cover up a rough edging, or put a pretty border around a cake. Once you learn the skill, you won't forget it, practise with mashed potato. Here we're using a small fluted tube in a piping bag to edge a frosted cake.

ROASTING NUTS

Roast nuts on an oven tray in a moderate oven, or in a heavy-based frying pan on the stove top. Both methods require stirring the nuts, so they brown evenly, the oven method needs a couple of stirrings, the pan method needs constant stirring. Remove the nuts from the tray or pan as soon as they're browned, or they'll burn.

TOFFEE-DIPPING

Strawberries are the most popular fruit to toffee-dip, you can also dip mandarin segments, tiny bunches of grapes etc. Be careful you don't burn yourself with the hot toffee. A bamboo skewer, inserted into the fruit piece, makes the job easy and safer. Drain the toffee away from the fruit, then place the fruit on a baking-paper-lined tray to set.

SUGAR-COATING

Some fruit and edible flowers can be sugar-coated. Brush the fruit or flower sparingly with unbeaten egg white then sprinkle lightly with caster sugar — the coating will dry to a light "crust".

PIPING SHAPES

Coloured melted white chocolate is ideal for piping small shapes to use for decorations. Pipe shapes onto baking-paper-lined trays and let them set at room temperature. Peel the shapes off the paper and use as you like.

USING FONDANT

Commercially-made fondant (aka soft or prepared icing) is mostly used as a covering for cakes. It can be rolled out, shapes cut out from it, the shapes are then dried, ready to be used as you like.

CRYSTALLISING RIND

Finely shredded citrus rind tastes and looks good as a decoration. Shred the rind with a zester, or, peel the rind thinly from the fruit, then cut it finely. Blanch the rind twice (in and out of boiling then iced water), then add the rind to a citrus-flavoured sugar syrup. Boil the syrup until it's thick, then remove the rind to a wire rack to cool before using.

TOFFEE STRANDS

Toffee-making takes a bit of practice to get it to the right stage you need. Drizzle the toffee (after the bubbles have subsided) from the tines of a fork in strands onto baking-paper-lined oven trays. Leave the toffee to set at room temperature, then lift them from the paper, snap them to the length you need, and use for a great effect on cakes and desserts.

TOFFEE SHAPES

If you want some curved toffee shapes for a decoration, cover a rolling pin with baking paper, drizzle the toffee (after the bubbles have subsided) over the pin. Let the shapes dry at room temperature, then lift them onto the cake or dessert.

Dark chocolate and almond torte

PREPARATION TIME 20 MINUTES **COOKING TIME** 55 MINUTES (PLUS STANDING TIME) **SERVES** 12

Vienna almonds are toffee-coated almonds available in nut and confectionery shops. If you can't find them, decorate this cake with fresh raspberries or strawberries. The ganache will take at least 30 minutes to set at a cool room temperature. You can refrigerate the cake if you're in a hurry, but the ganache will lose its gloss.

160g dark eating chocolate, chopped coarsely

160g butter

5 eggs, separated

¾ cup (165g) caster sugar

1 cup (125g) almond meal

⅔ cup (50g) roasted flaked almonds, chopped coarsely

⅓ cup (35g) coarsely grated dark eating chocolate

1 cup (140g) vienna almonds

DARK CHOCOLATE GANACHE

125g dark eating chocolate, chopped coarsely

⅓ cup (80ml) cream

1 Preheat oven to 180°C/160°C fan-forced. Grease deep 22cm-round cake pan; line base and side with baking paper.

2 Stir chopped chocolate and butter in small saucepan over low heat until smooth; cool.

3 Beat egg yolks and sugar in small bowl with electric mixer until thick and creamy. Transfer to large bowl; stir in chocolate mixture, almond meal, flaked almonds and grated chocolate.

4 Beat egg whites in small bowl with electric mixer until soft peaks form; fold into chocolate mixture, in two batches. Pour mixture into pan.

5 Bake cake about 45 minutes. Stand cake in pan 15 minutes; turn, top-side up, onto wire rack to cool.

6 Make dark chocolate ganache; spread over cake. Decorate cake with vienna almonds.

DARK CHOCOLATE GANACHE Stir ingredients in small saucepan over low heat until smooth.

Cumquat layer cake

PREPARATION TIME 30 MINUTES **COOKING TIME** 35 MINUTES (PLUS COOLING TIME) **SERVES** 10

Cumquats make wonderful liqueur and marmalade with their bitter/sweet taste. Here we've cooked them to a jam-like consistency then added them to a rich custard to make an unusual filling for this cake.

3 eggs

½ cup (110g) caster sugar

¼ cup (35g) plain flour

¼ cup (35g) self-raising flour

¼ cup (35g) cornflour

2 tablespoons orange-flavoured liqueur

300ml thickened cream

CUMQUAT FILLING

250g fresh cumquats

½ cup (110g) caster sugar

½ cup (125ml) water

1 tablespoon orange-flavoured liqueur

⅓ cup (75g) caster sugar, extra

1 tablespoon plain flour

1 tablespoon cornflour

3 egg yolks

1½ cups (375ml) milk

½ cup (125ml) thickened cream

1 Make cumquat filling.

2 Preheat oven to 180°C/160°C fan-forced. Grease deep 20cm round cake pan; line base with baking paper.

3 Beat eggs in small bowl with electric mixer until thick and creamy. Gradually add sugar; beat until dissolved between additions. Transfer mixture to large bowl; carefully fold in sifted flours. Spread mixture into pan.

4 Bake cake about 30 minutes. Turn, top-side up, onto wire rack to cool.

5 Cut cold cake into three layers. Brush each layer with liqueur. Sandwich layers with cumquat filling. Beat cream until soft peaks form. Cover cake with cream and decorate with reserved cooked cumquats.

CUMQUAT FILLING Slice unpeeled cumquats finely; discard seeds. Place cumquats, sugar and the water in medium saucepan; stir over heat, without boiling, until sugar is dissolved. Bring to the boil; reduce heat and simmer, uncovered, without stirring, 5 minutes. Remove from heat and stir in liqueur; cool to room temperature. Combine extra sugar and flours in medium saucepan; gradually stir in combined egg yolks and milk. Stir over high heat until custard mixture boils and thickens; remove from heat, cover, then cool to room temperature. Beat cream in small bowl until soft peaks form; fold into custard. Stir in three-quarters of the cumquat mixture; reserve remaining mixture.

Warm chocolate polenta cakes with chocolate sauce

PREPARATION TIME 20 MINUTES **COOKING TIME** 30 MINUTES **MAKES** 8

125g butter, softened

⅔ cup (150g) caster sugar

1¼ cups (150g) almond meal

¼ cup (25g) cocoa powder

50g dark eating chocolate, grated

2 eggs, beaten lightly

½ cup (85g) polenta

⅓ cup (80ml) milk

CHOCOLATE SAUCE

125g dark eating chocolate, chopped coarsely

½ cup (125ml) cream

1 Preheat oven to 160°C/140°C fan-forced. Grease 8 x ⅓-cup (80ml) individual oval pans; line bases with baking paper.

2 Beat butter and sugar in small bowl with an electric mixer until light and fluffy. Stir in almond meal, sifted cocoa and chocolate then egg; stir in combined polenta and milk. Divide mixture among pans.

3 Bake cakes about 30 minutes. Cool cakes in pans 5 minutes; turn, top-side up, onto wire rack to cool.

4 Meanwhile, make chocolate sauce; serve with warm cakes.

CHOCOLATE SAUCE Stir chocolate and cream in small saucepan over low heat until smooth.

Chocolate ganache and raspberry cake

PREPARATION TIME 25 MINUTES **COOKING TIME** 1 HOUR 25 MINUTES **SERVES** 10-12

⅓ cup (35g) cocoa powder

⅓ cup (80ml) water

150g dark eating chocolate, melted

150g butter, melted

1 ⅓ cups (300g) firmly packed brown sugar

1 cup (125g) almond meal

4 eggs, separated

200g dark eating chocolate, chopped coarsely

⅔ cup (160ml) thickened cream

300g raspberries

1 Preheat oven to 160°C/140°C fan-forced. Grease deep 22cm-round cake pan; line base and side with baking paper.

2 Blend sifted cocoa with the water in large bowl until smooth. Stir in melted chocolate, butter, sugar, almond meal and egg yolks.

3 Beat egg whites in small bowl with electric mixer until soft peaks fo·m. Fold egg whites into chocolate mixture, in two batches. Pour mixture ¡nto pan. Bake cake about 1¼ hours.

4 Stand cake in pan 15 minutes; turn, top-side up, onto wire rack to cool.

5 Stir chopped chocolate and cream in small saucepan over low heat until smooth.

6 Place raspberries on top of cake; drizzle chocolate mixture over raspberries. Stand cake at room temperature until chocolate sets.

Soft-centred chocolate cakes

PREPARATION TIME 20 MINUTES **COOKING TIME** 15 MINUTES **MAKES** 6

185g dark eating chocolate, chopped coarsely

185g butter, chopped coarsely

3 egg yolks

⅓ cup (50g) plain flour

4 eggs

⅓ cup (75g) caster sugar

350g jar sour cherry jam

To get just the right amount of gooey mixture in the middle of these cakes will take a little experimenting. Every oven has its own personality, and only you can work out the exact timing for these cakes — both in the baking and the standing. Be careful when you're removing the cakes from the pan, the gooey middle is uncooked — but very hot — cake mixture.

1 Preheat oven to 180°C/160°C fan-forced. Grease and flour 6-hole texas (¾-cup/180ml) muffin pan.

2 Stir chocolate and butter in small saucepan over low heat until smooth. Transfer mixture to large bowl; stir in egg yolks and sifted flour.

3 Beat eggs and sugar in small bowl with electric mixer until light and fluffy and sugar dissolved. Fold into chocolate mixture. Spoon mixture into pan holes.

4 Bake cakes about 10 minutes; cakes should be soft in the centre. Stand cakes in pan 5 minutes; remove carefully from pan.

5 Meanwhile, melt jam in small saucepan over low heat; blend until smooth, strain. Return jam to saucepan, add a little water to give pouring consistency; bring to the boil. Skim surface; stand 5 minutes. Drizzle warm sauce over warm cakes.

CHOCOLATE GANACHE AND RASPBERRY CAKE

Date, ricotta and polenta cake

PREPARATION TIME 30 MINUTES (PLUS STANDING TIME)

COOKING TIME 1 HOUR 55 MINUTES (PLUS COOLING TIME) **SERVES** 16

Polenta is made from coarsely or finely ground cornmeal. It originated in Italy and dates back to Roman times. Finely ground polenta is used in the recipe — it's available from supermarkets and health food stores — and gives the cake a pleasant granular texture.

1 cup (170g) finely chopped dried dates

⅓ cup (80ml) orange-flavoured liqueur

2 cups (300g) self-raising flour

1 teaspoon baking powder

⅔ cup (110g) polenta

1 cup (220g) caster sugar

1¼ cups (250g) ricotta cheese

125g butter, melted

¾ cup (180ml) water

½ cup (75g) coarsely chopped roasted hazelnuts

RICOTTA FILLING

1¼ cups (250g) ricotta cheese

2 tablespoons orange-flavoured liqueur

2 tablespoons icing sugar

1 tablespoon finely grated orange rind

1 Preheat oven to 160°C/140°C fan-forced. Grease deep 22cm-round cake pan; line base and side with baking paper.

2 Combine dates and liqueur in small bowl; stand 15 minutes.

3 Meanwhile, make ricotta filling.

4 Beat flour, baking powder, polenta, sugar, ricotta, butter and the water in large bowl on low speed with electric mixer until combined. Increase speed to medium; beat until mixture changes to a paler colour. Stir in nuts and undrained date mixture.

5 Spread half the cake mixture into pan; spread ricotta filling over cake mixture. Spread with remaining cake mixture.

6 Bake cake about 45 minutes. Cover tightly with foil; bake further 1 hour. Stand cake in pan 10 minutes; turn, top-side up, onto wire rack to cool.

RICOTTA FILLING Stir ingredients in medium bowl until combined.

Warm apple cake with brandy butterscotch sauce

PREPARATION TIME 30 MINUTES **COOKING TIME** 40 MINUTES **SERVES** 8

We've used granny smith apples in this recipe, golden delicious are also good.

125g butter, softened

½ cup (110g) caster sugar

2 eggs

⅔ cup (100g) self-raising flour

⅓ cup (50g) plain flour

1 tablespoon milk

3 medium granny smith apples (450g)

½ cup (160g) apricot jam, warmed

BRANDY BUTTERSCOTCH SAUCE

½ cup (100g) firmly packed brown sugar

½ cup (125ml) cream

100g butter, chopped

2 tablespoons brandy

1 Preheat oven to 160°C140°C fan-forced. Grease two 8cm x 25cm bar cake pans; line bases and sides with baking paper.

2 Beat butter and sugar in small bowl with electric mixer until light and fluffy. Beat in eggs, one at a time; stir in sifted flours and milk. Divide mixture between pans.

3 Peel, core and halve apples; slice halves thinly. Push apple slices gently into surface of cake mixture. Brush apple with strained jam. Bake cakes about 40 minutes.

4 Stand cakes in pans 10 minutes; turn, top-side up, onto wire rack to cool.

5 Make brandy butterscotch sauce. Drizzle sauce over pieces of warm cake.

BRANDY BUTTERSCOTCH SAUCE Stir ingredients in small saucepan over heat, without boiling, until sugar dissolves; bring to the boil. Reduce heat; simmer, uncovered, without stirring, about 3 minutes or until mixture thickens slightly.

Pineapple cake with coconut liqueur cream

PREPARATION TIME 25 MINUTES **COOKING TIME** 50 MINUTES **SERVES** 10-12

1 cup (75g) shredded coconut

450g can crushed pineapple in syrup

125g butter, softened

½ cup (110g) caster sugar

2 eggs

1½ cups (225g) self-raising flour

6 egg whites

½ cup (110g) caster sugar, extra

2 teaspoons icing sugar

COCONUT LIQUEUR CREAM

300ml thickened cream

¼ cup (40g) icing sugar

1 tablespoon coconut-flavoured liqueur

You will find that the meringue topping on this cake will stick to the baking paper lining. Simply use a small spatula or vegetable knife to free the meringue from the paper before unclipping the springform tin.

1 Toast coconut in medium frying pan, stirring constantly, about 2 minutes or until browned lightly. Remove from pan; cool.

2 Drain pineapple over small bowl; reserve ½ cup of the syrup, discard remainder.

3 Preheat oven to 180°C/160°C fan-forced. Grease two deep 20cm-round springform tins; line bases and sides with baking paper.

4 Beat butter and sugar in small bowl with electric mixer until light and fluffy. Beat in eggs, one at a time. Transfer mixture to large bowl; stir in sifted flour, pineapple, then reserved syrup. Divide mixture between tins; bake 20 minutes.

5 Meanwhile, beat egg whites in small bowl with electric mixer until soft peaks form; gradually add extra caster sugar, beat until sugar is dissolved. Fold in coconut.

6 Remove cakes from oven. Working quickly; divide coconut mixture over cakes in tins, using spatula to spread evenly so tops are completely covered. Bake about 30 minutes. Stand cakes in tins 5 minutes; carefully loosen meringue from baking paper around inside of tin. Release sides of tins; cool.

7 Meanwhile, make coconut liqueur cream.

8 Place one cake on serving plate; spread with liqueur cream. Top with remaining cake; dust with sifted icing sugar.

COCONUT LIQUEUR CREAM Beat cream, sifted icing sugar and liqueur in small bowl with electric mixer until soft peaks form.

Raspberry and almond mascarpone cake

PREPARATION TIME 45 MINUTES **COOKING TIME** 2 HOURS (PLUS STANDING AND COOLING TIME)
SERVES 24

500g butter, softened

3 cups (660g) caster sugar

8 eggs

2 cups (300g) plain flour

1½ cups (225g) self-raising flour

1 cup (125g) almond meal

1 cup (250ml) milk

1 cup (140g) slivered almonds,
roasted, chopped finely

400g fresh or frozen raspberries

400g vienna almonds

MASCARPONE CREAM

750g mascarpone cheese

300g sour cream

1 cup (160g) icing sugar

⅓ cup (80ml) orange-flavoured
liqueur

1 Preheat oven to 160°C/140°C fan-forced. Grease deep 30cm-round cake pan;
line base and side with baking paper, extending 5cm above side.

2 Beat butter and sugar in large bowl with electric mixer until light and fluffy. Beat in
eggs, one at a time; stir in sifted flours, almond meal and milk, in three batches. Stir in
chopped almonds and raspberries. Spread mixture into pan.

3 Bake cake 1 hour. Reduce oven to 150°C/130°C fan-forced; bake further 1 hour.
Stand cake in pan 20 minutes; turn, top-side up, onto wire rack to cool.

4 Make mascarpone cream.

5 Split cake into three layers. Place base layer on serving plate; spread with a third of
the mascarpone cream, repeat layering, ending with mascarpone cream. Decorate top
of cake with vienna almonds.

MASCARPONE CREAM Beat mascarpone, sour cream and sifted icing sugar on low speed
in large bowl with electric mixer until combined; stir in liqueur.

Chocolate roulade with coffee cream

PREPARATION TIME 20 MINUTES **COOKING TIME** 10 MINUTES (PLUS REFRIGERATION TIME) **SERVES** 10

200g dark eating chocolate, chopped coarsely

¼ cup (60ml) water

1 tablespoon instant coffee granules

4 eggs, separated

½ cup (110g) caster sugar

1 tablespoon caster sugar, extra

1 teaspoon hot water

300ml thickened cream

2 tablespoons coffee-flavoured liqueur

1 tablespoon icing sugar

1 Preheat oven to 180°C/160°C fan-forced. Grease 25cm x 30cm swiss roll pan; line base with baking paper, extending paper 5cm over long sides.

2 Stir chocolate, the water and half of the coffee in large heatproof bowl over large saucepan of simmering water until smooth. Remove from heat.

3 Beat egg yolks and sugar in small bowl with electric mixer until thick and creamy; fold into warm chocolate mixture.

4 Beat egg whites in small bowl with electric mixer until soft peaks form; fold into chocolate mixture, in two batches. Spread mixture into pan; bake about 10 minutes.

5 Meanwhile, place a piece of baking paper cut the same size as pan on bench; sprinkle evenly with extra caster sugar. Turn cake onto paper; peel lining paper away. Trim all sides of cake. Cover cake with tea towel; cool.

6 Dissolve remaining coffee in the hot water in small bowl. Add cream, liqueur and icing sugar; beat with electric mixer until firm peaks form.

7 Spread cake evenly with coffee cream mixture. Using paper as a guide, roll cake from long side. Cover roll; refrigerate 30 minutes before serving.

You'll notice this recipe doesn't contain flour, in fact the roulade has more the texture of a mousse than that of a cake. The "cake's" cooling process needs to be slowed down to let the mixture settle — we do this by covering it with a tea towel.

Choc-strawberry meringue gateau

PREPARATION TIME 40 MINUTES **COOKING TIME** 45 MINUTES **SERVES** 10

125g butter, softened

¾ cup (165g) caster sugar

4 eggs, separated

1 cup (150g) self-raising flour

⅓ cup (35g) cocoa powder

½ teaspoon bicarbonate of soda

1 cup (250ml) buttermilk

⅔ cup (150g) caster sugar, extra

¼ cup (30g) coarsely chopped roasted hazelnuts

⅔ cup (160ml) thickened cream

1 tablespoon icing sugar

250g strawberries, halved

Make sure you spread the meringue mixture over the cake mixture so that it clings to the side of the pan. If you don't have sandwich pans, deep 20cm cake pans will be fine, or, springform tins. Don't be nervous about turning the meringue-topped cakes upside-down onto wire racks, then right-side-up — they are surprisingly robust.

1 Preheat oven to 160°C/140°C fan-forced. Grease two 20cm sandwich pans; line bases and sides with baking paper.

2 Beat butter, caster sugar and egg yolks in medium bowl with electric mixer until light and fluffy. Stir in sifted flour, cocoa and soda, then buttermilk. Divide mixture between pans.

3 Beat egg whites in small bowl with electric mixer until soft peaks form; gradually add extra caster sugar, beating until sugar dissolves between additions. Divide meringue mixture over cake mixture in pans; spread meringue so cake mixture is completely covered. Sprinkle nuts over meringue on one of the cakes.

4 Bake cakes about 25 minutes. Cover pans loosely with foil; bake further 20 minutes. Stand cakes in pans 5 minutes; turn, top-side up, onto wire racks to cool.

5 Beat cream and icing sugar in small bowl with electric mixer until soft peaks form. Place cake without nuts on serving plate; spread with cream mixture. Sprinkle with strawberries; top with remaining cake.

Whipped cream cake with caramel icing

PREPARATION TIME 20 MINUTES **COOKING TIME** 50 MINUTES (PLUS COOLING TIME) **SERVES** 10

Cream takes the place of butter in this recipe, giving the cake a firm but fine texture.

600ml thickened cream	**CARAMEL ICING**
3 eggs	60g butter
1 teaspoon vanilla extract	½ cup (110g) firmly packed brown sugar
1¼ cups (275g) firmly packed brown sugar	2 tablespoons milk
2 cups (300g) self-raising flour	½ cup (80g) icing sugar

1 Preheat oven to 180°C/160°C fan-forced. Grease deep 22cm-round cake pan; line base with baking paper.

2 Beat half of the cream in small bowl with electric mixer until soft peaks form.

3 Beat eggs and extract in another small bowl with electric mixer until thick and creamy; gradually add sugar, beating until dissolved between additions. Transfer mixture to large bowl. Fold in a quarter of the whipped cream, then sifted flour, then remaining whipped cream. Spread mixture into pan.

4 Bake cake about 50 minutes. Stand cake in pan 5 minutes; turn, top-side up, onto wire rack to cool.

5 Meanwhile, beat remaining cream in small bowl with electric mixer until firm peaks form.

6 Make caramel icing.

7 Split cold cake in half; sandwich layers with cream. Spread cake with caramel icing.

CARAMEL ICING Melt butter in small saucepan, add brown sugar and milk; bring to the boil. Reduce heat immediately; simmer 2 minutes. Cool. Stir in sifted icing sugar.

Opera gateau

PREPARATION TIME 1 HOUR **COOKING TIME** 25 MINUTES (PLUS REFRIGERATION TIME) **SERVES** 24

4 eggs

1 ¼ cups (150g) almond meal

1 cup (160g) icing sugar

⅓ cup (50g) plain flour

25g unsalted butter, melted

4 egg whites

1 tablespoon caster sugar

COFFEE BUTTER CREAM

¼ cup (60ml) milk

¼ cup (55g) firmly packed brown sugar

2 teaspoons instant coffee granules

1 egg yolk

125g unsalted butter, softened

COFFEE SYRUP

⅓ cup (80ml) boiling water

2 tablespoons caster sugar

1 tablespoon instant coffee granules

GANACHE

160g dark eating chocolate, chopped coarsely

⅓ cup (80ml) cream

GLAZE

50g unsalted butter

75g dark eating chocolate

1 Preheat oven to 220°C/200°C fan-forced. Grease two 25cm x 30cm swiss roll pans; line bases with baking paper.

2 Beat eggs, almond meal and sifted icing sugar in another small bowl with electric mixer about 5 minutes or until creamy; beat in flour. Transfer mixture to large bowl; stir in butter.

3 Beat egg whites in small bowl with electric mixer until soft peaks form; add caster sugar, beat until meringue is thick and glossy. Fold into almond mixture, in two batches.

4 Divide mixture between pans. Bake cakes about 7 minutes. Cool in pans.

5 Make coffee butter cream, coffee syrup and ganache.

6 Cut each cake into a 20cm x 25cm rectangle and a 10cm x 25cm rectangle.

7 Place one of the large rectangles on a baking-paper-lined tray; brush with half of the coffee syrup. Spread cake with half of the butter cream; refrigerate 10 minutes. Top butter cream with two small rectangles of cake, side-by-side. Brush with the remaining coffee syrup; spread with ganache. Top with remaining cake; refrigerate 10 minutes. Spread top of cake with remaining butter cream; refrigerate 3 hours.

8 Meanwhile, make glaze. Working quickly, pour glaze over cake and spread evenly. Refrigerate 30 minutes or until glaze has set.

9 Using hot, dry knife, trim edges from cake before slicing and serving.

COFFEE BUTTER CREAM Stir milk, sugar and coffee in small saucepan until sugar dissolves. Whisk egg yolk in small bowl; gradually whisk in hot milk mixture. Return custard to pan; stir over low heat, without boiling, for about 5 minutes or until slightly thickened. Cool. Beat butter in small bowl with electric mixer until pale and fluffy; gradually beat in custard.

COFFEE SYRUP Stir ingredients in small bowl.

GANACHE Stir chocolate and cream in small heatproof bowl over small saucepan of simmering water until smooth. Refrigerate until spreadable.

GLAZE Stir ingredients in small saucepan over low heat until smooth. Use while warm.

Mocha truffle cake

PREPARATION TIME 35 MINUTES **COOKING TIME** 35 MINUTES (PLUS REFRIGERATION TIME) **SERVES** 16

3 eggs

½ cup (110g) caster sugar

¼ cup (35g) cornflour

¼ cup (35g) self-raising flour

¼ cup (35g) plain flour

2 tablespoons cocoa powder

2 tablespoons coffee-flavoured liqueur

2 tablespoons milk

600ml thickened cream, whipped

100g white eating chocolate, melted

200g dark eating chocolate, melted

MILK CHOCOLATE TOPPING

200g milk eating chocolate, chopped coarsely

90g unsalted butter, chopped coarsely

Use Tia Maria or Kahlua in the cake. When you're stirring the melted chocolate into the whipped cream, both mixtures should be of a similar temperature. If the cream is too cold, it will set the chocolate in a second. Use the tip of your finger to judge the temperature of the cream and chocolate.

1 Preheat oven to 180°C/160°C fan-forced. Grease deep 22cm-round cake pan; line base with baking paper.

2 Beat eggs in small bowl with electric mixer until thick and creamy. Gradually add sugar, beating until dissolved between each addition. Transfer mixture to large bowl; fold in sifted flours and cocoa. Spread mixture into pan.

3 Bake cake about 30 minutes. Stand cake in pan 5 minutes; turn, top-side up, onto wire rack to cool. Split cake in half, brush with combined liqueur and milk.

4 Divide whipped cream into two bowls; quickly stir cooled white chocolate into one bowl of the cream and cooled dark chocolate into remaining bowl of cream.

5 To assemble cake: place strips of foil to cover base of deep cake pan and extend over edge or use 23cm springform tin. Place one cake half into pan, spread cake with half the white chocolate cream, top with dark chocolate cream, then remaining white chocolate cream. Top with remaining cake. Refrigerate cake several hours or overnight, until firm.

6 Before serving, make milk chocolate topping.

7 Carefully remove cake from pan and transfer to serving plate; spread cake with topping.

MILK CHOCOLATE TOPPING Stir ingredients in small saucepan over low heat until smooth. Cool; stir occasionally until spreadable.

CUPCAKES

Cupcakes

It's not so long ago when cupcakes or patty cakes were considered children's party fare, quick to whip up and easy to pass around in convenient individual servings. If they were to grace the afternoon tea table they might be dressed up as fairy or butterfly cakes, with a scoop of cake from the centre cut in half to make wings and a dollop of jam and cream added to make them worthy of adult attention. In recent years however, cupcakes have grown up and become sophisticated stars of the cake kingdom.

The reasons for their popularity remain the same — they're portable, easy to serve and there will be no concerns about under-catering if you make one for every guest plus a few spares. What has changed is the way they are decorated and presented — clever cooks now know that what is basically a simple cake can be turned into a mini masterpiece with a few easy trimmings and presentation on a decorative plate. The French, of course, have known this for centuries — many of the elegant little confections known as petits fours are simply miniature cakes decorated with flair.

The term cupcake is probably a reference to the original recipe for the cake mixture — a cupful of butter, a cupful of flour, sugar... much as a pound cake used a pound of each of the core ingredients. Or it's possible that the name also refers to the small containers in which they were baked — most tea cups are fired at much higher temperatures than a domestic oven can ever achieve, so are quite safe as baking dishes. Either way, there are references to individual cakes in English cookbooks from the 18th century. Light fruit cakes known as queen cakes were also popular and baked in fluted or heart-shaped moulds.

These days, just about any cake mixture can be used to make the new-age cupcake. The butter cake recipe remains popular, but so too are chocolate and mud cake mixtures, flourless orange and almond cakes, gingerbread, fresh fruit and poppyseed recipes. Icings and decorations are limited only by your imagination and we're sure that the selection presented in this chapter will inspire a whole new generation of variations and adaptations.

BAKING TIPS

Each recipe specifies the baking time for the cake size we used, but there is no reason why you can't make these little cakes in different sizes as long as you adjust the baking times. You can now buy paper cases to fit most individual cake pans. Measured across the base a texas muffin case is 6.5cm, freeform 6cm, standard muffin 5cm, mini muffin 3cm and foil cases 2.5cm. Paper cases are available from supermarkets, cookware shops, chefs' supply shops and cake decorating suppliers.

If you don't have enough muffin pans, or your oven is not big enough to cook them all at once, don't worry, it's fine to cook in batches and stand the remaining mixture for the relatively short cooking times.

DECORATIVE TOUCHES

Sugared fruits and flowers, toffee decorations (see *Frills* page 203), coloured sprinkles, cachous, hundreds and thousands and the entire lolly shop of confectionery options can quickly elevate the simple cupcake to a work of art.

Coloured sugar, jelly crystals and desiccated coconut also provide a simple, but effective contrast to the icing on a cupcake. Place a small quantity of caster or granulated sugar (depending on the texture you prefer) or coconut in a plastic bag, add a tiny amount of colouring and work the colouring through by massaging the plastic bag between your fingers. As with all food colourings, start with a tiny drop of colour and add more if you need a deeper colour. Coloured sugar will keep in a jar at room temperature indefinitely. (See pages 226 & 227 for more decorating tips.)

COLOURINGS

Many varieties of food colourings are available from supermarkets, cake decorating suppliers and craft shops. They come in liquid, gel, powder and paste forms and should all be used in minute quantities first to determine strength. Concentrated pastes are more expensive than regular liquid colours, but they last longer, blend easily and are suitable for both pastel and strong colours. Coloured icing can become lighter or darker on standing, so if you plan to ice the cake a day in advance, test the colour-fastness of the colouring you plan to use by tinting a small quantity of icing beforehand. Lustre, or edible colour, is a powder available from cake decorating shops and craft shops in metallic shades. You apply it with a paintbrush. Edible glitter is a non-metallic decoration for cakes.

DECORATING TOOLS AND TECHNIQUES

The recipe for basic butter cream is included in *Kids' Birthday Cakes* on page 247 but you can also use cream cheese frosting, ready-made soft icing (fondant), marzipan, whipped cream or a host of other frostings and icings. A piping bag may be useful for decorating cupcakes and instructions for making one can be found in *Baking Techniques* (page 638). Other useful pieces of equipment include metal or plastic icing tubes that allow you to better control the flow of the icing as you pipe writing on the cake and non-stick rolling pins for rolling soft icing. Useful accessories to look out for in the supermarket include candy cake decorations, assorted lettering and shapes such as flowers and stars and tubes of piping gel which can be used to write or draw outlines on cakes.

PRESENTATION

For special occasions, such as weddings and birthdays, it's become popular to make a table centrepiece of cupcakes. A tiered cake stand is ideal for this, and you can decorate the spaces between the cakes with ribbon bows or fresh flowers. If you don't have a tiered cake stand, improvise by stacking three or four individual stands of varying sizes on top of each other.

Quick-mix patty cakes

PREPARATION TIME 20 MINUTES **COOKING TIME** 20 MINUTES **MAKES** 24

125g butter, softened

½ teaspoon vanilla extract

¾ cup (165g) caster sugar

3 eggs

2 cups (300g) self-raising flour

¼ cup (60ml) milk

1 Preheat oven to 180°C/160°C fan-forced. Line two 12-hole patty pans with paper cases.

2 Beat ingredients in medium bowl with electric mixer on low speed until ingredients are combined. Increase speed to medium; beat about 3 minutes or until mixture is smooth and paler in colour.

3 Drop rounded tablespoons of mixture into each case; bake about 20 minutes. Turn cakes, top-side up, onto wire racks to cool.

4 Top cakes with glacé icing of your choice.

VARIATIONS

CHOCOLATE & ORANGE Stir in 1 teaspoon finely grated orange rind and ½ cup (95g) dark Choc Bits at the end of step 2.

PASSIONFRUIT & LIME Stir in 1 teaspoon finely grated lime rind and ¼ cup (60ml) passionfruit pulp at the end of step 2.

BANANA & WHITE CHOCOLATE CHIP Stir in ½ cup overripe mashed banana and ½ cup (95g) white Choc Bits at the end of step 2.

MOCHA Blend 1 tablespoon sifted cocoa powder with 1 tablespoon strong black coffee; stir in at the end of step 2.

Glacé icing

2 cups (320g) icing sugar

2 teaspoons butter

2 tablespoons hot water, approximately

1 Place sifted icing sugar in small heatproof bowl; stir in butter and enough of the hot water to make a firm paste. Place over small saucepan of simmering water; stir until spreadable.

VARIATIONS

CHOCOLATE Stir in 1 teaspoon sifted cocoa powder.

COFFEE Dissolve 1 teaspoon instant coffee granules in the hot water.

PASSIONFRUIT Stir in 1 tablespoon passionfruit pulp.

Cloud cupcakes

PREPARATION TIME 25 MINUTES **COOKING TIME** 20 MINUTES **MAKES** 12

90g butter, softened

½ teaspoon vanilla extract

½ cup (110g) caster sugar

2 eggs

1 cup (150g) self-raising flour

2 tablespoons milk

2 tablespoons strawberry jam

¼ cup (55g) caster sugar, extra

pink food colouring

FLUFFY FROSTING

1 cup (220g) caster sugar

⅓ cup (80ml) water

2 egg whites

1 Preheat oven to 180°C/160°C fan-forced. Line 12-hole (⅓-cup/80ml) muffin pan with paper cases.

2 Beat butter, extract, sugar, eggs, flour and milk in small bowl with electric mixer on low speed until ingredients are combined. Increase speed to medium; beat until mixture is changed to a lighter colour.

3 Divide mixture among cases; smooth surface. Divide jam over tops of cakes; using a skewer swirl jam into cakes.

4 Bake cakes about 20 minutes. Turn cakes, top-side up, onto wire rack to cool.

5 Meanwhile, place extra sugar and a few drops food colouring in a small plastic bag. Seal bag; rub colouring into sugar until evenly coloured.

6 Make fluffy frosting. Spread frosting over cakes; sprinkle with coloured sugar.

FLUFFY FROSTING Stir sugar and the water in small saucepan over heat, without boiling, until sugar is dissolved. Boil, uncovered, without stirring about 5 minutes or until syrup reaches 116°C on a candy thermometer. Syrup should be thick but not coloured. Remove from heat, allow bubbles to subside. Beat egg whites in small bowl with electric mixer until soft peaks form. While mixer is operating, add hot syrup in thin stream; beat on high speed about 10 minutes or until mixture is thick and cool.

Spiced coffee cakes

PREPARATION TIME 25 MINUTES **COOKING TIME** 25 MINUTES **MAKES** 12

125g butter, chopped coarsely

¾ cup (180ml) milk

3 eggs

¾ cup (165g) caster sugar

1 ½ cups (225g) self-raising flour

2 tablespoons instant coffee granules

2 teaspoons hot water

ICING

60g butter

¾ cup (120g) icing sugar

1 tablespoon milk

1 tablespoon cocoa powder

¼ teaspoon ground cardamom

1 tablespoon instant coffee granules

1 teaspoon hot water

1 Preheat oven to 180°C/160°C fan-forced. Line 12-hole (⅓-cup/80ml capacity) muffin pan with paper cases.

2 Stir butter and milk in small saucepan over low heat until butter melts. Cool.

3 Beat eggs in small bowl with electric mixer until thick and creamy; gradually add sugar, beating until dissolved between additions. Transfer mixture to large bowl; stir in sifted flour and butter mixture, in two batches. Stir in combined coffee and hot water. Divide mixture among cases.

4 Bake cakes about 25 minutes. Turn cakes, top-side up, onto wire racks to cool.

5 Make icing; swirl both icings over each cake.

ICING Beat butter in small bowl with electric mixer until pale. Gradually beat in half the sifted icing sugar. Beat in milk and remaining sifted icing sugar. Divide mixture between two bowls. Stir sifted cocoa and cardamom into one bowl. Stir combined coffee and hot water into remaining bowl.

_____

Veryberry cupcakes

PREPARATION TIME 30 MINUTES **COOKING TIME** 35 MINUTES **MAKES** 12

125g butter, softened
½ teaspoon vanilla extract
⅔ cup (150g) caster sugar
2 eggs
1 cup (150g) dried mixed berries
½ cup (70g) slivered almonds
⅔ cup (100g) plain flour
⅓ cup (50g) self-raising flour
¼ cup (60ml) milk

SUGARED FRUIT
150g fresh blueberries
120g fresh raspberries
1 egg white, beaten lightly
2 tablespoons vanilla sugar

CREAM CHEESE FROSTING
30g butter, softened
80g cream cheese, softened
1½ cups (240g) icing sugar

1 Prepare sugared fruit.

2 Preheat oven to 160°C/140°C fan-forced. Line 12-hole (⅓-cup/80ml) muffin pan with paper cases.

3 Beat butter, extract, sugar and eggs in small bowl with electric mixer until light and fluffy. Stir in fruit and nuts, then sifted flours and milk. Divide mixture among cases; smooth surface.

4 Bake cakes about 35 minutes. Turn cakes, top-side up, onto wire racks to cool.

5 Make cream cheese frosting; spread over cakes. Decorate with sugared fruit.

SUGARED FRUIT Brush each berry lightly with egg white; roll fruit in sugar. Place fruit on baking-paper-lined tray. Leave about 1 hour or until sugar is dry.

CREAM CHEESE FROSTING Beat butter and cheese in small bowl with electric mixer until light and fluffy; gradually beat in sifted icing sugar.

Dried berries, especially strawberries, are easy to find in supermarkets. You can use any dried fruit you like. Sugared fruit is easy to do, looks effective and tastes good too. It takes a good hour for the sugar coating to set – if the weather is wet or humid it could take longer. Position the fruit on the frosting just before you're ready to serve the cakes. Vanilla sugar is available in supermarkets, usually amongst the spices. Or, you can make your own by putting a couple of vanilla beans into a jar of caster sugar – most cake cooks have one of these jars on the go.

Black forest cupcakes

PREPARATION TIME 25 MINUTES **COOKING TIME** 40 MINUTES (PLUS COOLING TIME) **MAKES** 12

425g can seeded cherries in syrup

165g butter, chopped coarsely

100g dark eating chocolate, chopped coarsely

1⅓ cups (295g) caster sugar

¼ cup (60ml) cherry brandy

1 cup (150g) plain flour

2 tablespoons self-raising flour

2 tablespoons cocoa powder

1 egg

⅔ cup (160ml) thickened cream, whipped

2 teaspoons cherry brandy, extra

100g dark eating chocolate, extra

1 Preheat oven to 160°C/140°C fan-forced. Line 12-hole (⅓-cup/80ml) muffin pan with paper cases.

2 Drain cherries; reserve syrup. Process ½ cup (110g) cherries with ½ cup (125ml) of the syrup until smooth. Halve remaining cherries; reserve for decorating cakes. Discard remaining syrup.

3 Stir butter, chocolate, sugar, brandy and cherry puree in small saucepan over low heat until chocolate is melted. Transfer mixture to medium bowl; cool 15 minutes. Whisk in sifted flours and cocoa, then egg. Divide mixture among cases; smooth surface.

4 Bake cakes about 40 minutes. Turn cakes, top-side up, onto wire racks to cool.

5 Top cakes with remaining cherries and combined cream and extra brandy. Using a vegetable peeler, make small chocolate curls from extra chocolate; sprinkle over cakes.

Use a vegetable peeler to make cute little chocolate curls — it's a quick and easy way to dress up cakes. See Chocolate tricks & techniques on pages 40 & 41.

Coffee caramel cakes

PREPARATION TIME 15 MINUTES **COOKING TIME** 20 MINUTES (PLUS COOLING TIME) **MAKES** 12

125g butter, softened

⅔ cup (150g) firmly packed brown sugar

2 tablespoons instant coffee granules

1 tablespoon boiling water

2 eggs

2 cups (300g) self-raising flour

½ cup (125ml) milk

18 (130g) jersey caramels, halved

1 Preheat oven to 180°C/160°C fan-forced. Grease 12-hole (⅓-cup/80ml) muffin pan.

2 Beat butter and sugar in small bowl with electric mixer until light and fluffy. Add combined coffee and the water; beat in eggs, one at a time. Transfer mixture to large bowl; stir in sifted flour and milk.

3 Spoon mixture into pan holes. Press 3 caramel halves into the centre of each cake; cover with batter.

4 Bake cakes about 20 minutes. Stand cakes in pan 5 minutes; turn, top-side up, onto wire racks to cool.

Jersey caramels are available in supermarkets and chain stores, they are on the soft side, caramel in colour with a white stripe in the middle. Be careful of the hot melted caramel in the centre of these cakes.

BLACK FOREST CUPCAKES

Cupcake decorations

Cupcakes can be as simple or as complicated as you like, let your imagination run riot.

CHOC SWIRL
Spread tops of cupcakes with melted dark chocolate, then before it sets, drizzle with melted white chocolate. Use a skewer to swirl the two chocolates together.

BITS OF CHOC
Choc Bits are usually used insides cakes and cookies etc, as they hold their shape during baking. They come in white, milk and dark, use them to outline various shapes, such as hearts, numbers, letters, stars etc.

PINK & PRETTY
Piped flowers are available in the baking aisle in supermarkets. They are sold on pieces of cardboard, in a range of colours. Position flowers on frosted cakes up to several hours before serving.

CARAMEL POPS
Buy caramel-flavoured popcorn from the supermarket, use the popcorn to decorate frosted cupcakes. The popcorn will become sticky if the weather is wet or humid, so top the cakes up to several hours before serving.

BO PEEPS
Buy these pretty little multi-coloured pillow-shaped sweets from special lolly shops, they come in 40g jars, and taste like boiled lollies. They will become sticky in wet or humid weather, so put them on the frosted cake an hour or so before serving.

POLKA MUSK DOTS
Use multi-coloured mini musks bought from a sweets shop. After frosting the cupcakes, push the musks into the frosting up to three hours before serving. If the weather is wet or humid, the colours from the sweets might bleed into the frosting.

CHAIN OF HEARTS

Pipe melted dark chocolate hearts directly onto frosted cakes. Pipe the first heart, then pull the tip of the tube through the chocolate to make a tail to link it with the second heart, and so on.

LIGHT & LEMONY

Small orange and lemon flavoured (and coloured) segments can be bought from supermarkets and sweets shops. They look good on matching coloured frosting. Try them on chocolate frosting as well.

CHOC-TOPPED

Break Flake bars into small pieces for an easy decoration, or make tiny chocolate curls (see page 41) using a vegetable peeler. Simply drag the peeler down the side of a block of chocolate.

BANCHOCOFFEE

Spread the tops of the cupcakes with thick caramel sauce or Top 'n' Fill caramel (see page 656), top with finely sliced banana, sprinkle with tiny dark chocolate curls made using a vegetable peeler (see page 41).

TOFFEE TOPS

Spread tops of cupcakes with melted dark, milk or white chocolate. When chocolate is almost set, top with toffee strands (see page 203). Or, top cupcakes with chocolate frosting, then top with toffee strands. Toffee will break down if the weather is wet or humid. Make the toffee several hours before you want to finish the cakes.

PAVLOVA TASTE-ALIKES

Spread the tops of the cupcakes with sweetened whipped thickened cream. Top with thin strawberry slices, top with tiny meringues (available in supermarkets), then drizzle with passionfruit. The cakes can be completed an hour before serving, keep them in the fridge.

Pineapple hibiscus cupcakes

PREPARATION TIME 25 MINUTES **COOKING TIME** 1 HOUR 40 MINUTES **MAKES** 6

You'll need a very sharp knife to slice the fresh pineapple into fine slices. If the pineapple slices are too thick, you won't be able to shape them into "flowers". Cut the pineapple from the centre of the fresh pineapple. See page 635 for tips on shaping pineapple flowers.

½ cup (125ml) vegetable oil

3 eggs

1½ cups (225g) self-raising flour

¾ cup (165g) caster sugar

½ teaspoon ground cinnamon

2 cups (440g) firmly packed coarsely grated carrot

¾ cup (160g) well-drained canned crushed pineapple

PINEAPPLE FLOWERS

1 tablespoon caster sugar

1 tablespoon water

12 wafer thin slices fresh pineapple

LEMON CREAM CHEESE FROSTING

30g butter, softened

80g cream cheese, softened

1 teaspoon finely grated lemon rind

1½ cups (240g) icing sugar

1 Preheat oven to 120°C/100°C fan-forced; make pineapple flowers.

2 Increase oven to 180°C/160°C fan-forced. Line 6-hole texas (¾-cup/180ml) muffin pan with paper cases.

3 Combine oil, eggs, sifted flour, sugar and cinnamon in medium bowl; stir until combined. Stir in carrot and pineapple. Divide mixture among cases.

4 Bake cakes about 40 minutes. Turn cakes, top-side up, onto wire racks to cool.

5 Make lemon cream cheese frosting; spread on top of cakes. Decorate cakes with pineapple flowers.

PINEAPPLE FLOWERS Stir sugar and the water in small saucepan over low heat until sugar has dissolved; boil 1 minute. Brush both sides of pineapple slices with sugar syrup. Place slices in a single layer on wire racks over oven trays. Dry pineapple in oven about 1 hour. Immediately remove slices from rack. Pinch centre of each slice; carefully shape into flowers. Dry over an upturned, foil-covered egg carton.

LEMON CREAM CHEESE FROSTING Beat butter, cream cheese and rind in small bowl with electric mixer until light and fluffy; gradually beat in sifted icing sugar.

Honeycomb cream cupcakes

PREPARATION TIME 25 MINUTES **COOKING TIME** 40 MINUTES **MAKES** 6

We've used chocolate-coated honeycomb here — for a more grown-up cake, you could use proper honeycomb instead. It's readily available in gourmet food stores and health food shops. Use the same weight, chop it coarsely before folding it through the cream.

½ cup (110g) firmly packed brown sugar

½ cup (75g) plain flour

½ cup (75g) self-raising flour

¼ teaspoon bicarbonate of soda

1 teaspoon ground ginger

½ teaspoon ground cinnamon

¼ teaspoon ground nutmeg

90g butter, softened

1 egg

¼ cup (60ml) buttermilk

2 tablespoons golden syrup

50g dark eating chocolate, chopped coarsely

300ml thickened cream, whipped

3 x 50g Violet Crumble bars, chopped coarsely

1 Preheat oven to 170°C/150°C fan-forced. Line 6-hole texas (¾-cup/180ml) muffin pan with paper cases.

2 Sift dry ingredients into small bowl, add butter, egg, buttermilk and syrup; beat mixture with electric mixer on low speed until ingredients are combined. Increase speed to medium; beat until mixture is changed to a lighter colour. Stir in chocolate. Divide mixture among cases; smooth surface.

3 Bake cakes about 40 minutes. Turn cakes, top-side up, onto wire racks to cool.

4 Spread cakes with whipped cream; top with Violet Crumble.

Choc-chip butterfly cupcakes

PREPARATION TIME 25 MINUTES **COOKING TIME** 20 MINUTES **MAKES** 12

60g butter, softened

1 teaspoon vanilla extract

⅓ cup (75g) caster sugar

¾ cup (110g) self-raising flour

¼ cup (60ml) milk

1 egg

¼ cup (45g) dark Choc Bits, chopped coarsely

⅔ cup (160ml) thickened cream

1 tablespoon icing sugar

2 red glacé cherries

1 Preheat oven to 180°C/160°C fan-forced. Line deep 12-hole patty pan with paper cases.

2 Beat butter, extract, sugar, flour, milk and egg in small bowl with electric mixer on low speed until combined. Increase speed to medium; beat until mixture is smooth and changed to a lighter colour. Stir in Choc Bits. Divide mixture among paper cases.

3 Bake cakes about 20 minutes. Turn cakes, top-side up, onto wire racks to cool.

4 Beat cream and sifted icing sugar in small bowl with electric mixer until soft peaks form. Cut each cherry into six slices.

5 Using sharp pointed vegetable knife, cut circle from top of each cake; cut circle in half to make two "wings". Fill cavities with whipped cream. Place wings in position on top of cakes; top with sliced cherries. Dust with a little extra sifted icing sugar.

Butterfly cakes

PREPARATION TIME 30 MINUTES **COOKING TIME** 20 MINUTES **MAKES** 24

125g butter, softened
1 teaspoon vanilla extract
⅔ cup (150g) caster sugar
3 eggs
1½ cups (225g) self-raising flour

¼ cup (60ml) milk
½ cup (160g) jam
300ml thickened cream, whipped
1 tablespoon icing sugar

1 Preheat oven to 180°C/160°C fan-forced. Line two deep 12-hole patty pans with paper cases.

2 Beat butter, extract, caster sugar, eggs, flour and milk in small bowl of electric mixer on low speed until ingredients are combined. Increase speed to medium; beat about 3 minutes or until mixture is smooth and changed to a lighter colour. Drop slightly rounded tablespoons of mixture into paper cases.

3 Bake cakes about 20 minutes. Turn cakes, top-side up, onto wire racks to cool.

4 Using sharp pointed vegetable knife, cut circle from top of each cake; cut circle in half to make two "wings". Fill cavities with jam and cream. Place wings in position on top of cakes; top with strawberry pieces and dust with sifted icing sugar.

Butterfly or fairy cakes, call them what you will, they both have wings. Use whatever jam you like, or some pureed fruit (like berries) or stewed fruit such as apple or any stone fruit of your choice. Lemon butter (or curd) is another popular filling favourite.

Mini passionfruit cakes

PREPARATION TIME 25 MINUTES **COOKING TIME** 20 MINUTES **MAKES** 16

2 tablespoons passionfruit pulp
60g butter, softened
1 teaspoon finely grated lemon rind
¼ cup (55g) caster sugar
1 egg
½ cup (75g) self-raising flour
¼ cup (60ml) buttermilk

ICING
½ cup (80g) icing sugar
1 teaspoon milk

1 Preheat oven to 180°C/160°C fan-forced. Grease 16 holes of two 12-hole mini (1 tablespoon/20ml) muffin pans.

2 Strain passionfruit pulp over small bowl; reserve seeds and juice separately.

3 Beat butter, rind and sugar in small bowl with electric mixer until light and fluffy; beat in egg. Stir in sifted flour, passionfruit juice and buttermilk. Spoon mixture into pan holes.

4 Bake cakes about 20 minutes. Turn cakes, top-side up, onto wire rack.

5 Meanwhile, make icing; spread icing over each warm cake.

ICING Sift icing sugar into small bowl; stir in milk and reserved passionfruit seeds.

1

2

3

4

Turkish delight cupcakes

PREPARATION TIME 25 MINUTES **COOKING TIME** 35 MINUTES **MAKES** 6

60g white eating chocolate, chopped roughly

2 tablespoons rose water

½ cup (125ml) water

⅓ cup (45g) pistachios

90g butter, softened

1 cup (220g) firmly packed brown sugar

2 eggs

⅔ cup (100g) self-raising flour

2 tablespoons plain flour

DECORATIONS

900g turkish delight, chopped coarsely

⅔ cup (90g) coarsely chopped pistachios

300g white eating chocolate, melted

1 Preheat oven to 180°C/160°C fan-forced. Line 6-hole texas (¾-cup/180ml) muffin pan with paper cases.

2 Stir chocolate, rose water and the water in small saucepan over low heat until smooth. Blend or process nuts until fine.

3 Beat butter, sugar and eggs in small bowl with electric mixer until combined. Stir in sifted flours, ground pistachios and warm chocolate mixture. Divide mixture among cases.

4 Bake cakes about 35 minutes. Turn cakes, top-side up, onto wire rack to cool.

5 Cut a 3cm deep hole in the centre of each cake; fill with chopped nuts. Drizzle with chocolate; replace lids. Decorate with pieces of turkish delight and chopped nuts dipped in chocolate.

Sugar & lace cupcakes

PREPARATION TIME 20 MINUTES (PLUS COOLING TIME) **COOKING TIME** 40 MINUTES **MAKES** 6

125g butter, chopped coarsely

100g white eating chocolate, chopped coarsely

⅔ cup (150g) firmly packed brown sugar

¼ cup (90g) golden syrup

⅔ cup (160ml) milk

1 cup (150g) plain flour

⅓ cup (50g) self-raising flour

1 egg

doily, lace or stencil

½ cup (80g) icing sugar

1 Preheat oven to 160°C/140°C fan-forced. Line 6-hole texas (¾-cup/180ml) muffin pan with paper cases.

2 Combine butter, chocolate, brown sugar, syrup and milk in small saucepan; stir over low heat, until smooth. Transfer mixture to medium bowl; cool 15 minutes. Whisk sifted flours into chocolate mixture, then egg. Divide mixture among cases.

3 Bake cakes about 40 minutes. Turn cakes, top-side up, onto wire rack to cool.

4 Place doily, lace or stencil over cake; sift a little icing sugar over doily, then carefully lift doily from cake. Repeat with remaining cakes and icing sugar.

Sifting icing sugar over a doily, stencil or a piece of lace sounds easier than it is. We found we needed a defined clear pattern to be able to keep the pattern created by the icing sugar once the doily was lifted away. If the doily has a tight pattern, use some sharp pointed scissors to cut pieces away to enlarge the pattern.

1 TURKISH DELIGHT CUPCAKES **2** SUGAR & LACE CUPCAKES
3 BANANA CARAMEL CAKES [P 234] **4** ROCKY ROAD CUPCAKES [P 234]

Banana caramel cakes

PREPARATION TIME 20 MINUTES **COOKING TIME** 25 MINUTES **MAKES** 6

90g butter, softened

½ cup (110g) firmly packed brown sugar

2 eggs

½ cup (75g) plain flour

½ cup (75g) self-raising flour

½ teaspoon bicarbonate of soda

½ teaspoon mixed spice

⅔ cup mashed banana

⅓ cup (80g) sour cream

2 tablespoons milk

380g can Top 'n' Fill caramel

½ cup (125ml) thickened cream, whipped

2 medium bananas (400g), sliced thinly

100g dark eating chocolate

1 Preheat oven to 180°C/160°C fan-forced. Line 6-hole texas (¾-cup/180ml) muffin pan with paper cases.

2 Beat butter, sugar and eggs in small bowl with electric mixer until light and fluffy. Stir in sifted dry ingredients, banana, sour cream and milk. Divide mixture among cases; smooth surface.

3 Bake cakes about 25 minutes. Turn cakes, top-side up, onto wire rack to cool. Remove paper cases from cakes.

4 Fold 2 tablespoons of the caramel into cream. Split cakes into three layers. Re-assemble cakes with remaining caramel and banana. Top cakes with caramel cream. Using a vegetable peeler, make small curls from the chocolate; sprinkle over cakes.

Rocky road cakes

PREPARATION TIME 25 MINUTES **COOKING TIME** 30 MINUTES **MAKES** 6

125g butter, softened

½ teaspoon vanilla extract

⅔ cup (150g) caster sugar

2 eggs

1¼ cups (185g) self-raising flour

⅓ cup (80ml) milk

pink food colouring

1 tablespoon cocoa powder

2 teaspoons milk, extra

50g milk chocolate Melts, melted

ROCKY ROAD TOPPING

½ cup (70g) unsalted roasted peanuts

1 cup (200g) red glacé cherries, halved

1 cup (100g) pink and white marshmallows, chopped coarsely

½ cup (25g) flaked coconut, toasted

200g milk eating chocolate, melted

1 Preheat oven to 180°C/160°C fan-forced. Line 6-hole texas (¾-cup/180ml) muffin pan with paper cases.

2 Beat butter, extract, sugar and eggs in small bowl with electric mixer until light and fluffy. Stir in sifted flour and milk in two batches.

3 Divide mixture evenly among three bowls. Tint one mixture pink. Blend sifted cocoa with extra milk in cup; stir into another mixture. Leave third mixture plain. Drop alternate spoonfuls of the mixtures into cases. Pull a skewer backwards and forwards through mixtures for a marbled effect; smooth surface.

4 Bake cakes about 30 minutes. Turn cakes, top-side up, onto wire rack to cool.

5 Combine ingredients for rocky road topping in medium bowl. Place topping on tops of cakes; drizzle with melted milk chocolate Melts.

Apple ginger cakes with lemon icing

PREPARATION TIME 15 MINUTES **COOKING TIME** 25 MINUTES (PLUS COOLING TIME) **MAKES** 12

250g butter, softened

1½ cups (330g) firmly packed dark brown sugar

3 eggs

¼ cup (90g) golden syrup

2 cups (300g) plain flour

1½ teaspoons bicarbonate of soda

2 tablespoons ground ginger

1 tablespoon ground cinnamon

1 cup (170g) coarsely grated apple

⅔ cup (160ml) hot water

LEMON ICING

1 cup (160g) icing sugar

1 teaspoon butter, softened

1 tablespoon lemon juice, approximately

You'll need one large apple for this recipe. If you work quickly you can get away with not bothering to warm the icing to a pouring consistency. As soon as you've turned the cakes the right-side up, and while the cakes are still hot, dollop each cake with the icing — the heat from the cakes will be enough to melt the icing. Help the icing along with a spatula for a more even result.

1 Preheat oven to 180°C/160°C fan-forced. Line 6-hole texas (¾-cup/180ml) muffin pan with paper cases.

2 Beat butter and sugar in small bowl with electric mixer until light and fluffy. Beat in eggs, one at a time. Stir in syrup. Transfer mixture to medium bowl; stir in sifted dry ingredients, then apple and the water. Divide mixture among cases; smooth surface.

3 Bake cakes about 25 minutes. Stand cakes in pan 5 minutes; turn, top-side up, onto wire racks.

4 Make lemon icing; drizzle icing over warm cakes.

LEMON ICING Sift icing sugar into small heatproof bowl; stir in butter and enough juice to form a paste. Place bowl over small saucepan of simmering water; stir until icing is a pouring consistency.

Apple custard teacakes

PREPARATION TIME 20 MINUTES (PLUS COOLING TIME) **COOKING TIME** 35 MINUTES **MAKES** 12

Try serving these cakes warm from the oven as a dessert. You could double the custard — use half in the cakes, then make the remaining custard more pourable with a little extra milk or cream, and serve over the teacakes.

90g butter

½ teaspoon vanilla extract

½ cup (110g) caster sugar

2 eggs

¾ cup (110g) self-raising flour

¼ cup (30g) custard powder

2 tablespoons milk

1 large unpeeled apple (200g), cored, sliced finely

30g butter, melted, extra

1 tablespoon caster sugar, extra

½ teaspoon ground cinnamon

CUSTARD

1 tablespoon custard powder

1 tablespoon caster sugar

½ cup (125ml) milk

¼ teaspoon vanilla extract

1 Make custard.

2 Preheat oven to 180°C/160°C fan-forced. Line 12-hole (⅓-cup/80ml) muffin pan with paper cases.

3 Beat butter, extract, sugar, eggs, sifted flour and custard powder, and milk in small bowl with electric mixer on low speed until ingredients are combined. Increase speed to medium; beat until mixture is changed to a paler colour.

4 Divide half the mixture among cases. Top with custard, then remaining cake mixture; spread mixture to cover custard. Top with apple slices, pressing slightly into cake.

5 Bake cakes about 30 minutes. Stand cakes in pan 5 minutes; turn, top-side up, onto wire racks. Brush hot cakes with extra butter; sprinkle with combined extra sugar and cinnamon.

CUSTARD Blend custard powder and sugar with milk and extract in small saucepan; stir over heat until mixture boils and thickens. Remove from heat; cover surface with plastic wrap; cool.

Banana blueberry cupcakes

PREPARATION TIME 20 MINUTES (PLUS COOLING TIME) **COOKING TIME** 30 MINUTES **MAKES** 12

Just two tips for these cakes — make sure you use overripe bananas and have the blueberries still frozen when you use them.

125g butter, chopped coarsely

½ cup (125ml) milk

2 eggs

1 cup (220g) caster sugar

½ cup mashed banana

1½ cups (225g) self-raising flour

½ cup (75g) frozen blueberries

1 Preheat oven to 180°C/160°C fan-forced. Grease 12-hole (⅓-cup/80ml) muffin pan.

2 Stir butter and milk in small saucepan over low heat until butter melts. Cool.

3 Beat eggs in small bowl with electric mixer until thick and creamy. Gradually add sugar, beating until dissolved between additions; stir in banana. Fold in sifted flour and cooled butter mixture, in two batches. Divide mixture among muffin holes.

4 Bake cakes 10 minutes. Remove from oven; press frozen blueberries into tops of cakes. Bake further 15 minutes. Stand cakes 5 minutes; turn, top-side up, onto wire racks to cool.

APPLE CUSTARD TEACAKES

Patience is required if you're going to master making curds — also known as butters. Homemade curd makes a great gift, if it's made correctly, and kept in the fridge, it will keep for months. Use a bowl (glass or china) that fits comfortably just inside the top of a saucepan. You're replicating a double saucepan. You need to stir the ingredients for the curd all the time, over simmering water. The water in the saucepan must not touch the bottom of the bowl containing the curd ingredients as it will make the curd too hot, causing it to curdle — you'll then have to start again. As soon as the curd thickens and starts to coat the back of a spoon, remove the bowl from the saucepan completely — you need to stop the cooking. See also page 527.

Passionfruit curd cupcakes

PREPARATION TIME 25 MINUTES **COOKING TIME** 25 MINUTES (PLUS REFRIGERATION TIME) **MAKES** 12

90g butter, softened

½ cup (110g) caster sugar

2 eggs

1 cup (150g) self-raising flour

¼ cup (60ml) passionfruit pulp

85g packet passionfruit jelly

1 cup (250ml) boiling water

1 cup (80g) desiccated coconut

½ cup (125ml) thickened cream, whipped

PASSIONFRUIT CURD

2 eggs

⅓ cup caster sugar

1 tablespoon lemon juice

¼ cup passionfruit pulp

60g butter, chopped coarsely

1 Make passionfruit curd.

2 Preheat oven to 180°C/160°C fan-forced. Line 12-hole (⅓-cup/80ml) muffin pan with paper cases.

3 Beat butter, sugar, eggs and flour in small bowl with electric mixer on low speed until ingredients are combined. Increase speed to medium; beat until mixture is changed to a lighter colour. Stir in passionfruit pulp. Divide mixture among cases; smooth surface.

4 Bake cakes about 20 minutes. Turn cakes, top-side up, onto wire rack to cool.

5 Meanwhile, dissolve jelly in the water in large shallow dish. Refrigerate about 30 minutes or until set to the consistency of unbeaten egg white.

6 Remove cases from cakes. Roll cakes in jelly; leave cakes to stand in jelly 15 minutes, turning occasionally. Roll cakes in coconut; place on wire rack over tray. Refrigerate 30 minutes. Split cakes in half; fill with curd and whipped cream.

PASSIONFRUIT CURD Stir ingredients in small heatproof bowl over small saucepan of simmering water until mixture thickens slightly and coats the back of a spoon. Remove from heat. Cover tightly; refrigerate curd until cold.

Neapolitan cupcakes

PREPARATION TIME 25 MINUTES **COOKING TIME** 20 MINUTES **MAKES** 12

125g butter, softened

½ teaspoon vanilla extract

⅔ cup (150g) caster sugar

2 eggs

1¼ cups (185g) self-raising flour

⅓ cup (80ml) milk

pink food colouring

1 tablespoon cocoa powder

2 teaspoons milk, extra

BUTTER CREAM

125g butter, softened

1½ cups (240g) icing sugar

2 tablespoons milk

pink food colouring

1 tablespoon cocoa powder

2 teaspoons milk, extra

1 Preheat oven to 180°C/160°C fan-forced. Line 12-hole (⅓-cup/80ml) muffin pan with paper cases.

2 Beat butter, extract, sugar and eggs in small bowl with electric mixer until light and fluffy. Stir in sifted flour and milk, in two batches.

3 Divide mixture evenly among three bowls. Tint one mixture pink. Blend sifted cocoa with extra milk in cup; stir into another mixture. Leave third mixture plain.

4 Drop alternate spoonfuls of the three mixtures into cases. Pull a skewer backwards and forwards through mixtures for a marbled effect; smooth surface.

5 Bake cakes about 20 minutes. Turn cakes, top-side up, onto wire rack to cool.

6 Make butter cream. Spread cakes with the three colours of butter cream.

BUTTER CREAM Beat butter in small bowl with electric mixer until as white as possible; beat in sifted icing sugar and milk, in two batches. Divide mixture evenly among three bowls. Tint one mixture pink. Blend sifted cocoa with extra milk in cup; stir into another mixture. Leave third mixture plain.

Coconut cupcake kisses

PREPARATION TIME 24 MINUTES **COOKING TIME** 40 MINUTES (PLUS COOLING TIME) **MAKES** 6

125g butter, chopped coarsely

80g white eating chocolate, chopped coarsely

1 cup (220g) caster sugar

½ cup (125ml) milk

½ cup (75g) plain flour

½ cup (75g) self-raising flour

½ teaspoon coconut essence

1 egg

3 x 150g boxes ferrero raffaelo chocolate truffles

WHIPPED WHITE CHOCOLATE GANACHE

¼ cup (60ml) cream

185g white eating chocolate, chopped coarsely

1 tablespoon coconut-flavoured liqueur

White chocolate mud cakes keep particularly well because of the high sugar — and fat — content. Small cakes will become staler faster than large cakes due to the smaller surface area. Mud cakes keep at room temperature in an airtight container for a week — longer in the fridge and for months in the freezer.

1 Preheat oven to 160°C/140°C fan-forced. Line 6-hole texas (¾-cup/180ml) muffin pan with paper cases.

2 Stir butter, chocolate, sugar and milk in small saucepan over low heat until smooth. Transfer mixture to medium bowl; cool 15 minutes. Whisk in sifted flours, then essence and egg. Divide mixture among cases; smooth surface.

3 Bake cakes about 40 minutes. Turn cakes, top-side up, onto wire rack to cool.

4 Meanwhile, make whipped white chocolate ganache.

5 Spread cakes with ganache. Top with halved truffles, then stack with whole truffles using a little ganache to secure truffles.

WHIPPED WHITE CHOCOLATE GANACHE Bring cream to the boil in small saucepan; pour over chocolate and liqueur in small bowl of electric mixer, stir until smooth. Cover; refrigerate 30 minutes. Beat with an electric mixer until light and fluffy.

Pear butterfly cupcakes

PREPARATION TIME 40 MINUTES   **COOKING TIME** 1 HOUR 15 MINUTES   **MAKES** 6

1 medium fresh pear (230g), grated coarsely

60g butter, softened

¼ cup (35g) self-raising flour

¾ cup (110g) plain flour

1 teaspoon ground cinnamon

½ cup (110g) firmly packed brown sugar

¼ cup (60ml) maple-flavoured syrup

2 eggs

⅓ cup (40g) coarsely chopped pecans

⅓ cup (55g) finely chopped dried pear

PEAR BUTTERFLIES

1 tablespoon caster sugar

1 tablespoon water

1 medium brown pear (230g) (eg. beurre bosc), sliced thinly

FONDANT ICING

500g white ready-made soft icing, chopped coarsely

1 egg white

blue, pink and yellow food colouring

1 Preheat oven to 120°C/100°C fan-forced; make pear butterflies.

2 Increase oven to 180°C/160°C fan-forced. Line 6-hole texas (¾-cup/180ml) muffin pan with paper cases.

3 Drain fresh pear, squeezing out as much juice as possible. You need ⅔ cup grated pear.

4 Beat butter, sifted flours and cinnamon, sugar, syrup and eggs in small bowl with electric mixer on low speed until ingredients are combined. Beat on medium speed until mixture is changed to a paler colour.

5 Stir in fresh pear, nuts and dried pear. Divide mixture among cases; smooth surface.

6 Bake cakes about 35 minutes. Turn cakes, top-side up, onto wire rack to cool.

7 Make fondant icing. Divide icing into three small bowls; using colourings, tint icing pale blue, pink and yellow. Spoon icing quickly over cupcakes, level with tops of cases; allow to set.

8 Top cupcakes with pear slices.

PEAR BUTTERFLIES Stir sugar and the water in small saucepan over medium heat, without boiling, until sugar is dissolved. Bring to the boil. Reduce heat; simmer, without stirring, 1 minute. Brush pear slices both sides with sugar syrup. Place slices in single layer on wire rack over tray. Dry in oven about 40 minutes. While pears are still warm, shape into butterfly wings by pinching the narrow end. Cool on wire rack.

FONDANT ICING Place soft icing in medium bowl over medium saucepan of simmering water; stir until smooth. Stir in egg white; stand at room temperature about 10 minutes or until thickened slightly.

Lemon pavlova cupcakes

PREPARATION TIME 30 MINUTES **COOKING TIME** 1 HOUR 15 MINUTES **MAKES** 6

90g butter, softened

90g cream cheese, softened

2 teaspoons finely grated lemon rind

²⁄₃ cup (150g) caster sugar

2 eggs

¹⁄₃ cup (50g) self-raising flour

½ cup (75g) plain flour

MERINGUE CASES

3 egg whites

¾ cup (165g) caster sugar

1 tablespoon cornflour

1 teaspoon white vinegar

½ teaspoon vanilla extract

DECORATIONS

300ml thickened cream, whipped

125g strawberries, quartered

1 tablespoon passionfruit pulp

½ cup (75g) blueberries

1 medium banana (230g), sliced thickly

Make the cakes and meringues up to a day before you need them. Store them separately in airtight containers. Position and fill the meringue cases no more than 30 minutes before serving the cakes.

1 Preheat oven to 120°C/100°C fan-forced; make meringue cases.

2 Increase oven to 180°C/160°C fan-forced. Line 6-hole texas (¾-cup/180ml) muffin pan with paper cases.

3 Beat butter, cheese, rind, sugar and eggs in small bowl with electric mixer until light and fluffy. Add sifted flours; beat on low speed until combined. Divide mixture among cases; smooth surface.

4 Bake cakes about 30 minutes. Turn cakes, top-side up, onto wire rack to cool.

5 Drop a teaspoon of cream on each cake; top with meringue cases. Spoon remaining cream into cases and decorate with fruit.

MERINGUE CASES Grease oven tray; line with baking paper, trace six 8.5cm circles onto paper for large cakes. Beat egg whites in small bowl with electric mixer until soft peaks form. Gradually add sugar, a tablespoon at a time, beating until sugar dissolves between additions. Fold in cornflour, vinegar and extract. Spoon meringue inside circles on tray; hollow out slightly. Bake 45 minutes or until cases are firm. Cool in oven with door ajar.

Carrot cupcakes with maple frosting

PREPARATION TIME 30 MINUTES **COOKING TIME** 30 MINUTES **MAKES** 12

You need four medium carrots in order to get enough grated carrot for this recipe. Use a bland flavourless vegetable oil from the supermarket. If you don't have unsalted butter for the frosting, just use regular salted table butter. Use proper maple syrup for the best flavour.

½ cup (125ml) vegetable oil

3 eggs

1 ½ cups (225g) self-raising flour

1 cup (220g) firmly packed brown sugar

2 teaspoons mixed spice

2 cups (480g) firmly packed coarsely grated carrot

¾ cup (90g) coarsely chopped roasted pecans

12 roasted pecan halves

MAPLE CREAM CHEESE FROSTING

30g unsalted butter, softened

80g cream cheese, softened

2 tablespoons maple syrup

1 ¼ cups (200g) icing sugar

1 Preheat oven to 180°C/160°C fan-forced. Line 12-hole (⅓-cup/80ml) muffin pan with paper cases.

2 Combine oil, eggs, sifted flour, sugar and spice in medium bowl; stir in carrot and chopped pecans. Divide mixture among paper cases.

3 Bake cakes about 30 minutes. Stand cakes 5 minutes before turning, top-side up, onto wire rack to cool.

4 Meanwhile, make maple cream cheese frosting. Spread frosting over cupcakes; top each with a nut half.

MAPLE CREAM CHEESE FROSTING Beat butter, cream cheese and syrup in small bowl with electric mixer until light and fluffy. Gradually beat in sifted icing sugar, beating until frosting is spreadable.

Lace wedding cake

PREPARATION TIME 1 HOUR **COOKING TIME** 50 MINUTES **MAKES** 36

250g butter, softened

1 ¼ cups (250g) firmly packed brown sugar

4 eggs

2 tablespoons orange marmalade

1.5kg (7 ¾ cups) mixed dried fruit, chopped finely

1 ½ cups (225g) plain flour

½ cup (75g) self-raising flour

2 teaspoons mixed spice

½ cup (125ml) sweet sherry

¼ cup (30g) blanched whole almonds

2 tablespoons sweet sherry, extra

DECORATIONS

½ cup (80g) icing sugar

750g white ready-made soft icing

filigree textured plate

½ cup (160g) orange marmalade, warmed, strained

silver lustre

1 Preheat oven to 150°C/130°C fan-forced. Line three 12-hole (⅓-cup/80ml) muffin pans with silver foil and paper cases.

2 Beat butter, sugar and eggs in small bowl with electric mixer until just combined.

3 Transfer mixture to large bowl. Add marmalade and fruit; mix well. Sift flours and spice over mixture, add sherry; mix well.

4 Place 2 level tablespoons of mixture into each case; smooth surface.

5 Bake cakes about 50 minutes. Remove cakes from oven; brush tops with extra sherry. Cover pan tightly with foil; cool cakes in pan.

6 On surface dusted with sifted icing sugar, knead soft icing until smooth. Roll out to a thickness of 5mm. Using a 7cm round fluted cutter cut out 36 rounds.

7 Using a filigree textured plate, gently press an imprint onto each icing round.

8 Brush cakes with marmalade; top with icing rounds. Carefully brush silver lustre over pattern on icing.

If your oven won't hold three sets of muffin pans, it's fine to leave the mixture standing at room temperature while the first batch bakes. We used three cake stands stacked on top of each other to display the cakes. They measured 17cm, 24cm and 34cm in diameter. We used a plastic filigree textured plate to mark the icing, available from craft or haberdashery shops. There is a trend towards using cupcakes for wedding cakes. This cake — when assembled as a whole on three cake stands — looks fabulous. Mix and match the colours of the plates, cakes and flowers to suit the occasion.

KIDS' BIRTHDAY CAKES

Kids' Birthday Cakes

With the possible exception of Christmas it is hard to imagine a more important event in a child's life than his or her birthday. Regardless of whether the event is shared with just close family or an extended group of friends and their families, the anticipation reaches fever pitch as the big day approaches and another year is added to the birthday card. The cake is usually the star attraction of the birthday feast and we hope the suggestions on these pages make choosing the "perfect" cake a little easier.

Choose a cake that suits the theme of the party — a fairy princess or sweetheart cake for the dolly crowd or perhaps a party piñata or play pool for the outdoorsy types. Make sure the cake is big enough to serve all the guests. Cupcakes make a great deal of sense as they ensure every child gets a serving and avoids the messy business of cutting the cake. With a little creative thought, cupcakes can become funny faces or a bouquet of flowers. Or for a personal touch, use lollies or piping gel to write the initial of each guest on the top.

PREPARING THE CAKE

You don't need any experience as a cake decorator to make the cakes in this chapter; just follow our instructions and you'll end up with picture-perfect results. The lolly shop is your greatest ally and we've devised lots of colourful ways to use sweets to creative effect. If you're short of time or not sure of your cake-making skills, by all means use a packet mix — our recipes specify how many quantities you'll need. Or buy a ready made un-iced cake from the supermarket or cake shop and save your energies for the decorating. Most of these cakes use the smooth base as the top of the finished cake; in this case, it's a good idea to cool the cake upside-down.

Icings and frostings are a decorative covering for the cake. It makes it more attractive and provides a protective coating which traps the moisture and improves its keeping qualities.

The most commonly used icing is a butter or vienna cream (recipe opposite). The flavour can be varied by adding finely grated citrus rind or any extract or essence to your taste. Butter cream is a very forgiving icing in terms of achieving a smooth finish. Once the icing has been applied, dip a knife in a jug of hot water, wipe it dry and run it across the top of the icing for a polished look. To prevent crumbs from mixing with the icing, bake the cake the day before you ice it and refrigerate overnight in an airtight container. Decorate the cake while it is still cold. If you think it will take longer than half an hour to decorate, freeze it, uncovered, for about 30 minutes before decorating.

BUTTER CREAM Beat 125g softened butter in a small bowl with electric mixer until it is as white as possible. Gradually beat in 1 ½ cups (240g) sfited icing sugar and 2 tablespoons milk, in two batches. Flavour and colour as required.

CHOCOLATE VARIATION Sift ⅓ cup (35g) cocoa powder in with the first batch of icing sugar.

Ready-made soft icing or fondant is a pliable, mouldable icing made from icing sugar and glucose. The traditional Christmas cake icing, it can be coloured for use on children's cakes. The best way to do this is by kneading the icing until smooth. Dip the tip of a skewer into the colouring then dab colouring onto the icing. You have to keep kneading until the icing is a uniform colour — at first it will look streaky. To cover a cake with fondant, brush the cake lightly and evenly with sieved jam. Roll the icing out to the desired thickness and lift it onto the cake using your hands or a rolling pin. Smooth the surface with your hands dusted with icing sugar and shape the icing around the sides of the cake. Trim the excess with a sharp knife.

For more information on the tools and techniques for cake decorating, see *Cupcakes* on page 219.

CAKE BOARDS

Most of these cakes are presented on cake boards which become part of the decoration. You can buy cake boards from craft shops and cake decorating suppliers or you can make your own using masonite or any other strong board. Cut the covering (greaseproof) paper about 5cm to 10cm larger than the board; place on the board, fold the surplus to the wrong side and secure with adhesive tape or glue. To cover a round board neatly, you will need to make incisions in the overlap so it folds back without requiring tucks.

FORWARD PLANNING

Organisation is the key to a smooth party, and we suggest involving your child/ren as much as possible in the planning. Decide on how many guests you are going to have — a good rule of thumb seems to be the same number of guests as the age of the birthday person. Send out the invitations several weeks in advance. If your child has a special friend it's probably worth consulting the parents before setting the date to make sure s/he can attend. Make the RSVP date and contacts (phone numbers and an email address) clear as there's nothing worse than not knowing how many people you're catering for. Give start and finish times, so parents know exactly when to pick up their children and you're not left with rowdy extras while you're trying to clear up. If the party is to include a meal, make that clear on the invitation and if it's just nibbles and cake, schedule it well between meals, say 9.30am to 11.30am or 2pm to 4pm.

Your child will probably be very clear on whatever the "essential ingredients" of a successful party are (from the experience of attending other parties) so prepare whatever games, prizes and activities are deemed important well in advance. If you are to give take-home bags, make sure you have them prepared and on a table or in a basket by the front door well before the party begins or you're bound to forget them in the confusion of everyone leaving.

Lollies

Lollies are the key to easy party cake decorating, bringing your creations alive. Secure to cake with butter cream.

SMARTIES
In cake decorating, Smarties make excellent eyes or can be sorted into colours for a striking effect. Stick to butter cream close to presentation time to prevent colours running.

MARSHMALLOWS
Their pastel colours and malleability make them a wonderful decorating tool. Cut lengthways and pinch the ends to make perfect petals. Secure to cake and finish with a fruit stick stem and some spearmint leaves.

FRUIT STICKS
Cut colourful fruit sticks to any length for a variety of uses. They can be legs or arms, or form a colourful outline of a shape on your cake. Available from the supermarket.

SPEARMINT LEAVES
The green colouring of spearmint lends them the look of foliage on a cake. By cutting them lengthways, through the centre, a shiny and a rough side can be used to create texture in the green.

CACHOUS
Available at supermarkets, cachous add some magnificent metallic to a party cake. Elegantly spell out letters, or use them to represent jewels. Use lavishly for an over-the-top look, or sparingly on a simple, special cupcake.

CRAZY COLOURS
Use lollies with a crazy collection of colours like these rainbow choc-chips for almost any use. A cake simply covered in a thick layer of these looks spectacular.

COLOUR COORDINATION

Sort different lollies into colour groups such as these Ripe Raspberries, jubes and jelly babies. They can have a great impact when used together on a themed cake.

PARTY SPRINKLES

Coloured sprinkles and hundreds and thousands are indispensible party products. Dust over chocolate crackles and sprinkle over crustless buttered bread for fairy bread. On a party cake, they become magical fairy dust.

LICORICE STRAPS

Party cakes wouldn't be the same without licorice straps. Cut to any shape or size, roll, stretch or flatten them to define edges and to make features such as eyelashes or whiskers.

FRECKLES

Freckles are kiddie favourites and fantastic for party cakes. Their large round shape makes them perfect to use as pompoms for hats, buttons, wheels or even surprised mouths.

FLAKE BAR

Break Flake Bars into small pieces and scatter across a mud cake for an extra chocolate hit. They make excellent bark, roofs, racing tracks or logs on boys cakes.

CANDY LOVE HEARTS

The high gloss and rich colour on these make them striking additions to your cake decorating palette. Use them as a hem to a skirt or as the nose of a kitten. Nestle into butter cream to secure to cake.

Pudding steamers are always in shops around Christmas time, but can be hard to get at other times. We use aluminium steamers for cakes such as this one. If you are likely to be making cakes for children, buy the steamers in various sizes when you see them. They're not expensive and are useful for many things. The heart-shaped lollies we used on this cake are available from chain stores and some supermarkets. They have words on one side — we have used them word-side down. Make sure you have enough fairies — one for each guest.

Magic toadstool

2 x 340g packets buttercake mix

35cm x 50cm prepared board

1 ½ quantities butter cream (see page 247)

yellow and pink food colouring

15cm-round cardboard

DECORATIONS

4 pink Fruit Sticks

2 spearmint leaves

8 mini heart lollies

1 yellow Fruit Stick

25 large heart lollies

24 silver cachous

3 large white marshmallows

3 white marshmallows

1 teaspoon cocoa powder

assorted mini fairy statues

1 Preheat oven to 180°C/160°C fan-forced. Grease 1.25-litre (5 cup) and 2.25-litre (9 cup) pudding steamers.

2 Make cakes according to directions on packets; pour mixture into steamers until three-quarters full. Bake smaller pudding about 35 minutes and larger pudding about 55 minutes. Stand cakes in steamers 5 minutes; turn onto wire rack to cool. Using serrated knife, level cake tops.

3 Place small cake on board. Tint half of the butter cream with yellow colouring; spread all over cake for toadstool stem.

4 Position large cake on cardboard round, cut-side down. Position large cake on toadstool stem for toadstool cap. Tint remaining butter cream with pink colouring; spread all over cap.

5 Place pink Fruit Sticks, side by side, on flat surface; trim tops of sticks to make rounded door. Position on toadstool stem for door.

6 Split spearmint leaves in half through centre; slice halves into three pieces. Use centre pieces for stems and side pieces as leaves; position around toadstool stem. Position two mini heart lollies at top of each spearmint stem for flowers.

7 Cut yellow Fruit Stick into thin strips; using a little water, position on two large heart lollies; position on toadstool stem for windows.

8 Position six large heart lollies on board at front of toadstool for path. Decorate toadstool cap with cachous and remaining large heart lollies.

9 Using a little butter cream, attach large marshmallows on top of smaller marshmallows, sprinkle with sifted cocoa powder; position around toadstool. Decorate toadstool with fairy statues.

Whirlipop

340g packet buttercake mix

27cm x 60cm prepared board

1 quantity butter cream (see page 247)

yellow food colouring

DECORATIONS

icing sugar

500g ready-made soft icing

green and red food colouring

3.5cm x 85cm orange ribbon

38cm dowelling

1 Preheat oven to 180°C/160°C fan-forced. Grease deep 17cm-round cake pan; line base and side with baking paper, extending paper 5cm over sides.

2 Make cake according to directions on packet; pour mixture into pan. Bake cake about 45 minutes. Stand cake in pan 5 minutes; turn, top-side up, onto wire rack to cool. Using serrated knife, level cake top.

3 Place cake on board, cut-side down.

4 Tint butter cream with yellow colouring; spread all over cake.

5 On surface dusted with sifted icing sugar, knead icing until smooth. Knead green colouring into one-third of the icing; roll into 1cm-thick cord. Enclose remaining icing in plastic wrap; reserve. Cut cord in half; cover both halves with plastic wrap. Repeat with reserved icing, tinting half of the icing red and half of the icing yellow.

6 Pinch one cord of each colour together, twist the cords by rotating them; cover with plastic wrap. Repeat with remaining three cords.

7 Starting from centre of cake, spiral one length of twisted cord. Join end of remaining twisted cord to first twisted cord by gently pinching and moulding cords together; continue spiralling twisted cord to cover cake.

8 Tie ribbon into a bow around dowelling; insert dowelling slightly into cake to make lollipop stick.

Pinch the three cords together at one end, then twist cords together by rotating them.

Starting from centre of cake, spiral twisted cord to cover the top of cake.

The only tricky part of making this cake is keeping the icing soft and pliable, it starts to develop a crust and dry out as soon as it's exposed to air. So, work quickly and keep the icing covered with plastic wrap when you're not handling it.

Flower bouquet

340g packet buttercake mix

1 quantity butter cream (see page 247)

yellow and pink food colouring

40cm x 50cm prepared board

DECORATIONS

2 x 250g packets coloured marshmallows

5 purple Smarties

7 pink Smarties

icing sugar

350g ready-made soft icing

green food colouring

pink bow

16 spearmint leaves

1 Preheat oven to 180°C/160°C fan-forced. Line 12-hole (⅓-cup/80ml) muffin pan with paper cases.

2 Make cake according to directions on packet; pour ¼ cup mixture into each hole. Bake cakes about 20 minutes. Stand cakes in pan 5 minutes; turn, top-side up, onto wire rack to cool.

3 Tint half of the butter cream with yellow colouring; spread over five cakes. Tint remaining butter cream with pink colouring; spread over remaining cakes.

4 Using scissors, cut 24 yellow marshmallows and 18 pink marshmallows in half. Squeeze ends of each marshmallow together to form petals. Decorate yellow cakes with six or seven pink marshmallow petals and pink cakes with six or seven yellow marshmallow petals.

5 Position purple Smarties in pink flower centres; position pink Smarties in yellow flower centres. Position flowers on board.

6 On surface dusted with sifted icing sugar, knead icing until smooth. Knead green colouring into icing; divide icing into quarters. Roll one-quarter of the icing into 5mm thick cord. Enclose remaining icing in plastic wrap; reserve. Cut icing cord into three uneven lengths; position on board. Repeat with reserved icing to make 12 stems in total.

7 Pinch stems together near ends; secure bow with a little butter cream. Position spearmint leaves along stems; secure with a little butter cream.

Lazy ladybird

340g packet buttercake mix

25cm x 30cm prepared board

1 quantity butter cream (see page 247)

black and red food colouring

DECORATIONS

1 black licorice strap

14 chocolate freckles

2 x 15cm (3mm) black chenille sticks (pipe cleaners)

2 yellow Smarties

1 Preheat oven to 180°C/160°C fan-forced. Grease one hole of 12-hole (⅓-cup/80ml) muffin pan and 1.25-litre (5 cup) pudding steamer.

2 Make cake according to directions on packet; pour ¼ cup of mixture into muffin hole and remaining mixture into pudding steamer. Bake muffin about 20 minutes and steamer cake about 35 minutes. Stand cakes in pans 5 minutes; turn muffin, top-side up, onto wire rack to cool, leave steamer cake top-side down to cool. Using serrated knife, level steamer cake top.

3 Using serrated knife, cut segment from muffin so muffins sits snugly against the ladybird's body; trim bottom of steamer cake to make a more rounded body. Place cake on board, top-side down.

4 Tint ¼ cup of butter cream with black colouring and remaining butter cream with red colouring. Spread red butter cream all over body of ladybird.

5 Position muffin against body for head, secure with a little butter cream; spread all over with black butter cream. Pull an outside strip of licorice from the strap; position along centre of body. Position freckles on body.

6 Curl one end of each chenille stick; position on cake for antennae. Position Smarties on cake for eyes.

Using a serrated knife, trim the bottom of the steamer cake to make more rounded.

Using a large palette knife, spread the red butter cream all over the ladybird's body.

Position the muffin against the ladybird's body, for head, then spread with black butter cream.

Picture perfect

2 x 340g packets buttercake mix

35cm-square prepared board

2 quantities butter cream (see page 247)

DECORATIONS

11cm-square photograph, laminated

1kg mixed lollies

1 Preheat oven to 180°C/160°C fan-forced. Grease deep 23cm-square cake pan; line base and sides with baking paper, extending paper 5cm over sides.

2 Make cakes according to directions on packets; pour mixtures into pan. Bake cake about 1 hour. Stand cake in pan 5 minutes; turn, top-side up, onto wire rack to cool. Using serrated knife, level cake top.

3 Place cake on board, cut-side down. Spread butter cream all over cake.

4 Centre photograph carefully on top of cake. Scatter mixed lollies all over cake; press lollies gently into butter cream.

Parties are all about lollies, the combinations are endless — you could "go pretty" with just pink and white lollies, or go ghoulish with just black and red lollies — say bats, cats and snakes. Also, you can easily change the whole look by using a different shaped cake such as a heart, oval or round.

Sweetheart cake

2 x 340g packets buttercake mix

2 quantities butter cream (see page 247)

pink and red food colouring

48cm x 55cm prepared board

DECORATIONS

pink and white mallow bakes, halved

raspberry lollies

small red jubes, cut in half

red fruit rings

red jelly beans

pink and white marshmallows

pink jelly beans

musk sticks

1 Preheat oven to 180°C/160°C fan-forced. Line four 12-hole (⅓-cup/80ml) muffin pans with red paper cases.

2 Make cakes according to directions on packets; divide mixture evenly among cases. Bake cakes about 20 minutes. Stand cakes in pans 5 minutes; turn, top-side up, onto wire racks to cool.

3 Tint one-third of the butter cream pink, tint another third red; leave remaining third plain.

4 Spread one-third of the cakes with pink butter cream, another third with red butter cream and remaining cakes with plain butter cream.

5 Using picture as a guide, decorate cakes with lollies, as desired.

6 Arrange cupcakes, side by side, on prepared board, in the shape of a heart. Use musk sticks to outline the heart shape.

This cake is another one perfect to take to school, or picnic — or any outdoor party.

Party piñata

Using the markings as a guide and a small serrated knife, cut a deep hollow into the cake.

Spread the chocolate butter cream over the top and side of the cake, then fill the hollow.

Swirl the chocolate around the inside of the steamer until it is evenly coated.

340g packet buttercake mix

30cm-round prepared board

1 quantity chocolate butter cream (see page 247)

DECORATIONS

23 large chocolate coins

19 medium chocolate coins

13 small chocolate coins

150g rainbow choc-chips

½ teaspoon vegetable oil

450g milk chocolate Melts, melted

50g milk chocolate, melted

35g packet mini M&M's

200g packet Smarties

toy hammer

1 Preheat oven to 180°C/160°C fan-forced. Grease deep 15cm-round cake pan; line base and side with baking paper, extending paper 5cm over sides.

2 Make cake according to directions on packet; pour into pan until three-quarters full. Bake cake about 45 minutes. Stand cake in pan 5 minutes; turn, top-side up, onto wire rack to cool. Using serrated knife, level cake top.

3 Position cake on board, cut-side down. Using ruler and toothpicks, mark 11cm circle in centre of cake. Using markings as a guide, cut a deep hollow into cake.

4 Spread chocolate butter cream all over cake; fill hollow with coins and half of the rainbow choc-chips.

5 To make chocolate shell: grease 2.25-litre (9 cup) pudding steamer with oil; place bowl in freezer 10 minutes. Place melted chocolate Melts in steamer; swirl chocolate to coat inside of steamer evenly. Continue swirling until chocolate begins to set and stops flowing around the steamer; try to keep the chocolate a uniform thickness, particularly at the top edge of the steamer. Stand until chocolate is almost set. Freeze until chocolate sets completely.

6 Carefully place pudding steamer with set chocolate shell over cake; using hot cloth, briefly rub outside of steamer. Chocolate shell will slip from steamer to enclose the cake.

7 Using melted milk chocolate, secure remaining rainbow choc-chips, mini M&M's and Smarties to chocolate shell.

8 Allow birthday child to break chocolate shell open with toy hammer.

Friendly flutterfly

2 x 340g packets buttercake mix

40cm x 55cm prepared board

DECORATIONS

icing sugar

1.5kg ready-made soft icing

yellow, green, orange, pink and purple food colouring

½ cup (160g) apricot jam, warmed, sieved

2 pink Smarties

2 x 30cm (3mm) yellow chenille sticks (pipe cleaners)

1 Preheat oven to 180°C/160°C fan-forced. Grease and line two 18cm-heart pans and line four holes of 12-hole (⅓-cup/80ml) muffin pan with paper cases.

2 Make cakes according to directions on packets; place ¼ cup of the cake mixture into each paper case and divide remaining cake mixture between heart pans. Bake muffins about 20 minutes and heart cakes about 35 minutes. Stand cakes in pans 5 minutes; turn, top-side up, onto wire racks to cool.

3 On surface dusted with sifted icing sugar, knead 350g of the icing until smooth. Knead yellow colouring into icing; roll until 3mm thick. Using 7.5cm-round cutter, cut four rounds from icing; brush tops of muffins with one-quarter of the jam, top with rounds of icing. Enclose yellow trimmings in plastic wrap.

4 On surface dusted with icing sugar, knead 500g of the icing until smooth. Knead green colouring into icing; roll until 5mm thick. Brush top and sides of one heart cake with half of the remaining jam. Using rolling pin, lift icing over one heart cake; using sharp-pointed knife, neatly trim excess icing at base of cake. Using hands dusted with icing sugar, gently mould icing around heart cake. Repeat with another 500g of the icing, green colouring, jam and remaining heart cake.

5 Assemble icing-covered muffins and cakes on board to form butterfly.

6 On surface dusted with sifted icing sugar, knead remaining icing until smooth. Divide icing into three portions. Knead orange colouring into one portion of the icing; enclose remaining pieces of icing in plastic wrap. Roll orange icing until 3mm thick. Using cutters or sharp-pointed knife, cut heart and star shapes from icing; position on butterfly wings with a little dab of water. Repeat with reserved yellow trimmings and remaining icing portions, one portion tinted pink and one tinted purple.

7 Position Smarties for eyes on butterfly. Using scraps of pink icing, shape a small piece into mouth; position on butterfly. Twist tops of chenille sticks into curls; position on cake for antennae.

Ready-made soft icing is available in supermarkets and some delis. Cake decorator's suppliers also have it, but usually in large quantities. It is a type of fondant and, once you've handled it and gained confidence, you'll be converted to using it forever. It's great to shape, roll, mould or colour — and the finish looks professional — only you will know how easy it is to handle. Chenille sticks are available in craft shops, party shops and many chain stores. They come in many widths, lengths, colours and various degrees of fluffiness — a far cry from the pipe cleaners of yesteryear.

Funny faces

You can have fun decorating these funny faces. Piping gel is available in several colours in small manageable tubes from supermarkets. Invest in some good-quality food colourings from cake decorating suppliers, they're concentrated, so will last for years.

340g packet buttercake mix

1 quantity butter cream (see page 247)

yellow, red, green and blue food colouring

DECORATIONS

1 tablespoon apricot jam, warmed, sieved

icing sugar

250g ready-made soft icing

flesh colouring

cake decorating stars

cake decorating hearts

cake decorating moons

12 assorted coloured mini M&M's

red piping gel

black piping gel

1 Preheat oven to 180°C/160°C fan-forced. Line six holes of 12-hole (⅓-cup/80ml) muffin pan with paper cases.

2 Make cake according to directions on packet; pour ¼ cup mixture into each paper case. Bake cakes about 20 minutes. Stand cakes in pan 5 minutes; turn, top-side up, onto wire rack to cool.

3 Divide butter cream into quarters; tint one-quarter with yellow colouring, one-quarter with red colouring, one-quarter with green colouring and remaining with blue colouring.

4 Brush tops of cakes with jam. On surface dusted with sifted icing sugar, knead icing until smooth. Knead flesh colouring into icing; roll icing until 3mm thick. Using 7.5cm round cutter, cut six rounds from icing; cover each patty cake with one round.

5 Place yellow butter cream into piping bag fitted with a fluted tube; pipe random hairstyles onto one or two patty cakes. Repeat with red, green and blue butter creams, cleaning or replacing piping bag and tube between colours.

6 Decorate hairstyles with stars, hearts and moons. Position M&M's on each cake for eyes; secure with tiny dabs of butter cream.

7 Using piping gels, pipe pupils, eyebrows, noses, freckles, mouths, eyelashes, ears and glasses onto cakes.

Play pool

2 x 340g packets buttercake mix

35cm-round prepared board

DECORATIONS

85g packet bubblegum-flavoured jelly crystals

½ cup (160g) apricot jam, warmed, sieved

icing sugar

1kg ready-made soft icing

purple, green, yellow, pink and blue food colouring

2 toy dolls

Using the markings as a guide, cut a shallow hollow from the cake with a serrated knife.

1 Preheat oven to 180°C/160°C fan-forced. Grease deep 22cm-round cake pan; line base and side with baking paper, extending paper 5cm above side.

2 Make cakes according to directions on packets; pour mixtures into pan. Bake cake about 50 minutes. Stand cake in pan 5 minutes; turn, top-side up, onto wire rack to cool. Using serrated knife, level cake top.

3 Make jelly according to directions on packet; refrigerate until almost set.

4 Position cake on board, cut-side down. Using ruler and toothpicks, mark a 19cm circle in centre of cake. Using markings as a guide and small serrated knife, cut 2cm-deep hollow from cake. Brush top edge and side of cake with jam.

5 On surface dusted with sifted icing sugar, knead icing until smooth. Knead purple colouring into 200g of the icing; roll three-quarters of the purple icing into a rope long enough to reach around the bottom circumference of cake. Enclose remaining purple icing in plastic wrap; reserve. Position rope around cake. Repeat with 200g batches of icing and green, yellow and pink colouring, stacking the coloured ropes up around the outside of the cake.

6 Knead blue colouring into remaining white icing; roll half of the icing into a rope long enough to reach around the top edge of the cake. Flatten rope slightly with rolling pin; position on cake for top of pool. Roll remaining blue icing into a rope long enough to reach around the circumference of the cake; position on cake above pink rope.

7 When jelly is almost set, stir gently to break up; spoon into hollowed section of cake. Position dolls in pool.

8 On surface dusted with sifted icing sugar, shape reserved icings into pool toys; position in and around pool just before serving.

Roll the icing into a rope long enough to reach around the circumference of the cake.

Shape half of the blue icing around the top edge of the play pool.

Fairy princess

2 x 340g packets buttercake mix
25cm-round prepared board or plate
500g ready-made soft icing
1 cup (160g) icing sugar
purple food colouring
½ cup (160g) apricot jam, warmed, sieved

DECORATIONS
28cm dressed doll
butterfly wings on a stick
30cm ribbon
small butterfly decoration
small butterfly wand

1 Preheat oven to 180°C/160°C fan-forced. Grease 2.5-litre (10-cup) Dolly Varden pan.

2 Make cakes according to directions on packets; pour mixtures into pan. Place pan on oven tray; bake about 1 hour. Stand cake in pan 5 minutes; turn onto wire rack to cool.

3 Trim cake so it sits flat on board or plate. Remove legs from doll; trim bodice neatly around waist. Scoop out small hole from top of cake large enough to fit doll's body. Style doll's hair, as desired.

4 On surface dusted with icing sugar, knead icing until smooth. Knead purple colouring into icing to make a pale purple. Reserve a piece of icing about the size of a small apple; tint a darker shade of purple then wrap in plastic wrap (this is for the flowers on the dress).

5 Brush cake all over with jam.

6 To make skirt, roll large piece of icing into a circle almost large enough to cover cake (this allows for stretching), about 28cm in diameter. Using rolling pin, lift icing onto cake. To make flounces in skirt, position scrunched soft paper towel or tissues under hem of skirt, trim flounces to shape, if necessary, using scissors. Leave paper under flounces until icing becomes firm.

7 Cut a small hole in top of icing for doll; position doll.

8 Roll out reserved icing; cut out flower shapes (we used 1.5cm and 4cm flower-shaped cutters). Brush the backs of flowers with a tiny amount of water; position on skirt.

9 Push butterfly wings on stick into cake at back of doll. Make a sash from ribbon; wrap around doll's waist. Decorate sash with butterfly. Position butterfly wand in doll's hand.

Only remove the legs of the doll if she's too tall for the cake. Just push the doll, with legs, gently through the cake until the doll's body is in the right position. Dolly Varden cake pans (see pages 628 & 629) can be bought or hired from cake decorating suppliers. Alternatively make the cake in a pudding steamer. When it's cold, put it in the freezer for about 30 minutes, then "sculpt" the cake using a small sharp knife to make a good skirt shape. You might need to stack large and smaller pudding-shaped cakes to get the height, then "sculpt" it into shape.

Zappo the alien

2 x 340g packets buttercake mix

30cm x 46cm prepared board

2 quantities butter cream (see page 247)

green food colouring

DECORATIONS

2 yellow Skittles

2 giant Jaffas

27 green Skittles

1 red fruit ring

rainbow choc-chips

2 green lollipops

7 spearmint leaves

7 toothpicks

12 orange Cool Fruits

9 yellow Cool Fruits

You need a 200g packet of Skittles for Zappo. Oval cake pans can be bought from cake decorating suppliers, or make a cake in a baking dish and cut the oval shape from it — easy and cheaper. Remember to remove the toothpicks out of the reach of children.

1 Preheat oven to 180°C/160°C fan-forced. Grease and line deep 20cm-round cake pan and deep 18cm-oval cake pan.

2 Make cake according to directions on packet; divide mixture between pans so that both mixtures are the same depth. Bake round cake about 35 minutes and oval cake about 40 minutes. Stand cakes in pans 5 minutes; turn, top-side up, onto wire rack to cool.

3 Assemble cakes on board, using the oval cake for the head and the round cake for the body.

4 Tint butter cream with green colouring; use a little butter cream to attach oval cake to round cake. Spread remaining butter cream all over cakes.

5 Attach yellow Skittles to Jaffas with a little butter cream for eyes; position on cake. Position 1 green Skittle for nose; position fruit ring for mouth. Sprinkle rainbow choc-chips on cheeks and top of head; position lollipops on head for antennae.

6 Skewer each spearmint leaf with a toothpick; position on sides and top of head. Scatter Cool Fruits and remaining green Skittles on body of alien.

Cut a 2.5cm piece from one half of the square cake and trim a 3.5cm piece from the jam roll.

Assemble the cakes on the board to form the train; discard any remaining cake and jam roll.

When it comes to eating this cake, remember that a small segment of stick is still embedded in each Carnival Pop (used for wheels). You could easily make carriages to trundle along behind the express train – make another square cake, cut it into blocks for carriages, scoop out the centres, ice and decorate them, then fill them with "cargo".

Express train

2 x 340g packets buttercake mix
400g jam roll
22cm x 37cm prepared board
2 quantities butter cream (see page 247)
green food colouring

DECORATIONS
2 red licorice straps
8 Carnival Pops
1 red Super Rope licorice
2 green Smarties
1 large yellow Sour Ball
22 yellow Smarties
8 red Smarties
1 Screw Pop
artificial spider's web

1 Preheat oven to 180°C/160°C fan-forced. Grease and line deep 23cm-square cake pan.
2 Make cakes according to directions on packet; pour into pan. Bake about 1 hour. Stand cake in pan 5 minutes; turn, top-side up, onto wire rack to cool. Using serrated knife, level cake top.
3 Cut square cake in half; cut 2.5cm piece from one half of square cake.
4 Cut 3.5cm piece from jam roll. Assemble cakes on board to form train, as shown; discard remaining cake.
5 Tint butter cream with green colouring; spread all over train.
6 Cut licorice strap into thin strips; using licorice, outline train's edges and make window on train.
7 Trim and discard sticks from Carnival Pops; position as wheels. Cut eight 1.5cm pieces from Super Rope; position between wheels as axle.
8 Cut two 8cm pieces from Super Rope; position at front of train for bumper. Position green Smarties and Sour Ball at front of train for lights. Decorate train with yellow and red Smarties.
9 Place Screw Pop in position for funnel; place a little of the butter cream on top of funnel. Press the end of a piece of spider's web into the butter cream for smoke.

Lamington choo choo

8 x 6cm-square (3.5cm-deep) ready-made lamingtons

40cm x 50cm prepared board

DECORATIONS

3 green Fruit Sticks, halved

4 x 20g packets Five Flavours Life Savers

2 x 400g packets jelly beans

1 Place one lamington at front of board. Cut one-third from another lamington; position larger lamington piece in front of whole lamington for train's engine. Completely hollow out smaller lamington piece; top whole lamington with hollowed lamington piece.

2 Using small serrated knife, cut shallow hollows into remaining lamingtons.

3 Connect six lamingtons, hollow-side up, to train's engine with Fruit Sticks, to make train's carriages.

4 Position two Life Savers on top of engine; position remaining Life Savers on each carriage for wheels.

5 Stand two jelly beans in Life Savers on engine; place three black jelly beans at front of engine. Fill each carriage and hollow of engine with remaining jelly beans.

Place larger piece on board for engine then hollow out the smaller piece of the lamington.

Top the whole lamington with the hollowed smaller piece to make the front of the train.

Using a small serrated knife, cut shallow hollows into the remaining lamingtons.

ALLERGY-FREE BAKING

Allergy-free Baking

The heightened awareness of food allergies and intolerances thanks to new testing and diagnostic procedures means that it's highly likely someone you know is not allowed one or more of a basic food. That doesn't mean they have to lead a life of deprivation. This collection of recipes addresses the main food intolerances — to eggs, dairy and gluten. The proof of the pudding, as they say, is in the eating. These cakes may be egg-free, dairy-free or gluten-free but they're far from taste-free, so even if you aren't food intolerant, go ahead and give them a try. We're sure you won't even notice the missing ingredients.

Food intolerance is a condition where adverse effects occur after eating a particular food or food ingredient. Genuine food intolerance is different from a food aversion, where a person strongly dislikes a food and believes that a food produces a particular reaction. A lack or deficiency of enzymes responsible for the digestion of food can cause many types of food intolerance. For example, a deficiency in lactase, the enzyme responsible for digesting milk, causes intolerance to milk. Coeliac disease is a gut intolerance to a protein found in wheat, called gluten.

A genuine food allergy is when a specific immune reaction occurs in the body in response to consuming a particular food. While this is different from food intolerance, the symptoms can be very similar and the outcome — the need to avoid eating that food — is the same.

Cooking for people with food allergies and intolerances requires a bit of extra care because you have to be sure to avoid contamination, which can be as simple as butter or peanut butter left on a knife or spoon, or a sifter which has previously been used to sift wheat flour and not washed thoroughly in between uses. The situation is compounded because many small children have double or multiple intolerances, so perhaps have to avoid dairy foods as well as eggs. So be sure to ask exactly what your guests must avoid before you start cooking for them. The benefit of all the increased knowledge about intolerances and allergies is that commercial substitutes are becoming increasingly available and affordable in mainstream supermarkets and nutritionists, chefs and cookbook authors are more accustomed to devising recipes that avoid the troublesome ingredients. The cakes in this chapter are just the tip of the culinary iceberg. You can experiment with adaptations to your favourite recipes to devise your own treats to suit the food intolerance in your life.

COELIAC DISEASE AND GLUTEN INTOLERANCE

Gluten, the protein in wheat, is found in anything containing wheat flour. This includes bread, biscuits, cakes, pastries, puddings, pies and pasta. Couscous, burghul, flour-thickened gravies, sauces and soups, stuffing mixes, hamburgers and sausages which contain breadcrumbs also have to be avoided unless you are sure they are gluten-free. Proteins similar to gluten are also found in rye, barley, triticale and oats, so any foods containing these are off the menu as well. You should also use pure icing sugar rather than icing sugar mixture as the latter can contain wheat starch to stop it from going lumpy. Some commercial baking powders also contain wheat starch, so check the label or make your own by triple-sifting bicarbonate of soda and cream of tartar in the ratio of half to one (ie ½ teaspoon bicarbonate of soda to 1 teaspoon cream of tartar).

The good news is that packaged gluten-free bread and cake mixes are available and potato flour, arrowroot, cornflour, buckwheat flour, soy flour, ground rice flour and chickpea flour are all good substitutes for wheat flour. To obtain an informative list of gluten-free ingredients, contact The Coeliac Society in your state.

In many instances you can adapt recipes containing gluten. When substituting wheat flour with gluten-free flour, you usually get best results with recipes that have a small quantity of flour in them. Gluten is a sticky substance that stops baked goods from crumbling and improves the texture by trapping pockets of air. You can replicate the effects of gluten by adding xanthum/xanthan gum, pre-gel starch or guar gum in the approximate proportions of 1 teaspoon to 1 cup of flour. You can buy these gums from some health food shops and The Coeliac Society. In some recipes it's possible to avoid flour altogether by using ground nuts instead.

AVOIDING EGGS

You should avoid any products which are labelled as containing: albumin, dried egg, egg white, yolk, protein or solids, globulin, livetin, lysozyme, ovalbumin, ovoglobulin, ovomucin, ovomucid, ovovitellin or vitellin and pasteurised, powdered or whole egg.

Sometimes you can leave out the eggs in a recipe that calls for only one or two and replace the liquid by adding water. However this is not recommended with most baking recipes, so you will need to either use commercial egg substitutes (available from most supermarkets) or experiment with the substitutions suggested below.

If the purpose of the egg is to bind the ingredients, you can try substituting mashed banana, apple puree, soft tofu or gelatine dissolved in hot water. If the egg is required as a thickening or setting agent you could use wheat, rice, or corn flour blended to a paste with a little water to do the job.

DAIRY INTOLERANCES

If you can't tolerate dairy foods you need to avoid all products labelled as containing: milk, lactose, butter, margarine, cheese, cream, yogurt, whey, milk solids, non-fat milk products, skimmed milk powder, lactoglobulin, casein, lactalbumin or sodium caseinate. This usually applies to sheep, goat, buffalo and horse milk products as well as those made from cow's milk. Fortunately, you can substitute soy milk and any soy milk products. Sometimes fat from butter can be replaced with olive or other vegetable oils and on other occasions, fruit juice can make up the liquid component supplied by the milk.

Mandarin, polenta and macadamia cake

PREPARATION TIME 20 MINUTES (PLUS COOLING TIME) **COOKING TIME** 2 HOURS (PLUS STANDING TIME)
SERVES 12

4 small mandarins (400g)

2 cups (280g) macadamias

250g butter, softened

1 teaspoon vanilla extract

1 cup (220g) caster sugar

3 eggs

1 cup (170g) polenta

1 teaspoon gluten-free baking powder

1 tablespoon pure icing sugar

1 Cover whole mandarins in medium saucepan with cold water; bring to the boil. Drain then repeat process twice more. Cool mandarins to room temperature.
2 Preheat oven to 170°C/150°C fan-forced. Grease deep 22cm-round cake pan; line base with baking paper.
3 Blend or process nuts until coarsely ground. Halve mandarins; discard seeds. Blend or process mandarins until pulpy.
4 Beat butter, extract and caster sugar in small bowl with electric mixer until light and fluffy. Beat in eggs, one at a time. Transfer mixture to large bowl; stir in polenta, baking powder, ground nuts and mandarin pulp. Spread mixture into pan.
5 Bake cake about 1 hour. Stand cake in pan 15 minutes; turn, top-side up, onto wire rack to cool. Serve cake dusted with sifted icing sugar.

Non-dairy fruit cake

PREPARATION TIME 20 MINUTES (PLUS COOLING TIME) **COOKING TIME** 1 HOUR 40 MINUTES **SERVES** 16

2¾ cups (500g) mixed dried fruit

1 cup (150g) finely chopped dried apricots

440g can crushed pineapple in natural juice

¼ cup (60ml) orange juice

1 teaspoon mixed spice

¼ teaspoon ground clove

1 teaspoon bicarbonate of soda

2 egg whites

2 cups (320g) wholemeal self-raising flour

1 Preheat oven to 170°C/150°C fan-forced. Grease deep 20cm-round cake pan; line base and side with baking paper, extending paper 5cm above side.
2 Cook dried fruits, undrained pineapple, juice and spices in large saucepan, stirring until mixture comes to the boil. Reduce heat; simmer, stirring, 5 minutes. Transfer mixture to large bowl; cool.
3 Stir sifted soda and egg whites into fruit mixture; stir in flour. Spread mixture into pan.
4 Bake cake about 1½ hours. Cover cake tightly with foil; cool in pan.

MANDARIN, POLENTA AND MACADAMIA CAKE

1

2

3 4

Gluten-free berry cupcakes

PREPARATION TIME 20 MINUTES **COOKING TIME** 25 MINUTES **MAKES** 12

125g butter, softened

2 teaspoons finely grated lemon rind

¾ cup (165g) caster sugar

4 eggs

2 cups (240g) almond meal

½ cup (40g) desiccated coconut

½ cup (100g) rice flour

1 teaspoon bicarbonate of soda

1 cup (150g) frozen mixed berries

1 tablespoon desiccated coconut, extra

1 Preheat oven to 180°C/160°C fan-forced. Grease 12-hole (⅓-cup/80ml) muffin pan.

2 Beat butter, rind and sugar in small bowl with electric mixer until light and fluffy. Beat in eggs, one at a time. Transfer mixture to large bowl; stir in almond meal, coconut, sifted flour and soda, then the berries. Divide mixture among pan holes.

3 Bake cakes about 25 minutes. Stand cakes in pan 5 minutes; turn, top-side up, onto wire rack to cool. Sprinkle with extra coconut.

Gluten-free chocolate cake

PREPARATION TIME 20 MINUTES **COOKING TIME** 30 MINUTES (PLUS COOLING TIME) **SERVES** 12

1 cup (125g) soy flour

¾ cup (110g) maize cornflour

1¼ teaspoons bicarbonate of soda

½ cup (50g) cocoa powder

1¼ cups (275g) caster sugar

150g butter, melted

1 tablespoon white vinegar

1 cup (250ml) evaporated milk

2 eggs

½ cup mashed banana

2 tablespoons raspberry jam

300ml thickened cream, whipped

2 teaspoons pure icing sugar

Light and luscious describes this cake. The cake batter does need to be spread quite thinly to bake properly. If you haven't got two 22cm sandwich pans use two deep 22cm cake pans.

1 Preheat oven to 180°C/160°C fan-forced. Grease two 22cm-round sandwich cake pans; line bases with baking paper.

2 Sift flours, soda, cocoa and sugar into large bowl. Add butter, vinegar and milk; beat with electric mixer on low speed 1 minute. Add eggs, banana and jam; beat with electric mixer on medium speed 2 minutes. Pour cake mixture into pans.

3 Bake cakes about 30 minutes. Stand cakes in pans 5 minutes; turn, top-side up, onto wire racks to cool.

4 Sandwich cakes with whipped cream; dust with sifted icing sugar.

1 GLUTEN-FREE BERRY CUPCAKES **2** GLUTEN-FREE CHOCOLATE CAKE
3 EGG-FREE DATE AND NUT CAKE [P 284] **4** GLUTEN-FREE, DAIRY-FREE RASPBERRY MUFFINS [P 284]

Serve this cake sliced with a little butter.

Egg-free date and nut cake

PREPARATION TIME 15 MINUTES **COOKING TIME** 40 MINUTES (PLUS COOLING TIME) **SERVES** 24

1 cup (360g) honey

30g butter

1 cup (250ml) water

2¼ cups (360g) wholemeal self-raising flour

1 teaspoon mixed spice

½ teaspoon ground ginger

1½ cups (250g) coarsely chopped dates

¾ cup (90g) coarsely chopped walnuts

¼ cup (35g) coarsely chopped slivered almonds

1 tablespoon honey, extra

1 Preheat oven to 180°C/160°C fan-forced. Grease deep 19cm-square cake pan; line base with baking paper.
2 Stir honey, butter and the water in medium saucepan over low heat until butter melts.
3 Combine sifted flour and spices, dates and nuts in medium bowl; stir in warm honey mixture. Spread mixture into pan.
4 Bake cake about 40 minutes. Stand cake in pan 5 minutes; turn, top-side up, onto wire rack to cool. Glaze with extra honey warmed.

Demerara or raw sugar can be used instead of coffee crystals. All of these sugars add a crunchy texture to the muffins.

Gluten-free, dairy-free raspberry muffins

PREPARATION TIME 15 MINUTES **COOKING TIME** 20 MINUTES **MAKES** 12

2½ cups (375g) gluten-free plain flour

1 tablespoon gluten-free baking powder

½ teaspoon bicarbonate of soda

⅓ cup (40g) rice bran

⅔ cup (150g) firmly packed brown sugar

1½ cups (375ml) soy milk

1 teaspoon vanilla extract

60g dairy-free spread, melted

2 eggs

150g frozen raspberries

1 tablespoon coffee crystals

1 Preheat oven to 200°C/180°C fan-forced. Grease 12-hole (⅓-cup/80ml) muffin pan.
2 Sift flour, baking powder and soda into large bowl. Stir in bran, brown sugar and combined milk, extract, spread and eggs until almost combined. Stir in raspberries.
3 Divide mixture among muffin holes; sprinkle with coffee crystals.
4 Bake muffins about 20 minutes. Turn muffins, top-side up, onto wire rack to cool.

Egg-free ginger jumble cake

PREPARATION TIME 20 MINUTES **COOKING TIME** 45 MINUTES **SERVES** 20

185g butter, chopped coarsely

¾ cup (180ml) golden syrup

½ cup (100g) firmly packed brown sugar

¾ cup (180ml) water

2¼ cups (335g) plain flour

1½ teaspoons bicarbonate of soda

1½ tablespoons ground ginger

1½ teaspoons mixed spice

¼ teaspoon ground clove

1 Preheat oven to 180°C/160°C fan-forced. Grease 23cm-square slab cake pan; line base with baking paper.

2 Stir butter, golden syrup, sugar and the water in medium saucepan over heat, without boiling, until butter is melted; cool 10 minutes. Stir in sifted flour, soda and spices. Pour mixture into pan.

3 Bake cake about 40 minutes. Stand cake in pan 5 minutes; turn, top-side up, onto wire rack to cool.

Serve this cake at room temperature, or warm as a dessert with yogurt, cream or ice-cream. A deep 23cm square cake pan can be used in place of the slab pan, or, a 20cm x 30cm lamington pan will also do the job for you.

Egg-free fruit cake

PREPARATION TIME 25 MINUTES **COOKING TIME** 2 HOURS 25 MINUTES **SERVES** 24

2¾ cups (500g) dried mixed fruit

½ cup (100g) firmly packed brown sugar

60g butter

1 cup (250ml) water

⅓ cup (55g) coarsely chopped dates

1 cup (150g) plain flour

½ cup (75g) self-raising flour

1 teaspoon bicarbonate of soda

1 teaspoon mixed spice

¼ cup (60ml) sweet sherry

1 Preheat oven to 150°C/130°C fan-forced. Grease deep 19cm-square cake pan; line base and sides with three layers of baking paper, extending paper 5cm above sides.

2 Stir dried fruit, sugar, butter and the water in medium saucepan over heat, without boiling, until sugar dissolves. Simmer, uncovered, 3 minutes. Remove from heat, then stir in dates; cool.

3 Stir sifted flours, soda and spice, and sherry into fruit mixture, in two batches. Spread mixture into pan.

4 Bake cake about 2¼ hours. Cover cake tightly with foil; cool in pan.

Good eggless rich fruit cake recipes are hard to find. This recipe is also low in fat and sugar which means its keeping quality is quite low. Store the cake in an airtight container in the fridge, cut the cake while it's fridge-cold.

Teapots & coffee pots

Steeped in tradition, tea and coffee drinking and equipment is an expression of ritual and personal taste.

FINE BONE CHINA
Bone china is the mostly highly regarded of ceramics. It makes an excellent teapot as it is strong, durable, dishwasher-safe and has good heat retention for hot tea.

CHINESE TRADITION
The Chinese have been enjoying tea since at least AD 350, and according to legend, since 2700 BC. Tea is infused into Chinese history, economics, rituals, mythology and the day-to-day lives of its people.

MODERN DESIGN
Modern design is a nod to smooth, organic shapes and simple forms. This pot, forged from one piece and with a rounded, shapely figure, highlights this design aesthetic.

FEMININE FORMS
The elegant textural effect of white glaze falling over the dark, patterned clay and the rounded shape creates a feminine look perfect for afternoon tea with the girls.

FORM AND FUNCTION
This French press, or coffee plunger, exhibits form and function. The graphic metal sheath fits over the glass to keep the coffee warm and also looks unique and modern. Brew plunger coffee for several minutes before plunging, and serve immediately to avoid a bitter taste.

GLASS
Glass is an excellent tea brewing material; tea flavours are not retained as glass is non-porous. This teapot has a diffusing cage so tea need not be strained as it is poured into a cup.

NATURAL MATERIALS
Get back to nature with materials such as cork and walnut like this Swedish design teapot. A tea strainer allows free-flowing infusion without pesky leaves sneaking into your cup.

ENAMEL
Enamel coating over metal has long been a common material for teapots as it is cheap and durable. Find charmingly chipped relics of the depression era in flea markets or vintage stores.

BESPOKE
Quirky, imperfect, handmade tea sets make a gorgeous side table display or a special gift. The white clay used to make this set is the perfect material to show off the makers mark.

STAINLESS STEEL
The ultimate in modern materials, stainless steel makes a smooth, sophisticated look suitable for any home. This design by Arne Jacobsen is double-walled to keep in heat.

JAPANESE TEA CEREMONY
Founded in Zen Buddhism and as much about quiet refinement and ritual as it is about the tea. Ceremonies are performed with a powdered green tea and can be up to four hours long. This design of east meets west fusion is perfect for your own tea ceremony.

ENGLISH TRADITION
Britons celebrate the drinking of tea on a regular basis at afternoon tea where there is a pause in the day at about 4pm for tea poured from silver or antique teapots with dainty sandwiches or scones with cream and jam.

Flourless chocolate hazelnut cake

PREPARATION TIME 20 MINUTES **COOKING TIME** 1 HOUR (PLUS COOLING TIME) **SERVES** 10

⅓ cup (35g) cocoa powder

⅓ cup (80ml) water

150g dark eating chocolate, melted

150g butter, melted

1 ⅓ cups (295g) firmly packed brown sugar

1 cup (100g) hazelnut meal

4 eggs, separated

1 tablespoon cocoa powder, extra

1 Preheat oven to 180°C/160°C fan-forced. Grease deep 20cm-round cake pan; line base and side with baking paper.

2 Blend cocoa with the water in large bowl until smooth. Stir in chocolate, butter, sugar, hazelnut meal and egg yolks.

3 Beat egg whites in small bowl with electric mixer until soft peaks form; fold into chocolate mixture in two batches. Pour mixture into pan.

4 Bake cake about 1 hour. Stand cake in pan 15 minutes; turn, top-side up, onto wire rack to cool. Dust with sifted extra cocoa.

Flourless (making this recipe gluten-free) cakes have a delightful texture and are now very popular in restaurants. They are simple to make, we're not sure why more home-cooks don't make them. Almond meal can be used instead of hazelnut meal. Serve slim wedges of cake with whipped cream and some berries of your choice.

Gluten-free orange syrup cake

PREPARATION TIME 25 MINUTES **COOKING TIME** 1 HOUR 15 MINUTES **SERVES** 10

185g butter, softened

1 tablespoon finely grated orange rind

1 ¼ cups (275g) caster sugar

6 eggs

3 cups (375g) almond meal

¾ cup (60g) desiccated coconut

¾ cup (110g) rice flour

1 teaspoon gluten-free baking powder

ORANGE SYRUP

1 large orange (300g)

⅓ cup (75g) caster sugar

⅓ cup (80ml) water

1 Preheat oven to 180°C/160°C fan-forced. Grease 20cm baba cake pan well.

2 Beat butter, rind and sugar in medium bowl with electric mixer until light and fluffy. Beat in eggs, one at a time; stir in almond meal, coconut and sifted flour and baking powder. Spread mixture into pan.

3 Bake cake about 1 hour. Stand cake in pan 5 minutes; turn, top-side up, onto wire rack over tray.

4 Meanwhile, make orange syrup; pour hot syrup over hot cake. Serve warm or cold.

ORANGE SYRUP Peel rind thinly from orange; cut into thin strips. Squeeze ⅓ cup juice from orange into small saucepan; add rind, sugar and the water. Stir over heat, without boiling, until sugar dissolves. Simmer, uncovered, without stirring, 10 minutes.

FLOURLESS CHOCOLATE HAZELNUT CAKE

The secret to making this sponge successfully is in the beating. The eggs must be beaten in a small bowl for maximum volume and the eggs must be thick and holding their own shape before the sugar is added gradually. Make sure every grain of sugar is dissolved, then gently, carefully and quickly fold in the cornflour. The sponge will shrink a little in the pan. Either split the sponge, then re-join the halves with jam and whipped cream, or simply top the delicate sponge with jam and cream.

Wheat-free sponge

PREPARATION TIME 15 MINUTES **COOKING TIME** 20 MINUTES **SERVES** 8

3 eggs
½ cup (110g) caster sugar
¾ cup (110g) maize cornflour

1 Preheat oven to 180°C/160°C fan-forced. Grease 20cm-round cake pan; line base with baking paper.
2 Beat eggs in small bowl with electric mixer until thick and creamy. Add sugar, 1 tablespoon at a time, beating after each addition until sugar dissolves. Gently fold in triple-sifted cornflour. Spread mixture into pan.
3 Bake cake about 20 minutes. Turn cake onto wire rack to cool.

Egg-free chocolate cake

PREPARATION TIME 15 MINUTES (PLUS COOLING TIME) **COOKING TIME** 1 HOUR 20 MINUTES **SERVES** 8-10

125g butter, chopped coarsely
100g dark cooking chocolate, chopped coarsely
¾ cup (180ml) milk
¾ cup (165g) caster sugar
1 teaspoon vanilla extract
1 cup (150g) self-raising-flour
½ cup (75g) plain flour
2 tablespoons cocoa powder

FUDGE FROSTING
50g butter
¼ cup (55g) caster sugar
2 tablespoons water
¾ cup (120g) icing sugar
2 tablespoons cocoa powder

1 Preheat oven to 150°C/130°C fan-forced. Grease deep 20cm-round cake pan; line base and side with baking paper.
2 Stir butter, chocolate, milk and sugar in medium saucepan over low heat, without boiling, until smooth. Transfer mixture to large bowl; cool to warm. Whisk in extract, sifted flours and cocoa until smooth. Pour mixture into pan.
3 Bake cake about 1 hour 10 minutes. Stand cake in pan 5 minutes; turn, top-side up, onto wire rack to cool.
4 Meanwhile, make fudge frosting; spread over top of cake.

FUDGE FROSTING Stir butter, caster sugar and the water in small saucepan over heat, without boiling, until sugar is dissolved. Sift icing sugar and cocoa into heatproof bowl; gradually stir in hot butter mixture. Cover and refrigerate until thick. Beat with wooden spoon until frosting is spreadable.

Gluten-free carrot cake with orange frosting

PREPARATION TIME 25 MINUTES **COOKING TIME** 1 HOUR (PLUS COOLING TIME) **SERVES** 8-10

1 cup (125g) soy flour

¾ cup (110g) maize cornflour

2 teaspoons gluten-free baking powder

1 teaspoon bicarbonate of soda

2 teaspoons mixed spice

1 cup (220g) firmly packed brown sugar

1½ cups (360g) coarsely grated carrot

1 cup (120g) chopped coarsely walnuts

½ cup (125ml) extra light olive oil

½ cup (120g) sour cream

3 eggs

ORANGE FROSTING

125g cream cheese, softened

1 teaspoon finely grated orange rind

1½ cups (240g) pure icing sugar

1 Preheat oven to 160°C/140°C fan-forced. Grease deep 20cm-round cake pan; line base and side with baking paper.

2 Sift flours, baking powder, soda and spice into large bowl; stir in sugar, carrot and nuts. Stir in combined oil, sour cream and eggs. Pour mixture into pan.

3 Bake cake 1 hour. Stand cake in pan 5 minutes; turn, top-side up, onto wire rack to cool.

4 Meanwhile, make orange frosting. Top cake with frosting.

ORANGE FROSTING Beat cream cheese and rind in small bowl with electric mixer until light and fluffy. Gradually beat in sifted icing sugar until smooth.

Be sure to read the packaging of cornflour carefully. Maize is corn — so whichever word appears on the packet is right for you — it's the "wheat" word you need to avoid. You can also use besan flour (chickpea) rather than soy flour.

BISCUITS

Biscuits

Biscuits have existed almost as long as man has known how to grind grain to make flour. Most of the breads of ancient history probably resembled the hard, flat cakes we now know as biscuits. The word "biscuit" dates from Roman times. Their armies marched on *panis biscoctus* — *panis* meaning "bread", *bis* meaning "twice" and *coctus* meaning "cooked". The word travelled to France where it was translated as *biscuit*, Italy as *biscotti* and Spain as *biscochitos*.

Maintaining the military tradition, ship's biscuits and hard tack travelled the world as a hard, nutritionally filling foodstuff that kept well when stored in relatively airtight containers such as tins. Australian women went a few steps further towards palatability during World War I when they adapted Scottish oat cookies to invent the Anzac biscuit to send to their boys at the frontlines of Turkey, France and Germany. The recipe used only ingredients which were long lasting; bound together with golden syrup rather than butter, which was both in short supply and prone to deteriorate in the absence of refrigeration.

In the United States, biscuits are more likely to be called crackers or cookies. When Americans use the term biscuit, they are usually referring to scones.

America has also given the world the biscuit known as the tollhouse or chocolate chip cookie, perhaps invented, but certainly popularised by Ruth Wakefield who introduced it on the menu of her Whitman, Massachusetts Tollhouse restaurant in the 1930s. As the recipes that follow illustrate, biscuit variations are only limited by the imagination. We're sure you'll find some to stimulate yours in this collection of quick and easy tea-time treats.

OVEN TRAYS

It's important to use the correct trays to ensure even baking and browning. We use flat aluminium trays, which have little or no sides. This allows the heat to circulate properly and ensures even browning. Grease the trays lightly with cooking-oil spray or a light and even brushing with a pastry brush that has been dipped in melted butter.

You can bake two or more trays of biscuits at once, so long as the trays don't touch the sides of the oven or the door when it is closed. There should be at least 2cm of space around each tray to allow for heat circulation. To cook the biscuits evenly, you'll need to swap the trays around halfway through baking. Some ovens have hot spots, and if this is the case with yours, it's a good idea to rotate the trays as well, to help with even browning.

PREPARATION AND MIXING

Have all ingredients out on the bench at room temperature before you start. Take care not to over-beat the butter and sugar mixture; beat the butter until it's smooth then add the sugar and beat just until the ingredients are combined. Overbeating can give a too-soft mixture which can cause the biscuits to spread excessively. Add the sifted dry ingredients in two batches to make mixing easier. You may need to transfer the butter and sugar mixture to a larger bowl to make stirring in the dry ingredients easier.

PIPING BAGS

Some of our recipes use a piping bag to force the mixture into decorative shapes. There is also a device called a biscuit or cookie pusher which you can use, though the thickness of the biscuits will vary from ours and you'll need to adjust the baking times. You can also make a basic piping bag by snipping a small hole in the corner of a sturdy, clean plastic bag, though, without fancy tubes, you will only be able to pipe tubular and round shapes.

TESTING IF COOKED

Biscuits generally feel soft in the oven and become firmer as they cool. If they are very soft, loosen with a palette knife or spatula and lift on to a wire rack to cool. Some of the crisper varieties of biscuit are cooled on the oven trays; follow each recipe's instructions. A good test for most types of biscuit is to push the biscuit on the tray gently with your finger; if it moves without breaking, the biscuit is cooked.

STORAGE

Store biscuits in an airtight container. They must be completely cold before storing or they will soften in the container. Biscuits which are to be filled with jam, cream or icing are best filled on the day of serving. If unfilled un-iced biscuits soften, they can be re-crisped by placing them on oven trays and heating in a moderate oven for about 5 minutes.

FREEZING

To freeze un-iced or unfilled biscuits, place the cooked cooled biscuits in an airtight container, with sheets of baking paper between the layers.

TROUBLE SHOOTING

- If the biscuits spread on the tray, the mixture could be too soft due to over-beating the butter and sugar, or the ingredients were measured incorrectly, the wrong flour (such as self-raising when the recipe calls for plain flour) was used or the oven was not hot enough.
- If the biscuits are too hard, the ingredients may have been measured incorrectly, the biscuits baked too long or at too high a temperature or the wrong type of oven trays used.
- If the biscuits are too soft, they may not have been baked long enough, or they may have been stacked on top of each other during cooling. Most biscuits need air circulating around them to crisp. They generally need to rest on the trays for a few minutes to harden slightly before transferring to wire racks to cool completely.
- If the biscuits are too brown underneath, the trays may have been overgreased; excess greasing attracts heat to the base of the biscuit. Incorrect oven position and temperature could also be to blame. Excess sweetening (sugar, honey etc) will also cause overbrowning.

Golden pecan twists

PREPARATION TIME 25 MINUTES **COOKING TIME** 10 MINUTES **MAKES** 30

Walnuts, pistachios, almonds or hazelnuts could all be substituted for pecans in this recipe.

⅓ cup (40g) finely chopped pecans

2 tablespoons golden syrup

125g butter, softened

¼ teaspoon vanilla extract

⅓ cup (75g) caster sugar

1 egg yolk

1 cup (150g) plain flour

1 Preheat oven to 180°C/160°C fan-forced. Grease oven trays; line with baking paper.

2 Combine nuts and half of the golden syrup in small bowl.

3 Beat butter, extract, sugar, egg yolk and remaining golden syrup in small bowl with electric mixer until light and fluffy. Stir in sifted flour.

4 Shape rounded teaspoons of mixture into balls; roll each ball into 12cm log. Twist each log into a loop, overlapping one end over the other. Place twists about 3cm apart on oven trays; top each twist with ½ teaspoon nut mixture.

5 Bake twists about 10 minutes; cool on trays.

Orange, coconut and almond biscotti

PREPARATION TIME 25 MINUTES **COOKING TIME** 1 HOUR (PLUS COOLING TIME) **MAKES** 30

Biscotti (or "biscuit" in Italian) are favourites when served with coffee. Biscotti should be thoroughly dried out in the oven — second time around — they will keep for months in an airtight container at room temperature. For this reason, biscotti make great gifts.

2 eggs

1 cup (220g) caster sugar

1 teaspoon finely grated orange rind

1 ⅓ cups (200g) plain flour

⅓ cup (50g) self-raising flour

⅔ (50g) shredded coconut

1 cup (160g) blanched almonds

1 Preheat oven to 180°C/160°C fan-forced. Grease oven trays.

2 Whisk eggs, sugar and rind in medium bowl. Stir in sifted flours, coconut and nuts; mix to a sticky dough.

3 Knead dough on floured surface until smooth. Divide dough into two portions. Using floured hands, roll each portion into a 20cm log; place logs on oven tray.

4 Bake logs about 35 minutes. Cool logs on tray 10 minutes.

5 Reduce oven to 160°C/140°C fan-forced.

6 Using a serrated knife, cut logs diagonally into 1cm slices. Place slices, in single layer, on ungreased oven trays. Bake biscotti about 25 minutes or until dry and crisp, turning over halfway through cooking. Transfer to wire racks to cool.

GOLDEN PECAN TWISTS

Chocolate and cranberry checkerboard cookies

PREPARATION TIME 30 MINUTES (PLUS REFRIGERATION TIME) **COOKING TIME** 15 MINUTES **MAKES** 30

200g butter, softened

¾ cup (165g) caster sugar

½ teaspoon vanilla extract

1 egg

2 cups (300g) plain flour

1 tablespoon cocoa powder

1 teaspoon finely grated orange rind

¼ cup (40g) finely chopped dried cranberries

1 egg white

1 Beat butter, sugar, extract and egg in medium bowl with electric mixer until light and fluffy. Stir in sifted flour, in two batches.

2 Divide dough in half, knead sifted cocoa into one half; knead rind and cranberries into the other half. Using ruler, shape each batch of dough into 4.5cm x 4.5cm x 15cm rectangular bars. Wrap each in baking paper; refrigerate 30 minutes.

3 Cut each bar lengthways equally into three slices. Cut each slice lengthways equally into three; you will have nine 1.5cm x 1.5cm x 1.5cm slices from each bar of dough.

4 Brush each slice of dough with egg white, stack alternate flavours together in threes. Stick three stacks together to recreate the log; repeat with second log. Refrigerate 30 minutes.

5 Preheat oven to 180°C/160°C fan-forced. Grease oven trays; line with baking paper.

6 Using a sharp knife, cut each log crossways into 1cm slices. Place, cut-side up, onto oven trays about 3cm apart.

7 Bake biscuits about 15 minutes. Stand on trays 5 minutes; transfer to wire racks to cool.

For steps on assembling checkerboard cookies, see page 636. Checkerboard cookies look and taste wonderful. These biscuits make a perfect gift. Stack the cookies, then wrap securely in cellophane to keep airtight. They will keep fresh for a week or two.

Pistachio shortbread mounds

PREPARATION TIME 15 MINUTES **COOKING TIME** 25 MINUTES **MAKES** 35

⅔ cup (70g) roasted pistachios

250g butter, softened

1 cup (160g) icing sugar

1½ cups (225g) plain flour

2 tablespoons rice flour

2 tablespoons cornflour

¾ cup (90g) almond meal

⅓ cup (55g) icing sugar, extra

1 Preheat oven to 150°C/130°C fan-forced. Grease oven trays; line with baking paper.

2 Coarsely chop half the nuts.

3 Beat butter and sifted icing sugar in small bowl with electric mixer until light and fluffy. Transfer mixture to large bowl; stir in sifted flours, almond meal and chopped nuts.

4 Shape level tablespoons of mixture into mounds; place about 3cm apart on oven trays. Press one whole nut on each mound.

5 Bake mounds about 25 minutes. Stand mounds on tray 5 minutes; transfer to wire racks to cool. Serve dusted thickly with extra sifted icing sugar.

You will recognise the "look" of these mounds if you've ever been into a shop which sells middle eastern goodies. These little mounds will keep well in an airtight container for several weeks.

Peanut brittle cookies

PREPARATION TIME 25 MINUTES **COOKING TIME** 20 MINUTES **MAKES** 18

125g butter, softened

¼ cup (70g) crunchy peanut butter

½ cup (100g) firmly packed brown sugar

1 egg

1½ cups (225g) plain flour

½ teaspoon bicarbonate of soda

PEANUT BRITTLE

¾ cup (100g) roasted unsalted peanuts

½ cup (110g) caster sugar

2 tablespoons water

1 Make peanut brittle.

2 Preheat oven to 160°C/140°C fan-forced. Grease oven trays; line with baking paper.

3 Beat butter, peanut butter, sugar and egg in small bowl with electric mixer until combined. Stir in sifted dry ingredients and crushed peanut brittle.

4 Roll heaped teaspoons of mixture into balls with floured hands. Place about 5cm apart on oven trays; flatten slightly.

5 Bake cookies about 12 minutes. Cool on trays.

PEANUT BRITTLE Place nuts on baking-paper-lined oven tray. Stir sugar and the water in small frying pan over heat, without boiling, until sugar is dissolved; bring to the boil. Boil, uncovered, without stirring, until golden brown. Pour mixture over nuts; leave until set. Crush coarsely in food processor.

Why don't you make double the quantity of peanut brittle? Use a medium heavy-based frying pan for a large quantity — use half for these cookies, then keep the remaining brittle in an airtight jar for another use. Try the brittle sprinkled over vanilla ice-cream — maybe with chocolate topping — for a great quick dessert.

Coconut fortune cookies

PREPARATION TIME 25 MINUTES **COOKING TIME** 5 MINUTES **MAKES** 12

2 egg whites

⅓ cup (75g) caster sugar

⅓ cup (50g) plain flour

1 teaspoon coconut essence

30g butter, melted

½ teaspoon finely grated lime rind

2 tablespoons desiccated coconut

12 small paper messages

1 Preheat oven to 160°C/140°C fan-forced. Grease oven tray; line with baking paper. Mark two 9cm circles on paper.

2 Beat egg whites in small bowl with electric mixer until soft peaks form; gradually add sugar, beating until dissolved between additions. Fold in sifted flour, essence, butter and rind.

3 Drop one level tablespoon of mixture into centre of each circle on oven tray, spread evenly to cover circle completely; sprinkle with a little coconut. Bake about 5 minutes.

4 Working quickly, loosen cookies from tray, place message in the centre of cookies; fold in half then gently bend cookies over edge of a glass. Cool 30 seconds. Transfer to wire rack to cool. Repeat with remaining cookie mixture and coconut.

Fortune cookies can be personalised by using special messages for your loved ones. Use a sheet of A4 paper cut into narrow strips and either write a messafe using a ballpoint pen or print out a series of typed messages if you have access to a computer and printer. Bake the first two cookies, but have another tray ready to go into the oven when you remove the first two. You'll soon get into a rhythm.

Basic vanilla biscuits

PREPARATION TIME 20 MINUTES **COOKING TIME** 15 MINUTES **MAKES** 30

200g butter, softened
½ teaspoon vanilla extract
1 cup (160g) icing sugar
1 egg
1¾ cups (260g) plain flour
½ teaspoon bicarbonate of soda

1 Preheat oven to 170°C/150°C fan-forced. Grease oven trays; line with baking paper.
2 Beat butter, extract, sifted icing sugar and egg in small bowl with electric mixer until light and fluffy. Transfer mixture to medium bowl; stir in sifted flour and soda, in two batches.
3 Roll level tablespoons of dough into balls; place about 3cm apart on oven trays.
4 Bake biscuits about 15 minutes; cool on trays.

VARIATIONS

CRANBERRY & COCONUT Stir ½ cup (65g) dried cranberries and ½ cup (40g) shredded coconut into basic biscuit mixture before flour and soda are added.

PEAR & GINGER Stir ¼ cup (35g) finely chopped dried pears, ¼ cup (55g) coarsely chopped glacé ginger and ½ cup (45g) rolled oats into basic biscuit mixture before flour and soda are added.

CHOC CHIP Stir ½ cup (95g) dark Choc Bits into basic biscuit mixture before flour and soda are added. Roll level tablespoons of dough into balls then roll balls in a mixture of 1 tablespoon caster sugar, 2 teaspoons ground nutmeg and 2 teaspoons ground cinnamon.

BROWN SUGAR & PECAN Substitute 1 cup (220g) firmly packed brown sugar for the icing sugar in the basic biscuit mixture. Stir ½ cup (60g) coarsely chopped pecans into basic biscuit mixture before flour and soda are added.

If you're after a good basic buttery biscuit then look no further. We've suggested several variations here, but the sky's the limit. The biscuits can be flavoured with any essence, citrus rinds, many different varieties of finely chopped dried fruit and nuts. Not to mention a whole range of different flavoured icings to top these biscuits. Make tiny, bite-sized biscuits, join them with ganache or butter cream — the variations are endless.

1 CRANBERRY & COCONUT **2** PEAR & GINGER
3 CHOC CHIP **4** BROWN SUGAR & PECAN

1 2

3 4

Chocolate lace crisps

PREPARATION TIME 25 MINUTES (PLUS REFRIGERATION TIME) **COOKING TIME** 20 MINUTES **MAKES** 24

100g dark cooking chocolate, chopped coarsely

80g butter, chopped coarsely

1 cup (220g) caster sugar

1 egg

1 cup (150g) plain flour

2 tablespoons cocoa powder

¼ teaspoon bicarbonate of soda

¼ cup (40g) icing sugar

1 Melt chocolate and butter in small saucepan over low heat.

2 Transfer chocolate mixture to medium bowl; sir in caster sugar, egg and sifted flour, cocoa and soda. Cover; refrigerate 15 minutes or until mixture is firm enough to handle.

3 Preheat oven to 180°C/160°C fan-forced. Grease oven trays; line with baking paper.

4 Roll level tablespoons of mixture into balls; roll each ball in sifted icing sugar, place about 8cm apart on trays.

5 Bake crisps about 15 minutes; cool on trays.

Baking paper is your friend for most biscuit baking, nothing sticks or burns and washing up is a breeze. You only need to grease the oven tray in the middle to anchor the baking paper. Don't grease the oven tray out to the edges, the greasing will burn on and be difficult to wash off.

Oat and bran biscuits

PREPARATION TIME 15 MINUTES (PLUS REFRIGERATION TIME) **COOKING TIME** 15 MINUTES **MAKES** 30

1 cup (150g) plain flour

1 cup (60g) unprocessed bran

¾ cup (60g) rolled oats

½ teaspoon bicarbonate of soda

60g butter, chopped coarsely

½ cup (110g) caster sugar

1 egg

2 tablespoons water, approximately

1 Process flour, bran, oats, soda and butter until crumbly; add sugar, egg and enough of the water to make a firm dough. Knead dough on lightly floured surface until smooth. Cover; refrigerate 30 minutes.

2 Preheat oven to 180°C/160°C fan-forced. Grease oven trays; line with baking paper.

3 Divide dough in half; roll each half between sheets of baking paper to about 5mm thickness. Cut dough into 7cm rounds; place about 2cm apart on trays.

4 Bake biscuits about 15 minutes. Stand on trays 5 minutes; transfer to wire rack to cool.

CHOCOLATE LACE CRISPS

Date and walnut scrolls

PREPARATION TIME 30 MINUTES (PLUS REFRIGERATION TIME) **COOKING TIME** 30 MINUTES **MAKES** 28

If you're in a hurry and need to cool the date filling quickly, spread the filling, as soon as it becomes thick and pulpy, out thinly into a shallow cake pan — a lamington or swiss roll pan would be good. Put it in the fridge and it will cool down in 10 to 15 minutes.

125g butter, softened

⅓ cup (75g) caster sugar

1 teaspoon ground cardamom

1 egg

1½ cups (225g) plain flour

1 cup (100g) roasted walnuts, ground finely

DATE FILLING

2 cups (250g) coarsely chopped dried dates

¼ cup (55g) caster sugar

2 teaspoons finely grated lemon rind

⅓ cup (80ml) lemon juice

¼ teaspoon ground cardamom

½ cup (125ml) water

1 Make date filling.

2 Beat butter, sugar, cardamom and egg in small bowl with electric mixer until combined. Stir in sifted flour and nuts.

3 Knead dough on floured surface until smooth; divide into two portions. Roll each portion between sheets of baking paper to 15cm x 30cm rectangles; refrigerate 20 minutes.

4 Spread filling evenly over the two rectangles, leaving 1cm border. Using paper as a guide, roll rectangles tightly from short side to enclose filling. Wrap rolls in baking paper; refrigerate 30 minutes.

5 Preheat oven to 190°C/170°C fan-forced. Grease oven trays; line with baking paper.

6 Trim edges of roll; cut each roll into 1cm slices. Place slices cut-side up on oven trays; bake about 20 minutes.

DATE FILLING Stir ingredients in medium saucepan over heat, without boiling, until sugar is dissolved; bring to the boil. Reduce heat, simmer, uncovered, stirring occasionally, about 5 minutes or until mixture is thick and pulpy.

Maple-syrup butter cookies

PREPARATION TIME 20 MINUTES **COOKING TIME** 15 MINUTES **MAKES** 24

This mixture would work perfectly in a biscuit pusher or cookie press, or simply roll the mixture into balls, after flouring your hands, put the balls about 5cm apart on the trays then flatten them a little, either with your floured fingers or with a fork.

125g butter, softened

½ teaspoon vanilla extract

⅓ cup (80ml) maple syrup

¾ cup (110g) plain flour

¼ cup (35g) cornflour

1 Preheat oven to 180°C/160°C fan-forced. Grease oven trays; line with baking paper.

2 Beat butter, extract and maple syrup in small bowl with electric mixer until light and fluffy; stir in sifted flours.

3 Spoon mixture into piping bag fitted with 1cm fluted tube. Pipe stars about 3cm apart onto trays.

4 Bake cookies about 15 minutes. Cool on trays.

Almond and plum crescents

PREPARATION TIME 30 MINUTES (PLUS REFRIGERATION TIME) **COOKING TIME** 25 MINUTES **MAKES** 28

1½ cups (225g) plain flour

½ cup (60g) almond meal

¼ cup (55g) caster sugar

2 teaspoons finely grated
lemon rind

90g cream cheese,
chopped coarsely

90g butter, chopped coarsely

2 tablespoons buttermilk

1 egg white

¼ cup (20g) flaked almonds,
crushed lightly

FILLING

⅓ cup (60g) finely chopped
seeded prunes

¼ cup (80g) plum jam

¼ cup (55g) caster sugar

½ teaspoon ground cinnamon

*We love this recipe — sweet
and tart best describes
the flavour of the crescents.
Roll the dough as evenly
as you can, rolling from
the centre to the outside —
don't roll over the edge. Use
a plate or a cake pan as a
guide when you're cutting
out the 22cm rounds.*

1 Process flour, almond meal, sugar and rind until combined. Add cream cheese and butter, pulse until crumbly. Add buttermilk, process until ingredients come together.

2 Knead dough on floured surface until smooth. Divide dough in half. Roll each half between sheets of baking paper until large enough to be cut into 22cm rounds; refrigerate 30 minutes.

3 Preheat oven to 180°C/160°C fan-forced. Grease oven trays; line with baking paper.

4 Make filling by combining ingredients in small bowl.

5 Cut each round into eight wedges, spread wedges with filling; roll from wide end into crescents. Place on oven trays, brush with egg white, sprinkle with nuts.

6 Bake crescents about 25 minutes. Cool on trays.

Wholemeal rosemary butter rounds

PREPARATION TIME 20 MINUTES **COOKING TIME** 15 MINUTES **MAKES** 28

125g butter, softened

2 teaspoons finely grated
orange rind

1 cup (220g) firmly packed
brown sugar

1⅓ cups (200g) wholemeal
self-raising flour

⅔ cup (100g) raisins, halved

1 cup (100g) coarsely chopped
roasted walnuts

2 teaspoons dried rosemary

⅓ cup (80ml) orange juice

⅔ cup (50g) desiccated coconut

⅔ cup (60g) rolled oats

1 Preheat oven to 180°C/160°C fan-forced. Grease oven trays; line with baking paper.

2 Beat butter, rind and sugar in small bowl with electric mixer until combined. Transfer to medium bowl; stir in sifted flour then remaining ingredients.

3 Roll rounded tablespoons of mixture into balls, place about 5cm apart on oven trays; flatten slightly. Bake about 15 minutes. Cool biscuits on trays.

Chocolate chip cookies

PREPARATION TIME 15 MINUTES **COOKING TIME** 15 MINUTES **MAKES** 24

125g butter, softened

½ teaspoon vanilla extract

⅓ cup (75g) caster sugar

⅓ cup (75g) firmly packed brown sugar

1 egg

1 cup (150g) plain flour

½ teaspoon bicarbonate of soda

150g milk eating chocolate, chopped coarsely

½ cup (50g) coarsely chopped roasted walnuts

1 Preheat oven to 180°C/160°C fan-forced. Grease oven trays; line with baking paper.

2 Beat butter, extract, sugars and egg in small bowl with electric mixer until combined. Transfer mixture to medium bowl; stir in sifted flour and soda then chocolate and nuts.

3 Drop level tablespoons of mixture about 5cm apart onto oven trays.

4 Bake cookies about 15 minutes; cool on trays.

Don't overbeat the butter, sugar and egg mixture or the cookies will spread too much during baking. You can use dark or white chocolate in place of the milk chocolate if you like — or a mixture of any types of chocolate.

Macadamia anzacs

PREPARATION TIME 20 MINUTES **COOKING TIME** 20 MINUTES **MAKES** 32

125g butter, chopped coarsely

2 tablespoons golden syrup

½ teaspoon bicarbonate of soda

2 tablespoons water

1 cup (90g) rolled oats

1 cup (150g) plain flour

1 cup (220g) firmly packed brown sugar

¾ cup (60g) desiccated coconut

½ cup (65g) finely chopped macadamias

¼ cup (45g) finely chopped glacé ginger

1 Preheat oven to 180°C/160°C fan-forced. Grease oven trays; line with baking paper.

2 Stir butter and golden syrup in medium saucepan over low heat until smooth. Stir in soda, then remaining ingredients.

3 Roll level tablespoons of mixture into balls. Place about 5cm apart on oven trays; flatten slightly.

4 Bake biscuits about 15 minutes. Cool on trays.

Experiment by baking just two or three biscuits first until you determine how you want the texture of the Anzacs to be when they're cold. We like them a bit on the soft side — you might like them crisp all the way through. It's all in the baking time and oven temperature, make a note of the time and temperature for the next time you bake Anzacs. If you prefer, leave the nuts and ginger out of the recipe.

CHOCOLATE CHIP COOKIES

Pink macaroons

PREPARATION TIME 30 MINUTES **COOKING TIME** 25 MINUTES **MAKES** 18

3 egg whites

2 tablespoons caster sugar

pink food colouring

1 ¼ cups (200g) icing sugar

1 cup (120g) almond meal

2 tablespoons icing sugar, extra

WHITE CHOCOLATE GANACHE

100g white eating chocolate, chopped coarsely

2 tablespoons cream

1 Make white chocolate ganache.

2 Grease oven trays; line with baking paper.

3 Beat egg whites in small bowl with electric mixer until soft peaks form. Add caster sugar and food colouring, beat until sugar dissolves. Transfer mixture to large bowl; fold in sifted icing sugar and almond meal, in two batches.

4 Spoon mixture into large piping bag fitted with 1.5cm plain tube. Pipe 36 x 4cm rounds, 2cm apart, onto trays. Tap trays on bench top to help macaroons to spread slightly. Dust with sifted extra icing sugar; stand 15 minutes.

5 Meanwhile, preheat oven to 150°C/130°C fan-forced.

6 Bake macaroons 20 minutes. Stand on trays 5 minutes; transfer to wire rack to cool.

7 Sandwich macaroons with ganache.

WHITE CHOCOLATE GANACHE Stir chocolate and cream in small saucepan over low heat until smooth. Transfer mixture to small bowl. Cover; refrigerate until mixture is spreadable.

Crunchy muesli cookies

PREPARATION TIME 15 MINUTES **COOKING TIME** 25 MINUTES **MAKES** 36

1 cup (90g) rolled oats

1 cup (150g) plain flour

1 cup (220g) caster sugar

2 teaspoons ground cinnamon

¼ cup (35g) dried cranberries

⅓ cup (55g) finely chopped dried apricots

½ cup (70g) slivered almonds

125g butter, chopped coarsely

2 tablespoons golden syrup

½ teaspoon bicarbonate of soda

1 tablespoon boiling water

1 Preheat oven to 150°C/130°C fan-forced. Grease oven trays; line with baking paper.

2 Combine oats, flour, sugar, cinnamon, dried fruit and nuts in large bowl.

3 Melt butter with golden syrup in small saucepan over low heat; add combined soda and the boiling water. Stir warm butter mixture into dry ingredients.

4 Roll level tablespoons of mixture into balls, place about 5cm apart on oven trays; flatten slightly. Bake cookies about 20 minutes; cool on trays.

PINK MACAROONS

1

2

3

4

Scottish shortbread

PREPARATION TIME 20 MINUTES (PLUS REFRIGERATION TIME) **COOKING TIME** 40 MINUTES **MAKES** 16

250g butter, softened
⅓ cup (75g) caster sugar
¼ cup (35g) rice flour
2¼ cups (335g) plain flour
2 tablespoons white sugar

1 Preheat oven to 150°C/130°C fan-forced. Grease two oven trays.
2 Beat butter and caster sugar in medium bowl with electric mixer until light and fluffy; stir in sifted flours, in two batches. Knead on floured surface until smooth.
3 Divide mixture in half; shape into two 20cm rounds on oven trays. Mark each round into eight wedges, prick with fork, pinch edges with fingers. Sprinkle with white sugar.
4 Bake about 40 minutes. Stand 5 minutes then, using sharp knife, cut shortbread into wedges along marked lines; cool on trays.

We found — after much testing and tasting — that by using half regular (salted) and half unsalted butter in shortbread recipes we achieved the taste we liked best. Shortbread should be quite pale in colour after it's cooked. The rice flour (ground rice) is the ingredient that makes shortbread "short" — a particular hard-to-describe kind of mouth-feel.

Vanilla bean thins

PREPARATION TIME 20 MINUTES **COOKING TIME** 5 MINUTES **MAKES** 24

1 vanilla bean
30g butter, softened
¼ cup (55g) caster sugar
1 egg white, beaten lightly
¼ cup (35g) plain flour

1 Preheat oven to 200°C/180°C fan-forced. Grease oven trays; line with baking paper.
2 Halve vanilla bean lengthways; scrape seeds into medium bowl, discard pod. Add butter and sugar to bowl; stir until combined. Stir in egg white and sifted flour.
3 Spoon mixture into piping bag fitted with 5mm plain tube. Pipe 6cm-long strips (making them slightly wider at both ends) about 5cm apart on trays.
4 Bake biscuits about 5 minutes or until edges are browned lightly; cool on trays.

People who bake a lot usually have a large jar of caster sugar in the pantry containing at least two vanilla beans. Over time the beans impart a delicate vanilla flavour to the sugar. If you have some vanilla sugar on the go, you can happily omit vanilla beans and extract from our recipes when we call for caster sugar and vanilla.

1 SCOTTISH SHORTBREAD **2** VANILLA BEAN THINS
3 JAM DROPS [P 312] **4** ICED MARSHMALLOW BUTTERFLIES [P 312]

To make the "flowers" for these cookies dip the end of the handle of a wooden spoon in flour. Start the flower by pushing the spoon gently into the centres of the slightly flattened balls, then make five "petals" using the end of the spoon around the flower centres. You'll need to flour the end of the spoon quite often as you make the flowers.

Jam drops

PREPARATION TIME 15 MINUTES **COOKING TIME** 15 MINUTES **MAKES** 26

125g butter, softened

½ teaspoon vanilla extract

½ cup (110g) caster sugar

1 cup (120g) almond meal

1 egg

1 cup (150g) plain flour

1 teaspoon finely grated lemon rind

⅓ cup (110g) raspberry jam

2 tablespoons apricot jam

1 Preheat oven to 180°C/160°C fan-forced. Grease oven trays; line with baking paper.

2 Beat butter, extract, sugar and almond meal in small bowl with electric mixer until light and fluffy. Beat in egg; stir in sifted flour.

3 Divide rind between both jams; mix well.

4 Roll level tablespoons of mixture into balls; place about 5cm apart on oven trays, flatten slightly. Using end of a wooden spoon, press a flower shape (about 1cm deep) into dough; fill each hole with a little jam, using apricot jam for centres and raspberry jam for petals of flowers.

5 Bake drops about 15 minutes. Cool on trays.

Butterfly-shaped cutters can be bought from cookware shops and cake decorating suppliers.

Iced marshmallow butterflies

PREPARATION TIME 30 MINUTES (PLUS REFRIGERATION TIME) **COOKING TIME** 12 MINUTES **MAKES** 16

125g butter, softened

¾ cup (165g) caster sugar

1 egg

1½ cups (225g) plain flour

¼ cup (35g) self-raising flour

½ cup (40g) desiccated coconut

⅓ cup (25g) desiccated coconut, extra

TOPPING

¼ cup (80g) strawberry jam, warmed, strained, cooled

48 pink marshmallows

48 white marshmallows

1 Beat butter, sugar and egg in small bowl with electric mixer until light and fluffy. Stir in sifted flours and coconut, in two batches.

2 Knead dough on floured surface until smooth. Roll dough between sheets of baking paper until 5mm thick; refrigerate 30 minutes.

3 Preheat oven to 180°C/160°C fan-forced. Grease oven trays; line with baking paper.

4 Using 11.5cm butterfly cutter, cut 16 shapes from dough. Place about 3cm apart on oven trays. Bake about 12 minutes.

5 Meanwhile, using scissors, quarter marshmallows. Press marshmallows cut-side down onto hot butterfly wings; trim marshmallows to the shape of the wings if necessary. Brush marshmallows with a little water; sprinkle with extra coconut. Bake about 1 minute or until marshmallows soften slightly.

6 Pipe jam down centre of each butterfly. Cool on wire racks.

Orange hazelnut butter yoyo bites

PREPARATION TIME 15 MINUTES **COOKING TIME** 15 MINUTES **MAKES** 20

250g unsalted butter, softened

1 teaspoon vanilla extract

½ cup (80g) icing sugar

1½ cups (225g) plain flour

½ cup (75g) cornflour

ORANGE HAZELNUT BUTTER

80g unsalted butter, softened

2 teaspoons finely grated orange rind

⅔ cup (110g) icing sugar

1 tablespoon hazelnut meal

1 Preheat oven to 160°C/140°C fan-forced. Grease oven trays; line with baking paper.

2 Beat butter, extract and sifted icing sugar in small bowl with electric mixer until light and fluffy; stir in sifted flours, in two batches.

3 Roll rounded teaspoons of mixture into balls; place about 3cm apart on trays. Using fork dusted with flour, press tines gently onto each biscuit to flatten slightly.

4 Bake biscuits about 15 minutes; cool on trays.

5 Meanwhile, make orange hazelnut butter. Sandwich biscuits with the butter.

ORANGE HAZELNUT BUTTER Beat butter, rind and sifted icing sugar in small bowl with electric mixer until light and fluffy. Stir in meal.

Fill the yoyos just before you're ready to eat them, the butter will soften the biscuits quite fast. A little dusting of sifted sugar makes the yoyos even prettier.

Caramel ginger crunchies

PREPARATION TIME 20 MINUTES **COOKING TIME** 20 MINUTES **MAKES** 45

2 cups (300g) plain flour

½ teaspoon bicarbonate of soda

1 teaspoon ground cinnamon

2 teaspoons ground ginger

1 cup (220g) caster sugar

125g cold butter, chopped

1 egg

1 teaspoon golden syrup

2 tablespoons finely chopped glacé ginger

45 wrapped hard caramels

1 Preheat oven to 160°C/140°C fan-forced. Grease oven trays; line with baking paper.

2 Process sifted dry ingredients with butter until mixture is crumbly; add egg, golden syrup and ginger, process until ingredients come together. Knead on floured surface until smooth.

3 Roll rounded teaspoons of mixture into balls; flatten slightly. Place about 3cm apart on oven trays.

4 Bake biscuits 13 minutes. Place one caramel on top of each hot biscuit; bake further 7 minutes or until caramel begins to melt. Cool on trays.

Make sure you buy hard caramels, those which resemble boiled lollies.

Apple crumble custard creams

PREPARATION TIME 30 MINUTES (PLUS REFRIGERATION TIME) **COOKING TIME** 12 MINUTES **MAKES** 20

1 medium apple (150g), peeled, cored, chopped coarsely

2 teaspoons water

125g butter, softened

⅓ cup (75g) firmly packed brown sugar

2 tablespoons apple concentrate

1 cup (150g) self-raising flour

¾ cup (110g) plain flour

¼ cup (30g) oat bran

¼ cup (20g) desiccated coconut

1 teaspoon ground cinnamon

1 tablespoon icing sugar

CUSTARD CREAM

1 tablespoon custard powder

1 tablespoon caster sugar

½ cup (125ml) milk

¼ teaspoon vanilla extract

125g cream cheese, softened

1 Stew apple with the water in small saucepan, covered, over medium heat until tender. Mash with a fork; cool.

2 Beat butter, sugar and concentrate in small bowl with electric mixer until combined. Transfer mixture to medium bowl; stir in sifted flours, oat bran, stewed apple, coconut and cinnamon, in two batches.

3 Knead dough on floured surface until smooth. Roll dough between sheets of baking paper until 3mm thick; refrigerate 30 minutes.

4 Preheat oven to 180°C/160°C fan-forced. Grease oven trays; line with baking paper.

5 Using 6.5cm apple cutter, cut 40 shapes from dough. Place shapes about 3cm apart on oven trays.

6 Bake biscuits about 12 minutes. Cool on wire racks.

7 Meanwhile, make custard cream. Sandwich biscuits with custard cream. Serve dusted with sifted icing sugar.

CUSTARD CREAM Blend custard powder and sugar with milk and extract in small saucepan; stir over heat until mixture boils and thickens. Remove from heat, cover surface with plastic wrap; cool. Beat cream cheese in small bowl with electric mixer until smooth. Add custard; beat until combined.

Beautiful biscuits

We used plain oval biscuits, spread with royal icing (see recipe on page 592) topped with simple decorations.

CRITTERS
Cute little sugary critters can be bought from supermarkets, sweets shops and cake decorating suppliers. Position them on the icing before it sets.

HEARTS
Heart-shaped lollies can be bought from sweets shops. Position them on the icing before it sets. Use the hearts to outline various shapes, such as diamonds or stars, make numbers, or, the initial of each guest.

BUTTERFLY
Butterflies can be bought from supermarkets, position them before the icing sets. Use some of the royal icing to pipe flowers onto the set icing.

GHOSTS
These biscuits would be perfect for Halloween. Use fruit allsorts, sliced crossways for the eyes, and jelly beans for the mouths, position the lollies before the icing sets.

FLOWERS
Make the leaves and stems before you ice the biscuits. Cut fine slices of mint leaves to make the leaves and stems. Ice the biscuits, position the stems and leaves immediately, then position the flowers. The flowers can be found in the baking section of supermarkets.

ABC
Letters can be bought from sweets shops, like these pictured, or from supermarkets in the baking section, or, cut out of rolled-out ready-made soft icing or modelling paste. Position the lollies before the icing sets.

FUNNY FACES

Use Smarties or M&M's to make the eyes and noses, use rainbow choc chips to outline the mouths. Position the lollies before the icing sets.

ROCKET MAN

The two top sections are shaped from pieces taken from disassembled licorice allsorts, we used M&M's on the top section. The feet are made from fruit allsorts. Assemble the rocket man on the biscuit before the icing sets.

MINI MUSK DOTS

These little lollies come in various pastel shades, and are bought from sweets shops. Push the lollies into the icing straight after the biscuits have been iced.

SPRINKLES

Coloured sprinkles, hundreds and thousands — they come in all shapes, colours and sizes these days and are usually found in the baking section of supermarkets. They must be sprinkled on the icing straight after spreading it on the biscuits, or, they'll simply roll off. This icing gets a crust as soon as it's exposed to air.

RIBBONS & BOWS

We made the ribbons and bows by cutting very thin strips from red sour straps. Position the ribbons before the icing sets, secure the bows to the ribbons with a tiny dot of the icing.

RAINBOW STRIPES

Cut very fine strips from rainbow sour straps, then position the strips carefully on the icing before it sets.

Decadent mocha fingers

PREPARATION TIME 30 MINUTES (PLUS REFRIGERATION TIME) **COOKING TIME** 20 MINUTES **MAKES** 25

1 teaspoon instant coffee granules

2 teaspoons boiling water

125g butter, softened

¾ cup (165g) firmly packed brown sugar

1 egg

1½ cups (225g) plain flour

¼ cup (35g) self-raising flour

¼ cup (25g) cocoa powder

75 roasted coffee beans

MOCHA CUSTARD

2 tablespoons custard powder

2 tablespoons caster sugar

60g dark eating chocolate, chopped roughly

1 cup (250ml) milk

1 tablespoon coffee-flavoured liqueur

1 Blend coffee with the water. Beat butter, sugar and egg in small bowl with electric mixer until combined. Stir in coffee mixture, sifted flours and cocoa, in two batches.

2 Knead dough on floured surface until smooth; roll dough between sheets of baking paper until 4mm thick. Cover; refrigerate 30 minutes.

3 Preheat oven to 180°C/160°C fan-forced. Grease oven trays; line with baking paper.

4 Make mocha custard.

5 Using 8.5cm square cutter, cut out 25 shapes from dough. Halve squares to make 50 rectangles; place on oven trays. Press three coffee beans on half of the rectangles.

6 Bake biscuits about 12 minutes. Cool on wire racks. Spread custard over plain biscuits; top with coffee-bean topped biscuits.

MOCHA CUSTARD Blend custard powder, sugar and chocolate with milk in small saucepan; stir over heat until mixture boils and thickens. Remove from heat, stir in liqueur. Cover surface with plastic wrap; refrigerate until cold.

A square cutter will make it easier to make perfectly shaped biscuits. However, you can easily cut out well-shaped rectangles from the rolled out dough. Be fussy, roll the dough as evenly as you can, then use a ruler and a sharp knife to cut out the rectangles. Use Kahlua or Tia Maria in the custard.

Refrigerator cookies

PREPARATION TIME 20 MINUTES (PLUS REFRIGERATION TIME) **COOKING TIME** 10 MINUTES **MAKES** 50

250g butter, softened

1 cup (160g) icing sugar

2½ cups (375g) plain flour

1 Beat butter and sifted sugar in small bowl with electric mixer until light and fluffy. Transfer to large bowl; stir in sifted flour, in two batches.

2 Knead dough on floured surface until smooth. Divide dough in half; roll each half into a 25cm log. Enclose in plastic wrap; refrigerate about 1 hour or until firm.

3 Preheat oven to 180°C/160°C fan-forced. Grease oven trays.

4 Cut rolls into 1cm slices; place 2cm apart on trays. Bake about 10 minutes. Cool on trays.

The beauty of this recipe is that you can have the dough made and in the fridge, then just slice off as many cookies as you want and bake them. The dough can be flavoured with essences, extracts or citrus rinds and will keep in the fridge for about a week. Or, freeze the logs, for up to about three months.

DECADENT MOCHA FINGERS

Sesame snaps or bars are available from supermarkets either in the confectionery or biscuit section. They are basically sesame seeds set in toffee. If you don't have a square cutter, simply cut the dough into 4.5cm x 9cm rectangles. Use a ruler and a sharp knife to measure and cut the dough.

Lemon grass, ginger and sesame bars

PREPARATION TIME 20 MINUTES (PLUS REFRIGERATION TIME) **COOKING TIME** 15 MINUTES **MAKES** 32

125g butter, softened

⅔ cup (130g) firmly packed grated palm sugar

½ teaspoon ground cardamom

½ teaspoon ground cinnamon

pinch ground nutmeg

pinch ground clove

2 egg yolks

1½ cups (225g) plain flour

10cm stick fresh lemon grass (20g), chopped finely

2 tablespoons finely chopped glacé ginger

32 sesame snaps

1 Beat butter, sugar, spices and egg yolks in small bowl with electric mixer until smooth. Stir in sifted flour, lemon grass and ginger.

2 Knead dough on floured surface until smooth. Roll dough between sheets of baking paper until 5mm thick; refrigerate 30 minutes.

3 Preheat oven to 160°C/140°C fan-forced. Grease oven trays; line with baking paper.

4 Using 9cm square cutter, cut 16 shapes from dough; cut in half to make 32 rectangles. Place about 5cm apart on oven trays; bake 12 minutes.

5 Carefully trim edges of sesame snaps to fit the top of each biscuit. Top each hot biscuit with a sesame snap; bake further 3 minutes. Cool on trays.

There is no need to grease the oven trays for this recipe, the biscuits won't stick to the trays.

Snickerdoodles

PREPARATION TIME 25 MINUTES (PLUS REFRIGERATION TIME) **COOKING TIME** 15 MINUTES **MAKES** 50

250g butter, softened

1 teaspoon vanilla extract

½ cup (110g) firmly packed brown sugar

1 cup (220g) caster sugar

2 eggs

2¾ cups (410g) plain flour

1 teaspoon bicarbonate of soda

½ teaspoon ground nutmeg

1 tablespoon caster sugar, extra

2 teaspoons ground cinnamon

1 Beat butter, extract and sugars in small bowl with electric mixer until light and fluffy. Beat in eggs, one at a time. Transfer mixture to large bowl; stir in sifted flour, soda and nutmeg, in two batches. Cover; refrigerate dough 30 minutes.

2 Preheat oven to 180°C/160°C fan-forced.

3 Combine extra caster sugar and cinnamon in small shallow bowl.Roll level tablespoons of the dough into balls; roll balls in cinnamon sugar. Place balls about 7cm apart on ungreased oven trays.

4 Bake biscuits about 12 minutes. Cool on trays.

LEMON GRASS, GINGER AND SESAME BARS

Pistachio almond crisps

PREPARATION TIME 25 MINUTES **COOKING TIME** 1 HOUR 5 MINUTES (PLUS COOLING TIME) **MAKES** 65

3 egg whites
½ cup (110g) caster sugar
pinch ground cardamom
1 cup (150g) plain flour
½ cup (80g) blanched almonds
½ cup (70g) roasted unsalted pistachios

1 Preheat oven to 160°C/140°C fan-forced. Grease 30cm-square piece of foil.
2 Beat egg whites in small bowl with electric mixer until soft peaks form. Gradually add sugar, beating until dissolved between additions. Transfer mixture to medium bowl; fold in sifted dry ingredients and nuts.
3 Spoon mixture onto foil, shape into 7cm x 25cm log. Enclose firmly in foil; place on oven tray.
4 Bake log about 45 minutes or until firm. Turn log out of foil onto wire rack to cool.
5 Reduce oven to 120°C/100°C fan-forced.
6 Using serrated knife, slice log thinly. Place slices close together in single layer on oven trays. Bake about 20 minutes or until crisp; transfer to wire racks to cool.

If you store the crisps in an airtight container, in a cool dry place, they'll keep for months. The most important thing is to dry out the crisps completely at the second baking. If you have an electric knife you can cut the slices really finely.

Polenta and orange biscuits

PREPARATION TIME 15 MINUTES **COOKING TIME** 15 MINUTES **MAKES** 30

125g butter, softened
2 teaspoons finely grated orange rind
⅔ cup (110g) icing sugar
⅓ cup (55g) polenta
1 cup (150g) plain flour

1 Preheat oven to 180°C/160°C fan-forced. Grease oven trays; line with baking paper.
2 Beat butter, rind and sifted icing sugar in small bowl with electric mixer until combined; stir in polenta and sifted flour.
3 Shape mixture into 30cm-long rectangular log; cut log into 1cm slices. Place slices about 2cm apart on trays.
4 Bake biscuits about 15 minutes. Stand on trays 5 minutes; transfer to wire rack to cool.

1 PISTACHIO ALMOND CRISPS **2** POLENTA AND ORANGE BISCUITS
3 COFFEE HAZELNUT MERINGUES [P 324] **4** RHUBARB CUSTARD MELTING MOMENTS [P 324]

Coffee hazelnut meringues

PREPARATION TIME 10 MINUTES **BAKING TIME** 45 MINUTES (PLUS COOLING TIME) **MAKES** 30

2 teaspoons instant coffee granules

½ teaspoon hot water

3 teaspoons coffee-flavoured liqueur

2 egg whites

½ cup (110g) caster sugar

¼ cup (35g) roasted hazelnuts

1 Preheat oven to 120°C/100°C fan-forced. Grease oven trays; line with baking paper.

2 Dissolve coffee in the water in small jug; stir in liqueur.

3 Beat egg whites in small bowl with electric mixer until soft peaks form. Gradually add sugar, beating until dissolved between additions. Fold in coffee mixture.

4 Spoon mixture into piping bag fitted with 5mm fluted tube. Pipe meringues about 2cm apart on trays; top each meringue with a nut.

5 Bake meringues about 45 minutes. Cool in oven with door ajar.

A piping bag — available from cookware shops — is a really handy thing to have. They are easy to use, much easier than you'd expect, and make the dividing up of a mixture into trays quick and efficient. Buy a few different sizes and shapes of tubes — you'll be surprised how often you'll use them.

Rhubarb custard melting moments

PREPARATION TIME 25 MINUTES **COOKING TIME** 20 MINUTES **MAKES** 25

250g butter, softened

½ teaspoon vanilla extract

½ cup (80g) icing sugar

1 cup (125g) custard powder

1 cup (150g) plain flour

1 tablespoon icing sugar, extra

RHUBARB CUSTARD

1 tablespoon custard powder

1 tablespoon caster sugar

½ cup (125ml) milk

⅓ cup stewed rhubarb

1 Preheat oven to 160°C/140°C fan-forced. Grease oven trays; line with baking paper.

2 Make rhubarb custard.

3 Meanwhile, beat butter, extract and sifted icing sugar in small bowl with electric mixer until light and fluffy. Stir in sifted custard powder and flour, in two batches.

4 With floured hands, roll rounded teaspoons of mixture into balls. Place about 5cm apart on oven trays; flatten slightly with a floured fork.

5 Bake biscuits about 15 minutes. Stand on trays 5 minutes; transfer to wire racks to cool.

6 Sandwich biscuits with a little rhubarb custard.

RHUBARB CUSTARD Blend custard powder and sugar with milk in small saucepan; stir over heat until mixture boils and thickens. Remove from heat, stir in rhubarb. Cover surface of custard with plastic wrap; refrigerate until cold.

Sandwich the biscuits with the rhubarb custard just before serving them.

Honey jumbles

PREPARATION TIME 10 MINUTES (PLUS REFRIGERATION TIME) **COOKING TIME** 15 MINUTES **MAKES** 40

60g butter

½ cup (110g) firmly packed brown sugar

¾ cup (270g) golden syrup

1 egg

2½ cups (375g) plain flour

½ cup (75g) self-raising flour

½ teaspoon bicarbonate of soda

1 teaspoon ground cinnamon

½ teaspoon ground clove

2 teaspoons ground ginger

1 teaspoon mixed spice

ICING

1 egg white

1½ cups (240g) icing sugar

2 teaspoons plain flour

1 tablespoon lemon juice, approximately

pink food colouring

1 Stir butter, sugar and syrup in medium saucepan over low heat until sugar dissolves; cool 10 minutes. Transfer mixture to large bowl; stir in egg and sifted dry ingredients, in two batches. Knead dough on floured surface until dough loses stickiness, cover; refrigerate 30 minutes.

2 Preheat oven to 160°C/140°C fan-forced. Grease oven trays.

3 Divide dough into eight portions. Roll each portion into 2cm-thick sausage; cut each sausage into five 6cm lengths. Place about 3cm apart on oven trays; round ends with floured fingers, flatten biscuits slightly.

4 Bake biscuits about 15 minutes; cool on trays.

5 Meanwhile, make icing.

6 Spread jumbles with pink and white icing.

ICING Beat egg white lightly in small bowl; gradually stir in sifted icing sugar and flour, then enough juice to make icing spreadable. Place half the mixture in another small bowl; tint with colouring. Keep icings covered with a damp tea towel.

This recipe was devised in the Test Kitchen (by me) back in the 1970s. It took a lot of testing and tasting to get the balance of spices just right. The jumbles keep well in an airtight container, in fact, I like them better after a few days, when they soften slightly.

Lemon madeleines

PREPARATION TIME 15 MINUTES **COOKING TIME** 10 MINUTES **MAKES** 12

2 eggs

2 tablespoons caster sugar

2 tablespoons icing sugar

2 teaspoons finely grated
lemon rind

¼ cup (35g) self-raising flour

¼ cup (35g) plain flour

75g unsalted butter, melted

1 tablespoon lemon juice

2 tablespoons icing sugar, extra

1 Preheat oven to 200°C/180°C fan-forced. Grease 12-hole (1½-tablespoons/30ml) madeleine tin.

2 Beat eggs, caster sugar, sifted icing sugar and rind in small bowl with electric mixer until pale and thick.

3 Meanwhile, triple-sift flours; sift flour over egg mixture. Pour butter and juice down the side of the bowl then fold ingredients together. Drop rounded tablespoons of mixture into each hole of tin.

4 Bake madeleines about 10 minutes. Tap hot tin firmly on bench to release madeleines onto wire rack to cool. Dust with sifted extra icing sugar to serve.

Serious bakers whip these up in a flash, the electric mixer does the hard work. Madeleines are irresistible — they're light, sweet and perfect to have with a cup of tea or coffee. They are at their best eaten within an hour of baking, they simply don't keep well. Use butter for greasing the madeleine tin.

Amaretti

PREPARATION TIME 15 MINUTES (PLUS STANDING TIME) **COOKING TIME** 15 MINUTES **MAKES** 20

1 cup (125g) almond meal

1 cup (220g) caster sugar

2 egg whites

¼ teaspoon almond essence

20 blanched almonds (20g)

1 Lightly grease oven trays.

2 Beat almond meal, sugar, egg whites and essence in small bowl with electric mixer for 3 minutes; stand 5 minutes.

3 Spoon mixture into piping bag fitted with 1cm plain tube. Pipe directly onto trays in circular motion from centre out, to make biscuits about 4cm in diameter. Top each with a nut. Cover unbaked biscuits loosely with foil; stand at room temperature overnight.

4 Preheat oven to 180°C/160°C fan-forced.

5 Bake biscuits about 12 minutes. Stand on trays 5 minutes; transfer to wire rack to cool.

Amaretti will perform best for you if the mixture stands overnight — they do work if they're baked straight away, but they're not as good.

LEMON MADELEINES

Coffee almond biscuits

PREPARATION TIME 15 MINUTES   **COOKING TIME** 15 MINUTES   **MAKES** 24

1 tablespoon instant coffee granules

3 teaspoons hot water

3 cups (360g) almond meal

1 cup (220g) caster sugar

2 tablespoons coffee-flavoured liqueur

3 egg whites

24 coffee beans

1 Preheat oven to 180°C/160°C fan-forced. Grease oven trays; line with baking paper.

2 Dissolve coffee in the hot water in large bowl. Add almond meal, sugar, liqueur and egg whites; stir until mixture forms a firm paste.

3 Roll level tablespoons of mixture into balls; place about 3cm apart on trays; flatten slightly. Press coffee beans into tops of biscuits.

4 Bake biscuits about 15 minutes; cool on trays.

Choc nut biscotti

PREPARATION TIME 35 MINUTES   **COOKING TIME** 50 MINUTES (PLUS COOLING TIME)   **MAKES** 60

1 cup (220g) caster sugar

2 eggs

1⅔ cups (250g) plain flour

1 teaspoon baking powder

1 cup (150g) roasted pistachios

½ cup (70g) slivered almonds

¼ cup (25g) cocoa powder

1 Preheat oven to 180°C/160°C fan-forced. Grease oven trays.

2 Whisk sugar and eggs in medium bowl. Stir in sifted flour and baking powder and nuts; mix to a sticky dough.

3 Knead dough on lightly floured surface until smooth. Divide dough into two portions. Using floured hands, knead one portion on lightly floured surface until smooth, but still slightly sticky. Divide this portion into four pieces; roll each piece into 25cm log shape.

4 Knead cocoa into remaining portion of dough until smooth. Divide chocolate dough into two pieces; roll each piece into 25cm log shape.

5 Place one chocolate log on tray. Place a plain log on each side, press gently together to form a slightly flattened shape. Repeat with remaining logs.

6 Bake logs about 30 minutes. Cool on tray 10 minutes.

7 Reduce oven to 150°C/130°C fan-forced.

8 Using a serrated knife, cut logs diagonally into 5mm slices. Place slices, in single layer, on ungreased oven trays. Bake about 20 minutes or until dry and crisp, turning over halfway through cooking; transfer to wire racks to cool.

COFFEE ALMOND BISCUITS

Note the number of bliss bombs — that's right 280 — but they're tiny little mouthfuls of cherry, chocolate and coconut. Serve them in bowls, and just watch them disappear, people will want to eat them by the handful.

Choc-cherry bliss bombs

PREPARATION TIME 15 MINUTES **COOKING TIME** 15 MINUTES (PLUS COOLING TIME) **MAKES** 280

1 ⅓ cups (200g) milk chocolate Melts

60g butter

¼ cup (60ml) vegetable oil

⅓ cup (75g) caster sugar

2 eggs

1 cup (150g) self-raising flour

1 cup (150g) plain flour

3 x 55g Cherry Ripe bars, chopped finely

¼ cup (20g) desiccated coconut

1 Stir chocolate, butter, oil and sugar in medium saucepan over low heat until smooth. Cool 15 minutes.

2 Preheat oven to 180°C/160°C fan-forced. Grease oven trays; line with baking paper.

3 Stir eggs and sifted flours into chocolate mixture; stir in Cherry Ripe.

4 Roll level ½ teaspoons of mixture into balls; roll half the balls in coconut. Place about 2cm apart on oven trays.

5 Bake cookies about 10 minutes. Cool on trays.

Florentines make great gifts. They can be stacked, wrapped and ready to give away, especially at Christmas when someone is bound to turn up with an unexpected gift for you.

Tropical florentines

PREPARATION TIME 15 MINUTES **COOKING TIME** 12 MINUTES **MAKES** 25

⅔ cup (160ml) passionfruit pulp

¼ cup (55g) finely chopped glacé ginger

½ cup (55g) finely chopped glacé pineapple

½ cup (90g) finely chopped dried papaya

1 cup (75g) shredded coconut

1 cup (60g) coarsely crushed corn flakes

½ cup (70g) finely chopped macadamias

¾ cup (180ml) condensed milk

1 cup (150g) white chocolate Melts

1 Preheat oven to 180°C/160°C fan-forced. Grease oven trays; line with baking paper.

2 Strain passionfruit pulp; you need ⅓ cup (80ml) juice. Discard seeds.

3 Combine ginger, pineapple, papaya, coconut, corn flakes, nuts, milk and 2 tablespoons of the passionfruit juice in medium bowl. Drop rounded tablespoonfuls of mixture about 5cm apart onto oven trays; press down slightly.

4 Bake florentines about 12 minutes. Cool on trays.

5 Stir chocolate and remaining passionfruit juice in small heatproof bowl over small saucepan of simmering water until smooth. Spread chocolate over flat side of each florentine; mark with a fork. Set at room temperature.

Double chocolate freckles

PREPARATION TIME 20 MINUTES (PLUS REFRIGERATION TIME) **COOKING TIME** 12 MINUTES **MAKES** 42

125g butter, softened

¾ cup (165g) firmly packed brown sugar

1 egg

1½ cups (225g) plain flour

¼ cup (35g) self-raising flour

¼ cup (35g) cocoa powder

200g dark eating chocolate, melted

⅓ cup (85g) hundreds and thousands

We've made different sized freckles just for fun — make them to whatever size and shape suits you. This biscuit dough is firm — providing you don't overbeat the butter, sugar and egg mixture — and very easy to handle.

1 Beat butter, sugar and egg in small bowl with electric mixer until combined. Stir in sifted dry ingredients, in two batches.

2 Knead dough on floured surface until smooth; roll dough between sheets of baking paper until 5mm thick. Cover; refrigerate 30 minutes.

3 Preheat oven to 180°C/160°C fan-forced. Grease oven trays; line with baking paper.

4 Using 3cm, 5cm and 6.5cm round cutters, cut 14 rounds of each size from dough. Place 3cm rounds on one oven tray; place remainder on other oven trays.

5 Bake small cookies about 10 minutes; bake larger cookies about 12 minutes. Transfer to wire racks to cool.

6 Spread top of cookies with chocolate; sprinkle with hundreds and thousands. Set at room temperature

---

Hazelnut pinwheels

PREPARATION TIME 20 MINUTES (PLUS REFRIGERATION TIME) **COOKING TIME** 20 MINUTES **MAKES** 30

1¼ cups (185g) plain flour

100g butter, chopped coarsely

½ cup (110g) caster sugar

1 egg yolk

1 tablespoon milk, approximately

⅓ cup (110g) chocolate hazelnut spread

2 tablespoons hazelnut meal

1 Process flour, butter and sugar until crumbly. Add egg yolk; process with enough milk until mixture forms a ball. Knead dough on lightly floured surface until smooth; cover, refrigerate 1 hour.

2 Roll dough between sheets of baking paper to form 20cm x 30cm rectangle; remove top sheet of paper. Spread dough evenly with hazelnut spread; sprinkle with hazelnut meal. Using paper as a guide, roll dough tightly from long side to enclose filling. Enclose roll in plastic wrap; refrigerate 30 minutes.

3 Preheat oven to 180°C/160°C fan-forced. Grease oven trays; line with baking paper.

4 Remove plastic from dough; cut into 1cm slices. Place slices about 2cm apart on oven trays. Bake about 20 minutes. Stand on trays 5 minutes; transfer to wire rack to cool.

Chocolate shortbread stars

PREPARATION TIME 30 MINUTES (PLUS REFRIGERATION TIME) **COOKING TIME** 20 MINUTES **MAKES** 25

250g unsalted butter, softened

1 cup (160g) icing sugar

1 ¼ cups (185g) plain flour

½ cup (100g) rice flour

¼ cup (25g) cocoa powder

125 (60g) dark Choc Bits

2 tablespoons icing sugar, extra

1 tablespoon cocoa powder, extra

1 Beat butter and sugar in medium bowl with electric mixer until light and fluffy. Stir in sifted flours and cocoa in two batches. Knead on floured surface until smooth. Roll dough between sheets of baking paper until 1cm thick; refrigerate 30 minutes.

2 Preheat oven to 160°C/140°C fan-forced. Line oven trays with baking paper.

3 Cut 25 x 6.5cm stars from dough. Place stars about 4cm apart on oven tray. Decorate with Choc Bits.

4 Bake stars about 20 minutes. Cool on trays.

5 Sift extra icing sugar and cocoa over stars before serving.

Chocolate hazelnut thins

PREPARATION TIME 10 MINUTES **COOKING TIME** 15 MINUTES **MAKES** 24

1 egg white

¼ cup (55g) brown sugar

2 tablespoons plain flour

2 teaspoons cocoa powder

30g butter, melted

1 teaspoon milk

1 tablespoon hazelnut meal

1 Preheat oven to 180°C/160°C fan-forced. Grease oven trays.

2 Beat egg white in small bowl with electric mixer until soft peaks form; gradually add sugar, beating until dissolved between additions. Stir in sifted flour and cocoa, butter, milk and hazelnut meal.

3 Spread level teaspoons of mixture into 8cm circles, about 4cm apart.

4 Bake thins about 5 minutes. Remove from tray immediately using metal spatula, place over baking-paper-covered rolling pin to cool.

These are perfect to serve with ice-cream or coffee — or even better, both. You will be able to bake about four thins on one tray. After a while you'll get into the rhthym of handling the thins quickly — before and after baking. Once they're baked, slide a metal spatula under each thin, loosen it gently, then drape each one over a baking-paper-covered rolling pin.

Ginger chocolate creams

PREPARATION TIME 30 MINUTES (PLUS REFRIGERATION TIME) **COOKING TIME** 10 MINUTES **MAKES** 16

125g unsalted butter, softened

⅓ cup (75g) firmly packed brown sugar

2 tablespoons golden syrup

½ cup (75g) self-raising flour

⅔ cup (100g) wholemeal self-raising flour

1 teaspoon ground ginger

1 tablespoon cocoa powder

CHOCOLATE GINGER CREAM

¼ cup (60ml) cream

150g milk eating chocolate, chopped coarsely

¼ cup (55g) finely chopped glacé ginger

1 Beat butter and sugar in small bowl with electric mixer until light and fluffy. Beat in golden syrup. Stir in sifted dry ingredients in two batches.

2 Roll dough between sheets of baking paper until 5mm thick. Refrigerate 30 minutes.

3 Meanwhile, make chocolate ginger cream.

4 Preheat oven to 180°C/160°C fan-forced. Grease oven trays; line with baking paper.

5 Cut 32 x 5.5cm rounds from dough; place on oven trays.

6 Bake about 5 minutes; cool on trays. Sandwich biscuits with chocolate ginger cream.

CHOCOLATE GINGER CREAM Stir cream and chocolate in small heatproof bowl over small saucepan of simmering water. Stir in ginger; refrigerate until spreadable.

Fudgy choc-cherry biscuits

PREPARATION TIME 15 MINUTES **COOKING TIME** 12 MINUTES PER BATCH **MAKES** 40

250g butter, softened

1 teaspoon vanilla extract

¾ cup (165g) caster sugar

¾ cup (165g) firmly packed brown sugar

1 egg

2 cups (300g) plain flour

¼ cup (25g) cocoa powder

1 teaspoon bicarbonate of soda

½ cup (25g) shredded coconut

¼ cup (50g) coarsely chopped glacé cherries

200g dark eating chocolate, chopped coarsely

200g milk eating chocolate, chopped coarsely

The degree of fudginess in these biscuits is determined by the oven temperature and baking time. Bake only a few biscuits to start with, let them cool, then taste them. If you want them more gooey, bake them for less time and/or reduce the oven temperature to 170°C/150°C fan-forced.

1 Preheat oven to 180°C/160°C fan-forced. Line oven trays with baking paper.

2 Beat butter, extract, sugars and egg in small bowl with electric mixer until smooth and creamy. Transfer mixture large bowl; stir in sifted flour, cocoa and soda, in two batches. Stir in coconut, cherries and both chocolates.

3 Roll level tablespoons of dough into balls, place about 5cm apart on oven trays; flatten slightly.

4 Bake biscuits about 12 minutes. Cool on trays.

SLICES

Slices

Midway between a cake and a tart or a pie, slices, sometimes called slab cakes, make great prepare-ahead desserts, morning or afternoon teas or snacks to slip in the lunch box. Most of the slices in this chapter have a biscuit or pastry base covered with a filling and sometimes a topping or icing. Many will appeal to the busy cook as they can usually be made completely a day or so in advance, or at least the base and filling made and the finishing touches added on the day of serving.

The chocolate brownie, sometimes called a Boston brownie, is an American variation on the slice theme, probably invented when a cook forgot to add baking powder to a chocolate cake recipe. An intense chocolate hit, often studded with nuts and sometimes extra chunks of chocolate, a brownie becomes a blondie when white chocolate is used instead of milk or dark chocolate.

BAKING TIPS

As a general rule, the top half of a gas oven and the bottom half of an electric oven give the best baking results. As with all recipes in this book, we recommend preheating the oven to the desired temperature. This usually takes about 10 minutes and is particularly important with recipes such as slices, which often require less than 30 minutes baking. If you're cooking more than one slice at once, you may need to swap the pans around half way through the cooking time to ensure even browning. Fan-forced ovens distribute the heat more evenly, so you won't have to change the trays or pans around, but you may have to reduce the cooking time slightly. Slices and the bases for layered slices usually feel slightly soft when they first come out of the oven. They firm up as they cool.

PANS FOR SLICES

We used aluminium pans throughout this book as they conduct heat evenly and give the best baking results. Pans made from tin and stainless steel don't conduct heat as evenly. We've found that oven temperatures should be lowered slightly (by about 10°C) when using pans other than those made from aluminium. Pans with non-stick coatings only work well when the surface is not scratched. When making slices, you would only use a non-stick coated pan if you could turn the slice out before cutting it as otherwise you'd run the risk of damaging the surface of the pan.

The slices in this chapter were made using either a 19cm x 29cm slice pan, a 20cm x 30cm lamington pan, a 25cm x 30cm swiss roll pan or a 23cm-square slab cake pan. Generally the pans have low sides to allow for proper heat circulation and browning.

FILLING AND TOPPING TIPS

A number of the recipes featured here have a chocolate topping for a professional looking finish. Good quality eating chocolate can be melted with a little butter, vegetable oil or cream to make it spread easily, then iced or drizzled over the slice. You can make random zig zags of chocolate topping using a piping bag with a very thin piping tube. Or you can make a piping bag from greaseproof or baking paper or a small plastic bag. To make a paper piping bag cut a 30cm square of paper in half diagonally and twist into a cone shape. Staple or fold the cone to hold its shape (see page 638). Half fill the cone with icing, cooled melted chocolate or other topping then fold the top edges of the cone over themselves to keep the contents contained. Snip a tiny end from the point of the cone and pipe by holding the bag firmly and applying even pressure. Another simple but effective decorative finish can be achieved by dragging a comb, or zig zag tool, across the top of the chocolate as it cools and sets (see page 41).

If your condensed milk caramel doesn't set hard enough to cut, chances are the caramel hasn't been cooked long enough. The caramel needs to be a strong dark colour, not just golden. Whisk it continuously while it simmers for about 10 minutes or until it reaches the correct colour. Alternatively, take all the uncertainty out of the equation by buying the ready-made canned variety sold as Top 'n' Fill at many supermarkets.

Desiccated coconut is often used in the topping or filling of slices. This is finely shredded, concentrated, dried, unsweetened coconut flesh, not to be confused with shredded coconut which is thin strips of dried coconut and more coarsely textured than desiccated coconut. For toppings, you can probably use them interchangeably, though you may need to extend the cooking time to get shredded coconut to brown. If the recipe calls for toasted coconut, you can do this by spreading the coconut on to an oven tray and toasting it in a moderate oven for about 5 minutes or until it's lightly browned. Alternatively, place the coconut in a dry, heavy-based frying pan and stir over medium heat until the desired level of browning occurs. Remove the coconut from the tray or pan as soon as it's toasted as it will continue to brown from the heat of the tray or pan.

CUTTING SLICES NEATLY

Most recipes recommend cooling or refrigerating a slice in the pan to firm it before cutting. Cutting is best achieved using a sharp knife. Start in the middle of the long side of the pan, then cut each half into evenly-sized strips. Rotate the pan, find the mid-point on the short side and cut each side into evenly-sized squares or rectangles. Use a ruler if you're unsure of the accuracy of your eye. Dip the knife in hot water if the slice has a chocolate topping or creamy filling as the hot blade will cut more cleanly. Brush away crumbs with a pastry brush.

STORING, REFRIGERATING AND FREEZING SLICES

Most slices keep at room temperature for two or three days, provided they are stored in an airtight container. Slices containing condensed milk, cream or other dairy products such as cream cheese, must be refrigerated. Most slices freeze well provided you exclude as much air as possible from the container before freezing. Two months is about the maximum freezing time. Be warned, however, that slices with icings and cream fillings are liable to crack or change in appearance as they thaw. It won't affect their taste, but it could mean they don't look as pretty as they do in our pictures.

Vanilla passionfruit slice

PREPARATION TIME 25 MINUTES **COOKING TIME** 20 MINUTES (PLUS REFRIGERATION TIME) **MAKES** 12

1 sheet ready-rolled puff pastry, thawed
¼ cup (55g) caster sugar
¼ cup (35g) cornflour
1 ½ tablespoons custard powder
1 ¼ cups (310ml) milk
30g butter
1 egg yolk
½ teaspoon vanilla extract

PASSIONFRUIT ICING
¾ cup (110g) icing sugar
1 tablespoon passionfruit pulp
1 teaspoon water, approximately

1 Preheat oven to 240°C/220°C fan-forced. Grease 8cm x 26cm bar cake pan; line with strip of foil extending over long sides of pan.
2 Place pastry sheet on oven tray. Bake about 15 minutes or until puffed; cool. Split pastry in half horizontally; remove and discard any uncooked pastry from centre. Flatten pastry pieces gently with hand; trim both to fit pan. Place top half in pan, top-side down.
3 Meanwhile, combine sugar, cornflour and custard powder in medium saucepan; gradually stir in milk. Stir over heat until mixture boils and thickens. Reduce heat; simmer, stirring, about 3 minutes or until custard is thick and smooth. Remove pan from heat; stir in butter, egg yolk and extract.
4 Spread hot custard over pastry in pan; top with remaining pastry, bottom-side up, press down gently. Cool to room temperature.
5 Meanwhile, make passionfruit icing.
6 Spread pastry with icing; set at room temperature. Refrigerate 3 hours before cutting.

PASSIONFRUIT ICING Sift icing sugar into small heatproof bowl; stir in passionfruit and enough water to make a thick paste. Stir over small saucepan of simmering water until icing is spreadable.

Unsalted butter would be best — but not essential — in this recipe. Don't leave the caramel filling mixture for a second, it must be stirred from start to finish. The caramel won't be cuttable if you don't cook the caramel enough.

Hazelnut caramel slice

PREPARATION TIME 25 MINUTES **COOKING TIME** 40 MINUTES (PLUS REFRIGERATION TIME) **MAKES** 20

200g butter, chopped

½ cup (50g) cocoa powder

2 cups (440g) firmly packed brown sugar

1 teaspoon vanilla extract

2 eggs

1½ cups (225g) plain flour

200g dark eating chocolate, melted

1 tablespoon vegetable oil

CARAMEL FILLING

185g butter, chopped coarsely

½ cup (110g) caster sugar

2 tablespoons golden syrup

¾ cup (180ml) sweetened condensed milk

1¼ cups (175g) roasted hazelnuts

1 Preheat oven to 160°C/140°C fan-forced. Grease 20cm x 30cm lamington pan; line base with baking paper, extending paper 5cm over long sides.

2 Combine butter and sifted cocoa in medium saucepan; stir over low heat until smooth. Add sugar; stir until dissolved. Remove from heat; stir in extract, eggs and sifted flour. Spread mixture into pan; bake about 20 minutes. Cool.

3 Meanwhile, make caramel filling.

4 Quickly spread filling evenly over base. Refrigerate at least 30 minutes or until firm.

5 Combine chocolate and oil in small bowl, spread over filling; refrigerate until set before cutting.

CARAMEL FILLING Stir butter, sugar, syrup and condensed milk in medium saucepan over low heat until butter is melted. Increase heat to medium; simmer, stirring, about 10 minutes or until mixture is a dark caramel colour. Remove from heat; stir in nuts.

Marmalade almond coconut squares

PREPARATION TIME 25 MINUTES **COOKING TIME** 35 MINUTES **MAKES** 18

125g butter, softened

1 teaspoon almond essence

¼ cup (55g) caster sugar

1 cup (150g) plain flour

¼ cup (20g) desiccated coconut

⅓ cup (15g) flaked coconut

¼ cup (85g) marmalade, warmed

TOPPING

90g butter, softened

2 teaspoons finely grated orange rind

⅓ cup (75g) caster sugar

2 eggs

1 cup (90g) desiccated coconut

1 cup (125g) almond meal

1 Preheat oven to 200°C/180°C fan-forced. Grease 19cm x 29cm slice pan.

2 Beat butter, essence and sugar in small bowl with electric mixer until smooth; stir in flour and desiccated coconut. Press mixture into pan.

3 Bake base 15 minutes. Reduce oven to 180°C/160°C fan-forced.

4 Make topping. Spread topping over hot slice; sprinkle with flaked coconut.

5 Bake slice about 20 minutes. Brush hot slice with marmalade; cool in pan before cutting.

TOPPING Beat butter, rind and sugar in small bowl with electric mixer until smooth; add eggs, beat until combined (mixture will look curdled at this stage). Stir in coconut and almond meal.

When you make the topping, you'll find the butter, sugar and egg mixture will curdle, don't worry — both eggs are needed to "hold" the coconut and almond meal.

Fruit chews

PREPARATION TIME 25 MINUTES **COOKING TIME** 40 MINUTES **MAKES** 20

90g butter, chopped coarsely

⅓ cup (75g) firmly packed brown sugar

1¼ cups (185g) plain flour

1 egg yolk

TOPPING

2 eggs

1 cup (220g) firmly packed brown sugar

⅓ cup (50g) self-raising flour

½ cup (85g) coarsely chopped raisins

¾ cup (120g) sultanas

1¼ cups (185g) roasted unsalted peanuts

1 cup (90g) desiccated coconut

I love this slice — it has a biscuity base and a moist fruity top. Try changing the fruit and nuts to suit your own taste: 200g coarsely chopped dried apricots with 185g slivered almonds or roasted unsalted cashews would be delicious.

1 Preheat oven to 180°C/160°C fan-forced. Grease 20cm x 30cm lamington pan; line base with baking paper, extending paper 2cm over long sides.

2 Stir butter and sugar in medium saucepan over medium heat until butter is melted. Stir in sifted flour and egg yolk. Press mixture over base of pan.

3 Bake base about 10 minutes or until browned lightly; cool.

4 Meanwhile, make topping; spread over cold base.

5 Bake slice about 30 minutes. Cool in pan before cutting.

TOPPING Beat eggs and sugar in small bowl with electric mixer until changed to a paler colour and thickened slightly; stir in sifted flour. Transfer mixture to medium bowl; stir in remaining ingredients.

Date slice

PREPARATION TIME 1 HOUR (PLUS REFRIGERATION TIME) **COOKING TIME** 25 MINUTES **MAKES** 24

1 ½ cups (225g) plain flour
1 ¼ cups (185g) self-raising flour
150g butter, chopped coarsely
1 tablespoon honey
1 egg
⅓ cup (80ml) milk, approximately
1 tablespoon white sugar

DATE FILLING

3½ cups (500g) dried seeded dates, chopped coarsely
¾ cup (180ml) water
2 tablespoons finely grated lemon rind
2 tablespoons lemon juice

1 Make date filling.

2 Grease 20cm x 30cm lamington pan; line base with baking paper, extending paper 5cm over long sides.

3 Sift flours into medium bowl; rub in butter using fingertips. Stir in honey, egg and enough milk to make a firm dough. Knead on floured surface until smooth. Enclose with plastic wrap; refrigerate 30 minutes.

4 Preheat oven to 200°C/180°C fan-forced.

5 Divide dough in half. Roll one half large enough to cover base of pan; spread filling over dough. Roll remaining dough large enough to cover filling. Brush with a little milk; sprinkle with sugar. Bake about 20 minutes; cool in pan before cutting.

DATE FILLING Cook ingredients in medium saucepan, stirring, about 10 minutes or until thick and smooth. Cool.

Cranberry and pistachio muesli slice

PREPARATION TIME 20 MINUTES **COOKING TIME** 20 MINUTES **MAKES** 30

125g butter, chopped coarsely
⅓ cup (75g) firmly packed brown sugar
2 tablespoons honey
1 ½ cups (135g) rolled oats
½ cup (75g) self-raising flour
1 cup (130g) dried cranberries
1 cup (140g) roasted pistachios, chopped coarsely

1 Preheat oven to 180°C/160°C fan-forced. Grease 20cm x 30cm lamington pan; line base with baking paper, extending paper 2cm over long sides.

2 Stir butter, sugar and honey in medium saucepan over medium heat without boiling until sugar is dissolved. Stir in remaining ingredients. Press mixture firmly into pan.

3 Bake slice about 20 minutes. Cool in pan before cutting.

1

2

3

4

Fruit mince slice

PREPARATION TIME 20 MINUTES **COOKING TIME** 25 MINUTES **MAKES** 60

90g butter, softened

⅓ cup (75g) firmly packed brown sugar

1 cup (150g) plain flour

TOPPING

1 cup (340g) bottled fruit mince

2 eggs

½ cup (110g) firmly packed brown sugar

2 tablespoons brandy

1 tablespoon self-raising flour

1½ cups (120g) desiccated coconut

1 Preheat oven to 180°C/160°C fan-forced. Grease 20cm x 30cm lamington pan; line with baking paper, extending paper 2cm over long sides.

2 Beat butter and sugar in small bowl with electric mixer until pale in colour; stir in sifted flour, in two batches. Press dough over base of pan. Bake 10 minutes.

3 Meanwhile, make topping. Press topping gently over base.

4 Bake slice about 25 minutes or until golden brown. Cool in pan before cutting.

TOPPING Blend or process fruit mince until chopped finely. Beat eggs, sugar and brandy in small bowl with electric mixer until thick and creamy; stir in flour, coconut and mince.

Fruit mince can be bought throughout the year, or just maybe, you have some home-made fruit mince leftover from Christmas. Both will work well in this recipe. Serve the slice cut into small bars — it's rich. Dust the bars with a little sifted icing sugar, if you like.

Chocolate caramel slice

PREPARATION TIME 20 MINUTES **COOKING TIME** 25 MINUTES (PLUS REFRIGERATION TIME) **MAKES** 16

½ cup (75g) plain flour

½ cup (75g) self-raising flour

1 cup (80g) desiccated coconut

1 cup (220g) firmly packed brown sugar

125g butter, melted

30g butter, extra

395g can sweetened condensed milk

2 tablespoons golden syrup

200g dark eating chocolate, chopped coarsely

2 teaspoons vegetable oil

1 Preheat oven to 180°C/160°C fan-forced. Grease 20cm x 30cm lamington pan; line with baking paper, extending paper 2cm over long sides.

2 Combine sifted flours, coconut, sugar and butter in medium bowl; press mixture evenly over base of pan. Bake about 15 minutes or until browned lightly.

3 Meanwhile, make caramel filling by stirring extra butter, condensed milk and syrup in small saucepan over medium heat about for 10 minutes or until caramel is golden brown; pour over warm base. Bake 10 minutes; cool.

4 Stir chocolate and oil in small saucepan over low heat until smooth; pour over caramel. Refrigerate 3 hours or overnight before cutting.

1 FRUIT MINCE SLICE **2** CHOCOLATE CARAMEL SLICE
3 CHEWY CHOCOLATE SLICE [P 346] **4** APPLE AND RHUBARB STREUSEL SLICE [P 346]

Chewy chocolate slice

PREPARATION TIME 15 MINUTES (PLUS COOLING TIME) **COOKING TIME** 25 MINUTES **MAKES** 20

125g butter, melted

1 cup (220g) firmly packed brown sugar

1 egg

1 teaspoon vanilla extract

½ cup (75g) plain flour

¼ cup (35g) self-raising flour

2 tablespoons cocoa powder

½ cup (40g) desiccated coconut

1 tablespoon shredded coconut

CHOCOLATE ICING

1 cup (160g) icing sugar

2 tablespoons cocoa powder

2 teaspoons butter

1 tablespoon hot water

1 Preheat oven to 180°C/160°C fan-forced. Grease 19cm x 29cm slice pan; line with baking paper, extending paper 2cm over long sides.

2 Combine butter, sugar, egg and extract in medium bowl. Stir in sifted flours and cocoa then desiccated coconut. Spread mixture over base of pan.

3 Bake about 25 minutes or until firm.

4 Meanwhile, make chocolate icing.

5 Spread hot slice with icing; sprinkle with shredded coconut, cool. Cut into 15 squares; cut squares into triangles.

CHOCOLATE ICING Sift icing sugar and cocoa into small bowl; add butter and the water, stir until smooth.

Apple and rhubarb streusel slice

PREPARATION TIME 20 MINUTES (PLUS COOLING AND FREEZING TIMES) **COOKING TIME** 45 MINUTES **MAKES** 15

100g butter, softened

½ cup (110g) caster sugar

1 egg yolk

⅔ cup (100g) plain flour

¼ cup (35g) self-raising flour

1 tablespoon custard powder

4 cups (440g) coarsely chopped rhubarb

2 large granny smith apples (400g), sliced thinly

2 tablespoons honey

1½ teaspoons finely grated orange rind

STREUSEL

½ cup (75g) plain flour

¼ cup (35g) self-raising flour

⅓ cup (75g) firmly packed brown sugar

½ teaspoon ground cinnamon

80g butter, chopped coarsely

1 Make streusel.

2 Preheat oven to 180°C/160°C fan-forced. Line 20cm x 30cm lamington pan with baking paper, extending paper 2cm over long sides.

3 Beat butter, sugar and yolk in small bowl with electric mixer until light and fluffy. Stir in sifted flours and custard powder. Press mixture over base of pan.

4 Bake base about 20 minutes or until browned lightly. Cool 15 minutes.

5 Increase oven to 200°C/180°C fan-forced.

6 Meanwhile, cook rhubarb, apple, honey and rind in medium saucepan, stirring occasionally, about 5 minutes or until apples are just tender; cool 15 minutes.

7 Spread rhubarb mixture over base; coarsely grate streusel over fruit.

8 Bake slice about 15 minutes. Cool in pan before cutting.

STREUSEL Blend or process flours, sugar and cinnamon until combined. Add butter; process until ingredients come together. Enclose in plastic wrap; freeze 1 hour.

Cherry almond coconut slice

PREPARATION TIME 20 MINUTES **COOKING TIME** 30 MINUTES **MAKES** 20

60g butter, softened

⅓ cup (75g) caster sugar

1 egg yolk

2 tablespoons self-raising flour

½ cup (75g) plain flour

⅔ cup (220g) cherry jam

1 tablespoon cherry brandy

⅓ cup (25g) flaked almonds

TOPPING

2 eggs

¼ cup (55g) caster sugar

2 cups (160g) desiccated coconut

1 Preheat oven to 180°C/160°C fan-forced. Grease 19cm x 29cm slice pan; line with baking paper, extending paper 2cm over long sides.

2 Beat butter, sugar and egg yolk in small bowl with electric mixer until light and fluffy. Stir in sifted flours. Press mixture into pan; spread with combined jam and brandy.

3 Make topping.

4 Sprinkle topping over slice, then sprinkle topping with nuts; press down gently.

5 Bake about 30 minutes; cool in pan before cutting.

TOPPING Beat eggs and sugar together with fork in medium bowl; stir in coconut.

Change the flavour of the jam to suit yourself, leave the brandy out if you prefer, but you will need to use 1 tablespoon of some other liquid to make the jam spreadable. Whisky and marmalade would be a grown-up flavour.

Shredded or even flaked
coconut take longer to
toast than desiccated
coconut. You can toast it in
the oven or in a dry frying
pan — either way, you have
to watch it carefully. If you're
using the pan method, stir
the coconut the whole time,
then take it out of the pan
the second it's browned.

Choc-cherry macaroon slice

PREPARATION TIME 15 MINUTES **COOKING TIME** 45 MINUTES (PLUS COOLING AND REFRIGERATION TIME)
MAKES 16

3 egg whites

½ cup (110g) caster sugar

100g dark eating chocolate, grated coarsely

¼ cup (35g) plain flour

1⅓ cups (95g) shredded coconut, toasted

¾ cup (150g) glacé cherries, chopped coarsely

50g dark eating chocolate, melted

1 Preheat oven to 150°C/130°C fan-forced. Grease 19cm x 29cm slice pan; line with baking paper, extending paper 2cm over long sides.

2 Beat egg whites in small bowl with electric mixer until soft peaks form; gradually add sugar, beating until dissolved between additions. Fold in grated chocolate, sifted flour, coconut and cherries. Spread mixture into pan.

3 Bake slice about 45 minutes. Cool in pan.

4 Drizzle slice with melted chocolate; refrigerate until set before cutting.

Friands are usually baked
in oval-shaped pans,
but the mixture bakes
perfectly well in a slice pan.
Don't overmix the mixture
— you'll only create large
air pockets.

Cherry friand slice

PREPARATION TIME 15 MINUTES **COOKING TIME** 40 MINUTES **MAKES** 16

4 egg whites

100g butter, melted

1 tablespoon milk

½ teaspoon vanilla extract

1 cup (125g) almond meal

1 cup (160g) icing sugar

⅓ cup (50g) self-raising flour

1 vanilla bean

⅔ cup (100g) frozen cherries, chopped coarsely

1 Preheat oven to 170°C/150°C fan-forced. Grease 19cm x 29cm slice pan; line base with baking paper, extending paper 2cm over long sides.

2 Using fork, whisk egg whites in large bowl until combined. Add butter, milk, extract, almond meal and sifted icing sugar and flour; stir until combined. Split vanilla bean in half lengthways; scrape seeds from bean, stir seeds into mixture. Pour mixture into pan; sprinkle cherries over mixture.

3 Bake slice about 30 minutes. Stand 10 minutes; turn, top-side up, onto wire rack to cool.

CHOC-CHERRY MACAROON SLICE

Gift wrappings

Turn your homemade treats into special gifts that will surprise and delight.

GLASS JARS
These make an excellent gift and the jar lasts long after the cookies are gone. Buy them cheaply at discount stores. Sterilise with hot water before you fill them.

RUSTIC WRAPPING
Give two gifts at once. Wrap heavy cakes such as Christmas fruit cake, supported on a cake board, in a 100% linen teatowel. Secure with a rubber band and finish with wooden pegs found lying around the house.

PAPER SURPRISES
Use an unstuck envelope for a stencil and cut the shape out of a paper doily, insert a piece of card for stability and glue it together. Insert a few sweets for a gorgeous girlie gift.

CREATIVE THINKING
Eschew ribbon and pair soft, simple tissue paper or butchers paper with a detail borrowed from other applications. Try 100% mohair thread, coloured wool, or kitchen twine.

TIN TREATS
Use old chocolate or tea tins or buy tins from craft stores. Soften the look by wrapping in translucent patterned paper and adding a ribbon detail. Tins are great storage for keeping biscuits fresh and can be reused.

PERSONALISED GIFTS
Cut cellophane bags, available from craft stores, into rectangles. Place an initialled biscuit in the centre and wrap, twisting the ends into a wrapped sweet shape and securing with ribbon.

GIFT BOXES

Inspire tea and bikkies by filling one tissue paper-lined gift box with some home made biscuits and another with tea leaves tied into a muslin 'tea-bag'. Craft stores stock boxes and muslin.

GIFT BASKET

An old raspberry punnet box like this one can make a romantic, rustic home for fresh-baked biscuits. Use any reusable food package you can find in op shops or flea markets. Line and top with some greaseproof paper.

LOLLY BAGS

Make elegant lolly bags for grown-up kids out of paper bags sealed with a sticker. Add a vintage-sourced initial, or a sticker, available from craft shops, for a personal touch.

COLOUR COORDINATION

A simple colour scheme often carries the most punch. Work within tonal regions and use only one or two base colours. Make a statement by wrapping neatly, and tying ribbon in fresh ways.

FEATURE TREAT

A cello box, from craft stores, simply adorned, really lets the treat enclosed be the feature. Use white patty cases, and fill the box. Divide treats with a piece of baking paper. This ribbon was folded twice and secured with a pearl-headed pin for a different finish.

TRADITIONAL

A wax seal is a personal and quaint way to seal a paper bag of treats. Add a feeling of ceremony and importance to simple treats. Perfect for a wedding bonbonniere.

Fruity white chocolate bars

PREPARATION TIME 15 MINUTES **COOKING TIME** 45 MINUTES **MAKES** 24

²/₃ cup (90g) slivered almonds

1 ¼ cups (210g) brazil nuts, chopped coarsely

1 ½ cups (135g) desiccated coconut

1 cup (150g) chopped dried apricots

1 cup (150g) dried currants

¼ cup (35g) plain flour

250g white chocolate Melts, melted

½ cup (160g) apricot jam, warmed

½ cup (180g) honey

1 Preheat oven to 160°C/140°C fan-forced. Grease 19cm x 29cm slice pan; line base with baking paper.

2 Combine nuts, coconut, fruit and sifted flour in large bowl. Stir in chocolate, sieved jam and honey. Spread mixture evenly into pan.

3 Bake slice about 45 minutes. Cool in pan before cutting.

Cashew ginger squares

PREPARATION TIME 20 MINUTES **COOKING TIME** 20 MINUTES **MAKES** 30

125g butter, softened

¼ cup (55g) caster sugar

1 cup (150g) self-raising flour

1 teaspoon ground ginger

TOPPING

60g butter

2 tablespoons golden syrup

½ cup (80g) icing sugar

1 cup (150g) unsalted roasted cashews, chopped coarsely

¼ cup (50g) finely chopped glacé ginger

1 Preheat oven to 180°C/160°C fan-forced. Grease 20cm x 30cm lamington pan; line with baking paper, extending paper 2cm over long sides.

2 Beat butter and sugar in small bowl with electric mixer until light and fluffy; stir in sifted flour and ginger. Spread mixture over base of pan.

3 Bake base about 20 minutes or until browned lightly; cool in pan.

4 Meanwhile, make topping; spread hot topping over base. Cool.

TOPPING Stir butter, syrup and icing sugar in small saucepan over low heat until butter is melted. Stir in nuts and ginger.

The base for this slice is quite cakey, so, we found it necessary to spread the hot topping over the cooled base, so that the topping softened the base enough to cling to it. Otherwise the topping and base will part company when the slice was cut.

FRUITY WHITE CHOCOLATE BARS

Lemon meringue slice

PREPARATION TIME 20 MINUTES   **COOKING TIME** 1 HOUR (PLUS COOLING TIME)   **MAKES** 16

90g butter, softened

2 tablespoons caster sugar

1 egg

1 cup (150g) plain flour

¼ cup (80g) apricot jam

LEMON TOPPING

2 eggs

2 egg yolks

½ cup (110g) caster sugar

300ml cream

1 tablespoon finely grated lemon rind

2 tablespoons lemon juice

MERINGUE

3 egg whites

¾ cup (165g) caster sugar

1 Preheat oven to 200°C/180°C fan-forced. Grease base of 19cm x 29cm slice pan; line base with baking paper, extending paper 2cm over long sides.

2 Beat butter, sugar and egg in small bowl with electric mixer until pale in colour; stir in sifted flour, in two batches. Press dough over base of pan; prick dough all over with a fork.

3 Bake base about 15 minutes or until browned lightly. Cool 20 minutes; spread base with jam.

4 Reduce oven to 170°C/150°C fan-forced.

5 Make lemon topping; pour over base. Bake about 35 minutes or until set; cool 20 minutes. Roughen surface of topping with fork.

6 Increase oven to 220°C/200°C fan-forced.

7 Make meringue; spread evenly over topping.

8 Bake slice about 3 minutes or until browned lightly. Cool slice in pan 20 minutes before cutting.

LEMON TOPPING Whisk ingredients together in medium bowl until combined.

MERINGUE Beat egg whites in small bowl with electric mixer until soft peaks form; gradually add sugar, beating until dissolved between additions.

Everyone is short of time these days, but in a perfect world the base for this slice should be cooled to room temperature before the topping is poured over. Then once the topping has been baked, it should also be cooled to room temperature before topping with the meringue. The method we've given you does work and saves some time for you. If you've made meringue-topped pies or slices before, you'll have noticed that sometimes the meringue will pull away from the side of the pastry or pan — also, a moist layer develops between the topping and the meringue, causing the meringue to slip and slide — very annoying. Try roughing up the surface of the topping (see step 5) with a fork, it gives the meringue something to cling onto.

Tangy lemon squares

PREPARATION TIME 20 MINUTES **COOKING TIME** 35 MINUTES **MAKES** 25

125g butter, softened

¼ cup (40g) icing sugar

1¼ cups (185g) plain flour

3 eggs

1 cup (220g) caster sugar

2 teaspoons finely grated lemon rind

½ cup (125ml) lemon juice

1 Preheat oven to 180°C/160°C fan-forced. Grease 23cm-square slab cake pan; line base and two opposite sides with baking paper.

2 Beat butter and sifted icing sugar in small bowl with electric mixer until smooth. Stir in 1 cup (150g) of the flour. Press mixture over base of pan.

3 Bake base about 15 minutes.

4 Whisk eggs, caster sugar, remaining sifted flour, rind and juice in medium bowl until combined; pour over hot base.

5 Bake slice about 20 minutes. Cool in pan before cutting.

Berry sponge slice

PREPARATION TIME 20 MINUTES **COOKING TIME** 30 MINUTES **MAKES** 30

This is one of my favourite multi-purpose slices. It's great served as a slice or warm as a dessert. It doesn't last long (and why would it) as the berries soften the pastry. If you can't find the sweet ready-rolled puff pastry, just use the regular unsweetened pastry, the filling is sweet enough. Frozen rhubarb or cherries also work well.

2 sheets ready-rolled sweet puff pastry, thawed

3 eggs

½ cup (110g) caster sugar

½ cup (75g) self-raising flour

1½ cups (225g) frozen mixed berries

1 egg white

1 tablespoon caster sugar, extra

1 tablespoon icing sugar

1 Preheat oven to 220°C/200°C fan-forced. Grease 25cm x 30cm swiss roll pan.

2 Roll one pastry sheet until large enough to cover base of pan, extending pastry halfway up sides of pan. Prick pastry with fork at 2cm intervals; freeze 5 minutes.

3 Place another swiss roll pan on top of pastry; bake 5 minutes. Remove top pan; bake further 5 minutes or until pastry is browned lightly. Cool 5 minutes.

4 Meanwhile, beat eggs and caster sugar in small bowl with electric mixer until thick and creamy; fold in sifted flour. Spread mixture evenly over pastry; sprinkle evenly with berries.

5 Roll remaining pastry sheet large enough to fit pan; place over berries. Brush pastry with egg white, sprinkle with extra caster sugar; score pastry in crosshatch pattern.

6 Bake about 20 minutes; cool in pan. Dust with sifted icing sugar before cutting.

Raspberry coconut slice

PREPARATION TIME 25 MINUTES (PLUS COOLING TIME) **COOKING TIME** 40 MINUTES **MAKES** 20

90g butter, softened
½ cup (110g) caster sugar
1 egg
¼ cup (35g) self-raising flour
⅔ cup (100g) plain flour
1 tablespoon custard powder
⅔ cup (220g) raspberry jam

COCONUT TOPPING
2 cups (160g) desiccated coconut
¼ cup (55g) caster sugar
2 eggs, beaten lightly

1 Preheat oven to 180°C/160°C fan-forced. Grease 20cm x 30cm lamington pan; line base with baking paper, extending paper 2cm over long sides.

2 Beat butter, sugar and egg in small bowl with electric mixer until light and fluffy. Transfer mixture to medium bowl; stir in sifted flours and custard powder. Spread into pan; spread with jam.

3 Combine ingredients for topping in small bowl; sprinkle over jam.

4 Bake slice about 40 minutes; cool in pan before cutting.

Here's an old favourite, I'm sure all makers of this slice have their own favourite variation. For a change try this one: Replace the raspberry jam with marmalade. For the topping, combine 1 ½ cups desiccated coconut, ½ cup finely chopped pistachios, ¼ cup caster sugar, 2 eggs and 1 teaspoon finely grated orange rind in small bowl.

Semolina slice

PREPARATION TIME 15 MINUTES (PLUS REFRIGERATION TIME) **COOKING TIME** 1 HOUR 50 MINUTES
MAKES 28

1kg coarsely ground semolina
2½ cups (550g) white sugar
125g butter, chopped coarsely
1 cup (250ml) milk
¼ cup (40g) blanched almonds

SUGAR SYRUP
3 cups (750ml) water
2 teaspoons lemon juice
1½ cups (330g) caster sugar
2 teaspoons orange flower water

1 Make sugar syrup; cool.

2 Preheat oven to 160°C/140°C fan-forced. Grease 20cm x 30cm lamington pan.

3 Combine semolina and sugar in large bowl. Melt butter in milk in small saucepan over low heat; stir into semolina mixture. Spread mixture into pan; smooth top with wet hand. Mark slice into 4cm diamond shapes; place an almond in centre of each diamond.

4 Bake slice for 1 hour 20 minutes or until golden brown.

5 Cut through diamond shapes; gradually pour cooled syrup over hot slice. Cool in pan.

SUGAR SYRUP Bring the water, juice and sugar to the boil in medium saucepan. Reduce heat; simmer, uncovered, about 20 minutes or until slightly thickened and reduced to about 2½ cups. Cool. Add orange flower water.

White sugar is simply regular crystal or table sugar, the coarser grain of this sugar is best here.

Chocolate hazelnut slice

PREPARATION TIME 30 MINUTES **COOKING TIME** 40 MINUTES (PLUS COOLING AND REFRIGERATION TIME)
MAKES 24

Buy plain chocolate biscuits for this recipe, that is, chocolate biscuits without icing, filling or chocolate coating.

250g plain chocolate biscuits

60g butter, melted

4 eggs, separated

¾ cup (165g) caster sugar

½ cup (50g) hazelnut meal

2 tablespoons plain flour

TOPPING

125g butter, softened

½ cup (110g) caster sugar

1 tablespoon orange juice

200g dark eating chocolate, melted

1 tablespoon cocoa powder

1 Preheat oven to 180°C/160°C fan-forced. Grease 20cm x 30cm lamington pan; line with baking paper, extending paper 2cm over long sides.

2 Process biscuits until fine. Combine 1 cup of the biscuit crumbs with butter in medium bowl; press over base of pan. Refrigerate 10 minutes.

3 Beat egg whites in small bowl with electric mixer until soft peaks form. Gradually add sugar, beating until dissolved between additions; fold in hazelnut meal, remaining biscuit crumbs and sifted flour. Spread mixture over biscuit base.

4 Bake base about 20 minutes. Cool 20 minutes.

5 Reduce oven to 170°C/150°C fan-forced.

6 Meanwhile, make topping by beating butter, sugar, egg yolks and juice in small bowl with electric mixer until light and fluffy. Stir in chocolate. Spread topping over slice.

7 Bake slice about 20 minutes; cool in pan. Refrigerate until firm; dust with sifted cocoa before cutting.

Dutch ginger and almond slice

PREPARATION TIME 15 MINUTES **COOKING TIME** 35 MINUTES (PLUS STANDING TIME) **MAKES** 20

This shortbread-like slice can be marked into any size or shape pieces you like, diamonds and triangles look good. Do this before baking, then cut through the markings before the slice cools. Unsalted butter is best to use in this slice.

1¾ cups (255g) plain flour

1 cup (220g) caster sugar

⅔ cup (150g) coarsely chopped glacé ginger

½ cup (80g) coarsely chopped blanched almonds

1 egg

185g butter, melted

2 teaspoons icing sugar

1 Preheat oven to 180°C/160°C fan-forced. Grease 20cm x 30cm lamington pan; line with baking paper, extending paper 2cm over long sides.

2 Combine sifted flour, sugar, ginger, nuts and egg in medium bowl; stir in butter. Press mixture into pan. Mark slice into squares or rectangles.

3 Bake slice about 35 minutes. Stand slice in pan 10 minutes; cut into squares or rectangles, lift onto wire rack to cool. Dust with sifted icing sugar.

CHOCOLATE HAZELNUT SLICE

1 2

3 4

Chocolate fudge brownies

PREPARATION TIME 20 MINUTES **COOKING TIME** 1 HOUR 5 MINUTES **MAKES** 20

150g butter, chopped coarsely

300g dark eating chocolate, chopped coarsely

1½ cups (330g) firmly packed brown sugar

3 eggs

1 teaspoon vanilla extract

¾ cup (110g) plain flour

¾ cup (140g) dark Choc Bits

½ cup (120g) sour cream

¾ cup (110g) roasted macadamias, chopped coarsely

1 Preheat oven to 180°C/160°C fan-forced. Grease 19cm x 29cm slice pan;
line with baking paper, extending paper 2cm over sides.

2 Stir butter and dark chocolate in medium saucepan over low heat until smooth.
Cool 10 minutes.

3 Stir sugar, eggs and extract into chocolate mixture, then sifted flour, Choc Bits,
sour cream and nuts. Spread mixture into pan.

4 Bake brownies 40 minutes. Cover pan with foil; bake further 20 minutes. Cool in pan
before cutting.

Despite the richness of these seriously chocolatey brownies, nobody I know can stop at one. It's great to think that something so good is so easy to make — all in one pan. If you like your brownies really fudgy, bake them for less time. Dust the brownies with a little sifted cocoa powder or icing sugar, or both.

Triple choc brownies

PREPARATION TIME 20 MINUTES **COOKING TIME** 40 MINUTES **MAKES** 16

125g butter, chopped coarsely

200g dark eating chocolate, chopped coarsely

½ cup (110g) caster sugar

2 eggs

1¼ cups (185g) plain flour

150g white eating chocolate, chopped coarsely

100g milk eating chocolate, chopped coarsely

1 Preheat oven to 180°C/160°C fan-forced. Grease deep 19cm-square cake pan;
line with baking paper, extending paper 2cm over sides.

2 Stir butter and dark chocolate in medium saucepan over low heat until smooth.
Cool 10 minutes.

3 Stir sugar and eggs into chocolate mixture, then sifted flour and white and milk
chocolates. Spread mixture into pan.

4 Bake brownies about 35 minutes. Cool in pan before cutting.

If there is a trick to making brownies, there's only one we know of — don't overheat the chocolate mixture.

1 CHOCOLATE FUDGE BROWNIES 2 TRIPLE CHOC BROWNIES 3 WHITE CHOCOLATE
NUT AND BERRY BLONDIES [P 362] 4 CHOCOLATE RUM AND RAISIN SLICE [P 362]

White chocolate, nut and berry blondies

PREPARATION TIME 20 MINUTES **COOKING TIME** 45 MINUTES **MAKES** 25

Leave the nuts and berries out of this recipe if you just want a plain Blondie — obviously a paler relation of a Brownie. Dust the slice with a little sifted icing if you like.

125g butter, chopped coarsely

300g white eating chocolate, chopped coarsely

¾ cup (165g) caster sugar

2 eggs

¾ cup (110g) plain flour

½ cup (75g) self-raising flour

½ cup (75g) coarsely chopped roasted macadamias

150g fresh or frozen raspberries

1 Preheat oven to 180°C/160°C fan-forced. Grease 23cm-square slab cake pan; line with baking paper, extending paper 2cm over sides.

2 Stir butter and two-thirds of the chocolate in medium saucepan over low heat until smooth. Cool 10 minutes.

3 Stir sugar and eggs into chocolate mixture, then sifted flours, remaining chocolate, nuts and berries. Spread mixture into pan.

4 Bake blondies about 40 minutes. Cool in pan before cutting.

Chocolate rum and raisin slice

PREPARATION TIME 20 MINUTES **COOKING TIME** 35 MINUTES **MAKES** 32

Rum has a very distinctive taste, we like to use an underproof rum, but, if you like, use the stronger overproof variety.

125g butter, chopped coarsely

200g dark eating chocolate, chopped coarsely

½ cup (110g) caster sugar

1 cup (170g) coarsely chopped raisins

2 eggs, beaten lightly

1½ cups (225g) plain flour

1 tablespoon dark rum

1 Preheat oven to 160°C/140°C fan-forced. Grease 20cm x 30cm lamington pan.

2 Stir butter, chocolate, sugar and raisins in medium saucepan over low heat until chocolate is melted. Cool to room temperature.

3 Stir remaining ingredients into chocolate mixture. Spread into pan.

4 Bake slice about 30 minutes. Cool in pan before cutting.

Apple and prune slice

PREPARATION TIME 20 MINUTES **COOKING TIME** 1 HOUR 10 MINUTES (PLUS COOLING TIME) **MAKES** 24

4 medium apples (600g)

¾ cup (135g) coarsely chopped seeded prunes

2½ cups (625ml) water

½ teaspoon ground cinnamon

½ teaspoon ground nutmeg

2 tablespoons hazelnut meal

2 sheets ready-rolled shortcrust pastry, thawed

1 tablespoon caster sugar

1 Peel and core apples; slice thinly. Place apples, prunes and the water in medium saucepan; bring to the boil. Reduce heat; simmer, covered, 10 minutes or until apples are just tender. Drain well; cool 15 minutes.

2 Combine spices and hazelnut meal in medium bowl; gently stir in apple mixture.

3 Preheat oven to 200°C/180°C fan-forced. Grease 20cm x 30cm lamington pan; line base with baking paper.

4 Roll one pastry sheet large enough to cover base of pan; place in pan, trim edges. Cover pastry with baking paper, fill with dried beans or uncooked rice; bake 15 minutes. Remove paper and beans; bake further 5 minutes. Spread apple mixture over pastry.

5 Roll remaining pastry sheet large enough to fit pan; place over apple filling. Brush pastry with a little water, sprinkle with sugar; score pastry in crosshatch pattern.

6 Bake slice about 45 minutes. Cool in pan; cut into squares.

Use either granny smith or golden delicious apples. If you're not up to stewing the apples and prunes in the water, buy two cans of pie apple, put them in a bowl, stir in seeded dessert prunes, the spices and hazelnut meal. This will make a most acceptable substitute for the real thing. Check the level of sweetness of the apple mixture before you go ahead with the rest of the recipe.

Mint slice bites

PREPARATION TIME 20 MINUTES **COOKING TIME** 30 MINUTES **MAKES** 36

125g butter, chopped coarsely

200g dark eating chocolate, chopped coarsely

½ cup (110g) caster sugar

2 eggs

1¼ cups (185g) plain flour

1½ cups (240g) icing sugar

1 teaspoon butter, extra

¼ teaspoon peppermint essence

2 tablespoons milk, approximately

50g dark eating chocolate, melted, extra

1 Preheat oven to 180°C/160°C fan-forced. Grease deep 19cm-square cake pan; line base with baking paper.

2 Stir butter and chocolate in medium saucepan over low heat until chocolate melts. Stir in caster sugar, eggs, then flour. Spread mixture into pan.

3 Bake slice about 20 minutes. Stand 15 minutes; turn, top-side up, onto wire rack to cool.

4 Meanwhile, combine sifted icing sugar, extra butter and essence in small heatproof bowl; gradually stir in enough milk to make a thick paste. Stir mixture over small saucepan of simmering water until icing is spreadable.

5 Spread icing over slice; set at room temperature.

6 Using serrated knife, trim crisp edges from slice. Cut slice into 3cm squares; drizzle each square with extra chocolate.

Choc chip, fig and pecan slice

PREPARATION TIME 20 MINUTES **COOKING TIME** 30 MINUTES **MAKES** 24

185g unsalted butter, softened

¾ cup (75g) firmly packed brown sugar

1¼ cups (185g) plain flour

⅓ cup (65g) finely chopped dried figs

½ cup (60g) finely chopped roasted pecans

½ cup (95g) dark Choc Bits

100g dark eating chocolate, melted

1 Preheat oven to 180°C/160°C fan-forced. Grease 20cm x 30cm lamington pan; line with baking paper, extending paper 2cm over long sides.

2 Beat butter and sugar in small bowl with electric mixer until light and fluffy. Stir in sifted flour, then figs, nuts and Choc Bits. Press mixture into pan.

3 Bake slice about 25 minutes. Cool slice in pan. Drizzle with chocolate; cut when chocolate is set.

Hazelnut brownies

PREPARATION TIME 15 MINUTES **COOKING TIME** 35 MINUTES **SERVES** 12

125g butter

200g dark eating chocolate, chopped coarsely

½ cup (110g) caster sugar

2 eggs, beaten lightly

1¼ cups (185g) plain flour

½ cup (70g) roasted hazelnuts, chopped coarsely

1 cup (190g) white Choc Bits

1 Preheat oven to 180°C/160°C fan-forced. Grease deep 19cm-square cake pan; line base and two opposite sides with baking paper, extending paper 5cm above sides of pan.

2 Combine butter and chocolate in medium saucepan; stir over low heat until smooth. Stir in sugar; cook, stirring, 5 minutes. Cool 10 minutes.

3 Stir in eggs and flour then nuts and Choc Bits. Spread mixture into pan.

4 Bake brownies about 30 minutes. Cool brownies in pan.

Here's yet another brownie recipe, it seems people can't get enough of them. Chocolate mud cake and brownies are our two most-requested recipes in the Test Kitchen.

Black forest slice

PREPARATION TIME 10 MINUTES (PLUS STANDING TIME) **COOKING TIME** 25 MINUTES **MAKES** 20

2 eggs

2 egg yolks

⅓ cup (75g) caster sugar

85g dark eating chocolate, melted

1 cup (250ml) milk

1 cup (250ml) cream

1 cup (120g) almond meal

¼ cup (35g) plain flour

1 tablespoon cocoa powder

425g can seeded black cherries, drained

85g dark eating chocolate, grated coarsely

1 Preheat oven to 180°C/160°C fan-forced. Grease 23cm-square slab cake pan.

2 Beat eggs, egg yolks and sugar in medium bowl with electric mixer until combined; beat in cooled chocolate. Beat in milk and cream on low speed. Stir in almond meal, then sifted flour and cocoa. Pour mixture into pan; sprinkle with cherries and chopped chocolate.

3 Bake slice about 25 minutes. Stand slice in pan 15 minutes; turn onto wire rack.

Serve this slice as such, or warm from the oven as a dessert with cream or ice-cream.

Lemon butter almond slice

PREPARATION TIME 30 MINUTES (PLUS REFRIGERATION TIME)

COOKING 50 MINUTES (PLUS COOLING AND REFRIGERATION TIMES) **MAKES** 30

250g unsalted butter, softened

2 teaspoons vanilla extract

1¼ cups (275g) caster sugar

⅔ cup (80g) almond meal

2 cups (300g) plain flour

½ cup (40g) flaked almonds

LEMON BUTTER

1 teaspoon finely grated lemon rind

⅔ cup (160ml) lemon juice

1⅓ cups (300g) caster sugar

250g unsalted butter, chopped coarsely

4 eggs, beaten lightly

1 Make lemon butter; cover, refrigerate until cold.

2 Preheat oven to 200°C/180°C fan-forced. Grease 26cm x 32cm swiss roll pan; line with baking paper, extending paper 2cm over long sides.

3 Beat butter, extract and sugar in small bowl with electric mixer until light and fluffy. Transfer mixture to large bowl; stir in almond meal and sifted flour, mix well using hands.

4 Press two-thirds of the pastry evenly over base of pan. Wrap remaining pastry in plastic; refrigerate. Bake base about 12 minutes or until browned lightly; cool 10 minutes.

5 Spread base with lemon butter, crumble over the reserved pastry; sprinkle with flaked almonds.

6 Bake slice further 25 minutes or until browned; cool in pan. Refrigerate until cold. Remove from pan before cutting.

LEMON BUTTER Combine rind, strained juice, sugar, butter and strained eggs into medium heatproof bowl. Place bowl over medium saucepan of simmering water, stir about 10 minutes or until lemon butter coats the back of a spoon and thickens slightly.

Your hand is the best "utensil" for bringing the pastry ingredients together, handle it quickly and lightly. Lemon butter, like any custard without flour, can be cooked directly over the heat, that is, not over simmering water — the safe way. Chefs usually cook curds and custards by simply stirring the ingredients over a very low heat until they thicken. It is quicker, but the risk of failure is higher. (See also page 527 for tips on making curd.)

MUFFINS

Muffins

Originally a breakfast food, muffins are these days a popular snack to be enjoyed with a cup of tea or coffee or a cool drink at any time of day. Available in both sweet and savoury versions, they can be served with or without butter. With a dusting of icing sugar and a scoop of ice-cream, sweet muffins can be dressed up as desserts. Add a side salad or a complementary flavoured butter and a savoury muffin becomes a delicious light lunch. Team them with soup and you have a satisfying lunch, supper or winter's dinner. You might try cheesy pizza muffins with minestrone, bacon and chilli muffins with black bean soup or triple-cheese muffins with a chowder or creamy vegetable soup.

It should be noted that the muffin recipes in this chapter are American-style muffins, a variety of quick bread, leavened with egg and self-raising flour. They shouldn't be confused with English muffins, which are the small, round yeast-risen breads served with honey or jam at tea time or as the foundation for eggs Benedict.

MIXING

Muffins are quick and low-fuss to make and mostly require only a single bowl for the mixing. The butter is usually cubed and firm from the refrigerator when it is rubbed into the dry ingredients, then the flavourings lightly mixed in and finally the egg and milk or other liquid. Muffins toughen if the mixture is overhandled so the less mixing, the lighter the finished texture. Use a fork or a large metal spoon to cut the liquid through the dry ingredients and don't worry if the mix seems a bit lumpy — it will be fine when baked. If the recipe calls for berries, use frozen ones. If you add them straight from the freezer, there is less likelihood of them "bleeding" into the mixture as they bake. (See pages 376 & 377.)

MUFFIN PANS

We used a medium (⅓-cup/80ml) muffin pan and a texas (¾-cup/180ml) muffin pan. Other sized muffin pans, including mini muffin pans of about 1 tablespoon (20ml), are available and you will need to adjust cooking times if you choose a larger or smaller pan than the recipe specifies. Whatever sized pan you use, they should only be slightly more than half-filled with mixture to allow for rising. The pans should be lightly greased with a pastry brush dipped in melted butter or an even coating of cooking-oil spray. Or you can line the pans with paper cases — they come in every conceivable size these days. (See page 376.)

TESTING IF COOKED

Muffins should be browned, risen and firm to the touch and beginning to shrink from the sides of the pan when they are cooked. If in doubt, insert a metal skewer into the muffin. It should be clean and free of mixture when it comes out. Turn the muffins onto a wire rack as soon as they are baked to prevent them becoming steamy. The exception to this advice is when the muffins are filled with custard, caramel or jam. In this instance they should stand in the pans to cool for a few minutes before turning out. The fillings can be extremely hot.

KEEPING AND FREEZING

Muffins are at their best if eaten fresh from the oven while they are still warm. However, they can be kept in an airtight container for up to two days and frozen for up to three months. Place the cold muffins in a freezer bag or wrap individually in plastic wrap or foil (depending on how you intend to reheat them), expelling as much air as possible by wrapping as tightly as possible or pressing the bag gently.

To thaw in a conventional oven reheat foil-wrapped muffins by placing them in a single layer on an oven tray, in a moderate oven for about 20 minutes or until they are heated through. You can thaw muffins in a microwave oven, but as ovens vary in power, we can only give general guidelines for timing. Reheat plastic-wrapped muffins, one at a time on DEFROST, MEDIUM LOW or 30% according to your oven. Allow about 45 seconds for one muffin. Err on the conservative side with timing. You can always put them back in the microwave for a further short burst. Defrosted muffins should not feel hot to the touch. If they do, they are probably overheated and will toughen as they cool.

BUTTERMILK

Some of our recipes use buttermilk in place of milk. In spite of its name, buttermilk is actually low in fat, varying between 0.6 per cent and 2.0 per cent per 100ml. Originally the term given to the slightly sour liquid left after butter was churned from cream, today it is made from no-fat or low-fat milk to which specific bacterial cultures have been added during the manufacturing process. It is readily available from the dairy department in supermarkets. Buttermilk not only adds a tangy flavour to cooking, its acid content also reacts with raising agents, giving some baked goods a lighter texture.

FLAVOURED BUTTERS

Many people consider butter the natural accompaniment to the muffin and we tend to agree. You can take butter one step further by creating complementary flavoured butters. Bring the butter to room temperature and beat in a small quantity of the flavouring. You can mix in crushed berries to make a berry butter. Or combine the butter with a couple of spoons of jam, honey or maple syrup for a sweeter alternative. Crush some honeycomb with a rolling pin and fold it into the softened butter for a crunchy sweet addition to your choice of muffin. Savoury butters present just as many alternatives. Wrap unpeeled garlic cloves in foil and bake in a moderate oven until the garlic softens and can be squeezed from the clove. Mash it with a fork and mix into the softened butter. Or try finely chopped mixed herbs, olives, roasted capsicum or anchovies. Wrap the flavoured butter in plastic wrap, roll into a log shape and refrigerate until firm. Cut into rounds to serve with warmed muffins.

Triple-cheese muffins

PREPARATION TIME 10 MINUTES **COOKING TIME** 20 MINUTES **MAKES** 8

1 cup (150g) self-raising flour

½ teaspoon bicarbonate of soda

¼ teaspoon cayenne pepper

2 eggs

1¼ cups (310ml) milk

20g butter, melted

4 green onions, chopped finely

2 tablespoons finely grated mozzarella cheese

2 tablespoons finely grated parmesan cheese

2 tablespoons finely grated cheddar cheese

1 Preheat oven to 200°C/180°C fan-forced. Grease eight holes of 12-hole (⅓-cup/80ml) muffin pan.

2 Sift flour, soda and cayenne into medium bowl. Whisk egg, milk, butter and onion in small bowl. Pour egg mixture into flour mixture; whisk until combined. Do not over-mix.

3 Spoon half of the mixture into pan holes; sprinkle with combined cheeses. Top with remaining batter.

4 Bake muffins about 20 minutes. Stand muffins in pan 5 minutes; turn, top-side up, onto wire rack to cool.

Pesto salami muffins

PREPARATION TIME 15 MINUTES **COOKING TIME** 20 MINUTES **MAKES** 12

2 cups (300g) self-raising flour

1½ cups (210g) chopped salami

⅓ cup (80ml) bottled pesto

3 eggs

⅓ cup (80ml) vegetable oil

½ cup (125ml) buttermilk

⅔ cup (60g) finely grated gruyère cheese

PESTO CREAM

½ cup (125ml) sour cream

2 tablespoons bottled pesto

1 Preheat oven to 200°C/180°C fan-forced. Grease 12-hole (⅓-cup/80ml) muffin pan.

2 Sift flour into large bowl; stir in salami, pesto, eggs, oil and buttermilk. Do not over-mix. Spoon mixture into pan holes; sprinkle with cheese.

3 Bake muffins about 20 minutes. Stand muffins in pan 5 minutes; turn, top-side up, onto wire rack to cool.

4 Meanwhile, make pesto cream; serve with warm muffins.

PESTO CREAM Combine ingredients in small bowl.

TRIPLE-CHEESE MUFFINS

Cheesy pizza muffins

PREPARATION TIME 20 MINUTES **COOKING TIME** 35 MINUTES **MAKES** 6

Close your eyes while you eat these muffins, and you can just about taste pizza. Serve them with a green salad and you have a quick, tasty light lunch.

1 small red capsicum (150g)

2½ cups (375g) self-raising flour

1 egg

1¼ cups (310ml) milk

⅓ cup (80ml) olive oil

½ cup (60g) coarsely grated cheddar cheese

¼ cup (20g) finely grated parmesan cheese

½ cup (60g) seeded black olives, halved

¼ cup (35g) drained chopped sun-dried tomatoes

2 tablespoons finely chopped fresh basil

2 teaspoons finely chopped fresh rosemary

¼ cup (30g) coarsely grated cheddar cheese, extra

1 Preheat oven to 200°C/180°C fan-forced. Grease 6-hole texas (¾-cup/180ml) muffin pan.

2 Quarter capsicum; discard seeds and membranes. Roast under grill or in very hot oven, skin-side up, until skin blisters and blackens. Cover capsicum pieces with plastic or paper for 5 minutes; peel away skin, then cut capsicum into strips.

3 Sift flour into large bowl; stir in egg, milk, oil, cheeses, olives, tomatoes and herbs. Do not over-mix. Spoon mixture into pan holes; top with capsicum then extra cheese.

4 Bake muffins about 25 minutes. Stand muffins in pan 5 minutes; turn, top-side up, onto wire rack to cool.

Bacon and chilli muffins

PREPARATION TIME 10 MINUTES **COOKING TIME** 30 MINUTES **MAKES** 18

Buttermilk makes the texture of these muffins particularly delicious. Serve the muffins warm as a snack or make tiny one-bite muffins in mini muffin pans and serve them as finger food.

8 rashers rindless bacon (520g), chopped coarsely

2½ cups (375g) self-raising flour

80g butter, chopped coarsely

1 teaspoon sweet paprika

½ teaspoon dried chilli flakes

1½ cups (180g) coarsely grated cheddar cheese

310g can corn kernels, drained

1 egg

1 cup (250ml) buttermilk

1 Preheat oven to 200°C/180°C fan-forced. Grease three 6-hole (⅓-cup/180ml) muffin pans.

2 Cook bacon in heated medium frying pan, stirring, until crisp; drain on absorbent paper.

3 Process flour, butter, paprika and chilli until crumbly. Transfer mixture to medium bowl; stir in bacon, cheese, corn, egg and buttermilk. Do not over-mix. Spoon mixture into pan holes.

4 Bake muffins about 20 minutes. Stand muffins in pan 5 minutes; turn, top-side up, onto wire rack to cool.

Wholemeal fig muffins

PREPARATION TIME 10 MINUTES **COOKING TIME** 20 MINUTES **MAKES** 12

Try making this recipe in mini muffin pans and serving the muffins with cheese – particularly brie and camembert.

2 cups (320g) wholemeal self-raising flour

1 cup (150g) self-raising flour

½ cup (110g) raw sugar

125g butter, chopped coarsely

1 cup (190g) coarsely chopped dried figs

2 eggs

1 cup (250ml) milk

1 Preheat oven to 200°C/180°C fan-forced. Grease 12-hole (⅓-cup/80ml) muffin pan.
2 Sift flours and sugar into large bowl; rub in butter. Stir in figs, then eggs and milk. Do not over-mix. Spoon mixture into pan holes.
3 Bake muffins about 20 minutes. Stand muffins in pan 5 minutes; turn, top-side up, onto wire rack to cool.

Roasted capsicum and fetta muffins

PREPARATION TIME 20 MINUTES **COOKING TIME** 40 MINUTES **MAKES** 6

Fetta cheese is good and salty. Try making standard-sized muffins instead of the larger texas size and serve at a barbecue instead of bread.

1 medium red capsicum (200g)

1 medium yellow capsicum (200g)

2½ cups (375g) self-raising flour

100g fetta cheese, chopped

½ cup (40g) finely grated parmesan cheese

90g butter, melted

1 egg

1 cup (250ml) milk

1 tablespoon finely chopped fresh rosemary

1 tablespoon sesame seeds

1 Preheat oven to 200°C/180°C fan-forced. Grease 6-hole texas (¾-cup/180ml) muffin pan.
2 Quarter capsicums; discard seeds and membranes. Roast under grill or in very hot oven, skin-side up, until skin blisters and blackens. Cover capsicum pieces with plastic or paper for 5 minutes; peel away skin, then chop roughly.
3 Sift flour into large bowl, stir in capsicum, cheeses, butter, egg, milk and rosemary. Do not over-mix. Spoon mixture into pan holes; sprinkle with seeds.
4 Bake muffins about 25 minutes. Stand muffins in pan 5 minutes; turn, top-side up, onto wire rack to cool.

Cheese, corn and bacon muffins

PREPARATION TIME 20 MINUTES (PLUS STANDING TIME) **COOKING TIME** 25 MINUTES **MAKES** 12

½ cup (85g) polenta

½ cup (125ml) milk

3 rashers rindless bacon (195g), chopped finely

4 green onions, chopped finely

1½ cups (225g) self-raising flour

1 tablespoon caster sugar

310g can corn kernels, drained

125g can creamed corn

100g butter, melted

2 eggs

50g piece cheddar cheese

¼ cup (30g) coarsely grated cheddar cheese

1 Preheat oven to 200°C/180°C fan-forced. Grease 12-hole (⅓-cup/80ml) muffin pan.

2 Mix polenta and milk in small bowl; stand 20 minutes.

3 Meanwhile, cook bacon, stirring, in heated small frying pan for 2 minutes. Add onion; cook, stirring, another 2 minutes. Remove from heat; cool mixture about 5 minutes.

4 Sift flour and sugar into large bowl; stir in corn kernels, creamed corn and bacon mixture. Stir in butter, eggs and polenta mixture. Do not over-mix.

5 Spoon 1 tablespoon of the batter into each pan hole. Cut piece of cheese into 12 pieces; place one piece in the centre of each muffin. Top with remaining muffin mixture; sprinkle with grated cheese.

6 Bake muffins about 20 minutes. Stand muffins in pan 5 minutes; turn, top-side up, onto wire rack to cool.

Kids love the combination of bacon, cheese and corn — these muffins make a great addition to the lunch box or as an after-school snack.

Cranberry camembert muffins

PREPARATION TIME 15 MINUTES **COOKING TIME** 20 MINUTES **MAKES** 12

2 cups (300g) self-raising flour

2 tablespoons caster sugar

2 eggs

⅓ cup (80ml) cranberry sauce

125g camembert cheese, chopped finely

½ cup (125ml) yogurt

¼ (60ml) milk

60g butter, melted

½ cup (125ml) cranberry sauce, extra

⅓ cup (40g) finely chopped walnuts

1 Preheat oven to 200°C/180°C fan-forced. Grease 12-hole (⅓-cup/80ml) muffin pan.

2 Sift dry ingredients into large bowl; stir in eggs, sauce, cheese, yogurt, milk and butter. Do not over-mix.

3 Spoon half of the mixture into pan holes; drop rounded teaspoons of extra sauce into each pan hole. Top with remaining muffin mixture; sprinkle with nuts.

4 Bake muffins about 20 minutes. Stand muffins in pan 5 minutes; turn, top-side up, onto wire rack to cool.

Camembert cheese needs to be fridge-cold so it can be chopped finely. Leave the "skin" on during chopping.

CHEESE, CORN AND BACON MUFFINS

Muffin basics

American-style (yeast-free) muffins are quite versatile, bake the mixture in muffin pans or loaf pans.

PANS
There are several different-sized pans available, from supermarkets or kitchenware shops. The most common pans available are mini, texas and standard-sized.

LINING OR GREASING PANS
Muffin pans need to be greased or lined with paper cases to fit the various sized pans. Either coat the pan holes evenly with cooking oil spray, or brush the pan holes evenly with a little melted butter.

SIFTING
Sift the dry ingredients into a wide-topped bowl, this not only aerates the mixture, but mixes the ingredients together. Sometimes the sugar is sifted in at this stage too.

MIXING
Use a fork (some cooks like to use a slotted spoon), to barely mix the ingredients together, the mixture should look coarse and lumpy.

SPOONING MIXTURE
Using a spoon or two, or a spoon and one of your fingers, divide the mixture into the holes of the pan. The recipes will tell you how much to put into the pans, but, as a guide, they need to be about two-thirds full.

BAKING
Be guided by individual recipes, but generally, standard-sized muffins are baked in a moderately hot oven for about 20 minutes, the texas-sized muffins take longer, and the mini-sized muffins less time to bake. They are done when they shrink slightly from the side of the pan holes. Turn them onto a wire rack to cool.

RUBBING-IN

Most muffin recipes have a low fat content, which is why they don't keep well. Rub the diced cold butter into the dry ingredients with your fingertips.

ADDING INGREDIENTS

Any fruit dried, fresh or frozen etc, is usually added to the mixture now, along with the sugar. We prefer to add sugar at this stage, as rubbing the butter into the dry ingredients which includes the sugar, is a sticky business.

ADDING LIQUID

Most muffin recipes call for the wet ingredients, which includes eggs, honey etc, to be combined first then added to a well in the centre of the dry ingredients.

CREAMED METHOD

This is the method where the butter, sugar and egg are beaten together with an electric mixer, there's no need to beat the mixture until it's really light and creamy. These muffins will be more like a butter cake than a traditional coarser-textured muffin. Transfer the mixture from the small bowl to a larger one for easier mixing.

ADDING INGREDIENTS

Use a fork to stir the remaining ingredients through the beaten butter/sugar/egg mixture. As in the traditional method, don't over-mix the ingredients, the mixture should still look slightly coarse.

LOAF PAN

Most muffin mixtures can be baked in a loaf pan, a normal sized loaf will take about 45 minutes to bake in a moderate oven. Serve them sliced, either warm or cold, with butter. It's a good idea to line the base and two sides of the loaf pan with a strip of baking paper.

Berry and yogurt muffins

PREPARATION TIME 10 MINUTES **COOKING TIME** 25 MINUTES **MAKES** 6

1 ½ cups (225g) self-raising flour

⅓ cup (30g) rolled oats

3 eggs

¾ cup (165g) firmly packed brown sugar

¾ cup (200g) yogurt

⅓ cup (80ml) vegetable oil

180g fresh or frozen berries

1 Preheat oven to 200°C/180°C fan-forced. Grease six-hole texas (¾-cup/180ml) muffin pan.

2 Sift flour into medium bowl. Stir in oats, eggs, sugar, yogurt and oil, then berries. Do not over-mix. Spoon mixture into pan holes.

3 Bake muffins about 25 minutes. Stand muffins in pan 5 minutes; turn, top-side up, onto wire rack to cool.

Berry muffins

PREPARATION TIME 10 MINUTES **COOKING TIME** 20 MINUTES **MAKES** 12

2 ½ cups (375g) self-raising flour

90g butter, chopped coarsely

1 cup (220g) caster sugar

1 ¼ cups (310ml) buttermilk

1 egg

200g fresh or frozen mixed berries

1 Preheat oven to 200°C/180°C fan-forced. Grease 12-hole (⅓-cup/80ml) muffin pan.

2 Sift flour into large bowl; rub in butter. Stir in sugar, buttermilk and egg. Do not over-mix. Stir in berries. Spoon mixture into pan holes.

3 Bake muffins about 20 minutes. Stand muffins in pan 5 minutes; turn, top-side up, onto wire rack to cool.

This muffin recipe, to me, is the classic basic quick-to-make American-style muffin that I learnt to make in the 1960s. The recipe is low in fat and high in sugar. The result is much less refined than the muffins you buy in a coffee shop today. Eat them warm from the oven, split and served with a little butter.

Chocolate raspberry dessert muffins

Serve these muffins warm with cream or ice-cream for a delicious dessert.

PREPARATION TIME 15 MINUTES **COOKING TIME** 20 MINUTES **MAKES** 12

1 ¾ cups (255g) self-raising flour

¼ cup (35g) cocoa powder

¾ cup (165g) caster sugar

50g butter, melted

⅔ cup (160ml) milk

½ cup (120g) sour cream

2 eggs

½ cup (70g) coarsely chopped roasted hazelnuts

150g dark eating chocolate, chopped coarsely

1 cup (150g) frozen raspberries

1 Preheat oven to 200°C/180°C fan-forced. Line 12-hole (⅓-cup/80ml) muffin pan with paper cases.

2 Sift flour, cocoa and sugar in large bowl. Stir in butter, milk, sour cream and eggs. Do not over-mix. Stir in nuts, chocolate and raspberries. Spoon mixture into cases.

3 Bake muffins about 20 minutes. Stand muffins in pan 5 minutes; turn, top-side up, onto wire rack to cool.

Apricot and coconut muffins

Canned cherries, peaches or plums could be used instead of the apricots here. Change the flavour of the jam to suit the chosen fruit. Make sure you drain the canned fruit well.

PREPARATION TIME 30 MINUTES **COOKING TIME** 20 MINUTES **MAKES** 12

425g can apricot halves

2¼ cups (335g) self-raising flour

¾ cup (165g) firmly packed brown sugar

1 egg

⅔ cup (160ml) buttermilk

½ cup (125ml) vegetable oil

⅓ cup (110g) apricot jam

COCONUT TOPPING

¼ cup (35g) plain flour

1 tablespoon caster sugar

30g butter

⅓ cup (25g) shredded coconut

1 Preheat oven to 180°C/160°C fan-forced. Grease 12-hole (⅓-cup/80ml) muffin pan.

2 Drain apricots; discard syrup. Chop apricots coarsely.

3 Make coconut topping.

4 Sift flour and sugar into large bowl; stir in apricot, egg, buttermilk, oil and jam. Do not over-mix. Spoon mixture into pan holes; sprinkle each with coconut topping.

5 Bake muffins about 20 minutes. Stand muffins in pan 5 minutes; turn, top-side up, on wire rack to cool.

COCONUT TOPPING Sift flour and sugar into small bowl; rub in butter, stir in coconut.

Hazelnut plum muffins

PREPARATION TIME 15 MINUTES **COOKING TIME** 20 MINUTES **MAKES** 12

2½ cups (375g) self-raising flour

⅔ cup (150g) caster sugar

90g butter, melted

½ cup (55g) hazelnut meal

1 egg

1 cup (250ml) milk

½ cup (125ml) plum jam

1 Preheat oven to 200°C/180°C fan-forced. Grease 12-hole (⅓-cup/80ml) muffin pan.

2 Sift flour and sugar into large bowl, add butter, hazelnut meal, egg and milk; stir until combined. Do not over-mix.

3 Spoon half of the mixture into pan holes. Make a small well in centre of each muffin mixture, drop rounded teaspoons of jam into each well. Top with remaining muffin mixture.

4 Bake muffins about 20 minutes. Stand muffins in pan 5 minutes; turn, top-side up, onto wire rack to cool.

Apricot jam would be lovely with the hazelnut flavour too. Jam reaches a very high temperature while it's baking away in the middle of the muffin mixture — this is because of its high sugar content. Make sure you cool the muffins before you eat them.

Fruit and spice muffins

PREPARATION TIME 15 MINUTES **COOKING TIME** 20 MINUTES **MAKES** 12

3 cups (450g) self-raising flour

2 teaspoons mixed spice

½ cup (110g) caster sugar

125g butter, chopped

1 cup (250ml) milk

2 eggs

1 cup (190g) mixed dried fruit

1 Preheat oven to 200°C/180°C fan-forced. Grease 12-hole (⅓-cup/80ml) muffin pan.

2 Sift flour, spice and sugar into large bowl; rub in butter. Stir in milk, eggs and fruit until just combined. Do not over-mix. Spoon mixture into pan holes.

3 Bake muffins about 20 minutes. Stand muffins in pan 5 minutes; turn, top-side up, onto wire rack to cool.

1 2

3 4

White chocolate and macadamia muffins

PREPARATION TIME 10 MINUTES **COOKING TIME** 25 MINUTES **MAKES** 6

2 cups (300g) self-raising flour

⅔ cup (150g) caster sugar

¾ cup (140g) white Choc Bits

½ cup (75g) coarsely chopped roasted macadamias

60g butter, melted

¾ cup (180ml) milk

1 egg

1 Preheat oven to 200°C/180°C fan-forced. Grease 6-hole texas (¾-cup/180ml) muffin pan.

2 Sift flour and sugar into large bowl; stir in remaining ingredients. Do not over-mix. Spoon mixture into pan holes.

3 Bake muffins about 25 minutes. Stand muffins in pan 5 minutes; turn, top-side up, onto wire rack to cool.

Nuts can be bought already roasted, to save you a little time. Roasting brings out the flavour of the nuts.

Orange and date dessert muffins

PREPARATION TIME 10 MINUTES **COOKING TIME** 20 MINUTES **MAKES** 12

2 cups (300g) self-raising flour

½ cup (75g) plain flour

½ teaspoon bicarbonate of soda

1¼ cups (250g) firmly packed brown sugar

125g butter, melted

1 cup (250ml) buttermilk

1 egg

2 teaspoons finely grated orange rind

1 cup (160g) coarsely chopped seeded dried dates

ORANGE SAUCE

¾ cup (150g) firmly packed brown sugar

2 teaspoons cornflour

⅓ cup (80ml) orange juice

2 tablespoons orange-flavoured liqueur

125g butter, chopped coarsely

1 tablespoon finely grated orange rind

1 Preheat oven to 200°C/180°C fan-forced. Grease 12-hole (⅓-cup/80ml) muffin pan.

2 Sift flours, soda and sugar into large bowl. Stir in remaining ingredients. Do not over-mix. Spoon mixture into pan holes.

3 Bake muffins about 20 minutes. Stand muffins in pan 5 minutes; turn, top-side up, onto wire rack.

4 Meanwhile, make orange sauce; serve with warm muffins.

ORANGE SAUCE Combine sugar and cornflour in small saucepan, gradually stir in juice and liqueur; bring to the boil, stirring until sauce boils and thickens. Stir in butter and rind.

These muffins are delicious without the orange sauce. However, the rich buttery sauce transforms them into a dessert for grown-ups. Grand Marnier (or brandy) is the best liqueur to use. Remember to grate the rind of the oranges before you juice them. If the muffins need re-heating, 20 or 30 seconds in a microwave oven will do the trick.

1 WHITE CHOCOLATE AND MACADAMIA MUFFINS **2** ORANGE AND DATE DESSERT MUFFINS
3 OVERNIGHT DATE AND MUESLI MUFFINS [P 384] **4** CHOC BROWNIE MUFFINS [P 384]

Overnight date and muesli muffins

PREPARATION TIME 10 MINUTES (PLUS REFRIGERATION TIME) **COOKING TIME** 20 MINUTES **MAKES** 12

1 ¼ cups (185g) plain flour

1 ¼ cups (160g) toasted muesli

1 teaspoon ground cinnamon

1 teaspoon bicarbonate of soda

½ cup (110g) firmly packed brown sugar

½ cup (30g) unprocessed bran

¾ cup (120g) coarsely chopped seeded dried dates

1 ½ cups (375ml) buttermilk

½ cup (125ml) vegetable oil

1 egg

1 Stir ingredients in large bowl until combined. Do not over-mix. Cover; refrigerate overnight.

2 Preheat oven to 200°C/180°C fan-forced. Grease 12-hole (⅓-cup/80ml) muffin pan.

3 Spoon mixture into pan holes; bake about 20 minutes. Stand muffins in pan 5 minutes; turn, top-side up, onto wire rack to cool.

We love this recipe, the muffins are perfect to bring out hot from the oven — for a large gathering of friends and family at breakfast or brunch. A lot of busy people "entertain" at a late breakfast in the weekends. You can bake the muffins straight after they're mixed, but they are not as good. Serve them with butter.

Choc brownie muffins

PREPARATION TIME 15 MINUTES **COOKING TIME** 20 MINUTES **MAKES** 12

2 cups (300g) self-raising flour

⅓ cup (35g) cocoa powder

⅓ cup (75g) caster sugar

60g butter, melted

½ cup (95g) dark Choc Bits

½ cup (75g) coarsely chopped pistachios

½ cup (165g) chocolate hazelnut spread

1 egg

¾ cup (180ml) milk

½ cup (120g) sour cream

1 Preheat oven to 200°C/180°C fan-forced. Grease 12-hole (⅓-cup/80ml) muffin pan.

2 Sift dry ingredients into large bowl; stir in remaining ingredients. Do not over-mix. Spoon mixture into pan holes.

3 Bake muffins about 20 minutes. Stand muffins in pan 5 minutes; turn, top-side up, onto wire rack to cool.

Apple streusel muffins

PREPARATION TIME 20 MINUTES (PLUS FREEZING TIME) **COOKING TIME** 20 MINUTES **MAKES** 12

40g butter

3 large apples (600g), peeled, cut into 1cm pieces

⅓ cup (75g) firmly packed brown sugar

2 cups (300g) self-raising flour

1 teaspoon mixed spice

⅔ cup (150g) caster sugar

80g butter, melted, extra

¾ cup (180ml) buttermilk

1 egg

STREUSEL TOPPING

⅓ cup (50g) self-raising flour

⅓ cup (50g) plain flour

⅓ cup (75g) brown sugar

½ teaspoon ground cinnamon

80g butter, chopped

Streusel toppings can be made without using the food processor. Simply rub the butter into the dry ingredients using your fingertips. I prefer to add the sugar after the rubbing-in process as the sugar is sticky on your fingers.

1 Make streusel topping; freeze about 30 minutes or until firm.

2 Meanwhile, melt butter in large frying pan; cook apple, stirring, about 5 minutes or until browned lightly. Add brown sugar; cook, stirring, about 5 minutes or until mixture thickens. Cool.

3 Preheat oven to 200°C/180°C fan-forced. Grease 12-hole (⅓-cup/80ml) muffin pan.

4 Sift flour, spice and caster sugar into large bowl. Stir in extra butter, milk, and egg. Do not over-mix. Stir in half of the apple mixture. Spoon mixture into cases; top with remaining apple mixture. Coarsely grate streusel topping over muffins.

5 Bake muffins about 20 minutes. Stand muffins in pan 5 minutes; turn, top-side up, onto wire rack to cool.

STREUSEL TOPPING Process flours, sugar and cinnamon until combined. Add butter; process until combined. Roll dough into ball; wrap in plastic wrap.

Banana, cranberry and macadamia muffins

PREPARATION TIME 10 MINUTES **COOKING TIME** 20 MINUTES **MAKES** 12

2 ¼ cups (335g) self-raising flour

¾ cup (165g) caster sugar

½ cup (65g) dried cranberries

½ cup (70g) coarsely chopped roasted macadamias

⅔ cup mashed banana

2 eggs

1 cup (250ml) milk

½ cup (125ml) vegetable oil

The balance of the ingredients in this recipe relies on the natural sugars in the banana — make sure they're overripe.

1 Preheat oven to 200°C/180°C fan-forced. Grease 12-hole (⅓-cup/80ml) muffin pan.

2 Sift flour and sugar into large bowl, add cranberries and nuts; stir in banana, eggs, milk and oil. Do not over-mix. Spoon mixture into pan holes.

3 Bake muffins about 20 minutes. Stand muffins in pan 5 minutes; turn, top-side up, onto wire rack to cool.

Banana and cinnamon muffins

PREPARATION TIME 20 MINUTES **COOKING TIME** 20 MINUTES **MAKES** 12

Cream cheese frostings can easily be made by hand. The cream cheese needs to be at room temperature to make the beating easier. Just use a wooden spoon to beat the ingredients together. Spreadable cream cheese can be used here, if you like.

2 cups (300g) self-raising flour
⅓ cup (50g) plain flour
1 teaspoon ground cinnamon
½ teaspoon bicarbonate of soda
½ cup (110g) firmly packed brown sugar
1 cup mashed banana
2 eggs

¾ cup (180ml) buttermilk
⅓ cup (80ml) vegetable oil
½ teaspoon ground cinnamon, extra

CREAM CHEESE TOPPING
125g cream cheese, softened
¼ cup (40g) icing sugar

1 Preheat oven to 200°C/180°C fan-forced. Grease 12-hole (⅓-cup/80ml) muffin pan.

2 Sift flours, cinnamon, soda and sugar into large bowl; stir in banana, eggs, buttermilk and oil. Do not over-mix. Spoon mixture into pan holes.

3 Bake muffins about 20 minutes. Stand muffins in pan 5 minutes; turn, top-side up, onto wire rack to cool.

4 Meanwhile, make cream cheese topping.

5 Spread topping over muffins, sprinkle with extra cinnamon.

CREAM CHEESE TOPPING Beat cream cheese with sugar in small bowl with electric mixer until smooth.

Citrus poppy seed muffins

PREPARATION TIME 15 MINUTES **COOKING TIME** 20 MINUTES **MAKES** 12

If you look at the ingredients for this recipe, you'll notice they are close to the ingredients used in a butter cake — there is a little more flour. This is the kind of muffin served in coffee shops today, much more cakey than the original rough-textured American-style muffin.

125g butter, softened
2 teaspoons finely grated lemon rind
2 teaspoons finely grated lime rind
2 teaspoons finely grated orange rind

⅔ cup (150g) caster sugar
2 eggs
2 cups (300g) self-raising flour
½ cup (125ml) milk
2 tablespoons poppy seeds

1 Preheat oven to 200°C/180°C fan-forced. Grease 12-hole (⅓-cup/80ml) muffin pan.

2 Beat butter, rinds, sugar, eggs, flour and milk in medium bowl with electric mixer until combined. Increase speed to medium; beat until mixture is changed to a paler colour. Stir in poppy seeds. Spoon mixture into pan holes.

3 Bake muffins about 20 minutes. Stand muffins in pan 5 minutes; turn, top-side up, onto wire rack to cool.

BANANA AND CINNAMON MUFFINS

Rhubarb and custard muffins

PREPARATION TIME 20 MINUTES (PLUS COOLING TIME) **COOKING TIME** 25 MINUTES **MAKES** 12

2 cups (300g) self-raising flour

½ cup (75g) plain flour

¾ cup (165g) caster sugar

100g butter, melted

1 cup (250ml) milk

1 egg

3 cups (330g) finely chopped rhubarb

1 tablespoon demerara sugar

CUSTARD

2 tablespoons custard powder

¼ cup (55g) caster sugar

1 cup (250ml) milk

1 teaspoon vanilla extract

1 Make custard.

2 Preheat oven to 200°C/180°C fan-forced. Line 12-hole (⅓-cup/80ml) muffin pan with paper cases.

3 Sift flours and caster sugar into large bowl. Stir in butter, milk and egg. Do not over-mix. Stir in half of the rhubarb.

4 Spoon half of the mixture into cases; top with custard. Spoon in remaining mixture to cover custard. Sprinkle with remaining rhubarb and demerara sugar.

5 Bake muffins about 20 minutes. Stand muffins in pan 5 minutes; turn, top-side up, onto wire rack to cool.

CUSTARD Combine custard powder and sugar in small saucepan; gradually stir in milk. Stir custard over medium heat until mixture boils and thickens. Stir in extract. Cool.

Marmalade almond muffins

PREPARATION TIME 15 MINUTES **COOKING TIME** 20 MINUTES **MAKES** 12

2 cups (300g) self-raising flour

125g butter, chopped coarsely

1 cup (80g) flaked almonds

⅔ cup (150g) caster sugar

1 tablespoon finely grated orange rind

½ cup (170g) orange marmalade

2 eggs

½ cup (125ml) milk

¼ cup (20g) flaked almonds, extra

ORANGE SYRUP

¼ cup (85g) orange marmalade

2 tablespoons hot water

1 Preheat oven to 200°C/180°C fan-forced. Grease 12-hole (⅓-cup/80ml) muffin pan.

2 Sift flour into large bowl; rub in butter. Stir in nuts, sugar and rind, then marmalade, egg and milk. Do not over-mix. Spoon mixture into pan holes; sprinkle with extra nuts.

3 Bake muffins about 20 minutes. Stand muffins in pan 5 minutes; turn, top-side up, onto wire rack.

4 Meanwhile, combine orange syrup ingredients in small bowl; brush over warm muffins.

Chocolate beetroot muffins

PREPARATION TIME 20 MINUTES **COOKING TIME** 35 MINUTES **MAKES** 12

2 large beetroots (500g)

1 ¾ cups (260g) self-raising flour

⅓ cup (35g) cocoa powder

1 cup (220g) caster sugar

2 eggs

⅓ cup (80ml) vegetable oil

⅓ cup (80ml) buttermilk

1 Preheat oven to 200°C/180°C fan-forced. Grease 12-hole (⅓-cup/80ml) muffin pan.

2 Wash and trim beetroot and cut off leaves, leaving about 3cm of stem attached. Boil or steam unpeeled beetroot until tender. Drain, rinse under cold water and drain again. Peel beetroot while still warm. Blend or process until smooth. You will need 1 ⅓ cups (330ml) cooled beetroot puree.

3 Sift dry ingredients into large bowl; stir in beetroot puree and remaining ingredients. Do not over-mix. Spoon mixture into pan holes.

4 Bake muffins about 20 minutes. Stand muffins in pan 5 minutes; turn, top-side up, onto wire rack to cool.

Beetroot gives these muffins a wonderful colour and slightly earthy flavour which goes well with chocolate. I like these muffins each topped with a dark chocolate Melt as soon as they come out of the oven. The heat from the muffins will soften the chocolate enough to make it cling to the muffin. Use disposable gloves when you're peeling the beetroot (the skin just pops off smoothly) otherwise you'll have pink hands for days.

Blackberry streusel muffins

PREPARATION TIME 20 MINUTES (PLUS FREEZING TIME) **COOKING TIME** 20 MINUTES **MAKES** 12

2 cups (300g) self-raising flour

1 ¼ cups (170g) frozen blackberries

1 medium apple (150g), peeled, grated coarsely

¾ cup (150g) firmly packed brown sugar

3 eggs

⅓ cup (80ml) vegetable oil

⅓ cup (80ml) buttermilk

STREUSEL TOPPING

⅓ cup (50g) plain flour

2 tablespoons brown sugar

1 teaspoon mixed spice

30g butter

1 Make streusel topping; freeze until firm.

2 Preheat oven to 200°C/180°C fan-forced. Grease 12-hole (⅓-cup/80ml) muffin pan.

3 Sift flour into large bowl; stir in remaining ingredients. Do not over-mix. Spoon mixture into pan holes; coarsely grate streusel topping over muffins.

4 Bake muffins about 20 minutes. Stand muffins in pan 5 minutes; turn, top-side up, onto wire rack to cool.

STREUSEL TOPPING Sift flour, sugar and spice into small bowl; rub in butter. Roll dough into ball. Enclose in plastic wrap.

Warm malt truffle muffins

PREPARATION TIME 40 MINUTES (PLUS REFRIGERATION AND FREEZING TIME)
COOKING TIME 40 MINUTES **MAKES** 12

1 ¼ cups (185g) self-raising flour
2 tablespoons cocoa powder
¼ cup (30g) malted milk powder
pinch bicarbonate of soda
¼ cup (55g) brown sugar
60g unsalted butter
⅓ cup (125g) liquid barley malt
½ cup (125ml) milk
1 egg
¾ cup (180ml) cream

MALT TRUFFLES
200g milk eating chocolate, chopped coarsely
¼ cup (60ml) cream
½ cup (60g) malted milk powder

1 Make malt truffles.
2 Preheat oven to 180°C/160°C fan-forced. Line 12-hole (⅓-cup/80ml) muffin pan with paper cases.
3 Sift flour, cocoa, malt powder, soda and sugar into medium bowl.
4 Stir butter and malt in small saucepan over low heat until smooth; stir into flour mixture with milk, egg and soda. Do not over-mix. Divide half the mixture among pan holes. Place a truffle into each hole; top with remaining mixture.
5 Bake muffins about 20 minutes. Cool 2 minutes; remove paper cases.
6 Meanwhile, stir reserved malt truffle mixture and cream in small saucepan, over low heat, until malt sauce is smooth.
7 Serve warm muffins with warm sauce. Dust with extra cocoa, if desired.

MALT TRUFFLES Stir ingredients in small heatproof bowl over small saucepan of simmering water until smooth. Reserve ½ cup (125ml) mixture for malt sauce. Refrigerate remaining mixture about 30 minutes or until firm. Roll heaped teaspoons of mixture into balls; place on baking-paper-lined tray. Freeze until firm.

Butterscotch pecan muffins

PREPARATION TIME 15 MINUTES **COOKING TIME** 25 MINUTES **MAKES** 12

¾ cup (240g) Top 'n' Fill caramel
¼ cup (60ml) cream
2 cups (300g) self-raising flour
¾ cup (165g) firmly packed brown sugar
¾ cup (75g) coarsely chopped roasted pecans
80g butter, melted
1 cup (250ml) buttermilk
1 egg

1 Preheat oven to 200°C/180°C fan-forced. Line 12-hole (⅓-cup/80ml) muffin pan with paper cases.

2 Stir caramel and cream in small saucepan over low heat until smooth. Cool 5 minutes.

3 Meanwhile, sift flour and sugar into large bowl. Stir in nuts, butter, buttermilk and egg. Do not over-mix.

4 Spoon mixture into pan holes. Spoon caramel onto muffin mixture; using a skewer, gently swirl into top of muffin mixture.

5 Bake muffins about 20 minutes. Stand muffins in pan 5 minutes; turn, top-side up, onto wire rack to cool.

Pumpkin and fetta muffins

PREPARATION TIME 20 MINUTES **COOKING TIME** 25 MINUTES **MAKES** 12

1 tablespoon olive oil

200g pumpkin, cut into 1cm pieces

1 clove garlic, crushed

2 cups (300g) self-raising flour

80g butter, melted

1 egg

1 cup (250ml) buttermilk

50g fetta cheese, crumbled

¼ cup (20g) finely grated parmesan cheese

¼ cup finely chopped fresh chives

Use a firm dry type of pumpkin for this recipe — the type you'd use for your roast dinner — Ironbark, Queensland Blue etc.

1 Preheat oven to 200°C/180°C fan-forced. Grease 12-hole (⅓-cup/80ml) muffin pan.

2 Heat oil in small frying pan; cook pumpkin, stirring, about 5 minutes or until browned lightly and tender. Add garlic; cook 1 minute. Cool.

3 Sift flour into large bowl; stir in butter, egg and buttermilk. Stir in cheeses, chives and pumpkin mixture. Do not over-mix. Spoon mixture into pan holes.

4 Bake muffins about 20 minutes. Stand muffins in pan 5 minutes; turn, top-side up, onto wire rack. Serve muffins warm.

SCONES

Scones

Named for the Stone of Destiny or the Stone of Scone, a block of sandstone that has for centuries been associated with coronations in Scotland and England, the scone is the UK's gift to the afternoon tea table. Bearing absolutely no resemblance beyond shape to a block of stone, a scone is a light and airy baked combination of basically flour, raising agent and liquid.

The scone's ancestry is probably the girdle or griddle cake, in which the dough was placed on a hot plate over the fire and quickly baked. Ireland's soda bread and Australia's damper, originally cooked in the coals, but these days baked in a camp oven or aluminium foil, are siblings of this cake, which was mounded in a single round loaf with a cross on top to allow for expansion. Scones, on the other hand, are usually cut out from the rolled or pressed out dough and baked separately.

Gem scones are another variant in which the batter is poured into the cups of trays of heated cast iron gem scone irons and baked in a hot oven.

INGREDIENTS

FLOUR We generally use white self-raising flour, but you can use plain flour with baking powder or a combination of white and wholemeal self-raising flours. The amount of liquid you'll need to achieve the desired soft, sticky dough will depend on the type of flour you choose, its age and even the weather (humid/dry) on the day you are baking.

SUGAR Is not essential, but a little does take away the floury taste of the dough.

SALT Some cooks add a pinch to everything they bake, add it to the flour if you like.

BUTTER Another optional extra, it gives colour and flavour to the scone dough.

LIQUID We generally use a mixture of milk and water, which results in a lighter texture than plain milk. But you can also use cream, buttermilk or sour cream or yogurt that have been diluted to the consistency of milk with a little water.

MAKING THE DOUGH

You are aiming for a soft, sticky dough that just holds its shape when turned out of the bowl. Avoid overhandling and using too much flour which can upset the balance of ingredients. Lightly flour your hands and the work surface and shape the dough into a smooth ball by working it gently. Flatten the dough gently with your hands to about 2cm in depth all over, pressing from the centre outwards. Use a sharp metal cutter which has been dipped in flour to cut out the rounds. These "first pressings" will result in the lightest scones. When you work the offcuts together and press the dough out again, make it a little thicker than originally, to compensate for the second handling. (See pages 404 & 405.)

GLAZING

Is not essential, but it helps the tops to brown. Glaze with a brush dipped in water (for light brown colour), beaten egg (for dark golden brown) or milk (for somewhere in the middle).

BAKING

Scones need to rise quickly to have a light texture, so your oven needs to be very hot. Ovens vary greatly, so get to know the vagaries of yours and work out whether the top or the bottom is the hottest and adjust the shelves accordingly. Follow the oven manufacturer's instructions initially and make adjustments from there.

We prefer to cook scones barely touching each other in lightly greased shallow aluminium cake pans. The sides of the pans will stop your scones from listing as they rise, but you will need to cook them slightly longer than if you were cooking them on an oven tray. If you want a scone that is crusty all over, place them about 1 cm apart on an oven tray which has been lightly greased only where the scones are going to stand. If you prefer one that is crusty on the top and the bottom, but with soft sides, place the scones on the oven tray just touching each other. They should support each other as they rise, but some of the outer ones will topple over. Turn scones out of the pan or off the oven tray on to a wire rack to cool as soon as they come out of the oven. If you prefer crusty scones, cool the scones uncovered. If you wrap them in a tea towel the crust will soften.

TO TEST IF COOKED

Cooked scones sound hollow when they're tapped with your fingers. Test (tap) the scones in the middle of the pan or tray, as they will take the longest to cook through.

FREEZING

Scones are quick to make, but for the time-strapped cook, they also freeze well. To freeze uncooked scones, leave the scones in the pan or on the oven tray to freeze, then place in freezer bags expelling as much air as possible. Mark the bags with a use-by date, which, so long as you've made them airtight, should be about two months after making. To bake uncooked scones, remove from the freezer bag and cook in a hot oven for about 20 minutes.

Cooked scones can also be frozen. Place cold scones in a freezer bag and expel as much air as possible. Freeze for up to two months. To reheat, remove from the bag, wrap in foil and reheat in a moderate oven for about 20 minutes.

WHAT TO SERVE WITH SCONES

If you come from the English west counties, you will agree that the only thing to serve with scones is jam and clotted cream (made by heating milk and standing in the sun for the cream to rise to the surface). People from Cornwall are adamant that the jam goes on the scone first and the cream on top, while their neighbours in Devon argue just as vehemently that the cream is the bottom layer. We don't really think it matters, and find whipped cream a good substitute for clotted cream, which requires access to unpasteurised milk.

Basic scones

PREPARATION TIME 20 MINUTES **COOKING TIME** 25 MINUTES **MAKES** 20

4 cups (600g) self-raising flour
2 tablespoons icing sugar
60g butter, chopped coarsely
1½ cups (375ml) milk
¾ cup (180ml) water, approximately

1 Preheat oven to 220°C/200°C fan-forced. Grease 20cm x 30cm lamington pan.

2 Sift flour and sugar into large bowl; rub in butter with fingertips.

3 Make a well in centre of flour mixture; add milk and almost all the water. Use knife to "cut" the milk and water through the flour mixture, mixing to a soft, sticky dough. Knead dough on floured surface until smooth.

4 Press dough out to 2cm thickness. Dip 4.5cm round cutter in flour; cut as many rounds as you can from piece of dough. Place scones, side by side, just touching, in pan. Gently knead scraps of dough together; repeat pressing and cutting of dough, place in same pan. Brush tops with a little extra milk.

5 Bake scones about 15 minutes or until browned and scones sound hollow when tapped firmly on the top with fingers.

Wholemeal date scones

PREPARATION TIME 15 MINUTES **COOKING TIME** 15 MINUTES **MAKES** 16

1 cup (150g) white self-raising flour
1 cup (150g) wholemeal self-raising flour
1 cup (60g) unprocessed bran
¼ cup (25g) full cream milk powder

60g butter, chopped coarsely
1 cup (140g) finely chopped dried seeded dates
1 cup (250ml) water, approximately

1 Preheat oven to 200°C/180°C fan-forced. Grease 20cm x 30cm lamington pan.

2 Sift flours into medium bowl, return husks from sifter to bowl, mix in bran and milk powder; rub in butter with fingertips. Stir in dates.

3 Make a well in centre of flour mixture; add almost all the water. Use knife to "cut" the water through the flour mixture, mixing to a soft, sticky dough. Knead dough on floured surface until smooth.

4 Press dough out to 2cm thickness. Dip 4.5cm round cutter in flour; cut as many rounds as you can from piece of dough. Place scones, side by side, just touching, in pan. Gently knead scraps of dough together; repeat pressing and cutting of dough, place in same pan. Brush tops with a little extra milk.

5 Bake scones about 15 minutes or until browned and scones sound hollow when tapped firmly on the top with fingers.

BASIC SCONES

Kumara and gruyère scone wedges

PREPARATION TIME 35 MINUTES **COOKING TIME** 30 MINUTES **MAKES** 16

Use cooked cold mashed kumara or pumpkin. If it has been mashed with milk, butter, cream etc., then you'll probably have to use less milk than we suggested.

2½ cups (375g) self-raising flour

40g butter

350g gruyère cheese, cut into 1cm pieces

¼ cup finely chopped fresh chives

1 egg, beaten lightly

¾ cup mashed kumara

½ cup (125ml) milk, approximately

1 egg, beaten lightly, extra

SPICY TOPPING

2 teaspoons coriander seeds, crushed lightly

2 teaspoons cumin seeds

½ teaspoon crushed dried chilli

2 tablespoons finely chopped unsalted roasted cashews

1 Preheat oven to 220°C/200°C fan-forced. Grease deep 19cm-square cake pan.
2 Make spicy topping.
3 Sift flour into large bowl; rub in butter with fingertips. Stir in cheese and chives. Add egg and kumara; stir in enough milk to mix a soft sticky dough.
4 Knead dough on floured surface until smooth. Press dough into pan; brush with extra egg. Sprinkle with spicy topping; press topping firmly onto dough. Using a floured, serrated knife, cut dough into quarters, then diagonally into 16 triangles.
5 Bake scones 15 minutes. Reduce oven to 200°C/180°C fan-forced; bake further 15 minutes. Turn scones, top-side up, onto wire rack to cool.

SPICY TOPPING Combine ingredients in small bowl.

Bacon, egg and mustard scones

PREPARATION TIME 30 MINUTES **COOKING TIME** 20 MINUTES **MAKES** 16

If you don't have a 23cm sandwich cake pan, use a deep 22cm-round cake pan instead. The scones won't brown quite as well as they would in a sandwich pan.

2 rindless bacon rashers (140g), chopped finely

2¼ cups (335g) self-raising flour

90g butter, chopped coarsely

2 hard-boiled eggs, chopped finely

¼ cup (20g) finely grated parmesan cheese

2 tablespoons finely chopped fresh chives

1 tablespoon wholegrain mustard

1 cup (250ml) milk, approximately

2 tablespoons finely grated parmesan cheese, extra

1 Preheat oven to 220°C/200°C fan-forced. Grease 23cm-round sandwich cake pan.

2 Cook bacon in small frying pan, stirring, until crisp; drain, cool.

3 Sift flour into medium bowl; rub in butter with fingertips. Add bacon, eggs, cheese, chives and mustard; stir in enough milk to mix to a soft, sticky dough. Knead dough on floured surface until smooth.

4 Press dough out to 2cm thickness. Dip 5cm round cutter in flour; cut as many rounds as you can from dough. Place scones, side by side, just touching, in pan. Gently knead scraps of dough together; repeat pressing and cutting of dough, place in same pan. Brush tops with a little extra milk; sprinkle with extra cheese.

5 Bake scones about 15 minutes or until browned and scones sound hollow when tapped firmly on the top with fingers.

Carrot banana scones

PREPARATION TIME 30 MINUTES **COOKING TIME** 20 MINUTES **MAKES** 12

2 cups (300g) white
self-raising flour

½ cup (80g) wholemeal
self-raising flour

½ teaspoon ground cardamom

40g butter

⅓ cup (65g) firmly packed
brown sugar

½ cup mashed banana

⅓ cup finely grated carrot

¼ cup (30g) finely chopped
roasted walnuts

¼ cup (40g) finely chopped raisins

¾ cup (180ml) milk,
approximately

ORANGE CREAM

50g cream cheese, softened

50g butter, softened

½ teaspoon finely grated
orange rind

½ cup (80g) icing sugar

See note about the sandwich pan at left — the same applies for this recipe. The orange cream is a lovely spread for these scones, but it's not essential — a little butter will do instead.

1 Preheat oven to 220°C/200°C fan-forced. Grease 23cm-round sandwich cake pan.

2 Sift flours and cardamom into large bowl; rub in butter with fingertips. Add sugar, banana, carrot, nuts and raisins; stir in enough milk to mix to a soft, sticky dough. Knead dough on floured surface until smooth.

3 Press dough out to 2cm thickness. Dip 5cm cutter into flour; cut as many rounds as you can from the dough. Place scones side by side, just touching, in pan. Gently knead scraps of dough together; repeat pressing and cutting of dough. Place in same pan. Brush tops with a little extra milk.

4 Bake scones about 20 minutes or until just browned and scones sound hollow when tapped firmly on the top with fingers.

5 Meanwhile, make orange cream. Serve scones with orange cream

ORANGE CREAM Beat cheese, butter and rind in small bowl with electric mixer until as white as possible. Gradually beat in sifted icing sugar.

Cheese scones

PREPARATION TIME 10 MINUTES **COOKING TIME** 20 MINUTES **MAKES** 24

1 ½ cups (225g) self-raising flour

¼ teaspoon cayenne pepper

2 teaspoons caster sugar

⅓ cup (25g) finely grated parmesan cheese

1 cup (120g) coarsely grated cheddar cheese

1 cup (250ml) milk, approximately

40g butter, melted

CHIVE BUTTER

60g butter, softened

1 tablespoon finely chopped fresh chives

1 Preheat oven to 220°C/200°C fan-forced. Grease 20cm-round sandwich cake pan.

2 Sift flour, pepper and sugar into medium bowl, add parmesan and half of the cheddar; stir in enough milk to make a soft, sticky dough. Knead dough on floured surface until smooth.

3 Press dough out to 2cm thickness. Dip 3.5cm round cutter in flour; cut as many rounds as you can from dough. Place scones, side by side, just touching, in pan. Gently knead scraps of dough together; repeat pressing and cutting of dough, place in same pan. Brush tops with melted butter; sprinkle with remaining cheddar.

4 Bake scones about 20 minutes or until browned and scones sound hollow when tapped firmly on the top with fingers.

5 Meanwhile, make chive butter. Serve warm scones with chive butter.

CHIVE BUTTER Combine ingredients in small bowl.

Sage and prosciutto scones

PREPARATION TIME 30 MINUTES **COOKING TIME** 15 MINUTES **MAKES** 12

1 ½ cups (225g) white self-raising flour

½ cup (80g) wholemeal self-raising flour

15g butter

2 tablespoons chopped fresh sage

60g prosciutto, chopped finely

1 cup (250ml) milk, approximately

1 Preheat oven to 220°C/200°C fan-forced. Grease 20cm-round sandwich cake pan.

2 Sift flours into medium bowl; rub in butter with fingertips. Stir in sage and prosciutto; stir in enough milk to mix to a soft, sticky dough. Knead dough on floured surface until smooth.

3 Press dough out to 2cm thickness. Dip 5cm round cutter in flour; cut as many rounds as you can from piece of dough. Place scones, side by side, just touching, in pan. Gently knead scraps of dough together; repeat pressing and cutting of dough, place in same pan. Brush tops with a little extra milk.

4 Bake scones about 15 minutes or until browned and scones sound hollow when tapped firmly on the top with fingers.

CHEESE SCONES

Sultana and lemon scones

PREPARATION TIME 25 MINUTES **COOKING TIME** 15 MINUTES **MAKES** 16

2½ cups (375g) self-raising flour

1 tablespoon caster sugar

30g butter

½ cup (80g) sultanas

2 teaspoons finely grated lemon rind

¾ cup (180ml) milk

½ cup (125ml) water, approximately

1 Preheat oven to 220°C/200°C fan-forced. Grease deep 19cm-square cake pan.

2 Sift flour and sugar into large bowl; rub in butter with fingertips. Stir in sultanas and rind.

3 Make a well in centre of flour mixture; add milk and almost all the water. Using a knife, "cut" the milk and water through the flour mixture to mix to a soft, sticky dough. Knead dough on floured surface until smooth.

4 Press dough out to a 2cm thickness. Dip 4.5cm cutter into flour; cut as many rounds as you can from the piece of dough. Place scones side by side, just touching, in pan. Gently knead scraps of dough together; repeat pressing and cutting of dough. Place in same pan. Brush tops with a little extra milk.

5 Bake scones about 15 minutes or until just browned and scones sound hollow when tapped firmly on the top with fingers.

If you're troubled by tiny white specks on top of your scones — it's only undissolved sugar grains, use icing sugar instead of caster sugar.

Pistachio lime syrup gems

PREPARATION TIME 20 MINUTES **COOKING TIME** 15 MINUTES **MAKES** 24

cooking-oil spray

30g butter

1 teaspoon finely grated lime rind

⅓ cup (75g) caster sugar

1 egg

1¼ cups (185g) self-raising flour

⅔ cup (160ml) milk

¼ cup (35g) finely chopped pistachios

LIME SYRUP

2 tablespoons lime juice

2 tablespoons water

⅓ cup (75g) caster sugar

1 Preheat oven to 200°C/180°C fan-forced. Heat ungreased gem irons in oven for 5 minutes; coat with cooking-oil spray.

2 Meanwhile, beat butter, rind, sugar and egg in small bowl with electric mixer until combined. Stir in sifted flour and milk in two batches.

3 Drop tablespoons of mixture into gem irons; sprinkle with nuts. Bake about 12 minutes.

4 Meanwhile, make lime syrup. Turn gems onto a wire rack, brush with hot lime syrup.

LIME SYRUP Stir ingredients in small saucepan over heat, without boiling, until sugar dissolves. Simmer, uncovered, without stirring, 2 minutes.

Gem irons are made from cast iron and not readily available anymore. If you look around garage sales and second-hand shops you might be lucky enough to find some — or maybe there are some tucked away in the back of a cupboard somewhere. You can use mini muffin pans instead of the gem irons. The baking time and temperature will be about the same. Heat the pan for only a few minutes.

SULTANA AND LEMON SCONES

Scone basics

By the time the oven is preheated, you will have the dough ready to make the best-ever scones.

BAKING PANS
We like to bake scones in a pan with sides, the scones will take a little longer to bake in these pans than those baked on a flat oven tray. Grease the pans evenly.

SIFTING
Sift the dry ingredients into a wide-topped bowl. Most of our recipes use self-raising flour, add a pinch of salt if you like. We usually add a little sugar to the flour to take away the floury taste, even in savoury scone recipes.

RUBBING-IN BUTTER
Usually only a small amount — or even none at all — of butter is added to scone dough, it should be refrigerator-cold, diced, then rubbed into the flour with your fingertips.

TURNING DOUGH OUT
Turn the dough out onto a lightly floured surface, use either your hand or a plastic spatula. Soak the bowl in cold water for easier washing up later. If your fingers are sticky with dough, dry-clean them, away from the scone dough, by rubbing them with flour.

KNEADING THE DOUGH
The dough does require kneading to get smooth-topped scones. Turn the outside edges of the dough towards the centre of the dough, do this quickly and lightly, but don't panic, and don't work too much flour into the dough, you only need enough to stop the dough sticking to the work surface.

SHAPING THE DOUGH
Turn the dough smooth-side up, then pat it out evenly, working from the centre to the outside edge. Keep the dough an even thickness, there is always a tendency to press the dough out too thinly on the edge, leaving a hump in the middle. If you're making a large quantity of dough, use a floured rolling pin for this process.

ADDING LIQUID
Add most of the measured cold liquid to a well in the centre of the dry ingredients, leave a little back until you decide if it's needed or not to make a soft sticky dough.

CUTTING-IN LIQUID
Use a table knife to cut the liquid through the dry ingredients, don't keep mixing if the dough becomes stiff. Now is the time to decide if you need to add all or some of the remaining liquid to make a soft sticky dough.

ADDING REMAINING LIQUID
Add as much of the remaining liquid as you need to make a soft sticky dough, sometimes you need even more liquid, depending on how the flour absorbs the liquid.

CUTTING OUT
Use a sharp metal cutter for the best results. We cut shapes out, starting from the centre of the dough working towards the outside edge, but many champion scone-makers work in reverse, so try both ways. Lift the scone shapes into the prepared pan, position them so they are barely touching each other.

GLAZING
The purpose of glazing is to brush away any excess flour, and to draw the heat from the oven to the scones to brown the tops. Egg yolk will give the darkest colour, water the palest colour, milk will give a good middle of the road colour.

BAKING
Scones are done when they sound hollow, when they're tapped firmly on the top. Test the scones in the middle of the pan, as these take the longest to cook. As soon as they're out of the oven, shake the pan to free them from the base and sides; turn onto a tea towel, cover with another tea towel to soften scones. For crisp-sided scones, turn them onto a wire rack to cool.

Rock cakes

PREPARATION TIME 15 MINUTES **COOKING TIME** 15 MINUTES **MAKES** 18

2 cups (300g) self-raising flour

¼ teaspoon ground cinnamon

⅓ cup (75g) caster sugar

90g butter, chopped

1 cup (160g) sultanas

1 egg

½ cup (125ml) milk

1 tablespoon caster sugar, extra

1 Preheat oven to 200°C/180°C fan-forced. Grease oven trays.

2 Sift flour, cinnamon and sugar into medium bowl; rub in butter with fingertips. Stir in sultanas, egg and milk. Do not over mix.

3 Drop rounded tablespoons of mixture about 5cm apart onto trays; sprinkle with extra sugar.

4 Bake cakes about 15 minutes; cool on trays.

Rock cakes are not scones, but they're at least related. Be careful not to overcook rock cakes, they will firm up as they cool. Like biscuits — when they look brown and firmish — give one a gentle push, and, if it slides on the oven tray, they're done.

Choc florentine scones

PREPARATION TIME 25 MINUTES **COOKING TIME** 25 MINUTES **MAKES** 12

2 cups (300g) self-raising flour

¼ cup (25g) cocoa powder

2 tablespoons caster sugar

1 teaspoon ground cinnamon

30g butter

¼ cup (40g) blanched almonds, roasted, chopped finely

¼ cup (60g) finely chopped red glacé cherries

¼ cup (60g) finely chopped glacé apricots

¼ cup (55g) finely chopped glacé pineapple

1 cup (250ml) milk, approximately

150g dark eating chocolate, melted

1 Preheat oven to 220°C/ 200°C fan-forced. Grease 20cm-round sandwich pan.

2 Sift flour, cocoa, sugar and cinnamon into medium bowl; rub in butter with fingertips. Stir in nuts and fruit.

3 Make a well in centre of flour mixture; add almost all the milk. Use knife to "cut" the milk through the flour mixture, mixing to a soft, sticky dough. Knead dough on floured surface until smooth.

4 Press dough out to 2cm thickness. Dip 5.5cm round cutter in flour; cut as many rounds as you can from dough. Place scones, side by side, touching, in pan. Gently knead scraps of dough together; repeat pressing and cutting of dough, place in same pan. Brush tops with a little extra milk.

5 Bake scones about 25 minutes or until browned and scones sound hollow when tapped firmly on the top with fingers.

6 Spread tops of scones with chocolate, swirl with fork when almost set.

Rubbing butter in with fingertips is a much-used technique in baking. The idea is to quickly and lightly rub the fat into the flour using the tips of your fingers — hopefully the coolest part of your hands. Lift your fingers well above the bowl as you rub the butter in — this is to aerate the mixture a little. Shake the bowl quite firmly and any bits you've missed will come to the flour's surface (see page 404).

ROCK CAKES

Cranberry, oatmeal and cinnamon scones

PREPARATION TIME 10 MINUTES **COOKING TIME** 25 MINUTES **MAKES** 12

1 cup (160g) wholemeal
self-raising flour

1 cup (150g) white self-raising flour

1 teaspoon ground cinnamon

½ cup (70g) fine oatmeal

½ teaspoon finely grated
lemon rind

30g butter

¾ cup (105g) dried cranberries

1 cup (250ml) milk

2 tablespoons honey

1 tablespoon oatmeal, extra

1 Preheat oven to 220°C/200°C fan-forced. Grease and flour deep 19cm-square cake pan.

2 Sift flours and cinnamon into a medium bowl, add oatmeal and rind; rub in butter with fingertips. Stir in cranberries.

3 Make a well in centre of flour mixture; add combined milk and honey. Using a knife, "cut" the milk and honey through the flour mixture to mix to a soft, sticky dough. Knead dough on floured surface until smooth.

4 Press dough out to 2cm thickness. Dip 5.5cm cutter into flour; cut as many rounds as you can from the piece of dough. Place scones side by side, just touching, in pan. Gently knead scraps of dough together; repeat pressing and cutting of dough. Place in same pan. Brush tops with a little extra milk; sprinkle with extra oatmeal.

5 Bake scones about 15 minutes or until browned and scones sound hollow when tapped firmly on the top with fingers.

Fine oatmeal can be bought from health food stores, or, you could put some rolled oats into a blender and pulse it until they become fine. Return the husks from the wholemeal flour to the bowl. Serve these scones with butter, or for a healthier version, try ricotta cheese instead.

Pumpkin scones

PREPARATION TIME 20 MINUTES **COOKING TIME** 15 MINUTES **MAKES** 16

40g butter, softened

¼ cup (55g) caster sugar

1 egg

¾ cup cooked mashed pumpkin

2½ cups (375g) self-raising flour

½ teaspoon ground nutmeg

⅓ cup milk (125ml),
approximately

1 Preheat oven to 220°C/200°C fan-forced. Grease two 20cm-round sandwich pans.

2 Beat butter, sugar and egg in small bowl with electric mixer until light and fluffy. Stir in pumpkin, then sifted dry ingredients and enough milk to make a soft sticky dough. Knead dough on floured surface until smooth.

3 Press dough out to 2cm thickness. Dip 4.5cm round cutter in flour; cut as many rounds as you can from piece of dough. Place scones, side by side, just touching, in pan. Gently knead scraps of dough together; repeat pressing and cutting of dough, place in same pan. Brush tops with a little extra milk.

4 Bake scones about 15 minutes or until browned and scones sound hollow when tapped firmly on the top with fingers.

Don't worry if the butter, sugar and egg mixture curdles. The amount of milk you need to add to this scone dough depends entirely on the water content of the pumpkin — the amount you add will vary every time you make these scones.

CRANBERRY, OATMEAL AND CINNAMON SCONES

1   2

3   4

Buttermilk scones

PREPARATION TIME 20 MINUTES **COOKING TIME** 15 MINUTES **MAKES** 16

2½ cups (375g) self-raising flour

1 tablespoon caster sugar

30g butter

1¼ cups (310ml) buttermilk, approximately

1 Preheat oven to 220°C/200°C fan-forced. Grease deep 19cm-square cake pan.

2 Sift flour and sugar into large bowl; rub in butter with fingertips.

3 Make well in centre of flour mixture; add buttermilk. Using a knife, "cut" the buttermilk through the flour mixture to mix to a soft, sticky dough. Knead dough on floured surface until smooth.

4 Press dough out to a 2cm thickness. Dip 4.5cm cutter into flour; cut as many rounds as you can from the piece of dough. Place scones side by side, just touching, in pan. Gently knead scraps of dough together; repeat pressing and cutting of dough. Place in same pan. Brush tops with a little extra milk.

5 Bake scones about 15 minutes or until just browned and scones sound hollow when tapped firmly on the top with fingers.

This is one of our favourite scone recipes — it's particularly good for beginners as they always turn out well. The buttermilk gives the scones a lovely texture and lightness.

Honey and muesli scones

PREPARATION TIME 25 MINUTES **COOKING TIME** 15 MINUTES **MAKES** 16

2½ cups (375g) self-raising flour

1 teaspoon ground cinnamon

1 tablespoon caster sugar

30g butter

½ cup (65g) toasted muesli

¼ cup (90g) honey

¾ cup (180ml) milk

½ cup (125ml) water, approximately

1 Preheat oven to 220°C/200°C fan-forced. Grease deep 19cm-square cake pan.

2 Sift flour, cinnamon and sugar into large bowl; rub in butter with fingertips. Add muesli.

3 Make a well in centre of flour mixture; add honey and milk and almost all of the water. Using a knife, "cut" the milk and water through the flour mixture to mix to a soft, sticky dough. Knead dough on floured surface until smooth.

4 Press dough out to 2cm thickness. Dip 4.5cm cutter into flour; cut as many rounds as you can from the piece of dough. Place scones side by side, just touching, in pan. Gently knead scraps of dough together; repeat pressing and cutting of dough. Place in same pan. Brush tops with a little extra milk.

5 Bake scones about 15 minutes or until browned and scones sound hollow when tapped firmly on the top with fingers.

When a recipe says "cut" the liquid through the dry ingredients, it means don't stir, just use a knife quickly and lightly to draw the knife through the flour, so moistening the dry ingredients as lightly as possible. This is done to stop you overworking the flour — which causes tough scones.

1 BUTTERMILK SCONES **2** HONEY AND MUESLI SCONES
3 CARDAMOM MARMALADE SCONES [P 412] **4** BLUEBERRY GINGER SCONES [P 412]

A soft sticky dough should guarantee you really good results in the scone-making stakes. The dough shouldn't be so soft that it doesn't hold its shape, but should be tacky and want to stick to your fingers. Flour your hands and lightly knead the dough — really only turning it gently so that you end up with a smooth ball of dough.

Cardamom marmalade scones

PREPARATION TIME 25 MINUTES **COOKING TIME** 15 MINUTES **MAKES** 16

2½ cups (375g) self-raising flour

1 tablespoon caster sugar

30g butter

1 teaspoon ground cardamom

2 teaspoons finely grated orange rind

1 cup (250ml) milk

⅓ cup (115g) orange marmalade

1 Preheat oven to 220°C/200°C fan-forced. Grease deep 19cm-square cake pan.

2 Sift flour and sugar into large bowl; rub in butter with fingertips. Stir in cardamom and rind.

3 Make a well in centre of flour mixture; add combined milk and marmalade. Using a knife, "cut" the milk and marmalade through the flour mixture to mix to a soft, sticky dough. Knead dough on floured surface until smooth.

4 Press dough out to a 2cm thickness. Dip 4.5cm cutter into flour; cut as many rounds as you can from the piece of dough. Place scones side by side, just touching, in pan. Gently knead scraps of dough together; repeat pressing and cutting of dough. Place in same pan. Brush tops with a little extra milk.

5 Bake scones about 15 minutes or until browned and scones sound hollow when tapped firmly on the top with fingers.

Blueberry ginger scones

PREPARATION TIME 25 MINUTES **COOKING TIME** 15 MINUTES **MAKES** 16

2½ cups (375g) self-raising flour

1 tablespoon caster sugar

30g butter

3 teaspoons ground ginger

½ cup (75g) fresh or frozen blueberries

¾ cup (180ml) milk

½ cup (125ml) water, approximately

1 Preheat oven to 220°C/200°C fan-forced. Grease deep 19cm-square cake pan.

2 Sift flour and sugar into large bowl; rub in butter with fingertips. Stir in ginger and blueberries.

3 Make a well in centre of flour mixture; add combined milk and almost all of the water. Using a knife, "cut" the milk and water through the flour mixture to mix to a soft, sticky dough. Knead dough on floured surface until smooth.

4 Press dough out to a 2cm thickness. Dip 4.5cm cutter into flour; cut as many rounds as you can from the piece of dough. Place scones side by side, just touching, in pan. Gently knead scraps of dough together; repeat pressing and cutting of dough. Place in same pan. Brush tops with a little extra milk.

5 Bake scones about 15 minutes or until browned and scones sound hollow when tapped firmly on the top with fingers.

Apricot and almond scones

PREPARATION TIME 25 MINUTES **COOKING TIME** 15 MINUTES **MAKES** 16

2½ cups (375g) self-raising flour

1 tablespoon caster sugar

30g butter

1 teaspoon mixed spice

1 cup (150g) finely chopped
dried apricots

⅓ cup (45g) finely chopped
roasted slivered almonds

¾ cup (180ml) milk

½ cup (125ml) water,
approximately

1 Preheat oven to 220°C/200°C fan-forced. Grease deep 19cm-square cake pan.
2 Sift flour and sugar into large bowl; rub in butter with fingertips. Stir in spice, apricots
and nuts.
3 Make a well in centre of flour mixture; add combined milk and almost all of the water.
Using a knife, "cut" the milk and water through the flour mixture to mix to a soft, sticky
dough. Knead dough on floured surface until smooth.
4 Press dough out to a 2cm thickness. Dip 4.5cm cutter into flour; cut as many rounds
as you can from the piece of dough. Place scones side by side, just touching, in pan.
Gently knead scraps of dough together; repeat pressing and cutting of dough. Place in
same pan. Brush tops with a little extra milk.
5 Bake scones about 15 minutes or until just browned and scones sound hollow when
tapped firmly on the top with fingers.

Use a sharp metal cutter for the best scones. A blunt cutter will just squash the light dough. Always try to press out the dough as evenly as you can, using your floured hand. Press from the centre to the outside of the piece of dough. Scone dough is springy so try and keep it even — it will fight you.

Spicy fruit scones

PREPARATION TIME 20 MINUTES (PLUS STANDING TIME) **COOKING TIME** 15 MINUTES **MAKES** 16

1¼ cups (310ml) hot strong
strained black tea

¾ cup (135g) mixed dried fruit

3 cups (450g) self-raising flour

1 teaspoon ground cinnamon

1 teaspoon mixed spice

2 tablespoons caster sugar

20g butter

½ cup (125ml) sour cream,
approximately

1 Preheat oven to 220°C/200°C fan-forced. Grease 23cm-square slab cake pan.
2 Combine tea and fruit in small heatproof bowl. Cover; stand 20 minutes or until cold.
3 Sift dry ingredients into large bowl; rub in butter with fingertips. Stir in fruit mixture and
enough sour cream to mix to a soft, sticky dough. Knead on floured surface until smooth.
4 Press dough out to 2cm thickness. Dip 5.5cm cutter into flour; cut as many rounds
as you can from the piece of dough. Place scones side by side, just touching, in pan.
Gently knead scraps of dough together; repeat pressing and cutting of dough. Place in
same pan. Brush tops with a little extra milk.
5 Bake scones about 15 minutes or until just browned and scones sound hollow when
tapped firmly on the top with fingers.

FRIANDS

Friands

The darlings of the café set, friands are the perfectly-sized little cake to accompany a cup of coffee. With both a high nut and butter content, and any of a host of fruits for added flavour, they're dense and moist and incredibly more-ish.

In France, these oval- or rectangular-shaped cakes are better known as financiers, because they were originally baked in tiny, gold-bar shaped pans. You can buy these traditionally-shaped pans individually from specialty kitchen stores or as baking dishes with multiple holes from most supermarkets. You might also choose to make tiny friands containing a single berry or piece of fruit using a mini-muffin pan, or larger friands in a regular muffin pan. Friands can also be cut into shapes as the bases for the little decorated cakes known as petits fours. The basic mixture for most of these recipes will fill a 9 x ½-cup (125ml) oval friand pan or an 8 x ½-cup (125ml) rectangular friand pan.

Friands are best made on the day of serving, but they can be stored in an airtight container for two days, or frozen for up to three months. To defrost, wrap them individually in foil and heat in a moderate oven for about 15 minutes or in a microwave oven, unwrapped, on HIGH (100%) for about 30 seconds.

FRUIT

You can use frozen berries and other fruit quite successfully in friands. Don't defrost before use; if they are unthawed there is less likelihood of the fruit "bleeding" as the mixture cooks. You can buy frozen fruit at the supermarket or freeze it yourself when there is a surplus at the peak of their season.

If you're using peaches or nectarines, you may want to peel them before slicing. Cut a cross in the base of the fruit with a sharp knife and immerse the fruit in a saucepan of boiling water for about a minute. Remove the fruit using a slotted spoon and starting at the cross, peel the skin away. If it doesn't come off easily at first, you may need to use a sharp knife to get started. If the fruit is too hot to handle, put it in cold water to cool.

EGGS

Friands use a lot of egg whites. We use large (60g) eggs in all our recipes. You only want to break the egg whites with a fork, not to aerate them by beating them to peaks (see page 641). For a more closely-textured friand, stand the mixture in the pan for 30 minutes before baking. It's just fine to use thawed frozen egg whites in these recipes. You can buy them in packs at the supermarket. Pavlova mix also works well.

If you use fresh eggs, you can always freeze the leftover yolks for future use. Freeze them singly in the compartments of an ice cube tray, turn out and store in a sealed plastic bag in the freezer. Mark clearly with the date and use them within a couple of months. Defrost in the fridge. Or you can make mayonnaise, lemon curd, ice-cream, custard, scrambled eggs or frittata with the surplus yolks.

It's easiest to separate eggs when they are cold, but let the whites come to room temperature before you use them. The shell to shell method is the most common way of separating eggs. Break the egg against the edge of the bench or the rim of a bowl as close to the equator of the egg as possible, then gently pull the egg apart holding the yolk in one half of the shell and letting the white run out of the other half of the egg into a bowl or cup. Remove any remaining white surrounding the yolk by holding the two shell halves close together and tipping the yolk into the empty shell half, letting the white run off as you transfer the yolk. You may need to repeat the tipping process several times to remove all the egg white.

Or you can separate eggs with your hand by breaking the whole egg into the palm of your cupped hand and letting the white run out into a bowl by separating your fingers slightly. Place the yolk in another bowl or cup. There is also such a thing as an egg separator. This tool has a central bowl surrounded by a slotted rim. Place the separator over a bowl and break the egg into the bowl of the separator, which will hold the yolk while the white escapes into the bowl underneath through the slots.

NUTS

Hazelnuts, almonds, macadamias and shredded and desiccated coconut all have a place in the friand repertoire. We've also successfully substituted ground pine nuts and cashews. You can buy ready ground nuts at the supermarket or grind them yourself using a blender or food processor. Process the nuts in short bursts to avoid turning them to a paste.

You might like to toast or roast the nuts to enhance their flavour before grinding. Be vigilant, however, as they burn easily, so you need to stir and check them frequently. You can roast nuts in a small non-stick frying pan over low to moderate heat or roast them on an oven tray or cake pan in a moderate oven for 5 to 10 minutes, shaking the pan occasionally, until they brown. Whichever method you use, be sure to tip the roasted nuts onto another cold tray when they are done as they will continue to cook and might burn if left in the hot pan or oven tray.

The skins of almonds and hazelnuts are quite bitter so you will want to remove as much as possible before you grind them for use in friands. Skin almonds by blanching them. Place the nuts in a heatproof bowl and cover with boiling water for a couple of minutes. Drain and place them in a bowl of cold water. Drain again and the skins should slip off easily when the almond is squeezed between the thumb and the forefinger.

To skin hazelnuts, roast the nuts on an oven tray in a moderate oven for about 15 minutes, shaking the tray occasionally and checking to make sure they're not burning. Remove the tray from the oven and turn the nuts out onto a clean dry tea towel. Wrap the nuts in the towel and rub them together vigorously — the skins should flake off quite readily. You won't get all the skins off, but this is fine for most baking purposes.

Lime and berry friands

PREPARATION TIME 15 MINUTES **COOKING TIME** 10 MINUTES **MAKES** 24

Lime is a flavour that works really well in friands, the tartness of the lime counteracts the buttery sweetness of the cakes. Use the blueberries in their frozen state or the colour will "bleed" into the mixture.

3 egg whites

90g butter, melted

1 teaspoon finely grated lime rind

½ cup (60g) almond meal

¾ cup (120g) icing sugar

¼ cup (35g) plain flour

⅓ cup (50g) frozen blueberries

1 tablespoon icing sugar, extra

1 Preheat oven to 180°C/160°C fan-forced. Grease two 12-hole mini (1-tablespoon/20ml) muffin pans.

2 Place egg whites in medium bowl; beat with a fork. Stir in butter, rind, almond meal and sifted icing sugar and flour. Spoon mixture into pan holes; top each with a blueberry.

3 Bake friands about 10 minutes. Stand friands in pans 5 minutes; turn, top-side up, onto wire rack to cool. Dust with sifted extra icing sugar.

Little lime friands

PREPARATION TIME 20 MINUTES **COOKING TIME** 15 MINUTES **MAKES** 24

There are several different-sized mini muffin pans available. It doesn't matter which one you use, just be aware that the smaller-sized mini muffin pans will take less cooking time.

4 egg whites

125g butter, melted

⅔ cup (80g) almond meal

¾ cup (120g) icing sugar

¼ cup (35g) plain flour

2 teaspoons finely grated lime rind

1 tablespoon lime juice

24 (50g) whole blanched almonds

1 Preheat oven to 200°C/180°C fan-forced. Grease two 12-hole mini (2-tablespoons/40ml) muffin pans.

2 Place egg whites in medium bowl; beat with a fork. Stir in butter, almond meal, sifted icing sugar and flour, rind and juice. Spoon mixture into pan holes; top each with an almond.

3 Bake friands about 15 minutes. Stand friands in pans 5 minutes; turn, top-side up, onto wire rack to cool.

Chocolate hazelnut friands

PREPARATION TIME 20 MINUTES **COOKING TIME** 20 MINUTES **MAKES** 12

6 egg whites

185g butter, melted

1 cup (125g) hazelnut meal

1 ½ cups (240g) icing sugar

½ cup (75g) plain flour

100g dark eating chocolate, chopped coarsely

¼ cup (35g) coarsely chopped roasted hazelnuts

1 Preheat oven to 200°C/180°C fan-forced. Grease 12 x ½-cup (125ml) rectangular or oval friand pans; stand on oven tray.

2 Place egg whites in medium bowl; beat with a fork. Stir in butter, hazelnut meal and sifted icing sugar and flour; stir in chocolate. Spoon mixture into pan holes; sprinkle with nuts.

3 Bake friands about 20 minutes. Stand friands in pans 5 minutes; turn, top-side up, onto wire rack to cool.

Loaf and oval-shaped pans are available in racks, or as individual pans. It's the individual pans that need to be stood and baked on an oven tray, simply for easy handling.

Citrus and poppy seed friands

PREPARATION TIME 20 MINUTES **COOKING TIME** 20 MINUTES **MAKES** 12

6 egg whites

185g butter, melted

1 cup (125g) almond meal

1 ½ cups (240g) icing sugar

½ cup (75g) plain flour

1 tablespoon poppy seeds

1 teaspoon finely grated lemon rind

1 teaspoon finely grated orange rind

1 Preheat oven to 200°C/180°C fan-forced. Grease 12-hole (⅓-cup/80ml) muffin pan or 12 oval friand pans; stand on oven tray.

2 Place egg whites in medium bowl; beat with a fork. Stir in butter, almond meal, sifted icing sugar and flour, seeds and rinds. Spoon mixture into pan holes.

3 Bake friands about 20 minutes. Stand friands in pan 5 minutes; turn, top-side up, onto wire rack to cool.

Poppy seeds and citrus flavours complement each other beautifully. Here we've used lemon and orange, but use one or the other if you prefer.

1 CHOCOLATE HAZELNUT FRIANDS **2** CITRUS AND POPPY SEED FRIANDS
3 RASPBERRY AND WHITE CHOCOLATE FRIANDS [P 422] **4** PEAR AND HAZELNUT FRIANDS [P 422]

Raspberry and white chocolate friands

PREPARATION TIME 20 MINUTES **COOKING TIME** 25 MINUTES **MAKES** 12

We've taken the simple friand to a new level of decadence here by adding white chocolate. It needs to be chopped coarsely (about the size of a raisin will do nicely) but evenly.

6 egg whites

185g butter, melted

1 cup (125g) almond meal

1½ cups (240g) icing sugar

½ cup (75g) plain flour

100g white eating chocolate, chopped coarsely

100g fresh or frozen raspberries

1 Preheat oven to 200°C/180°C fan-forced. Grease 12 x ½-cup (125ml) rectangular or oval friand pans; stand on oven tray.

2 Place egg whites in medium bowl; beat with a fork. Stir in butter, almond meal and sifted icing sugar and flour. Stir in chocolate. Spoon mixture into pan holes; top each with raspberries.

3 Bake friands about 25 minutes. Stand friands in pans 5 minutes; turn, top-side up, onto wire rack to cool.

Pear and hazelnut friands

PREPARATION TIME 15 MINUTES **COOKING TIME** 20 MINUTES **MAKES** 12

If you need to remove the skins from hazelnuts, it's easy — read the simple instructions on page 417. Corella pears have only a short season, if they're not available use thinly sliced apple — red-skinned look best — instead.

6 egg whites

185g butter, melted

1 cup (100g) hazelnut meal

1½ cups (240g) icing sugar

½ cup (75g) plain flour

1 small corella pear (100g)

12 (10g) roasted hazelnuts, halved

1 Preheat oven to 200°C/180°C fan-forced. Grease 12-hole (⅓-cup/80ml) muffin pan or 12 oval friand pans; stand on oven tray.

2 Place egg whites in medium bowl; beat with a fork. Stir in butter, hazelnut meal, sifted icing sugar and flour.

3 Core pear; cut lengthways into 12 even slices.

4 Spoon mixture into pan holes; top each with one slice pear and two nut halves.

5 Bake friands about 20 minutes. Stand friands in pan 5 minutes; turn, top-side up, onto wire rack to cool.

Mocha walnut friands

PREPARATION TIME 15 MINUTES **COOKING TIME** 20 MINUTES **MAKES** 12

1¼ cups (125g) walnuts

3 teaspoons instant coffee granules

2 teaspoons cocoa powder

1 tablespoon boiling water

6 egg whites

185g butter, melted

1½ cups (240g) icing sugar

½ cup (75g) plain flour

12 dark chocolate Melts

1 Preheat oven to 200°C/180°C fan-forced. Grease 12 x ½-cup (125ml) oval friand pans; stand on oven tray.

2 Process nuts until ground finely. Blend coffee and cocoa in small jug with the water until smooth.

3 Place egg whites in medium bowl; beat with a fork. Stir in butter, sifted icing sugar and flour, ground walnuts and mocha mixture. Spoon friand mixture into pan holes.

4 Bake friands about 20 minutes. Top each friand with a chocolate Melt. Stand friands in pans 5 minutes; carefully turn, top-side up, onto wire rack to cool.

There will be enough heat in the just-baked friands to hold the chocolate Melts. If you'd rather have the friands "iced", you'll be able to spread the Melts after a few minutes.

Pistachio and lime friands

PREPARATION TIME 15 MINUTES **COOKING TIME** 20 MINUTES **MAKES** 12

125g pistachios

6 egg whites

185g butter, melted

1½ cups (240g) icing sugar

½ cup (75g) plain flour

1 tablespoon lime juice

2 teaspoons finely grated lime rind

1 Preheat oven to 200°C/180°C fan-forced. Grease 12 x ½-cup (125ml) oval friand pans; stand on oven tray.

2 Process nuts until ground finely.

3 Place egg whites in large bowl; whisk until frothy. Stir in butter, sifted sugar and flour, juice, rind and ground pistachios. Spoon mixture into pans.

4 Bake friands about 20 minutes. Stand friands in pans 5 minutes; turn, top-side up, onto wire rack to cool.

Sometimes limes are a bit reluctant to give up their juice. Roll each one on the bench with your hand, don't be gentle. A quick zap of about 10 seconds per lime in the microwave oven will also get the juice flowing for you.

Special equipment

If you're starting out as a home-baker, buy equipment as you need it — price is usually a guide to quality.

KITCHEN THERMOMETERS

There are many types, shapes and sizes available at cookware shops. The most commonly used thermometers are oven (left), meat (right) and candy/sweet.

CAKE PANS

Occasionally you'll need an unusual-shaped cake. Suitable pans are available for sale and hire at cake decorating suppliers. They are made from a good quality tin, so bake the cake 10°C lower than you normally would.

PUSHERS & PIPING TUBES

Icing can be forced through icing pushers with a tube on the end to achieve an endless variety of decorations. These are available in plastic and metal at cookware shops.

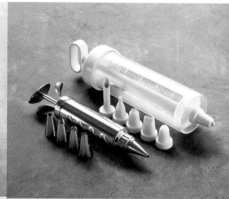

CROQUEMBOUCHE MOULD

These are used to create a croquembouche — the famous stack of cream puffs (made from choux pastry), held together with toffee or melted chocolate. The moulds are expensive to buy, but can be hired from cake decorating suppliers.

SPOONS & SPATULAS

You can't have too many of both of these utensils, you'll find you will use different spoons and spatulas for different jobs. Keep the wooden spoons you use for baking separate from the spoons you use for stirring savoury food as the wood will absorb flavours and fats.

CUTTERS

You get what you pay for with cutters. If you want the best available, buy them from chefs' suppliers — if you look after them, they will last you a lifetime. Metal cutters are far superior to plastic, simply because they cut cleanly through dough or icing etc.

PASTRY SCRAPERS

These spatula-like utensils are used for cutting and turning various types of dough, soft icing (fondant) etc, as a scraper for a bowl or board, or to transfer ingredients from a board to a pan.

ROLLING PINS

Bakers love their rolling pins, and usually look after them. If made from wood, they will mark and bruise easily. Rolling pins can be made from many different materials, and come in various shapes and sizes for different purposes.

GRATERS & ZESTERS

These come in a range of shapes and sizes, and vary hugely in cost and quality. If you buy a cheap grater, be prepared to throw it out when it gets blunt.

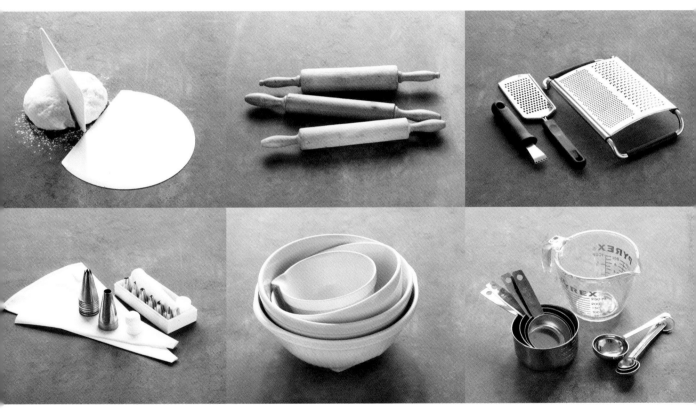

ICING BAGS & TUBES

Icing bags come in a variety of materials and sizes, they can be found in supermarkets, cake decorating suppliers, chefs' suppliers and cookware shops. Icing tubes/pipes are also available in many shapes and sizes. Screw on attachments are available so you can change tubes on the same bag of icing.

MIXING BOWLS

Like saucepans, there is no need to buy a "set" of bowls. Buy the size and shape of bowl that suits your needs. Stainless steel, glass and china are probably the most user-friendly types of bowls.

MEASURERS

Baking is a science, and it's vital that you weigh or measure ingredients accurately for success every time. Buy robust, easy-to-read metric measuring jugs, cups and spoons. Check that the tablespoon measure is 20ml. Australia is the only country in the world with a 20ml tablespoon.

If you don't have any coffee beans, don't worry — the flavour will be strong enough from the instant coffee. To make the friands look pretty, dust them either with sifted icing sugar, or a light dusting of good-quality cocoa powder (for a mocha twist) or a combination of both.

Coffee friands

PREPARATION TIME 15 MINUTES **COOKING TIME** 20 MINUTES **MAKES** 12

2 teaspoons instant coffee granules

2 teaspoons hot water

6 egg whites

185g butter, melted

1 cup (100g) hazelnut meal

1 ½ cups (240g) icing sugar

½ cup (75g) plain flour

24 coffee beans

1 Preheat oven to 200°C/180°C fan-forced. Grease 12 x ½-cup (125ml) rectangular or oval friand pans; stand on oven tray.

2 Dissolve coffee in the water in a small jug.

3 Place egg whites in medium bowl; beat with a fork. Stir in coffee mixture, then butter, hazelnut meal and sifted icing sugar and flour. Spoon mixture into pan holes; top each with two coffee beans.

4 Bake friands about 20 minutes. Stand friands in pans 5 minutes; turn, top-side up, onto wire rack to cool.

Coconut and pineapple friands

PREPARATION TIME 15 MINUTES **COOKING TIME** 20 MINUTES **MAKES** 12

6 egg whites

185g butter, melted

1 cup (120g) almond meal

1 ½ cups (240g) icing sugar

⅓ cup (50g) plain flour

150g finely chopped glacé pineapple

½ cup (40g) shredded coconut

1 Preheat oven to 200°C/180°C fan-forced. Line 12 x ½-cup (125ml) oval friand pans; stand on oven tray.

2 Place egg whites in medium bowl; beat with a fork. Stir in butter, almond meal, sifted icing sugar and flour, pineapple and ⅓ cup of the coconut. Spoon mixture into pan holes; sprinkle with remaining coconut.

3 Bake friands about 20 minutes. Stand friands in pans 5 minutes; turn, top-side up, onto wire rack to cool.

Mini choc-chip friands

PREPARATION TIME 20 MINUTES **COOKING TIME** 20 MINUTES **MAKES** 24

4 egg whites
125g butter, melted
²⁄₃ cup (80g) almond meal
¾ cup (120g) icing sugar
¼ cup (35g) plain flour
100g dark eating chocolate, chopped finely
¼ cup (60ml) cream
100g dark eating chocolate, chopped, extra

1 Preheat oven to 200°C/180°C fan-forced. Grease two 12-hole mini (2-tablespoons/40ml) muffin pans.
2 Place egg whites in medium bowl; beat with a fork. Stir in butter, almond meal, sifted icing sugar and flour and chopped chocolate. Spoon mixture into pan holes.
3 Bake friands about 15 minutes. Stand friands in pans 5 minutes; turn, top-side up, onto wire rack to cool.
4 Meanwhile, combine cream and extra chocolate in small heatproof bowl over small saucepan of simmering water; stir until smooth. Stand until thickened. Spoon chocolate mixture over friands.

The cream and chocolate make a rich frosting, almost like a ganache. These two-mouthful friands are perfect for an afternoon tea or to serve with good strong coffee.

Lemon and cranberry friands

PREPARATION TIME 15 MINUTES **COOKING TIME** 20 MINUTES **MAKES** 12

6 egg whites
185g butter, melted
1 cup (120g) almond meal
1½ cups (240g) icing sugar
½ cup (75g) plain flour
¾ cup (105g) dried cranberries
1 tablespoon finely grated lemon rind
1 tablespoon lemon juice

1 Preheat oven to 200°C/180°C fan-forced. Grease 12 x ½-cup (125ml) oval friand pans; stand on oven tray.
2 Place egg whites in medium bowl; beat with a fork. Stir in butter, almond meal, sifted icing sugar and flour, cranberries, rind and juice. Spoon mixture into pan holes.
3 Bake friands about 20 minutes. Stand friands in pans 5 minutes; turn, top-side up, onto wire rack to cool.

Most of the flavour comes from the lemon rind in this recipe. Always wash and dry the lemon before you grate it. Then, be sure to grate only the rind, not the white pith, which can be quite bitter in taste.

MINI CHOC-CHIP FRIANDS

Brandied cherry friands

PREPARATION TIME 15 MINUTES (PLUS STANDING TIME) **COOKING TIME** 20 MINUTES **MAKES** 12

150g frozen seeded cherries
2 tablespoons brandy
125g roasted pecans
6 egg whites
185g butter, melted
1 ½ cups (240g) icing sugar
½ cup (75g) plain flour

CHERRY SAUCE
¼ cup (55g) caster sugar
2 tablespoons water

1 Preheat oven to 200°C/180°C fan-forced. Grease 12 x ½-cup (125ml) oval friand pans; stand on oven tray.
2 Combine cherries and brandy in small bowl; stand 30 minutes. Process nuts until ground finely. Drain cherries; reserve juice.
3 Place egg whites in medium bowl; beat with a fork. Stir in butter, sifted icing sugar and flour and ground pecans. Spoon mixture into pan holes; top each with drained cherries.
4 Bake friands about 20 minutes. Stand friands in pans 5 minutes; turn, top-side up, onto wire rack to cool.
5 Meanwhile, make cherry sauce. Serve friands with sauce.

CHERRY SAUCE Stir sugar, water and reserved cherry juice in small saucepan over low heat until sugar dissolves; bring to the boil. Reduce heat; simmer, uncovered, about 3 minutes or until sauce thickens slightly.

Mandarin and poppy seed friands

PREPARATION TIME 15 MINUTES **COOKING TIME** 20 MINUTES **MAKES** 12

1 tablespoon poppy seeds
2 tablespoons mandarin juice
6 egg whites
185g butter, melted
1 cup (120g) almond meal

1 ½ cups (240g) icing sugar
½ cup (75g) plain flour
2 tablespoons finely grated mandarin rind

1 Preheat oven to 200°C/180°C fan-forced. Grease 12 x ½-cup (125ml) oval friand pans; stand on oven tray.
2 Combine poppy seeds and juice in small jug; stand 10 minutes.
3 Place egg whites in medium bowl; beat with a fork. Stir in butter, almond meal, sifted icing sugar and flour, then rind and poppy seed mixture. Spoon mixture into pan holes.
4 Bake friands about 20 minutes. Stand friands in pans 5 minutes; turn, top-side up, onto wire rack to cool.

Passionfruit friands

PREPARATION TIME 20 MINUTES   **COOKING TIME** 20 MINUTES   **MAKES** 12

6 egg whites
185g butter, melted
1 cup (125g) almond meal
1 ½ cups (240g) icing sugar
½ cup (75g) plain flour
2 medium passionfruit

1   Preheat oven to 200°C/180°C fan-forced. Grease 12 x ½-cup (125ml) rectangular or oval friand pans; stand on oven tray.
2   Place egg whites in medium bowl; beat with a fork. Stir in butter, almond meal and sifted icing sugar and flour. Spoon mixture into pan holes; drizzle with passionfruit.
3   Bake friands about 20 minutes. Stand friands in pans 5 minutes; turn, top-side up, onto wire rack to cool.

Plum friands

PREPARATION TIME 20 MINUTES   **COOKING TIME** 25 MINUTES   **MAKES** 12

6 egg whites
185g butter, melted
1 cup (125g) hazelnut meal
1 ½ cups (240g) icing sugar
½ cup (75g) plain flour
2 medium plums (200g), sliced thinly

1   Preheat oven to 200°C/180°C fan-forced. Grease 12 x ½-cup (125ml) rectangular or oval friand pans; stand on oven tray.
2   Place egg whites in medium bowl; beat with a fork. Stir in butter, hazelnut meal and sifted icing sugar and flour. Spoon mixture into pan holes; top each with sliced plums.
3   Bake friands about 25 minutes. Stand friands in pans 5 minutes; turn, top-side up, onto wire rack to cool.

If you're mad about passionfruit, make a thin glaze for these friands. You'll need ½ cup icing sugar, stir in enough fresh passionfruit juice or pulp to make a thin pourable mixture. Once the friands are on the wire rack, pour the glaze over them, it doesn't have to be neat or spread evenly. The heat from the friands will soften the glaze just enough. When the friands cool, the glaze will set.

Plums, peaches, apricots nectarines — all of these stone fruits work perfectly well in this recipe. The fruit needs to be ripe, but firm enough to slice thinly.

If you've read through this chapter looking for a recipe to make, you'll have realised that there is not much difference between any of the recipes. We have tried to push a lot of boundaries in the Test Kitchen by experimenting with the balance of ingredients for friands, and we've realised you simply can't do much — apart from adding small amounts of various flavourings. Anyway, why tamper with them, they're so delicious and so simple to make — usually in one bowl. And they require a minimum amount of mixing — a fork is all you need really. Friands are not meant to be light and airy, so the last thing you want to do is whisk air into the mixture.

Pear and almond friands

PREPARATION TIME 15 MINUTES **COOKING TIME** 20 MINUTES **MAKES** 12

6 egg whites

185g butter, melted

1 cup (120g) almond meal

1 ½ cups (240g) icing sugar

¾ cup (110g) plain flour

1 small pear (180g), peeled, cored, chopped finely

¼ cup (20g) flaked almonds

1 Preheat oven to 200°C/180°C fan-forced. Grease 12-hole (⅓-cup/80ml) muffin pan.

2 Place egg whites in medium bowl; beat with a fork. Stir in butter, almond meal, sifted icing sugar and flour, then pear.

3 Pour ¼-cups of mixture into pan holes; sprinkle with nuts.

4 Bake friands about 20 minutes. Stand friands in pan 5 minutes; turn, top-side up, onto wire rack to cool.

Lemon and coconut friands

PREPARATION TIME 15 MINUTES **COOKING TIME** 20 MINUTES **MAKES** 12

6 egg whites

185g butter, melted

1 cup (100g) hazelnut meal

1 ½ cups (240g) icing sugar

½ cup (75g) plain flour

2 teaspoons finely grated lemon rind

1 tablespoon lemon juice

¼ cup (20g) desiccated coconut

⅓ cup (15g) flaked coconut

1 Preheat oven to 200°C/180°C fan-forced. Grease 12-hole (⅓-cup/80ml) muffin pan.

2 Place egg whites in medium bowl; beat with a fork. Stir in butter, hazelnut meal, sifted icing sugar and flour, rind, juice and desiccated coconut.

3 Pour ¼-cups of mixture into pan holes; sprinkle with flaked coconut.

4 Bake friands about 20 minutes. Stand friands in pan 5 minutes; turn, top-side up, onto wire rack to cool.

PEAR AND ALMOND FRIANDS

TARTS & PASTRIES

Tarts & Pastries

Perhaps a little more refined than their pie siblings, tarts, flans and other pastry desserts have no upper crust and usually a thin filling. The exceptions of course are tarts that are called pies such as chiffon pie and lemon meringue which are often piled high with either clouds of whipped egg whites and/or cream.

Pecan pie is the signature tart of the American south, with a rich filling of the nuts of the pecan tree, which is native to the mid and southwest of the US. Canada's response is the maple syrup tart, which is filled with a thickened combination of maple syrup, sugar and cream. The French have contributed all manner of flans and tarts to the recipe books from the rich crème pâtissière (custard) filled and shiny fruit bedecked fruit flan to the upside-down tarte tatin. The invention of two sisters who ran a hotel in the Loire Valley, the original tarte tatin has caramelised apples with a pastry lid, which is turned out before serving. The recipe was popularised by the famous Paris restaurant, Maxim's, which is believed to have sent a chef disguised as a gardener to learn how to make the delicious tart. It remains on the menu today. Any fruit which can be baked can replace the apples in modern versions.

England gave us the custard tart, sprinkled with nutmeg, while the Portuguese invented the pasteis de nata with its puff pastry, rich custard filling and burnt sugar topping. Many people don't consider a Chinese meal complete without the yolky Cantonese version of the custard tart. Like the croissant, the Danish pastry, a yeast-risen pastry topped with fruit, custard, jam or marzipan, was devised by bakers in Vienna.

Flans and tarts are usually baked in a straight-sided or fluted-edged tin with a removable base. Some cooks maintain that shiny tart tins reflect heat and slow the baking process. Adherents to this school of thought prefer a flan tin with a black or at least, dark, base. Either way, flan and tart tins are usually placed on an oven tray to make getting them in and out of the oven easier. The term galette is used to describe a very thin rectangular or square tart which is topped with thinly sliced fruit sprinkled with sugar and usually baked directly on an oven tray.

PASTRY MAKING TIPS

More information on kneading and rolling pastry is in *Sweet Pies* on page 469.

Most tarts and flans have a shortcrust base which is made by first mixing the flour and butter together until the mixture resembles coarse breadcrumbs.

The amount of liquid required in pastry varies according to the temperature and humidity in the kitchen, the type of flour you are using, the temperature and amount of the butter or shortening in the recipe. Too much liquid will result in shrinkage during baking. For this reason, most recipes specify a quantity of water or liquid, followed by "approximately". We recommend adding two thirds of the specified amount first, then adding the remaining liquid only until the dough comes together. Using a round bladed knife, work the liquid through in a cutting motion before forming it into a ball and kneading.

When kneading and rolling pastry, the golden rules are to handle it quickly, lightly and as little as possible. Heavy handling develops the gluten (protein) in the flour, which can make the pastry tough. Also, if the butter gets too soft it will be absorbed by the flour, creating a crust that is heavy and tough. Pastry toughens each time it is rolled, so avoid re-rolling pastry scraps more than twice.

Making shortcrust pastry in the food processor is the preferred option of many cooks, but be careful not to overprocess. Use short, quick pulses when mixing the butter into the flour and be extra sparing with the water as it's harder to judge when the pastry is ready. (See pages 452 & 453.)

To line the flan tin, drape the pastry over a lightly floured rolling pin and position it on the tin. Gently ease the pastry into the tin, pressing with your fingers or thumb to ensure that no air pockets develop. Roll the rolling pin across the top edge of the flan tin to trim the pastry evenly. Rest the pastry as specified in the recipe to prevent it from shrinking during cooking. Where the recipe indicates, prick or "dock" the base of the pastry with a fork. This will help prevent the pastry developing air bubbles during baking. Keep an eye on it while it's cooking and if it does rise, you can flatten the bump by pressing gently with the back of a spoon or a ball of rolled up (clean) tea towel or a ball of floured scrap pastry.

BAKING BLIND

Pastry cases which are to be filled with a cold filling are usually baked "blind", that is empty. Cases in which the filling is cooked are often partially baked blind to ensure the pastry stays crisp when the filling is added. As a general rule of thumb to avoid a soggy base, add hot fillings to hot cases and cold fillings to cold, just before serving.

To bake blind, line the pastry case with a piece of baking paper, or unwaxed greaseproof paper cut a few centimetres larger than the circumference of the flan. Fill the paper with dried beans, uncooked rice, lentils or purpose-made ceramic pastry weights to stop the pastry from rising during cooking. Place the flan pan on an oven tray and bake in a moderately hot oven for 10 minutes or as the recipe specifies. Remove the paper and beans carefully. (Store the cooled beans in a container marked for future baking as you won't be able to cook them after they have been in the oven.) Either add the filling at this stage, or continue baking as directed by the recipe. For step-by-step instructions to blind baking, see *Savoury Pies & Tarts* pages 618 & 619.

Some cooks swear by lining their flan cases with foil which they maintain conducts heat well and results in a crisper base. Others sprinkle the case with dry cake crumbs or fine soft breadcrumbs before adding a fruit mixture, to soak up any excess liquid.

GLAZING PASTRIES

Many tarts and pastries are glazed to give them an attractive glossy finish. This can be achieved by a host of options ranging from sugar syrup or a flavoured syrup or fruit juice which has been thickened with cornflour or gelatine to warmed sieved jam.

Passionfruit curd tartlets

PREPARATION TIME 50 MINUTES (PLUS REFRIGERATION TIME)

COOKING TIME 40 MINUTES (PLUS REFRIGERATION TIME) **MAKES** 8

4 egg yolks

½ cup (110g) caster sugar

80g butter, softened

1 cup (250ml) passionfruit pulp

1 teaspoon gelatine

2 tablespoons water

½ cup (125ml) thickened cream

PASTRY

1⅔ cups (250g) plain flour

½ cup (110g) caster sugar

140g cold butter, chopped coarsely

1 egg, beaten lightly

2 teaspoons iced water, approximately

BERRY TOPPING

¼ cup (80g) raspberry jam

1 tablespoon water

150g blueberries

1 Make pastry.

2 Divide dough into eight portions; roll portions between sheets of baking paper, into rounds large enough to line eight 10cm-round loose-based flan tins. Lift rounds into tins; press into sides, trim edges, prick bases all over with fork. Refrigerate 20 minutes.

3 Preheat oven to 180°C/160°C fan-forced.

4 Place tins on oven tray. Line each with baking paper; fill with dried beans or rice. Bake 15 minutes. Remove paper and beans; bake further 7 minutes. Cool.

5 Meanwhile, combine yolks, sugar, butter and ⅓ cup of the pulp in medium heatproof bowl. Place bowl over medium saucepan of simmering water; cook, stirring, about 10 minutes or until curd coats the back of a spoon. Remove from heat, strain; discard seeds.

6 Sprinkle gelatine over the water in small heatproof jug. Stand jug in small saucepan of simmering water; stir until gelatine dissolves. Stir gelatine mixture and remaining pulp into warm curd. Cover; refrigerate 1 hour.

7 Meanwhile, make berry topping.

8 Beat cream in small bowl with electric mixer until soft peaks form; fold cream into curd mixture. Divide curd filling among pastry cases; refrigerate until firm. Serve tartlets with berry topping.

PASTRY Process flour, sugar and butter until crumbly. Add egg and enough of the water to process until ingredients come together. Knead pastry on floured surface until smooth. Enclose in plastic wrap; refrigerate 30 minutes.

BERRY TOPPING Combine jam and the water in small saucepan over medium heat; simmer, stirring, until mixture is reduced by half. Push jam mixture through sieve into small bowl, gently stir in blueberries.

Pear and frangipane tarts

PREPARATION TIME 30 MINUTES **COOKING TIME** 40 MINUTES **SERVES** 4

You can use well-drained canned peach, plum, apricot or pear halves instead of the fresh pear. Eliminate the fruit preparation and baking in steps 2 and 3, use the maple syrup and butter mixture to brush over the canned fruit of your choice.

2 corella pears (250g)

1 tablespoon maple syrup

30g butter, melted

1 sheet ready-rolled puff pastry, thawed

FRANGIPANE FILLING

40g butter

¼ teaspoon vanilla extract

2 tablespoons caster sugar

1 egg yolk

2 teaspoons plain flour

½ cup (60g) almond meal

1 Preheat oven to 180°C/160°C fan-forced.

2 Peel pears; cut in half lengthways; carefully remove core. Combine maple syrup and butter in small bowl.

3 Place pears in small baking dish, cut-side down; brush with butter mixture. Bake about 15 minutes or until pears are tender; reserve any juice in dish.

4 Meanwhile, make frangipane filling.

5 Cut pastry into four squares; place squares on greased oven tray. Spread rounded tablespoons of frangipane filling over each square, leaving 2cm border on all sides. Place one pear half, cut-side down, on each square; fold pastry edges over.

6 Brush pear and pastry with reserved juice. Bake about 25 minutes.

FRANGIPANE FILLING Beat butter, extract, sugar and egg yolk in small bowl with electric mixer until light and fluffy. Stir in flour and almond meal.

Apple and rhubarb turnovers

PREPARATION TIME 15 MINUTES **COOKING TIME** 25 MINUTES **SERVES** 4

It's fine to use red-skinned eating apples here. Trim any greenish parts of the rhubarb stalks away.

20g butter

2 medium apples (300g), peeled, cored, sliced thickly

2 cups (220g) coarsely chopped rhubarb

⅓ cup (75g) firmly packed brown sugar

1 tablespoon lemon juice

½ teaspoon ground cinnamon

2 sheets ready-rolled butter puff pastry, thawed

1 egg

1 tablespoon icing sugar

1 Preheat oven to 200°C/180°C fan-forced. Grease oven tray.

2 Melt butter in medium frying pan; cook apple, rhubarb, sugar and juice, stirring occasionally, until sugar dissolves and apple starts to caramelise. Stir in cinnamon; spread mixture on tray. Cool.

3 Cut two 14cm rounds from each pastry sheet. Place a quarter of the fruit mixture on each pastry round; brush around edges with egg. Fold pastry over to enclose filling; pinch edges together to seal. Place turnovers on tray; brush with egg.

4 Bake turnovers about 15 minutes. Dust with sifted icing sugar.

Roasted pear tart

PREPARATION TIME 20 MINUTES **COOKING TIME** 40 MINUTES **SERVES** 6

3 medium pears (700g)

1 tablespoon maple syrup

¼ cup (55g) raw sugar

40g butter

1 sheet ready-rolled butter puff pastry, thawed

1 egg

1 Preheat oven to 180°C/160°C fan-forced. Grease oven tray.

2 Peel pears, leaving stems intact; cut in half lengthways. Remove cores carefully. Place pears in baking dish, cut-side up; top with syrup and sugar, dot with butter.

3 Bake pears about 20 minutes or until tender, brushing occasionally with pan juices and turning pears over after 10 minutes.

4 Increase oven to 200°C/180°C fan-forced.

5 Cut pastry sheet in half; place pastry halves about 2cm apart on tray. Place three pear halves, cut-side down, on each pastry half. Brush pears and pastry with pan juices, then brush pastry only with a little of the egg.

6 Bake tarts about 20 minutes.

We've used butter puff pastry here for its extra richness, but regular puff pastry will work just as well. Use pears that are ripe, but still firm.

Portuguese custard tarts

PREPARATION TIME 25 MINUTES (PLUS STANDING TIME)

COOKING TIME 30 MINUTES (PLUS COOLING TIME) **MAKES** 12

½ cup (110g) caster sugar

2 tablespoons cornflour

3 egg yolks

¾ cup (180ml) cream

½ cup (125ml) water

strip of lemon rind

1 teaspoon vanilla extract

1 sheet ready-rolled butter puff pastry, thawed

1 Preheat oven to 220°C/200°C fan-forced. Grease 12-hole (⅓-cup/80ml) muffin pan.

2 Combine sugar and cornflour in medium saucepan; whisk in egg yolks, cream and the water until smooth.

3 Add lemon rind; stir over medium heat until mixture comes to the boil. Remove from heat; discard rind. Stir in extract.

4 Cut pastry sheet in half; stack halves on top of each other. Stand about 5 minutes or until thawed. Roll pastry up tightly from short side; cut log into 12 x 1cm rounds.

5 Roll out pastry rounds on lightly floured board to about 10cm. Press rounds into pan holes with your fingers. Spoon custard into pastry cases.

6 Bake tarts about 20 minutes. Stand 5 minutes. Transfer to wire rack to cool.

Use a vegetable peeler to peel a strip of rind — about 5cm long and 1cm wide — from a washed and dried lemon. Avoid the white pith, and use a rough-skinned lemon for the best flavour.

Lime meringue tartlets

PREPARATION TIME 25 MINUTES (PLUS REFRIGERATION TIME) **COOKING TIME** 15 MINUTES **MAKES** 20

2 eggs, separated

2 tablespoons caster sugar

1 teaspoon finely grated lime rind

1½ tablespoons lime juice

20g butter

20 x 4cm pastry cases

½ cup (110g) caster sugar, extra

⅔ cup (50g) shredded coconut

1 Combine egg yolks, sugar, rind, juice and butter in small heatproof bowl. Stir over small saucepan of simmering water until mixture thickens slightly and coats the back of a spoon; remove from heat. Cover; refrigerate curd until cold.

2 Preheat oven to 220°C/200°C fan-forced.

3 Divide curd among pastry cases; place on oven tray.

4 Beat egg whites in small bowl with electric mixer until soft peaks form; gradually beat in extra sugar until dissolved. Fold in ½ cup (35g) of the coconut. Spoon meringue evenly over curd to enclose filling; sprinkle with remaining coconut.

5 Bake tarts about 3 minutes or until meringue is browned lightly.

See note about making curd on page 438. Make sure you spread the meringue right out to the pastry – where the curd meets the side of the cases. The pastry gives the meringue something to cling to, during its short burst in the oven. The meringue should be barely browned, just kissed by the heat. Pastry cases are available in delis and some supermarkets.

Pear, rhubarb and ricotta tarts

PREPARATION TIME 15 MINUTES **COOKING TIME** 25 MINUTES (PLUS REFRIGERATION TIME) **MAKES** 4

1¼ cups (250g) low-fat ricotta cheese

2 egg yolks

2 tablespoons caster sugar

2 teaspoons plain flour

½ cup (55g) finely chopped rhubarb

1 small pear (180g), quartered, sliced thinly lengthways

1 tablespoon caster sugar, extra

1 Preheat oven to 200°C/180°C fan-forced. Grease four 10cm-round deep fluted tins; place on oven tray.

2 Beat ricotta, egg yolks, sugar and flour in small bowl with electric mixer until smooth; stir in rhubarb. Spread mixture into tins; top each with pear, sprinkle with extra sugar.

3 Bake tarts about 25 minutes. Cool 10 minutes. Refrigerate until cold.

If you're watching your weight, eating a light and lovely tart will make you feel virtuous. The pear and rhubarb flavours marry well with the velvety texture of the baked ricotta.

1 LIME MERINGUE TARTLETS **2** PEAR, RHUBARB AND RICOTTA TARTS
3 FRUIT SCROLLS [P 444] **4** BERRY CUSTARD PASTRIES [P 444]

Fruit scrolls

PREPARATION TIME 10 MINUTES **COOKING TIME** 25 MINUTES **SERVES** 4

40g butter

¼ teaspoon ground nutmeg

1½ tablespoons brown sugar

1 tablespoon ground cinnamon

½ cup (125ml) orange juice

1 small apple (130g), peeled, cored, grated coarsely

⅓ cup (50g) finely chopped dried apricots

1 sheet ready-rolled puff pastry, thawed

½ cup (140g) yogurt

1 tablespoon honey

2 teaspoons icing sugar

1 Preheat oven to 200°C/180°C fan-forced. Grease oven tray.

2 Melt half of the butter in small saucepan; add nutmeg, sugar and half of the cinnamon. Cook, stirring, over low heat, until sugar dissolves. Stir in half of the juice, then apple and apricot; bring to the boil. Reduce heat; simmer, uncovered, 2 minutes. Remove from heat; stir in remaining juice. Cool.

3 Spread fruit mixture over pastry sheet; roll into log. Cut log into quarters; place on tray, 5cm apart, brush with remaining melted butter. Bake scrolls about 20 minutes.

4 Meanwhile, combine yogurt, honey and remaining cinnamon in small bowl.

5 Serve hot scrolls with spiced yogurt, dusted with sifted icing sugar.

Berry custard pastries

PREPARATION TIME 40 MINUTES **COOKING TIME** 12 MINUTES **SERVES** 8

2 sheets ready-rolled butter puff pastry, thawed

1 tablespoon icing sugar

700g mixed fresh berries

1 tablespoon icing sugar, extra

CUSTARD CREAM

300ml thickened cream

300g thick vanilla custard

¼ cup (40g) icing sugar

1 Preheat oven to 220°C/200°C fan-forced. Grease three oven trays; line with baking paper.

2 Make custard cream; cover, refrigerate 30 minutes or until firm.

3 Meanwhile, cut one pastry sheet in half. Sprinkle one half with half of the sugar; place other pastry half on top. Roll pastry up tightly from short side; cut log into eight rounds. Repeat with remaining pastry sheet and remaining sugar.

4 Place pastry rounds, cut-side up, on board dusted lightly with icing sugar; roll each round into an oval about 8cm x 10cm. Place ovals on trays.

5 Bake pastries about 12 minutes.

6 Place a drop of the custard cream on each of eight serving plates; top each with a pastry. Divide half of the berries over pastries, then top with custard cream, remaining berries and remaining pastries. Dust with extra sifted icing sugar.

CUSTARD CREAM Beat cream, custard and sifted icing sugar in small bowl with electric mixer until soft peaks form.

This recipe is such a good use of a commercially-made product. The pastry — thanks to the rolling-up process — ends up being really crisp, light and flaky. Use the pastry idea then make your own fillings. Imagine the flavour combination of a citrus-flavoured curd folded through some whipped cream, maybe with a passionfruit glaze on the top piece of pastry — or passionfruit drizzled over the cream. Let your imagination run riot.

Roast nectarine tart

PREPARATION TIME 40 MINUTES (PLUS REFRIGERATION TIME)

COOKING TIME 50 MINUTES (PLUS COOLING AND REFRIGERATION TIMES) **SERVES** 8

1⅔ cups (250g) plain flour

⅔ cup (110g) icing sugar

125g cold butter, chopped coarsely

1 egg yolk

1 tablespoon iced water, approximately

1.6kg small firm nectarines, halved

½ cup (110g) firmly packed brown sugar

¼ cup (60ml) orange juice

CREME PATISSIERE

1 cup (250ml) cream

1½ cups (375ml) milk

½ cup (110g) caster sugar

1 vanilla bean, split lengthways

2 eggs

¼ cup (35g) cornflour

90g butter, chopped coarsely

1 Process flour, icing sugar, butter and egg yolk until crumbly. Add enough of the water to process until ingredients come together. Knead dough on floured surface until smooth. Enclose in plastic wrap; refrigerate 30 minutes.

2 Roll pastry between sheets of baking paper until large enough to line base and sides of 19cm x 27cm rectangular loose-based flan tin. Lift pastry into tin; press into base and sides. Place tin on oven tray; refrigerate 30 minutes.

3 Preheat oven to 180°C/160°C fan-forced.

4 Line pastry with baking paper; fill with dried beans or rice. Bake 10 minutes. Remove paper and beans; bake further 10 minutes or until browned lightly. Cool.

5 Increase oven to 220°C/200°C fan-forced.

6 Place nectarines in large baking dish; sprinkle with brown sugar and juice. Roast, uncovered, about 20 minutes or until nectarines are soft.

7 Meanwhile, make crème pâtissiére.

8 Spoon crème pâtissiére into pastry case; refrigerate tart about 30 minutes or until firm. Top with nectarines.

CREME PATISSIERE Bring cream, milk, sugar and vanilla bean to the boil in medium saucepan. Whisk eggs in medium bowl; whisk in sifted cornflour. Gradually whisk in hot milk mixture. Strain mixture back into same pan; stir over heat until mixture boils and thickens. Remove from heat; whisk in butter. Cover surface of custard with plastic wrap; cool.

The rectangular flan tin we've used here is a favourite of ours, the whole tart looks good and it's easy to serve. A 24cm round flan tin will do the job as well. It's worth mastering the art of making a crème pâtissiére — it's easy and tastes divine — there's nothing quite like it.

Pear, chocolate and almond galette

PREPARATION TIME 5 MINUTES **COOKING TIME** 15 MINUTES **SERVES** 4

80g dark eating chocolate, chopped finely

¼ cup (30g) almond meal

1 sheet ready-rolled puff pastry, thawed

1 tablespoon milk

1 medium pear (230g)

1 tablespoon raw sugar

1 Preheat oven to 220°C/200°C fan-forced. Line greased oven tray with baking paper.

2 Combine chocolate and 2 tablespoons of the almond meal in small bowl.

3 Cut pastry sheet into quarters; place quarters on oven tray, prick each with a fork, brush with milk. Divide chocolate mixture over pastry squares, leaving 2cm border.

4 Peel and core pear; cut into quarters. Cut each pear quarter into thin slices then spread one sliced pear quarter across each pastry square; sprinkle with sugar then remaining almond meal. Bake about 15 minutes.

Rhubarb galette

PREPARATION TIME 10 MINUTES **COOKING TIME** 20 MINUTES **SERVES** 4

20g butter, melted

2½ cups (275g) coarsely chopped rhubarb

⅓ cup (75g) firmly packed brown sugar

1 teaspoon finely grated orange rind

1 sheet ready-rolled puff pastry, thawed

2 tablespoons almond meal

10g butter, melted, extra

1 Preheat oven to 220°C/200°C fan-forced. Line greased oven tray with baking paper.

2 Combine butter, rhubarb, sugar and rind in medium bowl.

3 Cut 24cm round from pastry, place on oven tray; sprinkle almond meal evenly over pastry. Spread rhubarb mixture over pastry, leaving a 4cm border. Fold 2cm of pastry edge up and around filling.

4 Brush pastry edge with extra butter; bake about 20 minutes.

PEAR, CHOCOLATE AND ALMOND GALETTE

Apple tarte tatin

PREPARATION TIME 40 MINUTES (PLUS REFRIGERATION TIME) **COOKING TIME** 1 HOUR 45 MINUTES
SERVES 8

100g unsalted butter, chopped coarsely

6 large apples (1.2kg), peeled, cored, quartered

1 cup (220g) firmly packed brown sugar

2 tablespoons lemon juice

PASTRY

1 cup (150g) plain flour

2 tablespoons caster sugar

80g cold unsalted butter, chopped coarsely

2 tablespoons sour cream

1 Melt butter in large heavy-based frying pan; add apple, sprinkle with sugar and juice.
Cook, uncovered, over low heat, for about 1 hour, turning apples as they caramelise.

2 Meanwhile, make pastry; refrigerate 30 minutes.

3 Preheat oven to 200°C/180°C fan-forced.

4 Place apple, rounded-sides down, in 23cm pie dish; drizzle with 1 tablespoon of
the caramel. Reserve remaining caramel.

5 Roll pastry between sheets of baking paper until large enough to cover apple. Peel
away one sheet of baking paper; invert pastry, carefully over hot apple. Remove remaining
paper; tuck pastry carefully around apple.

6 Bake tarte tatin about 30 minutes or until pastry is browned. Carefully turn onto
serving plate, apple-side up; drizzle apple with reheated reserved caramel.

PASTRY Process flour, sugar, butter and sour cream until ingredients come together.
Knead pastry on floured surface until smooth. Enclose in plastic wrap.

Quince tarte tatin

PREPARATION TIME 20 MINUTES (PLUS REFRIGERATION TIME) **COOKING TIME** 3 HOURS **SERVES** 6

4 medium quinces (1.2kg)

1 cup (220g) caster sugar

1 litre (4 cups) water

¼ cup (60ml) orange juice

1 teaspoon finely grated
orange rind

40g butter

PASTRY

1 cup (150g) plain flour

¼ cup (40g) icing sugar

100g butter, chopped coarsely

1 egg yolk

1 tablespoon iced water,
approximately

1   Peel, quarter and core quinces.

2   Combine quince, sugar, the water, juice and rind in large saucepan; bring to the boil. Reduce heat; simmer, covered, about 2½ hours or until quince is rosy in colour. Remove quince from syrup; bring syrup to the boil. Boil, uncovered, until syrup reduces to ¾ cup. Stir in butter.

3   Meanwhile, make pastry; refrigerate 30 minutes.

4   Preheat oven to 200°C/180°C fan-forced. Line base of greased deep 22cm-round cake pan with baking paper.

5   Place quince, rounded-sides down, in pan; pour syrup over quince.

6   Roll pastry between sheets of baking paper until large enough to cover the quince in the pan. Peel away one sheet of baking paper; invert pastry over quince. Remove remaining paper; tuck pastry around quince.

7   Bake tarte tatin about 30 minutes. Cool tart in pan 5 minutes; turn onto serving plate.

PASTRY Process flour, sugar and butter until crumbly. Add egg yolk and enough of the water to process until ingredients come together. Shape dough into ball. Enclose with plastic wrap.

Bakewell tart

PREPARATION TIME 20 MINUTES (PLUS REFRIGERATION TIME) **COOKING TIME** 25 MINUTES **SERVES** 8

We love this old-fashioned recipe. Try different flavoured jams to suit your own taste. I love plum jam in this recipe.

100g butter, softened

2 tablespoons caster sugar

1 egg yolk

1 cup (150g) plain flour

½ cup (80g) almond meal

2 tablespoons raspberry jam

2 tablespoons apricot jam, warmed, strained

FILLING

125g butter, softened

½ teaspoon finely grated lemon rind

½ cup (110g) caster sugar

2 eggs

¾ cup (120g) almond meal

2 tablespoons rice flour

LEMON ICING

⅓ cup (55g) icing sugar

2 teaspoons lemon juice

1   Beat butter, sugar and egg yolk in small bowl with electric mixer until combined. Stir in sifted flour and almond meal, in two batches. Knead dough on floured surface until smooth. Enclose in plastic wrap; refrigerate 30 minutes.

2   Meanwhile, make filling.

3   Preheat oven to 200°C/180°C fan-forced.

4   Roll dough between sheets of baking paper until large enough to line 24cm flan tin. Lift pastry into tin, ease into base and side; trim edge. Spread raspberry jam over base; spread filling over jam. Bake about 25 minutes.

5   Brush top of hot tart with apricot jam; cool. Make lemon icing; pipe or drizzle over tart.

FILLING Beat butter, rind and sugar in small bowl with electric mixer until light and fluffy. Beat in eggs, one at a time. Stir in almond meal and rice flour.

LEMON ICING Sift icing sugar into small bowl; stir in juice until smooth.

Caramelised apple tarts

PREPARATION TIME 10 MINUTES **COOKING TIME** 20 MINUTES **SERVES** 4

50g butter

¼ cup (55g) firmly packed
brown sugar

½ teaspoon ground cinnamon

4 small apples (520g),
peeled, cored, sliced thinly

½ cup (50g) roasted pecans

¼ cup (75g) apple sauce

2 teaspoons lemon juice

2 sheets ready-rolled butter
puff pastry, thawed

1 egg

1 Stir butter, sugar and cinnamon in large frying pan over low heat until sugar dissolves. Add apple; cook, stirring occasionally, over low heat, until apple softens. Drain apple mixture over medium bowl; reserve caramel syrup.

2 Meanwhile, blend or process nuts, apple sauce and juice until smooth.

3 Preheat oven to 200°C/180°C fan-forced. Line greased oven tray with baking paper.

4 Cut eight 11cm rounds from pastry sheets. Place four of the rounds on oven tray; brush with egg. Using 9cm cutter, remove centres from four remaining rounds; centre pastry rings on the 11cm rounds. Spread nut mixture in centre of rounds; top with apple.

5 Bake tarts about 15 minutes. Serve tarts warm with reheated reserved caramel syrup.

Apple sauce can be bought from supermarkets. However, you can stew and puree your own apples if you like, or, buy canned apple usually sold for babies. Any of the above will be fine for this recipe.

Almond pear flan

PREPARATION TIME 30 MINUTES (PLUS REFRIGERATION TIME) **COOKING TIME** 45 MINUTES **SERVES** 10

1¼ cups (185g) plain flour

¼ cup (55g) caster sugar

90g butter

2 egg yolks

3 firm ripe medium pears (690g),
peeled, cored, quartered

2 tablespoons apricot jam,
warmed, strained

ALMOND FILLING

125g butter, softened

⅓ cup (75g) caster sugar

2 eggs

1 cup (120g) almond meal

1 tablespoon plain flour

1 Process flour, sugar and butter until crumbly. Add egg yolks, process until combined. Knead on floured surface until smooth. Enclose in plastic wrap; refrigerate 30 minutes.

2 Meanwhile, make almond filling.

3 Preheat oven to 180°C/160°C fan-forced. Grease 23cm-round loose-based flan tin.

4 Roll dough between sheets of baking paper until large enough to line tin. Lift pastry into tin, ease into base and side; trim edge.

5 Spread filling into pastry case; place pears over filling.

6 Bake flan about 45 minutes. Brush flan with jam.

ALMOND FILLING Beat butter and sugar in small bowl with electric mixer until combined. Beat in eggs, one at a time. Stir in almond meal and flour.

Eggs yolks are the only "liquid" in this pastry, so be quick about mixing them into the flour/butter mixture. Pulse the ingredients until they barely come together.

CARAMELISED APPLE TARTS

Shortcrust pastry step-by-step

This is the most commonly used of all pastries. Here, we've walked you through making it by hand and processor.

SIFTING
Sifting isn't essential, but it's what we pastry-makers do. Use a sifter or a strainer to sift the dry ingredients into a wide-topped bowl. Chill the bowl if making pastry on a hot day.

RUBBING-IN BUTTER
Chop chilled butter into cubes, use your fingertips (the coolest part of your hands) to squash butter cubes through the flour. Do this quickly to keep the butter cold. Shake the bowl so any large lumps come to the surface.

ADDING EGG YOLK
Egg yolks are not always added to shortcrust pastry, but they do add colour and richness from the added fat. Egg yolks are best if refrigerator-cold. Add it now, but don't mix it in yet.

KNEADING DOUGH
Turn the dough onto a cold surface, then barely knead the dough until the ingredients are gathered together, and almost smooth. Don't over-handle the dough, it will toughen the dough and make it difficult to handle.

RESTING DOUGH
It's important to rest the dough in the refrigerator for about 30 minutes. Pat the dough into a flat shape, this will make it easier to roll out later, enclose the dough in a piece of plastic wrap, and put it in the fridge. Put the timer on, too long in the fridge will make the dough hard to roll out, you will have to let it stand a while before rolling.

PROCESSOR PASTRY
Food processors make really good pastry, and are particularly useful, if the pastry-maker has hot hands. Put the dry ingredients into the bowl of the processor, no need for sifting, add the chopped chilled butter.

ADDING LEMON JUICE

If you're adding egg yolk to the dough, most recipes will use lemon juice to counteract the richness of the egg yolk. Use freshly squeezed lemon juice, then strain it.

ADDING LIQUID

If you want a shortcrust pastry that is not so rich, use chilled water in place of the egg yolk and lemon juice. Follow whatever the recipe suggests. Most recipes will suggest an approximate amount of water.

COMBINING INGREDIENTS

Use the fingertips of one hand to gently, lightly and quickly pull the ingredients together. You should have just enough liquid to moisten the dry ingredients.

PROCESSING

Pulse the ingredients until the butter has barely cut through the flour. Don't walk away and leave the processor on, as the blade will continue to cut the butter through the flour, and the ingredients will come together. It's important to add some liquid to the dough.

PULSING

Add enough of the liquid to the flour/butter mixture, only experience will teach you how much to add – the same as if you were making pastry by hand. Too much liquid and the dough will be too soft, too little liquid and the dough will be too firm, both will result in the dough being difficult to roll out. Pulse the ingredients until the processor works the ingredients into a ball. Remove the dough from the processor.

RESTING PROCESSOR PASTRY

Knead the dough until it's smooth, as above. It's just as important to rest the processor-made pastry, as it is to rest the hand-made pastry. Processor pastry usually looks smoother than hand-made pastry because the butter has been cut through the flour more evenly.

Chocolate jaffa tart

PREPARATION TIME 30 MINUTES (PLUS REFRIGERATION TIME) **COOKING TIME** 55 MINUTES **SERVES** 8

1½ cups (225g) plain flour

¼ cup (40g) icing sugar

125g cold butter, chopped coarsely

2 egg yolks

2 teaspoons iced water, approximately

140g dark eating chocolate, chopped coarsely

¼ cup (60ml) thickened cream

FILLING

3 eggs

1 tablespoon finely grated orange rind

⅔ cup (160ml) thickened cream

¾ cup (165g) caster sugar

60g dark eating chocolate, melted

2 tablespoons cocoa powder, sifted

2 tablespoons orange-flavoured liqueur

1 Grease 24cm-round loose-based flan tin.

2 Process flour, icing sugar and butter until crumbly. Add egg yolks and enough of the water to process until ingredients come together. Knead dough on floured surface until smooth. Enclose in plastic wrap; refrigerate 30 minutes.

3 Roll pastry between sheets of baking paper until large enough to line tin. Lift pastry into tin, ease into base and side; trim edge. Refrigerate 30 minutes.

4 Preheat oven to 200°C/180°C fan-forced.

5 Line pastry case with baking paper; fill with dried beans or rice. Place tin on oven tray; bake 10 minutes. Remove paper and beans; bake further 10 minutes. Cool.

6 Meanwhile, make filling.

7 Reduce oven to 180°C/160°C fan-forced.

8 Pour filling into pastry case; bake about 30 minutes. Cool.

9 Stir chocolate and cream in small saucepan over low heat until smooth; spread warm mixture over cold tart. Refrigerate until set.

FILLING Whisk ingredients together in medium bowl.

Palmiers with honey cream

PREPARATION TIME 25 MINUTES **COOKING TIME** 15 MINUTES **MAKES** 30

2 tablespoons raw sugar

1 sheet ready-rolled puff pastry, thawed

1 teaspoon ground nutmeg

300ml thickened cream

2 teaspoons honey

I've been making palmiers for years, I always have some frozen puff pastry in the freezer for an emergency. They're at their best baked and eaten warm, I don't like them cold at all. Generally, I turn the palmiers over half-way through baking time. See pages 634 & 635 for tips on palmiers.

1 Preheat oven to 180°C/160°C fan-forced. Grease two oven trays; line with baking paper.

2 Sprinkle board lightly with a little of the sugar. Roll pastry on sugared board into a 20cm x 40cm rectangle; trim edges. Sprinkle pastry with nutmeg and remaining sugar.

3 Starting from long side, loosely roll one side at a time into the middle of the rectangle, so the two long sides meet.

4 Cut pastry into 5mm-thick pieces. Place, cut-side up, about 5cm apart, on trays. Spread pastry open slightly at folded ends to make a V-shape.

5 Bake palmiers about 15 minutes or until golden brown; transfer to wire rack to cool.

6 Beat cream and honey in small bowl with electric mixer until firm peaks form.

7 Serve palmiers with honey cream.

Pistachio and rosewater palmiers

PREPARATION TIME 30 MINUTES (PLUS REFRIGERATION TIME) **COOKING TIME** 15 MINUTES **MAKES** 32

Rosewater, cinnamon and pistachio give these syrup palmiers a distinct Middle-Eastern flavour.

¾ cup (110g) roasted shelled pistachios

¼ cup (55g) caster sugar

2 teaspoons rosewater

½ teaspoon ground cinnamon

20g butter, softened

2 tablespoons demerara sugar

2 sheets ready-rolled puff pastry, thawed

1 egg

½ cup (175g) honey

1 teaspoon rosewater, extra

1 Blend or process nuts, sugar, rosewater, cinnamon and butter until mixture forms a coarse paste.

2 Sprinkle board with half of the demerara sugar; place one sheet of pastry on the sugar. Using rolling pin, press pastry gently into demerara sugar. Spread half of the nut mixture on pastry; fold two opposing sides of the pastry inwards to meet in the middle. Flatten folded pastry slightly; brush with a little of the egg. Fold each side in half to meet in the middle; flatten slightly. Fold the two sides in half again so they touch in the middle, flattening slightly. Repeat process with remaining demerara sugar, pastry sheet, nut mixture and egg. Enclose rolled pastry pieces, separately, with plastic wrap; refrigerate 30 minutes.

3 Preheat oven to 200°C/180°C fan-forced. Grease two oven trays.

4 Cut pastry rolls into 1cm slices; place slices, cut-side up, on trays about 1.5cm apart. Bake about 12 minutes or until palmiers are browned lightly both sides.

5 Meanwhile, combine honey and extra rosewater in small frying pan; bring to the boil. Reduce heat; simmer, uncovered, 3 minutes. Remove from heat.

6 Add hot palmiers, one at a time, to honey mixture, turning to coat all over; drain on greased wire rack. Serve cold.

Danish pastries

PREPARATION TIME 1 HOUR 30 MINUTES (PLUS STANDING AND REFRIGERATION TIMES)
COOKING TIME 25 MINUTES **MAKES** 24

Good-quality Danish pastries can be bought at any good patisserie, cake shop or bakery, but, if you want to make them yourself, here's the recipe. The process of rolling, buttering and folding is important to create light flaky layers in the pastry.

1 cup (250ml) warm milk
¼ cup (55g) caster sugar
1 tablespoon (14g) dried yeast
20g butter, melted
1 egg
2¼ cups (335g) plain flour
1 teaspoon salt
200g cold butter
825g can whole dark plums, drained, halved, seeded
1 egg, extra

2 tablespoons milk
⅓ cup (110g) apricot jam, warmed, strained

CREME PATISSIERE
2 egg yolks
¼ cup (55g) caster sugar
2 tablespoons cornflour
¾ cup (180ml) milk
½ cup (125ml) cream
1 vanilla bean
30g butter

1 Whisk milk, sugar and yeast in medium jug until yeast dissolves, cover; stand in warm place about 15 minutes or until mixture is frothy. Whisk butter and egg into yeast mixture. Sift flour and salt into large bowl; stir in yeast mixture, mix to a soft dough. Knead dough on floured surface about 10 minutes or until smooth. Place dough in oiled large bowl, turning once to coat in oil. Cover; stand at room temperature 1 hour. Refrigerate overnight.

2 Turn dough onto floured surface; knead until smooth and elastic.

3 Roll out dough into 25cm x 40cm rectangle, keeping corners square. Cut butter into small pieces; scatter half of the butter over two-thirds of the dough. Fold unbuttered section of dough over half of the buttered dough; fold remaining buttered section over it. With seam facing right, roll dough to form 25cm x 40cm rectangle again; fold one third of the dough onto centre third, fold remaining third on top. Cover; refrigerate 30 minutes.

4 Unwrap dough; with seam facing right, repeat step 3 with remaining butter.

5 Meanwhile, make crème pâtissière.

6 Unwrap dough; with seam facing right, repeat step 3 with no added butter.

7 Preheat oven 220°C/200°C fan-forced. Divide dough in half; roll each half into 30cm x 40cm rectangle. Cut each rectangle into 10cm squares; you will have 24 squares.

8 Centre 1 heaped teaspoon of the cold crème pâtissière on each square; top each with one plum half. Brush dough around plum with combined extra egg and milk; bring opposite corners together, pinch gently. Place pastries 5cm apart on ungreased oven trays; brush dough again with egg mixture. Bake about 12 minutes.

9 Brush hot pastries with warm jam; transfer to wire rack to cool.

CREME PATISSIERE Whisk egg yolks, sugar and cornflour in medium bowl until light and fluffy. Combine milk and cream in medium saucepan. Split vanilla bean in half lengthways; scrape seeds into pan, then add pod. Bring mixture almost to the boil; discard pod. Whisking constantly, gradually pour milk mixture into egg mixture; return custard mixture to same pan. Cook over low heat, stirring constantly, until mixture boils and thickens; remove from heat. Return to same cleaned medium bowl; stir in butter until smooth. Cover; cool to room temperature.

Rosewater baklava

PREPARATION TIME 15 MINUTES **COOKING TIME** 35 MINUTES **MAKES** 16

1 cup (160g) blanched almonds

1 cup (140g) shelled pistachios

2 teaspoons ground cinnamon

1 teaspoon ground clove

1 teaspoon ground nutmeg

18 sheets fillo pastry

80g butter, melted

ROSEWATER SYRUP

1 cup (250ml) water

1 cup (220g) caster sugar

¼ cup (90g) honey

1 teaspoon rosewater

1 Preheat oven to 180°C/160°C fan-forced. Grease deep 23cm-square cake pan.

2 Process nuts and spices until chopped finely; spread nut mixture onto oven tray. Roast about 10 minutes or until browned lightly.

3 Increase oven to 200°C/180°C fan-forced.

4 Cut pastry sheets to fit base of pan; layer three pastry squares, brushing each with butter; place in pan, sprinkle with ⅓ cup of the nut mixture. Repeat layering with remaining pastry, butter and nut mixture, ending with pastry.

5 Using sharp knife, cut baklava into quarters; cut each quarter in half on the diagonal, then cut each triangle in half. Bake 25 minutes.

6 Reduce oven to 150°C/130°C fan-forced; bake baklava further 10 minutes.

7 Meanwhile, combine ingredients for rosewater syrup in small saucepan. Stir over heat, without boiling, until sugar dissolves; bring to the boil. Simmer, uncovered, without stirring, about 5 minutes or until thickened slightly.

8 Pour hot syrup over hot baklava; cool in pan.

Honey-almond pastries

PREPARATION TIME 45 MINUTES **COOKING TIME** 15 MINUTES **MAKES** 32

1½ cups (240g) roasted blanched almonds

½ cup (110g) caster sugar

1 teaspoon ground cinnamon

30g butter, softened

1 tablespoon orange flower water

8 sheets fillo pastry

100g butter, melted

1 cup (360g) honey

1 tablespoon toasted sesame seeds

1 Preheat oven to 180°C/160°C fan-forced. Grease two oven trays.

2 Blend or process nuts, sugar, cinnamon, softened butter and 3 teaspoons of the orange flower water until mixture forms a paste.

3 Cut fillo sheets in half lengthways, then in half crossways; cover fillo rectangles with baking paper, then with damp tea towel. Brush one fillo rectangle with melted butter; roll 1 level tablespoon of the nut mixture into log shape. Place log at short end of fillo rectangle; roll to enclose mixture, folding in sides after first complete turn. Brush with melted butter. Repeat with remaining fillo, melted butter and nut mixture.

4 Place pastries, seam-side down, on oven trays. Bake about 15 minutes.

5 Meanwhile, bring honey and remaining orange flower water to the boil in medium frying pan. Reduce heat; simmer, uncovered, 3 minutes.

6 Add hot pastries, in batches, to honey mixture, turning until well coated; drain on greased wire rack. Sprinkle with seeds; cool before serving.

Gourmet chocolate tart

PREPARATION TIME 40 MINUTES (PLUS REFRIGERATION TIME) **COOKING TIME** 30 MINUTES **SERVES** 12

2 eggs

2 egg yolks

¼ cup (55g) caster sugar

250g dark eating chocolate, melted

200g butter, melted

PASTRY

1½ cups (225g) plain flour

½ cup (110g) caster sugar

140g cold butter, chopped coarsely

1 egg

1 Make pastry.

2 Grease 24cm-round loose-based flan tin. Roll dough between sheets of baking paper until large enough to line tin. Lift pastry into tin, ease into base and side; trim edge, prick base all over with fork. Refrigerate 30 minutes.

3 Preheat oven to 200°C/180°C fan-forced.

4 Place tin on oven tray. Line pastry case with baking paper; fill with dried beans or rice. Bake 10 minutes. Remove paper and beans; bake 5 minutes. Cool.

5 Reduce oven to 180°C/160°C fan-forced.

6 Whisk eggs, egg yolks and sugar in medium heatproof bowl over medium saucepan of simmering water about 15 minutes or until light and fluffy. Gently whisk chocolate and butter into egg mixture; pour into pastry shell.

7 Bake tart about 10 minutes or until filling is set; cool 10 minutes. Refrigerate 1 hour.

PASTRY Process flour, sugar and butter until crumbly. Add egg; process until ingredients come together. Knead pastry on floured surface until smooth. Enclose in plastic wrap; refrigerate 30 minutes.

Use unsalted butter in this tart and good-quality eating chocolate. Give a light dusting of good-quality cocoa powder to the tart just before serving in slender wedges. A small dollop of cream on each wedge — despite its added richness, somehow cuts through the rich chocolate filling.

Profiteroles

PREPARATION TIME 30 MINUTES **COOKING TIME** 30 MINUTES **MAKES** 24

20g butter

¼ cup (60ml) water

¼ cup (35g) plain flour

1 egg

PASTRY CREAM

1 cup (250ml) milk

½ vanilla bean, split

3 egg yolks

⅓ cup (75g) caster sugar

2 tablespoons cornflour

TOFFEE

1 cup (220g) caster sugar

½ cup (125ml) water

1 Preheat oven to 220°C/200°C fan-forced. Grease two oven trays.

2 Combine butter with the water in small saucepan; bring to the boil. Add flour; beat with wooden spoon over heat until mixture comes away from base and side of saucepan and forms a smooth ball. Transfer mixture to small bowl; beat in egg with electric mixer until mixture becomes smooth and glossy.

3 Spoon mixture into piping bag fitted with 1cm plain tube; pipe small dollops of pastry 5cm apart onto trays. Bake 7 minutes. Reduce oven to 180°C/160°C fan-forced; bake further 10 minutes or until profiteroles are browned lightly and crisp. Cut small opening in side of each profiterole; bake further 5 minutes or until profiteroles are dried out. Cool.

4 Meanwhile, make pastry cream and toffee.

5 Spoon pastry cream into piping bag fitted with 1cm plain tube; pipe cream through cuts into profiteroles. Place profiteroles on foil-covered tray; drizzle with toffee.

PASTRY CREAM Bring milk and vanilla bean to the boil in small saucepan. Discard vanilla bean. Meanwhile, beat egg yolks, sugar and cornflour in small bowl with electric mixer until thick. With motor operating, gradually beat in hot milk mixture. Return custard mixture to saucepan; stir over heat until mixture boils and thickens.

TOFFEE Combine sugar with the water in medium heavy-based frying pan. Stir over heat, without boiling, until sugar dissolves; bring to the boil. Reduce heat; simmer, uncovered, without stirring, until golden-brown. Remove from heat; stand until bubbles subside.

Profiteroles or puffs are made from choux pastry — choux means "little cabbage", which does describe cream puffs quite accurately. Choux pastry sends some home-bakers into a tail-spin, but once you've mastered it, you'll wonder what the fuss was about. Follow the recipe carefully and all will be well. The proper French name for pastry cream is crème pâtissière, this is one of many variations. There's no need to pipe the pastry if you don't have a pipe and a bag (but it's neater). You can just put small amounts of the pastry well-apart on the oven tray, using a teaspoon. The pastry will more than triple in size in the oven. (See page 637 for choux pastry tips.)

1 PROFITEROLES **2** MINI CHOCOLATE ECLAIRS [P 462]
3 PARIS-BREST [P 462] **4** PRUNE AND CUSTARD TART [P 463]

Mini chocolate éclairs

PREPARATION TIME 25 MINUTES **COOKING TIME** 25 MINUTES **MAKES** 16

20g butter
¼ cup (60ml) water
¼ cup (35g) plain flour

1 egg
300ml thickened cream, whipped
100g dark eating chocolate, melted

1 Preheat oven to 220°C/200°C fan-forced. Grease two oven trays.

2 Combine butter with the water in small saucepan; bring to the boil. Add flour; beat with wooden spoon over heat until mixture comes away from base and side of saucepan and forms a smooth ball. Transfer mixture to small bowl; beat in egg with electric mixer until mixture becomes glossy.

3 Spoon mixture into piping bag fitted with 1cm plain tube. Pipe 5cm lengths of pastry mixture 3cm apart onto oven trays; bake 7 minutes. Reduce oven to 180°C/160°C fan-forced; bake further 10 minutes or until éclairs are browned lightly and crisp. Carefully cut éclairs in half, remove any soft centre; bake further 5 minutes or until éclairs are dried out. Cool.

4 Spoon cream into piping bag fitted with 1cm plain tube; pipe cream onto 16 éclair halves; top with remaining halves. Place éclairs on foil-covered tray; spread with chocolate.

Eclairs are log-shaped pieces of choux pastry, split open, filled with pastry cream or whipped cream (sometimes flavoured) and topped with melted chocolate, or a chocolate, coffee or mocha glacé icing. Fill the éclairs just before serving; you can have the éclair-tops already iced, ready for filling and joining.

Paris-brest

PREPARATION TIME 10 MINUTES **COOKING TIME** 30 MINUTES **MAKES** 16

20g butter
¼ cup (60ml) water
¼ cup (35g) plain flour
1 egg
¼ cup (20g) flaked almonds

TOFFEE
1 cup (220g) caster sugar
½ cup (125ml) water

PASTRY CREAM
1 cup (250ml) milk
½ vanilla bean, split
3 egg yolks
⅓ cup (75g) caster sugar
2 tablespoons cornflour

1 Preheat oven to 220°C/200°C fan-forced. Line two oven trays with baking paper; draw eight 4cm-circles on each tray.

2 Combine butter with the water in small saucepan; bring to the boil. Add flour; beat with wooden spoon over heat until mixture comes away from base and side of saucepan and forms a smooth ball. Transfer mixture to small bowl; beat in egg with electric mixer until mixture becomes glossy.

3 Spoon mixture into piping bag fitted with 1cm plain tube; pipe pastry mixture around edge of each circle. Bake 7 minutes. Reduce heat to 180°C/160°C fan-forced; bake further 10 minutes or until pastry rings are browned lightly and crisp. Cut each in half horizontally; bake further 5 minutes or until rings are dried out. Cool.

4 Meanwhile, make toffee and pastry cream.

Paris-Brest was created by a French chef in the shape of a wheel in honour of the famous annual bicycle race run between Paris and Brest.

5 Spoon pastry cream into piping bag fitted with 1cm plain tube; pipe cream into 16 ring halves, top with remaining halves. Place paris-brest on foil-covered tray; drizzle with toffee, top with nuts.

TOFFEE Combine sugar with the water in medium heavy-based frying pan. Stir over heat, without boiling, until sugar dissolves; bring to the boil. Reduce heat; simmer, uncovered, without stirring, until golden-brown. Remove from heat; stand until bubbles subside.

PASTRY CREAM Bring milk and vanilla bean to the boil in small saucepan. Discard vanilla bean. Meanwhile, beat egg yolks, sugar and cornflour in small bowl with electric mixer until thick. With motor operating, gradually beat in hot milk mixture. Return custard mixture to saucepan; stir over heat until mixture boils and thickens.

Prune and custard tart

PREPARATION TIME 20 MINUTES (PLUS REFRIGERATION TIME)
COOKING TIME 35 MINUTES (PLUS COOLING AND STANDING TIME) **SERVES** 12

1½ cups (250g) seeded prunes	**PASTRY**
2 tablespoons brandy	1¼ cups (175g) plain flour
300ml cream	⅓ cup (55g) icing sugar
3 eggs	¼ cup (30g) almond meal
⅔ cup (150g) caster sugar	125g cold butter, chopped coarsely
1 teaspoon vanilla extract	1 egg yolk
	1 tablespoon iced water, approximately

Not only is the flavour delicious in this tart, but the texture combinations are good too. Use good dessert prunes in this recipe. Dust the tart with sifted icing sugar just before serving.

1 Make pastry.
2 Grease 26cm-round loose-based flan tin. Roll pastry between sheets of baking paper until large enough to line tin. Lift pastry into tin, ease into base and side; trim edge, prick base all over with fork. Refrigerate 20 minutes.
3 Preheat oven to 200°C/180°C fan-forced. Place tin on oven tray. Line pastry with baking paper; fill with dried beans or rice. Bake 10 minutes. Remove paper and beans; bake about 5 minutes. Cool.
4 Reduce oven to 150°C/130°C fan-forced.
5 Blend or process prunes and brandy until combined; spread into pastry cases.
6 Bring cream to the boil in small saucepan; remove from heat. Whisk eggs, sugar and extract in small bowl, whisk in cream. Pour custard into pastry case; bake about 20 minutes or until custard sets. Stand 10 minutes before serving.

PASTRY Process flour, sugar, almond meal and butter until crumbly. Add egg yolk and enough of the water to process until ingredients come together. Enclose in plastic wrap; refrigerate 30 minutes.

Lemon tart

PREPARATION TIME 30 MINUTES (PLUS REFRIGERATION TIME) **COOKING TIME** 55 MINUTES **SERVES** 10

1 ¼ cups (185g) plain flour
⅓ cup (55g) icing sugar
¼ cup (30g) almond meal
125g cold butter, chopped coarsely
1 egg yolk

LEMON FILLING
1 tablespoon finely grated lemon rind
½ cup (125ml) lemon juice
5 eggs
¾ cup (165g) caster sugar
1 cup (250ml) cream

Lemon tart appears on almost every restaurant menu, with varying degrees of quality. We guarantee this recipe is as good, if not better, than any lemon tart you've ever tasted. Don't overcook the filling — the custard should feel firm around the outside of the tart, but still a bit wobbly in the middle. The middle will set as the tart cools. It's best made a day ahead, keep the tart in the fridge. Dust with a little sifted icing sugar just before serving.

1 Blend or process flour, icing sugar, almond meal and butter until crumbly. Add egg yolk; process until ingredients come together. Knead dough on floured surface until smooth. Enclose in plastic wrap; refrigerate 30 minutes.

2 Roll pastry between sheets of baking paper until large enough to line 24cm-round loose-based flan tin. Lift pastry into tin, ease into base and side; trim edge. Refrigerate 30 minutes.

3 Meanwhile, preheat oven to 200°C/180°C fan-forced.

4 Place flan tin on oven tray. Line pastry case with baking paper, fill with dried beans or rice. Bake 15 minutes. Remove paper and beans; bake further 10 minutes or until browned lightly.

5 Meanwhile, whisk ingredients for lemon filling in medium bowl; stand 5 minutes.

6 Reduce oven to 180°C/160°C fan-forced.

7 Strain lemon filling into pastry case; bake about 30 minutes or until filling has set slightly, cool. Refrigerate until cold.

Chocolate, quince and hazelnut tartlets

PREPARATION TIME 25 MINUTES (PLUS REFRIGERATION TIME) **COOKING TIME** 10 MINUTES **MAKES** 24

Quince paste can be bought from delis and gourmet food shops. Dust the tartlets with a little sifted cocoa powder just before serving.

150g dark eating chocolate, chopped coarsely
⅓ cup (80ml) cream
40g unsalted butter
100g quince paste
¼ cup (30g) finely chopped roasted hazelnuts

PASTRY
¾ cup (110g) plain flour
¼ cup (25g) cocoa powder
¼ cup (40g) icing sugar
90g unsalted butter, chopped coarsely
1 egg yolk
1 tablespoon iced water, approximately

1 Make pastry.

2 Grease two 12-hole (¼-cup/60ml) shallow round-based patty pans with butter. Roll rounded teaspoons of pastry into balls, press into pan holes. Prick pastry all over with a fork. Refrigerate 30 minutes.

3 Preheat oven to 180°C/160°C fan-forced.

4 Bake pastry cases 10 minutes.

5 Meanwhile, stir chocolate, cream and butter in small heatproof bowl over small saucepan of simmering water until smooth. Cool 15 minutes.

6 Soften paste in microwave oven on MEDIUM (75%) for about 20 seconds.

7 Divide paste among pastry cases; top with half of the nuts. Top with chocolate mixture, then remaining nuts. Refrigerate 1 hour.

PASTRY Process flour, cocoa, icing sugar and butter until crumbly. Add egg yolk and enough of the water to process until ingredients come together. Knead dough on floured surface until smooth. Enclose in plastic wrap; refrigerate 30 minutes.

Baklava cigars

PREPARATION TIME 45 MINUTES **COOKING TIME** 25 MINUTES **MAKES** 36

1 cup (160g) blanched almonds

½ cup (70g) pistachios

1 teaspoon ground cinnamon

1 teaspoon ground nutmeg

½ teaspoon ground clove

1 cup (250ml) water

1 cup (220g) white sugar

1 teaspoon finely grated lemon rind

2 teaspoons rosewater

16 sheets fillo pastry

150g butter, melted

1 Preheat oven to 180°C/160°C fan-forced. Grease two oven trays.

2 Process nuts and spices until finely chopped; spread mixture onto oven tray. Roast about 10 minutes or until browned lightly.

3 Meanwhile, stir the water and sugar in small saucepan over heat, without boiling, until sugar dissolves; bring to the boil. Simmer, uncovered, without stirring, about 5 minutes or until slightly thickened. Add rind and rosewater. Combine ¼ cup rosewater syrup with nut mixture in small bowl; reserve remaining syrup.

4 Increase oven to 220°C/200°C fan-forced.

5 Cut one pastry sheet crossways into three strips, brush each strip with butter (cover remaining sheets with baking paper then damp tea towel). Spoon heaped teaspoon of nut mixture on one end of each strip, leaving 3.5cm border from short edge. Roll pastry tightly into cigar shape; brush with butter. Place on oven tray; cover with dry tea towel. Repeat with remaining pastry, butter and nut mixture.

6 Bake cigars about 15 minutes.

7 Meanwhile, heat remaining syrup. Place cigars, in single layer, in large shallow dish; pour hot syrup over hot cigars. Cool in dish.

Another sweet sticky middle-eastern speciality. They aren't hard to make, and very rewarding to be able to turn out goodies that look just as good as those that are commercially made.

SWEET PIES

Sweet Pies

A slice of homemade pie is a passport to deep comfort territory but it's a sad sign of our busy lives that pie-making is becoming something of a lost art. It doesn't have to be so because if you break the preparation into stages and make the pastry and filling on one day and assemble and bake the next, the task becomes more manageable. Ready-rolled frozen pastry sheets also make the job a whole lot easier.

TYPES OF PASTRY

Shortcrust pastry is the classic pastry used for most sweet pies. Work the butter into the flour and sugar using the fingertips until it resembles breadcrumbs, then add the liquid, usually egg and water, until the mixture forms a dough. (See pages 452 & 453.)

SWEET SHORT-CRUST PASTRY is, as the name implies, a pastry with sugar added. If you use icing sugar instead of caster sugar you'll end up with a crisper pastry and avoid the possibility of the granular effect that occurs when sugar isn't dissolved. Pâte sablée is another sweetened pastry, though more like a biscuit dough, in that the butter and sugar are beaten together before the flour and liquid are added. The word sablée means sandy or grainy and this effect is sometimes enhanced by the addition of ground almonds.

PUFF PASTRY is truly a labour of love as it requires working the butter into the dough by repeated folding and rolling and resting the dough in the refrigerator between rolls to firm the butter (to keep the layers separate) and relax the gluten in the flour (to stop the pastry shrinking). If this sounds like too much hard work, the good news is that ready-rolled sheets of puff pastry are available in most supermarkets. Reduced-fat puff pastry is also available, though it tends not to brown as well as the higher-fat version.

FILLO PASTRY Your life is probably too short to make your own fillo pastry, but thankfully, there are good examples of these fine sheets of pastry in the freezer section of the supermarket. It is important to keep fillo covered while you are working with it as the thin sheets tend to dry out quickly and crumble or break. We have found the best way to prevent this happening is to cover the pastry completely with a piece of plastic wrap or greaseproof paper, then a well wrung-out damp tea towel. If the pastry does break up a bit during handling, don't panic. It's actually quite forgiving and as you are usually working in layers, the next layer will cover any minor tears and not be visible in the finished product.

CHOUX PASTRY is not as intimidating as it initially sounds, as piping is actually one of those skills that grow with confidence. (And if you do make a wonky shape, you can always scrape the dough back into the bag and pipe it again.) This cooked pastry is used to make puffs for chocolate éclairs and the custard filled puffs of the towering toffee-glazed croquembouche. It's made by making a panada (thick paste) by melting butter and water in a saucepan, stirring in flour over the heat until it leaves the sides of the pan, then removing from the heat and beating in eggs to form a smooth paste. The pastry is piped into the desired shape, then baked. The puff can collapse if it is not dry and cooked right through. To prevent this from happening, make a slit with the point of a knife in the cooked puff to allow steam to escape, then return it to the turned-off oven to cool.

TYPES OF PIE DISHES

Practically any ovenproof vessel with raised sides can be used as a pie dish. Traditional pie dishes are usually made of ceramic, thin enamelled metal or heat-resistant glass. Ceramic dishes are ideal for pies that have lots of filling as they take up the heat gradually and heat the filling slowly and evenly. Free-form or rustic pies require no dish at all as they are simply baked on an oven tray. The filling is placed in the centre of the pastry with an overlap on all sides which is folded over to partially enclose the filling.

HANDLING PASTRY

Further information is also in *Tarts & Pastries* pages 436 & 437.

KNEADING This really means turning the outside edges of the dough into the centre. When applied to most pastries it's not the heavy action you might apply to breadmaking, just lightly working the dough into a manageable shape.

ROLLING We find it's best to roll out pastry between sheets of baking or greaseproof paper or plastic wrap. If you work on a floured surface with a floured rolling pin, there's always the risk that you'll upset the balance of ingredients by working in too much flour. Besides, it's easier to pick up a sheet of pastry and transfer it to the pie dish when there's a sheet of paper or plastic supporting it. Start rolling with short light strokes from the centre outwards, each time rolling the pastry towards you then away from you. Reduce the pressure towards the edges and don't roll over the edges. Pastry is best rolled on a cold surface; marble is perfect, but your benchtop will be fine, so long as it's smooth and clean.

RESTING Always rest pastry, wrapped in plastic, in the refrigerator for up to 30 minutes before rolling and after lining the dish and covering the pie. This allows the gluten (protein) in the flour to relax and prevents the pastry from shrinking too much during baking.

STORING AND FREEZING

Pastry can be stored, wrapped securely in plastic wrap or a plastic bag in the refrigerator for one or two days, or frozen for up to two months. When freezing, be sure to label with a use-by date. To defrost, place overnight in the refrigerator and return to room temperature before rolling. You can also freeze, lined, unbaked pastry cases. Thaw as above.

FROZEN PIES

To reheat a frozen or refrigerated pie: Defrost in the refrigerator, then bring to room temperature before baking. If the pie has already been baked and you only want to reheat it, place it in a slow oven until it is warmed through.

Banoffee pie

PREPARATION TIME 45 MINUTES (PLUS REFRIGERATION TIME) **COOKING TIME** 35 MINUTES **SERVES** 10

395g can sweetened condensed milk

80g butter, chopped

½ cup (110g) firmly packed brown sugar

2 tablespoons golden syrup

2 large bananas (460g), sliced thinly

300ml thickened cream, whipped

PASTRY

1½ cups (225g) plain flour

1 tablespoon icing sugar

140g cold butter, chopped coarsely

1 egg yolk

2 tablespoons iced water, approximately

1 Make pastry.

2 Grease 24cm-round loose-based fluted flan tin. Roll dough between sheets of baking paper until large enough to line tin. Ease dough into tin; press into base and side. Trim edge; prick base all over with fork. Cover; refrigerate 30 minutes.

3 Preheat oven to 200°C/180°C fan-forced.

4 Place tin on oven tray; line pastry with baking paper, fill with dried beans or rice. Bake 10 minutes. Remove paper and beans; bake further 10 minutes. Cool.

5 Meanwhile, combine condensed milk, butter, sugar and syrup in medium saucepan; stir over medium heat about 10 minutes or until mixture is caramel-coloured. Stand 5 minutes; pour into pie shell, cool.

6 Top caramel filling with banana then whipped cream.

PASTRY Process flour, sugar and butter until crumbly. Add egg yolk and the water; process until ingredients come together. Knead dough on floured surface until smooth. Enclose in plastic wrap; refrigerate 30 minutes.

It is believed that this dessert, originally called banoffi pie (the sound of the made-up word coming from a mix of banana and toffee), was developed by an East Sussex restaurateur in 1971.

If cherries are in season, then use them — they need to be ripe, halved and seeded.

Old-fashioned cherry pie

PREPARATION TIME 30 MINUTES (PLUS REFRIGERATION AND COOLING TIMES)
COOKING TIME 1 HOUR 15 MINUTES **SERVES** 10

600g frozen seeded cherries

2 tablespoons cornflour

1 tablespoon lemon juice

$\frac{1}{3}$ cup (75g) white sugar

$\frac{1}{2}$ teaspoon ground cinnamon

20g butter

1 egg white

PASTRY

$2\frac{1}{4}$ cups (335g) plain flour

$\frac{2}{3}$ cup (110g) icing sugar

185g cold butter, chopped coarsely

1 egg

2 teaspoons iced water, approximately

1 Make pastry.

2 Meanwhile, stand thawed cherries in colander over bowl 30 minutes to drain well.

3 Grease 23cm pie dish. Roll two-thirds of the pastry between sheets of baking paper until large enough to line dish. Lift pastry into dish; trim edge. Refrigerate 30 minutes.

4 Preheat oven to 180°C/160°C fan-forced.

5 Place pie dish on oven tray; line pastry with baking paper, fill with dried beans or rice. Bake 10 minutes. Remove paper and beans; bake further 10 minutes. Cool.

6 Combine drained cherries, cornflour, juice, $\frac{1}{4}$ cup of the sugar and cinnamon in a medium bowl. Spoon filling into pastry case. Dot with butter.

7 Roll out remaining pastry until large enough to cover pie. Brush edges with a little egg, place pastry over filling. Press edges together to seal. Brush pastry with a little more egg; sprinkle with remaining sugar. Bake about 40 minutes.

PASTRY Process flour, sugar and butter until crumbly. Add egg yolk and enough of the water to process until ingredients come together. Knead dough on floured surface until smooth. Enclose in plastic wrap; refrigerate 30 minutes.

Jalousie is a French cake made from flaky pastry and almond paste usually with a lattice top. You can buy frozen rhubarb if it's out of season. But, fresh is best, choose dark and red stalks for the most flavour.

Rhubarb and almond jalousie

PREPARATION TIME 20 MINUTES **COOKING TIME** 40 MINUTES **SERVES** 8

2 cups (250g) chopped rhubarb

$\frac{1}{3}$ cup (75g) caster sugar

2 sheets ready-rolled puff pastry, thawed

1 tablespoon apricot jam

1 egg white

1 tablespoon caster sugar, extra

FRANGIPANE FILLING

30g butter, softened

$\frac{1}{4}$ teaspoon vanilla extract

$\frac{1}{4}$ cup (55g) caster sugar

1 egg

1 tablespoon plain flour

$\frac{2}{3}$ cup (80g) almond meal

1 Cook rhubarb and sugar in medium saucepan over low heat, stirring, until sugar dissolves and rhubarb softens.

2 Preheat oven to 200°C/180°C fan-forced. Grease oven tray.

3 Make frangipane filling.

4 Cut one pastry sheet into 14cm x 24cm rectangle; place on oven tray, spread with jam. Cut remaining pastry sheet into 16cm x 24cm rectangle; leaving 2cm border around all sides, make about eight evenly spaced cuts across the width of the pastry.

5 Spread frangipane filling over pastry with jam, leaving 2cm border around edges; top evenly with rhubarb mixture. Brush around border with egg white. Place the pastry sheet with cuts over filling; press edges of pastry together to seal. Brush with egg white; sprinkle with extra sugar. Bake about 35 minutes.

FRANGIPANE FILLING Beat butter, extract and sugar in small bowl with electric mixer until creamy. Beat in egg; stir in flour and almond meal.

Apple pie

PREPARATION TIME 30 MINUTES (PLUS REFRIGERATION TIME) COOKING TIME 50 MINUTES **SERVES** 8

2 cups (300g) self-raising flour

¼ cup (40g) icing sugar

125g cold butter, chopped coarsely

½ cup (125ml) milk, approximately

1 egg white

1 tablespoon caster sugar

FILLING

10 medium apples (1.5kg)

⅓ cup (80ml) water

2 tablespoons brown sugar

½ teaspoon ground cinnamon

1 Make filling.

2 Process flour, icing sugar and butter until crumbly. Add enough of the milk to process until ingredients come together. Knead dough on floured surface until smooth. Enclose in plastic wrap; refrigerate 30 minutes.

3 Grease 23cm pie dish. Roll two-thirds of the pastry between sheets of baking paper until large enough to line dish. Lift pastry into dish; trim edge. Refrigerate 30 minutes.

4 Preheat oven to 200°C/180°C fan-forced.

5 Brush pastry case all over with egg white. Spread filling into pastry case.

6 Roll out remaining pastry large enough to cover pie; position over filling. Pinch edges of pastry together. Brush pastry with egg white; sprinkle with caster sugar. Slash several holes in pastry.

7 Bake pie about 40 minutes. Stand 10 minutes before serving.

FILLING Peel, core and thinly slice apples. Combine apples and the water in large saucepan; bring to the boil. Reduce heat; simmer, covered, about 5 minutes or until apples are tender. Drain apples well; discard liquid. Transfer apples to large bowl; stir in sugar and cinnamon. Cool.

My mother made wonderful apple pies, usually in the form of a slice. Strictly speaking an all self-raising flour pastry is incorrect, but this pastry is deliciously cakey — just like mum used to make. The apples need to be drained really well and must be cooled to room temperature. Brushing the inside of the pastry case with egg white will stop the apples from making the pastry soggy.

Apricot and almond apple pie

PREPARATION TIME 45 MINUTES (PLUS REFRIGERATION TIME) **COOKING TIME** 1 HOUR 10 MINUTES **SERVES** 8

10 medium granny smith apples (1.5kg), peeled, cored, sliced thickly

½ cup (125ml) water

1 tablespoon caster sugar

⅔ cup (220g) apricot jam

1 teaspoon finely grated lemon rind

¼ cup (20g) flaked almonds

PASTRY

1 cup (150g) plain flour

½ cup (75g) self-raising flour

¼ cup (35g) cornflour

¼ cup (30g) custard powder

1 tablespoon caster sugar

100g cold butter, chopped coarsely

1 egg, separated

¼ cup (60ml) iced water, approximately

1 Make pastry.

2 Meanwhile, combine apple and the water in large saucepan; bring to the boil. Reduce heat; simmer, covered, about 10 minutes or until apples soften. Drain well; transfer apples to medium bowl, stir in sugar, jam and rind. Cool.

3 Preheat oven to 220°C/200°C fan-forced. Grease deep 25cm pie dish.

4 Roll two-third of the pastry between sheets of baking paper until large enough to line dish. Lift pastry into dish; trim edge. Spoon apple mixture into dish; brush edge with egg white.

5 Roll out remaining pastry large enough to cover pie. Place pastry over filling; press edge together to seal. Brush pastry with egg white; sprinkle with nuts.

6 Bake pie 20 minutes. Reduce oven to 180°C/160°C fan-forced; bake 25 minutes.

PASTRY Process flours, custard powder, sugar and butter until crumbly. Add egg yolk and enough of the water to process until ingredients come together. Knead dough on floured surface until smooth. Enclose in plastic wrap; refrigerate 30 minutes.

Apple, date and orange pie

PREPARATION TIME 45 MINUTES (PLUS REFRIGERATION TIME) **COOKING TIME** 1 HOUR 10 MINUTES

SERVES 10

8 medium granny smith apples (1.2kg), peeled, cored, sliced thickly

½ cup (125ml) water

1½ cups (210g) coarsely chopped seeded dried dates

¼ cup (55g) caster sugar

2 teaspoons finely grated orange rind

1 tablespoon demerara sugar

PASTRY

1 cup (150g) plain flour

½ cup (75g) self-raising flour

¼ cup (35g) cornflour

¼ cup (30g) custard powder

1 tablespoon caster sugar

100g cold butter, chopped coarsely

1 egg, separated

¼ cup (60ml) iced water, approximately

1 Make pastry.

2 Meanwhile, combine apple and the water in large saucepan; bring to the boil. Reduce heat; simmer, covered, about 5 minutes. Add dates; cook further 5 minutes or until apples soften. Drain well; transfer apple mixture to medium bowl, stir in caster sugar and rind. Cool.

3 Preheat oven to 220°C/200°C fan-forced. Grease deep 25cm pie dish.

4 Roll two-thirds of the pastry between sheets of baking paper until large enough to line dish. Lift pastry into dish; trim edge. Spoon apple mixture into dish; brush edge with egg white.

5 Roll out remaining pastry large enough to cover pie. Place pastry over filling; press edge together to seal. Brush pastry with egg white; sprinkle with demerara sugar.

6 Bake 20 minutes. Reduce oven to 180°C/160°C fan-forced; bake further 25 minutes.

PASTRY Process flours, custard powder, sugar and butter until crumbly. Add egg yolk and enough of the water to process until ingredients come together. Knead dough on floured surface until smooth. Enclose in plastic wrap; refrigerate 30 minutes.

Apple cranberry pie

PREPARATION TIME 45 MINUTES (PLUS REFRIGERATION TIME)

COOKING TIME 1 HOUR 10 MINUTES **SERVES** 8

2 cups (300g) plain flour

150g butter, chopped coarsely

½ cup (125ml) iced water, approximately

1 egg white

1 tablespoon caster sugar

CRANBERRY FILLING

½ cup (110g) caster sugar

2 tablespoons water

300g frozen cranberries

APPLE FILLING

10 medium apples (1.5kg)

½ cup (125ml) water

⅓ cup (75g) caster sugar

1 Process flour and butter until crumbly; add enough of the water to process until ingredients come together. Press dough into a smooth ball. Enclose in plastic wrap; refrigerate 1 hour.

2 Make apple filling. Make cranberry filling.

3 Preheat oven to 220°C/200°C fan-forced.

4 Roll two-thirds of the pastry between sheets of baking paper until large enough to line base of deep 25cm pie dish. Lift pastry into dish; trim edge. Spoon cranberry filling into pastry case; top with apple filling. Brush edge with egg white.

5 Roll remaining pastry until large enough to cover top of pie; press edges together. Brush with egg white; sprinkle with sugar.

6 Bake pie 15 minutes. Reduce oven to 180°C/160°C fan-forced; bake 30 minutes.

CRANBERRY FILLING Combine sugar, the water and cranberries in medium saucepan; simmer, stirring, about 10 minutes or until syrupy. Remove from heat; cool.

APPLE FILLING Peel, quarter, core and slice apples thinly; combine in large saucepan with the water; simmer, stirring occasionally, about 10 minutes or until apple is tender. Drain well; transfer apples to medium bowl, stir in sugar. Cool.

Blueberry apple crumble pies

PREPARATION TIME 30 MINUTES (PLUS FREEZING AND REFRIGERATION TIMES)
COOKING TIME 20 MINUTES **MAKES** 24

1 cup (150g) plain flour

⅓ cup (55g) icing sugar

90g cold butter, chopped coarsely

1 egg yolk

3 teaspoons iced water, approximately

2 tablespoons roasted slivered almonds

FILLING

1 small apple (130g), grated coarsely

½ cup (75g) frozen blueberries

1 teaspoon ground cinnamon

2 teaspoons finely grated lemon rind

Pastry purists usually use unsalted butter, as it does give a slightly better result. But we're leaving the decison to you – do your own taste test, you'll find there is a difference.

1 Preheat oven to 180°C/160°C fan-forced. Grease two 12-hole (1-tablespoon/20ml) mini muffin pans.

2 Pulse flour, sugar and butter in food processor until crumbly. Add egg yolk and enough of the water to process until ingredients come together.

3 Shape one-quarter of the dough into thick sausage. Enclose in plastic wrap; freeze 45 minutes.

4 Meanwhile, roll remaining dough to 4mm thickness, cut out 24 x 6cm rounds; press rounds into pan holes. Refrigerate 15 minutes.

5 Make filling; divide filling among pastry cases. Coarsely grate frozen dough evenly over filling; sprinkle with nuts.

6 Bake pies about 20 minutes. Stand pies in pans 5 minutes; transfer to wire rack to cool.

FILLING Combine ingredients in small bowl.

Apple and marmalade freeform pie

PREPARATION TIME 40 MINUTES (PLUS REFRIGERATION TIME) **COOKING TIME** 30 MINUTES **SERVES** 6

2½ cups (375g) plain flour

185g cold butter, chopped coarsely

2 egg yolks

½ cup (60g) finely grated cheddar cheese

¼ cup (60ml) iced water, approximately

2 tablespoons marmalade

1 egg white

FILLING

6 medium apples (900g), peeled and cored

2 tablespoons water

2 tablespoons brown sugar

1 Make filling.

2 Process flour and butter until crumbly. Add egg yolks, cheese and enough of the water to process until ingredients come together. Knead on floured surface until smooth. Enclose in plastic wrap; refrigerate 30 minutes.

3 Preheat oven to 200°C/180°C fan-forced.

4 Roll pastry between sheets of baking paper to 40cm round. Remove top sheet of paper; turn pastry onto oven tray, remove remaining paper.

5 Spread filling over pastry, leaving a 5cm border. Dollop teaspoons of marmalade about 2cm apart over filling. Fold and pleat pastry up and over to partly enclose fruit; brush pastry with egg white. Bake about 30 minutes.

FILLING Halve apples; cut each half into six wedges. Cook apple with the water and sugar in medium saucepan, covered, stirring occasionally, 5 minutes or until apple softens. Cool.

Apple pie made with cheese pastry is much loved in the USA — use a sharp-tasting cheese. Adding cheese makes the pastry more "short" — it is adding fat content to the pastry after all. Use any marmalade you like here — we can't think of one that wouldn't work flavour-wise. If you don't happen to have an egg white for brushing the pastry before baking, use a little milk. Finish the pie off with a light dusting of sifted icing sugar.

Impossible pie

PREPARATION TIME 10 MINUTES **COOKING TIME** 45 MINUTES **SERVES** 8

½ cup (75g) plain flour

1 cup (220g) caster sugar

¾ cup (60g) desiccated coconut

4 eggs

1 teaspoon vanilla extract

125g butter, melted

½ cup (40g) flaked almonds

2 cups (500ml) milk

1 Preheat oven to 180°C/160°C fan-forced. Grease deep 24cm pie dish.

2 Combine sifted flour, sugar, coconut, eggs, extract, butter and half of the nuts in large bowl; gradually stir in milk. Pour mixture into dish.

3 Bake pie 35 minutes. Sprinkle pie with remaining nuts; bake further 10 minutes.

The reason this pie is "impossible" is because the ingredients separate into three layers while baking. The heavy flour sinks to the bottom of the dish and pretends it's pastry, the lighter coconut floats to the top of the mixture to make a kind of crust or topping. The egg and milk stay happily in the middle making a delicious custard. The result is loved by all. Serve it warm or cold, as is or with fresh, canned or stewed fruit.

1 APPLE AND MARMALADE FREEFORM PIE 2 IMPOSSIBLE PIE
3 SPICED APRICOT AND PLUM PIE [P 480] 4 MINI PECAN, MACADAMIA AND WALNUT PIES [P 480]

Spiced apricot and plum pie

PREPARATION TIME 30 MINUTES   **COOKING TIME** 45 MINUTES (PLUS COOLING TIME)   **SERVES** 8

2 x 825g cans dark plums in light syrup

2 cups (300g) dried apricots

1 cinnamon stick

3 cloves

½ teaspoon mixed spice

½ teaspoon ground ginger

2 sheets ready-rolled puff pastry

1 egg

SPICED YOGURT CREAM

½ cup (140g) yogurt

½ cup (120g) sour cream

1 tablespoon ground cinnamon

¼ teaspoon ground ginger

1 Preheat oven to 200°C/180°C fan-forced. Grease 26cm pie dish.

2 Drain plums; reserve 1 cup of the syrup. Halve plums, discard stones; place plums in dish.

3 Combine reserved syrup, apricots, cinnamon, cloves, mixed spice and ginger in medium saucepan, simmer, uncovered, until liquid is reduced to ½ cup. Remove and discard cinnamon stick and cloves; cool to room temperature. Pour mixture over plums.

4 Cut pastry into 2.5cm strips. Brush edge of dish with a little of the egg; press pastry strips around edge of dish. Twist remaining strips, place over filling in lattice pattern; trim ends, brush top with egg.

5 Bake pie about 40 minutes. Serve with spiced yogurt cream.

SPICED YOGURT CREAM Combine ingredients in small bowl.

Mini pecan, macadamia and walnut pies

PREPARATION TIME 20 MINUTES (PLUS REFRIGERATION TIME)   **COOKING TIME** 25 MINUTES   **MAKES** 4

1¼ cups (185g) plain flour

⅓ cup (55g) icing sugar

¼ cup (30g) almond meal

125g cold butter, chopped coarsely

1 egg yolk

1 teaspoon iced water, approximately

FILLING

⅓ cup (50g) roasted macadamias

⅓ cup (35g) roasted pecans

⅓ cup (35g) roasted walnuts

2 tablespoons brown sugar

1 tablespoon plain flour

40g butter, melted

2 eggs

¾ cup (180ml) maple syrup

1 Process flour, sugar and almond meal with butter until crumbly. Add egg yolk and enough of the water to process until ingredients come together. Knead on floured surface until smooth. Enclose in plastic wrap; refrigerate 30 minutes.

2 Grease four 10cm-round loose-based flan tins. Divide pastry into quarters. Roll out each piece, between sheets of baking paper, into rounds large enough to line tins. Ease pastry into tins, press into base and side; trim edge. Cover; refrigerate 1 hour.

3 Preheat oven to 200°C/180°C fan-forced.

4 Place tins on oven tray; line each tin with baking paper then fill with dried beans or rice. Bake 10 minutes. Remove paper and beans; bake further 7 minutes. Cool.

5 Reduce oven to 180°C/160°C fan-forced.

6 Make filling; divide among cases. Bake about 25 minutes; cool.

FILLING Combine ingredients in medium bowl.

Pecan pie

PREPARATION TIME 25 MINUTES (PLUS REFRIGERATION TIME) **COOKING TIME** 1 HOUR **SERVES** 10

1 cup (120g) pecans, chopped coarsely

2 tablespoons cornflour

1 cup (220g) firmly packed brown sugar

60g butter, melted

2 tablespoons cream

1 teaspoon vanilla extract

3 eggs

1/3 cup (40g) pecans, extra

2 tablespoons apricot jam, warmed, sieved

PASTRY

1 1/4 cups (185g) plain flour

1/3 cup (55g) icing sugar

125g cold butter, chopped coarsely

1 egg yolk

1 teaspoon iced water, approximately

1 Make pastry.

2 Grease 24cm-round loose-based flan tin. Roll pastry between sheets of baking paper until large enough to line tin. Ease pastry into tin, press into base and side; trim edge. Cover; refrigerate 30 minutes.

3 Preheat oven to 180°C/160°C fan-forced.

4 Place tin on oven tray. Line pastry with baking paper, fill with dried beans or rice. Bake 10 minutes. Remove paper and beans; bake further 5 minutes. Cool.

5 Reduce oven to 160°C/140°C fan-forced.

6 Combine chopped nuts and cornflour in medium bowl. Stir in sugar, butter, cream, extract and eggs. Pour mixture into pastry shell; sprinkle with extra nuts.

7 Bake about 45 minutes. Cool; brush pie with jam.

PASTRY Process flour, icing sugar and butter until crumbly. Add egg yolk and enough of the water to process until ingredients come together. Knead dough on floured surface until smooth. Enclose in plastic wrap; refrigerate 30 minutes.

Pecan pie, like the mini pies on the opposite page, don't have a topping of any kind, but for some reason it's always been pecan pie — pecan tart just doesn't sound right. Nuts are expensive so store them in the fridge, or even better, in the freezer. The natural oils will turn rancid quite quickly in a warm cupboard. Pecan pieces can be bought more cheaply than the whole nuts — they are fine to use, but the whole nut looks best on top of the pie.

Pastry decorations

Pies and tarts of all shapes and sizes can be finished off with some simple decorations.

TRIMMING PUFF PASTRY
Hold the pie plate up in one hand, and, using a large sharp knife, cut any overhanging pastry away from the plate edge, at a 45° angle.

FLAKING PUFF PASTRY
To help the puff pastry flake, use the blade of a sharp knife to "cut" the side surface of the joined pastry edge. This will encourage the pastry to flake, after the slightly squashing effect of trimming the edge.

SHORTCRUST PASTRY FRILL
There are a few ways to do this, but basically use your fingers on both hands to pinch the edges of the pastry together to form a frilled edge.

LEAVES
Use a leaf cutter, or cut leaf shapes, freehand, out of any type of pastry, using a sharp pointed vegetable knife. Mark veins on leaves, secure them to the pie with a little water.

CUT-OUTS
Use any size or shape you like to do this. It looks good, and lets steam escape from the filling during the baking. Use a sharp metal cutter, dipped in flour. The shapes can be cut from any type of pastry, either before or after the pastry is in place on the dish.

MORE CUT-OUTS
Personalise the pies with cut-out letters. Use a template, or cut the letters out freehand, using a sharp pointed vegetable knife, secure them to the pies with a little water.

SHORTCRUST PASTRY EDGING

The quickest, easiest and the best of all edgings is simply done with the floured tines of a fork. Press the fork quite firmly onto the pastry edge.

MORE EDGING

This frill is made by using the floured handle of a small spoon, such as a teaspoon. Press the handle firmly onto the pastry edge. The tip of the bowl of a teaspoon or dessert spoon makes a scalloped pattern on the edge.

PASTRY WHEEL

These are available from supermarkets, cookware and hardware shops. Flour the wheel, then run it around the edge of the plate, to join and decorate the pastry.

PASTRY ROSE

These are best made from shortcrust pastry. Make a petal shape, roll it into a cylinder, press it upright onto the bench to make a bud. Make another petal, secure it to the bud with water.

FINISHING THE ROSE

Make another petal and secure it to the bud opposite the last petal. Make another three petal shapes in the same way, position them, each slightly overlapping each other, around the bud shape. Cut the rose from its base, secure the rose to the pie with a little water.

LATTICE TOPS

Using a floured pastry wheel, cut narrow strips of shortcrust pastry. "Weave" the pastry strips directly over the pie filling, trim the pastry so it sits inside the pie plate, or, position a narrow strip of pastry around the edge of the pie plate, brush with a little water to hold the lattice strips in position. Don't stretch the pastry.

Pumpkin pie

PREPARATION TIME 30 MINUTES (PLUS REFRIGERATION TIME)
COOKING TIME 1 HOUR 10 MINUTES (PLUS COOLING TIME) **SERVES** 8

1 cup (150g) plain flour

¼ cup (35g) self-raising flour

2 tablespoons cornflour

2 tablespoons icing sugar

125g cold butter, chopped coarsely

2 tablespoons cold water, approximately

FILLING

2 eggs

¼ cup (50g) firmly packed brown sugar

2 tablespoons maple syrup

1 cup cooked mashed pumpkin

⅔ cup (160ml) evaporated milk

1 teaspoon ground cinnamon

½ teaspoon ground nutmeg

pinch ground allspice

1 Sift flours and sugar into medium bowl; rub in butter. Add enough water to make ingredients come together. Knead dough on floured surface until smooth. Enclose in plastic wrap; refrigerate 30 minutes.

2 Preheat oven to 200°C/180°C fan-forced. Grease 23cm pie dish.

3 Roll pastry between sheets of baking paper until large enough to line dish. Ease pastry into dish, press into base and side; trim edge. Use scraps of pastry to make a double edge of pastry; trim and decorate edge.

4 Place pie dish on oven tray; line pastry with baking paper, fill with dried beans or rice. Bake 10 minutes. Remove paper and beans; bake further 10 minutes. Cool.

5 Reduce oven to 180°C/160°C fan-forced.

6 Make filling; pour into pastry case.

7 Bake pie about 50 minutes; cool.

FILLING Beat eggs, sugar and maple syrup in small bowl with electric mixer until thick. Stir in pumpkin, milk and spices.

Step 1 is the classic way to make pastry, but you can make this pastry in the food processor if you'd rather. The processor does a good job, as long as you don't overdo the processing at any stage. Pulsing the processor will give you the best results, particularly at the liquid-adding stage. If your fingertips are on the warm side, the processor is a better option for you. Good pastry is made from cold ingredients. Some bakers put the flour bowl, rolling pin, the lot in the fridge to cool down, particularly if the kitchen is warm. Pumpkin pie is best served with cream or ice cream. Dust it with a little sifted icing sugar.

Cornflour will "hold" a lot
of the moisture in the fruit.
The consistency of the
filling will remind you a
little of commercially made
fruit pies — but minus the
glugginess. You can use raw
or white sugar sprinkled
over the pastry if you don't
have any demerara sugar.
The slits cut into the top
pastry crust will allow any
build up of steam to escape.
Remember to do this after
any glazing and sugaring,
or else the sugar will
simply clog any vents
you've made.

Blackberry and apple pie

PREPARATION TIME 50 MINUTES (PLUS REFRIGERATION TIME) **COOKING TIME** 1 HOUR 5 MINUTES
SERVES 10

9 medium apples (1.4kg), peeled, cored, sliced thickly

2 tablespoons caster sugar

1 tablespoon cornflour

1 tablespoon water

300g frozen blackberries

1 tablespoon cornflour, extra

1 egg white

1 tablespoon demerara sugar

PASTRY

2 cups (300g) plain flour

⅔ cup (110g) icing sugar

185g cold butter, chopped coarsely

2 egg yolks

1 tablespoon iced water, approximately

1 Make pastry.

2 Meanwhile, cook apple and caster sugar in large saucepan, covered, over low heat, about 10 minutes or until apples soften. Strain over small saucepan; reserve cooking liquid. Blend cornflour with the water; stir into reserved cooking liquid over heat until mixture boils and thickens. Place apples in large bowl, gently stir in cornflour mixture.

3 Preheat oven to 220°C/200°C fan-forced. Grease deep 23cm pie dish.

4 Roll out two-thirds of the pastry between sheets of baking paper until large enough to line dish. Ease pastry into dish; trim edge.

5 Toss blackberries in extra cornflour; stir gently into apple mixture. Spoon fruit mixture into pastry case; brush pastry edge with egg white.

6 Roll remaining pastry large enough to cover pie. Place pastry over filling; press edges together to seal. Brush pastry with egg white; sprinkle with demerara sugar. Using knife, make three cuts in top of pastry.

7 Bake pie 20 minutes. Reduce oven to 180°C/160°C fan-forced; bake 30 minutes.

PASTRY Process flour, sugar and butter until crumbly. Add egg yolks and enough of the water to process until ingredients come together. Knead on floured surface until smooth. Enclose in plastic wrap; refrigerate 30 minutes.

Lemon meringue pie

PREPARATION TIME 30 MINUTES (PLUS REFRIGERATION TIME) **COOKING TIME** 35 MINUTES **SERVES** 10

½ cup (75g) cornflour

1 cup (220g) caster sugar

½ cup (125ml) lemon juice

1¼ cups (310ml) water

2 teaspoons finely grated lemon rind

60g butter, chopped coarsely

3 eggs, separated

½ cup (110g) caster sugar, extra

PASTRY

1½ cups (225g) plain flour

1 tablespoon icing sugar

140g cold butter, chopped coarsely

1 egg yolk

2 tablespoons iced water, approximately

1 Make pastry.

2 Grease 24cm-round loose-based fluted flan tin. Roll out pastry between sheets of baking paper until large enough to line tin. Ease pastry into tin, press into base and side; trim edge. Cover; refrigerate 30 minutes.

3 Preheat oven to 220°C/200°C fan-forced.

4 Place tin on oven tray. Line pastry case with baking paper; fill with dried beans or rice. Bake 10 minutes. Remove paper and beans; bake further 10 minutes. Cool. Turn oven off.

5 Meanwhile, combine cornflour and sugar in medium saucepan. Gradually stir in juice and the water until smooth; cook, stirring, over high heat, until mixture boils and thickens. Reduce heat; simmer, stirring, 1 minute. Remove from heat; stir in rind, butter and egg yolks. Cool.

6 Spread filling into pastry case.

7 Preheat oven to 240°C/220°C fan-forced.

8 Beat egg whites in small bowl with electric mixer until soft peaks form; gradually add extra sugar, beating until sugar dissolves.

9 Roughen surface of filling with fork before spreading with meringue mixture. Bake about 2 minutes or until browned lightly.

PASTRY Process flour, icing sugar and butter until crumbly. Add egg yolk and enough of the water to process until ingredients come together. Knead dough on floured surface until smooth. Enclose in plastic wrap; refrigerate 30 minutes.

There are many versions of lemon fillings around, experiment until you find one you like. The tartness depends on the lemons — the flavour will vary slightly every time you make the filling. Remember to grate the rind before you juice the lemons. To counteract the cornflour taste, it's important to simmer the boiled and thickened filling for a minute or so, you must stir from start to finish — it is thick and will burn if you're not careful. It's not vital to the success of the pie, but try using unsalted butter in the filling and the pastry — taste the subtle difference.

Orange curd meringue pies

PREPARATION TIME 15 MINUTES **COOKING TIME** 30 MINUTES **MAKES** 12

½ cup (110g) caster sugar

2 tablespoons cornflour

⅔ cup (180ml) blood orange juice

2 tablespoons water

2 teaspoons finely grated blood orange rind

80g unsalted butter, chopped coarsely

2 eggs, separated

½ cup (110g) caster sugar, extra

PASTRY

1¼ cups (185g) plain flour

¼ cup (55g) caster sugar

125g cold butter, chopped coarsely

1 egg

1 Make pastry.

2 Grease 12-hole (⅓-cup/80ml) muffin pan. Roll pastry between two sheets of baking paper to 4mm thickness; cut 12 rounds using 8cm cutter. Press rounds into pan holes; prick bases all over with fork. Refrigerate 30 minutes.

3 Preheat oven to 200°C/180°C fan-forced. Bake pastry cases 10 minutes. Cool.

4 Meanwhile, combine sugar and cornflour in small saucepan; gradually stir in juice and the water until smooth. Cook, stirring, over high heat, until mixture boils and thickens. Reduce heat; simmer, stirring, 1 minute. Remove from heat; stir in rind, butter and egg yolks. Cool.

5 Preheat oven to 220°C/200°C fan-forced.

6 Spread filling into pastry cases.

7 Beat egg whites in small bowl with electric mixer until soft peaks form; gradually add extra sugar, beating until sugar dissolves.

8 Roughen surface of filling with fork; pipe or spoon meringue over filling. Bake about 3 minutes or until browned lightly.

PASTRY Process flour, sugar and butter until crumbly. Add egg; process until combined. Knead on floured surface until smooth. Enclose in plastic wrap; refrigerate 30 minutes.

Blood oranges have a wonderful taste and give a unique colour to whatever they're used in. However, they have a short season, so, you can use regular full-flavoured oranges in this recipe. Keep an eye on the pastry cases while they're baking, even though the pastry is well-pricked to prevent it rising, it's easy enough to trap air pockets under the pastry. At the first sign of puffiness, squash the air bubble using a floured ball of pastry dough made from leftover scraps. Be careful not to burn your fingers. You could bake the cases "blind" (see pages 618 & 619) but the process is a bit fiddly in muffin pans.

Berry and rhubarb pies

PREPARATION TIME 30 MINUTES (PLUS REFRIGERATION TIME) **COOKING TIME** 35 MINUTES **MAKES** 6

2 cups (220g) coarsely chopped rhubarb

¼ cup (55g) caster sugar

2 tablespoons water

1 tablespoon cornflour

300g frozen mixed berries

1 egg white

2 teaspoons caster sugar, extra

PASTRY

1⅔ cups (250g) plain flour

⅓ cup (75g) caster sugar

150g cold butter, chopped coarsely

1 egg

1 Make pastry.

2 Combine rhubarb, sugar and half of the water in medium saucepan; bring to the boil. Reduce heat; simmer, covered, about 3 minutes or until rhubarb is tender. Stir in blended cornflour and remaining water; stir gently until mixture boils and thickens. Reduce heat; simmer, stirring 1 minute. Remove from heat; stir in berries. Cool.

3 Grease 6-hole texas (¾-cup/180ml) muffin pan. Roll two-thirds of the pastry between sheets of baking paper to 4mm thickness; cut six rounds using 12cm cutter. Press rounds into pan holes. Refrigerate 20 minutes.

4 Preheat oven to 200°C/180°C fan-forced.

5 Roll remaining pastry between sheets of baking paper to 4mm thickness; cut six rounds using 9cm cutter. Spoon fruit mixture into pastry cases. Brush edges of pastry tops with egg white; place over filling. Press edges together to seal. Brush tops with egg white; sprinkle with extra sugar.

6 Bake pies about 30 minutes. Stand pies in pan 10 minutes; gently turn, top-side up, onto wire racks to cool.

PASTRY Process flour, sugar and butter until crumbly. Add egg; process until combined. Knead on floured surface until smooth. Enclose in plastic wrap; refrigerate 30 minutes.

Berry (particularly strawberry) and rhubarb flavours are great together — use fresh or frozen, whatever is available. If you're using fresh rhubarb, you'll need about 4 large stems — look for darkest red stalks for the unique taste only rhubarb can deliver.

BREADS & BUNS

Breads & Buns

While flat bread has been around since prehistoric times when man first discovered that grinding grain made it more palatable, archaeologists tell us that the earliest examples of leavened breads come from Egyptian remains from around 4000BC. In those days bread was risen by what we today recognise as the sourdough method in which leavening is started by adding a "starter", or piece of dough in which yeast is already growing, to the dough.

SPECIALTY BREADS

Sourdough is a flavour-packed and long-lasting bread thanks to the acidity in the starter which comes from the same lactic acid bacteria that makes milk into yogurt and buttermilk. Bagels, from the Yiddish word for "ring", are small, round breads that are boiled or steamed before being baked. Rye remains a popular northern European flour and rye bread usually contains about 20 per cent rye flour and the rest wheat flour. Wholemeal or whole wheat bread contains about half wholemeal flour while pumpernickel bread, which originated in Westphalian Germany, is a dense, dark bread made with rye flour and a sourdough starter. Sweet breads such as brioche, panettone and pandoro contain substantial amounts of both sugar and fat in the form of butter and eggs. The sugar in the dough means they brown quickly, so sweet breads are usually baked at slightly lower temperatures than regular bread and may need to be covered with foil to prevent burning. Pizza, the Neopolitan Italians' gift to the culinary world, is a flat, though yeast-risen, bread topped with tomato and cheese and any number of other ingredients limited only by the imagination and what is to hand. Pita, or pocket breads of the Middle East and Indian naan are yeast-risen flat breads, while others, such as Indian chapati and roti and Mexican tortillas, contain no yeast. Yet others, such as dampers and cornbreads, rely on baking powder for their rising action.

FLOUR

Flour is graded according to the gluten content. Gluten, the protein in flour, is what the Chinese call "the muscle of flour" and gives bread dough its elasticity. The higher the gluten content the harder the flour. Soft or winter wheat produces a soft, velvety flour which is clear white in colour and is preferred for making cakes and biscuits. Hard flour has a higher protein content, is creamier in colour and is preferred for bread and puff pastry.

YEAST

Yeast provides the enzymes which react with the sugar in bread to form gas (carbon dioxide) which causes the dough to rise. Breads rise to the point where as much as 80 per cent of their volume is empty space (gas). Yeast also adds flavour to bread.

You can use dry (dried) or fresh compressed yeast. We use dry yeast packaged in five 7g (2 teaspoon) sachets. Generally one sachet of dried yeast is equivalent to 15g of compressed yeast, but follow the instructions on the packaging. Fresh yeast has a limited shelf life and must be stored in an airtight container in the refrigerator. Dried yeast keeps well in the pantry. Liquid added to the yeast should be warm, about 26°C. As a rule of thumb if you don't have a thermometer, add one third boiling liquid to two thirds cold. If the liquid is too cold, it will retard the yeast growth; if it's too hot, it will kill the yeast.

KNEADING

Mix the ingredients to a dough then turn out on to a lightly floured surface to knead it until it is smooth and pliable. Press the middle of the dough with the heel of your hand and push the dough away from you. Then lift the furthest edge of the dough a little, give it a quarter turn and fold the dough in half towards you. Repeat the press and push motion kneading for the time specified, when the dough will spring back if pressed with a finger.

PROVING

Proving is the time when bread rests and rises. Place the dough in an oiled bowl, turn the dough lightly to grease the top and stop a skin forming. Cover the bowl with a clean tea towel or plastic wrap and stand the bowl in a warm place away from draughts until it rises.

BAKING

To test if bread is cooked, turn it out of the pan and tap the loaf firmly on the bottom crust. It should sound hollow. If it doesn't, return it to the pan and continue baking.

FREEZING

Small breads such as dinner rolls and pizza bases freeze well if baked for half the specified time before cooling and freezing in airtight bags. To complete baking, return to room temperature and continue baking. To freeze baked bread, cool as quickly as possible and freeze in airtight bags. Slice it before freezing. Bread freezes well for up to two months.

TROUBLE SHOOTING

- If your loaf is small and heavy, it could be caused by insufficient kneading, stale yeast or if the dough was too stiff, dough was left to prove too long.
- If the loaf is too large, or bulges over the pan, the mixture could be too soft or the pan was the wrong size, or the oven temperature too low.
- If the bread tastes too "yeasty", it could be because it was made in hot weather, or the dough risen in too warm a place, resulting in too quick rising. Or, too much yeast was used.
- If the bread is coarse in texture, it could be the dough was too wet, or because it was proved too long, or cooked at the wrong temperature. If it crumbles, the dough could have been too dry, or proved in too warm a place.

Dinner rolls

PREPARATION TIME 30 MINUTES (PLUS STANDING TIME) **COOKING TIME** 15 MINUTES **MAKES** 20

2 teaspoons (7g) dried yeast

1 teaspoon caster sugar

2 cups (500ml) warm water

4 cups (640g) baker's flour

2 teaspoons salt

cooking-oil spray

1 Whisk yeast, sugar and the water in medium jug until yeast dissolves. Cover; stand in warm place about 15 minutes or until mixture is frothy.

2 Sift flour and salt into large bowl; stir in yeast mixture. Turn dough onto floured surface; knead about 15 minutes or until dough is smooth and elastic. Place dough in large oiled bowl, turning dough once to coat in oil. Cover; stand in warm place about 1 hour or until dough doubles in size.

3 Preheat oven to 200°C/180°C fan-forced. Oil two oven trays.

4 Knead dough on floured surface about 1 minute or until smooth. Divide dough into quarters; divide each quarter into five pieces.

5 Shape each piece into a ball; place balls 5cm apart on trays. Cut small cross in top of each ball; coat lightly with cooking-oil spray. Cover loosely with plastic wrap; stand in warm place about 20 minutes or until dough doubles in size.

6 Bake rolls about 15 minutes; transfer to wire rack to cool.

Basic white bread

PREPARATION TIME 30 MINUTES (PLUS STANDING TIME) **COOKING TIME** 45 MINUTES **MAKES** 18 SLICES

3 teaspoons (10g) dried yeast

2 teaspoons caster sugar

½ cup (125ml) warm water

2½ cups (375g) plain flour

1 teaspoon salt

30g butter, melted

½ cup (125ml) warm milk

1 Whisk yeast, sugar and the water in small bowl until yeast dissolves. Cover; stand in warm place about 10 minutes or until mixture is frothy.

2 Sift flour and salt into large bowl; stir in butter, milk and yeast mixture. Turn dough onto floured surface; knead about 10 minutes or until dough is elastic. Place dough in large oiled bowl, turning dough once to coat in oil. Cover; stand in warm place about 1 hour or until dough doubles in size.

3 Preheat oven to 200°C/180°C fan-forced. Oil oven tray.

4 Knead dough on floured surface until smooth. Roll dough to 18cm x 35cm rectangle; roll up from short side like a swiss roll. Place on tray; cut four diagonal slashes across top. Cover; stand in warm place 20 minutes or until risen. Bake 45 minutes; turn onto wire rack to cool.

Rosemary damper

PREPARATION TIME 20 MINUTES **COOKING TIME** 45 MINUTES **SERVES** 8

60g butter

1 medium brown onion (150g), chopped finely

3 cups (450g) self-raising flour

2 tablespoons finely chopped fresh rosemary

1 cup (125g) grated tasty cheese

1¼ cups (310ml) water, approximately

1 Melt 15g of the butter in small frying pan; cook onion, stirring, over medium heat about 2 minutes or until onion is soft. Cool.

2 Sift flour into large bowl; rub in remaining butter. Stir in onion mixture, rosemary and ⅔ cup of the cheese; make well in centre. Stir in enough of the water to mix to a soft dough. Knead dough on floured surface until smooth.

3 Preheat oven to 180°C/160°C fan-forced. Oil oven tray.

4 Place dough onto tray; pat into 16cm circle. Using sharp knife, cut 1cm deep cross in top of dough. Brush with a little water or milk; sprinkle with remaining cheese.

5 Bake damper about 40 minutes or until golden brown and sounds hollow when tapped.

Rosemary pumpkin bread

PREPARATION TIME 20 MINUTES **COOKING TIME** 1 HOUR 40 MINUTES **SERVES** 8

500g pumpkin, diced into 1cm pieces

1 tablespoon vegetable oil

1 tablespoon finely chopped fresh rosemary

1¾ cups (260g) self-raising flour

¾ cup (125g) polenta

½ cup (40g) finely grated parmesan cheese

2 eggs

300g sour cream

⅓ cup (55g) pepitas

1 Preheat oven to 200°C/180°C fan-forced. Oil 14cm x 21cm loaf pan; line base and long sides with baking paper.

2 Place combined pumpkin, oil and half of the rosemary, in single layer, on oven tray; roast about 20 minutes or until pumpkin is tender. Cool 10 minutes; mash mixture in medium bowl.

3 Reduce oven to 180°C/160°C fan-forced.

4 Stir flour, polenta, cheese and remaining rosemary into pumpkin mixture. Whisk eggs and sour cream in medium jug; pour into mixture, stirring until combined. Spread mixture into pan; top with pepitas, pressing gently into surface.

5 Cover pan with a piece of foil folded with a pleat; bake 1 hour. Remove foil; bake about 20 minutes. Stand in pan 5 minutes; turn onto wire rack to cool.

Olive bread with oregano

PREPARATION TIME 25 MINUTES (PLUS STANDING TIME)
COOKING TIME 45 MINUTES (PLUS COOLING TIME) **SERVES** 10

1 tablespoon (14g) dried yeast

1 teaspoon white sugar

2¼ cups (560ml) skim milk

5½ cups (825g) plain flour

⅓ cup (80ml) olive oil

1¼ cups (150g) seeded black olives, halved

2 tablespoons coarsely chopped fresh oregano

1 Combine yeast, sugar and milk in large bowl; stir in 3 cups (450g) of the sifted flour. Cover; stand in warm place 30 minutes or until foamy.

2 Stir oil into yeast mixture, then remaining sifted flour. Knead dough on floured surface about 10 minutes or until smooth and elastic. Place dough in large oiled bowl, turning dough once to coat in oil. Cover; stand in warm place until doubled in size.

3 Preheat oven to 200°C/180°C fan-forced. Oil large oven tray.

4 Turn dough onto floured surface; knead in olives and oregano. Roll dough into 30cm x 35cm oval; fold almost in half. Place on tray; sift a little plain flour over dough.

5 Bake bread about 45 minutes; turn onto wire rack to cool.

Onion focaccia

PREPARATION TIME 20 MINUTES (PLUS STANDING TIME)
COOKING TIME 25 MINUTES (PLUS COOLING TIME) **SERVES** 8

2½ cups (375g) plain flour

2 teaspoons (7g) dried yeast

¼ cup (20g) finely grated parmesan cheese

2 tablespoons coarsely chopped fresh sage

3 teaspoons sea salt flakes

1 cup (250ml) warm water

¼ cup (60ml) olive oil

1 small white onion (80g), sliced thinly

1 Sift flour into large bowl; stir in yeast, cheese, sage and 1 teaspoon of the salt. Gradually stir in the water and 2 tablespoons of the oil. Knead on floured surface about 10 minutes or until dough is smooth and elastic.

2 Place dough on oiled oven tray; press into a 24cm-round. Cover with oiled plastic wrap; stand in warm place until dough doubles in size.

3 Preheat oven to 220°C/200°C fan-forced.

4 Meanwhile, combine onion, remaining salt and remaining oil in small bowl. Remove plastic wrap from dough; sprinkle dough with onion mixture.

5 Bake focaccia about 25 minutes; slide onto wire rack to cool.

Once you start making yeast doughs you will realise that it's not difficult. The rewards far outweigh the time and effort. Your friends and family will be amazed at your new found skills.

Hot cross buns

PREPARATION TIME 1 HOUR (PLUS STANDING TIME) **COOKING TIME** 25 MINUTES (PLUS COOLING TIME)

MAKES 16

1 tablespoon (14g) dried yeast

¼ cup (55g) caster sugar

1½ cups (375ml) warm milk

4 cups (600g) plain flour

1 teaspoon mixed spice

½ teaspoon ground cinnamon

60g butter

1 egg

¾ cup (120g) sultanas

FLOUR PASTE

½ cup (75g) plain flour

2 teaspoons caster sugar

⅓ cup (80ml) water, approximately

GLAZE

1 tablespoon caster sugar

1 teaspoon gelatine

1 tablespoon water

1 Combine yeast, sugar and milk in small bowl or jug. Cover; stand in warm place about 10 minutes or until mixture is frothy.

2 Sift flour and spices into large bowl; rub in butter. Stir in yeast mixture, egg and sultanas; mix to a soft sticky dough. Cover; stand in warm place about 45 minutes or until dough has doubled in size.

3 Grease 23cm-square slab cake pan or deep 23cm-square cake pan.

4 Turn dough onto floured surface; knead about 5 minutes or until smooth. Divide dough into 16 pieces, knead into balls. Place balls into pan; cover, stand in warm place about 10 minutes or until buns have risen to top of pan.

5 Meanwhile, preheat oven to 220°C/200°C fan-forced.

6 Make flour paste for crosses; place in piping bag fitted with small plain tube, pipe crosses on buns.

7 Bake buns about 20 minutes. Turn buns, top-side up, onto wire rack.

8 Make glaze; brush hot buns with hot glaze. Cool on wire rack.

FLOUR PASTE Combine flour and sugar in cup. Gradually blend in enough of the water to form a smooth firm paste.

GLAZE Stir ingredients in small saucepan over heat, without boiling, until sugar and gelatine are dissolved.

Home-made hot cross buns have a much stronger yeasty flavour than commercially made buns and, they won't keep for more than a day or so. You'll notice hot cross buns appearing in supermarkets weeks before Easter — that's because they have preservatives added. Rather than slaving over the buns on Easter Sunday, make them the day before — put the shaped buns in the pan, then cover them loosely with oiled plastic wrap. Put them in the fridge overnight. They will prove in the fridge. All you have to do the next day is make the crosses, then bake the buns. See pages 500 & 501 for illustrated step-by-step instructions to making hot cross buns.

Hot cross buns step-by-step

Unglazed buns freeze well, so get organised, and make your own, they're easy and taste wonderful.

YEAST

Compressed (or baker's) yeast can be bought from some health food stores — dried or granular yeast can be bought from supermarkets, making it the most popular to use.

SPONGE MIXTURE

Most recipes start by mixing the yeast, sugar and warmed liquid together. It is then stood in a warm place for 10 to 15 minutes to rise. Be fussy about measuring the yeast — it's important for success.

RUBBING-IN BUTTER

Sift the dry ingredients into a large wide-topped bowl, rub the chopped butter through the ingredients with your fingertips. Butter is best used at room temperature.

SHAPING

Divide the dough as evenly as you can into the number of buns suggested in the recipe. If you can be bothered, weigh each portion of dough for even-sized buns. Knead each portion until smooth, and place in the prepared pan, smooth-side up.

PROVING

Cover the buns loosely with a light tea towel, stand them in a warm place until they double in size — this will take about 15 minutes, depending on the temperature of the dough and the kitchen.

PIPING CROSSES

The paste for crosses is usually made from blended plain flour and water. Make sure it's smooth as any lumps will block the piping tube. Pipe the crosses over the buns, being generous with the paste as the buns will rise even more in the oven so will stretch the crosses.

ADDING INGREDIENTS

Mix in the fruit and sugar, then use a wooden spoon to stir in the egg and sponge mixture. When the mixture becomes too stiff to stir, use your hand to mix.

PROVING

Cover the bowl with plastic wrap, then a tea towel. Stand the bowl in a warm place until the dough has doubled in size. This will take about an hour, depending on the temperature of the dough and the kitchen.

KNEADING

Turn the dough onto a floured surface, and knead for 5 to 10 minutes (as directed in the recipe) until the dough is smooth, elastic and the fruit appears to be popping out.

BAKING

Buns are baked quickly (about 20 minutes) at a moderately high temperature to arrest the rising of the yeast. They should be well-browned, and when turned out, should sound hollow when tapped on the bottom with your fingers. Turn them top-side up onto a wire rack to cool.

GLAZE

Combine the ingredients for the glaze in a small saucepan. Stir with a wooden spoon over a medium heat, without boiling, until the sugar and gelatine are completely dissolved. Then follow the recipe's instructions.

GLAZING

Glaze the warm buns as close to serving time as possible, the glaze is sticky. You might have baked, cooled then frozen the unglazed buns, they will need to be thawed and reheated in the oven, then glazed. You can use warmed sieved jam as a glaze, but it's not as shiny as a gelatine-based glaze.

Chilli corn bread

PREPARATION TIME 20 MINUTES **COOKING TIME** 1 HOUR (PLUS COOLING TIME) **SERVES** 10

This is a full-flavoured non-yeast type of bread, perfect to serve at a barbecue with steaks and salads. You can use well-drained canned corn kernels (or fresh/cooked) instead of the frozen corn if you like. Finely chopped fresh chilli can be used instead of sambal oelek.

1 cup (150g) self-raising flour

1 teaspoon salt

1 cup (170g) cornmeal

½ cup (100g) kibbled rye

1 tablespoon brown sugar

1 teaspoon ground cumin

½ cup (60g) finely grated cheddar cheese

2 tablespoons finely chopped fresh flat-leaf parsley

1 teaspoon finely chopped fresh thyme

310g can creamed corn

⅔ cup (90g) frozen corn kernels, thawed

⅔ cup (160ml) buttermilk

⅓ cup (80ml) milk

2 teaspoons sambal oelek

2 eggs

50g butter, melted

1 Preheat oven to 200°C/180°C fan-forced. Oil deep 19cm-square cake pan; line base with baking paper.

2 Sift flour and salt into large bowl; stir in cornmeal, rye, sugar, cumin, cheese and herbs. Combine remaining ingredients in medium bowl; stir into dry ingredients. Spread mixture into pan.

3 Bake bread about 1 hour. Stand 10 minutes; turn onto wire rack to cool.

Naan

PREPARATION TIME 45 MINUTES (PLUS STANDING TIME) **COOKING TIME** 15 MINUTES **MAKES** 6

Naan is a flat bread (from India) traditionally cooked in a tandoor oven, but the heat from a good griller will do a quite good job of puffing and browning the naan. Kalonji are black onion seeds.

1 teaspoon (3g) dried yeast

1 teaspoon white sugar

⅔ cup (160ml) warm water

2 cups (300g) plain white flour

1 teaspoon salt

⅓ cup ghee, melted

2 tablespoons yogurt

2 teaspoons kalonji

1 Whisk yeast, sugar and the water in small bowl until yeast is dissolved. Cover; stand in warm place 10 minutes.

2 Sift flour and salt into large bowl; add yeast mixture, half the ghee and yogurt. Mix to a soft dough. Knead on floured surface about 5 minutes or until smooth and elastic.

3 Place dough in large oiled bowl, turning once to coat in oil. Cover; stand in warm place about 1½ hours or until doubled in size.

4 Knead dough on floured surface for 5 minutes. Divide dough into 6 pieces; roll each piece into a 20cm round naan.

5 Preheat grill to highest heat possible. Cover oven tray with foil; grease foil.

6 Cook naan, one at a time, under grill for about 2 minutes each side or until puffed and browned. Brush naan with a little of the remaining ghee, sprinkle with some of the kalonji; grill further 30 seconds. Keep naan warm while cooking remainder.

CHILLI CORN BREAD

Basic pizza dough

PREPARATION TIME 15 MINUTES (PLUS STANDING TIME) **MAKES** 4 X 15CM OR 2 X 30CM PIZZA BASES

2 teaspoons (7g) dried yeast

1 teaspoon caster sugar

1 cup (250ml) warm water

2½ cups (375g) plain flour

1 teaspoon salt

1 Combine yeast, sugar and the water in small jug; cover, stand in warm place about 10 minutes or until mixture is frothy.

2 Combine yeast mixture with sifted flour and salt in large bowl. Turn dough onto floured surface; knead about 10 minutes or until smooth and elastic.

3 Place dough in large oiled bowl; turn once to coat in oil. Stand in warm place, covered, about 1 hour or until doubled in size. Knead dough on floured surface until smooth.

Onion, anchovy and olive pizzetta

PREPARATION TIME 15 MINUTES **COOKING TIME** 20 MINUTES **MAKES** 4

1 tablespoon olive oil

3 medium brown onions (450g), sliced thinly

2 tablespoons dry sherry

1 quantity basic pizza dough (see recipe above)

2 tablespoons tomato paste

12 drained anchovy fillets, chopped coarsely

¼ cup (40g) thinly sliced seeded black olives

2 tablespoons fresh oregano leaves

1 Heat oil in large frying pan; cook onion, stirring, until browned lightly. Add sherry; cook, stirring, until sherry evaporates.

2 Preheat oven to 240°C/220°C fan-forced. Grease oven or pizza trays.

3 Divide basic pizza dough into four portions; roll each portion to 15cm-round pizzetta base. Place bases on trays; spread with tomato paste. Top with onion mixture, anchovies, olives and oregano.

4 Bake pizzetta about 15 minutes or until base is crisp.

Making pizza is fun, kids in particular love it. We recently included pizza-making as part of a kids' birthday party theme. If you want to include some wholemeal flour into this recipe, use about half wholemeal for a good not-too-heavy result. You will almost certainly need to add a little more warm water to the dough as wholemeal flour absorbs more liquid than white flour. Let your imagination run riot with topping; let kids choose from a range of their favourite foods. For inspiration check out menus from gourmet-pizza places. Pizza bases can be frozen — preferably untopped, as a lot of toppings simply don't freeze well. Freeze each round of dough unwrapped until it's solid, then the bases can be stacked with some freezer wrap between each one and made airtight, freeze for up to 3 months.

1 BASIC PIZZA DOUGH **2** ONION, ANCHOVY AND OLIVE PIZZETTA **3** SEMI-DRIED TOMATO, BASIL PESTO AND RICOTTA PIZZETTA [P 506] **4** FIG, PROSCIUTTO AND GOAT CHEESE PIZZETTA [P 506]

Semi-dried tomato, basil pesto and ricotta pizzetta

PREPARATION TIME 20 MINUTES **COOKING TIME** 15 MINUTES **MAKES** 4

1 cup firmly packed fresh basil leaves

1 tablespoon pine nuts

1 clove garlic, quartered

¼ cup (20g) coarsely grated parmesan cheese

¼ cup (60ml) olive oil

1 quantity basic pizza dough (see page 505)

1 fresh long red chilli, sliced thinly

1 cup (200g) ricotta cheese

½ cup (75g) drained semi-dried tomatoes

⅓ cup loosely packed fresh small basil leaves, extra

1 Blend or process basil, nuts, garlic, parmesan and oil until pesto forms a smooth paste.

2 Preheat oven to 240°C/220°C fan-forced. Grease oven or pizza trays.

3 Divide basic pizza dough into four portions; roll each portion to 15cm-round pizzetta base. Place bases on trays; spread with pesto. Top with chilli, ricotta and tomato.

4 Bake pizzetta about 15 minutes or until base is crisp.

Fig, prosciutto and goat cheese pizzetta

PREPARATION TIME 10 MINUTES **COOKING TIME** 15 MINUTES **MAKES** 4

1 quantity basic pizza dough (see page 505)

⅓ cup (85g) bottled tomato pasta sauce

100g goat cheese, crumbled

2 large figs (160g), cut into thin wedges

4 slices prosciutto (60g), chopped coarsely

25g baby rocket leaves

1 Preheat oven to 240°C/220°C fan-forced. Grease oven or pizza trays.

2 Divide dough into four portions; roll each portion to 15cm-round pizzetta base. Place bases on trays; spread with pasta sauce. Top with cheese, fig and prosciutto.

3 Bake pizzetta about 15 minutes or until base is crisp. Serve topped with rocket.

Potato, garlic and oregano pizza

PREPARATION TIME 25 MINUTES **COOKING TIME** 20 MINUTES **SERVES** 4

1 quantity basic pizza dough
(see page 505)

2 tablespoons polenta

⅓ cup loosely packed fresh
oregano leaves

6 small potatoes (720g),
sliced thinly

3 cloves garlic, crushed

2 tablespoons olive oil

sea salt flakes

1 tablespoon fresh oregano
leaves, extra

1 Preheat oven to 240°C/220°C fan-forced. Grease two oven trays.

2 Divide basic pizza dough in half; roll halves to 20cm x 30cm rectangle. Place dough on trays; sprinkle with polenta, prick all over with fork.

3 Divide oregano leaves between bases then layer with potato, overlapping slightly. Brush combined garlic and oil over potato.

4 Bake pizzas about 20 minutes or until potato is tender and bases are crisp. Sprinkle pizzas with sea salt and extra oregano before serving.

This is one of our favourite pizza toppings. The polenta (corn meal) will absorb some moisture from the potato. Use rosemary instead of oregano if you like. If you have a mandoline or V-slicer, use it to slice the potatoes really finely.

Pizza scrolls

PREPARATION TIME 20 MINUTES **COOKING TIME** 30 MINUTES **MAKES** 12

2 cups (300g) self-raising flour

1 tablespoon caster sugar

30g butter

¾ cup (180ml) milk

¼ cup (70g) tomato paste

2 teaspoons dried italian
herb blend

100g sliced salami,
cut into thin strips

1 medium green capsicum (200g),
cut into thin strips

2 cups (200g) pizza cheese

1 Preheat oven to 180°C/160°C fan-forced. Grease 19cm x 29cm slice pan.

2 Sift flour and sugar into medium bowl; rub in butter. Stir in milk; mix to a soft, sticky dough. Knead dough lightly on floured surface; using rolling pin, roll dough out to 30cm x 40cm rectangle.

3 Spread tomato paste all over base, sprinkle with herbs; top with salami, capsicum then cheese.

4 Starting from one of the long sides, roll dough tightly; trim edges. Cut roll into 12 even slices; place slices, cut-side up, in single layer, in pan. Bake about 30 minutes.

Scone dough makes a good base for pizzas. Roll it firmly as it will want to keep shrinking back. Pull the corners of the rectangle into shape as you go. You have to let scone dough know who's the boss. The Italian herb blend and pizza cheese (a mix of cheddar, mozzarella and parmesan) are both available from supermarkets. Use hot or mild salami, whatever you like best.

Cheese and bacon rolls

PREPARATION TIME 30 MINUTES (PLUS STANDING TIME) **COOKING TIME** 20 MINUTES **MAKES** 16

1 tablespoon (14g) dry yeast
1 teaspoon caster sugar
1½ cups (375ml) warm water
5 cups (750g) plain flour
1 teaspoon salt
½ cup (125ml) milk
2 tablespoons caster sugar, extra

60g butter, melted
1 egg
1 tablespoon milk, extra
1¼ cups (155g) grated tasty cheddar cheese
4 rindless bacon rashers (260g), chopped finely

1 Whisk yeast, sugar and the water in small bowl until yeast dissolves. Cover; stand in warm place about 10 minutes or until mixture is frothy.
2 Sift flour and salt into large bowl. Stir in yeast mixture, milk, extra sugar and butter; mix to a soft dough. Knead on floured surface about 5 minutes or until smooth and elastic. Place dough in large oiled bowl; turn once to coat in oil. Cover; stand in warm place about 30 minutes or until dough has doubled in size.
3 Turn dough onto floured surface, knead until smooth. Divide dough into 16 portions, roll each to a 10cm x 12cm oval. Place on oiled oven trays, cover with oiled plastic wrap; stand in warm place about 15 minutes or until rolls have risen well.
4 Preheat oven to 200°C/180°C fan-forced.
5 Remove plastic wrap. Brush rolls with combined egg and extra milk; sprinkle evenly with cheese and bacon. Bake about 20 minutes.

Banana and oat bread

PREPARATION TIME 20 MINUTES **COOKING TIME** 55 MINUTES **SERVES** 10

185g butter, softened
¾ cup (165g) caster sugar
3 eggs
1 cup mashed banana
¼ cup (20g) quick-cooking oats
1½ cups (225g) self-raising flour
2 tablespoons quick-cooking oats, extra

1 Preheat oven to 180°C/160°C fan-forced. Grease 14cm x 21cm loaf pan; line base with baking paper, extending paper 5cm over two long sides.
2 Beat butter and sugar in small bowl with electric mixer until light and fluffy. Beat in eggs, one at a time. Transfer mixture to large bowl; stir in banana and oats, then sifted flour. Spread mixture into pan; sprinkle top with extra oats.
3 Bake bread about 55 minutes. Stand bread in pan 5 minutes; turn, top-side up, onto wire rack to cool.

Café-style banana bread

PREPARATION TIME 15 MINUTES **COOKING TIME** 1 HOUR **SERVES** 10

1 cup mashed banana

1 cup (220g) firmly packed dark brown sugar

2 eggs

40g butter, melted

½ cup (125ml) buttermilk

¼ cup (90g) treacle

1 ½ cups (225g) plain flour

1 cup (150g) self-raising flour

2 teaspoons mixed spice

1 teaspoon bicarbonate of soda

1 Preheat oven to 180°C/160°C fan-forced. Grease 14cm x 21cm loaf pan; line base with baking paper, extending paper 5cm over two long sides.

2 Combine banana, sugar, eggs, butter, buttermilk and treacle in large bowl; stir in sifted dry ingredients. Spoon mixture into pan.

3 Bake bread about 1 hour. Stand bread in pan 10 minutes; turn, top-side up, onto wire rack to cool.

Dark brown sugar, though not essential to the bread's success, does improve the flavour and colour of the bread. You can use golden syrup or honey instead of the treacle, but like the sugar, treacle will produce the best colour and flavour. Don't over-mix the batter — lumpy is good in this case. Serve the bread as it is, or toasted with butter.

Brioche

PREPARATION TIME 40 MINUTES (PLUS STANDING TIME) **COOKING TIME** 15 MINUTES **MAKES** 12

2½ cups (375g) plain flour

1½ teaspoons (5g) dried yeast

½ teaspoon salt

¼ cup (55g) caster sugar

¾ cup (180ml) warm milk

5 egg yolks

125g butter

1 egg yolk, extra

2 teaspoons white sugar

1 Combine flour, yeast and salt in large bowl. Combine caster sugar and milk in small jug; stir until sugar dissolves. Stir milk mixture into flour mixture, then stir in egg yolks. Stir until mixture stiffens, then, using hand, mix to a firm dough.

2 Divide butter into 10 portions. Turn dough onto floured surface; work each portion of butter into dough, kneading well after each addition, until all of the butter is incorporated and the dough is smooth and glossy. Place dough in oiled large bowl. Cover; stand in warm place about 2 hours or until dough doubles in size.

3 Grease 12 x ⅓ cup (80ml) fluted ovenproof moulds or 12-hole (⅓-cup/80ml) muffin pan. Divide dough into 12 portions; remove about a quarter of each portion. Roll both the small and the large portions into balls. Place large balls in moulds; make small indentation in top of each with fingertip, sit small round in each indentation. Brush each brioche with extra egg yolk; sprinkle with sugar. Stand, uncovered, in warm place about 1 hour or until dough doubles in size.

4 Meanwhile, preheat oven to 180°C/160°C fan-forced.

5 Bake brioche about 15 minutes.

Brioche is seriously rich (and wonderful) with butter. Use unsalted butter for a slightly better result. The butter should be firm, but not too cold when it comes to working the butter into the dough. Use only as much flour as is necessary during the process of working in the butter — try and be quick, as you have to avoid breaking the butter down.

Carrot raisin bread

PREPARATION TIME 30 MINUTES (PLUS COOLING TIME) **COOKING TIME** 1 HOUR **SERVES** 10

1 cup (170g) coarsely chopped raisins

1 cup coarsely grated carrot

¾ cup (180ml) water

¾ cup (165g) sugar

30g butter

¾ cup (110g) self-raising flour

¾ cup (110g) plain flour

1 teaspoon ground cinnamon

½ teaspoon bicarbonate of soda

½ cup (60g) coarsely chopped roasted walnuts

1 Preheat oven to 160°C/140°C fan-forced. Grease 14cm x 21cm loaf pan; line base with baking paper.

2 Stir raisins, carrot, the water, sugar and butter in medium saucepan over heat, without boiling, until sugar dissolves. Bring to the boil. Reduce heat; simmer, covered, 10 minutes. Cool. Stir in sifted dry ingredients and nuts. Spread mixture into pan.

3 Bake bread about 1 hour. Stand bread in pan 5 minutes; turn, top-side up, onto wire rack to cool.

Potato and dried fruit bread

PREPARATION TIME 15 MINUTES **COOKING TIME** 40 MINUTES **SERVES** 10

2 cups (300g) self-raising four

1 cup (220g) mashed potato

½ cup (110g) caster sugar

1 cup (190g) mixed dried fruit

½ cup (125ml) milk

1 Preheat oven to 200°C/180°C fan-forced. Grease 14cm x 21cm loaf pan.

2 Combine ingredients in medium bowl. Knead on floured surface until smooth. Press mixture into pan.

3 Bake bread about 30 minutes. Turn, top-side up, onto wire rack to cool.

Pumpkin, kumara or any sweet potato can be used in place of potato here. This is really a scone dough, the potato will keep the bread moist for a day or so. The chosen vegetables will determine how much milk is needed to make this dough just right. The dough should be firm, but with a little stickiness left in it.

Chocolate banana bread

PREPARATION TIME 15 MINUTES **COOKING TIME** 1 HOUR **SERVES** 12

1 cup mashed banana

¾ cup (165g) caster sugar

2 eggs

¼ cup (60ml) extra light olive oil

¼ cup (60ml) milk

⅔ cup (100g) self-raising flour

⅔ cup (100g) wholemeal self-raising flour

¾ cup (90g) coarsely chopped roasted walnuts

¼ cup (45g) finely chopped dark eating chocolate

WHIPPED NUT BUTTER

100g butter

¼ cup (30g) finely chopped roasted walnuts

1 Preheat oven to 180°C/160°C fan-forced. Grease 14cm x 21cm loaf pan; line base and long sides with baking paper, extending paper 5cm over sides.

2 Combine banana and sugar in large bowl; stir in eggs, oil and milk. Stir in remaining ingredients until combined. Spread mixture into pan.

3 Bake bread about 1 hour. Stand bread in pan 5 minutes; turn onto wire rack to cool.

4 Meanwhile, make whipped nut butter. Serve bread warm with whipped nut butter.

WHIPPED NUT BUTTER Beat butter in small bowl with electric mixer until light and fluffy; stir in nuts.

The whipped butter is good with the bread, (particularly when it's toasted) but not essential to the popularity of the bread. Use either the extra light olive oil we specify, or a light generic type of vegetable oil. Don't forget to return the husks from the wholemeal flour to the mixture.

Chocolate fruit and nut bread

PREPARATION TIME 30 MINUTES **COOKING TIME** 1 HOUR (PLUS COOLING TIME) **SERVES** 14

3 egg whites

½ cup (110g) caster sugar

1 cup (150g) plain flour

¾ cup (105g) roasted hazelnuts

⅓ cup (85g) finely chopped glacé apricots

¼ cup (45g) dark Choc Bits

1 Preheat oven to 180°C/160°C fan-forced. Grease 8cm x 26cm bar cake pan.

2 Beat egg whites in small bowl with electric mixer until soft peaks form; gradually add sugar, beating until dissolved after each addition. Fold in sifted flour, hazelnuts, apricots and Choc Bits. Spread mixture into pan.

3 Bake bread about 30 minutes. Cool in pan. Turn off oven.

4 Preheat oven to 120°C/100°C fan-forced.

5 Cut bread into wafer thin slices; place in single layer on oven trays. Bake about 30 minutes or until dry and crisp. Stand on trays for 10 minutes. Carefully remove from trays to wire racks to cool.

CHEESECAKES

Cheesecakes

The history books tell us that cheesecake has been around since ancient times and that the Greeks, who are credited with inventing the combination of cheese and honey on an oaten base, served cheesecake at ceremonial events such as the Olympics. Cheesecake spread to the rest of Europe with the rise of the Roman empire and a written recipe for "placenta" was included in Roman historian Cato the Elder's treatise on agriculture in the second century BC. Along with reams of good advice on tending vines and making wine, harvesting figs and olives and looking after stock and crops, he provided instructions for a massive "placenta" cake that involved 14 pounds of goat cheese and four and a half pounds of honey.

These days cheesecake is a canvas upon which many countries have imprinted their own national character. The modern Greeks make theirs with mizithra and mascarpone cheeses, Italians with ricotta cheese and candied fruit, Germans use a fresh curd called quark; the French, gelatine and delicate Neufchatel cheese. English cheesecakes are not usually baked, whereas American ones generally are.

Since Americans invented Philadelphia cream cheese in the late 1800s cheesecake has become something of a national dish, with most regions creating a variation of their own. New Yorkers claim their baked cheesecake, containing nothing more than cream cheese, cream, eggs, sugar and maybe a little lemon rind, as the best. Arnold Reuben, owner of the legendary New York City Turf Restaurant is credited with popularising this cheesecake in the 1920s and '30s after he was first served it at a private dinner.

Let your tastebuds take a world tour and, as you work your way through the recipes in this chapter, we're sure you'll find your own personal best.

SPRINGFORM TINS

The cheesecake maker's greatest ally is the springform tin as it eliminates all the uncertainties of turning the cheesecake out. If you want to transfer the cake from the tin's base to a serving plate it's a good idea to reverse the base of the springform tin before pressing in the crust. It's the slight ridge on the base which makes it difficult to separate the base from the cheesecake and the underside doesn't have that ridge. To make doubly certain of being able to remove the cake from the base, line the base with aluminium foil cut to the diameter of the tin.

Every brand of springform tin gives a different measurement; the measurement we use is the one stamped on the bottom of the tin. If the crumb mixture is lining the base and side of the springform tin, there is no need to grease the tin. If it's only covering the base of the tin, you should grease the side. For an extra smooth side to an unbaked "biscuit base-only" cheesecake remove the base of the tin then drape a piece of plastic wrap over the lightly greased sides of the tin. Position and secure the base back into the tin, stretching the wrap neatly and leaving a little of the wrap hanging over the edge.

TO ACHIEVE A GOOD CRUMB CRUST

For a crumb crust that holds its shape without crumbling and cuts well, the ideal proportions are half the amount of butter to the weight of biscuit crumbs. For example, a crumb crust that uses 250g of biscuit crumbs will hold together well with 125g of melted butter. The exception to this ratio is if you're using biscuits, such as shortbread, which already have a high fat content. In this case you will need to reduce the amount of butter. We recommend using plain, sweet un-iced biscuits to make the crumbs.

You need fine, evenly-sized crumbs to make a good crust. This can be achieved by using a blender or food processor or by crushing them in a plastic bag with a rolling pin. When you've added the remaining ingredients to the crumb mixture and combined them well, press the crumbs over the base of the tin first. Scatter about one third of the crumbs over the base and press them firmly using a tablespoon or your fingers wrapped in plastic wrap or a small plastic bag. When the base is covered, turn the tin on its side and put large spoonfuls of crumbs on to the side. Press in firmly with the spoon and neaten the finish by rolling with a straight sided glass. Pour the filling in and bake and refrigerate according to the recipe. See *Cheesecake techniques* on pages 526 & 527 for more information.

MAKING, BAKING AND COOLING

For a smooth-textured filling, have the cream cheese and all the other ingredients at room temperature before you start to mix. Use the correct sized tin and other equipment such as measuring cups and add the ingredients in the order the recipe recommends. Don't overbeat mixtures that contain cream and mascarpone cheese as the mixture can curdle.

Follow cooking times carefully; don't overcook. At the end of the specified cooking time, the cake might appear a bit soft in the centre; it will firm as it cools. An overbaked cheesecake has a grainy texture and is inclined to shrink, crack and become dry as it cools.

You can help prevent the cheesecake from shrinking, sinking in the middle or cracking as it cools, by cooling it in the oven. Turn the oven heat off, leave the oven door ajar and let the cake stand undisturbed in the oven until it is cool. When cool, refrigerate it until it sets firmly. In the case of a larger cheesecake, this is best done overnight. Not only is the cheesecake easier to cut, its flavour is also better developed.

REMOVING FROM THE TIN

Release the catch on the side of the tin and remove the outer ring. Slip a large spatula or egg slice under the crust so you can slide the chilled cheesecake onto a plate. Neaten the crumb crust by trimming with a sharp knife; work carefully to avoid breaking the crust and, using a pastry brush, sweep off any crumbs that drop on to the filling. Decorate according to the recipe or your personal whim. Use a hot, dry, sharp knife to cut the cheesecake.

Sour cream cheesecake

PREPARATION TIME 20 MINUTES (PLUS REFRIGERATION TIME)

COOKING TIME 1 HOUR 15 MINUTES (PLUS COOLING TIME) **SERVES** 12

250g plain sweet biscuits	3 eggs
125g butter, melted	1 cup (240g) sour cream
250g cottage cheese	¼ cup (60ml) lemon juice
250g cream cheese, softened	300g fresh blueberries
2 teaspoons finely grated lemon rind	2 teaspoons icing sugar
¾ cup (165g) caster sugar	

1 Process biscuits until fine. Add butter, process until combined. Press mixture over base and side of 22cm springform tin. Place tin on oven tray; refrigerate 30 minutes.

2 Preheat oven to 160°C/140°C fan-forced.

3 Push cottage cheese through a sieve into medium bowl. Add cream cheese, rind and sugar; beat with electric mixer until smooth. Beat in eggs, one at a time, then sour cream and juice. Pour mixture into tin.

4 Bake cheesecake about 1¼ hours. Cool in oven with door ajar. Refrigerate cheesecake 3 hours or overnight.

5 Before serving, top cheesecake with blueberries; dust with sifted icing sugar.

Bistro cheesecake

PREPARATION TIME 20 MINUTES (PLUS REFRIGERATION TIME)

COOKING TIME 50 MINUTES (PLUS COOLING TIME) **SERVES** 10

250g plain sweet biscuits

125g butter, melted

4 eggs

¾ cup (165g) caster sugar

500g cream cheese, softened

1 tablespoon finely grated lemon rind

1 Process biscuits until fine. Add butter, process until combined. Press mixture over base and side of 20cm springform tin. Place tin on oven tray; refrigerate 30 minutes.

2 Preheat oven to 160°C/140°C fan-forced.

3 Beat eggs and sugar in small bowl with electric mixer until thick and creamy. Beat cheese and rind in medium bowl with electric mixer until smooth. Add egg mixture to cheese mixture; beat until combined. Pour mixture into tin.

4 Bake cheesecake about 50 minutes. Cool in oven with door ajar. Refrigerate cheesecake 3 hours or overnight.

SOUR CREAM CHEESECAKE

Sticky date cheesecake

PREPARATION TIME 25 MINUTES **COOKING TIME** 1 HOUR 10 MINUTES (PLUS COOLING TIME) **SERVES** 14

Sticky date pudding (or cake) became popular in the 1980s, so we've taken the flavours and incorporated them into a cheesecake to make a winning combination.

2 cups (280g) seeded dried dates

¾ cup (180ml) water

½ teaspoon bicarbonate of soda

750g cream cheese, softened

½ cup (110g) firmly packed brown sugar

¼ teaspoon ground cinnamon

¼ teaspoon mixed spice

2 eggs

CARAMEL SAUCE

25g butter

⅓ cup (75g) firmly packed brown sugar

⅓ cup (80ml) cream

1 Preheat oven to 160°C/140°C fan-forced. Grease 24cm springform tin; line base and side with baking paper. Place tin on oven tray.

2 Combine dates, the water and soda in small saucepan; bring to the boil. Simmer 5 minutes. Cool mixture 5 minutes; blend or process until almost smooth.

3 Beat cheese and sugar in medium bowl with electric mixer until smooth. Add spices, eggs and date mixture; beat until combined. Pour mixture into tin.

4 Bake cheesecake about 1 hour. Cool in oven with door ajar. Refrigerate cheesecake 3 hours or overnight.

5 Make caramel sauce. Turn cheesecake onto serving plate, drizzle with warm or cold sauce.

CARAMEL SAUCE Stir ingredients in small saucepan over low heat until smooth. Bring to the boil; remove from heat.

New York cheesecake

PREPARATION TIME 25 MINUTES (PLUS REFRIGERATION TIME)

COOKING TIME 1 HOUR 35 MINUTES (PLUS COOLING TIME) **SERVES** 14

This famous cheesecake completes the most popular trio of recipes (see notes on page 516). We've added some orange rind as well as the lemon rind. If you prefer the lemon flavour you can increase the amount of finely grated lemon rind up to 1 tablespoon and leave the orange rind out completely — or add 1 teaspoon vanilla extract instead of the orange rind, for that lovely lemon/vanilla combination.

250g plain sweet biscuits

125g butter, melted

750g cream cheese, softened

2 teaspoons finely grated orange rind

1 teaspoon finely grated lemon rind

1 cup (220g) caster sugar

3 eggs

¾ cup (180g) sour cream

¼ cup (60ml) lemon juice

SOUR CREAM TOPPING

1 cup (240g) sour cream

2 tablespoons caster sugar

2 teaspoons lemon juice

1 Process biscuits until fine. Add butter, process until combined. Press mixture over base and side of 24cm springform tin. Place tin on oven tray; refrigerate 30 minutes.

2 Preheat oven to 180°C/160°C fan-forced.

3 Beat cheese, rinds and sugar in medium bowl with electric mixer until smooth; beat in eggs, one at a time, then cream and juice. Pour mixture into tin.

4 Bake cheesecake 1¼ hours. Remove from oven; cool 15 minutes.

5 Combine ingredients for sour cream topping in small bowl; spread over cheesecake.

6 Bake cheesecake further 20 minutes; cool in oven with door ajar. Refrigerate cheesecake 3 hours or overnight.

Italian ricotta cheesecake

PREPARATION TIME 30 MINUTES (PLUS REFRIGERATION TIME)
COOKING TIME 1 HOUR 15 MINUTES (PLUS COOLING TIME) **SERVES** 16

90g butter, softened

¼ cup (55g) caster sugar

1 egg

1¼ cups (185g) plain flour

¼ cup (35g) self-raising flour

FILLING

1kg ricotta cheese, drained

1 tablespoon finely grated lemon rind

¼ cup (60ml) lemon juice

1 cup (220g) caster sugar

5 eggs

¼ cup (40g) sultanas

¼ cup (80g) finely chopped glacé fruit salad

1 Beat butter, sugar and egg in small bowl with electric mixer until combined. Stir in sifted flours. Knead pastry on floured surface until smooth. Enclose in plastic wrap; refrigerate 30 minutes.

2 Grease 28cm springform tin. Press pastry over base of tin; prick with fork. Place on oven tray; refrigerate 30 minutes.

3 Preheat oven to 200°C/180°C fan-forced.

4 Cover pastry with baking paper, fill with dried beans or rice. Bake 10 minutes. Remove paper and beans; bake further 15 minutes or until browned lightly. Cool.

5 Meanwhile, make filling.

6 Reduce oven to 160°C/140°C fan-forced.

7 Pour filling into tin; bake cheesecake about 50 minutes. Cool in oven with door ajar. Refrigerate cheesecake 3 hours or overnight.

FILLING Process cheese, rind, juice, sugar and eggs until smooth; stir in fruit.

Pastry bases seem to go well topped with ricotta cheesecake mixtures. This pastry makes a slightly cakey/biscuity base. It does need to be pricked well with a fork, as it contains some raising agent, before baking blind (see pages 618 & 619). Do not overbeat the butter, sugar and egg mixture, or the pastry will become too soft and hard to handle. When you've worked in most of the flour using a spoon, use one hand to quickly and lightly gather the ingredients together. Drain the ricotta cheese in a fine sieve, press it with the back of a spoon to get rid of any excess moisture. Use whatever combination of glacé fruit takes your fancy.

1   2

3   4

Cinnamon and apple cheesecake

PREPARATION TIME 30 MINUTES **COOKING TIME** 1 HOUR 10 MINUTES (PLUS COOLING TIME) **SERVES** 14

1 sheet ready-rolled shortcrust pastry, thawed

750g cream cheese, softened

¾ cup (165g) caster sugar

1 teaspoon ground cinnamon

3 eggs, separated

¾ cup (180ml) cream

2 medium apples (300g), unpeeled, sliced thinly

1 tablespoon lemon juice

1 tablespoon demerara sugar

1 Preheat oven to 180°C/160°C fan-forced. Grease 24cm springform tin.

2 Cut pastry into 24cm round, press into base of tin; prick well with a fork. Place tin on oven tray; bake about 20 minutes or until browned lightly. Cool 5 minutes.

3 Beat cheese, caster sugar, cinnamon and egg yolks in medium bowl with electric mixer until smooth; beat in cream. Beat egg whites in small bowl with electric mixer until soft peaks form; fold into cheese mixture in two batches. Pour filling mixture into tin.

4 Combine apple slices and lemon juice in small bowl. Arrange slices, slightly overlapping, over filling; sprinkle with demerara sugar.

5 Bake cheesecake about 50 minutes. Cool in oven with door ajar. Refrigerate cheesecake 3 hours or overnight.

Ready-rolled shortcrust pastry is a common product for time-poor people, however, if you want to make your own shortcrust pastry, use the pastry from the Italian ricotta cheesecake [page 519]. Golden delicious apples would be my first choice in this recipe, with granny smith being second choice. If you have a mandoline or V-slicer use it for uniformly thin apple slices. The lemon juice will help prevent the apples turning brown. Use brown or raw sugar instead of demerara if you like. Use un-iced unfilled plain chocolate biscuits for this recipe.

Butterscotch pecan cheesecake

PREPARATION TIME 25 MINUTES (PLUS REFRIGERATION TIME)
COOKING TIME 45 MINUTES (PLUS COOLING TIME) **SERVES** 10

150g plain chocolate biscuits

50g butter, melted

500g cream cheese, softened

1 teaspoon vanilla extract

¾ cup (165g) caster sugar

2 eggs

1 tablespoon plain flour

½ cup (60g) finely chopped roasted pecans

BUTTERSCOTCH TOPPING

⅓ cup (75g) firmly packed brown sugar

40g butter

1 tablespoon cream

1 Process biscuits until fine. Add butter, process until combined. Press mixture over base of 20cm springform tin. Place tin on oven tray; refrigerate 30 minutes.

2 Preheat oven to 160°C/140°C fan-forced.

3 Beat cheese, extract and sugar in medium bowl with electric mixer until smooth; beat in eggs. Stir in flour and nuts. Pour mixture into tin.

4 Bake cheesecake about 45 minutes. Cool in oven with door ajar.

5 Make butterscotch topping by stirring ingredients in small saucepan over low heat until smooth; spread over cheesecake. Refrigerate cheesecake 3 hours or overnight.

1 CINNAMON AND APPLE CHEESECAKE **2** BUTTERSCOTCH PECAN CHEESECAKE **3** WHITE CHOCOLATE AND CRANBERRY CHEESECAKE [P 522] **4** DOUBLE CHOC RUM AND RAISIN CHEESECAKE [P 522]

White chocolate and cranberry cheesecakes

PREPARATION TIME 25 MINUTES (PLUS REFRIGERATION TIME)
COOKING TIME 35 MINUTES (PLUS COOLING TIME) **MAKES** 6

100g plain sweet biscuits

50g butter, melted

150g frozen cranberries

50g white eating chocolate, melted

FILLING

¼ cup (60ml) cream

130g white eating chocolate, chopped coarsely

375g cream cheese, softened

1 teaspoon finely grated orange rind

½ cup (110g) caster sugar

1 egg

1 Line 6-hole texas (¾-cup/180ml) muffin pan with paper cases.

2 Process biscuits until fine. Add butter, process until combined. Divide mixture among paper cases; press firmly over bases of pan holes. Refrigerate 30 minutes.

3 Preheat oven to 150°C/130°C fan-forced.

4 Meanwhile, make filling.

5 Divide filling among cases; sprinkle with cranberries.

6 Bake cheesecakes about 30 minutes. Cool in oven with door ajar. Refrigerate 3 hours or overnight. Drizzle cheesecakes with melted chocolate.

FILLING Stir cream and chocolate in small saucepan over low heat until smooth. Cool. Beat cheese, rind, sugar and egg in small bowl with electric mixer until smooth; stir in cooled chocolate mixture.

Double choc rum and raisin cheescake

PREPARATION TIME 25 MINUTES (PLUS STANDING TIME) **COOKING TIME** 1 HOUR (PLUS COOLING TIME)
SERVES 18

⅓ cup (80ml) dark rum

1 cup (160g) coarsely chopped raisins

150g butter, chopped coarsely

100g dark eating chocolate, chopped coarsely

1 cup (220g) caster sugar

⅔ cup (160ml) water

1 cup (150g) plain flour

2 tablespoons cocoa powder

2 egg yolks

1 tablespoon cocoa powder, extra

FILLING

500g cream cheese, softened

½ cup (110g) caster sugar

3 eggs

250g dark eating chocolate, melted

1 Combine rum and raisins in small bowl. Cover; stand 3 hours or overnight.

2 Preheat oven to 180°C/160°C fan-forced. Grease 20cm x 30cm lamington pan; line base with baking paper, extending paper 5cm over two long sides.

3 Stir butter, chocolate, sugar and the water in medium saucepan over low heat until smooth. Remove from heat; stir in sifted flour and cocoa, then egg yolks. Pour mixture into pan; bake about 15 minutes. Cool in pan.

4 Meanwhile, make filling. Pour filling over base.

5 Bake cheesecake about 45 minutes. Cool in oven with door ajar. Refrigerate cheesecake 3 hours or overnight. Serve cheesecake dusted with extra cocoa.

FILLING Beat cheese and sugar in medium bowl with electric mixer until smooth. Beat in eggs, one at a time. Stir in cooled chocolate, then raisin mixture.

Jaffa liqueur cheesecake slice

PREPARATION TIME 25 MINUTES (PLUS REFRIGERATION TIME)
COOKING TIME 30 MINUTES (PLUS COOLING TIME) **SERVES** 12

Orange and chocolate flavours fall into the love and hate area — I've never met anyone who was half-hearted about the flavour combination. Grand Marnier will give you the best orange taste in this recipe.

250g plain chocolate biscuits

150g butter, melted

3 eggs

¾ cup (165g) caster sugar

500g cream cheese, softened

100g dark eating chocolate, melted

1 tablespoon finely grated orange rind

2 tablespoons orange-flavoured liqueur

CHOCOLATE GANACHE
150g dark eating chocolate, chopped coarsely

¼ cup (60ml) cream

1 Grease 19cm x 29cm slice pan; line base with baking paper, extending paper 5cm over two long sides.

2 Process biscuits until fine. Add butter, process until combined. Press mixture over base of pan; refrigerate 30 minutes.

3 Preheat oven to 160°C/140°C fan-forced.

4 Beat eggs and sugar in small bowl with electric mixer until thick and creamy. Beat cheese in medium bowl with electric mixer until smooth; beat in egg mixture, in two batches.

5 Pour half the mixture into another medium bowl. Stir cooled chocolate into one bowl; stir rind and liqueur into other bowl. Pour both mixtures into pan; swirl with skewer.

6 Bake cheesecake about 25 minutes. Cool in oven with door ajar.

7 Meanwhile, make chocolate ganache; spread over cheesecake. Refrigerate cheesecake 3 hours or overnight.

CHOCOLATE GANACHE Stir ingredients in small saucepan over low heat until smooth. Cool 10 minutes.

Low-fat lemon and blackberry cheesecake

PREPARATION TIME 20 MINUTES **COOKING TIME** 1 HOUR (PLUS COOLING TIME) **SERVES** 10

200g low-fat cottage cheese

250g light spreadable cream cheese

2 teaspoons finely grated lemon rind

¾ cup (165g) caster sugar

2 eggs

⅓ cup (55g) semolina

¼ cup (35g) self-raising flour

¼ cup (60ml) buttermilk

200g fresh or frozen blackberries

1 teaspoons icing suagr

1 Preheat oven to 160°C/140°C fan-forced. Grease 20cm springform tin; line base with baking paper. Place tin on oven tray.

2 Beat cheeses, rind and sugar in medium bowl with electric mixer until smooth; beat in eggs, one at a time. Stir in semolina and sifted flour, then buttermilk. Pour mixture into tin, sprinkle with blackberries.

3 Bake cheesecake about 1 hour. Cool in oven with door ajar. Refrigerate cheesecake 3 hours or overnight. Serve dusted with sifted icing sugar.

Lemon curd cheesecake

PREPARATION TIME 25 MINUTES (PLUS REFRIGERATION TIME)

COOKING TIME 1 HOUR (PLUS COOLING TIME) **SERVES** 12

250g plain sweet biscuits

125g butter, melted

750g cream cheese, softened

2 teaspoons finely grated lemon rind

½ cup (110g) caster sugar

3 eggs

LEMON CURD

45g butter

½ cup (110g) caster sugar

1 egg, beaten lightly, strained

1 teaspoon finely grated lemon rind

2 tablespoons lemon juice

1 Process biscuits until fine. Add butter, process until combined. Press mixture over base and side of 22cm springform tin. Place tin on oven tray; refrigerate 30 minutes.

2 Preheat oven to 160°C/140°C fan-forced.

3 Beat cheese, rind and sugar in medium bowl with electric mixer until smooth; beat in eggs, one at a time. Pour mixture into tin.

4 Bake cheesecake about 1 hour. Cool in oven with door ajar.

5 Meanwhile, make lemon curd.

6 Spread cheesecake with lemon curd; refrigerate 3 hours or overnight.

LEMON CURD Combine ingredients in small heatproof bowl. Place bowl over small saucepan of simmering water; cook, stirring, about 20 minutes or until mixture coats the back of a spoon. Remove bowl from saucepan immediately; cover surface of curd with plastic wrap. Cool.

LOW-FAT LEMON AND BLACKBERRY CHEESECAKE

Cheesecake techniques

Cheesecakes involve a few techniques — here are the finer points of a crumb crust, folding-in egg whites and making curd.

SPRINGFORM TINS
These tins come in a large range of sizes and finishes. Check the sizes carefully, in our recipes, we refer to the size that is stamped onto the base of the tin.

TIN PREPARATION
If the tin is new, undo the clip, wash and dry the base and side. For most of our recipes, we use the base upside-down, to make the cake easier to cut and serve. Line the tin with plastic wrap for a smooth-sided non-bake cheesecake.

CRUMB CRUST
Blend, process or crush the biscuits finely for the best cutting results. Melt the butter, without overheating it, then stir the butter evenly through the crumbs.

BEATING EGG WHITES
Some recipes call for beaten egg whites to be folded through a cheesecake mixture, they must be beaten only until soft peaks form, use a small bowl for volume, and an electric mixer.

FOLDING EGG WHITES
You need a wide-topped bowl for folding-in. Usually recipes direct you to fold in egg whites in two batches, fold about half (or even less) in first, to break down the mixture to a more manageable state, then fold the rest of the egg whites in gently and lightly.

CUTTING CHEESECAKE
Remove the cake from the tin by unclipping the side, then slide a long-bladed spatula or egg slide under the base, to move the cake. Cut the cake with a large sharp, heated dry knife.

CRUMB CRUST BASE

Tip the biscuit mixture into the tin, press about one-third of the mixture over the base, and the remaining mixture up the side of the tin, using a straight-sided glass to firm the crumbs.

CREAM CHEESE

The cream cheese must be at room temperature before mixing — if it's too hard, it will form small lumps during beating. Soften the cheese slightly in a microwave oven, or by standing it in the mixing bowl in hot water.

BEATING CREAM CHEESE

Most cheesecake recipes direct you to beat the cheese, flavouring and sugar etc, in a small bowl with an electric mixer. The mixture must be smooth at this stage.

CITRUS-FLAVOURED CURD

Some recipes use a citrus-flavoured curd (also know as butter or cheese), usually lemon, as part of a cheesecake recipe.

MAKING CURD

Basically, a curd consists of eggs, sugar, butter and citrus rind and juice. The ingredients are stirred constantly, in a bowl, over a pan of simmering water. The bottom of the bowl must not touch the simmering water.

THICKENING CURD

The curd thickening process takes 10 to 15 minutes, depending on the type of bowl used, the heat, and the quantity of curd. The curd is done when it coats the back of a spoon. Remove the bowl from the pan immediately the curd has thickened, to stop the cooking process.

Spiced fig and orange cheesecake

PREPARATION TIME 30 MINUTES (PLUS REFRIGERATION TIME)
COOKING TIME 1 HOUR 25 MINUTES (PLUS COOLING TIME) **SERVES** 12

½ cup (80g) brazil nuts

125g plain sweet biscuits

80g butter, melted

1 cup (250ml) orange juice

1 ¼ cups (250g) finely chopped dried figs

1 cinnamon stick

pinch ground clove

2 teaspoons icing sugar

FILLING

250g cream cheese, softened

1 tablespoon finely grated orange rind

¾ cup (165g) caster sugar

1 cup (250g) mascarpone cheese

2 eggs, separated

1 Grease 22cm springform tin.

2 Process nuts and biscuits until fine. Add butter, process until combined. Press mixture over base of tin. Place tin on oven tray; refrigerate 30 minutes.

3 Preheat oven to 160°C/140°C fan-forced.

4 Simmer juice, figs, cinnamon and cloves in small saucepan, uncovered, 10 minutes or until most of the juice has been absorbed. Discard cinnamon stick. Spread fig mixture over crumb base in tin.

5 Meanwhile, make filling; pour over fig mixture.

6 Bake cheesecake about 1 ¼ hours. Cool in oven with door ajar. Refrigerate cheesecake 3 hours or overnight.

7 Serve cheesecake dusted with sifted icing sugar.

FILLING Beat cream cheese, rind and sugar in medium bowl with electric mixer until smooth. Add mascarpone and egg yolks; beat only until combined. Beat egg whites in small bowl with electric mixer until soft peaks form; fold into cheese mixture.

We don't use brazil nuts often, yet when we do we wonder why we've forgotten them. They are a lovely flavour and go well with fig and orange. Buy the best quality cinnamon sticks (or quills) you can, as so often so-called cinnamon is really cassia bark sticks or quills. The best quality cinnamon is available from specialised spice shops.

Spicy carrot and walnut cheesecake

PREPARATION TIME 35 MINUTES **COOKING TIME** 1 HOUR 5 MINUTES (PLUS COOLING TIME) **SERVES** 16

⅓ cup (80ml) vegetable oil

⅓ cup (75g) firmly packed brown sugar

1 egg

¾ cup (110g) self-raising flour

½ teaspoon mixed spice

1 cup (40g) coarsely grated carrot

½ cup (55g) coarsely chopped roasted walnuts

FILLING

750g cream cheese, softened

2 teaspoons finely grated orange rind

¾ cup (165g) caster sugar

3 eggs

2 tablespoons plain flour

½ teaspoon mixed spice

½ teaspoon ground cardamom

1 cup (40g) finely grated carrot

1 Preheat oven to 160°C/140°C fan-forced. Grease 23cm-square slab cake pan; line base and sides with baking paper, extending paper 5cm above edges of pan.
2 Beat oil, sugar and egg in small bowl with electric mixer until thick and creamy. Stir in sifted flour and spice, carrot and nuts. Spread mixture into pan.
3 Bake base 15 minutes. Remove from oven; stand 15 minutes.
4 Meanwhile, make filling; pour over cake base.
5 Bake cheesecake about 40 minutes. Cool in oven with door ajar. Refrigerate cheesecake 3 hours or overnight.

FILLING Beat cheese, rind and sugar in medium bowl with electric mixer until smooth; beat in eggs, one at a time. Stir in sifted flour and spices, then carrot.

Mixed spice cheesecake with honey syrup

PREPARATION TIME 25 MINUTES (PLUS REFRIGERATION TIME)
COOKING TIME 50 MINUTES (PLUS COOLING TIME) **SERVES** 9

250g plain sweet biscuits

125g butter, melted

500g cream cheese, softened

½ cup (110g) firmly packed brown sugar

2 teaspoons vanilla extract

1 teaspoon mixed spice

½ cup (125ml) cream

3 egg yolks

2 egg whites

HONEY SYRUP

2 cinnamon sticks

4 strips lemon rind

⅓ cup (120g) honey

1 tablespoon water

¾ teaspoon gelatine

1 Grease deep 19cm square cake pan; line base and sides with baking paper, extending paper 5cm above edges of pan.

2 Process biscuits until fine. Add butter, process until combined. Press mixture over base of pan; refrigerate 30 minutes.

3 Preheat oven to 160°C/140°C fan-forced.

4 Beat cheese, sugar, extract and spice in medium bowl with electric mixer until smooth; beat in cream and egg yolks.

5 Beat egg whites in small bowl with electric mixer until soft peaks form; fold into cream cheese mixture. Pour filling into pan.

6 Bake cheesecake about 50 minutes. Cool in oven with door ajar. Refrigerate cheesecake 3 hours or overnight.

7 Make honey syrup; serve warm with cheesecake.

HONEY SYRUP Stir ingredients in small saucepan over high heat; bring to the boil. Remove from heat.

Vanilla spice cheesecake

PREPARATION TIME 25 MINUTES (PLUS REFRIGERATION TIME)
COOKING TIME 55 MINUTES (PLUS COOLING TIME) **SERVES** 14

¾ cup (110g) plain flour

¼ teaspoon ground cinnamon

pinch ground nutmeg

⅓ cup (75g) caster sugar

80g butter, melted

½ teaspoon vanilla extract

⅓ cup (45g) coarsely chopped roasted hazelnuts

¼ cup (80g) apricot jam, warmed, strained

1 vanilla bean

250g cream cheese, softened

500g ricotta cheese

2 tablespoons lemon juice

⅔ cup (150g) caster sugar

2 eggs

Remember to secure the base of the tin upside-down (flat bottom-side up) to make it easier to remove the cheesecake.

1 Grease 24cm springform tin.

2 Sift flour, spices and sugar into medium bowl; stir in butter, extract and nuts. Press mixture over base of tin. Place tin on oven tray; refrigerate 30 minutes.

3 Preheat oven to 180°C/160°C fan-forced.

4 Bake base about 20 minutes or until browned lightly. Spread with jam.

5 Reduce oven to 150°C/130°C fan-forced.

6 Split vanilla bean in half lengthways; scrape seeds into medium bowl. Add cheeses, juice and half of the sugar; beat with electric mixer until combined. Beat remaining sugar and eggs in small bowl with electric mixer about 5 minutes or until thick and creamy; fold into cheese mixture. Pour mixture into tin.

7 Bake cheesecake about 35 minutes. Cool in oven with door ajar. Refrigerate cheesecake 3 hours or overnight.

Cheesecake brownies

PREPARATION TIME 25 MINUTES **COOKING TIME** 30 MINUTES (PLUS COOLING TIME) **SERVES** 16

125g butter, chopped

150g dark eating chocolate, chopped coarsely

1 egg

⅔ cup (150g) caster sugar

¾ cup (110g) plain flour

¼ cup (35g) self-raising flour

TOPPING

250g cream cheese, softened

1 teaspoon vanilla extract

⅓ cup (75g) caster sugar

1 egg

½ cup (125ml) cream

1 Preheat oven to 180°C/160°C fan-forced. Grease deep 19cm-square cake pan; line base and sides with baking paper, extending paper 5cm over edges of pan.

2 Stir butter and chocolate in small saucepan over low heat until smooth. Cool.

3 Beat egg and sugar in small bowl with electric mixer until thick and creamy. Stir in chocolate mixture and sifted flours. Spread mixture into pan; bake 10 minutes.

4 Make topping by beating cheese, extract, sugar and egg in small bowl with electric mixer until smooth; beat in cream. Pour topping over brownie base.

5 Bake cheesecake about 15 minutes. Cool in oven with door ajar. Refrigerate 3 hours.

Cherry chocolate cheesecake

PREPARATION TIME 20 MINUTES (PLUS REFRIGERATION TIME)
COOKING TIME 50 MINUTES (PLUS COOLING TIME) **SERVES** 14

125g plain chocolate biscuits

75g butter, melted

425g can seeded black cherries in syrup, drained

500g cream cheese, softened

⅓ cup (75g) caster sugar

2 eggs

200g dark eating chocolate, melted

3 x 55g Cherry Ripe bars, chopped coarsely

1 Grease 24cm springform tin.

2 Process biscuits until fine. Add butter, process until combined. Press mixture over base of tin. Place tin on oven tray; refrigerate 30 minutes.

3 Preheat oven to 180°C/160°C fan-forced.

4 Place cherries on absorbent paper. Beat cheese and sugar in medium bowl with electric mixer until smooth; beat in eggs, one at a time. Gradually beat in cooled chocolate; stir in Cherry Ripe and cherries. Spread mixture into tin.

5 Bake cheesecake about 50 minutes. Cool in oven with door ajar. Refrigerate cheesecake 3 hours or overnight.

CHEESECAKE BROWNIES

Glacé ginger and pineapple cheesecake

PREPARATION TIME 25 MINUTES (PLUS REFRIGERATION TIME)

COOKING TIME 50 MINUTES (PLUS COOLING TIME) **SERVES** 14

150g butternut snap biscuits

75g butter, melted

¼ cup (60g) finely chopped glacé ginger

½ cup (115g) finely chopped glacé pineapple

FILLING

500g cream cheese, softened

½ cup (110g) caster sugar

½ cup (120g) sour cream

2 tablespoons plain flour

3 eggs

1 Grease 24cm springform tin; line base and side with baking paper.

2 Process biscuits until fine. Add butter, process until combined. Press mixture over base of tin. Place tin on oven tray; refrigerate 30 minutes.

3 Preheat oven to 160°C/140°C fan-forced.

4 Meanwhile, make filling.

5 Combine glacé fruit; sprinkle one-third over base. Pour filling over fruit; bake 15 minutes. Sprinkle with remaining fruit; bake about 35 minutes. Cool in oven with door ajar.

6 Refrigerate cheesecake 3 hours or overnight.

FILLING Beat cheese, sugar, cream and flour in medium bowl with electric mixer until smooth; beat in eggs, one at a time.

Triple coconut cheesecake

PREPARATION TIME 30 MINUTES (PLUS REFRIGERATION TIME)

COOKING TIME 1 HOUR 5 MINUTES (PLUS COOLING TIME) **SERVES** 16

90g coconut macaroons

125g plain sweet biscuits

125g butter, melted

250g cream cheese, softened

½ cup (110g) caster sugar

300g sour cream

2 tablespoons coconut-flavoured rum

2 x 140ml cans coconut milk

½ cup (40g) desiccated coconut, toasted

¼ cup (35g) cornflour

3 eggs

GLAZE

100g dark eating chocolate, chopped coarsely

60g unsalted butter, chopped coarsely

We used Malibu for the coconut-flavoured rum. You can leave the alcohol out of this cheesecake if you like, although it does make the flavour a bit more grown-up. Make a little effort to toast the coconut perfectly to a golden brown colour. The toasting brings out the flavour of the coconut. See Roasting on page 659 for the perfect and easiest method of toasting coconut.

1 Preheat oven to 160°C/140°C fan-forced.

2 Process macaroons and biscuits until fine. Add butter, process until combined. Press mixture over base and side of 26cm springform tin. Place tin on oven tray; refrigerate 30 minutes.

3 Beat cheese, sugar, sour cream, rum, coconut milk, coconut and cornflour in medium bowl with electric mixer until smooth; beat in eggs, one at a time. Pour mixture into tin.

4 Bake cheesecake about 1 hour. Cool in oven with door ajar. Refrigerate cheesecake 3 hours or overnight.

5 Make glaze; spread over cheesecake. Stand cheesecake 20 minutes before serving.

GLAZE Stir ingredients in small saucepan over low heat until smooth. Refrigerate until mixture is spreadable.

Black forest cheesecake

PREPARATION TIME 20 MINUTES (PLUS REFRIGERATION TIME) **COOKING TIME** 35 MINUTES **SERVES** 8

425g can seedless black cherries in syrup

200g dark eating chocolate, melted

125g cream cheese, softened

125g mascarpone cheese

½ cup (110g) caster sugar

⅔ cup (160ml) cream

1 egg, separated

CHERRY TOPPING

85g packet cherry flavoured jelly crystals

⅔ cup (160ml) boiling water

Don't overbeat the filling mixture. If the cream cheese is softened correctly (that is at room temperature), the ingredients will combine easily. Overbeating could cause the mascarpone to split (curdle).

1 Preheat oven to 160°C/140°C fan-forced. Grease 19cm x 29cm slice pan; line base with baking paper, extending paper 5cm over long sides.

2 Drain cherries; reserve syrup.

3 Make cherry topping.

4 Meanwhile, spread chocolate over base of pan; refrigerate until set.

5 Beat cheese, mascarpone, sugar, cream and egg yolk in small bowl with electric mixer until smooth; stir in cherries.

6 Beat egg white in small bowl with electric mixer until soft peaks form; fold into cream cheese mixture. Pour over chocolate base.

7 Bake cheesecake about 35 minutes; cool in oven with door ajar.

8 Pour topping over cheesecake. Refrigerate overnight.

CHERRY TOPPING Stir jelly crystals and the water in small bowl until jelly is dissolved. Stir in ⅔ cup reserved cherry syrup; cool. Refrigerate jelly until thickened to the stage where it resembles unbeaten egg whites before pouring over the cheesecake.

Lemon cheesecake with chocolate glaze

PREPARATION TIME 25 MINUTES (PLUS REFRIGERATION TIME)

COOKING TIME 55 MINUTES (PLUS REFRIGERATION TIME) **SERVES** 10

125g plain chocolate biscuits

75g butter, melted

½ cup (125ml) cream

150g white chocolate Melts, melted

500g cream cheese, softened

1 cup (220g) caster sugar

3 eggs

2 teaspoons finely grated lemon rind

¼ cup (60ml) lemon juice

CHOCOLATE GLAZE

200g dark eating chocolate, melted

2 tablespoons light corn syrup

60g unsalted butter, melted

1 Grease 20cm springform tin; line base with foil, grease foil.

2 Process biscuits until fine. Add butter, process until combined. Press mixture evenly over base of tin; refrigerate 30 minutes.

3 Preheat oven to 180°C/160°C fan-forced.

4 Stir cream and Melts in small saucepan over low heat until smooth. Cool.

5 Beat cheese and sugar in medium bowl with electric mixer until smooth. Beat in chocolate mixture; then eggs, rind and juice. Pour mixture into tin.

6 Bake cheesecake about 50 minutes. Cool in oven with door ajar. Remove cheesecake from tin; refrigerate 1 hour.

7 Make chocolate glaze.

8 Place cheesecake on wire rack over tray. Spread warm glaze all over cheesecake; refrigerate until set.

CHOCOLATE GLAZE Stir ingredients in small bowl until smooth.

Mixed berry baked cheesecake

PREPARATION TIME 25 MINUTES (PLUS REFRIGERATION TIME) **COOKING TIME** 35 MINUTES **SERVES** 10

250g plain chocolate biscuits

125g butter, melted

500g cream cheese, softened

½ cup (110g) caster sugar

1 tablespoon lemon juice

2 eggs

⅓ cup (80g) sour cream

1 tablespoon plain flour

1½ cups (225g) frozen mixed berries, thawed

1 Grease and line 20cm x 30cm lamington pan; line base with baking paper, extending paper 5cm over long sides.

2 Process biscuits until fine. Add butter, process until combined. Press mixture over base of pan. Refrigerate 30 minutes.

3 Preheat oven to 150°C/130°C fan-forced.

4 Beat cheese, sugar and juice in medium bowl with electric mixer until smooth. Beat in eggs, sour cream and flour. Spread mixture into pan; sprinkle with berries.

5 Bake cheesecake about 35 minutes. Cool; refrigerate until firm.

Celebration cheesecake

PREPARATION TIME 40 MINUTES (PLUS REFRIGERATION TIME) **COOKING TIME** 1 HOUR 15 MINUTES
SERVES 16

500g fruit cake, cut into 1cm slices

1 medium pink grapefruit (425g), segmented

2 large oranges (600g), segmented

250g strawberries, halved

120g fresh raspberries

150g fresh blueberries

FILLING

750g cream cheese, softened

300g sour cream

1 teaspoon vanilla extract

1 cup (220g) caster sugar

¼ cup (60ml) brandy

½ teaspoon ground nutmeg

3 eggs

TOFFEE

1 cup (220g) caster sugar

1 cup (250ml) water

1 Preheat oven to 180°C/160°C fan-forced. Grease 26cm springform tin; line base with baking paper.

2 Cover base of tin with cake slices; bake 10 minutes.

3 Reduce oven to 150°C/130°C fan-forced.

4 Meanwhile, make filling; pour into tin.

5 Bake cheesecake about 45 minutes. Cool in oven with door ajar. Refrigerate cheesecake 3 hours or overnight.

6 Make toffee.

7 Remove cheesecake from tin to serving plate; top with fruit. Drizzle toffee over fruit.

FILLING Beat cheese, sour cream, extract, sugar, brandy and nutmeg in large bowl with electric mixer until smooth; beat in eggs, one at a time.

TOFFEE Stir sugar and the water in medium heavy-based frying pan over high heat until sugar dissolves. Boil, without stirring, uncovered, about 10 minutes or until mixture is golden brown. Remove from heat; stand until bubbles subside before using.

Use a good-quality fruit cake – bought or even home-made. This dessert would be perfect to serve at Christmas. Toffee finishes this cheesecake in a glamorous way; once you've mastered toffee you'll find it a quick and easy way to decorate a cake or dessert (see page 203 for the finer details). Toffee will stand up well at room temperature for several hours, providing the weather is dry – toffee hates humidity and wet weather.

DESSERTS

Desserts

The notion of a baked dessert is a relatively recent one, as it's only come to the table since sugar became widely available in the late 18th and early 19th centuries. A whole world of crumbles, sponges, meringues and custard-based desserts has opened up since then, popularised by thrifty cooks who knew that to put a pudding in the oven after or while the roast was cooking not only made the most of precious heat and fuel, but also provided a low-maintenance dessert which required little attention beyond mixing and placing in the oven.

Although the custom of eating a daily baked dessert has become a victim of today's busy lifestyle, it still remains a great option when entertaining. The cook can pop the dessert in the oven as the main course is served and it will be ready before anyone even starts thinking about afters. The word pudding can be traced to a Germanic word meaning "sausage" or "swollen" and this connection exists to the present with sausages such as blood pudding. But by and large, pudding these days means a luscious sweet treat, with all the comforting connotations of meals from a less stressful age when cooks were judged by their ability to serve hearty, nourishing fare and built lasting reputations for their delicious desserts.

BAKING TIPS

We can't emphasise enough how important it is to get to know your oven. Every oven bakes differently but as a rule of thumb it's good to position the dish so the top of the cooked dessert is at the centre of the oven. You can check the accuracy of your oven's temperature gauge by checking it against an oven thermometer. Most domestic ovens have hotspots, so don't be nervous about opening the over door — and giving the dish a turn. But any dessert or cake full of air, like soufflés or sponges, should be treated with respect. They just might deflate if you turn them at the wrong time.

You may think a timer is an unnecessary accessory, but in today's world it's a rare cook who doesn't get distracted, so a timer, preferably with a bell, can be a great asset. Set the timer to the minimum cooking time specified in the recipe and check when it goes off. If the dish is not done, reset the timer for a couple of minutes more and continue cooking and checking until it's right. It's often at this final cooking stage that a timer is most useful. Five minutes can easily morph into 10 when you're busy getting a meal, so the alarm can make the difference between perfection and "not your best effort".

A bain marie or water bath is sometimes used to insulate baked desserts and make the baking process more gentle. The water in the base dish also adds humidity which can prevent the top of the dessert or custard from cracking. Place the pudding dish in a larger baking dish or ovenproof dish and pour boiling water into the bottom pan until the water comes half way up the sides of the dessert dish. Do this while they are sitting on a shelf in the oven. It's safer than trying to get both dishes in the oven with the boiling water splashing about. The bottom pan should be able to hold enough water so that the water doesn't evaporate during the cooking time. Keep an eye on the bottom pan and if it looks like drying out, top it up with extra boiling water.

MERINGUE TIPS

A number of the desserts in this chapter involve making meringue. It's not a difficult process, but it does help if you follow a few basic guidelines.

Beat egg whites only until soft peaks form before you start adding the sugar; if you beat the whites until they are stiff and dry, the sugar will take longer to dissolve. If the sugar doesn't dissolve properly the meringue can "weep" droplets of moisture during and after baking. To make sure the sugar is properly dissolved rub a small quantity of the egg white mixture between your fingertips. If it feels smooth, the sugar is dissolved; if it's granular you need to keep beating for a while longer. "Weeping" isn't the end of the world however, it's just an appearance thing. The meringue will still taste as yummy, it just mightn't look as good as it does in the photograph.

Egg whites won't whip if they come into contact with any fat and that's why it's so important to make sure you don't end up with any yolk in the egg whites when you separate them. If it does, you can usually scoop out the offending scrap of yolk by dipping the shell in the whites — this is also the best way to extricate any bit of shell which might accidentally end up in your bowl during separation. Make sure there's no grease on your bowl or mixer, by wiping them with a piece of absorbent paper that has been dipped in lemon juice or vinegar. Egg whites are beaten to either soft or firm peak stage. Soft peaks mean the whites barely support themselves and the peak will usually lean over and curl to one side. Firm peak is the stage where the egg white is glossy and smooth and will hold its shape. In the case of a bombe or baked alaska, egg whites beaten to firm peaks are used to cover the ice-cream and cake shape to insulate it so the dessert can be baked without the ice-cream melting. For a pavlova, the firm peaks are shaped into large or small circles which will become the base for an ethereally light dessert. (See page 641.)

ACCOMPANIMENTS

Most baked desserts can stand alone. However, you might like to multiply the pleasure by serving the dish with a scoop of ice-cream, custard studded with vanilla seeds or a decadent dollop of crème fraîche, mascarpone or double or heavy cream. Whipped cream is a perennial favourite and the secret to its success is to have everything — the cream, the bowl and beaters or whisk — very cold before you start. Cold cream holds on to the air that's whipped into it and whips more readily, so you should put the utensils in the fridge for about half an hour before you want to whip. Use thin or pouring cream or gelatine-thickened cream (both have a fat content of at least 35 per cent) and start by beating slowly, then increasing the speed as the cream begins to thicken and gain volume.

Crème caramel

PREPARATION TIME 20 MINUTES (PLUS REFRIGERATION TIME) **COOKING TIME** 40 MINUTES **SERVES** 8

¾ cup (165g) caster sugar

½ cup (125ml) water

300ml cream

1¾ cups (430ml) milk

6 eggs

1 teaspoon vanilla extract

⅓ cup (75g) caster sugar, extra

1 Preheat oven to 160°C/140°C fan-forced.

2 Stir sugar and the water in medium frying pan over heat, without boiling, until sugar dissolves. Bring to the boil; boil, uncovered, without stirring, until mixture is deep caramel in colour. Remove from heat; allow bubbles to subside. Pour toffee into deep 20cm-round cake pan.

3 Meanwhile, bring cream and milk in medium saucepan to the boil. Whisk eggs, extract and extra sugar in large bowl; whisking constantly, pour hot milk mixture into egg mixture. Strain mixture into cake pan.

4 Place pan in medium baking dish; add enough boiling water to come half way up side of pan. Bake about 40 minutes or until firm. Remove custard from baking dish. Cover; refrigerate overnight.

5 Gently ease crème caramel from side of pan; invert onto deep-sided serving plate.

VARIATIONS

VANILLA BEAN Omit vanilla extract. Add 1 split vanilla bean to cream and milk mixture before bringing to the boil; strain, remove vanilla bean before adding to egg mixture.

CINNAMON Add 1 cinnamon stick to cream and milk mixture before bringing to the boil; strain, remove cinnamon stick before adding to egg mixture.

ORANGE Stir 2 teaspoons finely grated orange rind into custard mixture before baking.

HAZELNUT Add 1 cup coarsely chopped roasted hazelnuts to cream and milk mixture; bring to the boil. Cover; stand 20 minutes then strain through muslin-lined sieve. Discard nuts. Bring cream and milk mixture back to the boil before whisking into egg mixture.

Baked custard

PREPARATION TIME 5 MINUTES **COOKING TIME** 45 MINUTES **SERVES** 6

6 eggs

1 teaspoon vanilla extract

⅓ cup (75g) caster sugar

1 litre (4 cups) hot milk

¼ teaspoon ground nutmeg

1 Preheat oven to 160°C/140°C fan-forced. Grease shallow 1.5-litre (6-cup) ovenproof dish.

2 Whisk eggs, extract and sugar in large bowl; gradually whisk in hot milk. Pour custard mixture into dish; sprinkle with nutmeg.

3 Place dish in larger baking dish; add enough boiling water to come halfway up sides of dish. Bake about 45 minutes. Remove custard from larger dish; stand 5 minutes before serving.

VARIATIONS

CITRUS Omit nutmeg. Stir ½ teaspoon each of finely grated orange, lime and lemon rind into hot milk mixture.

CHOCOLATE Omit nutmeg. Whisk ⅓ cup cocoa powder and ⅓ cup dark Choc Bits with eggs, extract and sugar.

COCONUT AND CARDAMOM Omit hot milk; bring 2⅓ cups milk, 400ml can coconut milk, 3 bruised cardamom pods and 5cm strip lime rind to the boil. Remove from heat, stand 10 minutes. Strain; discard solids. Whisk milk mixture into egg mixture.

Queen of puddings

PREPARATION TIME 20 MINUTES **COOKING TIME** 40 MINUTES **SERVES** 6

2 cups (140g) stale breadcrumbs

1 tablespoon caster sugar

1 teaspoon vanilla extract

1 teaspoon finely grated lemon rind

2½ cups (625ml) milk

60g butter

4 eggs, separated

¼ cup (80g) raspberry jam, warmed

¾ cup (165g) caster sugar, extra

1 Preheat oven to 180°C/160°C fan-forced. Grease six ¾-cup (180ml) ovenproof dishes; stand on oven tray.

2 Combine breadcrumbs, sugar, extract and rind in medium bowl. Heat milk and butter in medium saucepan until almost boiling, pour over breadcrumb mixture; stand 10 minutes. Stir in yolks. Divide mixture among dishes.

3 Bake puddings about 30 minutes. Carefully spread top of hot puddings with jam.

4 Beat egg whites in small bowl with electric mixer until soft peaks form; gradually add extra sugar, beating until sugar dissolves. Spoon meringue over puddings; bake 10 minutes.

Brandy snap and rhubarb stacks

PREPARATION TIME 10 MINUTES **COOKING TIME** 15 MINUTES **SERVES** 4

3¼ cups (400g) coarsely chopped rhubarb

2 tablespoons water

¼ cup (55g) caster sugar

30g butter

2 tablespoons brown sugar

1 tablespoon golden syrup

½ teaspoon ground ginger

2 tablespoons plain flour

¼ cup (70g) yogurt

1 Preheat oven to 180°C/160°C fan-forced. Grease two oven trays.

2 Combine rhubarb, the water and caster sugar in medium saucepan; bring to the boil. Reduce heat; simmer, uncovered, stirring occasionally, about 5 minutes or until rhubarb softens. Drain rhubarb mixture through sieve over medium bowl; reserve liquid. Spread rhubarb mixture onto metal tray; cover with foil, place in freezer.

3 Meanwhile, combine butter, brown sugar, syrup and ginger in same cleaned pan; stir over low heat until butter has melted. Remove from heat; stir in flour.

4 Drop level teaspoons of mixture about 6cm apart onto trays. Bake about 7 minutes or until brandy snaps bubble and become golden brown; cool on trays for 2 minutes then transfer to wire rack to cool completely.

5 Place rhubarb mixture in small bowl; add yogurt, pull skewer backwards and forwards through rhubarb mixture for marbled effect.

6 Sandwich three brandy snaps with a quarter of the rhubarb mixture; repeat with remaining brandy snaps and rhubarb mixture.

7 Place stacks on serving plates; drizzle with reserved rhubarb liquid.

Brandy snaps are much loved, but regarded as difficult to make. It's all about getting the oven temperature and timing right. If you're a first-time brandy snap maker, bake one first, note the time and adjust either your oven temperature or the baking time to comply with our recipe.

Rhubarb and pear sponge pudding

PREPARATION TIME 15 MINUTES **COOKING TIME** 50 MINUTES **SERVES** 6

825g can pear slices in natural juice

800g rhubarb, trimmed, cut into 4cm pieces

2 tablespoons caster sugar

2 eggs

⅓ cup (75g) caster sugar, extra

2 tablespoons plain flour

2 tablespoons self-raising flour

2 tablespoons cornflour

1 Preheat oven to 180°C/160°C fan-forced.

2 Drain pears; reserve ¾ cup (180ml) of the juice. Combine reserved juice, rhubarb and sugar in large saucepan; cook, stirring occasionally, about 5 minutes or until rhubarb is tender. Stir in pears. Pour mixture into deep 1.75-litre (7-cup) ovenproof dish.

3 Meanwhile, beat eggs in small bowl with electric mixer until thick and creamy. Gradually add extra sugar, 1 tablespoon at a time, beating until sugar dissolves between additions. Fold in sifted flours.

4 Spread sponge mixture over hot rhubarb mixture. Bake about 45 minutes.

Sponge-topped fruit-based puddings are easy to make. Any type of canned and/or stewed fruit can be used. The fruit mixture needs to be quite moist and must be hot — just under boiling — before being topped with the sponge mixture. The hot moist fruit mixture creates steam in the oven, which forces the sponge mixture to rise beautifully.

Berry pavlova tower

PREPARATION TIME 20 MINUTES **COOKING TIME** 25 MINUTES (PLUS COOLING AND REFRIGERATION TIME)
SERVES 8

6 egg whites

1 cup (220g) caster sugar

1 tablespoon cornflour

600ml thickened cream

⅓ cup (75g) caster sugar, extra

300g fresh blueberries

360g fresh raspberries

250g strawberries, sliced thinly

2 tablespoons icing sugar

MIXED BERRY COULIS

120g fresh blueberries

120g fresh raspberries

120g fresh blackberries

¼ cup (55g) caster sugar

1 Preheat oven to 180°C/160°C fan-forced. Grease three oven trays; line with baking paper. Mark a 23cm-diameter circle on each piece of paper.

2 Beat egg whites in medium bowl with electric mixer until soft peaks form. Add sugar, 1 tablespoon at a time, beating until sugar dissolves between each addition; beat in cornflour. Spread meringue over circles on trays.

3 Bake meringues 10 minutes. Reduce oven to 150°C/130°C fan-forced; bake further 15 minutes. Cool meringues in oven with door ajar.

4 Meanwhile, make mixed berry coulis.

5 Beat cream and extra sugar in small bowl with electric mixer until firm peaks form.

6 Place one meringue on serving plate; flatten slightly. Layer with half of the cream mixture then top with half of the combined berries. Repeat layering with a second meringue, remaining cream and three-quarters of remaining berries, reserving remaining berries. Cover pavlova; refrigerate 3 hours.

7 Top pavlova with reserved berries, dust with sifted icing sugar; serve with coulis.

MIXED BERRY COULIS Combine ingredients in medium saucepan, simmer, uncovered, over low heat, about 10 minutes or until berries have softened. Push coulis mixture through sieve into medium bowl; cool. Discard seeds.

Most ovens only have two oven racks. In fan-forced ovens, it's fine to bake the third meringue layer on the floor of the oven. After the first 19 minutes of baking, alternate the top meringue layer to the oven floor position and lower the oven temperature. Then alternate the top two meringue layers after the next 10 minutes of baking. The need to rotate the meringue layers depends entirely on your oven and how evenly it bakes. Use your hand to flatten the meringue layers slightly. Mix and match the berry combinations to suit what's available and your taste. Blend or process the berries for the coulis if you like, but, it's better pushed through a sieve.

Marshmallow pavlova

PREPARATION TIME 25 MINUTES (PLUS COOLING TIME) **COOKING TIME** 1 HOUR 30 MINUTES **SERVES** 8

4 egg whites
1 cup (220g) caster sugar
½ teaspoon vanilla extract
¾ teaspoon white vinegar
300ml thickened cream, whipped
250g strawberries, halved

1 Preheat oven to 120°C/100°C fan-forced. Line oven tray with foil; grease foil, dust with a little cornflour, shake away excess. Mark 18cm-circle on foil.
2 Beat egg whites in small bowl with electric mixer until soft peaks form; gradually add sugar, beating until sugar dissolves. Add extract and vinegar; beat until combined.
3 Spread meringue into circle on foil, building up at the side to 8cm in height. Smooth side and top of pavlova gently. Using spatula blade, mark decorative grooves around side of pavlova; smooth top again.
4 Bake pavlova about 1½ hours. Turn oven off; cool pavlova in oven with door ajar. When pavlova is cold, cut around top edge (the crisp meringue top will fall slightly on top of the marshmallow).
5 Serve pavlova topped with whipped cream and strawberries.

Warm chocolate pavlovas

PREPARATION TIME 5 MINUTES **COOKING TIME** 35 MINUTES **SERVES** 4

2 egg whites
1⅓ cups (215g) icing sugar
⅓ cup (80ml) boiling water
1 tablespoon cocoa powder
500ml chocolate ice-cream

CHOCOLATE CUSTARD SAUCE
1 tablespoon cornflour
1 tablespoon cocoa powder
1 tablespoon caster sugar
1 cup (125ml) milk
2 egg yolks

1 Preheat oven to 180°C/160°C fan-forced. Line large oven tray with baking paper.
2 Beat egg whites, sifted icing sugar and the water in small bowl with electric mixer about 10 minutes or until firm peaks form. Fold sifted cocoa into mixture.
3 Drop six equal amounts of mixture onto tray; use the back of a spoon to quickly make a well in the centre of the mounds.
4 Bake pavlovas about 25 minutes or until firm to touch.
5 Meanwhile, make chocolate custard sauce.
6 Serve pavlovas hot, straight from the oven, topped with ice-cream and custard sauce.

CHOCOLATE CUSTARD SAUCE Blend cornflour, sifted cocoa and sugar with milk in small saucepan; stir in egg yolks. Stir over heat until sauce boils and thickens.

Peach and raspberry meringue roll

PREPARATION TIME 25 MINUTES **COOKING TIME** 20 MINUTES **SERVES** 8

4 egg whites

¾ cup (165g) caster sugar

1 teaspoon cornflour

1 teaspoon white vinegar

⅓ cup (25g) flaked almonds

3 medium peaches (450g)

300ml thickened cream

1 tablespoon peach schnapps

120g raspberries

1 Preheat oven to 180°C/160°C fan-forced. Grease 25cm x 30cm swiss roll pan; line base with baking paper, extending paper 5cm over long sides.

2 Beat egg whites in small bowl with electric mixer until soft peaks form. Gradually add sugar, 1 tablespoon at a time, beating until sugar dissolves between additions. Fold in cornflour and vinegar. Spread mixture into pan; sprinkle with nuts.

3 Bake meringue about 20 minutes or until browned lightly.

4 Meanwhile, place piece of baking paper cut the same size as pan on bench. Turn meringue onto paper; peel lining paper away. Cool.

5 Cut small cross in stem end of each peach; place in medium heatproof bowl. Cover with boiling water; stand 30 seconds, drain. Peel skin from peaches; slice flesh thinly.

6 Beat cream and schnapps in small bowl with electric mixer until soft peaks form; spread evenly over meringue. Top with peach and raspberries. Using paper as a guide, roll meringue firmly, from the long side.

Peaches and raspberries look and taste wonderful together. If you don't have any peach-flavoured schnapps, leave it out or use brandy instead. The fruit needs to be fully ripe and flavoursome. Berries and passionfruit are my favourite.

Plum clafoutis

PREPARATION TIME 15 MINUTES **COOKING TIME** 30 MINUTES **SERVES** 4

825g can plums, drained, pitted

½ cup (75g) self-raising flour

¼ cup (55g) caster sugar

2 eggs

½ cup (125ml) milk

100g butter, melted

1 Preheat oven to 200°C/180°C fan-forced. Place plums in greased shallow 3-cup ovenproof dish.

2 Sift flour and sugar into medium bowl; make well in centre. Gradually whisk in combined eggs, milk and butter until smooth. Spoon mixture evenly between plums.

3 Bake clafoutis about 30 minutes. Serve hot with cream, ice-cream or custard.

See the information on page 547 for how to bake three layers of meringue. *Unsalted butter will give the butter cream a smooth velvety taste and texture. Beat the butter until it's as white as possible. The chocolate and cream filling will only take a short time to beat. You can do the beating with a wooden spoon if you like, as long as the mixture is spreadable. Three hours is a minimum refrigerating time, overnight is best.*

Chocolate mocha dacquoise terrine

PREPARATION TIME 20 MINUTES (PLUS REFRIGERATION TIME) **COOKING TIME** 45 MINUTES **SERVES** 12

4 egg whites

1 cup (220g) caster sugar

2 tablespoons cocoa powder

200g dark eating chocolate, chopped coarsely

¾ cup (180ml) cream

2 teaspoons cocoa powder, extra

MOCHA BUTTER CREAM

1 tablespoon instant coffee granules

2 tablespoons boiling water

100g unsalted butter, softened

2¼ cups (360g) icing sugar

1 Preheat oven to 150°C/130°C fan-forced. Line three oven trays with baking paper. Mark a 10cm x 25cm rectangle on each piece of paper.

2 Beat egg whites in small bowl with electric mixer until soft peaks form. Gradually add sugar, beating after each addition until sugar dissolves; fold in sifted cocoa. Spread meringue mixture evenly over rectangles.

3 Bake meringues about 45 minutes or until dry. Turn off oven; cool in oven with door ajar.

4 Meanwhile, stir chocolate and cream in small saucepan over low heat until smooth, transfer to small bowl; refrigerate until firm. Beat chocolate mixture with electric mixer until changed to a paler colour.

5 Make mocha butter cream.

6 Place one meringue layer on serving plate; spread with half of the chocolate mixture, then top with half of the butter cream. Top with another meringue layer; spread with remaining chocolate mixture, then remaining butter cream. Top with last meringue layer, cover; refrigerate 3 hours or overnight. To serve, dust with sifted extra cocoa powder.

MOCHA BUTTER CREAM Dissolve coffee in the boiling water in small bowl; cool 10 minutes. Beat butter in small bowl with electric mixer until pale in colour; gradually beat in sifted icing sugar. Beat in coffee mixture.

Modelling a rose

Hand-made roses are not all that difficult to make, they just need patience and practice.

INGREDIENTS
Modelling paste makes the best roses, but it is possible to use prepared soft icing. You need pure sifted icing sugar, colourings, a fine artists brush and lots of patience.

MAKING A PETAL
Dust your fingers with icing sugar, work a small ball of the paste until it's smooth, shape it into a petal shape. Keep the rest of the paste tightly covered with plastic wrap, as it will develop a crust and dry out quickly in the air.

SHAPING A PETAL
Shape the petal by placing the shape into the lightly icing-sugared, slightly cupped palm of your hand, and gently rub the petal shape with your finger until it's smooth.

SECOND PETAL
Make the second petal the same size as the first petal. Secure it to the upright bud with water, opposite the first petal. Gently touch and pinch the edge of the petal for a natural look.

OUTER PETALS
Make the outer petals larger than the first and second petals — you need at least three outer petals. Secure each one separately to the upright bud with a tiny amount of water, so that each of these outer petals slightly overlap each other. Gently touch and pinch the edge of each petal after you position it.

REMOVING ROSE FROM BASE
Pinch each rose gently and slowly from its base. This has to be done before the icing in the centre is set, and while the outer petals are still drying.

MAKING A BUD

Use you finger to roll the petal, while still in the palm of your hand, into a cylinder shape. You can pinch off the pointy end, and use this shape as a small bud if you like.

FIRST PETAL

Stand the bud upright by pushing the pointy end of the bud down onto the bench to form the base of the rose. Make another petal the same way as that under Making A Petal. Brush base of the bud with a tiny amount of water.

POSITIONING FIRST PETAL

Gently wrap the petal around the upright bud, then, use your icing-sugared finger to gently touch and pinch the edge of the petal, to make it resemble a rose petal.

DRYING ROSES

Leave the roses to dry on a flat surface, they will take at least several hours to dry thoroughly. If some of the petals look a bit droopy, support them with pieces of crumpled tissue until they dry out completely.

LEAVES

Knead some green colouring into the modelling paste. We use edible concentrated gels for colouring, these are available from some craft shops and cake decorating suppliers, they are more expensive than colourings from supermarkets, but you will use much less of them.

SHAPING LEAVES

Roll the paste out thinly, use a leaf-shaped cutter, or cut the leaves out freehand using a sharp pointed vegetable knife. Mark the veins with a wooden skewer, then dry the leaves on a flat surface. Give each leaf a twist so that they look more natural when they're used.

Crème brûlée

PREPARATION TIME 15 MINUTES (PLUS REFRIGERATION TIME) **COOKING TIME** 40 MINUTES **SERVES** 6

1 vanilla bean

3 cups (750ml) thickened cream

6 egg yolks

¼ cup (55g) caster sugar

¼ cup (40g) pure icing sugar

1 Preheat oven to 180°C/160°C fan-forced. Grease six ½-cup (125ml) ovenproof dishes.
2 Split vanilla bean in half lengthways; scrape seeds into medium heatproof bowl. Place pod in saucepan with cream; heat, without boiling.
3 Add egg yolks and caster sugar to seeds in bowl; gradually whisk in hot cream mixture. Set bowl over medium saucepan of simmering water; stir over heat about 10 minutes or until custard mixture thickens slightly and coats the back of a spoon. Discard pod.
4 Place dishes in large baking dish; divide custard among dishes. Add enough boiling water to baking dish to come halfway up sides of ovenproof dishes. Bake about 20 minutes or until custard sets. Remove custards from baking dish; cool. Cover; refrigerate overnight.
5 Preheat grill. Place custards in shallow flameproof dish filled with ice cubes; sprinkle custards evenly with sifted icing sugar. Using finger, spread sugar over the surface of each custard, pressing in gently; grill until tops of crème brûlée caramelise.

Making the custard is the easy part of making crème brûlée, getting the crunchy caramel crust just right in a domestic kitchen without a blow-torch (used by chefs) is the tricky bit. We've found using pure icing sugar, pressed gently into the surface of the custard, then exposed to the highest possible heat from a domestic grill, will give the closest to the restaurant's version. You do need to keep the custard as chilled as possible during the grilling process — as this takes longer than a zap with a blow-torch — hence the use of ice.

Lemon delicious puddings

PREPARATION TIME 20 MINUTES **COOKING TIME** 45 MINUTES **SERVES** 6

125g butter, melted

2 teaspoons finely grated lemon rind

1½ cups (330g) caster sugar

3 eggs, separated

½ cup (75g) self-raising flour

⅓ cup (80ml) lemon juice

1⅓ cups (330ml) milk

1 Preheat oven to 180°C/160°C fan-forced. Grease six 1-cup (250ml) ovenproof dishes.
2 Combine butter, rind, sugar and yolks in large bowl; stir in sifted flour, then juice. Gradually stir in milk; mixture should be smooth and runny.
3 Beat egg whites in small bowl with electric mixer until soft peaks form; fold into lemon mixture, in two batches.
4 Place ovenproof dishes in large baking dish; divide lemon mixture among dishes. Add enough boiling water to baking dish to come halfway up sides of ovenproof dishes.
5 Bake puddings about 45 minutes.

Lemon delicious is wonderful when it's light, fluffy and spongy on top with lots of lemony sauce underneath. This recipe is the best lemon delicious I've ever tasted.

CRÈME BRULEE

Chocolate soufflé with raspberry coulis

PREPARATION TIME 15 MINUTES **COOKING TIME** 20 MINUTES **SERVES** 4

1 tablespoon caster sugar	**RASPBERRY COULIS**
50g butter	150g frozen raspberries, thawed
1 tablespoon plain flour	2 tablespoons caster sugar
200g dark eating chocolate, melted	4 cloves
2 egg yolks	½ cup (125ml) dry red wine
4 egg whites	
¼ cup (55g) caster sugar, extra	

1 Preheat oven to 200°C/180°C fan-forced. Grease four ¾-cup (180ml) soufflé dishes. Sprinkle insides of dishes evenly with sugar; shake away excess. Place dishes on oven tray.
2 Melt butter in small saucepan, add flour; cook, stirring, until mixture thickens and bubbles. Remove from heat; stir in chocolate and egg yolks. Transfer to large bowl.
3 Beat egg whites in small bowl with electric mixer until soft peaks form. Gradually add extra sugar, 1 tablespoon at a time, beating until sugar dissolves between additions. Fold egg white mixture into chocolate mixture, in two batches.
4 Divide mixture among dishes; bake about 15 minutes or until soufflés are puffed.
5 Meanwhile, make raspberry coulis. Serve soufflés with coulis.

RASPBERRY COULIS Cook raspberries and sugar in small saucepan, without boiling, until sugar dissolves. Add cloves and wine; bring to the boil. Reduce heat; simmer, uncovered, about 5 minutes or until coulis thickens. Strain coulis into medium jug.

Apricot and honey soufflés

PREPARATION TIME 15 MINUTES **COOKING TIME** 30 MINUTES **SERVES** 6

¼ cup (55g) caster sugar	2 tablespoons honey
4 apricots (200g)	4 egg whites
¼ cup (60ml) water	

1 Preheat oven to 180°C/160°C fan-forced. Grease six ¾-cup (180ml) soufflé dishes. Sprinkle inside of dishes with a little of the caster sugar. Place dishes on oven tray.
2 Place apricots in small heatproof bowl, cover with boiling water; stand 2 minutes. Drain; cool 5 minutes. Peel and seed apricots; chop flesh finely.
3 Combine apricot in small saucepan with remaining caster sugar, the water and honey; bring to the boil. Reduce heat; simmer, uncovered, about 10 minutes or until apricots soften to a jam-like consistency.
4 Beat egg whites in small bowl with electric mixer until soft peaks form. With motor operating, gradually add hot apricot mixture, beating until combined.
5 Divide soufflé mixture among dishes; bake 15 minutes. Dust with sifted icing sugar.

CHOCOLATE SOUFFLE WITH RASPBERRY COULIS

Raspberry soufflés

PREPARATION TIME 15 MINUTES **COOKING TIME** 25 MINUTES **SERVES** 4

½ cup (110g) caster sugar

300g frozen raspberries, thawed

1 tablespoon water

4 egg whites

300ml thickened cream

2 teaspoons caster sugar, extra

1 Preheat oven to 180°C/160°C fan-forced. Grease four 1-cup (250ml) ovenproof dishes; sprinkle inside of dishes evenly with a little of the sugar. Place dishes on oven tray.

2 Combine 250g of the raspberries and the water in small saucepan; bring to the boil. Reduce heat; simmer, uncovered, until raspberries soften. Add sugar, stir over medium heat, without boiling, until sugar dissolves; bring to the boil. Reduce heat; simmer, uncovered, about 5 minutes or until mixture is thick and pulpy. Remove from heat; push mixture through fine sieve over small bowl, discard seeds.

3 Beat egg whites in small bowl with electric mixer until soft peaks form. With motor operating, gradually beat in hot raspberry mixture.

4 Spoon soufflé mixture into dishes; bake about 15 minutes or until puffed.

5 Meanwhile, beat remaining raspberries, cream and extra sugar in small bowl with electric mixer until thickened slightly. Serve hot soufflés with raspberry cream.

Sprinkling the greased dishes with sugar gives the mixture a little traction as it increases in volume during baking. Be careful not to overcook soufflés, they should be slightly soft in the middle, particularly those containing flour. Some cooks like the centres to be soft, resembling lightly scrambled eggs. Make sure the diners, and any sauces, ice-cream, cream etc., are ready to eat as soon as the soufflés come out of the oven. Soufflés — especially those made with flour — will not wait for anyone before they sink.

Sticky banana macadamia pudding with butterscotch sauce

PREPARATION TIME 20 MINUTES **COOKING TIME** 1 HOUR 10 MINUTES **SERVES** 10

150g butter, softened

1 cup (200g) firmly packed brown sugar

3 eggs

2 cups (300g) self-raising flour

½ teaspoon bicarbonate of soda

1 teaspoon mixed spice

1½ cups mashed banana

⅓ cup (80g) sour cream

⅓ cup (80ml) milk

½ cup (70g) coarsely chopped roasted macadamias

2 tablespoons finely chopped glacé ginger

BUTTERSCOTCH SAUCE

1 cup (200g) firmly packed brown sugar

1 cup (250ml) cream

125g butter, chopped coarsely

You need to use overripe bananas for this. Don't worry if the butter, sugar and egg mixture curdles.

1 Preheat oven to 180°C/160°C fan-forced. Grease deep 22cm-round cake pan; line base and side with baking paper.

2 Beat butter and sugar in small bowl with electric mixer until combined. Beat in eggs, one at a time. Transfer mixture to large bowl; stir in half of the sifted dry ingredients, half of the banana then sour cream and milk. Stir in remaining flour and banana, nuts and ginger. Spread mixture into pan.

3 Bake pudding about 1 hour 10 minutes. Stand pudding in pan 10 minutes; turn, top-side up, onto wire rack to cool.

4 Meanwhile, make butterscotch sauce.

5 Serve warm pudding with butterscotch sauce.

BUTTERSCOTCH SAUCE Stir ingredients in medium saucepan over heat, without boiling, until sugar has dissolved. Simmer, stirring occasionally, for 3 minutes.

Coffee and pecan puddings with caramel sauce

PREPARATION TIME 15 MINUTES **COOKING TIME** 40 MINUTES **SERVES** 6

¾ cup (90g) coarsely chopped roasted pecans

300ml cream

1½ cups (330g) firmly packed brown sugar

100g cold butter, chopped coarsely

125g butter, softened

½ cup (110g) caster sugar

1 teaspoon vanilla extract

2 eggs

1 cup (150g) self-raising flour

¼ cup (35g) plain flour

¼ cup (60ml) milk

1 tablespoon finely ground espresso coffee

These buttery-rich self-saucing puddings are best served warm with cream or ice-cream.

1 Preheat oven to 180°C/160°C fan-forced. Grease six ¾-cup (180ml) metal moulds or ovenproof dishes; line bases with baking paper.

2 Divide nuts among moulds; place moulds on oven tray.

3 Stir cream, brown sugar and chopped butter in small saucepan over heat, without boiling, until sugar dissolves. Bring to the boil. Reduce heat; simmer, uncovered, without stirring, about 5 minutes or until mixture thickens slightly. Spoon 2 tablespoons of the sauce over nuts in each mould; reserve remaining sauce.

4 Beat softened butter, caster sugar and extract in small bowl with electric mixer until light and fluffy. Beat in eggs, one at a time; stir in sifted flours, milk and coffee. Spoon mixture into moulds.

5 Bake puddings about 30 minutes. Stand puddings in moulds 5 minutes; turn onto serving plates.

6 Reheat reserved caramel sauce; serve with puddings.

1

2

3

4

Bread and butter pudding

PREPARATION TIME 20 MINUTES **COOKING TIME** 50 MINUTES **SERVES** 6

6 slices white bread (270g)
40g butter, softened
½ cup (80g) sultanas
¼ teaspoon ground nutmeg

CUSTARD
1 ½ cups (375ml) milk
2 cups (500ml) cream
⅓ cup (75g) caster sugar
1 teaspoon vanilla extract
4 eggs

1 Preheat oven to 160°C/140°C fan-forced. Grease shallow 2-litre (8-cup) ovenproof dish.
2 Make custard.
3 Trim crusts from bread. Spread each slice with butter; cut into 4 triangles. Layer bread, overlapping, in dish; sprinkle with sultanas. Pour custard over bread; sprinkle with nutmeg.
4 Place ovenproof dish in large baking dish; add enough boiling water to come halfway up sides of ovenproof dish.
5 Bake pudding about 45 minutes or until set. Remove pudding from baking dish; stand 5 minutes before serving.

CUSTARD Combine milk, cream, sugar and extract in medium saucepan; bring to the boil. Whisk eggs in large bowl; whisking constantly, gradually add hot milk mixture.

Use a good firm bread if you can, some of the sliced bread we get now turns spongy the moment the custard is poured over it. Bread and butter pud is at its best eaten warm, but a close second-best is after a day in the fridge. You can leave the crusts on the bread if you like. The recipe is also good using wholemeal bread. The chocolate pecan recipe is really just a variation of the pudding above it, but it's so good, we had to include it for you.

Chocolate pecan bread pudding

PREPARATION TIME 20 MINUTES **COOKING TIME** 50 MINUTES **SERVES** 6

200g ciabatta bread, sliced thickly
100g dark eating chocolate, chopped coarsely
⅓ cup (40g) coarsely chopped roasted pecans

CUSTARD
1 ½ cups (375ml) milk
2 cups (500ml) cream
⅓ cup (75g) caster sugar
1 teaspoon vanilla extract
4 eggs

1 Preheat oven to 160°C/140°C fan-forced. Grease shallow 2-litre (8-cup) ovenproof dish.
2 Make custard.
3 Layer bread, chocolate and nuts, overlapping slices slightly, in dish. Pour custard over bread. Place ovenproof dish in large baking dish; add enough boiling water to come halfway up sides of ovenproof dish.
4 Bake pudding about 45 minutes or until set. Remove pudding from baking dish; stand 5 minutes before serving.

CUSTARD Combine milk, cream, sugar and extract in medium saucepan; bring to the boil. Whisk eggs in large bowl; whisking constantly, gradually add hot milk mixture.

1 BREAD AND BUTTER PUDDING **2** CHOCOLATE PECAN BREAD PUDDING
3 FRUIT MINCE AND BRIOCHE PUDDING [P 562] **4** GOLDEN SYRUP DUMPLINGS [P 562]

Fruit mince and brioche pudding

PREPARATION TIME 20 MINUTES **COOKING TIME** 50 MINUTES **SERVES** 6

475g jar fruit mince
2 tablespoons brandy
300g brioche, sliced thickly
1 tablespoon demerara sugar

CUSTARD
1½ cups (375ml) milk
2 cups (500ml) cream
⅓ cup (75g) caster sugar
½ teaspoon vanilla extract
4 eggs

1 Preheat oven to 160°C/140°C fan-forced. Grease shallow 2-litre (8-cup) ovenproof dish.

2 Make custard.

3 Combine fruit mince and brandy in small bowl.

4 Layer brioche slices and half of the fruit mixture, overlapping brioche slightly, in dish. Dollop spoonfuls of remaining fruit mixture over brioche. Pour custard over brioche; sprinkle with sugar.

5 Place ovenproof dish in large baking dish; add enough boiling water to come halfway up sides of ovenproof dish.

6 Bake pudding about 45 minutes or until set. Remove pudding from baking dish; stand 5 minutes before serving.

CUSTARD Combine milk, cream, sugar and extract in medium saucepan; bring to the boil. Whisk eggs in large bowl; whisking constantly, gradually add hot milk mixture.

Golden syrup dumplings

PREPARATION TIME 10 MINUTES **COOKING TIME** 25 MINUTES **SERVES** 4

1¼ cups (185g) self-raising flour
30g butter
⅓ cup (115g) golden syrup
⅓ cup (80ml) milk

SAUCE
30g butter
¾ cup (165g) firmly packed brown sugar
½ cup (175g) golden syrup
1⅔ cups (410ml) water

1 Sift flour into medium bowl; rub in butter. Gradually stir in combined syrup and milk.

2 Make sauce.

3 Drop rounded tablespoonfuls of mixture into simmering sauce; simmer, covered, about 20 minutes.

4 Serve dumplings with sauce.

SAUCE Stir ingredients in medium saucepan over heat, without boiling, until sugar dissolves. Bring to the boil; without stirring. Reduce heat; simmer, uncovered, 5 minutes.

Mini apple charlottes with caramel sauce

PREPARATION TIME 25 MINUTES **COOKING TIME** 30 MINUTES **SERVES** 4

4 large apples (800g), peeled,
cored, sliced thickly

¼ cup (50g) firmly packed
brown sugar

¼ cup (60ml) orange juice

1 loaf sliced raisin bread (560g)

80g butter, melted

CARAMEL SAUCE

50g butter

½ cup (100g) firmly packed
brown sugar

⅓ cup (80ml) orange juice

1 Grease four 1-cup (250ml) metal moulds.

2 Cook apple with sugar and juice in large frying pan, stirring until apple browns and mixture bubbles and thickens.

3 Preheat oven to 220°C/200°C fan-forced.

4 Remove crusts from bread slices. Cut one 5.5cm round from each of four bread slices; cut remaining bread slices into three strips each. Brush one side of each round and strip with butter. Place one round, buttered-side down, in each mould; line side of each mould with bread strips, buttered-side against side of mould, slightly overlapping edges. Firmly pack warm apple mixture into moulds. Fold end of each bread strip down into centre of charlotte to enclose filling; press firmly to seal.

5 Bake charlottes about 15 minutes or until golden brown. Turn onto serving plates.

6 Meanwhile, make caramel sauce; drizzle over charlottes.

CARAMEL SAUCE Melt butter in small frying pan. Add sugar; stir until dissolved. Add juice; cook, stirring, until sauce thickens slightly.

Charlottes are a bit fiddly to make — especially individual ones, but, they're an inexpensive old-fashioned dessert, which everyone will love. Use the regular sliced raisin bread, not the thicker variety suitable for toasting.

Chocolate self-saucing pudding

PREPARATION TIME 20 MINUTES **COOKING TIME** 45 MINUTES **SERVES** 6

60g butter

½ cup (125ml) milk

½ teaspoon vanilla extract

¾ cup (165g) caster sugar

1 cup (150g) self-raising flour

1 tablespoon cocoa powder

¾ cup (165g) firmly packed
brown sugar

1 tablespoon cocoa powder, extra

2 cups (500ml) boiling water

1 Preheat oven to 180°C/160°C fan-forced. Grease 1.5-litre (6-cup) ovenproof dish.

2 Melt butter with milk in medium saucepan. Remove from heat; stir in extract and caster sugar then sifted flour and cocoa. Spread mixture into dish.

3 Sift brown sugar and extra cocoa over mixture; gently pour boiling water over mixture.

4 Bake pudding about 40 minutes or until centre is firm. Stand 5 minutes before serving.

This is a good saucy dessert — even when the pudding has gone cold. You can cook this dessert in a microwave oven in a microwave-proof dish, on MEDIUM (50%) for about 10 minutes — depending on the energy rating of your oven.

Date and butterscotch self-saucing pudding

PREPARATION TIME 20 MINUTES **COOKING TIME** 45 MINUTES **SERVES** 6

1 cup (150g) self-raising flour

½ cup (110g) firmly packed brown sugar

20g butter, melted

½ cup (125ml) milk

½ cup (70g) finely chopped dried seedless dates

CARAMEL SAUCE

½ cup (110g) firmly packed brown sugar

1¾ cups (430ml) boiling water

50g butter

1 Preheat oven to 180°C/160°C fan-forced. Grease 2-litre (8-cup) shallow ovenproof dish.

2 Combine flour, sugar, butter, milk and dates in medium bowl. Spread mixture into dish.

3 Make caramel sauce.

4 Pour caramel sauce slowly over back of spoon onto mixture in dish.

5 Bake pudding about 45 minutes or until centre is firm. Stand 5 minutes before serving.

CARAMEL SAUCE Stir ingredients in medium heatproof jug until sugar is dissolved.

Mocha, pear and nut self-saucing pudding

PREPARATION TIME 35 MINUTES **COOKING TIME** 35 MINUTES **SERVES** 8

100g dark eating chocolate, chopped coarsely

150g butter, chopped coarsely

⅔ cup (160ml) milk

1½ tablespoons instant coffee granules

⅔ cup (70g) hazelnut meal

¾ cup (165g) firmly packed brown sugar

1 cup (150g) self-raising flour

1 egg

2 medium pears (460g), sliced thinly

1¾ cups (430ml) water

¾ cup (165g) firmly packed brown sugar, extra

½ cup (50g) cocoa powder

1 Preheat oven to 180°C/160°C fan-forced. Grease eight 1¼-cup (310ml) ovenproof dishes or a shallow 2.5-litre (10-cup) ovenproof dish.

2 Stir chocolate, 50g of the butter, milk and coffee in small saucepan over low heat until smooth. Transfer to large bowl; stir in almond meal, sugar, then sifted flour and egg.

3 Place pear slices, slightly overlapping, in dishes; top with chocolate mixture.

4 Stir the water, extra sugar, sifted cocoa and remaining butter in small saucepan over low heat until smooth; pour over chocolate mixture.

5 Bake pudding about 30 minutes (or 45 minutes for larger pudding). Stand 5 minutes before serving.

DATE AND BUTTERSCOTCH SELF-SAUCING PUDDING

Quince and apple crumble

PREPARATION TIME 30 MINUTES **COOKING TIME** 2 HOURS 10 MINUTES **SERVES** 6

4 quince (1.4kg)
3 cups (660g) sugar
1.5 litres (6 cups) water
2 strips lemon rind
4 medium apples (800g)

CRUMBLE
½ cup (75g) plain flour
80g butter, chopped coarsely
¾ cup (60g) flaked almonds
⅓ cup (75g) firmly packed brown sugar
½ teaspoon ground cinnamon

1 Peel, halve and core quinces. Cut each half into four wedges.

2 Place sugar and the water in large saucepan, stir over low heat until sugar is dissolved. Add quince and rind; bring to the boil. Simmer, covered, 1¾ hours.

3 Meanwhile, peel, halve and core apples. Cut each half into four wedges. Add apples to quince mixture; simmer, covered, further 15 minutes or until fruit is tender. Cool in syrup.

4 Preheat oven to 180°C/160°C fan-forced. Grease shallow 1.5-litre (6-cup) ovenproof dish.

5 Make crumble.

6 Drain fruit mixture, reserving ⅓ cup (80ml) of syrup. Spoon fruit mixture and reserved syrup into dish. Sprinkle crumble evenly over fruit mixture; bake about 25 minutes.

CRUMBLE Place flour in medium bowl; rub in butter. Stir in remaining ingredients.

Use regular white or caster sugar here, it doesn't matter. Quince should be cooked until they turn a deep rosy colour. If this hasn't happened after 1¾ hours — keep going, they won't break up.

Pear and plum amaretti crumble

PREPARATION TIME 10 MINUTES **COOKING TIME** 15 MINUTES **SERVES** 4

825g can plums in syrup, drained, halved, stoned
825g can pear halves in natural juice, drained, halved
1 teaspoon ground cardamom
125g amaretti, crushed
⅓ cup (50g) plain flour
⅓ cup (35g) almond meal
½ cup (70g) slivered almonds
100g butter, chopped coarsely

1 Preheat oven to 200°C/180°C fan-forced. Grease deep 1.5-litre (6-cup) ovenproof dish.

2 Combine plums, pears and cardamom in dish.

3 Combine amaretti, flour, almond meal and nuts in medium bowl; rub in butter. Sprinkle evenly over plum mixture.

4 Bake crumble about 15 minutes.

Amaretti are almond-flavoured biscuits — you could use macaroons instead if you like, or even a combination of both.

Plum cobbler

PREPARATION TIME 15 MINUTES **COOKING TIME** 40 MINUTES **SERVES** 4

825g can plums in syrup

¾ cup (110g) self-raising flour

¼ cup (55g) caster sugar

1 teaspoon ground cinnamon

60g butter, chopped coarsely

1 egg yolk

¼ cup (60ml) buttermilk

2 tablespoons coarsely chopped roasted hazelnuts

2 tablespoons icing sugar

1 Preheat oven to 180°C/160°C fan-forced.

2 Drain plums over medium saucepan. Halve plums; discard stones. Add plums to pan; bring to the boil. Reduce heat; simmer, uncovered, about 5 minutes or until plums soften.

3 Strain plums; reserve ½ cup syrup. Place plums and reserved syrup in 1-litre (4-cup) ovenproof dish; place dish on oven tray.

4 Sift flour, caster sugar and cinnamon into medium bowl; rub in butter. Stir in egg yolk and enough of the buttermilk to make a soft, sticky dough. Drop heaped teaspoons of the mixture over hot plums; sprinkle with nuts.

5 Bake cobbler about 30 minutes; serve dusted with sifted icing sugar.

A cobbler is a fruit pie with a thick crust on top and no bottom crust.

Raspberry bombe alaska

PREPARATION TIME 20 MINUTES (PLUS FREEZING AND COOLING TIME) **COOKING TIME** 10 MINUTES **SERVES** 4

1.5 litres vanilla ice-cream, softened slightly

1 cup (135g) frozen raspberries

1 tablespoon caster sugar

200g madeira cake

4 egg whites

1 cup (220g) firmly packed brown sugar

1 teaspoon vanilla extract

1 teaspoon cornflour

1 Line four ¾-cup (180ml) moulds with plastic wrap. Press quarter of the ice-cream firmly up and around inside of each mould to form a cavity. Cover with foil; freeze 2 hours or until firm.

2 Combine raspberries and caster sugar in small saucepan; stir gently over low heat about 5 minutes or until sugar dissolves. Cool 15 minutes.

3 Preheat oven to 240°C/220°C fan-forced.

4 Cut cake into four thick slices; cut one round from each quarter, each large enough to cover top of each mould. Place slices, about 5cm apart, on oven tray.

5 Beat egg whites in small bowl with electric mixer until soft peaks form. Gradually add brown sugar, 1 tablespoon at a time, beating until sugar dissolves between additions. Fold in extract and cornflour.

6 Spoon a quarter of the raspberry sauce into one mould; turn mould onto one cake round, peel away plastic wrap. Spread a quarter of the meringue mixture over cake to enclose bombe completely; repeat with remaining sauce, moulds, cake rounds and meringue mixture. Bake about 3 minutes or until browned lightly.

This is a good do-ahead dessert — a quick zap in a hot oven just before serving is all it needs to set and brown the meringue. Use any kind of sponge or buttercake for the bases of the bombes. Home-made would of course be best of all.

Meringue layers can be made three days ahead; store in an airtight container. It is best to assemble the gateau the day before it's needed — keep it covered, in the refrigerator. For a really decadent dessert, the gateau can be completely covered in whipped cream. This also helps soften the meringue, making it easier to cut. The butter stops the chocolate from shattering when the gateau is cut.

Strawberry hazelnut gateau

PREPARATION TIME 1 HOUR **COOKING TIME** 35 MINUTES (PLUS COOLING AND REFRIGERATION TIME)
SERVES 8

4 egg whites

1 ¼ cups (275g) caster sugar

1 cup (100g) hazelnut meal

1 teaspoon white vinegar

½ teaspoon vanilla extract

185g dark eating chocolate, melted

20g butter, melted

1 ¾ cup (430ml) thickened cream, whipped

125g strawberries, halved

1 Preheat oven to 180°C/160°C fan-forced. Grease two 20cm springform tins; line base and sides with baking paper, grease paper, sprinkle with a little cornflour, shake away excess.
2 Beat egg whites in small bowl with electric mixer until soft peaks form. Gradually add sugar, beating until sugar is dissolved between additions. Fold in hazelnut meal, vinegar and extract. Spread meringue mixture evenly into tins.
3 Bake meringues about 35 minutes or until crisp. Release sides of tins; cool meringues on bases of tins.
4 Combine chocolate and butter in small bowl.
5 Remove meringue layers from bases. Place one layer on plate, flat-side down; spread with half of the chocolate mixture, top with half of the cream and the strawberries.
6 Spread flat side of second meringue layer with remaining chocolate mixture, place on top of strawberry layer, chocolate-side down. Cover top of cake with remaining cream. Refrigerate 3 hours or overnight.

Coffee anglaise can be stirred over a large saucepan of boiling water until the mixture is thickened slightly. This is the safe method. If the mixture overheats, it will curdle.

Chocolate mousse cake with coffee anglaise

PREPARATION TIME 45 MINUTES

COOKING TIME 30 MINUTES (PLUS STANDING, COOLING AND REFRIGERATION TIME) **SERVES** 10

6 eggs, separated

½ cup (80g) icing sugar

¼ cup (25g) cocoa powder

2 tablespoons cornflour

150g dark eating chocolate, melted

1 tablespoon water

1 litre (4 cups) thickened cream

600g dark eating chocolate, melted, extra

1 tablespoon cocoa powder, extra

COFFEE ANGLAISE

3 cups (750ml) milk

1 ½ cups (135g) coffee beans

8 egg yolks

¾ cup (165g) caster sugar

1 Make coffee anglaise.

2 Preheat oven to 180°C/160°C fan-forced. Grease 25cm x 30cm swiss roll pan; line base and short sides of pan with baking paper, extending paper 5cm above edges.

3 Beat egg yolks and sifted icing sugar in small bowl with electric mixer until light and creamy. Transfer mixture to large bowl; fold in sifted cocoa powder and cornflour, then cooled chocolate. Stir in the water.

4 Beat egg whites in medium bowl with electric mixer until soft peaks form; fold into chocolate mixture in two batches. Spread mixture into pan.

5 Bake cake 15 minutes. Turn onto baking-paper-lined wire rack; cool to room temperature.

6 Cut out circle of cake large enough to fit 26cm springform tin, using smaller pieces to fit, if necessary. Beat cream in large bowl with electric mixer until slightly thickened. Fold in slightly cooled extra melted chocolate in four batches. Pour mixture over cake base; refrigerate until set.

7 Remove cake from tin, dust withextra sifted cocoa; serve with coffee anglaise.

COFFEE ANGLAISE Bring milk and beans to the boil in large saucepan; remove from heat, cover, stand 1 hour. Whisk egg yolks and sugar in large bowl; whisk in milk mixture. Return mixture to same pan, stir over heat, without boiling, until slightly thickened, strain; cool to room temperature. Cover; refrigerate until cold.

Hot passionfruit soufflé with raspberry cream

PREPARATION TIME 25 MINUTES **COOKING TIME** 10 MINUTES **SERVES** 4

1 tablespoon caster sugar

2 eggs, separated

½ cup passionfruit pulp

2 tablespoons lemon juice

¾ cup (120g) icing sugar

4 egg whites

RASPBERRY CREAM

125g frozen raspberries, thawed

300ml thickened cream

1 tablespoon icing sugar

1 tablespoon orange-flavoured liqueur

You will need about six passionfruit for this recipe. We used Grand Marnier in this recipe, but you can use any citrus-flavoured liqueur, such as Curaçao or Cointreau.

1 Make raspberry cream. Refrigerate until required.

2 Preheat oven to 220°C/200°C fan-forced. Grease four 1-cup (250ml) soufflé dishes, sprinkle inside each one with caster sugar; shake away excess. Place dishes on oven tray.

3 Combine yolks, passionfruit, juice and half of the sifted icing sugar in large bowl.

4 Beat all the egg whites in small bowl with electric mixer until soft peaks form; add remaining sifted icing sugar and continue beating until firm peaks form. Gently fold a quarter of the whites into passionfruit mixture, then fold in remaining whites.

5 Spoon soufflé mixture into dishes; bake about 10 minutes or until puffed.

6 Dust soufflés with extra sifted icing sugar. Serve immediately with raspberry cream.

RASPBERRY CREAM Push raspberries through sieve to remove seeds. Whip cream and sifted icing sugar until soft peaks form; fold in raspberry puree and liqueur.

CHRISTMAS BAKING

Christmas Baking

Christmas baking doesn't have to be a labour of love, as most Christmas goodies can be made well in advance, which lightens, rather than adds to, the cook's load during the festive season.

Apart from having some home baked goodies on hand for the inevitable guests at this time of year, it's fun to make edible gifts and decorations to hang on the tree, over the mantelpiece or pretty much anywhere you'd place a factory-made decoration. Cookie cut-outs with guests' names piped on them make great place cards, gift tags or take-home mementos. The tradition of gingerbread dates back to medieval times but it was the German brothers Grimm who popularised the gingerbread house in their tale of Hansel and Gretel in the 19th century. Like any building, a gingerbread house can be as fancy or plain as its owners choose.

The rich dark fruit cake is an English tradition, which grew out of an oat pudding served on Christmas morning from the 16th century onwards. Gradually it evolved into a dense, fruit- and nut-laden treat which was considered so sinfully delicious that it could only be served at Christmas, weddings and other festive occasions.

FRUIT CAKE ADVICE
PREPARING THE FRUIT
It is important to cut the fruit into evenly-sized pieces (about the same size as a sultana is good), so the mixture can support it and the cake will cut well. Combine all the fruit in a large bowl with the alcohol (fruit juice can be substituted, but don't soak the fruit in juice as it won't keep as well as alcohol) and rinds. Mix it well, your hand is the best tool for this job. At this stage the fruit can be transferred to an airtight container and stored for three to seven days. It will absorb the alcohol during this time; don't add more as it will upset the balance of ingredients. Soaking the fruit in advance is more a matter of convenience to the time-poor cook as it only makes a slight difference to the cooked cake. The fruit appears plumper and the flavour slightly more developed, but much the same result will be achieved if the cake is baked six weeks before cutting, assuming it is stored correctly.
PREPARING THE CAKE PAN
To ensure a well-shaped cake the pan must be lined correctly. Lining with several sheets of greaseproof, baking or brown paper is especially important to protect the cake during the long cooking time. See instructions for lining the pan on page 643.

MIXING THE CAKE

Have butter and eggs at room temperature and beat the butter until it clings to the side of the bowl, not until it's pale in colour. Add the sugar and beat only until combined; overbeating will make the mixture too soft to support the fruit. Beat in eggs one at a time until the egg has been absorbed by the butter mixture (note advice in the Trouble Shooting section below). Add the butter mixture to the fruit mixture, mix with your hand. Mix in the sifted flour and spices. Place dollops of the cake mixture into the corners of the pan, then add the rest of the mixture. Drop the pan from a height of about 15cm to break large air bubbles and settle the mixture. Smooth the mixture with a spatula.

KEEPING AND STORING

When the cake is cooked, tear away the lining paper from around the top of the pan leaving the cake in the pan. While the cake is hot, brush the top with the specified extra alcohol; cover the top of the pan tightly with foil to trap the steam and give the cake a softer surface. Wrap the cake, still in the pan, in a towel and leave it until it's cold.

If the cake is to be decorated, you need a flat surface, so turn the hot, foil-covered cake still in its pan upside-down on a flat surface. The cake's weight will level the top.

When the cake is cold, remove it from the pan, leaving the lining paper intact; wrap the cake tightly in plastic wrap, then in aluminium foil. It can then be stored in a cool, dry place for up to six months, or in the refrigerator for up to a year or frozen indefinitely in a container to protect it. Slices can be cut from the cake as required (refrigerator-cold cake cuts perfectly) and brought to room temperature before serving. If there is a danger of the cake being discovered by insects, then the refrigerator (or freezer) is the best place to keep it. Humidity too can be a problem (causing mould) but if the cake is rich in sugar and fruit, and stored correctly, it should keep indefinitely.

TROUBLE SHOOTING

- If the fruit sinks to the bottom of the cake it could be because the fruit was washed, but not dried. Or that the cake mixture was too soft to support the weight of the fruit due to overbeating the butter and sugar. Or because you used self-raising, instead of plain flour.
- If the cake is doughy in the centre it's probably because it hasn't been cooked long enough or because the oven temperature was too low.
- If the bottom is burned, you may have used the wrong oven position, or cooked the cake at too high a temperature. Most fruit cakes require protection during the long cooking times, see Preparing the Cake Pan (opposite).
- Cracks on top of the cake also indicate that the oven temperature was too high.
- If the cake is uneven it could be that the oven is not level or that you've not levelled the mixture evenly in the pan.
- If the cake sinks in the middle it could be because self-raising flour was used, or too much bicarbonate of soda added. Or the cake may not have been baked long enough and may not be cooked through. To test, push the blade of a sharp-pointed knife through the centre of the cake to the base of the pan; the blade surface helps distinguish between the uncooked mixture or fruit and cooked mixture. Test after the minimum cooking time.
- If the butter, sugar and egg mixture curdles it could be for any of the reasons listed in *Butter Cakes* on page 61. If it's because the eggs are larger than the 60g eggs we specify, cut back on the number of eggs, or use only the yolk of one.

Mini fruit mince pies

PREPARATION TIME 30 MINUTES (PLUS REFRIGERATION TIME) **COOKING TIME** 30 MINUTES **MAKES** 24

FRUIT MINCE

⅓ cup (50g) finely chopped dried dates

⅓ cup (55g) dried currants

⅓ cup (55g) finely chopped raisins

½ cup (80g) sultanas

2 tablespoons finely chopped glacé cherries

1 teaspoon finely grated lemon rind

2 tablespoons dark rum

2 tablespoons finely chopped roasted pecans

2 tablespoons brown sugar

20g butter

2 teaspoons plum jam

PASTRY

2 cups (300g) plain flour

⅓ cup (55g) icing sugar

150g butter, chopped

1 egg, separated

1 tablespoon iced water

1 tablespoon white sugar

1 Combine ingredients for fruit mince in small saucepan; stir over low heat until sugar is dissolved. Transfer mixture to small bowl; cover, cool.

2 Make pastry.

3 Preheat oven to 180°C/160°C fan-forced.

4 Roll pastry between sheets of baking paper until 3mm thick. Using a 6.5cm plain cutter, cut 24 rounds from pastry for the bases; using a 4.5cm fluted cutter, cut 24 rounds for the tops. Gently press pastry bases into two 12-hole (1-tablespoon/20ml) mini muffin pans; fill each with a heaped teaspoon of fruit mince filling.

5 Brush edges of pastry in pan with lightly beaten egg white, cover with pastry tops, pressing edges gently together. Using remaining pastry, cut out 24 stars. Brush tops of pies with egg white, place a star in centre of each pie; sprinkle with white sugar.

6 Bake pies about 25 minutes. Stand pies in pans 5 minutes; turn onto wire rack to cool.

PASTRY Process sifted flour and icing sugar, and butter until crumbly. Add egg yolk and enough water to process to a soft dough. Enclose in plastic wrap; refrigerate 30 minutes.

Hazelnut shortbread trees

PREPARATION TIME 25 MINUTES (PLUS REFRIGERATION TIME) **COOKING TIME** 15 MINUTES **MAKES** 12

250g butter, softened

2 teaspoons finely grated orange rind

½ cup (80g) icing sugar

2 tablespoons rice flour

2 cups (300g) plain flour

2 teaspoons mixed spice

¼ cup (75ml) hazelnut meal

silver cachous

1 tablespoon icing sugar, extra

BRANDY BUTTER CREAM

60g butter, softened

½ teaspoon finely grated orange rind

¾ cup (120g) icing sugar

2 teaspoons brandy

1 Beat butter, rind and sifted icing sugar in small bowl with electric mixer until light and fluffy. Transfer mixture to large bowl; stir in sifted flours and spice, and hazelnut meal, in two batches.

2 Knead dough on floured surface until smooth. Roll dough between sheets of baking paper until 5mm thick; refrigerate 30 minutes.

3 Preheat oven to 180°C/160°C fan-forced. Grease oven trays; line with baking paper.

4 Using 3cm, 5cm and 7cm star-shaped cutters, cut 24 of each size star from dough. Place small stars, about 1cm apart, on an oven tray; place remaining stars, about 2cm apart, on other oven trays.

5 Bake small stars about 10 minutes; bake larger stars about 15 minutes. Stand cookies on trays 5 minutes; cool on wire racks.

6 Meanwhile, make brandy butter cream.

7 Sandwich two of each size cookie with butter cream. Assemble trees by joining three different size stars together with butter cream.

8 Decorate trees by joining cachous to stars with a tiny dot of butter cream. Dust trees with extra sifted icing sugar.

BRANDY BUTTER CREAM Beat butter, rind, sifted icing sugar and brandy in small bowl with electric mixer until light and fluffy.

Stained-glass Christmas cookies

PREPARATION TIME 1 HOUR (PLUS REFRIGERATION TIME) **COOKING TIME** 1 HOUR (PLUS COOLING TIME) **MAKES** 36

250g butter, softened

2 teaspoons finely grated lemon rind

½ teaspoon almond essence

¾ cup (165g) caster sugar

1 egg

1 tablespoon water

2¼ cups (335g) plain flour

90g individually wrapped sugar-free fruit drops, assorted colours

1 Preheat oven to 180°C/160°C fan-forced. Line two oven trays with baking paper.

2 Beat butter, rind, essence, sugar, egg and the water in small bowl with electric mixer until smooth. Transfer mixture to large bowl; stir in sifted flour, in two batches. Knead dough on floured surface until smooth. Enclose in plastic wrap; refrigerate 30 minutes.

3 Meanwhile, using rolling pin, gently tap wrapped lollies to crush slightly. Unwrap lollies; separate by colour into small bowls.

4 Roll dough between sheets of baking paper until 4mm thick. Cut shapes from dough using medium-sized cookie cutters; use very small cookie cutters to cut out the centre of each cookie.

5 Place cookies on trays; bake 5 minutes. Remove trays from oven; fill cut-out centre of each cookie with a different lolly colour. Return to oven for 5 minutes. Cool on trays.

Christmas angel cookies

PREPARATION TIME 20 MINUTES (PLUS REFRIGERATION TIME) **COOKING TIME** 15 MINUTES **MAKES** 16

125g butter, softened

¾ cup (165g) caster sugar

1 egg

1½ cups (225g) plain flour

¼ cup (35g) self-raising flour

½ cup (40g) desiccated coconut

⅓ cup (110g) apricot jam, warmed, strained

MACAROON TOPPING

3 egg whites

¾ cup (165g) caster sugar

¼ cup (35g) plain flour

2¼ cups (180g) desiccated coconut

These angels would make a lovely Christmas gift, but they're too heavy (thanks to the topping) to be hung from a tree or mantelpiece.

1 Beat butter, sugar and egg in small bowl with electric mixer until light and fluffy. Stir in sifted flours and coconut, in two batches.

2 Knead dough on floured surface until smooth. Roll dough between sheets of baking paper until 5mm thick; refrigerate 30 minutes.

3 Preheat oven to 180°C/160°C fan-forced. Grease oven trays; line with baking paper.

4 Make macaroon topping.

5 Using 11cm angel cutter, cut 16 angel shapes from dough. Place, about 3cm apart, on oven trays.

6 Bake cookies 8 minutes. Spread each hot cookie with jam; divide macaroon topping among angels. Cover with foil (like a tent so foil does not touch surface of macaroon); bake further 7 minutes. Cool on wire racks.

MACAROON TOPPING Beat egg whites in small bowl with electric mixer until soft peaks form. Gradually add sugar, beating until dissolved between additions. Fold in sifted flour and coconut, in two batches.

Grand Marnier fruit cake

PREPARATION TIME 2 HOURS (PLUS STANDING TIME)

COOKING TIME 3 HOURS 40 MINUTES (PLUS COOLING TIME) **SERVES** 36

3 cups (500g) sultanas

1½ cups (250g) mixed peel

¾ cup (120g) coarsely chopped raisins

¾ cup (120g) coarsely chopped dried seeded dates

⅔ cup (140g) coarsely chopped seeded prunes

½ cup (125g) coarsely chopped glacé apricots

⅔ cup (150g) coarsely chopped glacé pineapple

½ cup (70g) slivered almonds

½ cup (60g) coarsely chopped roasted walnuts

1 tablespoon finely grated orange rind

½ cup (110g) caster sugar

¼ cup (60ml) orange juice

½ cup (125ml) Grand Marnier

250g butter, softened

½ cup (110g) firmly packed brown sugar

5 eggs

2 cups (300g) plain flour

2 tablespoons Grand Marnier, extra

1kg ready-made soft icing

1 egg white, beaten lightly

½ cup (80g) icing sugar, sifted

25cm-round covered cake board

decorative ribbon

13g packet silver cachous

1 Combine fruit, nuts and rind in large bowl. Heat caster sugar in large heavy-based frying pan over low heat, without stirring, until it begins to melt then stir until sugar is melted and browned lightly. Remove from heat, slowly stir in juice; return to low heat, stir until toffee dissolves (do not boil). Add liqueur; pour over fruit mixture, cover tightly with plastic wrap. Store mixture in cool, dark place for 10 days, stirring every day.

2 Preheat oven to 150°C/130°C fan-forced. Line base and side of deep 22cm-round cake pan (or deep 10cm-square cake pan) with one thickness of brown paper and two thicknesses of baking paper, extending papers 5cm above side.

3 Beat butter and brown sugar in small bowl with electric mixer until combined; beat in eggs, one at a time. Stir butter mixture into fruit mixture, mix in sifted flour; spread mixture into pan. Tap pan firmly on bench to settle mixture into pan; level mixture with wet spatula.

4 Bake cake about 3½ hours. Remove cake from oven, brush with extra liqueur; cover hot cake with foil then turn upside down to cool overnight. Cover pan with a towel.

5 Trim top of cake with sharp knife to ensure it sits flat when turned upside down. Mix a little fondant and cold boiled water to a sticky paste. Spread about 2 tablespoons of this mixture into centre of baking paper cut 5cm larger than cake; position cake upside down on paper. Using spatula and small pieces of fondant, patch any holes on cake.

6 Brush egg white evenly over cake. Knead fondant on surface dusted with icing sugar until smooth; roll to 7mm thickness. Lift fondant onto cake with rolling pin, smoothing fondant all over with hands dusted with icing sugar. Cut excess fondant away from base of cake.

7 Mix scraps of fondant and cold boiled water to a sticky paste. Spread about 2 tablespoons of paste in centre of board; position cake on board. Cut away excess baking paper extending around base of cake. Secure ribbon around cake using pins (remove to a safe place before cutting cake). Push cachous gently into fondant in the design of your choice.

I created this recipe for the makers of Grand Marnier and The Australian Women's Weekly back in 1982. Since then it has become one of our most-requested fruit-cake recipes. I make it every year, often "playing" with the balance of fruit. Mostly, I leave the nuts out the mix, only because I think they interfere with the cutting of the cake.

Golden glacé fruit cake

PREPARATION TIME 35 MINUTES **COOKING TIME** 2 HOURS (PLUS COOLING TIME) **SERVES** 36

250g butter, softened

1 cup (220g) caster sugar

4 eggs

1 cup (190g) mixed dried fruit

¾ cup (185g) quartered glacé cherries

½ cup (125g) coarsely chopped glacé apricots

⅓ cup (85g) coarsely chopped glacé peaches

½ cup (115g) coarsely chopped glacé pineapple

¾ cup (125g) blanched almonds, roasted, halved

1 cup (150g) plain flour

1 cup (150g) self-raising flour

¼ cup (60ml) citrus-flavoured liqueur

¼ cup (60ml) apricot jam

Use Cointreau, Grand Marnier or Curaçao here – brandy would also work just as well.

1 Preheat oven to 160°C/140°C fan-forced. Grease deep 22cm-round cake pan or deep 19cm-square cake pan; line base and side(s) with three layers baking paper, extending paper 5cm above side(s).

2 Beat butter and sugar in large bowl with electric mixer until changed to a lighter colour. Beat in eggs, one at a time; stir in fruit, nuts, sifted flours, liqueur and jam.

3 Spread mixture into pan; bake about 2 hours. Cover hot cake with foil; cool in pan.

Lemon-glazed Christmas wreath cookies

PREPARATION TIME 20 MINUTES **COOKING TIME** 15 MINUTES **MAKES** 30

3 cups (450g) self-raising flour

125g butter, chopped coarsely

¼ cup (60ml) milk

⅔ cup (110g) caster sugar

1 teaspoon vanilla extract

2 eggs

LEMON ICING

3 cups (480g) icing sugar

2 tablespoons lemon juice

Edible glitter will give these wreaths a Christmas sparkle. Edible glitter is available from some craft shops, cake decorating suppliers and gourmet food stores. The glazed wreaths can easily be tied onto a tree, or into a gift-sized bundle, using festive ribbon.

1 Preheat oven to 180°C/160°C fan-forced. Grease oven trays; line with baking paper.

2 Sift flour into medium bowl; rub in butter. Combine milk and sugar in small saucepan, stir over low heat until sugar is dissolved, add extract; cool 5 minutes. Stir combined warm milk mixture and egg into flour mixture.

3 Knead dough on floured surface until smooth. Roll rounded teaspoons of dough into 13cm sausages. Twist two sausages together, form into circles; press edges together. Place about 3cm apart on oven trays. Bake about 15 minutes. Cool on wire racks.

4 Meanwhile, make lemon icing. Drizzle wreaths with icing; set at room temperature.

LEMON ICING Sift sugar into small heatproof bowl; stir in enough juice to make a firm paste. Stir over small saucepan of simmering water until pourable.

1 GOLDEN GLACE FRUIT CAKE **2** LEMON-GLAZED CHRISTMAS WREATH COOKIES
3 IRISH PUDDING CAKE [P 582] **4** CHRISTMAS PUDDING COOKIES [P 582]

Irish pudding cake

PREPARATION TIME 25 MINUTES (PLUS STANDING TIME) **COOKING TIME** 3 HOURS (PLUS COOLING TIME)
SERVES 30

1 ¼ cups (200g) seeded prunes, chopped coarsely

1 ½ cups (250g) raisins, chopped coarsely

1 cup (150g) dried currants

¾ cup (125g) sultanas

1 large apple (200g), grated coarsely

1 ½ cups (375ml) Irish whiskey

1 ¼ cups (275g) firmly packed dark brown sugar

185g butter, softened

3 eggs

½ cup (50g) hazelnut meal

1 ½ cups (225g) plain flour

1 teaspoon ground nutmeg

½ teaspoon ground ginger

½ teaspoon ground clove

½ teaspoon bicarbonate of soda

1 Combine fruit and 1 cup of the whiskey in large bowl, cover tightly with plastic wrap; stand at room temperature overnight.

2 Preheat oven to 120°C/100°C fan-forced. Line deep 20cm-round cake pan with two thicknesses of baking paper, extending paper 5cm above side.

3 Stir remaining whiskey and ½ cup of the sugar in small saucepan over heat until sugar dissolves; bring to the boil. Remove from heat; cool syrup 20 minutes.

4 Meanwhile, beat butter and remaining sugar in small bowl with electric mixer until combined; beat in eggs, one at a time. Add to fruit mixture; stir in hazelnut meal, sifted dry ingredients and ½ cup of the cooled syrup. Spread mixture into pan.

5 Bake cake about 3 hours. Brush cake with remaining hot syrup, cover with foil; cool in pan.

Christmas pudding cookies

PREPARATION TIME 25 MINUTES (PLUS REFRIGERATION TIME) **COOKING TIME** 15 MINUTES **MAKES** 30

1 ⅔ cups (250g) plain flour

⅓ cup (40g) almond meal

⅓ cup (75g) caster sugar

1 teaspoon mixed spice

1 teaspoon vanilla extract

125g cold butter, chopped coarsely

2 tablespoons water

700g rich dark fruit cake

⅓ cup (80ml) brandy

1 egg white

400g dark eating chocolate, melted

½ cup (75g) white chocolate Melts, melted

30 red glacé cherries

1 Process flour, almond meal, sugar, spice, extract and butter until crumbly. Add the water, process until ingredients come together.

2 Knead dough on floured surface until smooth; roll dough between sheets of baking paper until 5mm thick. Refrigerate 30 minutes.

3 Preheat oven to 180°C/160°C fan-forced. Grease oven trays; line with baking paper.

4 Using 5.5cm round cutter, cut 30 rounds from dough. Place about 3cm apart on trays. Bake about 10 minutes.

5 Meanwhile, crumble fruit cake into medium bowl; add brandy. Press mixture firmly into round metal tablespoon measures. Brush partially baked cookies with egg white, top with cake domes; bake further 5 minutes. Cool on wire racks.

6 Place wire racks over tray, coat cookies with dark chocolate; set at room temperature.

7 Spoon white chocolate over cookies; top with cherries.

Celebration fruit cake

PREPARATION TIME 20 MINUTES (PLUS STANDING TIME)
COOKING TIME 3 HOURS 30 MINUTES (PLUS COOLING TIME) **SERVES** 36

3 cups (500g) sultanas

1¾ cups (300g) raisins, halved

1¾ cups (300g) dried seeded dates, chopped finely

1 cup (150g) dried currants

⅔ cup (110g) mixed peel

⅔ cup (150g) glacé cherries, halved

¼ cup (55g) coarsely chopped glacé pineapple

¼ cup (60g) coarsely chopped glacé apricots

½ cup (125ml) dark rum

250g butter, softened

1 cup (220g) firmly packed brown sugar

5 eggs

1½ cups (225g) plain flour

⅓ cup (50g) self-raising flour

1 teaspoon mixed spice

2 tablespoons dark rum, extra

Every Christmas, countless readers phone us for this recipe, they rarely know the name, but identify it as "the cake with the glacé apricots and pineapple". It really is a very good quality cake, cuts and keeps well — and tastes good too.

1 Combine fruit and rum in large bowl; mix well. Cover tightly with plastic wrap. Store mixture in cool, dark place overnight or up to a week stirring every day.

2 Preheat oven to 150°C/130°C fan-forced. Line deep 22cm-round cake pan with three thicknesses of baking paper, extending paper 5cm above side.

3 Beat butter and sugar in small bowl with electric mixer until combined; beat in eggs, one at a time. Add butter mixture to fruit mixture; mix well. Mix in sifted dry ingredients; spread mixture evenly into pan.

4 Bake cake about 3½ hours. Brush hot cake with extra rum. Cover hot cake, in pan, tightly with foil; cool overnight.

Gingerbread house

PREPARATION TIME 2 HOURS 30 MINUTES (PLUS REFRIGERATION TIME)

COOKING TIME 45 MINUTES (PLUS STANDING TIME)

4½ cups (675g) self-raising flour

3 teaspoons ground ginger

2 teaspoons ground cinnamon

1½ teaspoons ground clove

1 teaspoon ground nutmeg

185g butter, chopped coarsely

1 cup (220g) firmly packed dark brown sugar

½ cup (180g) treacle

2 eggs, beaten lightly

35cm round or square board

assorted lollies

ROYAL ICING

2 egg whites

3 cups (480g) pure icing sugar

1 Process flour, spices and butter until mixture is crumbly (you may have to process in two batches). Add sugar, treacle and enough egg for mixture to combine. Knead dough on floured surface until smooth. Enclose in plastic wrap; refrigerate 1 hour.

2 Meanwhile, cut paper patterns for gingerbread house: cut two 12cm x 19cm rectangles for roof; two 10.5cm x 16cm rectangles for side walls of house; and two 16cm x 18cm rectangles for front and back walls of house. Trim front and back walls to form two 11cm-high gables.

3 Preheat oven to 180°C/160°C fan-forced.

4 Roll dough between sheets of baking paper until 5mm thick. Peel away top layer of paper; use patterns to cut shapes from dough. Pull away excess dough; slide baking paper with shapes onto oven tray; bake about 12 minutes. Re-roll dough scraps into one 5mm-thick piece; cut out trees and chimney.

5 While shapes are still warm and soft, use tip of sharp knife to cut out small windows from side walls of house, then cut out door from front wall; reserve cut-out door piece. Trim shapes to straighten sides; transfer all shapes to wire racks to cool.

6 Make royal icing. Cover board with foil or silver paper.

7 Secure two crossed bamboo skewers to back of each roof piece with icing. Allow to dry before assembling house.

8 Assemble house, securing roof and walls together with icing. If possible, stand house several hours or overnight, supporting sides with four cans, so that it is thoroughly dry before decorating. Decorate board around house with remaining icing to resemble fallen snow.

9 Secure door to house with icing; decorate house with lollies, securing with icing. Secure trees to board and chimney to roof with icing.

ROYAL ICING Beat egg whites in small bowl with electric mixer until frothy; gradually beat in sifted icing sugar. Cover icing with damp cloth while not using.

Christmas cake step-by-step

Here are step-by-step instructions for a really pretty, but easy Christmas cake decoration.

PATCHING THE CAKE
Turn the cake upside-down onto a sheet of baking or greaseproof paper, use a spatula to smooth small pieces of almond paste into any holes in the cake's surface.

GLAZING THE CAKE
Roll sausage-shaped pieces of almond paste, using a spatula, push the sausage shapes around the base of the cake to make the side of the cake smooth. Brush the cake evenly, all over, with warmed sieved apricot jam.

ALMOND PASTE
Knead the almond paste with sifted icing sugar until it's smooth. Roll the paste on an icing-sugared surface until it's large enough to cover the cake.

COVERING WITH SOFT ICING
Use the rolling pin to lift the icing onto the cake, gently smooth out any folds or pleats in the icing with your icing-sugared hands.

TRIMMING SOFT ICING
Use your icing-sugared hands to gently smooth and rub the top and side(s) of the cake. Use a sharp knife to cut away the excess soft icing from the base of the cake until it's smooth. Enclose the scraps of icing in plastic wrap.

PLACING THE CAKE ON BOARD
Take a small piece of the soft icing, moisten it well with water, and position it in the centre of the board. Carefully lift the cake from the paper, and centre it on the board.

COVERING THE CAKE

Use the rolling pin to lift the paste onto the cake, smooth the paste with your icing-sugared hands, then trim away any excess paste at the base of the cake.

GLAZING THE PASTE

If you have time, stand the cake at a cool room temperature overnight to let the almond paste develop a crust. Just before you're ready to cover the cake with soft icing, brush the paste evenly with warmed, sieved, apricot jam.

SOFT ICING

Knead the soft icing with sifted icing sugar until it's smooth. Roll the icing on an icing-sugared surface until it's almost large enough to cover the cake — the icing will stretch.

STAR-SHAPED CUT-OUTS

While the soft icing is still soft, use star-shaped cutters to cut out star shapes from the soft icing layer. Lift the stars out with a spatula.

FILLING STAR SHAPES

Re-position the star cutters on the cake (we used three different-sized star cutters), fill the star-shaped cavities with a single layer of cachous. We used a mixture of silver and blue cachous, but you could use any colour combination you like or just one colour.

FINISHING THE CAKE

Secure a band of ribbon around the base of the cake with a pin (we used wedding pins with large plastic tops, for easy removal later). Make a bow from a piece of the ribbon, secure it to the cake, over the join, with another pin. Remove the ribbon and pins before cutting the cake.

Christmas tree cupcakes

PREPARATION TIME 30 MINUTES **COOKING TIME** 35 MINUTES **MAKES** 12

125g butter, softened

1 teaspoon coconut essence

²⁄₃ cup (150g) caster sugar

2 eggs

1 cup (180g) finely chopped dried tropical fruit salad

½ cup (75g) coarsely chopped macadamias

²⁄₃ cup (100g) plain flour

⅓ cup (50g) self-raising flour

⅓ cup (25g) desiccated coconut

¼ cup (60ml) milk

COCONUT ICE FROSTING

2 egg whites

1 teaspoon coconut essence

1½ cups (240g) icing sugar

1 cup (90g) desiccated coconut

DECORATIONS

10 star fruit, approximately

1 Preheat oven to 170°C/150°C fan-forced. Line 12-hole (⅓-cup/80ml) muffin pan with paper cases.

2 Beat butter, essence, sugar and eggs in small bowl with electric mixer until light and fluffy. Stir in dried fruit and nuts, then sifted flours, coconut and milk. Spoon mixture into cases; smooth surface.

3 Bake cakes about 35 minutes. Turn cakes, top-side up, onto wire racks to cool.

4 Make coconut ice frosting; top cakes with frosting.

5 Cut star fruit into 5mm slices. Arrange slices to make Christmas tree shapes of varying heights and sizes. Use toothpicks or trimmed bamboo skewers to hold star fruit in position. Sprinkle with edible glitter, if desired.

COCONUT ICE FROSTING Beat egg whites and essence in small bowl with electric mixer until foamy. Beat in sifted icing sugar in about four batches; stir in coconut.

Dried tropical fruit salad usually consists of mango, pawpaw, pineapple and banana — if you can't find it in a health food store, mix your own. The undecorated cakes will freeze for months, but will keep at room temperature in an airtight container, for about a week. The frosting can be made a day ahead, but the star fruit must be sliced and stacked as close to serving as possible. Star fruit have a high water content and would soften the frosting and cake after a couple of hours. To add some extra sparkle for Christmas, sprinkle the fruit with green or silver edible glitter — it looks stunning. However, it will soon disappear on the moist star fruit.

Last-minute fruit cake

PREPARATION TIME 20 MINUTES **COOKING TIME** 2 HOURS (PLUS COOLING TIME) **SERVES** 30

We've all been caught out at Christmas — it's suddenly here and you find yourself cake-free. This is just the cake for you. It's made by the boiled method but contains the components of a rich fruit cake. The cake cuts and keeps well and has become one of our all-time favourite recipes.

1½ cups (240g) sultanas

1 cup (170g) coarsely chopped raisins

1 cup (150g) dried currants

½ cup (85g) mixed peel

⅓ cup (70g) glacé cherries, halved

2 tablespoons coarsely chopped glacé pineapple

2 tablespoons coarsely chopped glacé apricots

185g butter, chopped coarsely

¾ cup (165g) firmly packed dark brown sugar

⅓ cup (80ml) brandy

⅓ cup (80ml) water

2 teaspoons finely grated orange rind

1 teaspoon finely grated lemon rind

1 tablespoon treacle

3 eggs, beaten lightly

1¼ cups (185g) plain flour

¼ cup (35g) self-raising flour

½ teaspoon bicarbonate of soda

½ cup (80g) blanched almonds

1 Line deep 20cm-round cake pan with three thicknesses of baking paper, extending paper 5cm above side.

2 Combine fruit, butter, sugar, brandy and the water in medium saucepan, stir over medium heat until butter is melted and sugar is dissolved; bring to the boil. Remove from heat; transfer to large bowl. Cool.

3 Preheat oven to 150°C/130°C fan-forced.

4 Stir rinds, treacle and eggs into fruit mixture then sifted dry ingredients. Spread mixture into pan; decorate with nuts.

5 Bake cake about 2 hours. Cover hot cake with foil; cool in pan overnight.

Glacé fruit cupcakes

PREPARATION TIME 45 MINUTES **COOKING TIME** 40 MINUTES **MAKES** 24

1 cup (220g) caster sugar

150g marzipan, chopped coarsely

150g butter, softened

4 eggs

¾ cup (110g) self-raising flour

¾ cup (110g) plain flour

1 cup (160g) sultanas

½ cup (85g) finely chopped glacé apricots

¼ cup (25g) finely chopped red glacé cherries

¼ cup (25g) finely chopped green glacé cherries

silver cachous

ROYAL ICING

3 cups (480g) pure icing sugar

2 egg whites

¼ cup (60ml) water

1 Preheat the oven to 160°C/140°C fan-forced. Line two 12-hole (⅓-cup/80ml) muffin pans with foil patty cases.

2 Process ½ cup (110g) of the caster sugar with the marzipan until crumbly. Add butter and remaining sugar; process until combined. Add eggs, one at a time; pulse until combined between each addition. Add flours; pulse until combined.

3 Transfer mixture to large bowl; stir in fruit. Spoon mixture into cases.

4 Bake cakes about 40 minutes. Stand cakes in pans 5 minutes; turn, top-side up, onto wire rack to cool.

5 Meanwhile, make royal icing.

6 Spread the tops of the cakes with royal icing and decorate with cachous.

ROYAL ICING Lightly beat egg whites in small bowl with electric mixer. Beat in sifted icing sugar, a heaped tablespoon at a time. Stir in the water, a little at a time until icing is spreadable.

Boiled pineapple rum cake

PREPARATION TIME 20 MINUTES (PLUS COOLING TIME) **COOKING TIME** 2 HOURS **SERVES** 20

440g can crushed pineapple in syrup

1kg (5 cups) mixed dried fruit

250g butter, chopped coarsely

1 cup (200g) firmly packed brown sugar

2 tablespoons orange marmalade

2 tablespoons dark rum

4 eggs

1⅔ cups (250g) plain flour

⅓ cup (50g) self-raising flour

½ teaspoon bicarbonate of soda

1 tablespoon dark rum, extra

1 Drain pineapple over large jug; discard ½-cup (125ml) of the syrup.

2 Combine pineapple, remaining syrup, fruit, butter, sugar, marmalade and rum in large saucepan. Stir over heat until butter melts and sugar dissolves; bring to the boil. Reduce heat; simmer, covered, 10 minutes. Cool.

3 Preheat oven to 150°C/130°C fan-forced. Line base and side of deep 20cm-round cake pan with three thicknesses baking paper, extending paper 5cm above edge.

4 Stir eggs and sifted dry ingredients into fruit mixture. Pour mixture into pan.

5 Bake cake about 2 hours. Brush hot cake with extra rum. Cover with foil; cool cake in pan.

Festive fruit and nut cake

PREPARATION TIME 20 MINUTES **COOKING TIME** 1 HOUR 45 MINUTES (PLUS STANDING TIME) **SERVES** 20

½ cup (115g) coarsely chopped glacé pineapple

½ cup (125g) coarsely chopped glacé apricots

1½ cups (250g) seeded dried dates

½ cup (110g) red glacé cherries

½ cup (110g) green glacé cherries

1 cup (170g) brazil nuts

½ cup (75g) macadamia nuts

2 eggs

½ cup (110g) firmly packed brown sugar

1 tablespoon dark rum

100g butter, melted

⅓ cup (50g) plain flour

¼ cup (35g) self-raising flour

FRUIT AND NUT TOPPING

⅓ cup (75g) coarsely chopped glacé pineapple

¼ cup (55g) red glacé cherries, halved

¼ cup (55g) green glacé cherries, halved

¼ cup (40g) brazil nuts

¼ cup (35g) macadamia nuts

TOFFEE TOPPING

½ cup (110g) caster sugar

¼ cup (60ml) water

This cake has many names and variations — it's rich, with large chunks of fruit and nuts, but despite that, cuts well with a sharp knife. Ring, bar or loaf-shaped pans cook this mixture the best, simply because of the narrow areas of these pans. You can leave both toppings off this cake if you like — they do make it look extra festive though.

1 Preheat oven to 150°C/130°C fan-forced. Grease 20cm-ring pan; line base and side with baking paper, extending paper 5cm above side.

2 Combine fruit and nuts in large bowl.

3 Beat eggs and sugar in small bowl with electric mixer until thick. Add rum, butter and sifted flours; beat until just combined. Stir egg mixture into fruit mixture. Press mixture firmly into pan.

4 Make fruit and nut topping; gently press topping evenly over cake mixture.

5 Bake cake, covered, for 1 hour. Uncover; bake 45 minutes. Stand cake in pan 10 minutes.

6 Meanwhile, make toffee topping. Turn cake, top-side up, onto wire rack; drizzle with toffee.

FRUIT AND NUT TOPPING Combine ingredients in medium bowl.

TOFFEE TOPPING Stir ingredients in small saucepan over heat, without boiling, until sugar dissolves; bring to the boil. Reduce heat; simmer, uncovered, without stirring, 10 minutes or until mixture is golden. Remove from heat; stand until bubbles subside before using.

Rich sherried fruit cake

PREPARATION TIME 30 MINUTES (PLUS STANDING TIME)
COOKING TIME UP TO 3 HOURS 15 MINUTES DEPENDING ON CAKE PAN SIZE (PLUS COOLING TIME)
SERVES 36

We get asked all the time for the baking times needed for various different-sized cake pans. The list below can be applied to all the rich fruit cakes in this chapter that contain 250g butter.

1 x deep 22cm-round or deep 19cm-square cake pan — cook 3¼ hours

2 x deep 17cm-round or deep 15cm-square cake pans — cook 2 hours

4 x deep 12.5cm-round or deep 9.5cm-square cake pans — cook 1¾ hours

250g butter, softened

2 tablespoons plum jam

2 teaspoons finely grated orange rind

1¼ cups (275g) firmly packed brown sugar

5 eggs

¾ cup (180ml) sweet sherry

1½ cups (225g) plain flour

½ cup (75g) self-raising flour

2 teaspoons mixed spice

1kg (5 cups) mixed dried fruit

½ cup (125ml) sweet sherry, extra

1 Preheat oven to 150°C/130°C fan-forced. Grease base of chosen pan (see left); line base and side(s) with four thicknesses of baking paper, extending paper 5cm above edge(s).
2 Beat butter, jam, rind and sugar in medium bowl with electric mixer until combined. Beat in eggs, one at a time. Stir in ½ cup of the sherry, sifted dry ingredients and fruit.
3 Spread mixture into pan; bake for time specified (see left).
4 Brush top of hot cake with remaining sherry, cover hot cake with foil; cool in pan overnight.
5 Remove cake from pan; remove paper from cake. Brush cake all over with 2 tablespoons of the warmed extra sherry each week for 3 weeks.

Super-rich chocolate Drambuie fruit cake

PREPARATION TIME 50 MINUTES (PLUS STANDING TIME)
COOKING TIME 4 HOURS 30 MINUTES (PLUS COOLING TIME) **SERVES** 36

Drambuie is a whisky-based liqueur and goes well with the honey flavour in this cake. You could use an orange-flavoured liqueur instead, such as Cointreau or Grand Marnier. Don't worry when the butter, sugar and egg mixture curdles — this is an egg-rich mixture.

2⅓ cups (375g) sultanas

2¼ cups (375g) raisins, chopped coarsely

1⅔ cups (230g) dried currants

1½ cups (250g) seeded prunes, chopped coarsely

1½ cups (210g) dried seeded dates, chopped coarsely

¾ cup (120g) mixed peel

⅔ cup (140g) red glacé cherries, quartered

1⅓ cups (330ml) Drambuie

⅓ cup (115g) honey

1 tablespoon finely grated lemon rind

250g butter, softened

1½ cups (330g) firmly packed dark brown sugar

6 eggs

90g dark eating chocolate, grated coarsely

1¼ cups (150g) coarsely chopped roasted pecans

2 cups (300g) plain flour

1 cup (150g) self-raising flour

¼ cup (25g) cocoa powder

1 Combine fruit, 1 cup (250ml) of the Drambuie, honey and rind in large bowl. Cover tightly with plastic wrap; store in cool, dark place overnight or up to a week, stirring every day.

2 Preheat oven to 120°C/100°C fan-forced. Grease six-hole texas (¾-cup/180ml) muffin pan. Grease deep 22cm-round or deep 19cm-square cake pan; line base and side(s) with four thicknesses of baking paper, extending paper 5cm above edge(s).

3 Beat butter and sugar in medium bowl with electric mixer until combined. Beat in eggs, one at a time. Stir butter mixture into fruit mixture with chocolate and nuts. Stir in sifted dry ingredients, in two batches.

4 Fill each hole of muffin pan with fruit cake mixture, level to the top; spread remaining mixture into cake pan.

5 Bake muffins 1½ hours (cake can stand while muffins are baking). Brush hot muffins with some of the remaining Drambuie; cover with foil, cool in pan.

6 Increase oven to 150°C/130°C fan-forced. Bake large cake about 3 hours. Brush hot cake with remaining Drambuie; cover hot cake with foil, cool in pan overnight.

Gluten-free fruit and almond loaves

PREPARATION TIME 35 MINUTES (PLUS STANDING TIME) **COOKING TIME** 2 HOURS **MAKES** 2

1kg mixed dried fruit

1 tablespoon finely grated orange rind

⅔ cup (160ml) sweet sherry

150g butter, softened

⅔ cup (150g) firmly packed dark brown sugar

4 eggs

100g marzipan, chopped coarsely

1 small apple (130g), grated coarsely

¾ cup (100g) almond meal

1¼ cups (185g) gluten-free plain flour

1 cup (160g) blanched almonds

¼ cup (60ml) sweet sherry, extra

1 Combine fruit, rind and sherry in large bowl. Cover tightly with plastic wrap; store in cool, dark place overnight or for several days, stirring every day.

2 Preheat oven to 150°C/130°C fan-forced. Line base and sides of two 8cm x 26cm loaf pans with two thicknesses of baking paper, bringing paper 5cm above sides.

3 Beat butter and sugar in small bowl with electric mixer until just combined. Beat in eggs, one at a time. Stir butter mixture into fruit mixture. Stir in marzipan, apple, almond meal and sifted flour. Spread mixture into pans; decorate with nuts.

4 Bake loaves about 2 hours. Brush hot loaves with extra sherry; cover hot loaves with foil, cool in pans.

Check all labels to ensure the products you're using do not contain gluten. There is a big demand for gluten-free recipes, particularly cakes and biscuits. This is a very good recipe.

SAVOURY
PIES & TARTS

Savoury Pies & Tarts

The beauty of savoury pastry is its adaptability. A pastry case can enclose all manner of cooked meats and vegetables and is a great way of both extending, and giving a new lease on life to leftovers. When made in single serving portions, pies make great picnic or outdoor eating fare that can be eaten with the hands without the need for plates or cutlery. The cornish pasty is typical of this genre, its shape allegedly devised to fit in the pockets of tin miners in 19th-century Cornwall. The elongated pasty encloses vegetables and meat, though in the original, one end may have contained a sweet filling such as cooked apple or apricot and the other, a savoury one.

TYPES OF PIES

Just about any ovenproof casserole or baking dish can be used to contain a pie, though the traditional shape is round and has slightly sloping sides with a rim to anchor the pastry base to the lid. A traditional Australian meat pie dish is usually made from thin sheet metal, which conducts heat well and ensures a good crisp crust on the bottom. This pie typifies the variety called a double or two-crust pie, that is, it has a pastry base and lid, in this case, shortcrust on the bottom and puff pastry for the lid.

Roll out the bottom layer to allow about a 2cm overhang on the dish. Drape the pastry over the rolling pin and transfer it to the dish, easing it in gently to avoid stretching it. If it does happen to break, don't panic — you can usually patch up a pastry tear with an offcut. Press the pastry evenly over the base of the pie dish, make sure that no air is trapped between the pastry and the dish by using your fingers or a small ball of pastry dipped in flour. Fill with prepared filling. Roll out the pastry lid to about 2cm larger than the pie dish, moisten the outer edge of the base pastry, then drape the lid over the filling. Press the edges together firmly without stretching the pastry. Holding the pie dish in one hand and a sharp knife in the other, trim off the overhanging pastry, angling the knife slightly under the rim as you turn the dish around. Pie lids are often brushed with egg, or an egg and milk mixture to glaze and help brown the tops.

One-crust pies have a lid but no base. The filling is placed in a container just large enough to hold it. If the filling is not firm enough to mound, you can support the lid by placing a pie funnel or upsidedown egg cup in the centre of the pie. A pie funnel, aka a pastry bird will serve the added role of venting the pie — through the bird's "mouth". Alternatively, cut a few slashes in the pastry to allow the steam to escape.

To cover a one-crust pie, roll out the pastry to about 4cm larger than the top of the dish; cut a 1cm strip from the outside of the pastry and place the strip around the rim of the pie dish. Moisten the pastry rim, using the rolling pin, lay the pastry lid over the pie dish, pressing together the pastry strip and lid, without stretching the pastry. Trim away any excess using the method described for two-crust pies.

One or two-crust pies can be decorated using pastry trimmings or by a decorative edge. See *Pastry decorations* on pages 482 & 483.

English-style raised pies, such as pork or veal and ham pies use hot water pastry, which is made by mixing melted lard in hot water into the flour mixture. When cooled, this pastry sets strong enough to stand by itself before baking. To make the pub lunch and picnic classic pie, the pastry is usually placed into a decorative heavy ceramic mould. If you don't have a suitable mould, a springform tin makes a good substitute.

OTHER TOPPINGS

Not all pies have pastry lids. Shepherd's and cottage pies use mashed potato as the topping. Variants include mashed pumpkin, kumara, celeriac and jerusalem artichoke, sometimes combined with mashed potato. Some pies have dumplings as a topping, in which case the moist balls of dough are gently rested on top of the meat or vegetable filling. The pot is then covered, so the steam cooks the dumplings. Other pies use a damper or scone mixture as a crust which is baked, uncovered, in a hot oven. The addition of polenta or cornmeal to this kind of dough can provide an interesting contrast, while herbs, spices and cheese can be used as complementary flavours to the filling.

OTHER SAVOURY PASTRIES

The quiche, basically a savoury custard contained in an open pastry case, is France's gift to the pie world. It's thought to have originated in Germany, in the medieval kingdom of Lothringen, under German rule, and which the French later renamed Lorraine. Classic quiche lorraine contains eggs, cream and smoked pork or bacon; cheese is a modern addition. Add onions and you have quiche alsacienne, add spinach for florentine. You can also add mushrooms, capsicum, carrot, salmon, herbs, pretty much whatever combination of fillings you fancy. The English have their own rustic egg and bacon pie, which has a thicker crust and a chunkier filling than its French cousin.

Turnovers are basically pastry pockets with a savoury (or sweet) filling. The cook starts with a square or round of pastry and folds it over to enclose the filling in a triangular or semi-circular pie which is either baked or fried. The cornish pasty is one variant; in the countries of the former Ottoman empire they use fillo pastry with minced meat, cheese and vegetables to make bureks; in Greece spinach and fetta cheese in fillo forms spanakopita. The Spanish, Portuguese and Latin Americans enclose meat, chicken, vegetables, cheese and sometimes raisins or sultanas to make empanadas while the Indians use a spicy vegetable and/or meat mixture to make curry puffs or samosas.

Roulades are made by rolling puff, or fillo, pastry swiss-roll style, to enclose a savoury filling. Some roulades are baked whole; others are cut into slices and baked flat as spirals. This chapter wouldn't be complete without mention of the sausage roll. While inferior versions deserve the scorn which is so often poured on them, a good sausage roll is a delight. The secrets are good puff pastry and a quality sausage meat.

Caramelised onion and beetroot tart

PREPARATION TIME 20 MINUTES (PLUS FREEZING TIME) **COOKING TIME** 45 MINUTES **SERVES** 6

50g butter

4 medium red onions (680g), halved, sliced thinly

1 tablespoon red wine vinegar

1 teaspoon fresh thyme leaves

3 medium beetroot (500g), trimmed

1 sheet ready-rolled butter puff pastry, thawed

cooking-oil spray

120g baby rocket leaves

CHIVE OIL

½ cup coarsely chopped fresh chives

¾ cup (180ml) olive oil

1 ice cube

HORSERADISH CREAM

¾ cup (180ml) cream

1 tablespoon horseradish cream

1 Melt butter in medium frying pan; cook onion, stirring occasionally, over medium heat about 30 minutes or until caramelised. Stir in vinegar and thyme.

2 Meanwhile, boil or steam unpeeled beetroot until tender; drain. When cool enough to handle, peel beetroot; slice thinly.

3 Preheat oven to 220°C/200°C fan-forced. Grease oven tray.

4 Place pastry sheet on flat surface; cut a 24cm circle out of pastry. Place on tray, prick all over with fork; freeze 10 minutes. Bake about 5 minutes or until browned lightly.

5 Make chive oil. Make horseradish cream.

6 Spread onion mixture over pastry; top with slightly overlapping beetroot slices. Spray tart lightly with oil; bake about 10 minutes.

7 Meanwhile, combine rocket in medium bowl with half of the chive oil; divide among serving plates.

8 Cut tart into six wedges. Place each wedge on rocket, drizzle with remaining chive oil; serve with horseradish cream.

CHIVE OIL Blend or process ingredients until smooth.

HORSERADISH CREAM Beat cream in small bowl with electric mixer until soft peaks form; fold in horseradish cream.

Antipasto puff pastry tarts

PREPARATION TIME 20 MINUTES **COOKING TIME** 20 MINUTES **SERVES** 4

¼ cup (60ml) olive oil

2 cloves garlic, crushed

1 small red capsicum (150g), chopped coarsely

1 small yellow capsicum (150g), chopped coarsely

1 medium zucchini (120g), sliced thinly

2 baby eggplants (120g), sliced thinly

1 small red onion (100g), sliced thickly

100g semi-dried tomatoes

150g baby bocconcini cheese, halved

½ cup (40g) finely grated parmesan cheese

½ cup firmly packed fresh basil leaves

2 sheets ready-rolled puff pastry, thawed

⅓ cup (85g) bottled tomato pasta sauce

2 tablespoons olive tapenade

1 Preheat oven to 220°C/200°C fan-forced. Grease oven trays.

2 Combine oil and garlic in large bowl. Add capsicums, zucchini, eggplant and onion; turn gently to coat vegetables in oil mixture.

3 Cook vegetables, in batches, on heated oiled grill plate (or grill or barbecue) until browned lightly and tender; transfer to large bowl. Mix in tomatoes, cheeses and basil.

4 Cut pastry sheets in half; fold edges 1cm inward, place on trays. Divide sauce among pastry pieces; top with vegetable mixture.

5 Bake tarts about 15 minutes or until browned lightly; serve topped with tapenade.

Serve these as a snack or cut crossways into smaller pieces to have with drinks. You could add chopped salami to the topping.

Vegetarian tarts

PREPARATION TIME 20 MINUTES **COOKING TIME** 25 MINUTES **SERVES** 4

1kg potatoes, peeled, chopped coarsely

½ cup (125ml) hot vegetable stock

30g butter

2 cloves garlic, crushed

200g mushrooms, sliced thickly

2 tablespoons finely shredded fresh basil

2 green onions, chopped finely

⅔ cup (80g) coarsely grated cheddar cheese

3 sheets fillo pastry

30g butter, melted

Don't worry if the fillo breaks up a little while you're handling it — no one will know once the tarts are cooked. The baking paper strips will make it easier to lift the tarts out of the pie dishes.

1 Boil, steam or microwave potato until tender; drain. Mash potato in large bowl with stock.

2 Meanwhile, melt butter in small frying pan; cook garlic and mushrooms, stirring, until mushroom softens. Stir mushroom mixture, basil, onion and half of the cheese into potato mixture.

3 Preheat oven to 200°C/180°C fan-forced. Grease four 1-cup (250ml) metal pie dishes. Place a 2.5cm x 30cm strip of baking paper over base of each dish, extending 5cm over side of dishes.

4 Stack fillo sheets; cut stack in half crossways. Brush between layers with melted butter, then cut stack into four squares. Line dishes with squares, place dishes on oven trays. Spoon potato mixture into dishes; sprinkle with remaining cheese.

5 Bake tarts about 15 minutes.

Vegetable and fetta freeform tarts

PREPARATION TIME 30 MINUTES (PLUS STANDING TIME) **COOKING TIME** 50 MINUTES **SERVES** 4

1 small eggplant (230g), chopped coarsely

coarse cooking salt

1 tablespoon olive oil

1 medium brown onion (150g), sliced thinly

2 medium zucchini (240g), sliced thinly

4 sheets ready-rolled shortcrust pastry, thawed

¼ cup (65g) bottled pesto

120g fetta cheese, crumbled

8 cherry tomatoes, halved

1 tablespoon finely chopped fresh basil

1 egg, beaten lightly

Most eggplants (particularly small eggplants) grown these days don't need disgorging with salt. The salt extracts any bitter liquid from the vegetable. Use a plate or the base of a cake pan as a guide to cut out the pastry rounds.

1 Place eggplant in sieve or colander; sprinkle all over with salt, then stand sieve over sink or large bowl for about 15 minutes. Rinse eggplant well under cold running water, drain; pat dry with absorbent paper.

2 Preheat oven to 180°C/160°C fan-forced.

3 Heat oil in large frying pan; cook onion, stirring, until softened. Add eggplant and zucchini to pan; cook, stirring, until vegetables are softened.

4 Cut a 20cm round from each pastry sheet; place rounds on oven trays. Spread equal amounts of pesto onto each round, leaving a 4cm border around the outside edge.

5 Divide vegetables over pesto; top each with equal amounts of cheese, tomato and basil. Turn the 4cm edge on each round over filling; brush around pastry edge with egg.

6 Bake tarts about 40 minutes.

Onion and anchovy tartlets

PREPARATION TIME 45 MINUTES **COOKING TIME** 35 MINUTES **SERVES** 6

1 tablespoon olive oil

60g butter

3 medium brown onions (450g), halved, sliced thinly

2 cloves garlic, crushed

1 bay leaf

3 sprigs fresh thyme

⅓ cup coarsely chopped fresh flat-leaf parsley

8 anchovy fillets, drained, chopped finely

2 tablespoons coarsely chopped seeded black olives

¾ cup (110g) self-raising flour

¾ cup (110g) plain flour

¾ cup (180ml) buttermilk

1 Heat oil and half of the butter in large frying pan; cook onion, garlic, bay leaf and thyme, stirring occasionally, about 20 minutes or until onion caramelises. Discard bay leaf and thyme; stir in parsley, anchovy and olives.

2 Meanwhile, blend or process flours and remaining butter until fine. Add buttermilk; process until ingredients come together. Knead dough on floured surface until smooth.

3 Preheat oven to 220°C/200°C fan-forced. Grease two oven trays.

4 Divide dough into six pieces; roll each piece of dough on floured surface into 14cm squares. Fold edges over to form 1cm border. Place squares on trays; place rounded tablespoons of the onion mixture on each square.

5 Bake tartlets about 15 minutes.

The base for the tartlets is really a "strong" scone dough. The plain flour in the dough will help the dough maintain the square shape. Kalamata olives are good for this recipe, but are not as easy to seed as regular black olives.

Tapenade and tomato pastries

PREPARATION TIME 10 MINUTES **COOKING TIME** 10 MINUTES **SERVES** 4

2 sheets ready-rolled puff pastry

½ cup (60g) seeded black olives

2 teaspoons drained rinsed capers

2 teaspoons olive oil

2 teaspoons fresh lemon thyme leaves

2 teaspoons coarsely chopped fresh flat-leaf parsley

2 medium tomatoes (380g), sliced thinly

30g fetta cheese, crumbled

1 tablespoon fresh oregano leaves

1 Preheat oven to 200°C/180°C fan-forced. Line greased oven tray with baking paper.

2 Cut six 8.5cm rounds from each pastry sheet. Place on tray; using fork, prick rounds about five times, cover with baking paper, top pastry rounds with another oven tray.

3 Bake pastries about 10 minutes or until golden brown.

4 Meanwhile, process olives, capers, oil, thyme and parsley until tapenade is combined.

5 Divide tomato among pastry bases; top each with 1 rounded teaspoon of the tapenade. Sprinkle with cheese and oregano.

Lemon thyme goes well with salty ingredients such as olives, capers and fetta cheese. If you can't find it, use regular thyme and a little finely grated lemon rind instead.

1 ONION AND ANCHOVY TARTLETS 2 TAPENADE AND TOMATO PASTRIES 3 CARAMELISED ONION AND GOAT CHEESE TARTLETS [P 606] 4 VEGETABLE PITHIVIERS WITH ROASTED TOMATO SAUCE [P 606]

SAVOURY PIES & TARTS **BAKE** 605

Caramelised onion and goat cheese tartlets

PREPARATION TIME 25 MINUTES (PLUS REFRIGERATION TIME) **COOKING TIME** 45 MINUTES **SERVES** 4

1 cup (150g) plain flour

80g cold butter,
chopped coarsely

1 egg yolk

2 tablespoons iced water,
approximately

100g soft goat cheese

2 tablespoons coarsely chopped
fresh chives

CARAMELISED ONION

2 tablespoons olive oil

4 large brown onions (800g),
sliced thinly

⅓ cup (80ml) port

2 tablespoons red wine vinegar

2 tablespoons brown sugar

1 Process flour and butter until crumbly. Add egg yolk and enough of the water to process until ingredients come together. Enclose in plastic wrap; refrigerate 30 minutes.

2 Meanwhile, make caramelised onion.

3 Preheat oven to 200°C/180°C fan-forced. Grease four 10.5cm loose-based flan tins.

4 Divide pastry into four portions. Roll each portion of pastry between sheets of baking paper until large enough to line tins. Lift pastry into tins, press into base and side; trim edge, prick base all over with fork.

5 Place tins on oven tray; line pastry with baking paper, fill with dried beans or rice. Bake 10 minutes. Remove paper and beans; bake further 5 minutes or until tart cases brown lightly.

6 Divide onion mixture and cheese among tartlets. Bake about 5 minutes or until heated through. Sprinkle tartlets with chives.

CARAMELISED ONION Heat oil in large frying pan; cook onion, stirring, until onion softens. Add port, vinegar and sugar; cook, stirring occasionally, about 25 minutes or until onion caramelises.

Vegetable pithiviers with roasted tomato sauce

PREPARATION TIME 45 MINUTES **COOKING TIME** 2 HOURS 5 MINUTES **SERVES** 4

10 large egg tomatoes (900g),
quartered

2 teaspoons brown sugar

⅓ cup (80ml) olive oil

2 tablespoons red wine vinegar

2 large red capsicums (700g),
halved

30g butter

2 large green zucchini (300g),
sliced thinly

7 flat mushrooms (560g),
sliced thinly

1 clove garlic, crushed

1 tablespoon port

5 sheets ready-rolled puff pastry,
thawed

1 egg yolk

1 tablespoon milk

50g baby spinach leaves

1 Preheat oven to 180°C/160°C fan-forced. Grease oven trays.

2 Combine tomato, sugar, half of the oil and half of the vinegar in large bowl; place tomato pieces, skin-side down, on oven tray. Roast 1 hour 40 minutes. Remove from oven; return to same bowl; crush with potato masher. Cover to keep warm; reserve tomato sauce.

3 While tomato is roasting, place capsicum, skin-side up, on oven tray. Roast 40 minutes or until softened. Place capsicum in plastic bag; close tightly, cool. Discard skin, membrane and seeds; slice thinly.

4 Meanwhile, melt butter in large frying pan; cook zucchini, stirring, about 5 minutes or until softened. Place zucchini in small bowl; cover to keep warm. Place mushrooms and garlic in same pan; cook, stirring, about 5 minutes or until mushrooms soften. Add port; cook, stirring, until liquid evaporates.

5 Cut four of the pastry sheets into 16cm squares; cut remaining sheet into quarters. Place one of the small squares on oven tray; centre 9cm cutter on pastry. Layer a quarter of the mushroom mixture, a quarter of the zucchini and a quarter of the capsicum on pastry; remove cutter. Brush border with combined egg yolk and milk; top with one of the large squares, press edges together to seal.

6 Using sharp knife, cut around pithiviers, leaving 5mm border; mark pastry with swirl design from centre to side, taking care not to cut through pastry. Brush lightly with egg mixture. Repeat with remaining pastry, vegetables and egg mixture.

7 Bake pithiviers about 25 minutes.

8 Place spinach, remaining oil and remaining vinegar in small bowl; toss gently to combine. Divide salad among serving plates; serve with pithivier and roasted tomato sauce.

Leek and fetta triangles

PREPARATION TIME 15 MINUTES **COOKING TIME** 15 MINUTES **SERVES** 4

50g butter

2 cloves garlic, crushed

2 medium leeks (700g), sliced thinly

1 tablespoon caraway seeds

150g fetta cheese, chopped coarsely

⅓ cup (40g) coarsely grated cheddar cheese

4 sheets fillo pastry

50g butter, melted, extra

2 teaspoons sesame seeds

1 Heat half of the butter in large frying pan; cook garlic and leek, stirring occasionally, until leek softens. Stir in caraway seeds; cook, stirring, 2 minutes.

2 Combine leek mixture in medium bowl with cheeses.

3 Preheat oven to 200°C/180°C fan-forced. Grease oven tray.

4 Brush one sheet of fillo with extra butter; fold in half lengthways. Place a quarter of the leek mixture at bottom of one narrow edge of fillo, leaving a 1cm border. Fold opposite corner of fillo diagonally across filling to form a triangle; continue folding to end of fillo. Place on tray, seam-side down. Repeat with remaining fillo and filling to make four triangles in total. Brush triangles with butter; sprinkle with sesame seeds.

5 Bake triangles about 10 minutes.

Leeks take quite a long time to soften. Buy the smallest leeks you can find – they will take the least time to cook. Be fussy about washing the leeks, grit hides between the layers. Cut off the root end and most of the green part, split the leeks down the centre, lengthways, then wash between the layers (under cold water) by fanning the layers out with your fingers.

Tomato tarte tatins with crème fraîche sauce

PREPARATION TIME 40 MINUTES **COOKING TIME** 30 MINUTES **SERVES** 6

9 small firm tomatoes (800g), peeled, quartered

30g butter

1 clove garlic, crushed

1 tablespoon brown sugar

2 tablespoons balsamic vinegar

1½ sheets ready-rolled butter puff pastry, thawed

1 egg

vegetable oil, for deep-frying

6 sprigs fresh baby basil

CREME FRAICHE SAUCE

20g butter

2 shallots (50g), chopped finely

1 cup (240g) crème fraîche

⅓ cup (80ml) water

1 Preheat oven to 220°C/200°C fan-forced.

2 Discard pulp and seeds from tomato quarters; gently flatten flesh.

3 Melt butter in large frying pan; cook garlic, stirring, over low heat, until fragrant. Add sugar and vinegar; cook, stirring, until sugar dissolves. Place tomato in pan, in single layer; cook, covered, turning once, about 5 minutes or until tomato softens.

4 Grease six 1-cup (250ml) metal pie dishes; cut six 11cm rounds from pastry sheets. Divide tomato among dishes; top each with one pastry round, pressing down gently. Brush pastry with egg; bake about 15 minutes or until pastry is browned lightly.

5 Meanwhile, heat oil in small saucepan; place thoroughly dry basil sprigs, one at a time, in pan. Deep-fry about 3 seconds or until basil is crisp. Drain on absorbent paper.

6 Make crème fraîche sauce.

7 Divide sauce among serving plates; turn tarts onto sauce, top with basil.

CREME FRAICHE SAUCE Melt butter in small saucepan; cook shallot, stirring, about 3 minutes or until softened. Add crème fraîche; cook, stirring, over low heat, until heated through. Stir in the water.

Deep-frying basil brings out a delicious flavour in it, but you have to be careful with the frying. First, be fanatical about drying the sprigs — water and oil don't mix — there will be much splattering if the basil is wet at frying time. Heat the oil — it should be about 4cm deep in a small saucepan with high sides — use long tongs to carefully lower one sprig at a time into the oil. Stand back in case the oil spits and splutters. The frying takes only a few seconds, quickly but carefully remove the basil, with tongs, to drain on absorbent paper.

Sausage rolls

PREPARATION TIME 15 MINUTES **COOKING TIME** 30 MINUTES **MAKES** 24

2 teaspoons vegetable oil

1 small brown onion (80g), grated coarsely

1 slice stale white bread, crusts removed

200g sausage mince

200g beef mince

2 teaspoons tomato paste

½ teaspoon dried mixed herbs

1 tablespoon finely chopped fresh flat-leaf parsley

2 sheets ready-rolled puff pastry, thawed

1 egg

1 Preheat oven to 220°C/200°C fan-forced. Line two oven trays with baking paper.

2 Heat oil in small frying pan; cook onion until soft.

3 Dip bread quickly in and out of a small bowl of cold water; discard water.

4 Combine onion and bread in medium bowl with minces, tomato paste, mixed herbs and parsley.

5 Cut pastry sheets in half. Spoon or pipe mince mixture along centre of each pastry piece. Turn one long side of pastry over mince mixture; brush pastry flap with egg. Turn other long side of pastry over to enclose mince mixture.

6 Cut each roll into six pieces. Place rolls, seam-side down, on trays; brush with egg. Make two cuts in top of each roll; bake rolls about 30 minutes or until browned.

7 Stand 10 minutes before serving with tomato sauce.

Chicken and vegetable rolls

PREPARATION TIME 15 MINUTES **COOKING TIME** 30 MINUTES **MAKES** 48

500g chicken mince

1 clove garlic, crushed

1 medium brown onion (150g), chopped finely

1 medium carrot (120g), grated finely

100g green beans, trimmed, chopped finely

125g can creamed corn

1 egg

⅓ cup (25g) stale breadcrumbs

1 tablespoon tomato sauce

4 sheets ready-rolled puff pastry, thawed

1 egg, extra

1 Preheat oven to 200°C/180°C fan-forced. Line oven trays with baking paper.

2 Combine mince, garlic, onion, carrot, beans, corn, egg, breadcrumbs and sauce in medium bowl.

3 Cut pastry sheets in half. Spoon or pipe mince mixture down centre of each pastry piece. Turn one long side of pastry over mince mixture; brush pastry flap with extra egg. Turn other long side of pastry over to enclose mince mixture.

4 Cut each roll into six pieces. Place rolls, seam-side down, on trays; brush with extra egg. Make two cuts in top of each roll; bake rolls about 30 minutes or until browned.

5 Stand 10 minutes before serving with tomato sauce.

Beef samosas with peach and raisin chutney

PREPARATION TIME 50 MINUTES **COOKING TIME** 1 HOUR 25 MINUTES (PLUS REFRIGERATION TIME)

MAKES 36

2 teaspoons vegetable oil

1 small brown onion (80g), chopped finely

2 cloves garlic, crushed

2cm piece fresh ginger (10g), grated

1 tablespoon ground cumin

1 tablespoon ground coriander

1 fresh small red thai chilli, chopped finely

250g beef mince

1 small kumara (250g), chopped finely

⅓ cup (80ml) water

4 sheets ready-rolled shortcrust pastry, thawed

1 egg

PEACH AND RAISIN CHUTNEY

3 medium peaches (450g)

⅓ cup (110g) finely chopped raisins

½ cup (125ml) cider vinegar

2 tablespoons lemon juice

1 small brown onion (80g), chopped finely

¼ teaspoon ground cinnamon

½ teaspoon ground allspice

1 cup (220g) white sugar

The chutney can be made as a stand-alone recipe. If you want to keep it long-term, pour it while it's still hot into sterilised jars; seal while hot. The samosas can be prepared, then frozen uncooked.

1 Make peach and raisin chutney.

2 Heat oil in large frying pan; cook onion, garlic, ginger and spices, stirring, until onion softens. Add chilli and mince; cook, stirring, until mince browns. Add kumara and the water; bring to the boil. Reduce heat; simmer, uncovered, stirring occasionally, until kumara softens. Stir in ⅓ cup of the chutney. Refrigerate beef filling until cold.

3 Preheat oven to 200°C/180°C fan-forced. Grease oven trays.

4 Using 7.5cm cutter, cut nine rounds from each pastry sheet. Place rounded teaspoons of beef filling in centre of each round; brush edge of round with egg, press edges together to enclose filling. Repeat with remaining rounds and filling.

5 Place samosas on trays; brush tops with egg.

6 Bake samosas about 20 minutes.

PEACH AND RAISIN CHUTNEY Cover peaches with boiling water in medium heatproof bowl for about 30 seconds. Peel, seed, then chop peaches finely. Place in medium saucepan with remaining ingredients; bring to the boil. Reduce heat; simmer, uncovered, stirring occasionally, about 45 minutes or until chutney thickens.

Chicken and olive empanadas

PREPARATION TIME 25 MINUTES **COOKING TIME** 40 MINUTES **MAKES** 24

2 cups (500ml) chicken stock

1 bay leaf

3 chicken thigh fillets (330g)

1 tablespoon olive oil

1 small brown onion (80g), chopped finely

2 cloves garlic, crushed

2 teaspoons ground cumin

½ cup (80g) sultanas

⅓ cup (40g) coarsely chopped seeded green olives

5 sheets ready-rolled shortcrust pastry, thawed

1 egg

1 Place stock and bay leaf in medium frying pan; bring to the boil. Add chicken, reduce heat; poach chicken, covered, about 10 minutes or until cooked through. Cool chicken in liquid 10 minutes; shred chicken finely. Reserve 1 cup of the poaching liquid; discard remainder.

2 Meanwhile, heat oil in large frying pan; cook onion, stirring, until softened. Add garlic and cumin; cook, stirring, until fragrant. Add sultanas and reserved poaching liquid; bring to the boil. Reduce heat; simmer, uncovered, about 15 minutes or until liquid is almost evaporated. Stir in chicken and olives.

3 Preheat oven to 200°C/180°C fan-forced. Grease two oven trays.

4 Using 9cm cutter, cut 24 rounds from pastry sheets. Place 1 level tablespoon of the filling in centre of each round; fold round in half to enclose filling, pinching edges to seal. Using fork, press around edges of empanadas. Place on trays; brush tops with egg.

5 Bake empanadas about 25 minutes. Serve with yogurt.

Drain the silver beet as well as you possibly can. Spinach can be used instead of silver beet. Whichever vegetable you choose to use, make sure you trim the stalks away and wash the leaves well.

Spanakopita

PREPARATION TIME 40 MINUTES **COOKING TIME** 30 MINUTES **MAKES** 16

1.5kg silver beet, trimmed

1 tablespoon olive oil

1 medium brown onion (150g), chopped finely

2 cloves garlic, crushed

1 teaspoon ground nutmeg

200g fetta cheese, crumbled

1 tablespoon finely grated lemon rind

¼ cup chopped fresh mint

¼ cup chopped fresh flat-leaf parsley

¼ cup chopped fresh dill

4 green onions, chopped finely

16 sheets fillo pastry

125g butter, melted

2 teaspoons sesame seeds

1 Boil, steam or microwave silver beet until wilted; drain. Squeeze out excess liquid; drain on absorbent paper. Chop silver beet coarsely; spread out on absorbent paper.

2 Heat oil in small frying pan; cook brown onion and garlic, stirring, until onion is soft. Add nutmeg; cook, stirring, until fragrant. Combine onion mixture and silver beet in large bowl with cheese, rind, herbs and green onion. Grease oven tray.

3 Preheat oven to 180°C/160°C fan-forced.

4 Brush one sheet of fillo with butter; fold lengthways into thirds, brushing with butter between each fold. Place rounded tablespoon of silver beet mixture at the bottom of one narrow edge of folded fillo sheet, leaving a border. Fold opposite corner of fillo diagonally across filling to form large triangle; continue folding to end of fillo sheet, retaining triangular shape. Place on tray, seam-side down; repeat with remaining ingredients.

5 Brush spanakopita with remaining butter; sprinkle with sesame seeds.

6 Bake spanakopita about 15 minutes.

Kids love cottage pie and it's easy to hide vegies in the mixture. Sebago potatoes make a good topping, but just about any common potato will do. Pizza cheese is handy because it's available from supermarkets already grated, ready for sprinkling.

Cottage pie

PREPARATION TIME 20 MINUTES **COOKING TIME** 1 HOUR 35 MINUTES **SERVES** 8

1 tablespoon olive oil

2 cloves garlic, crushed

1 large brown onion (200g), chopped finely

2 medium carrots (240g), chopped finely

1kg beef mince

1 tablespoon worcestershire sauce

2 tablespoons tomato paste

2 x 425g cans crushed tomatoes

1 teaspoon dried mixed herbs

200g mushrooms, quartered

1 cup (120g) frozen peas

1kg potatoes, chopped coarsely

¾ cup (180ml) hot milk

40g butter, softened

½ cup (50g) pizza cheese

1 Heat oil in large saucepan; cook garlic, onion and carrot, stirring, until onion softens. Add mince; cook, stirring, about 10 minutes or until mince changes colour.

2 Add sauce, tomato paste, undrained tomatoes and herbs; bring to the boil. Reduce heat; simmer, uncovered, about 30 minutes or until mixture thickens slightly. Stir in mushrooms and peas.

3 Meanwhile, preheat oven to 180°C/160°C fan-forced

4 Boil, steam or microwave potato until tender; drain. Mash potato in large bowl with milk and butter.

5 Pour beef mixture into deep 3-litre (12-cup) ovenproof dish; top with mashed potato mixture, sprinkle with cheese.

6 Bake pie about 45 minutes or until heated through and top is browned lightly.

Chicken, bacon and mushroom pies

PREPARATION TIME 15 MINUTES **COOKING TIME** 45 MINUTES **SERVES** 4

1 tablespoon vegetable oil

1 medium leek (350g), sliced thinly

2 rindless bacon rashers (130g), sliced thinly

200g mushrooms, halved

1 tablespoon plain flour

1 cup (250ml) chicken stock

$\frac{1}{3}$ cup (80ml) cream

1 tablespoon dijon mustard

3 cups (480g) coarsely chopped barbecued chicken

1 sheet ready-rolled puff pastry, thawed, quartered

1 Preheat oven to 200°C/180°C fan-forced.

2 Heat oil in medium saucepan; cook leek, bacon and mushrooms, stirring, until leek softens. Stir in flour; cook, stirring, until mixture thickens and bubbles. Gradually add stock; cook, stirring, until mixture boils and thickens. Stir in cream, mustard and chicken.

3 Divide chicken mixture among four 1-cup (250ml) ovenproof dishes; top each with a pastry quarter.

4 Bake pies about 20 minutes.

You need to purchase a large barbecued chicken weighing about 900g for this recipe. It's a good idea to buy a few barbecued chickens when they're on special, remove and shred the meat then freeze it in 1-cup parcels — ready for use at another time, and effectively saving time and money. Discard the chicken skin, but use the bones, along with any slightly worse-for-wear carrots, celery or herbs in your vegetable crisper to make stock and freeze it in 1-cup amounts

Pumpkin and fetta pies

PREPARATION TIME 10 MINUTES **COOKING TIME** 20 MINUTES **SERVES** 4

500g pumpkin, cut into 2cm pieces

3 eggs

200g fetta cheese,
cut into 2cm pieces

2 tablespoons finely grated
parmesan cheese

2 tablespoons sour cream

⅓ cup (80g) drained char-grilled
capsicum in oil, sliced thinly

2 tablespoons halved seeded
black olives

4 green onions, sliced thinly

1 sheet ready-rolled puff pastry,
thawed

1 teaspoon finely shredded
fresh basil

1 Preheat oven to 220°C/200°C fan-forced. Grease four 11cm pie dishes.

2 Boil, steam or microwave pumpkin until tender; drain.

3 Meanwhile, combine eggs, cheeses, sour cream, capsicum, olives and green onion in large bowl. Add pumpkin; mix gently.

4 Cut pastry sheet into four squares; press each square into a dish, allowing pastry to hang over edge. Place dishes on oven tray; divide filling among dishes.

5 Bake pies about 15 minutes or until filling sets. Sprinkle with basil before serving.

Char-grilled capsicum can be bought in jars from supermarkets, but you can do your own quickly and easily if you prefer — see page 607. Use whatever type of black olives you like — kalamata are good.

Roast potato and bacon quiche

PREPARATION TIME 20 MINUTES **COOKING TIME** 1 HOUR 5 MINUTES **SERVES** 4

300g potatoes, chopped coarsely

1 tablespoon olive oil

1 sheet ready-rolled puff pastry,
thawed

2 teaspoons olive oil, extra

1 small brown onion (80g),
sliced thinly

2 cloves garlic, crushed

3 rindless rashers bacon (195g),
chopped coarsely

⅓ cup (80ml) milk

⅓ cup (80ml) cream

2 eggs

¼ cup (25g) coarsely grated
mozzarella cheese

1 Preheat oven to 200°C/180°C fan-forced.

2 Combine potato and oil in medium baking dish. Roast about 30 minutes or until browned and cooked through.

3 Meanwhile, cut pastry into four squares; press one square into each of four 1-cup (250ml) ovenproof dishes. Place dishes on oven tray; bake 10 minutes.

4 Heat extra oil in medium frying pan; cook onion, garlic and bacon, stirring, until onion softens and bacon is crisp. Drain on absorbent paper.

5 Divide potato among pastry cases; top with bacon mixture. Pour combined milk, cream, eggs and cheese into dishes. Bake about 30 minutes or until filling sets. Stand 5 minutes; carefully remove quiches from dishes.

PUMPKIN AND FETTA PIES

Baking blind

This is a term used for pastry, where the pastry case is partly or fully baked before filling.

ROLLING
Roll the chilled rested pastry from the centre to the edge between sheets of baking or greaseproof paper or plastic wrap. This method is clean, neat and easy.

LINING
Peel away the top layer of paper, then turn the pastry into the tin etc. Gently peel away the remaining sheet of paper, allowing the pastry to fall into the tin. Ease the pastry into the shape of the tin without stretching it.

SHAPING
Use a small scrap of pastry, pressed into a ball, then lightly floured, to gently push the pastry around the inside of the pie tin — don't stretch the pastry.

WEIGHTING
Use enough dried beans (or any kind of pulse) or uncooked rice to fill the pastry case and weigh the pastry down. These ingredients cannot be used for any other purpose, other than blind baking. Keep the beans etc., in a glass jar until next time.

BAKING
Recipes will tell you how long the pastry case needs to bake, this is done in two stages: the first with the paper and beans, and the second without the paper and beans.

AIR BUBBLES
If the pastry develops an air bubble during the first 5 to 10 minutes of baking, press the bubble gently with a ball of scrap pastry. Some recipes will direct you to bake the docked case without paper and beans etc. — watch these cases carefully for air bubbles. If you leave if too long to squash the bubble(s), the pastry will cook too much and break on squashing.

TRIMMING

If the tin has a sharp edge, like a fluted flan tin, simply roll the rolling pin over the top edge of the tin, the pressure from the rolling pin will cut the excess pastry away cleanly.

DOCKING

Some pastry cases, depending on the type of filling to be used, are docked to stop them rising when they're baked. Do this by pricking the pastry all over with a fork, or by rolling a pastry docker (as shown) over the pastry case.

LINING

Line the pastry case with a piece of baking or greaseproof paper, or foil, strong enough to hold the weight of the beans or rice etc, and large enough to hold and remove from the tin.

COVERING

Some recipes will direct you to blind bake a pastry case, then fill it, then top it with another layer of pastry. This method is good for pies with a wet filling, such as fruit and meat pies — it decreases the chance of a soggy pastry case.

TRIMMING

Hold the pie plate, flat on one hand, at eye level, then, using a sharp knife, and a downward cutting action, trim away the excess pastry, at a 45° angle.

SEALING

Use a fork, spoon etc to decorate the edge of the pie (see pages 482 & 483 for more ideas). Glaze the pastry as directed in the recipe, then slash some holes in the top of the pastry to allow steam to escape.

Beef bourguignon pies

PREPARATION TIME 30 MINUTES **COOKING TIME** 1 HOUR 50 MINUTES **SERVES** 6

12 pickling onions (480g)

6 rindless rashers bacon (390g), sliced thinly

2 tablespoons olive oil

400g mushrooms

1kg gravy beef, trimmed, cut into 2cm pieces

¼ cup (35g) plain flour

1 tablespoon tomato paste

2 teaspoons fresh thyme leaves

1 cup (250ml) dry red wine

2 cups (500ml) beef stock

2 sheets ready-rolled butter puff pastry, thawed

cooking-oil spray

½ cup finely chopped fresh flat-leaf parsley

1 Peel onions, leaving roots intact; halve lengthways.

2 Cook bacon in heated large heavy-based saucepan, stirring, until crisp; drain. Cook onion, stirring, in same pan until browned all over; remove from pan. Heat 2 teaspoons of the oil in same pan; cook mushrooms, stirring, until browned. Remove from pan.

3 Coat beef in flour; shake off excess. Heat remaining oil in same pan; cook beef, in batches, until browned all over. Add bacon and onion with tomato paste and thyme; cook, stirring, 2 minutes. Add wine and stock; stir, over heat, until mixture boils and thickens. Reduce heat; simmer, covered, 1 hour. Add mushrooms; simmer, uncovered, about 40 minutes or until beef is tender, stirring occasionally.

4 Preheat oven to 220°C/200°C fan-forced. Oil oven tray.

5 Place pastry sheets on board; using 1 ¼-cup (310ml) ovenproof dish, cut lid for one pie by tracing around upper-rim of dish with tip of sharp knife. Repeat until you have six lids. Place lids on tray, coat with cooking-oil spray; bake about 7 minutes or until browned.

6 Meanwhile, stir parsley into beef bourguignon then divide among six 1 ¼-cup (310ml) ovenproof dishes; top each with a pastry lid.

Shepherd's pie

PREPARATION TIME 20 MINUTES **COOKING TIME** 45 MINUTES **SERVES** 4

30g butter

1 medium brown onion (150g), chopped finely

1 medium carrot (120g), chopped finely

½ teaspoon dried mixed herbs

4 cups (750g) chopped cooked lamb

¼ cup (70g) tomato paste

¼ cup (60ml) tomato sauce

2 tablespoons worcestershire sauce

2 cups (500ml) beef stock

2 tablespoons plain flour

⅓ cup (80ml) water

POTATO TOPPING

5 medium potatoes (1kg), chopped

60g butter, softened

¼ cup (60ml) hot milk

1 Preheat oven to 200°C/180°C fan-forced. Grease shallow 2.5-litre (10 cup) ovenproof dish.

2 Make potato topping.

3 Meanwhile, heat butter in large saucepan; cook onion and carrot, stirring, until tender. Add mixed herbs and lamb; cook, stirring, 2 minutes. Stir in tomato paste, sauces and stock, then blended flour and water; stir over heat until mixture boils and thickens. Pour mixture into dish. Place heaped tablespoons of potato topping on lamb mixture.

4 Bake pie about 20 minutes or until browned lightly and heated through.

POTATO TOPPING Boil, steam or microwave potatoes until tender; drain. Mash with butter and milk until smooth.

Meat pies

PREPARATION TIME 35 MINUTES (PLUS REFRIGERATION TIME)
COOKING TIME 1 HOUR (PLUS COOLING TIME) **MAKES** 6

1 ½ cups (225g) plain flour

90g butter, chopped coarsely

1 egg

1 tablespoon iced water, approximately

2 sheets ready-rolled puff pastry, thawed

1 egg, extra

BEEF FILLING

1 tablespoon vegetable oil

1 medium brown onion (150g), chopped finely

700g beef mince

425g can diced tomatoes

2 tablespoons tomato paste

¼ cup (60ml) worcestershire sauce

1 cup (250ml) beef stock

2 tablespoons cornflour

2 tablespoons water

We love this recipe. By all means use bought shortcrust pastry for the pastry cases — but there's nothing like home-made shortcrust. Use the pastry scraps to make some decorations for the pies.

1 Process flour and butter until crumbly. Add 1 egg and enough water to process until ingredients come together; knead dough on floured surface until smooth. Roll into a ball. Enclose in plastic wrap; refrigerate 30 minutes.

2 Meanwhile, make beef filling.

3 Grease six ½-cup (125ml) pie tins. Turn a pie tin upside down on puff pastry, cut around tin. Repeat to make six pastry tops; refrigerate.

4 Divide dough into six portions; roll between sheets of baking paper until large enough to line tins. Lift pastry into tins, ease into sides; trim edges. Lightly prick bases with fork; refrigerate 30 minutes.

5 Preheat oven to 200°C/180°C fan-forced.

6 Place tins on oven trays, line each with baking paper; fill with dried beans or rice. Bake 10 minutes. Remove paper and beans; bake further 7 minutes or until browned. Cool.

7 Spoon beef filling into pastry cases. Brush edges with extra egg; top with puff pastry lids, gently press edges together to seal. Brush pies with a little more egg; bake about 20 minutes or until browned.

BEEF FILLING Heat oil in medium saucepan; cook onion, stirring, until soft. Add mince; cook until browned. Add undrained tomatoes, paste, sauce and stock; simmer, uncovered, 20 minutes. Add blended cornflour and water; stir until mixture boils and thickens. Cool.

Lamb and rosemary pies

PREPARATION TIME 20 MINUTES **COOKING TIME** 25 MINUTES **SERVES** 4

Buy lamb already diced from the butcher or trim and dice the lamb yourself. Lamb cut from the leg or shoulder will give you the best flavour.

2 tablespoons olive oil

400g diced lamb

4 pickling onions (100g), quartered

1 tablespoon plain flour

¼ cup (60ml) dry red wine

¾ cup (180ml) beef stock

1 tablespoon tomato paste

1 tablespoon fresh rosemary leaves

2 sheets ready-rolled puff pastry, thawed

1 egg

4 fresh rosemary sprigs

1 Heat half of the oil in large saucepan; cook lamb, in batches, until browned all over. Heat remaining oil in same pan; cook onion, stirring, until soft. Add flour; cook, stirring, until mixture bubbles and thickens. Gradually stir in wine, stock, paste and rosemary leaves; stir until mixture boils and thickens. Stir in lamb; cool 10 minutes.

2 Preheat oven to 200°C/180°C fan-forced. Oil four holes of 6-hole texas (¾-cup/180ml) muffin pan.

3 Cut two 13cm rounds from opposite corners of each pastry sheet; cut two 9cm rounds from remaining corners of each sheet. Place larger rounds in pan holes to cover bases and sides; trim any excess pastry, prick bases with fork.

4 Spoon lamb mixture into pastry cases; brush around edges with egg. Top pies with smaller pastry rounds; press edges together to seal. Brush pies with egg; press one rosemary sprig into top of each pie.

5 Bake pies about 15 minutes or until browned lightly. Stand pies in pan 5 minutes before serving.

Mini beef and guinness pies

PREPARATION TIME 20 MINUTES **COOKING TIME** 2 HOURS (PLUS REFRIGERATION TIME) **MAKES** 36

Stout will give a deep rich flavour and colour to the pie filling. For a lighter filling, you can use beer instead. Mini pies make perfect finger food — make sure they're served hot, but not so hot that they'll burn your guests' mouths.

1 tablespoon vegetable oil

500g beef skirt steak, chopped finely

1 medium brown onion (150g), chopped finely

2 tablespoons plain flour

375ml bottle guinness stout

1 cup (250ml) beef stock

5 sheets ready-rolled shortcrust pastry, thawed

1 egg

1 Heat oil in large saucepan; cook beef, stirring, until browned all over. Add onion; cook, stirring, until softened. Add flour; cook, stirring, until mixture is well browned.

2 Gradually stir in stout and stock, stirring, until gravy boils and thickens slightly. Cover, reduce heat; simmer, stirring occasionally for 1 hour. Uncover; simmer, stirring occasionally, about 30 minutes. Refrigerate filling until cold.

3 Preheat oven to 220°C/200°C fan-forced. Grease three 12-hole mini (1-tablespoon/ 20ml) muffin pans.

4 Using 6cm cutter, cut 36 rounds from pastry sheets; place one round in each pan hole. Using 5cm pastry cutter, cut 36 rounds from remaining pastry sheets.

5 Spoon 1 heaped teaspoon of the filling into pastry cases; brush around edges of pastry with egg. Top each pie with smaller pastry round; press gently around edges to seal, brush with egg. Cut two small slits in top of each pie.

6 Bake pies about 15 minutes or until browned. Stand pies in pans 5 minutes before serving.

Mini chicken and leek pies

PREPARATION TIME 40 MINUTES **COOKING TIME** 40 MINUTES **MAKES** 16

Don't throw the excess poaching liquid away, freeze it for another use.

1 cup (250ml) chicken stock

170g chicken breast fillet

1 tablespoon olive oil

1 small leek (200g), sliced thinly

½ trimmed celery stick (50g), chopped finely

2 teaspoons plain flour

2 teaspoons fresh thyme leaves

¼ cup (60ml) cream

1 teaspoon wholegrain mustard

2 sheets ready-rolled shortcrust pastry, thawed

1 sheet ready-rolled puff pastry, thawed

1 egg yolk

2 teaspoons sesame seeds

1 Bring stock to the boil in small saucepan. Add chicken; return to the boil. Reduce heat; simmer, covered, about 10 minutes or until chicken is cooked. Remove from heat; stand chicken in poaching liquid 10 minutes. Remove chicken; chop finely. Reserve ¼ cup of the poaching liquid.

2 Heat oil in medium saucepan; cook leek and celery, stirring, until leek softens. Add flour and half of the thyme; cook, stirring, until mixture bubbles and thickens. Gradually stir in reserved liquid and cream; cook, stirring, until mixture boils and thickens. Stir in chicken and mustard. Cool 10 minutes.

3 Preheat oven to 220°C/200°C fan-forced. Oil eight holes in each of two 12-hole (⅓-cup/80ml) muffin pans.

4 Using 7cm cutter, cut 16 rounds from shortcrust pastry; press 1 round into each pan hole. Spoon 1 tablespoon of the chicken mixture into each pastry case. Using 6cm cutter, cut 16 rounds from puff pastry; top chicken pies with puff pastry lids. Brush lids with egg yolk; sprinkle with remaining thyme and sesame seeds. Cut two small slits in each lid.

5 Bake pies about 20 minutes or until browned lightly.

Curried chicken pie

PREPARATION TIME 30 MINUTES **COOKING TIME** 1 HOUR 15 MINUTES **SERVES** 8

2 tablespoons olive oil

750g chicken thigh fillets, cut into 1.5cm pieces

1 large kumara (500g), chopped finely

¾ cup (225g) butter chicken simmer sauce

½ cup (125ml) cream

⅓ cup coarsely chopped fresh coriander leaves

15 sheets fillo pastry

100g butter, melted

Simmer sauces are readily available in supermarkets, in many flavours and varying degrees of spiciness and heat — any of these would be suitable for this recipe.

1 Heat half of the oil in large saucepan; cook chicken, in batches, until browned. Heat remaining oil in same pan; cook kumara until browned. Return chicken to pan.

2 Add simmer sauce and cream to chicken mixture; bring to the boil. Reduce heat; simmer, partially covered, about 15 minutes or until sauce thickens and chicken and kumara are cooked. Stir in coriander; cool.

3 Preheat oven to 200°C/180°C fan-forced. Grease 24cm springform tin.

4 Meanwhile, layer three sheets of pastry, brushing each with some of the butter. Fold in half lengthways, place across the base and up the side of tin with edges overhanging. Repeat with another nine sheets, overlapping strips clockwise around pan until covered.

5 Spoon chicken mixture into tin, trim pastry to be level with top edge of the tin. Layer remaining three pastry sheets, brushing with butter. Fold in half crossways. Place pastry on top of pie, trim pastry to a round a little larger than the tin. Tuck pastry edge down sides of tin, brush top with butter. Place pie on an oven tray.

6 Bake pie about 45 minutes or until browned. Stand pie in tin 15 minutes before cutting.

Hungarian veal goulash pies

PREPARATION TIME 25 MINUTES **COOKING TIME** 1 HOUR 15 MINUTES (PLUS COOLING TIME) **MAKES** 6

600g diced veal shoulder

2 tablespoons plain flour

1 tablespoon ground
sweet paprika

¼ teaspoon ground
cayenne pepper

¼ cup (60ml) olive oil

1 small brown onion (80g),
chopped finely

1 clove garlic, crushed

2 teaspoons caraway seeds

400g can diced tomatoes

¼ cup (60ml) beef stock

1 medium red capsicum (200g)
cut into 2cm pieces

1 medium unpeeled potato
(200g), cut into 2cm pieces

¼ cup (60g) sour cream

¼ cup coarsely chopped
fresh flat-leaf parsley

2 sheets ready-rolled shortcrust
pastry, thawed

1 sheet ready-rolled puff pastry,
thawed

1 egg

1 Coat veal in combined flour, paprika and pepper; shake off excess. Heat 2 tablespoons of the oil in large saucepan; cook veal, in batches, until browned all over.

2 Heat remaining oil in same pan; cook onion and garlic until soft. Return veal to pan with seeds, tomatoes and stock; bring to the boil. Simmer, covered, 25 minutes. Add capsicum and potato; simmer, uncovered, further 15 minutes or until veal is tender and sauce has thickened. Stir in sour cream; cook until heated through. Cool; stir in parsley.

3 Preheat oven to 200°C/180°C fan-forced. Grease 6-hole texas (¾-cup/180ml) muffin pan.

4 Cut six rounds from shortcrust pastry using 12cm cutter; press into pan holes. Cut six rounds from puff pastry using 9cm cutter.

5 Spoon goulash into pastry cases; top with puff pastry rounds. Press edges to seal. Brush tops with egg. Cut a small slit in top of each pie.

6 Bake pies about 25 minutes. Stand pies in pan 5 minutes before serving.

Caramelised leek and brie tartlets

PREPARATION TIME 10 MINUTES **COOKING TIME** 15 MINUTES **MAKES** 24

1 tablespoon olive oil

25g butter

2 medium leeks (700g), sliced thinly

1 clove garlic, crushed

1 tablespoon brown sugar

1 tablespoon white wine vinegar

2 sheets ready-rolled puff pastry, thawed

200g wheel brie cheese

24 sprigs lemon thyme

Camembert cheese would do just as well as brie in this recipe. If you can't find lemon thyme, ordinary thyme or even rosemary would work just as well.

1 Preheat oven to 200°C/180°C fan-forced. Grease two 12-hole (⅓-cup/80ml) muffin pans.

2 Heat oil and butter in large frying pan; cook leek, stirring, about 5 minutes or until soft. Add garlic, sugar and vinegar; cook, stirring, further 5 minutes or until leek caramelises.

3 Cut pastry into 24 x 6cm-squares; press a square of pastry into each pan hole. Spoon leek into pastry cases. Cut cheese into quarters; cut each quarter into six thin wedges. Place a wedge of cheese and a sprig of thyme on top of each tartlet.

4 Bake tartlets about 15 minutes. Stand tartlets in pan for 5 minutes before serving.

Lamb masala pies with raita

PREPARATION TIME 25 MINUTES **COOKING TIME** 1 HOUR (PLUS COOLING TIME) **MAKES** 6

2 tablespoons vegetable oil

1 medium brown onion (150g), chopped finely

600g diced lamb

⅓ cup (100g) tikka masala paste

400g can diced tomatoes

¼ cup (60ml) water

½ cup (125ml) cream

¼ cup coarsely chopped fresh coriander

2 sheets ready-rolled shortcrust pastry, thawed

1 sheet ready-rolled puff pastry, thawed

1 egg

RAITA

200g yogurt

1 small lebanese cucumber (130g), seeded, chopped finely

2 tablespoons finely chopped fresh mint

The cucumber seeds will make the raita too watery. The quickest and most efficient way to seed a cucumber is by using a teaspoon. Cut the cucumber (peeled or unpeeled) in half lengthways, then using the tip of a teaspoon, scratch out the seeds from the centre of the two halves.

1 Heat oil in large saucepan; cook onion, stirring, until soft. Add lamb; cook, stirring, until browned lightly. Add paste; cook, stirring, until fragrant. Add tomatoes, water and cream; bring to the boil. Simmer, uncovered, about 25 minutes or until lamb is tender and sauce is thickened. Cool; stir in coriander.

2 Preheat oven to 200°C/180°C fan-forced. Grease 6-hole texas (¾-cup/180ml) muffin pan.

3 Cut six rounds from shortcrust pastry using 12cm cutter; press into pan holes. Cut six rounds from puff pastry using 9cm cutter.

4 Spoon lamb curry into pastry cases; top with puff pastry rounds. Press edges together to seal. Brush tops with egg. Cut a small slit in top of each pie.

5 Bake pies about 25 minutes. Stand pies in pan 5 minutes before serving.

6 Meanwhile, make raita.

7 Serve lamb masala pies with raita.

RAITA Combine ingredients in small bowl.

Equipment

They are made from a vast array of materials, they all have their good and not-so good points.
Price is a guide to quality, so choose carefully. Good cake pans should last you a lifetime.

1 Dolly Varden pans are mostly used for making cakes which become the skirt of a doll. The doll is inserted (often without legs) into the top of the cake. The pans are available in cookware shops and cake decorating suppliers.

2 Square cake pans like the ones pictured can be bought or hired from cake decorating suppliers, they are made from good quality tin, they need to be lined well, and the cakes baked 10°C lower than if the mixture was baked in an aluminium cake pan.

3 Non-stick jelly moulds come in all shapes and sizes. Can be used for making various chilled desserts and small cakes.

4 Muffin pans can be found in many different finishes and sizes, non-stick pans are good if the finish is not scratched.

5 Fluted ring pans cook cake mixtures well as the cakes cook from the centre and the outside. Bundt, gugelhupf and tube pans are all types of ring pans.

6 Round cake pans pictured, are the same type as the square pans, see number 2 for information.

7 Bar cake pans are a handy size and great to freeze. Most cakes baked in bar pans will crack, this is because the mixture is in a narrow area, which forces the mixture up quite quickly, causing the cakes to crack.

8 Shallow, slice, slab or sandwich pans are multi-purpose mostly used for recipes that bake quickly, usually under 30 minutes.

9 Small round pans can be used for muffins, puddings, cakes, jellies, desserts etc.

Baking Techniques

MEASURING

All our measures are level. To use a measuring cup properly for dry ingredients, shake the ingredient loosely into the cup, don't pack it in, unless the recipe directs you to do this. Level off the surface with the blade of a knife or metal spatula.

GREASING & FLOURING PANS

Cake pans need greasing, even non-stick surfaces need a light greasing. You can use cooking oil spray, or melted butter or margarine. Use a pastry brush to grease the pans evenly. Sprinkle a little flour into the pan.

FLOURING PANS

Shake, tap and then turn the pan until the surface is evenly floured. Tap the pan, upside-down, to get rid of the excess flour.

MARBLING

For a marbled effect in a cake (or frosting), dollop the various coloured mixtures into the cake pan, then pull a skewer through the mixtures.

TESTING CAKES

Use a skewer to test most cakes (not sponges or fruit cakes). Take the cake out of the oven, close the oven door, push a skewer gently through the thickest part of the cake to the bottom of the pan. Pull the skewer out: if the skewer is clean the cake is done; if the skewer has uncooked mixture on it, cook the cake further.

COOLING CAKES

Most cakes are turned out of their pans, (after a few minutes of standing) onto wire racks to cool. Sponges are always turned out of their pans as soon as they come out of the oven. Rich fruit cakes are usually cooled in their pans.

INVERTING CAKES

Place another wire rack on top of the cake, sandwiching the cake between the two racks, then turn the cake right way up.

SYRUPING CAKES

Syrup cakes almost always have hot syrup poured over them when they're hot. Sometimes the syrup is poured over them while they're still in their cake pans, sometimes the cakes are turned out. In this case, the wire rack has a tray placed under it to catch the drips of syrup. This overflow should be poured back over the cake.

LINING ROUND CAKE PANS
Grease the cake pan evenly, with either cooking-oil spray or melted butter or margarine. The greasing will ensure that the cake turns out of the pan nicely, also, it will hold the lining paper in place.

TRACING BASE-LINING PAPER
Use the base of the pan as a guide to trace around the pan onto the lining paper. Cut out the shape, slightly inside the tracing.

CUTTING SIDE-LINING PAPER
Cut a strip of paper long enough to cover the side of the pan in one piece, and overlap a little at the ends. The strip needs to be wide enough to cover the side, plus about 2cm for the base, plus about 5cm to extend the paper above the side of the pan.

SNIPPING SIDE-LINING PAPER
Make a fold about 2cm wide, along one of the long sides of the strip of paper. Snip along the strip, up to the fold, at about 2cm intervals.

LINING SIDE OF PAN
Position the long strip of paper around the inside of the pan.

LINING BASE OF PAN
Position the base-lining paper in the pan.

LINING SQUARE CAKE PANS
Cut strips of baking or greaseproof paper long enough to cover the base and sides of the pan. Also long enough to give you some paper to hold, in case you need to lift the cake from the pan. Mostly, the pans are greased before they're lined, this method is usually used when mixtures are very wet or sticky.

LINING LAMINGTON OR BAR PANS
Cut a strip of baking or greaseproof paper long enough to cover the base and sides of the pan, also long enough to give you some paper to hold, in case you need to lift the cake from the pan. The recipes will tell you to line the pan lengthways or crossways, whatever is necessary.

BISCUITS

Always allow some space for biscuits to spread during cooking. The amount of spreading depends on the raising agent in the recipe and the consistency of the mixture. Bake biscuits either on a greased tray or baking-paper-lined tray. We grease under the baking paper to hold the paper in position, but this isn't really necessary.

FLATTENING BISCUITS

A lot of recipes call for biscuits to be flattened slightly in some way. This can be done by hand, or, like the picture, done with the floured tines of a fork.

TO TEST IF BISCUITS ARE COOKED

Inexperienced bakers tend to overcook biscuits. The best and easiest way to make sure they're done, is to check the cooking time, then, look at them to see if they're browned and firm, then, give one biscuit a gentle push on the tray with your thumb or finger. If the biscuit moves, even if it's still soft, they're done, they'll firm as they cool.

PALMIERS

These are so easy to make, with store-bought frozen puff pastry, which takes only a little time to thaw, ready to roll and shape. Follow recipes for any flavourings, fillings, etc. Roll one side of the pastry towards the middle of the sheet, then roll the other side to meet in the middle.

MORE ON PALMIERS

Press the two rolled up sides together so they join in the middle.

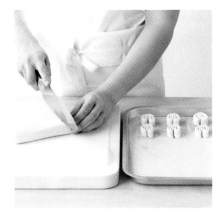

CUTTING PALMIERS

Cut palmier shapes crossways into about 1cm pieces, place them on baking-paper-lined oven trays, allowing room for them to spread. Bake as directed in the recipe.

DRIED PINEAPPLE

Place a wire rack over an oven tray. Brush the thinly sliced fresh pineapple, both sides, with the sugar syrup (see recipe page 228). Dry the pineapple in the oven as directed in the recipe.

SHAPING DRIED PINEAPPLE

As soon as the pineapple is dried, it should have some suppleness left, use tongs to lift the slices carefully from the tray, pinch the centre of each slice with your fingers, then gently shape the flowers, place over an upturned egg carton, (they will be cool enough to handle), then leave them to cool completely.

CHECKERBOARD COOKIES
This is easier than it looks, check the recipe on page 298. Turn the bars out of the pans onto a chopping board.

SLICING BARS
Using a long-bladed sharp knife, cut each bar into three slices, re-stack the slices, then cut each bar into three slices, giving you a total of nine slices from each bar.

ASSEMBLING BARS
Re-stack the slices, alternating the colours, (brush each slice with egg white) in a checkerboard pattern, refrigerate for 30 minutes.

SLICING COOKIES
Cut the bars crossways into 1cm slices, place them on prepared trays, bake as directed in the recipe.

CHOUX PASTRY

Choux pastry is used to make profiteroles (cream puffs), éclairs etc. After the butter and water (see recipe page 461) have been brought to the boil, the flour is immediately added to the saucepan, and stirred vigorously (the mixture is quite stiff) over the heat until the ingredients come together and pull away from the side and base of the pan.

MORE ON CHOUX PASTRY

Transfer the hot mixture to a small high-sided bowl, the beaters need to be right in the mixture. Use an electric mixer to gradually beat in the egg(s), do this on a medium speed. It can be done by hand, but it's hard work. The mixture is ready when all the eggs have been added and the mixture becomes smooth and glossy.

TARTE TATIN

Pack the fruit as tightly as you can into the dish, cut-side up, pour the caramel over the fruit.

PASTRY FOR TARTE TATIN

The pastry should be rolled out a little larger than the dish to allow for the pastry to shrink during the cooking. Tuck the excess pastry down between the side of the dish and the fruit.

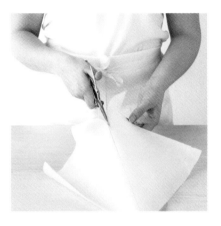

PAPER PIPING BAG
Cut a square of baking or greaseproof paper in half diagonally, be fussy about cutting the paper neatly and cleanly with sharp scissors.

MAKING A PAPER PIPING BAG
Hold the triangle of paper so the apex is pointing towards you, fold one corner over and around to form a cone, then fold the other corner over and around to finish the cone shape.

SHAPING A PAPER PIPING BAG
Make sure the three points of the triangle are together, and the two sides of the paper are aligned as straight as possible. If you've made a good bag, you should not be able to see through it at the pointy end. Wriggle the paper around until it's all straight.

FINISHING A PAPER PIPING BAG
Fold a little of the top of the bag over to hold the points together, then staple it, this is the best way to hold the bag together. Half-fill the bag with icing, cream, melted chocolate etc, fold the top of the bag over to enclose the icing. Use sharp scissors to snip a tiny hole at the pointy end, you can always make the hole bigger if you need to.

GINGERBREAD HOUSE

Follow the recipe on page 584, cut out the patterns for the roof and walls of the house. Make the royal icing, this makes wonderful mortar, as it dries really hard.

ROOF FOR THE HOUSE

Reinforce the two roof pieces with wooden skewers. Pipe or drizzle lines of royal icing from corner to corner on the underneath surface of each roof piece. Position a skewer from one corner to another, then pieces of another skewer across the other line to butt up against the whole skewer. Leave the icing to dry completely.

ASSEMBLING THE HOUSE

Pipe or drizzle royal icing around the side and bottom edges of all the walls, assemble on a board, support the walls inside and out with cans; leave to set and dry. Pipe or drizzle more royal icing on the top sections of the walls, to hold the roof on. Position the roof pieces, leave to set and dry before decorating with royal icing and lollies.

BUTTERFLY CAKES

Use a sharp pointed vegetable knife to cut a small round cavity out of the centres of patty cakes. Cut the small pieces of cake in half to make the butterfly's wings. Fill the cavities of the cakes with jam and cream (or the fillings of your choice). Position the wings on the cream, then dust the cakes with a little sifted icing sugar.

SUGAR SYRUP

Sugar syrup can be used as is, or can be caramelised to various strengths and colours by further boiling. Use a heavy-based pan. Add sugar and the water to the pan, stir over a high heat, without boiling, until the grains of sugar have dissolved. Use a brush dipped in water to brush grains from the side of the pan.

CANDY THERMOMETER

To use a candy thermometer correctly, put it in a small saucepan of cold water, bring it to the boil, when the syrup begins to boil, put the thermometer in the syrup. Leave the thermometer in the syrup until the temperature is reached, return it to the pan of boiling water, turn the heat off, cool.

MORE ON SUGAR SYRUP

The colour this sugar syrup has become is right for all sorts of uses, for making decorations, toffees for the kids, for coating fruit etc. If you're not using a thermometer, the water test is perfect. Before you test the toffee, remove it from the heat and let the bubbles subside completely.

THE TOFFEE WATER TEST

Drop about a teaspoon of the hot toffee into a glass of tap-cold water, it will set immediately it touches the water. There are different stages, the first stage is called "small crack", then it goes to "hard crack", and of course there are stages in between. The important thing is to make sure the toffee will set enough for your needs.

MORE ON TESTING TOFFEE

Take the toffee out of the water, and snap it with your fingers, if you want the toffee even harder, return it to the heat and boil it some more. It won't take long to become darker and harder — allow for the fact that it will continue to cook, even after it comes off the heat, while the bubbles subside.

CREME BRULEE

For the best brûlée topping, you really need a blow torch like chefs use. In the absence of a blow torch, preheat a grill to its highest setting, stand the dishes in an ice-filled flameproof dish, gently press sifted brown sugar over the custards. Grill as fast as possible to caramelise the sugar.

BEATING EGG WHITES

To beat egg whites, the beaters and bowl must be clean and dry, whites will not beat up if they're in touch with fat. Use a deep, not wide, bowl so the beaters can get into the whites to create volume. Start beating on a low speed, gradually increasing the speed as the whites thicken to the correct stage for the recipe.

FRIANDS

Egg whites used for friands must not be beaten too much at all, use a whisk, or a fork, it doesn't really matter. The important thing is not to beat air into the whites, they simply need to be broken up evenly. Air only creates pockets, bubbles and tunnels in the dense friand mixture.

MELTING CHOCOLATE

Chocolate must be melted carefully and gently. This method is the safest: place a heatproof bowl (preferably glass or china) containing the roughly chopped chocolate, over a pan of barely simmering water. The water mustn't touch the base of the bowl. Stir chocolate occasionally until smooth, remove from the pan as soon as it's melted.

GANACHE

Ganache is mostly used for frosting or filling. It can be used as a coating, in this case, the mixture is cooled but used before it thickens. When it's used as a frosting or filling, the ganache is cooled, sometimes in the fridge, it needs an occasional stir with a wooden spoon to mix the ingredients. It can also be whipped after it has been refrigerated.

FOLDING-IN EGG WHITES

This is a skill you must learn if you're going to become a good baker. It can be tricky when folding whites into a heavy mixture (such as chocolate or cake batter), or a lot of mixture. To loosen such mixtures, fold about a quarter of the whites through, using a spatula or whisk, then fold half the remaining whites through.

MORE ON FOLDING

The action of folding means that you have to pull the ingredients together in such a way that you keep the air in the mixture. We prefer to use a rubber spatula for this, as you can scrape the side of the bowl, as you fold the ingredients together.

RICH FRUIT CAKE

It's important to line the cake pan properly for a good shaped cake, also, the lining paper protects the cake during the long slow cooking time. We use one or two sheets of brown paper, and two or three sheets of baking or greaseproof paper. See pages 632 & 633 for how to line a round cake pan — use this for square pans too.

FRUIT CAKE MIXTURE

Dollop, then push large spoonfuls (or handfuls) into the corners of the pan, to hold the paper firmly in position, this helps to minimise air bubbles. When all the mixture is in the pan, level it with your hand or spoon, then drop the pan from about a height of 20cm onto the bench to settle the mixture into the pan.

LEVELLING FRUIT CAKE MIXTURE

Use a wet spatula to level the top of the mixture as evenly as you can. If you want to decorate the top of the cake with nuts or cherries etc, do it now, before you bake the cake.

ROLLING ROULADES

The most common method is to turn the cake from the pan, trim all sides, roll the hot cake loosely with sugared paper, unroll, then re-roll it without the paper, cool; unroll, fill it, then re-roll it. Another method is to cool the hot cake flat before filling and rolling. Another method is to roll the trimmed hot cake, unroll it, and cool it flat before filling.

Conversion Charts

One Australian metric measuring cup or jug holds approximately 250ml; one Australian metric tablespoon holds 20ml; one Australian metric teaspoon holds 5ml.

The difference between one country's measuring cups and another's is within a two- or three-teaspoon variance, which is only 10 or 15ml and will not affect your cooking results. Most countries, including the US, the UK and New Zealand, use a 15ml tablespoon.

All cup and spoon measurements are level. The most accurate way of measuring dry ingredients is to weigh them. When measuring liquids, use a clear glass or plastic jug with metric markings at eye level.

In this book we used large eggs with an average weight of 60g each. Please note that those who might be at risk from the effects of salmonella poisoning (such as pregnant women, the elderly or young children) should consult their doctor before eating raw eggs.

OVEN TEMPERATURES

These oven temperatures are only a guide for conventional ovens. For fan-forced ovens, check the manufacturer's manual.

	°C (CELSIUS)	°F (FAHRENHEIT)	GAS MARK
Very slow	120	250	½
Slow	150	275-300	1-2
Moderately slow	160	325	3
Moderate	180	350-375	4-5
Moderately hot	200	400	6
Hot	220	425-450	7-8
Very hot	240	475	9

DRY MEASURES

METRIC	IMPERIAL
15g	½oz
30g	1oz
60g	2oz
90g	3oz
125g	4oz (¼lb)
155g	5oz
185g	6oz
220g	7oz
250g	8oz (½lb)
280g	9oz
315g	10oz
345g	11oz
375g	12oz (¾lb)
410g	13oz
440g	14oz
470g	15oz
500g	16oz (1lb)
750g	24oz (1½lb)
1kg	32oz (2lb)

LIQUID MEASURES

METRIC	IMPERIAL
30ml	1 fluid oz
60ml	2 fluid oz
100ml	3 fluid oz
125ml	4 fluid oz
150ml	5 fluid oz (¼ pint/1 gill)
190ml	6 fluid oz
250ml	8 fluid oz
300ml	10 fluid oz (½ pint)
500ml	16 fluid oz
600ml	20 fluid oz (1 pint)
1000ml (1 litre)	1¾ pints

LENGTH MEASURES

METRIC	IMPERIAL
3mm	⅛in
6mm	¼in
1cm	½in
2cm	¾in
2.5cm	1in
5cm	2in
6cm	2½in
8cm	3in
10cm	4in
13cm	5in
15cm	6in
18cm	7in
20cm	8in
23cm	9in
25cm	10in
28cm	11in
30cm	12in (1ft)

GLOSSARY

Glossary

ALLSPICE also known as pimento or jamaican pepper; so-named because it tastes like a combination of nutmeg, cumin, clove and cinnamon. Available whole (a dark-brown berry the size of a pea) or ground, and used in both sweet and savoury dishes.

ALMONDS flat, pointy-tipped nuts having a pitted brown shell enclosing a creamy white kernel which is covered by a brown skin.

blanched brown skins removed.

essence made with almond oil and alcohol or another agent. *see essence/extract*

flaked paper-thin slices.

meal also known as ground almonds; nuts are powdered to a coarse flour texture for use in baking or as a thickening agent.

slivered small pieces cut lengthways.

vienna toffee-coated almonds.

AMARETTI small Italian-style macaroons (biscuit or cookie) made with ground almonds.

APPLE CONCENTRATE made from apples; juice is extracted from the fruit then pasteurised and evaporated under vacuum. Available at health food stores.

ARROWROOT a starch made from the rhizome of a Central American plant, used mostly as a thickening agent. Cornflour can be substituted but does not make as clear a glaze and imparts its own taste.

BACON RASHERS also known as bacon slices; made from cured and smoked pork side. *Middle rashers* are thin strips of belly pork having a lean, rather round piece of loin at one end; *streaky bacon* is the same cut minus the round loin section.

BAGEL small ring-shaped bread roll; yeast-based but egg-less, with a dense, chewy texture and shiny crust. A true bagel is boiled in water before it's baked.

BAKE BLIND a cooking term to describe baking a pie shell or pastry case before filling is added. If a filling does not need to be baked or is very wet, you may need to "blind-bake" the unfilled shell. To bake blind, ease the pastry into a pan or dish, place on an oven tray; line the pastry with baking paper then fill with dried beans, uncooked rice or "baking beans" (also called pie weights). Bake according to the recipe's directions then cool before adding the suggested filling. *see also pages 618 & 619*

BAKING PAPER also known as parchment, silicon paper or non-stick baking paper; not to be confused with greaseproof or waxed paper. Used to line pans before cooking and baking; also to make piping bags (*see page 638*).

BAKING POWDER a raising agent consisting mainly of two parts cream of tartar to one part bicarbonate of soda (baking soda). The acid and alkaline combination, when moistened and heated, gives off carbon dioxide which aerates and lightens a mixture during baking.

BAR CAKE PAN *see pages 628 & 629*

BASIL, SWEET the most common type of basil; used extensively in Italian dishes and one of the main ingredients in pesto.

BEEF

gravy boneless stewing beef cut from shin; slow-cooked, imbues stocks, soups and casseroles with a gelatine richness. Cut crossways, with bone in, is osso buco.

minced also known as ground beef.

skirt steak lean, flavourful coarse-grained cut from the inner thigh. Needs slow-cooking; good for stews or casseroles.

BEETROOT also known as red beets; firm, round root vegetable. Can be grated or finely chopped; boiled or steamed then diced or sliced; or roasted then mashed.

BESAN *see flour*

BICARBONATE OF SODA also known as baking soda; a mild alkali used as a leavening agent in baking.

BISCUITS also known as cookies; almost always an "eat-in-your-hand"-sized soft or crisp sweet cake.

butternut snap crunchy biscuit made from rolled oats, coconut and golden syrup.

plain chocolate crunchy biscuit made from cocoa.

plain sweet crisp, sweet and vanilla flavoured.

BLANCHING a cooking term to describe the act of plunging an ingredient, usually vegetables, briefly into boiling water, draining then placing it into a bowl of iced water, or rinsing under cold water, to immediately halt the cooking process. Blanching is used when the cooking time is to be minimal; when it is to precede another cooking process, as with certain hard vegetables before stir-frying; or to loosen the skin on fruit before peeling.

BLOOD ORANGE a virtually seedless citrus fruit with blood-red-streaked rind and flesh; sweet, non-acidic, salmon-coloured pulp and juice having slight strawberry or raspberry overtones. Thought to have occurred in nature by accident in 17th-century Sicily. The juice can be drunk straight or used in cocktails, sauces, sorbets and jellies; can be frozen for use in cooking when the growing season finishes. The rind is not as bitter as that of an ordinary orange; grated or finely sliced, it can be strewn over salads, puddings or cakes.

BRAN the outer casing (the husk of various cereal grains such as wheat or oats) made up of several layers to protect the inner kernel; rich in vitamin B and carbohydrates and a valuable source of fibre. Usually removed when a grain is milled for flour, but is added to many breakfast cereals or eaten sprinkled over food as a dietary supplement.

BRANDY short for brandywine, the translation of the Dutch "brandwijn", burnt wine. A general term for a liqueur distilled from wine grapes (usually white), it is used as the basis for many sweet-to-dry spirits made with fruits. Cognac and Armagnac are two of the finest aged brandies available.

BRAZIL NUT native to South America, a triangular-shelled oily nut with an unusually tender white flesh and a mild, rich flavour. Good for eating as well as cooking, the nuts can be eaten raw or cooked, or can be ground into meal for baking.

BREADCRUMBS, STALE crumbs made by grating, blending or processing 1- or 2-day-old bread.

BRIOCHE French in origin; a rich, yeast-leavened, cake-like bread made with butter and eggs. Most common form is the *brioche à tête*, a round fluted roll topped with a much smaller ball of dough. Eaten freshly baked or toasted; available from cake or specialty bread shops. *see also page 509*

BRUISE a cooking term to describe the slight crushing given to aromatic ingredients, particularly herbs, with the flat side of a heavy knife or cleaver to release flavour and aroma.

BUNDT PAN *see fluted ring pans on pages 628 & 629*

BUTTER this book uses salted butter unless stated otherwise; 125g is equal to 1 stick (4 ounces) in other recipes. Butter is basically churned pasteurised cream with salted being the most popular one sold in supermarkets. Unsalted or "sweet" butter has no salt added to the churned cream and is perhaps the most popular butter among pastry-chefs.

BUTTERMILK *see milk*

CACHOUS also called dragées in some countries; minuscule (3mm to 5mm) metallic-looking-but-edible confectionery balls used in cake decorating; available in silver, gold or various colours. *see also page 248*

CAPERS the grey-green buds of a warm climate (usually Mediterranean) shrub, sold either dried and salted or pickled in a vinegar brine; tiny young ones, called baby capers, are also available both in brine or dried in salt. Their pungent taste adds piquancy to a classic steak tartare, tapenade, sauces and condiments.

CAPSICUM also known as pepper or bell pepper. Native to central and South America; found in red, green, yellow, orange or purplish-black varieties. Discard seeds and membranes before use.

CARAWAY SEEDS the small, half-moon-shaped dried seed from a member of the parsley family; adds a sharp anise flavour when used in both sweet and savoury dishes. Used widely, in such different

foods as rye bread, harissa and the classic Hungarian fresh cheese, liptauer.

CARDAMOM a spice native to India and used extensively in its cuisine; can be purchased in pod, seed or ground form. Has a distinctive aromatic, sweetly rich flavour and is one of the world's most expensive spices. Used to flavour curries, rice dishes, sweet desserts and cakes.

CASHEWS plump, kidney-shaped, golden-brown nuts having a distinctive sweet, buttery flavour and containing about 48 per cent fat. Because of this high fat content, they should be kept, sealed tightly, under refrigeration to avoid becoming rancid. We use roasted unsalted cashews in this book, unless otherwise stated; they're available from health-food stores and most supermarkets. Roasting cashews brings out their intense nutty flavour.

CAYENNE PEPPER *see chilli*

CHEESE

bocconcini from the diminutive of "boccone", meaning mouthful in Italian; walnut-sized, baby mozzarella, a delicate, semi-soft, white cheese traditionally made from buffalo milk. Sold fresh, it spoils rapidly so will only keep, refrigerated in brine, for 1 or 2 days at the most.

brie often referred in France as the queen of cheeses; soft-ripened cow-milk cheese with a delicate, creamy texture and a rich, sweet taste that varies from buttery to mushroomy. Best served at room temperature after a brief period of ageing, brie should have a bloomy white rind and creamy, voluptuous centre which becomes runny with ripening.

cheddar the most common cow-milk tasty cheese; should be aged, hard and have a pronounced bite. We use a version having no more than 20 per cent fat when calling for low-fat cheese.

cottage fresh, white, unripened curd cheese with a lumpy consistency and mild, sweet flavour. Fat content ranges between 15 per cent to 55 per cent, determined by whether it is made from whole, low-fat or fat-free cow milk.

cream commonly known as philadelphia or philly; a soft cow-milk cheese with a fat content ranging from 14 per cent to 33 per cent.

fetta Greek in origin; a crumbly textured goat- or sheep-milk cheese having a sharp, salty taste. Ripened and stored in salted whey; particularly good cubed and tossed into salads. We use a version having no more than 15 per cent fat when calling for low-fat cheese.

goat made from goat milk, has an earthy, strong taste. Available in soft, crumbly and firm textures, in various shapes and sizes, and sometimes rolled in ash or herbs.

gruyère a hard-rind Swiss cheese with small holes and a nutty, slightly salty flavour. A popular cheese for soufflés.

mascarpone an Italian fresh cultured-cream product made in much the same way as yogurt. Whiteish to creamy yellow in colour, with a buttery-rich, luscious texture. Soft, creamy and spreadable, it is used in many Italian desserts and as an accompaniment to a dessert of fresh fruit.

mozzarella soft, spun-curd cheese; originating in southern Italy where it was traditionally made from water-buffalo milk. Now generally manufactured from cow milk, it is the most popular pizza cheese because of its low melting point and

elasticity when heated (used for texture rather than flavour). We use a version having no more than 17.5 per cent fat when calling for low-fat cheese.

parmesan also known as parmigiano, parmesan is a hard, grainy cow-milk cheese which originated in the Parma region of Italy. The curd for this cheese is salted in brine for a month before being aged for up to 2 years, preferably in humid conditions. Parmesan is grated or flaked and used for pasta, salads and soups; it is also eaten on its own with fruit. Reggiano is the best parmesan, aged for a minimum 2 years and made only in the Italian region of Emilia-Romagna.

pizza cheese a commercial blend of varying proportions of processed grated mozzarella, cheddar and parmesan.

ricotta a soft, sweet, moist, white cow-milk cheese with a low fat content (about 8.5 per cent) and a slightly grainy texture. The name roughly translates as "cooked again" and refers to ricotta's manufacture from a whey that is itself a by-product of other cheese making.

tasty generic name for a variety of processed and naturally made cheddar-like table cheeses.

CHERRY small, soft stone fruit varying in colour from yellow to dark red. Sweet cherries are eaten whole and in desserts while sour cherries such as the morello variety are used for jams, preserves, pies and savoury dishes (particularly good with game birds and meats).

glacé also known as candied cherries; boiled in heavy sugar syrup and then dried. Used in cakes, breads and sweets. *see also page 120*

CHICKEN

barbecued we use already-cooked whole barbecued chickens weighing about 900g apiece in our recipes. Skin discarded and bones removed, this size chicken provides 4 cups (400g) shredded meat or about 3 cups (400g) coarsely chopped meat.

breast fillet breast halved, skinned and boned.

thigh fillet thigh with skin and centre bone removed; makes flavoursome mince.

CHILLI always use rubber gloves when seeding and chopping fresh chillies as they can burn your skin. We use unseeded chillies in our recipes because the seeds contain the heat; use fewer chillies rather than seeding the lot.

cayenne also known as cayenne pepper; a thin-fleshed, long, extremely hot, dried red chilli native to South America, usually purchased ground.

flakes also sold as crushed chilli; dehydrated deep-red extremely fine slices and whole seeds; good in cooking or for sprinkling over a dish as one does with salt and pepper.

thai also known as "scuds"; tiny, very hot and bright red in colour.

CHIVES related to the onion and leek; has a subtle onion flavour. Used more for flavour than as an ingredient; chopped finely, they're good in sauces, dressings, omelettes or as a garnish. Chinese (or garlic) chives have rougher, flatter leaves than simple chives, and possess a pink-tinged teardrop-shaped flowering bud at the end; used as a salad green, or steamed and eaten as a vegetable.

CHOCOLATE

cherry ripe dark chocolate bar made with coconut and cherries; standard size bar weighs 55g.

Choc Bits also known as chocolate chips or chocolate morsels; available in milk, white and dark chocolate. Made of cocoa liquor, cocoa butter, sugar and an emulsifier, these hold their shape in baking and are ideal for decorating.

cocoa *see cocoa powder*

couverture a term used to describe a fine quality, very rich chocolate high in both cocoa butter and cocoa liquor. Requires tempering when used to coat but not if used in baking, mousses or fillings.

dark cooking also known as compounded chocolate; good for cooking as it doesn't require tempering and sets at room temperature. Made with vegetable fat instead of cocoa butter so it lacks the rich, buttery flavour of eating chocolate. Cocoa butter is the most expensive component in chocolate, so the substitution of a vegetable fat means that compounded chocolate is much cheaper to produce.

dark eating also known as semi-sweet or luxury chocolate; made of a high percentage of cocoa liquor and cocoa butter, and little added sugar. Unless stated otherwise, we use dark eating chocolate in this book as it's ideal for use in desserts and cakes.

Melts small discs of compounded milk, white or dark chocolate ideal for melting and moulding.

milk most popular eating chocolate, mild and very sweet; similar in make-up to dark with the difference being the addition of milk solids.

white contains no cocoa solids but derives its sweet flavour from cocoa butter. Very sensitive to heat.

CHOCOLATE HAZELNUT SPREAD also known as Nutella; made of cocoa powder, hazelnuts, sugar and milk.

CIABATTA in Italian, the word means slipper, the traditional shape of this popular crisp-crusted, open-textured white sourdough bread. A good bread to use for bruschetta.

CINNAMON available both in the piece (called sticks or quills) and ground into powder; one of the world's most common spices, used universally as a sweet, fragrant flavouring for both sweet and savoury foods. The dried inner bark of the shoots of the Sri Lankan native cinnamon tree; much of what is sold as the real thing is in fact cassia, Chinese cinnamon, from the bark of the cassia tree. Less expensive to process than true cinnamon, it is often blended with Sri Lankan cinnamon to produce the type of "cinnamon" most commonly found in supermarkets.

CLOVES dried flower buds of a tropical tree; can be used whole or in ground form. They have a strong scent and taste so should be used sparingly.

COCOA POWDER also known as unsweetened cocoa; cocoa beans (cacao seeds) that have been fermented, roasted, shelled, ground into powder then cleared of most of the fat content. Unsweetened cocoa is used in hot chocolate drink mixtures; milk powder and sugar are added to the ground product.

COCONUT

cream obtained commercially from the first pressing of the coconut flesh alone, without the addition of water; the second pressing (less rich) is sold as coconut milk. Available in cans and cartons at most supermarkets.

desiccated concentrated, dried, unsweetened and finely shredded coconut flesh.

essence synthetically produced from flavouring, oil and alcohol. *see essence/extract*

flaked dried flaked coconut flesh.

milk not the liquid found inside the fruit, which is called coconut water, but the diluted liquid from the second pressing of the white flesh of a mature coconut (the first pressing produces coconut cream). Available in cans and cartons at most supermarkets.

shredded unsweetened thin strips of dried coconut flesh.

COINTREAU *see liqueurs*

CORIANDER also known as cilantro, pak chee or chinese parsley; bright-green-leafed herb having both pungent aroma and taste. Used as an ingredient in a wide variety of cuisines from Mexican to South-East Asian. Often stirred into or sprinkled over a dish just before serving for maximum impact as, like other leafy herbs, its characteristics diminish with cooking. Both the stems and roots of coriander are used in Thai cooking: wash well before chopping. Coriander seeds are dried and sold either whole or ground, and neither form tastes remotely like the fresh leaf but rather like an acrid combination of sage and caraway. Seeds and ground are both used in garam masala, mixed spice, Indian and Thai curry pastes and sauces, sausages, and some breads and desserts.

CORN FLAKES commercially manufactured cereal made of dehydrated then baked crisp flakes of corn. Also available is a prepared finely ground mixture used for coating or crumbing food before frying or baking, sold as "crushed corn flakes" in 300g packages in most supermarkets.

CORN SYRUP is a sweet syrup made by heating cornstarch with water under pressure. It comes in light and dark types and is used in baking and in confectionery. It is sometimes mixed with other sugars such as honey.

CORNFLOUR also known as cornstarch. Available made from corn or wheat (wheaten cornflour, gluten-free, gives a lighter texture in cakes); used as a thickening agent in cooking.

CRANBERRY SAUCE a manufactured product made of cranberries cooked in sugar syrup; the astringent flavour goes beautifully with roast poultry and barbecued meats.

CREAM we use fresh pouring cream, also known as pure cream. It has no additives, and contains a minimum fat content of 35 per cent.

thickened a whipping cream that contains a thickener. Has a minimum fat content of 35 per cent.

CREAM OF TARTAR the acid ingredient in baking powder; added to confectionery mixtures to help prevent sugar from crystallising. Keeps frostings creamy and improves volume when beating egg whites.

CREME DE CACAO *see liqueurs*

CREME FRAICHE a mature, naturally fermented cream (minimum fat content 35 per cent) having a velvety texture and slightly tangy, nutty flavour. Crème fraîche, a French variation of sour cream, can boil without curdling and can be used in both sweet and savoury dishes.

CUMIN also known as zeera or comino; resembling caraway in size, cumin is the dried seed of a plant related to the parsley family. Its spicy, almost curry-like flavour is essential to the traditional foods of Mexico, India, North Africa and the Middle East. Available dried as seeds or ground. Black cumin seeds are smaller than standard cumin, and dark brown rather than true black; they are mistakenly confused with kalonji.

CUMQUATS orange-coloured citrus fruit about the size of walnuts. Usually preserved or used for making jam, the skin is always retained.

CURACAO *see liqueurs*

CURRANTS dried tiny, almost black raisins so-named from the grape type native to Corinth, Greece; most often used in jams, jellies and sauces (the best-known of which is the English cumberland sauce). These are not the same as fresh currants, which are the fruit of a plant in the gooseberry family.

CUSTARD POWDER instant mixture used to make pouring custard; similar to North American instant pudding mixes.

DATES fruit of the date palm tree, eaten fresh or dried, on their own or in prepared dishes. About 4cm to 6cm in length, oval and plump, thin-skinned, with a honey-sweet flavour and sticky texture. Best known, perhaps, for their inclusion in sticky toffee pudding; also found in muesli; muffins, scones and cakes; compotes and stewed fruit desserts. *see also page 120*

DILL also known as dill weed; used fresh or dried, in seed form or ground. Its anise/celery sweetness flavours the food of the Scandinavian countries, and Germany and Greece. Distinctive feathery, frond-like fresh leaves are grassier and more subtle than the dried version or the seeds (which slightly resemble caraway in flavour). Use dill leaves with smoked salmon and sour cream, poached fish or roast chicken; use the seeds with simply cooked vegetables, or home-baked dark breads.

DISGORGING (or degorging) describes how to rid an uncooked eggplant of its bitter juices. Slice or chop the eggplant as required, place the pieces in a colander or on a sloping surface and sprinkle them, both sides, with enough salt to cover the surface of each piece. Stand for at least half an hour; the salt will turn slightly brown as it absorbs the bitter liquid. Rinse the eggplant well under cold running water then pat dry with absorbent paper before using. This process also helps reduce the amount of oil eggplant will absorb when being fried.

DOCKING PASTRY *see page 619*

DOLLY VARDEN PAN *see pages 628 & 629*

DRAMBUIE *see liqueurs*

DRIED CRANBERRIES dried sweetened cranberries; used in cooking sweet or savoury dishes. Can usually be substituted for or with other dried fruit in most recipes.

DRIED MIXED HERBS a commercial blend of dried crushed thyme, rosemary, marjoram, basil, oregano and sage; available in supermarkets.

EGGPLANT also called aubergine; often thought of as a vegetable but actually a fruit and belongs to the same family as the tomato, chilli and potato. Ranging in size from tiny to very large and in colour from pale green to deep purple. Can be purchased char-grilled, packed in oil, in jars.

EGGS we use large chicken eggs having an average weigh of 60g in our recipes unless stated otherwise. Shell colour is determined by the breed of hen and what it has been fed on; it has nothing to do with quality. As far as the differences between cage, barn-laid and free-range eggs is concerned, nutrient content, value for money and taste have all got to be factored into the equation; in the end, the decision is left to individual preference. Store eggs, in the carton they come in, under refrigeration as soon as you bring them home to slow down deterioration. This helps reduce water loss and protects them from absorbing flavour from other fridge items. Most eggs can be kept, in their carton, in the fridge, for up to 4 weeks. Some recipes in this book call for raw or barely cooked eggs; exercise caution if there is a salmonella problem in your community, particularly in food eaten by children and pregnant women.

EGGWASH beaten egg (white, yolk or both) and milk or water; often brushed over pastry or bread to impart colour or gloss.

EQUIPMENT *see pages 628 & 629*

ESSENCE/EXTRACT an essence is either a distilled concentration of a food quality or an artificial creation of it. Coconut and almond essences are synthetically produced substances used in small amounts to impart their respective flavours to foods. An extract is made by actually extracting the flavour from a food product. In the case of vanilla, pods are soaked, usually in alcohol, to capture the authentic flavour. Both extracts and essences will keep indefinitely if stored in a cool dark place.

FIGS originally from the countries that border the eastern Mediterranean; are best eaten in peak season, at the height of summer. Vary in skin and flesh colour according to type not ripeness: the purple-black mission or black mission fig, with pink flesh, is a rich-flavoured, good all-rounder; the thick-skinned, pale green kadota, another all-purpose fruit, is good canned or dried as well as fresh; the yellow smyrna has nutty-tasting flesh; and the pale olive, golden-skinned adriatic has honey-sweet, light pink flesh. When ripe, figs should be unblemished and bursting with flesh; nectar beads at the base indicate when a fig is at its best. Figs are also glacéd (candied), dried or canned in sugar syrup; these are usually sold at health-food stores, Middle Eastern food shops or specialty cheese counters. *see also page 121*

FIVE-SPICE although the ingredients vary from country to country, five-spice is usually a fragrant mixture of ground cinnamon, cloves, star anise, sichuan pepper and fennel seeds. Used in Chinese and other Asian cooking; available from most supermarkets or Asian food shops.

FLOUR

baker's also known as gluten-enriched, strong or bread-mix flour. Produced from a variety of wheat that has a high gluten (protein) content and is best suited for pizza and bread making: the expansion caused by the yeast and the stretchiness imposed by kneading require a flour that is "strong" enough to handle these stresses. Since domestic breadmakers entered the marketplace, it has become easier to find strong flour; look for it at your supermarket or a health-food store.

besan also known as chickpea flour or gram; made from ground chickpeas so is gluten-free and high in protein. Used in Indian cooking to make dumplings, noodles and chapati; for a batter coating for deep-frying; and as a sauce thickener.

maize milled from maize (corn); finely ground polenta (cornmeal) can be substituted in some instances.

plain also known as all-purpose; unbleached wheat flour is the best for baking: the gluten content ensures a strong dough, which produces a light result. Also used as a thickening agent in sauces and gravies.

rice very fine, almost powdery, gluten-free flour; made from ground white rice. Used in baking, as a thickener, and in some Asian noodles and desserts.

self-raising all-purpose plain or wholemeal flour with baking powder and salt added; can be made at home with plain or wholemeal flour sifted with baking powder in the proportion of 1 cup flour to 2 teaspoons baking powder.

semolina coarsely ground flour milled from durum wheat; the flour used in making gnocchi, pasta and couscous.

wholemeal also known as wholewheat flour; milled with the wheat germ so is higher in fibre and more nutritional than plain flour.

FLUTED RING PAN *see pages 628 & 629*

FOOD COLOURING vegetable-based substance available in liquid, paste or gel form.

FRANGELICO *see liqueurs*

FRUIT MINCE also known as mincemeat. A mixture of dried fruits such as raisins, sultanas and candied peel, nuts, spices, apple, brandy or rum. Is used as a filling for cakes, puddings and fruit mince pies.

GANACHE pronounced gah-nash, a creamy chocolate filling or frosting for cakes. Depending on its intended use, it is made from varying proportions of good-quality chocolate and pouring cream. Other ingredients can be added for flavour, or to increase its richness or gloss. Ganache can be whipped, piped or poured like a glaze, and can be frozen for up to 3 months. *see also page 642*

GARAM MASALA literally meaning blended spices in its northern Indian place of origin; based on varying proportions of cardamom, cinnamon, cloves, coriander, fennel and cumin, roasted and ground together.

GARLIC like onion, a member of the lily family with the edible bulb growing underground. Each bulb is made up of many cloves which, uncooked, can be crushed, sliced, chopped, or used whole, peeled or unpeeled. Garlic powder is the ground product made from dehydrated garlic flakes and is used mostly for convenience purposes.

GELATINE we use dried (powdered) gelatine in the recipes in this book; it's also available in sheet form known as leaf gelatine. A thickening agent made from either collagen, a protein found in animal connective tissue and bones, or certain algae (agar-agar). Three teaspoons of dried gelatine (8g or one sachet) is roughly equivalent to four gelatine leaves. Professionals use leaf gelatine because it generally results in a smoother, clearer consistency; it is also most

commonly used throughout Europe. The two types are interchangable but leaf gelatine gives a much clearer mixture than dried gelatine; it's perfect in dishes where appearance really counts.

GINGER

fresh also known as green or root ginger; the thick gnarled root of a tropical plant. Can be kept, peeled, covered with dry sherry in a jar and refrigerated, or frozen in an airtight container.

glacé fresh ginger root preserved in sugar syrup; crystallised ginger (sweetened with cane sugar) can be substituted if rinsed with warm water and dried before using.

ground also known as powdered ginger; used as a flavouring in baking but cannot be substituted for fresh ginger.

GLACE FRUIT fruit such as pineapple, apricots, peaches and pears that are cooked in a heavy sugar syrup then dried. *see also pages 120 & 121*

GLUCOSE SYRUP also known as liquid glucose, made from wheat starch; used in jam and confectionery making. Available at health-food stores and supermarkets.

GLUTEN-FREE BAKING POWDER used as a leavening agent in bread, cake, pastry or pudding mixtures. Suitable for people having an allergic response to glutens or seeking an alternative to everyday baking powder. *see also baking powder*

GOLDEN SYRUP a by-product of refined sugarcane; pure maple syrup or honey can be substituted. Golden syrup and treacle (a thicker, darker syrup not unlike molasses), also known as flavour syrups, are similar sugar products made by partly breaking down sugar into its component

parts and adding water. Treacle is more viscous, and has a stronger flavour and aroma than golden syrup (which has been refined further and contains fewer impurities, so is lighter in colour and more fluid). Both can be use in baking and for making certain confectionery items.

GRAND MARNIER *see liqueurs*

GRAPEFRUIT one of the largest citrus fruits, grapefruit is available both seedless or with seeds; the seeded variety has more flavour. There are pink seedless and ruby or ruby red varieties in addition to the ordinary yellow fruit. Eat on its own or in salads, sorbets and granitas.

GREASING PANS use butter, margarine, oil or cooking-oil spray to grease baking pans; over-greasing pans can cause food to overbrown. Use absorbent paper or a pastry brush to spread the oil or butter over the pan. Try covering your hand with a small plastic bag then swiping it into the butter or margarine. *see also page 630*

HAZELNUTS also known as filberts; plump, grape-sized, rich, sweet nut having a brown skin that is removed by rubbing heated nuts together vigorously in a tea-towel.

meal is made by grounding the hazelnuts to a coarse flour texture for use in baking or as a thickening agent.

HERBS we specify when to use fresh or dried herbs in this book. Dried (not ground) herbs can be used in the proportion of one to four, ie, use 1 teaspoon dried herbs instead of 4 teaspoons (1 tablespoon) chopped fresh herbs.

HONEY the variety sold in a squeezable container is not suitable for the recipes in this book.

HORSERADISH a vegetable having edible green leaves but mainly grown for its long, pungent white root. Occasionally found fresh in specialty greengrocers and some Asian food shops, but commonly purchased in bottles at the supermarket in two forms: prepared horseradish and horseradish cream. These cannot be substituted one for the other in cooking but both can be used as table condiments. Horseradish cream is a commercially prepared creamy paste consisting of grated horseradish, vinegar, oil and sugar, while prepared horseradish is the preserved grated root.

HUNDREDS AND THOUSANDS also known as 100's & 1000's; tiny sugar-syrup-coated sugar crystals that come in a variety of colours. *see also page 249*

ICE-CREAM we use a good quality ice-cream having 5g of fat per 100ml for the recipes in this book.

ICING SUGAR *see sugar*

IRISH CREAM *see liqueurs*

JAM also known as preserve or conserve; a thickened mixture of a fruit (and occasionally, a vegetable) and sugar. Usually eaten on toast for breakfast, it's also used as a filling or icing for sweet biscuits and cakes.

JELLY CRYSTALS a combination of sugar, gelatine, colours and flavours; when dissolved in water, the solution sets as firm jelly.

JELLY MOULDS *see pages 628 & 629*

JERSEY CARAMELS confectionery made from sugar, glucose, condensed milk, flour, oil and gelatine.

KAFFIR LIME also known as magrood, leech lime or jeruk purut. The wrinkled, bumpy-skinned green fruit of a small citrus tree originally grown in South Africa and South-East Asia. As a rule, only the rind and leaves are used.

KAHLUA *see liqueurs*

KALONJI also known as nigella or black onion seeds. Tiny, angular seeds, black on the outside and creamy within, with a sharp nutty flavour that can be enhanced by frying briefly in a dry hot pan before use. Typically sprinkled over Turkish bread immediately after baking or as an important spice in Indian cooking, kalonji can be found in most Asian and Middle Eastern food shops. Often erroneously called black cumin seeds.

KIRSCH *see liqueurs*

KIWIFRUIT also known as Chinese gooseberry; having a brown, somewhat hairy skin and bright-green flesh with a unique sweet-tart flavour. Used in fruit salads, desserts and eaten (peeled) as is.

KUMARA the polynesian name of an orange-fleshed sweet potato often confused with yam; good baked, boiled, mashed or fried similarly to other potatoes.

LAMB

diced cubed lean meat.

minced ground lamb.

LAMINGTON PAN *see page 633*

LEBANESE CUCUMBER short, slender and thin-skinned. Probably the most popular variety because of its tender, edible skin, tiny, yielding seeds, and sweet, fresh and flavoursome taste.

LEEKS a member of the onion family, the leek resembles a green onion but is much larger and more subtle in flavour. Tender baby or pencil leeks can be eaten whole with minimal cooking but adult leeks are usually trimmed of most of the green tops then chopped or sliced and cooked as an ingredient in stews, casseroles and soups.

LEMON BUTTER a commercial lemon curd or lemon-flavoured spread.

LEMON GRASS also known as takrai, serai or serah. A tall, clumping, lemon-smelling and tasting, sharp-edged aromatic tropical grass; the white lower part of the stem is used, finely chopped, in much of the cooking of South-East Asia. Can be found, fresh, dried, powdered and frozen, in supermarkets and greengrocers as well as Asian food shops.

LEMON THYME *see thyme*

LIMONCELLO *see liqueurs*

LINING A FRUIT CAKE PAN *see page 643 and pages 632 & 633*

LIQUEURS

cointreau citrus-flavoured liqueur.

crème de cacao chocolate-flavoured liqueur.

curaçao orange-flavoured liqueur.

drambuie whisky-based liqueur.

frangelico hazelnut-flavoured liqueur.

grand marnier orange-flavoured liqueur based on cognac-brandy.

irish cream we used Baileys, a smooth and creamy natural blend of fresh Irish cream, the finest Irish spirits, Irish whiskey, cocoa and vanilla.

kahlua coffee-flavoured liqueur.

kirsch cherry-flavoured liqueur.

limoncello Italian lemon-flavoured liqueur; originally made from the juice and peel of lemons grown along the Amalfi coast.

malibu coconut-flavoured rum.

tia maria coffee-flavoured liqueur.

LOAF PAN *see pages 170 & 171*

MACADAMIAS native to Australia; fairly large, slightly soft, buttery rich nut. Used to make oil and macadamia butter; equally good in salads or cakes and pastries; delicious eaten on their own. Should always be stored in the fridge to prevent their high oil content turning them rancid.

MACAROONS a chewy biscuit made with egg white, sugar and coconut or almond meal.

MALIBU *see liqueurs*

MANDARIN also known as tangerine; a small, loose-skinned, easy-to-peel, sweet and juicy citrus fruit, prized for its eating qualities more than for juicing. Segments in a light syrup are available canned.

MANDOLINE a hand-operated implement with adjustable blades for thick to very thin slicing, shredding, dicing and cutting into match- or straw-sized sticks with speed and precision; ideal for shredding carrot and making french fries. Similar results can be achieved with a food processor or V-slicer and, as a last resort, the coarse side of a grater. Take care as this is an extremely sharp instrument.

MANGO tropical fruit originally from India and South-East Asia. With skin colour ranging from green to yellow and deep red; fragrant, deep yellow flesh surrounds a large flat seed. Slicing off the cheeks, cross-hatching them with a knife then turning them inside out shows the sweet, juicy flesh at its best. Mangoes can also be used in curries and salsas, or pureed for ice-cream, smoothies or mousse. Mango cheeks in light syrup are available canned. Sour and crunchy, green mangoes are just the immature fruit that is used as a vegetable in salads, salsas and curries.

MAPLE-FLAVOURED SYRUP is made from sugar cane and is also known as golden or pancake syrup. It is not a substitute for pure maple syrup.

MAPLE SYRUP distilled from the sap of sugar maple trees found only in Canada and about ten states in the USA. Most often eaten with pancakes or waffles, but also used as an ingredient in baking or in preparing desserts. Maple-flavoured syrup or pancake syrup is not an adequate substitute for the real thing.

MARJORAM an aromatic herb that is a member of the mint family; has long, thin, oval-shaped, pale-green leaves and a sweet taste similar to oregano. Used fresh or dried with lamb, seafood, vegetables and eggs. Usually added at the end of cooking so as not to lose its mild and delicate flavour.

MARMALADE a preserve, usually based on citrus fruit and its rind, cooked with sugar until the mixture has an intense flavour and thick consistency. Orange, lemon and lime are some of the commercially prepared varieties available.

MARSALA a fortified Italian wine produced in the region surrounding the Sicilian city of Marsala; recognisable by its intense amber colour and complex aroma. Often used in cooking, especially in sauces, risottos and desserts.

MARSHMALLOWS *see page 248*

MARZIPAN a paste made from ground almonds, sugar and water. Similar to almond paste but sweeter, more pliable and finer in texture. Easily coloured and rolled into thin sheets to cover cakes, or sculpted into shapes for confectionery.

MILK we use full-cream homogenised milk unless otherwise specified.

buttermilk in spite of its name, buttermilk is actually low in fat, varying between 0.6 per cent and 2.0 per cent per 100 ml. Originally the term given to the slightly sour liquid left after butter was churned from cream, today it is intentionally made from no-fat or low-fat milk to which specific bacterial cultures have been added during the manufacturing process. It is readily available from the dairy department in supermarkets. Because it is low in fat, it's a good substitute for dairy products such as cream or sour cream in some baking and salad dressings.

evaporated unsweetened canned milk from which water has been extracted by evaporation. Evaporated skim or low-fat milk has 0.3 per cent fat content.

full-cream powder instant powdered milk made from whole cow milk with liquid removed and emulsifiers added.

malted milk powder a blend of milk powder and malted cereal extract.

skim sometimes labelled "no-fat"; both have 0.1 per cent fat content.

skim-milk powder dried milk powder with 1 per cent fat content when dry and 0.1 per cent when reconstituted with water.

sweetened condensed a canned milk product consisting of milk with more than half the water content removed and sugar added to the remaining milk.

top 'n' fill caramel a canned milk product made of condensed milk that has been boiled to a caramel.

MINCED MEAT also known as ground meat, as in beef, pork, lamb and veal.

MIXED DRIED FRUIT a combination of sultanas, raisins, currants, mixed peel and cherries. *see also page 120*

MIXED PEEL candied citrus peel. *see also page 120*

MIXED SPICE a classic mixture generally containing caraway, allspice, coriander, cumin, nutmeg and ginger, although cinnamon and other spices can be added. It is used with fruit and in cakes.

MOLASSES a thick, dark brown syrup, the residue from the refining of sugar; available in light, dark and blackstrap varieties. Its slightly bitter taste is an essential ingredient in American cooking, found in foods such as gingerbread, shoofly pie and boston baked beans.

MUESLI also known as granola; a combination of grains (mainly oats), nuts and dried fruits. Some manufacturers toast their product in oil and honey, adding crispness and kilojoules.

MUFFIN PANS *see pages 376 and 628 & 629*

MUSCAT also known as muscatel; refers to both the grape variety and the sweet dessert wine made from them. The grape is superb eaten fresh; when dried, its distinctively musty flavour goes well with cheese, chocolate, pork and game. In winemaking, the grape is used for Italian Asti Spumante, a range of Australian fortifieds, Metaxa from Greece and so on.

MUSHROOMS

button small, cultivated white mushrooms with a mild flavour. When a recipe in this book calls for an unspecified type of mushroom, use button.

flat large, flat mushrooms with a rich earthy flavour, ideal for filling and barbecuing. They are sometimes misnamed field mushrooms which are wild mushrooms.

MUSTARD

dijon also known as french. Pale brown, creamy, distinctively flavoured, fairly mild French mustard.

wholegrain also known as seeded. A French-style coarse-grain mustard made from crushed mustard seeds and dijon-style french mustard. Works well with cold meats and sausages.

NAAN the rather thick, leavened bread associated with the tandoori dishes of northern India, where it is baked pressed against the inside wall of a heated tandoor (clay oven). Now available prepared by commercial bakeries and sold in most supermarkets. *see also page 507*

NASHI a member of the pear family but resembling an apple with its pale-yellow-green, tennis-ball-sized appearance; more commonly known as the Asian pear to much of the world. The nashi is different from other pears in that it is crisp, juicy and ready to eat as soon as it is picked and for several months thereafter, unlike its European cousins. These very qualities are more apple- than pear-like, which probably accounts for the widespread misconception that the nashi is a cross between an apple and a pear. Its distinctive texture and mildly sweet taste make it perfect for use raw in salads, or as part of a cheese platter.

NECTAR thick, undiluted fruit juice or a mixture of fruit juices (most commonly apricot, peaches and pears); found in cans in supermarkets.

NECTARINES smooth-skinned, slightly smaller cousin to the peach; juicy, with a rich and rather spicy flavour. Good for desserts peeled and sliced with a little cinnamon sugar and lemon.

NUT ROLL TINS *see pages 170 & 171*

NUTMEG a strong and pungent spice ground from the dried nut of an evergreen tree native to Indonesia. Usually found ground but the flavour is more intense from a whole nut, available from spice shops, so it's best to grate your own. Used most often in baking and milk-based desserts, but also works nicely in savoury dishes. Found in mixed spice mixtures.

OATBRAN the hard and rather woody protective coating of oats which serves to protect the grain before it germinates.

OIL

cooking spray we use a cholesterol-free cooking spray made from canola oil.

olive made from ripened olives. Extra virgin and virgin are the first and second press, respectively, of the olives and are therefore considered the best; the "extra light" or "light" name on other types refers to taste not fat levels.

vegetable any of a number of oils sourced from plant rather than animal fats.

ONIONS

green also known as scallion or (incorrectly) shallot; an immature onion picked before the bulb has formed, having a long, bright-green edible stalk.

leek *see leek*

pickling also known as baby or cocktail onions. These small brown onions have an average weight of 25g.

red also known as spanish, red spanish or bermuda onion; a sweet-flavoured, large, purple-red onion.

shallots also called french shallots, golden shallots or eschalots. Small and elongated, with a brown-skin, they grow in tight clusters similar to garlic.

spring crisp, narrow green-leafed tops and a round sweet white bulb larger than green onions.

ORANGE-FLAVOURED LIQUEUR brandy-based liqueur such as Grand Marnier or Cointreau.

ORANGE FLOWER WATER concentrated flavouring made from orange blossoms.

PANCETTA an Italian unsmoked bacon, pork belly cured in salt and spices then rolled into a sausage shape and dried for several weeks. Used, sliced or chopped, as an ingredient rather than eaten on its own; can also be used to add taste and moisture to tough or dry cuts of meat. Hot pancetta is lean pork belly first salted and cured then spiced and rolled into a fat loaf; used in pasta sauces and meat dishes except in its place of origin, Corsica, where it is eaten on its own.

PAPAYA also known as pawpaw, is a large, pear-shaped red-orange tropical fruit. Sometimes used unripe (green) in cooking.

PAPRIKA ground dried sweet red capsicum (bell pepper); there are many grades and types available, including sweet, hot, mild and smoked.

PARSLEY a versatile herb with a fresh, earthy flavour. There are about 30 varieties of curly parsley; the flat-leaf variety (also called continental or Italian parsley) is stronger in flavour and darker in colour.

PASTA SAUCE a prepared tomato-based sauce (sometimes called ragu or sugo on the label); comes in varying degrees of thickness and with different flavourings.

PASTRY For steps on handling pastry, see *Pastry decorations* pages 482 & 483, and *Baking blind* pages 618 & 619.

PASTRY WHEEL *see page 483*

PEANUTS, also known as groundnut, not in fact a nut but the pod of a legume. We mainly use raw (unroasted) or unsalted roasted peanuts.

PAWPAW *see papaya*

PECANS native to the US and now grown locally; pecans are golden brown, buttery and rich. Good in savoury as well as sweet dishes; walnuts are a good substitute.

PEPITAS are the pale green kernels of dried pumpkin seeds; they can be bought plain or salted.

PESTO a classic uncooked sauce made from basil, garlic, pine nuts, parmesan and olive oil; often served over pasta.

PINE NUTS also known as pignoli; not in fact a nut but a small, cream-coloured kernel from pine cones. They are best roasted before use to bring out the flavour.

PISTACHIO green, delicately flavoured nuts inside hard off-white shells. Available salted or unsalted in their shells; you can also get them shelled.

POACH a cooking term to describe gentle simmering of food in liquid (generally water or stock); spices or herbs can be added to impart their flavour.

POLENTA also known as cornmeal; a flour-like cereal made of dried corn (maize). also the name of the dish made from it.

POMEGRANATE dark-red, leathery-skinned fresh fruit about the size of an orange filled with hundreds of seeds, each wrapped in an edible lucent-crimson pulp having a unique tangy sweet-sour flavour.

POMELO similar to grapefruit but sweeter, somewhat more conical in shape and slightly larger, about the size of a small coconut. The firm rind peels away easily and neatly, like a mandarin, and the segments are easy to separate.

POPPY SEEDS

black small, dried, bluish-grey seeds of the poppy plant, with a crunchy texture and a nutty flavour. Can be purchased whole or ground in delicatessens and most supermarkets.

white also known as kas kas. Quite dissimilar to the black variety, these seeds from the white poppy are used, ground, as a thickening agent in sauces. Toasted, they take on a nutty flavour so are also used as a substitute for ground almonds.

PROSCIUTTO a kind of unsmoked Italian ham; salted, air-cured and aged, it is usually eaten uncooked. There are many styles of prosciutto, one of the best being parma ham, from Italy's Emilia Romagna region, traditionally lightly salted, dried then eaten raw.

PRUNES commercially or sun-dried plums; store in the fridge. *see also pages 120 & 121*

PUMPKIN often used interchangeably with the word squash, the pumpkin is a member of the gourd family and comes in a variety of sizes, shapes and colours. Used in sweet and savoury dishes, pumpkin can be boiled, steamed, mashed or roasted.

QUINCE yellow-skinned fruit with hard texture and astringent, tart taste; eaten cooked or as a preserve. Long, slow cooking makes the flesh a deep rose pink.

RAISINS dried sweet grapes (traditionally muscatel grapes).

READY-ROLLED PUFF PASTRY packaged sheets of frozen puff pastry, available from supermarkets.

READY-ROLLED SHORTCRUST PASTRY packaged sheets of frozen shortcrust pastry, available from supermarkets.

RHUBARB a plant with long, green-red stalks; becomes sweet and edible when cooked.

ROASTING nuts and dried coconut can be roasted in the oven to restore their fresh flavour and release their aromatic essential oils. Spread them evenly onto an oven tray then roast in a moderate oven for about 5 minutes. Desiccated coconut, pine nuts and sesame seeds roast more evenly if stirred over low heat in a heavy-based frying pan; their natural oils will help turn them golden brown. *see also page 202*

ROCKET also known as arugula, rugula and rucola; peppery green leaf eaten raw in salads or used in cooking. Baby rocket leaves are smaller and less peppery.

ROLLED OATS flattened oat grain rolled into flakes and traditionally used for porridge. Instant oats are also available, but use traditional oats for baking.

ROLLED RICE flattened rice grain rolled into flakes; looks similar to rolled oats.

ROLLED RYE flattened rye grain rolled into flakes and similar in appearance to rolled oats.

ROSEMARY pungent herb with long, thin pointy leaves; use large and small sprigs, and the leaves are usually chopped finely.

ROSEWATER extract made from crushed rose petals, called gulab in India; used for its aromatic quality in many sweetmeats and desserts.

ROUND CAKE PAN *see pages 628 & 629*

RUM we use a dark underproof rum (not overproof) for a more subtle flavour in cooking. White rum is almost colourless, sweet and used mostly in mixed drinks.

SAFFRON stigma of a member of the crocus family, available ground or in strands; imparts a yellow-orange colour to food once infused. The quality can vary greatly; the best is the most expensive spice in the world.

SAGE pungent herb with narrow, grey-green leaves; slightly bitter with a slightly musty mint aroma. Dried sage comes whole, crumbled or ground.

SALT unless specified otherwise, we use normal iodised table salt. Because we believe cooks salt as they like or not at all, the vast majority of our recipes do not list it as one of the ingredients.

SAMBAL OELEK also ulek or olek; Indonesian in origin, this is a salty paste made from ground chillies and vinegar.

SANDWICH PAN *see pages 628 & 629*

SAVOIARDI SPONGE FINGERS also known as savoy biscuits, lady's fingers or sponge fingers, they are Italian-style crisp fingers made from sponge cake mixture.

SEGMENTING a cooking term to describe cutting citrus fruits in such a way that the pieces contain no pith, seed or membrane.

The peeled fruit is cut towards the centre inside each membrane, forming wedges.

SEMOLINA *see flour*

SESAME SEEDS black and white are the most common of this small oval seed, however there are also red and brown varieties. The seeds are used in cuisines the world over as an ingredient and as a condiment. Roast the seeds in a heavy-based frying pan over low heat.

SESAME SNAPS sesame seeds set in honey-toffee; sold in thin bar-shapes and available in supermarkets.

SHALLOTS *see onions*

SHERRY fortified wine consumed as an aperitif or used in cooking. Sherries differ in colour and flavour; sold as fino (light, dry), amontillado (medium sweet, dark) and oloroso (full-bodied, very dark).

SILVER BEET also known as swiss chard and incorrectly, spinach; has fleshy stalks and large leaves, both of which can be prepared as for spinach.

SKEWERS metal or bamboo skewers can be used.

SLAB PAN *see pages 628 & 629*

SLICE PAN *see pages 628 & 629*

SOUR CREAM thick, commercially-cultured sour cream with a minimum fat content of 35 per cent.

SPINACH also known as english spinach and incorrectly, silver beet. Baby spinach leaves are best eaten raw in salads; the larger leaves should be added last to soups, stews and stir-fries, and should be cooked until barely wilted.

SPRINGFORM TINS *see page 526*

SQUARE CAKE PANS *see pages 628 & 629*

STAR ANISE a dried star-shaped pod whose seeds have an astringent aniseed flavour; commonly used to flavour stocks and marinades.

STAR FRUIT also known as carambola, five-corner fruit or Chinese star fruit; pale green or yellow colour, it has a clean, crisp texture. Flavour may be either sweet or sour, depending on the variety and when it was picked. There is no need to peel or seed it and they're slow to discolour.

STOCK cubes, powder or concentrated liquid can be used. As a guide, 1 small stock cube or 1 teaspoon of stock powder or 1 portion of stock concentrate mixed with 1 cup (250ml) water will give a fairly strong stock. Also available in ready-to-use bottles, cans or tetra packs.

SUGAR we use coarse, granulated table sugar, also known as crystal sugar, unless otherwise specified.

brown an extremely soft, fine granulated sugar retaining molasses for its characteristic colour and flavour.

caster also known as superfine or finely granulated table sugar. The fine crystals dissolve easily so it is perfect for cakes, meringues and desserts.

cinnamon combination of ground cinnamon and caster sugar. Most commonly sprinkled over buttered toast.

coffee crystals large golden-coloured crystal sugar made to enhance the flavour of coffee.

demerara small-grained golden-coloured crystal sugar.

icing also known as confectioners' sugar or powdered sugar; pulverised granulated sugar crushed together with a small amount (about 3 per cent) of cornflour.

palm also known as nam tan pip, jaggery, jawa or gula melaka; made from the sap of the sugar palm tree. Light brown to black in colour and usually sold in rock-hard cakes; substitute with brown sugar if unavailable.

pure icing also known as confectioners' sugar or powdered sugar.

raw natural brown granulated sugar.

SULTANAS also known as golden raisins; dried seedless white grapes.

SUNFLOWER SEED grey-green, slightly soft, oily kernels; a nutritious snack.

TANGELOS a cross between a grapefruit and a tangerine, it's eaten like an orange.

TAPENADE a thick paste made from black or green olives, capers, anchovies, olive oil and lemon juice.

TEMPERING the process by which chocolate is melted at a specific temperature that enables it to set with a glossy finish.

THYME a member of the mint family; there are many types of this herb but two that we use most. The "household" variety, simply called thyme in most shops, is French thyme; it has tiny grey-green leaves that give off a pungent minty, light-lemon aroma. Dried thyme comes in both leaf and powdered form. Lemon thyme's scent is due to the high level of citral in its leaves, an oil also found in lemon, orange, verbena and lemon grass. The citrus scent is enhanced by crushing the leaves in your hands before using the herb.

TIA MARIA *see liqueurs*

TOMATOES

canned whole peeled tomatoes in natural juices; available crushed, chopped or diced, sometimes unsalted or reduced salt. Use in recipes undrained.

cherry also known as tiny tim or tom thumb tomatoes; small and round.

egg also called plum or roma, these are smallish, oval-shaped tomatoes much used in Italian cooking or salads.

grape small, long oval-shaped tomatoes with a good tomato flavour.

paste triple-concentrated tomato puree used to flavour soups, stews, sauces and casseroles.

puree canned pureed tomatoes (not tomato paste); substitute with fresh peeled and pureed tomatoes.

semi-dried partially dried tomato pieces in olive oil; softer and juicier than sun-dried, these are not a preserve thus do not keep as long as sun-dried.

sun-dried tomato pieces that have been dried with salt; this dehydrates the tomato and concentrates the flavour. We use sun-dried tomatoes packaged in oil, unless otherwise specified. Also available in flavoured oil, such as chilli or herbs.

TOMATO SAUCE also known as ketchup or catsup; a flavoured condiment made from tomatoes, vinegar and spices.

TREACLE thick, dark syrup not unlike molasses. *see golden syrup*

V-SLICER cheaper and simpler to use than the Italian mandoline (but just as dangerously sharp), the V-slicer combines German efficiency and performance with its razor-sharp, flexible thin blades that slice, dice, shred and julienne.

VANILLA

bean dried, long, thin pod from a tropical golden orchid grown in central and South America and Tahiti; the minuscule black seeds inside the bean are used to impart a luscious vanilla flavour in baking and desserts. Place a whole bean in a jar of sugar to make the vanilla sugar often called for in recipes; a bean can be used three or four times.

essence obtained from vanilla beans infused in alcohol and water.

extract obtained from vanilla beans infused in water; a non-alcoholic version of essence.

sugar *see page 223*

VINEGAR

balsamic originally from Modena, Italy, there are now many balsamic vinegars on the market ranging in pungency and quality depending on how, and for how long, they have been aged. Quality can be determined up to a point by price; use the most expensive sparingly.

brown malt made from fermented malt and beech shavings.

cider made from fermented apples.

red wine made from red wine.

rice a colourless vinegar made from fermented rice and flavoured with sugar and salt. Also known as seasoned rice vinegar; sherry can be substituted.

sherry natural vinegar aged in oak according to the traditional Spanish system; a mellow wine vinegar named for its colour.

white made from distilled grain alcohol.

white wine made from white wine.

VIOLET CRUMBLE a honeycomb bar coated in milk chocolate.

WALNUTS as well as being a good source of fibre and healthy oils, nuts contain a range of vitamins, minerals and other beneficial plant components called phytochemicals. Each type of nut has a special make-up and walnuts contain the beneficial omega-3 fatty acids, which is terrific news for people who dislike the taste of fish.

WHEAT BRAN *see bran*

WINE the adage that you should never cook with wine you wouldn't drink holds true in this book; unless specified otherwise, we use good-quality dry white and red wines in our recipes.

WORCESTERSHIRE SAUCE thin, dark-brown spicy sauce developed by the British when in India; used as a seasoning for meat, gravies and cocktails, and as a condiment.

YEAST (dried and fresh), a raising agent used in dough making. A microscopic living organism that grows best in warm, moist conditions; over-hot conditions or dissolving liquid will kill yeast and keep the dough from rising. Granular (7g sachets) and fresh compressed (20g blocks) yeast can almost always be substituted one for the other when yeast is called for.

YOGURT we use plain full-cream yogurt in our recipes unless specifically noted otherwise. If a recipe in this book calls for low-fat yogurt, we use one with a fat content of less than 0.2 per cent.

ZUCCHINI also known as courgette; small, pale- or dark-green, yellow or white vegetable belonging to the squash family.

INDEX

Index

A

General manager *Christine Whiston*
Editorial director *Susan Tomnay*
Creative director and designer *Hieu Chi Nguyen*
Senior editor *Stephanie Kistner*
Sidebars written by *Pamela Clark*
Features writer *Kirsty McKenzie*
Food director *Pamela Clark*
Food editor *Cathie Lonnie*

Director of sales *Brian Cearnes*
Marketing manager *Bridget Cody*
Business analyst *Ashley Davies*
Operations manager *David Scotto*
International rights enquiries *Laura Bamford*
lbamford@acpuk.com

ACP Books are published by ACP Magazines
a division of PBL Media Pty Limited
Group publisher, Women's lifestyle *Pat Ingram*
Director of sales, Women's lifestyle *Lynette Phillips*
Commercial manager, Women's lifestyle *Seymour Cohen*
Marketing director, Women's lifestyle *Matthew Dominello*
Public relations manager, Women's lifestyle *Hannah Deveraux*
Creative director, Events, Women's lifestyle *Luke Bonnano*
Research Director, Women's lifestyle *Justin Stone*
ACP Magazines, Chief Executive officer *Scott Lorson*
PBL Media, Chief Executive officer *Ian Law*

The publishers would like to thank the following for props used
in photography *Bodum; Crowley & Gouch; Empire Vintage;
The Essential Ingredient; Iced Affair; Mokum Textiles; No Chintz;
Rebecca Neill Paint Effects; T2; The Bronte Tram; Tres Fabu!*

Photographers *Alan Benson, Sarah Callister, Gerry Colley,
Joshua Dasey, Ben Dearnley, Joe Filshie, Louise Lister,
Andre Martin, Rob Palmer, Con Poulos, Brett Stevens,
John Paul Urizar, Ian Wallace, Andrew Young.*
Stylists *Wendy Berecry, Julz Beresford, Janelle Bloom, Margot
Braddon, Kate Brown, Kirsty Cassidy, Marie-Helene Clauzon,
Kelly Cruickshanks, Sarah DeNardi, Carolyn Fienberg, Kay Francis,
Jane Hann, Mary Harris, Amber Keller, Michaela Le Compte,
David Morgan, Sarah O'Brien, Justine Osborne, Louise Pickford,
Stephanie Souvlis.*

Chapter openers and special features
Photographer *Louise Lister*
Stylist *Lynsey Fryers*
Food preparation *Belinda Farlow, Angela Muscat*

Produced by ACP Books, Sydney. Published by ACP Books, a division of ACP Magazines Ltd.
54 Park St, Sydney NSW Australia 2000. GPO Box 4088, Sydney, NSW 2001.
Phone +61 2 9282 8618 Fax +61 2 9267 9438
acpbooks@acpmagazines.com.au www.acpbooks.com.au
Printed by C&C Offset Printing, China.

Australia Distributed by Network Services, GPO Box 4088, Sydney, NSW 2001.
Phone +61 2 9282 8777 Fax +61 2 9264 3278 networkweb@networkservicescompany.com.au
United Kingdom Distributed by Australian Consolidated Press (UK),
10 Scirocco Close, Moulton Park Office Village, Northampton, NN3 6AP.
Phone +44 1604 642 200 Fax +44 1604 642 300 books@acpuk.com www.acpuk.com
Canada Distributed by Publishers Group Cananda, 559 College Street, Unit 402, Toronto, Ontario
M6G 1A9. Phone (416) 934 9900 or (800) 747 8147 Fax (416) 9341410 www.pgcbooks.ca
Order Desk & Customer Service, 9050 Shaughnessy Street, Vancouver, BC V6P 6E5
Phone (800) 663 5714 Fax (800) 565 3770 service@raincoast.com
New Zealand Distributed by Netlink Distribution Company, ACP Media Centre, Cnr Fanshawe
and Beaumont Streets, Westhaven, Auckland. PO Box 47906, Ponsonby, Auckland, NZ.
Phone +64 9 366 9966 Fax 0800 277 412 ask@ndc.co.nz
South Africa Distributed by PSD Promotions, 30 Diesel Road Isando, Gauteng Johannesburg.
PO Box 1175, Isando 1600, Gauteng Johannesburg.
Phone +27 11 392 6065/6/7 Fax +27 11 392 6079/80 orders@psdprom.co.za

Title: Bake: the Australian women's weekly/editor, Pamela Clark.
Publisher: Sydney: ACP Books, 2008.
ISBN: 978-1-86396-789-1
Subjects: Baked products.
Other authors: Clark, Pamela.
Also titled: Australian women's weekly.
Dewey number: 641.815

© ACP Magazines Ltd 2008
ABN 18 053 273 546
This publication is copyright. No part of it may be reproduced or
transmitted in any form without the written permission of the publishers.

To order books, phone 136 116 (within Australia).
Send recipe enquiries to: recipeenquiries@acpmagazines.com.au